Essential Psychopathology and Its Treatment

FOURTH EDITION

Essential Psychopathology and Its Treatment

FOURTH EDITION

Mark D. Kilgus

Jerrold S. Maxmen

Nicholas G. Ward

W. W. Norton & Company

New York • London

Copyright © 2016 by Mark D. Kilgus, the Estate
of Jerrold S. Maxmen, and the Estate of Nicholas G. Ward.
Copyright © 2009 by the Estate of Jerrold S. Maxmen,
Nicholas G. Ward, and Mark D. Kilgus.
Copyright © 1995 by Nicholas G. Ward and the Estate of Jerrold S. Maxmen.
Copyright © 1986 by Jerrold S. Maxmen.

All rights reserved
Printed in the United States of America

For information about permission to reproduce selections from this book, write to
Permissions, W. W. Norton & Company, Inc., 500 Fifth Avenue, New York, NY 10110

For information about special discounts for bulk purchases, please contact
W. W. Norton Special Sales at specialsales@wwnorton.com or 800-233-4830

Manufacturing by: Lake Book Manufacturing
Production manager: Christine Critelli

Library of Congress Cataloging-in-Publication Data

Kilgus, Mark D.
    Essential psychopathology & its treatment / Mark D. Kilgus, Jerrold S.
Maxmen, Nicholas G. Ward. — 4th edition.
        pages cm
    Revision of: Essential psychopathology and its treatment / Jerrold S.
Maxmen, Nicholas G. Ward, Mark D. Kilgus. 3rd ed. c2009.
    Includes bibliographical references and index.
    ISBN 978-0-393-71064-9 (hardcover)
1. Psychology, Pathological.   2. Psychiatry.   I. Maxmen, Jerrold S.
II. Ward, Nicholas G.   III. Title.   IV. Title: Essential psychopathology
and its treatment.
    RC454.M3   2016
    616.89—dc23   2015024746

ISBN: 978-0-393-71064-9

W. W. Norton & Company, Inc., 500 Fifth Avenue, New York, N.Y. 10110
www.wwnorton.com
W. W. Norton & Company Ltd., 15 Carlisle Street, London W1D 3BS

6 7 8 9 0

Contents

Acknowledgments

This revision of the text is largely necessitated by substantive changes in classifying mental disorders as presented in the *DSM-5*. *ICD-10* is used by most of the world (and for billing purposes in the United States) and within the next few years will update to the 11th edition. There is probably not a compelling reason to retain separate diagnostic nosologies but much merit in unification toward a single system of classification. With this in mind an attempt has been made in this edition to blend *ICD-10* and *DSM-5* in a way that minimizes confusion for the reader. The international criteria are presented in a familiar format with essential criteria in bold font. Wherever possible parallels between the two classification systems are demonstrated and differences are highlighted.

The new edition of this text also incorporates suggestions for improvement by those who took the time to provide feedback. Clinicians, educators, and students are encouraged to share their ideas for future editions so that this volume will continue to accomplish its intended purpose: to establish essential foundational knowledge in psychopathology and a framework for a lifetime of discovery. As in previous editions, older references of evidence that has stood the test of time are retained and provide a valuable perspective alongside the latest advances. For the 5th edition, anticipated progress in computational neuroscience and functional neuroimaging may allow a presentation of the essential neuroanatomical and neurophysiological correlates for each disorder.

Major contributors to the 4th edition include Bill Rea (Psychopharmacology), Andy Pumariega (Systems-Based Practice), and Frank Biscardi (Sleep Disorders). Last year faculty in the Department of Psychiatry and Behavioral Medicine at Virginia Tech Carilion School of Medicine authored a new resource to more thoroughly teach clinical decision making. *Essential Psychopathology Casebook* (2014) serves as a useful companion to this text and we hope that both will contribute to your understanding.

—Mark D. Kilgus, MD, PhD
Chair, Department of Psychiatry and Behavioral Medicine
Virginia Tech Carilion School of Medicine

List of Contributors
to the Previous Edition

FELICITY ADAMS, M.D.—Neurodevelopmental Disorders; Impulse Control Disorders

VISHAL S. ANAND, M.D.—Legal, Ethical, and Multicultural Issues

TRACEY CRISS, M.D.—Mood Disorders

DAVID A. DOWNS, JR., M.D.—Neurocognitive Disorders

WILLIAM S. ELIAS, M.D.—Sleep Disorders

BENJAMIN T. GRIFFETH, M.D.—Adjustment Disorders

DAVID W. HARTMAN, M.D.—Personality Disorders

ANN E. HEDBERG, M.D.—Assessment; Diagnosis and Prognosis

BUSH KAVURU, M.D.—Psychopathology

J. THOMAS NOGA, M.D.—Etiology; Schizophrenia and Other Thought Disorders

KIMBERLY BARNETT ORAM, PSY.D.—Legal, Ethical, and Multicultural Issues

ANDRES J. PUMARIEGA, M.D.—Systems-Based Practice; Eating Disorders

WILLIAM S. REA, M.D.—Psychopharmacology; Substance-Related Disorders

ANURADHA REDDY, M.D., M.P.H.—Dissociative Disorders; Neurodevelopmental Disorders

GEORGE A. REKERS, PH.D., TH.D.—Sexual and Gender Identity Disorders

RICHARD W. SEIDEL, PH.D.—Treatment; Sample Case History

DAVID B. TRINKLE, M.D.—Neurocognitive Disorders

SACHINDER VASUDEVA, M.D.—Anxiety Disorders

GEBREHANA W. ZEBRO, M.D.—Somatoform Disorders

Preface

A "nosology" is a system for naming and classifying diseases. In the early 1960s the World Health Organization (WHO) began the process of improving the diagnosis and classification of mental disorders through stimulating and conducting research to establish reliable and valid diagnostic criteria. Scientists from different disciplines, psychiatric traditions, nations, and cultures conferred and contributed to the diagnostic categories and criteria for the *International Classification of Diseases* (ICD) now in its 10th revision. Each revision is produced by careful consultation with clinical and research experts in addition to the membership of professional psychiatric societies across the globe. The proposed modifications are exhaustively studied in field trials in multiple countries before finalizing the guidelines. In much of the world, the *ICD* nosology is used for psychiatric diagnosis. The most recent version, *ICD-10*, was released in 1993, and clinical modifications were added in 2007 (*ICD-10-CM*). In the United States, The American Psychiatric Association, publishes its own classification system as the *Diagnostic and Statistical Manual of Mental Disorders* (DSM). *DSM-5*, the 2013 revision, attempts to be harmonious with *ICD-10*, so that when clinicians from different countries discuss a particular diagnosis, they are really talking about the same disorder or disease. Also, billing for clinical services in the United States requires the use of *ICD* diagnostic codes.

Psychiatric diagnosis has become the cornerstone for *all* clinical practice. In the most recent revisions of the *ICD* and *DSM*, major conceptual and practical shifts in making diagnoses favored scientific evidence over theoretical speculation. The respect for rigorous scientific thought has spread throughout clinical practice. Psychotherapy, once a strictly intuitive affair, is now researched with standards similar to other sciences. Mental health professionals now ask once ill-mannered questions such as "Where's the evidence?" and "What are the data?" No longer are things true simply because a professor or some other authority says so. Today, diagnostic common sense necessitates proof. Of course there are gaps in scientific knowledge and therefore deficiencies in our nosologies that motivate ongoing revisions. The clinician must also know how to interpret the available evidence and understand its limitations.

Some people consider a *scientific* psychiatry to be a dehumanized psychiatry. We could not disagree more. As long as therapists treat *people* with illnesses, instead of *illnesses* that happen to be in people, clinical practice necessitates artistry, intuition, philosophy, ethics, and science—each with its own contribution. The distinct contribution of science is that, when properly conducted, it yields the most likely predictions, and therefore affords patients the greatest chance of receiving treatments most likely to work. Offering patients anything less is hardly humanistic.

There is, of course, far more to proper clinical assessment than diagnosis, and any clinician who evaluates a patient's condition *solely* in terms of whether it meets *DSM* or *ICD* criteria is gravely misinformed and shows a disturbing misunderstanding of the diagnostic process. Proper clinical assessments must address the patient's context, including his or her family, friends, upbringing, genetic patterns, physical health, current stressors, psychodynamics, and so on. Still, good care begins with accurate diagnosis.

The essentials of psychopathology, including diagnosis and treatment, should be understood not just by psychiatrists, but by all physicians, psychologists, nurses, social workers, psychotherapists, and counselors. In 2004, conservative estimates established that diagnosable mental disorders afflict greater than one out of every four adults, or nearly 58 million Americans (Kessler et al., 2005). Nearly half of these individuals meet criteria for two or more mental disorders. Mental disorders are the leading cause of disability. Aside from the emotional toll, these disorders annually cost the United States over $200 billion in lost earnings and many billions more in direct health care expenditures. These amounts are similar to those for heart disease and cancer. We should remember that those with physical illness are also more likely to have co-occurring mental illness that affects outcomes. Of all patients with mental disorders, about half are treated by primary-care physicians, a quarter by mental-health professionals, and another quarter go untreated. Thus recognizing and healing psychopathology are everyday tasks for every helping professional. *Essential Psychopathology and Its Treatment* presents the current evidence and collective thinking of experts. Although stressing the new, the book does not abrogate the old. Time-tested concepts and practices are included. But psychiatric diagnosis is open to question as a dynamic and evolving endeavor. When Robert Spitzer, the chief architect of *DSM-III*, was asked, "What happens if a clinician doesn't want to diagnose using *DSM* criteria?" he replied, "Then don't! It's a free country. People wrote the *DSM*, not God." And that goes for the latest revisions of the *DSM* and *ICD* as well.

Essential Psychopathology and Its Treatment is a "no-nonsense" book. Many introductory psychiatric texts are an overly simplified collection of the "most basic facts." They do not lay a solid conceptual framework for an understanding of these psychiatric facts. This text will not pander. Diagnostic psychopathology is essential to clinical evaluation and to effective clinical care. The "essential" in *Essential Psychopathology and Its Treatment* does not refer to the "essence" of psychiatry or to "all the psychiatry you'll ever need to know." Reality dictates that in psychiatry, as in everything else, choices must be made—choices that eliminate some good stuff in the process. For better or worse, the "essential" in *Essential Psychopathology and Its Treatment* reflects these choices. Some information is *relatively* more critical than other information. To save space, smaller type is used for less important material, and fewer references are cited. The downside of this "essential trimming" is that major works in diagnostic psychopathology don't appear, significant details are omitted, and controversial material is mostly excluded.

In this book, people with *major* mental disorders are called "patients" instead of "clients." Referring to patients with *severe* mental disorders as "clients" is not only euphemistic, but may unwittingly trivialize the burden of having a disorder such as schizophrenia. Calling these people "patients" is purely descriptive and certainly no sign of disrespect. It is not intended as a reference to a strictly traditional medical model of care. "Patient" is derived from the Latin word *patiens*, meaning "one who endures" or "one who suffers," and the actual definition of "patient" does not itself connote passivity. In contrast, those who seek help for problems other than serious mental disorders (e.g., adjustment reactions, marital difficulties) are often called "clients." "Client" originates from the Latin root *cliens*, which means "follower" and suggests dependency rather than empowerment. This book employs "he" and "she" randomly, except when discussing a mental disorder more common in men or women. Any resemblance between the pseudonyms we've assigned to patients in case examples and to actual individuals with the same name is purely coincidental.

This text aims to be concise, to give students of all ages and levels of experience a brief, relatively jargon-free, and readable blend of the newest and most fundamental information in this rapidly evolving field. We hope that this revision of *Essential Psychopathology and Its Treatment* fascinates students about the subject and encourages them to question whatever they read, to pursue the topic further, to chuckle every now and then, and most of all, to help their patients. We intend this to be a teaching text that assists with discovery and not just a compendium of information on psychopathology. Hopefully it reads as well and is as thoroughly integrated as previous editions.

A word of caution: Do yourself a big favor and avoid self-diagnosis. With "medical student's disease," future physicians "catch" diabetes while studying medicine, cancer while studying surgery, and schizophrenia while studying psychiatry. Everybody has some features of a mental disorder, but that hardly means one has a mental disorder. Hemophiliacs bruise, but everyone who bruises isn't a hemophiliac. The same applies to mental disorders. If you are concerned that you, or a loved one, has a mental disorder, consult an expert.

References

American Psychiatric Association. (2013). *Diagnostic and statistical manual of mental disorders*, 5th ed. Washington, DC: American Psychiatric Association.

Insel, Thomas R. (2008). Assessing the economic costs of serious mental illness. *American Journal of Psychiatry, 165*, 663–665.

Kessler, R.C., Chiu, W.T., Demler, O., & Walters, E.E. (2005). Prevalence, severity, and comorbidity of twelve-month *DSM-IV* disorders in the National Comorbidity Survey Replication (NCS-R). *Archives of General Psychiatry, 62*(6), 617–627.

Kessler, R.C., Berglund, P.A., Demler, O., Jin, R., & Walters, E.E. (2005). Lifetime prevalence and age-of-onset distributions of DSM-IV disorders in the National Comorbidity Survey Replication (NCS-R). *Archives of General Psychiatry, 62*(6), 593–602.

National Institute of Mental Health, available online at www.nimh.nih.gov.

Riegleman, R.K. (2013). *Studying a study and testing a test*, 6th ed. Philadelphia: Lippincott.

Sartorius, N., et al. (1993). Progress towards achieving a common language in psychiatry: Results from the field trials of the clinical guidelines accompanying the WHO Classification of Mental and Behavioural Disorders in *ICD-10*. *Archives of General Psychiatry, 50*, 115–124.

Sartorius, N., et al. (Ed.). (1990). *Sources and traditions in classification in psychiatry*. Toronto: Hogrefe and Huber.

World Health Organization. (1992). *The ICD–10 classification of mental and behavioural disorders: Clinical descriptions and diagnostic guidelines*. Geneva: World Health Organization (WHO).

Essential Psychopathology and Its Treatment

FOURTH EDITION

DIAGNOSTIC PSYCHOPATHOLOGY

1

Psychopathology

Such is man that if he has a name for something it ceases to be a riddle.

—I. B. Singer, "Property"

At 58, Amy's life stopped. Although cancer-free for 5 months since her mastectomy, she remained paralyzed by depression and insomnia. Amy had withdrawn from family and friends, quit work, become addicted to sleeping pills, and contemplated suicide. Once a film buff, now she hid in bed ruminating about "it" (she was afraid to say *cancer*). Diligently, she attempted relaxation exercises to overcome insomnia, yet she was unable to concentrate—the harder she tried, the more she failed, and the less she slept. Her demoralization was pervasive.

The reasons for her symptoms were understandable and Amy "knew" that only time could heal her. To be sure, having cancer and a mastectomy are understandable reasons for sadness and insomnia. But this thinking misses the point: Amy had an additional problem—a mental disorder called "major depressive disorder."

Only after Amy's psychopathology was recognized and the proper antidepressant medication prescribed did her life return to normal. She still worried about her mastectomy—who wouldn't?—but she worried as a "normal" person, not as a depressed one. Now, at least, she could get her mind off the cancer. Without major depression impeding her concentration, she was able to perform the relaxation exercises, stop taking sleeping pills, sleep well, socialize, and return to work. No matter how "understandable" her symptoms, Amy was helped only *after* her major depression was diagnosed.

Critics would charge that to diagnose Amy's condition is to label and thus to dehumanize her. Yet it was only after a therapist recognized that Amy was suffering from more than the normal postmastectomy demoralization that her humanity returned. Explained Amy, "For months I'd assumed that there wasn't *really* anything wrong with me, and that if I only had the 'right' attitude, I'd feel fine. After all, other women get over their mastectomies. Why couldn't I? It had to be my fault—or so I thought. As soon as I learned that there really *was* something wrong with me, and that it had a name, my self-blame vanished. At last, something could be done: My depression could be treated. But you can't treat what you can't name." When used with clear goals in mind, psychiatric diagnosis avoids the pitfalls of labeling, the meaninglessness of academic exercise, and the distortions of an arrogant clinician's ego. Indeed, when diagnostic evaluation is thus abused, the culprit is the therapist, not the process.

THE PURPOSES OF A PSYCHIATRIC DIAGNOSIS

Psychiatric diagnosis serves two main purposes. The first is to *define clinical entities* so that clinicians have the same understanding of what a diagnostic category means. Patients with a particular (medical or psychiatric) diagnosis need not exhibit identical features, although they should present with certain cardinal *symptoms* (e.g., for major depression, these include diminished interest in pleasurable activities, insomnia, diminished concentration, or thoughts of suicide). The disorder should have a similar *natural history*—a typical age of onset, life course, prognosis, and complications. A diagnosis should reflect the *etiology* and *pathogenesis* of the condition. *Etiology* refers to the origins of a disorder; *pathogenesis* refers to its course of development. Although the same disorder can arise in more than one way, a diagnostic category should indicate whether the disorder consistently runs in families, is genetically transmitted, is initiated by psychosocial forces, and is exacerbated or aggravated by specific biological and environmental conditions.

The second goal of psychiatric diagnosis is to *determine treatment*. Having diagnosed Amy's condition as "major depression," the clinician knew to provide antidepressants; if the diagnosis had been unhappiness and insomnia, he may not have prescribed antidepressants but rather psychotherapy and sleep aids. Diagnosis not only influences biological treatments but also shapes the choice of particular psychotherapies.

How well a diagnosis defines a disorder and guides treatment depends on its validity and reliability. When a diagnostic category represents a genuine entity—that is, when patients with the same diagnosis have similar clinical features, natural histories, etiologies, pathogeneses, and responses to treatment—the category is said to have high *validity*. The more clinicians agree on a diagnosis when examining the same patient, the greater its *interrater reliability*. It is possible for a diagnostic category to have high validity without reliability, and vice versa. For example, a professor could conceive of the "Abominable Snowman syndrome" with very specific diagnostic features. It then would be easy to get clinical agreement (high reliability) on who did or did not fit the diagnosis—but the diagnosis itself is meaningless (low validity) as a syndrome. The diagnostic category of "codependent personality" exemplifies the reverse situation: Such people probably exist and share clinical features, history, and so on (high validity), but the diagnostic criteria are so vague or varied that clinicians have trouble agreeing on who has it (low reliability). Prior to the more recent *ICD* and *DSM* diagnostic manuals, the standard joke was that if 10 psychiatrists examined the same patient, they would come up with 12 different diagnoses—another example of very low reliability!

> In psychiatry the validity of the diagnostic categories must be established. Validity (accuracy) of the diagnostic criteria is the degree to which they define a discrete category of psychopathology. This is not the same as reliability, which is the extent to which the criteria gives consistent results. Validity and reliability are never perfect but rather are a matter of degrees. There are many different types of validity.
> - Face validity refers to whether the criteria appear to describe or measure what is intended.
> - Concurrent validity is based upon comparison with an already established criterion or test. It may come from psychological tests or from neurochemistry, neuroanatomy, or neurophysiological correlates.
> - Criterion-oriented or predictive validity is based upon a measure or criterion (familial aggregation, molecular genetics, premorbid personality, or other precipitating factors) that predicts future performance (diagnostic stability over time, rates of relapse and recovery, or treatment response)
> - Discriminant validity may involve clinical descriptors that distinguish from other disorders. Clinical description validators comprise distinct signs and symptoms that prove to be discrete identifiable entities with natural boundaries that distinguish from other disorders
> - Construct validity is the degree to which the diagnostic criteria or other tests measure an intended hypothetical construct
> - Content validity may refer to the logical representation of the disorder or construct in the diagnostic criteria or measure. A criterion must be sensi-

tive enough to validate most syndromes that are true disorders, while also being specific enough to invalidate most syndromes that are not true disorders.

DEFINING PSYCHOPATHOLOGY

Who in the rainbow can draw the line where the violet tint ends and the orange tint begins . . . so with sanity and insanity.
—Herman Melville, *Billy Budd*

Pathology is the study of diseases and the produced changes that deviate from an assumed normal condition. The *psyche* or *soul* refers to the mind, will, and emotions of a person. So *psychopathology* would be the *manifestations* of mental illness. It also refers to the *study* of mental disorders—their problems, causes, and processes. Psychopathology involves *impairments, deviance,* and *distress,* but not all impairments, deviance, and distress are psychopathological. Being ugly (not gorgeous), inefficient (not active), and thoughtless (not considerate) are all impairments, but they do not constitute psychopathology. Being an atheist, punker, crook, or drag queen is deviant, but not psychopathological. Being starved, broke, or lonely is distressing, but not psychopathological.

Distinguishing psychopathology from normality is usually easy, although on occasion it can be difficult. Critics argue that because the line between psychopathology and normality is hazy, psychopathology is a myth. That's nonsense. Day and night clearly exist, even though at dusk it is hard to know which it is. Psychopathology is no less real for its relativity. The definition of a mental disorder in the *DSM-5* does not suggest that there are sharp distinctions between psychopathology and normality or between different mental disorders. According to *DSM-5,* mental disorders must produce clinically significant *impairment* or *distress* in one's personal, social, or occupational life. Biological changes may or may not be involved. Also, it is possible to have psychopathology by being functionally impaired but not meeting all of the criteria for an established mental disorder. For such instances there are more general diagnostic categories with less specific criteria. *DSM-5* states:

A mental disorder is a syndrome characterized by clinically significant disturbance in an individual's cognition, emotion regulation, or behavior that reflects a dysfunction in the psychological, biological, or developmental processes underlying mental functioning. Mental disorders are usually associated with significant distress or disability in social, occupational, or other important activities. An expectable or culturally approved response to a common stressor or loss, such as the death of a loved one, is not a mental disorder. Socially deviant behavior (e.g., political, religious, or sexual) and conflicts that are primarily between the individual and society are not mental disorders unless the deviance or conflict results from a dysfunction in the individual. (p. 20)

In addition to the required distress or functional impairment, one should not diagnose most mental disorders if the psychopathology is exclusively caused by the physiological effects from a medical condition or substance.

DSM and ICD classify *mental disorders*; they do not classify *individuals* with mental disorders. Patients who receive the same diagnosis are not the same in every important respect. Just as the only similarity among people with diabetes is having symptoms of diabetes, the only similarity among people with schizophrenia is having symptoms of schizophrenia, such as delusional thoughts, hallucinations, or catatonic symptoms. Otherwise, some people with schizophrenia are delightful, some obnoxious, some brilliant, and some dull. When, for the sake of brevity, a patient with schizophrenia is called a "schizophrenic," it should be done with the understanding that a disorder is an attribute of a person and never his or her totality.

Many terms resemble "mental disorder." A *syndrome* refers to any cluster of signs and symptoms. Clinicians often use *mental disease* and *mental illness* as synonyms for mental disorder, especially for the more severe ones clearly involving biological changes, such as schizophrenia and bipolar disorder. Technically, this usage is inaccurate. In medicine, *disease* refers to the specific physical disturbances of a condition, whereas *illness* refers to the total experience of a condition, including physical disturbances. In the *DSM* and *ICD* diagnostic categories are always called *disorders*.

Laypeople often use terms such as *insanity* and *nervous breakdown* to mean mental disorder. Neither term has psychiatric meaning. *Insanity*, which is a legal term (the definition of which varies among states), establishes a defendant's lack of criminal responsibility due to a mental disorder or defect. *Nervous breakdown* is a popular term for any severe incapacitation due to emotional or psychiatric difficulties.

The term *problems in living* is often a euphemism for mental disorder. To have a mental disorder is surely a problem in living, but it is far more than that, and to equate the two is to err in categorization and to trivialize the pain of mental disorders. "Problems in living" connote the difficulties of everyday life: losing a job, squabbling with children, undergoing a divorce, fearing rejection, evading the bill collector, and dealing with low self-esteem. Problems in living can be miserable, yet they are vastly different in magnitude and type from mental disorders. Problems in living consist of "issues," whereas mental disorders consist of psychopathology.

Symptoms, Signs, and Issues

Psychopathology manifests as *symptoms* and *signs*. Symptoms are experienced subjectively, cannot be observed, and must be reported by the patient; signs can be observed and documented objectively. Symptoms include pain, hallucinations, appetite loss, paranoid thinking, and anxiety, whereas signs include avoidant behavior, restlessness, weight loss, and rapid speech. Depressed mood is a symptom, crying a sign; chest pain is a symptom, heart failure a sign. Mental-health professionals sometimes ignore this distinction and refer to signs as symptoms. For literary convenience, this book does likewise, except when lumping them together clouds clinical thinking.

People may have a symptom (e.g., anxiety, insomnia) without having a mental disorder. By itself, a symptom rarely constitutes a mental disorder. A symptom only reflects a mental disorder when it is a part of a specific symptom constellation. Most symptoms exceed the boundaries of routine experience; unlike issues (or problems in living), symptoms are not everyday occurrences. Everybody contends with issues, only some with symptoms. Patients with mental disorders have both symptoms *and* issues, whereas clients with problems in living have only issues.

Issues contain ideas; symptoms do not. However, just as mail transmits ideas, symptoms can express issues. The ideas patients communicate when they manifest symptoms reflect the issues concerning them. For instance, two men with the severe mental disorder of major depression may have the symptom of overwhelming hopelessness. The first, an elderly, devout Catholic, insists he is hopeless "because I sinned 20 years ago by cheating on my wife." The second, a young up-and-coming actor, feels equally hopeless because "I'm not a star." Both patients have psychopathology—that is, hopelessness—yet, because their issues are so different, each expresses hopelessness quite differently.

As very broad generalizations, *biological factors* primarily cause symptoms, whereas *psychosocial factors* primarily determine issues. Because most symptoms usually arise from an altered *brain*, biological therapies usually correct them; because issues mainly derive from an altered *mind*, psychosocial therapies usually rectify them. Since patients with mental disorders present with both symptoms and issues, their treatment frequently involves medication as well as psychotherapy. Since clients with problems in living present with issues but not symptoms, they only receive psychotherapy. Psychological symptoms such as negative thinking in depression or panic reactions in panic disorder fall between these two: They often stem from a combination of psychological and biological causes and are effectively treated by medication and/or psychotherapy.

Phenomenology is the aspect of psychopathology that deals with a person's consciously reported experiences (Jaspers, 1923/1972). Phenomenological investigation focuses on the form of experience, that is, the *way* in which the content is experienced, while the content itself is of secondary importance (Burgy, 2008). It is also a branch of philosophy that posits that behavior is determined not by an objective external reality, but by a person's subjective perception of that reality. Phenomenology is an important aspect of both existential and descriptive psychiatry. From a phenomenological point of view, psychopathology is the study of the nature and evolution of psychiatric symptoms.

TWO DIAGNOSTIC APPROACHES

There are two major approaches to diagnostic psychopathology. The first is called *descriptive* because diagnoses are based on relatively objective phenomena that require nominal clinical inference; these phenomena include signs, symptoms, and natural history. The second is called *psychological* because diagnoses are based primarily on inferred causes and mechanisms. The psychological approach also considers descriptive phenomena, but as merely superficial manifestations of more profound underlying forces.

The descriptive approach focuses on the *what* of behavior, the psychological on its *why*. Amy's case illustrates the common mistake of confusing the two. *What* was wrong (major depression) had been ignored because people focused on *why* things were wrong (having cancer and a mastectomy). Failing to distinguish the what from the why of psychopathology is the novice's first big mistake. An example: A hallucinating, disheveled youth, convinced he was Jesus Christ, told beginning medical students that his parents stifled his creativity, poisoned his food, and stole his Nintendo. Once he left the room, the students were asked, "What do you think is wrong with him?" "Nothing," they replied, "the problem is that he has lousy parents." Yet, even assuming he has dreadful parents (the why), he is no less delusional and hallucinatory (the what).

Both descriptive and psychological approaches are valuable, since each addresses a different aspect of psychopathology. Take a delusion. The descriptive approach would detail its characteristics: Is it fixed? Vague? Paranoid? Circumscribed? The psychological approach would focus on inner mechanisms (e.g., projection), which might produce the delusion.

> Emil Kraepelin (1856–1926) is virtually synonymous with descriptive psychiatry—sometimes called "Kraepelinian psychiatry"—because he devised the first major psychiatric nosology based on descriptive criteria (Kraepelin, 1915/1921). Examining thousands of delusional and hallucinating patients, he divided those without obvious brain damage into two groups according to prognosis and age of onset. The first he diagnosed as "dementia praecox": *Dementia* referred to the progressively downhill course of the disorder and *praecox* referred to the appearance of symptoms during the teens or twenties. He diagnosed the second group as "maniacal depression"—today called "bipolar disorder." These patients were initially hospitalized in their 30s and 40s and typically returned to normal. Thus, in creating a descriptively based nosology, Kraepelin added natural (or longitudinal) history to current (or cross-sectional) symptoms. His textbook is *the* classic in descriptive psychiatry, and his approach has dominated European psychiatry to this day.
>
> The psychological approach was launched by the Swiss psychiatrist Eugen Bleuler (1857–1939). In *Dementia Praecox, or the Group of Schizophrenias* (1911/1950), Bleuler introduced the term *schizophrenia* to signify the disorder's basic defect of splitting of psychic functions—that is, disorganization and incongruency between thought, emotion, and behavior (not a split or multiple personality, as popularly believed). Bleuler believed that these splits gave rise to the fundamental symptoms of schizophrenia: flat or inappropriate *affect*, profound *ambivalence, autism,* and disturbed *associations* of thought—the "4 A's." These splits are inferred psychological mechanisms of causation and thus fundamentally different from Kraepelin's observed, descriptive criteria.

Until *DSM-III* (1980), the psychological approach dominated American psychiatry, largely because it dovetailed with Freudian thought, which has always enjoyed more popularity in the United States than anyplace else. Indeed, Bleuler's psychological approach paved the way for diagnoses based on psychoanalytic criteria, such as "poor ego boundaries," "oral regression," "polymorphous perversity," "projection," and "primary process." The more psychiatrists focused on these inferred phenomena, the more they recognized that *everybody* had them to various degrees. This belief helps to explain three key differences between psychological and descriptive diagnoses.

First, the psychological view holds that everyone has some degree of psychopathology; with the descriptive approach, only a minority has psychopathology. Second, psychologically derived diagnoses follow a *unitary model,* in which there is essentially one mental disorder whose name is a matter of degree, not type—from the least severe to the most: neuroses, personality disorders, manic–depression, and schizophrenia. As in physical medicine, the descriptive approach follows a *multiple model,* in which disorders are distinct and numerous. Third, the psychological view often considers patients to have more severe psychopathology than does the descriptive view. Patients diagnosed as "neurotic" by psychological criteria might have "no mental disorder" by descriptive criteria, whereas those diagnosed as "schizophrenic" by psychological criteria might be diagnosed as "manic" or "depressive" by descriptive criteria.

THE DESCRIPTIVE REVIVAL

A purely psychological approach pervaded *DSM-I* (1952), the first official psychiatric nomenclature for the United States. All *Diagnostic and Statistical Manual of Mental Disorders (DSMs),* are created by the American Psychiatric Association. In the first edition, *DSM-I,* the diagnoses were loosely defined and emphasized psychological etiologies in the terminology (e.g., "schizophrenic reactions," "paranoid reactions," and "psychoneurotic reactions").

The main reason for writing *DSM-II* (1968) was to rectify *DSM-I*'s failure to conform to the World Health Organization's *International Classification of Diseases. DSM-II* eliminated "reactive" from most diagnostic labels, thereby inching away from an etiologically based nosology. *DSM-II* suffered from low interrater reliability. The "U.S./U.K." study (Cooper et al., 1972) showed that, unlike the descriptively oriented British psychiatrists, American psychiatrists frequently reached different diagnoses after observing the same videotape of the same patient being interviewed by the same psychiatrist. *DSM-II*'s diagnoses also lacked validity: The categories did not define disorders having predictable symptoms, natural histories, or responses to treatment.

In trying to be flexible, *DSM-II's* diagnostic categories were often vague, idiosyncratic, and susceptible to bias. For example, studies revealed that patients with the same clinical features would receive the more benign diagnosis of manic–depression if they were Caucasian but the more ominous diagnosis of schizophrenia if they were African American. Without objective diagnostic standards, a nosology based on inferred psychological phenomena often said more about the clinician's orientation than about the patient's attributes. In theory, the chief virtue of the psychological approach was that it indicated a disorder's cause, but since the etiologies of most mental disorders were unknown, American psychiatry was moving away from the psychological tradition and returning to Kraepelin.

Additional factors contributed to this descriptive revival and to the emergence of *DSM-III*. Different classes of medications were discovered that alleviated or eliminated symptoms of one disorder but not another. As a result, correct diagnosis became essential for choosing the correct medication. Researchers increasingly applied the same scientific methods (e.g., standardized interviews, double-blind conditions, matched controls, statistical proof) used in other branches of medicine to study mental disorders. Data began to show which mental disorders ran in families, which had predictable life courses, which afflicted various populations, which improved with specific therapies, and so on. To ensure that they were studying patients with similar disorders, researchers devised explicit, readily verifiable, and specific diagnostic criteria, which, after adjustment for clinical purposes, became *DSM-III's* most distinctive innovation.

DSM-IV (1994) and its text revision (TR) in 2000 continued the descriptive approach of *DSM-III* and *DSM-III-R* (1987). Changes in criteria that have occurred with the two revisions since *DSM-III* have been based largely on field testing of diagnostic criteria for validity, reliability, and stability. Each diagnostic manual is a work in progress that incorporates changes based on new information.

INNOVATIONS AND LIMITATIONS OF
DSM-III THROUGH *DSM-IV-TR*

Beginning with *DSM-III*, there were seven major departures from the earlier diagnostic manuals:

1. Whenever possible, *scientific evidence*, not theoretical hypotheses, determines diagnostic categories.

2. A *descriptive* rather than psychological approach is the foundation for diagnosis. Consequently, the *DSM* employs a largely non-etiological framework and a multiple rather than a unitary nosological model.
3. Diagnoses are defined by clearly delineated, objective, and readily verifiable criteria.
4. The diagnostic definitions recognize that most patients with the same mental disorder do not have identical clinical characteristics. Patients usually share one or two core features, but beyond that, have a variety of different symptoms that are all consistent with the disorder. Thus, *DSM* diagnoses often require some core diagnostic criteria, but offer a choice among others.
5. The *DSM* presents multiaxial diagnosis, allowing separate listings for the personality disorders, contributing medical diagnoses, etc.
6. Technical terms are defined.
7. The *DSM* was extensively field-tested prior to publication.

Table 1-1 compares *DSM-II*, *DSM-IV*, and *DSM-5/ICD-10* definitions of what is essentially the same kind of depression: *DSM-II* calls it a "depressive neurosis," *DSM-IV*, a "major depressive disorder," and *DSM-5/ICD-10* a "depressive episode." Whereas *DSM-II* explains the psychological cause of the depression, *DSM-IV* specifies the symptoms of this type of depression and shows how major depression differs from normality (criteria A–C) and from other mental conditions (criteria D–E). *ICD-10* is similarly descriptive with minor differences in symptom criteria. Because *DSM-IV* criteria (e.g., decrease in appetite, insomnia) are relatively objective and explicit, they are far easier for clinicians to identify and agree on; in contrast, *DSM-II*'s inferred psychological mechanisms (e.g., internal conflict) produce a much lower interrater reliability. Whether or not *DSM-IV* criteria for a major depression are optimal or valid can be disputed; yet because they are precise, when a therapist states that a specific patient meets *DSM-IV* criteria for major depressive disorder, clinicians reliably know what is meant.

Despite the exactness of *DSM-IV* criteria, their application still necessitates clinical judgment. For instance, in criterion A for depressive episode how much sleep loss (#4) constitutes "insomnia"? How much diminished interest or pleasure (#2) is "marked"? In practice, as clinicians gain experience, they develop internal norms to answer such questions. In addition, both recent history—for example, two-week requirement in criterion A for an episode—and past history—two or more episodes in criterion A for major depressive disorders, recurrent—are included. *DSM-II* says nothing about time.

TABLE 1-1
Definitions of Depression: DSM-II, DSM-IV, and DSM-5/ICD-10
DSM-II: DEPRESSIVE NEUROSIS

This disorder is manifested by an excessive reaction of depression due to an internal conflict or to an identifiable event such as the loss of a love object [i.e., a person] or cherished possession.

DSM-IV: MAJOR DEPRESSIVE EPISODE

A. Five (or more) of the following symptoms have been present during the same 2-week period and represent a change from previous functioning; at least one of the symptoms is either (1) depressed mood or (2) loss of interest or pleasure. **Note:** Do not include symptoms that are clearly due to a general medical condition, or mood-incongruent delusions or hallucinations.

   (1) depressed mood most of the day, nearly every day, as indicated by either subjective report (e.g., feels sad or empty) or observation made by others (e.g., appears tearful). **Note:** In children and adolescents, can be irritable mood.

   (2) markedly diminished interest or pleasure in all, or almost all, activities most of the day, nearly every day (as indicated by either subjective account or observation made by others)

   (3) significant weight loss or weight gain when not dieting (e.g., a change of more than 5% of body weight in a month), or decrease or increase in appetite nearly every day. Note: In children, consider failure to make expected weight gains.

   (4) insomnia or hypersomnia nearly every day

   (5) psychomotor agitation or retardation nearly every day (observable by others, not merely subjective feelings of restlessness or being slowed down)

   (6) fatigue or loss of energy nearly every day

   (7) feelings of worthlessness or excessive or inappropriate guilt (which may be delusional) nearly every day (not merely self-reproach or guilt about being sick)

   (8) diminished ability to think or concentrate, or indecisiveness, nearly every day (either by subjective account or as observed by others)

   (9) recurrent thoughts of death (not just fear of dying), recurrent suicidal ideation without a specific plan, or a suicide attempt or a specific plan for committing suicide

B. The symptoms do not meet criteria for a Mixed Episode.

C. The symptoms cause clinically significant distress or impairment in social, occupational, or other important areas of functioning.

D. The symptoms are not due to the direct physiological effects of a substance (e.g., a drug of abuse, a medication) or a general medical condition (e.g., hypothyroidism).

E. The symptoms are not better accounted for by Bereavement, i.e., after the loss of a loved one, the symptoms persist for longer than 2 months or are characterized by marked functional impairment, morbid preoccupation with worthlessness, suicidal ideation, psychotic symptoms, or psychomotor retardation.

ICD-10 AND DSM-5: DEPRESSIVE EPISODE

A. **Depressed mood, loss of interest and enjoyment, and increased fatigability** are usually regarded as the most typical symptoms of depression, and **at least 2 of these, plus at least 2 of the other symptoms** should usually be present for a definite diagnosis. **Minimum duration of the whole episode is about 2 weeks** (shorter periods may be reasonable if symptoms are unusually severe and of rapid onset).

TABLE 1-1
Continued

1. depressed mood
2. loss of interest and enjoyment
3. reduced energy leading to increased fatigability (marked tiredness after only slight effort is common)
4. disturbed sleep
5. diminished activity or agitation
6. significant changes in appetite and weight
7. ideas of guilt and unworthiness (even in a mild type of episode)
8. indecision, reduced concentration, and inattention
9. ideas or acts of self-harm or suicide
10. bleak and pessimistic views of the future (*not specified in DSM-5*)
11. reduced self-esteem and self-confidence (*not specified in DSM-5*)

Note: DSM-5 specifies that at least 5 of the first 9 symptoms above have been present during the same 2-week period and represent a change from previous functioning; at least one of the symptoms must be either (1) depressed mood or (2) loss of interest or pleasure.

B. The symptoms result in **significant distress or significant impairment** in personal, family, social, educational, occupational, or other important area of functioning.

C. The disturbance is **not better explained by the direct physiological effects of a substance or another medical condition.**

D. The symptoms **are not better explained by another mental disorder**, particularly psychotic thought disorders such as schizophrenia, delusional disorder, and schizoaffective disorder.

The presence of dementia or mental retardation does not rule out the diagnosis of a treatable depressive episode, but communication difficulties are likely to make it necessary to rely more than usual for the diagnosis upon objectively observed somatic symptoms, such as psychomotor retardation, loss of appetite and weight, and sleep disturbance.

E. The sufferer **must not meet the criteria for a manic, hypomanic, or mixed mood episode**.

Note: From *DSM-II*, p. 40; *DSM-IV*, pp. 327; and adapted from *ICD-10* and *DSM-5*: Depressive episode (p. 100)

In regard to etiology, the *DSM-IV* is largely atheoretical. Except in obvious cases (e.g., "cocaine abuse," "adjustment reaction," "posttraumatic stress"), its diagnostic criteria are free of etiological considerations—be they biological, psychoanalytic, social, or behavioral. In contrast, *DSM-II* requires an internal conflict or major loss to define depressive neurosis.

The *DSM-III*, and revisions through *DSM-IV-TR*, adopted a *multiaxial* system, so that a diagnosis could reflect more than a primary clinical syndrome, such as schizophrenia or phobic disorder. *DSM-IV-TR* uses five axes, as described in Table 1-2. Axes I–III are required; axes IV and V are optional.

TABLE 1-2
Multiaxial Diagnostic System

DIAGNOSTIC AXIS	CONTENT	EXAMPLE
I	Clinical disorders (more acute)	Major depressive disorder, recurrent
	Other conditions that may be a focus of clinical attention	
II	Personality disorders (more enduring)	Obsessive–compulsive personality disorder
III	General medical conditions	Diabetes
IV	Psychosocial and environmental problems	Problems with primary support group; divorce
V	Global Assessment of Functioning (GAF): currently and at highest level the past year	Current GAF: 55 Highest GAF last year: 80

The major reason *DSM-III* introduced *multiaxial* diagnosis was to underscore the distinction between personality disorders and traits from other mental disorders. *Personality*, or *character*, refers to a person's longstanding, deeply ingrained patterns of thinking, feeling, perceiving, and behaving. Everybody has personality *traits*, which are prominent behavioral features and not necessarily psychopathological. In contrast, only some people have *personality disorders*—that is, when personality traits are so excessive, inflexible, and maladaptive that they cause significant distress or impairment. Other mental disorders (Axis I) tend to be more acute, florid, and responsive to treatment than personality disorders (Axis II), which are more chronic, consistent, developmental, and resistant to treatment. When patients manifest both mental and personality disorders, the multiaxial system helps clinicians focus on the diagnostic and therapeutic differences between the disorders.

BACK TO THE FUTURE

Advances in neuroscience have once again prompted the deliberate incorporation of etiology into nosology. The *DSM-5* is a major departure from the more descriptive approach to classifying mental disorders. However, unlike the psychological approach, there is the acknowledgement of neurobiological, social, and other causes of psychopathology. The new direction in classifying mental disorders is reflected in the reduction in number of diagnoses guided by the emerging scientific evidence for lifting artificial boundaries between some disorders and pulling together a spectrum of previously separate disorders. This approach is in contrast to former editions that emphasized "splitting" disorders into multiple separate conditions. Fifty disorders were integrated into 22 new spectra or combined disorders for a net decrease of 28 disorders. So DSM-5 is moving back toward a more unitary rather than the multiple model of classification.

One of the challenges going forward is that most of the evidence on which to guide clinical practice is based on studies using the nosology of previous versions. Fortunately the vast majority of diagnoses are similar in the new DSM. The conceptual changes include:

- Moving toward an etiologically based classification versus clinical consensus and organizing disorders according to a developmental perspective. This is based on evidence from cognitive, behavioral, and neurological science, along with genetics and functional neuroimaging.
- Boundaries between disorders over the life course are more fluid and on a spectrum with dimensional measures that cross traditional diagnostic boundaries.
- Emphasizing less the reliability and more the validity of the diagnostic categories
- Removal of the multiaxial format so that all diagnoses are listed together including the former Axis IV stressors as V, Z, or T codes.

Approaches to validating diagnostic criteria for discrete categorical mental disorders include antecedent evidence (similar genetic markers, family traits, temperament, and environmental exposure), concurrent evidence (similar neural substrates, biomarkers, emotional and cognitive processing, and symptom similarity), and predictive evidence (similar clinical course and treatment response). Until incontrovertible etiological or pathophysiological mechanisms are identified to fully validate specific disorders or disorder spectrums, the most important standard for the DSM-5 criteria will be their clinical utility. The diagnosis of a mental disorder should assist clinicians in determining prognosis, treatment plans, and potential outcomes for their patients.

Despite many advances, DSM-5 and ICD-10 are not diagnostic dogma but *guides*. Remember—before DSM-5 was published, many were already planning the next revision. Controversies rage over whether some of the diagnostic categories describe genuine disorders in people or are nothing more than meaningless labels on paper. This text will provide the more universal *ICD-10* diagnostic criteria and guidelines with reference to how the new *DSM-5* differs. *ICD-11* will be completed within the next few years, in time for the next revision of this book. Any differences between the latest *ICD* and *DSM* classification systems are not based on real differences in neurobiology, genetics, or epidemiology. Rather they represent different preferences and approaches by the separate committees where evidence was scanty or debatable.

Although improved diagnoses have improved treatment planning, they remain insufficient, partly due to their variable validity. Yet, even if totally valid, no psychiatric (or medical) diagnosis would be sufficient by itself to establish the treatment. Other factors must be considered: the patient's ability to introspect, his or her defenses, family relationships, current stressors, compliance with therapy, and so on. Clinical evaluations that ignore such factors in favor of checklists of *DSM* or *ICD* criteria cannot lead to effective treatment plans, because they overlook that it is patients, not diagnoses, who are being treated. There may be substantial differences between two people who receive the same diagnosis and these differences will have a major impact on treatment approaches. It is actually more important to know the person and context than the actual diagnosis. The process of understanding (formulating) the present illness is the primary goal of the clinician—to determine why this diagnosis, why now, why this person. This text certainly stresses diagnosis, but clinical assessment clearly entails much more than a diagnosis.

AN OVERVIEW OF PSYCHIATRIC EPIDEMIOLOGY

Psychiatric epidemiology is the science that studies the frequency and distribution of mental disorders within various populations. By identifying the presence or absence of a mental disorder in a specific group, defined by age, sex, race, socioeconomic class, inpatient status, health, diet, other illnesses, etc., the epidemiologist compiles clues about a disorder's etiology, pathogenesis, prevention, and treatment.

Most often cited are measures of *incidence* and *prevalence*. For a specific time interval and population, incidence refers to the number of *new* cases, whereas *prevalence* refers to the number of *existing* cases. These terms are usually expressed as percentages and calculated as follows:

$$\text{Incidence Rate} = \frac{\text{Number of persons developing the disorder during a period of time}}{\text{Total number of persons at risk}}$$

$$\text{Prevalence} = \frac{\text{Number of persons with the disorder during a period of time}}{\text{Total number of persons in the group}}$$

As an example, if 2,000 new cases of a disorder arise in 1 year in a population of 100,000, the *incidence rate* is 2% (2,000/100,000). *Prevalence* reflects how widespread a disease or disorder is during a specified period of time, which can vary from a moment (called "point prevalence"), to 1 year ("1-year prevalence"), to a lifetime ("lifetime prevalence").

Incidence and prevalence can convey very different pictures of a disorder's frequency. Treatment does not affect incidence (new cases), but it *does* affect prevalence (existing cases). Prevention may reduce incidence (and consequently prevalence). Unlike incidence, prevalence is a factor of a disorder's duration, frequency of recovery, and death rate. That's why acute disorders generally have a higher incidence than point prevalence, whereas it is just the reverse for chronic disorders. For example, if an average person gets three colds per winter, the 6-month incidence rate may be over 90%; however, the point prevalence rate for a cold may only be 20%. For AIDS, a long-lasting illness, the point prevalence rate (existing cases) is much higher than the 6- or 12-month incidence rate (new cases).

The value of an epidemiologic study depends on the sensitivity and specificity of its diagnostic instruments. A test is *sensitive* when it accurately detects the *presence* of a disorder in a person who *has* the disorder. A test is *specific* when it accurately detects the *absence* of a disorder in a person who does *not* have the disorder. Remember when a "handwriting expert" would examine a person's writing and then say, "Underneath you have feelings of insecurity"? Of course he has some feelings of insecurity! Who doesn't? This test demonstrates high sensitivity but low specificity. A test (or the diagnostic criteria) must be sensitive enough to detect the disorder if it is present (so as to avoid many false negative results), but specific enough not to include other disorders (to avoid many false positive results).

	Disorder Present	Disorder Absent
Positive Test or Criterion	A	B
Negative Test or Criterion	C	D

Sensitivity = A/(A + C)
Specificity = D/(B + D)
Positive Predictive Value = A/(A + B)
Negative Predictive Value = D/(C + D)

The frequency of a mental disorder varies enormously, depending on how the disorder is defined, which populations are polled, and which assessment instruments are employed. For instance, pre–*DSM-III*, definition of mental disorders varied so widely that older surveys generated prevalence rates ranging from 11% to 81%.

> More accurate epidemiologic investigations resulted from a major advance in defining mental disorders. Feighner et al. (1972) first listed specific signs and symptoms as diagnostic criteria. Called the "Feighner criteria," they were used primarily by researchers. Adding duration, severity, and life course, Spitzer and colleagues (Spitzer, Williams, & Skodal, 1980) refined Feighner's criteria into the Research Diagnostic Criteria (RDC). These two diagnostic tools led to the more clinically oriented *DSM-III.*
>
> The Feighner and RDC approaches developed *structured interviews* that greatly facilitated data collection. A series of preset, standardized questions systematically determined if the subject met specific diagnostic criteria. Two structured interviews widely applied in research are the "Schedule for Affective Disorders and Schizophrenia" (SADS) and the *DSM-III*-based "Diagnostic Interview Schedule" (DIS).

Using the DIS, researchers from the National Institute of Mental Health (NIMH) interviewed almost 20,000 adults to establish the 1-year and lifetime prevalence of 30 mental disorders (Robins & Regier, 1991). The major concern regarding this project, known as the Epidemiologic Catchment Area (ECA) study, was that it may not have been a true national sample. This concern was addressed in the newer National Comorbidity Survey (NCS) in which 8,098 adults were interviewed to establish 1-year and lifetime prevalences of 17 "common" mental disorders (Kessler et al., 1994). The NCS used *DSM-III-R* diagnoses and an improved version of the DIS that had more thorough lists of symptoms than the ECA. The NCS yielded much higher rates of mental disorders than the ECA. Trained clinicians interviewed a subset of the respondents and found that most of the diagnoses were accurate.

The ECA and NCS reported that mental disorders had affected 20–30% of adult Americans during the preceding year and 32–50% of them throughout life. The primary focus of the ECA and the NCS studies was upon making categorical assessment of mental disorders without regard to severity. To address this limitation, the NCS Replication study (NCS-R) was conducted between 2001 and 2003. The NCS-R surveyed 9,282 respondents 18 years and older from across the United States, using *DSM-IV* criteria, a substan-

TABLE 1-3
Lifetime Prevalence of Mental Disorders in Percentage by Age in Years

MENTAL DISORDERS	ALL AGES*	18–29 YR	30–44 YR	45–49 YR	≥60 YR
Any disorder	**46.4** (26.2)	52.4	55.0	46.5	26.1
Any anxiety Disorder	**28.8** (18.1)	30.2	35.1	30.8	15.3
Panic disorder	**4.7** (2.7)	4.4	5.7	5.9	2.0
Agoraphobia without panic	**1.4** (0.8)	1.1	1.7	1.6	1.0
Specific phobia	**12** (8.7)	13.3	13.9	14.1	7.5
Social phobia	**5** (6.8)	13.6	14.3	12.4	6.6
Generalized anxiety disorder	**5.7** (3.1)	4.1	6.8	7.7	3.6
Posttraumatic stress disorder	**6.8** (3.5)	6.3	8.2	9.2	2.5
Obsessive–compulsive disorder	**1.6** (1.0)	2.0	2.3	1.3	0.7
Separation anxiety disorder	**5.2** (0.9)	5.2	5.1		
Any mood disorder	**20.8** (9.5)	21.4	24.6	22.9	11.9
Major depressive disorder	**16.6** (6.7)	15.4	19.8	18.8	10.6
Dysthymia	**2.5** (1.5)	1.7	2.9	3.7	1.3
Bipolar I–II disorders	**3.9** (2.6)	5.9	4.5	3.5	1.0
Any impulse-control disorder	**24.8** (8.9)	26.8	23.0	—	—
Oppositional-defiant disorder	**8.5** (1.0)	9.5	7.5	—	—
Conduct disorder	**9.5** (1.0)	10.9	8.2	—	—
Attention-deficit/hyperactivity	**8.1** (4.1)	7.8	8.3	—	—
Intermittent explosive disorder	**5.2** (2.6)	7.4	5.7	4.9	1.9
Any substance abuse disorder	**14.6** (3.8)	16.7	18.0	15.3	6.3
Alcohol abuse	**13.2** (3.1)	14.3	16.3	14.0	6.2
Alcohol dependence	**5.4** (1.3)	6.3	6.4	6.0	2.2
Drug abuse	**7.9** (1.4)	10.9	11.9	6.5	0.3
Drug dependence	**3.0** (0.4)	3.9	4.9	2.3	0.2
Two or more disorders	**27.7** (5.8)	33.9	34.0	27.0	11.6

*Twelve-month prevalence in parentheses
Adapted from Kessler et al., 2005a, 2005b

tially expanded interview process, and a broader range of mental disorders. Unfortunately, there is not much epidemiological information about childhood mental disorders and longitudinal studies are needed to understand the association between childhood mental disorders and adult mental disorders (Kessler & Wang, 2008).

Table 1-3 is based on the NCS-R findings and shows the lifetime prevalence of some of the common mental disorders. About 46.4% of respondents in the study had a history of at least one mental disorder. Among the mental disorders, anxiety disorders (28.8%) are the most common, followed by impulse control disorders (24.8%) and mood disorders (20.8%). The most common individual mental disorder was major depressive disorder. There was a general trend of higher prevalence among the middle age groups followed by a decline in the oldest. Of the 12-month prevalence estimates of the NCS-R, 22.3% were classified serious, 37.3% moderate, and 40.4% mild. Among disorder classes, mood disorders had the highest percentage of serious cases (45.0%) and anxiety disorders the lowest (22.8%). That almost half of all Americans suffer or have suffered from some type of mental disorder is startling and underscores the need for all health care professionals to understand the essentials of psychopathology. Most mentally ill patients are treated by non-psychiatrists including general practitioners, internists, nurses, psychologists, social workers, and counselors.

> Because people who have one disorder frequently (about 60% of the time) have two or more disorders (not mutually exclusive), the total percentage for classes of disorders in Table 1-3 is less than the sum of each separate disorder. Having coexisting or multiple diagnoses is referred to as comorbidity or co-occurring disorders. Factors leading to erroneous assumptions of true comorbidity include symptoms arising from the same underlying cause; diagnostic procedures failing to discriminate; diagnostic criteria not discriminating; higher-order pattern of the same diagnostic entity; incorrect placement of the border between the normal and pathological or between disorders (Achenbach, 1991).

References

Achenbach, T. M. (1991). "Comorbidity" in child and adolescent psychiatry: Categorical and quantitative perspectives. *Journal of Child and Adolescent Psychopharmacology, 1,* 271–278.

American Psychiatric Association. (1952). *Diagnostic and statistical manual of mental disorders,* 1st ed. Washington, DC: American Psychiatric Association.

American Psychiatric Association. (1968). *Diagnostic and statistical manual of mental disorders,* 2nd ed. Washington, DC: American Psychiatric Association.

American Psychiatric Association. (1980). *Diagnostic and statistical manual of mental disorders,* 3rd ed. Washington, DC: American Psychiatric Association.

American Psychiatric Association. (1994). *Diagnostic and statistical manual of mental disorders,* 4th ed. Washington, DC: American Psychiatric Association.

American Psychiatric Association. (2000). *Diagnostic and statistical manual of mental disorders,* text rev. Washington, DC: American Psychiatric Association.

American Psychiatric Association. (2013). *Diagnostic and statistical manual of mental disorders,* 5th ed. Arlington, VA: American Psychiatric Association.

Bleuler, E. (1950). *Dementia praecox, or the group of schizophrenias*. New York: International Universities Press. (Original work published 1911)

Burgy, M. (2008). The concept of psychosis: Historical and phenomenological aspects. *Schizophrenia Bulletin, 34*, 1200–1210.

Cooper, J.E., Kendell, R.E., Gurland, B.J., Sharpe, L., Copeland, J.R.M., & Simon, R. (1972). *Psychiatric diagnosis in New York and London*. New York: Oxford University Press.

Feighner, J.P., Robins, E., Guze, S.B., Woodruff, R.A., Winokur, G., & Munoz, R. (1972). Diagnostic criteria for use in psychiatric research. *Archives of General Psychiatry, 26*, 57–63.

Jaspers, K. (1972). *General psychopathology*. Chicago: University of Chicago Press. (Original work published 1923)

Kessler, R.C., Berglund, P., Demler, O., Jin, R., Merikangas, K.R., & Walters, E.E. (2005a). Lifetime prevalence and age-of-onset distributions of DSM-IV disorders in the National Comorbidity Survey Replication. *Archives of General Psychiatry, 62*, 593–602.

Kessler, R.C., Chiu, W.T., Demler, O., & Walters, E.E. (2005b). Prevalence, severity, and comorbidity of 12-month DSM-IV disorders in the National Comorbidity Survey Replication. *Archives of General Psychiatry, 62*, 617–627.

Kessler, R.C., McGonagle, K.A., Ahzo, S., Nelson, C.H., Hughes, M., Eshleman, S., et al. (1994). Lifetime and 12-month prevalence of DSM-III-R psychiatric disorders in the United States: Results from the National Comorbidity Survey. *Archives of General Psychiatry, 51*, 8–19.

Kessler, R.C., & Wang, P.S. (2008). The descriptive epidemiology of commonly occurring mental disorders in the United States. *Annual Review of Public Health, 29*, 115–129.

Kraepelin, E. (1921). *Clinical psychiatry: A text-book for students and physicians*. Translated and adapted from the 7th German Edition by A. Ross Diefendorf. New York: Macmillan. (Original work published 1915)

Robins, L.N., Helzer, J.E., Weissman, M.M., Orvaschel, H., Gruenberg, E., Burke, J.D., et al. (1984). Lifetime prevalence of specific psychiatric disorders in three sites. *Archives of General Psychiatry, 41*, 949–958.

Robins, L.N., & Regier, D.A. (Eds.). (1991). *Psychiatric disorders in America: The Epidemiologic Catchment Area study*. New York: Free Press.

Spitzer, R.L., Williams, J.B.W., & Skodal, A.E. (1980). DSM-III: The major achievements and an overview. *American Journal of Psychiatry, 137*, 151–164.

World Health Organization. (1992). *The ICD-10 classification of mental and behavioural disorders: clinical descriptions and diagnostic guidelines*. Geneva: World Health Organization (WHO).

2

Assessment

Would a patient with severe stomach pain undergo surgery or be given medication without first obtaining an evaluation? Hopefully not. Yet in psychiatry, many patients had chosen and received treatment without being formally assessed or diagnosed. The unitary model of mental illness rendered diagnosis almost academic since there was basically a single recommended treatment—psychoanalytic psychotherapy. If performed at all, assessments blended imperceptibly into psychotherapy. Today, however, the growing number and efficacy of contemporary biological and psychosocial treatments demands that *every* patient must receive a formal diagnostic assessment (evaluation) *before* treatment begins.

Assessment may be defined as *a time-limited, formal process that collects clinical information from many sources in order to reach a diagnosis, to make a prognosis, to render a biopsychosocial formulation, and to determine treatment.* This definition emphasizes that assessment is a specific task that is distinct from therapy. Indeed, some superb therapists are poor diagnosticians, and vice versa. Clinicians continue to reassess patients as treatment proceeds, but the *formal* assessment ends before *formal* treatment begins.

The psychiatric examination provides a cross-section of how the patient is functioning at a given time including his difficulties and symptoms. The interview is a unique kind of social transaction and its technique can only be learned through repeated practice and experience. During the interview the physician should avoid psychiatric jargon. He should begin with the usual courtesy and etiquette of identifying oneself and asking for similar information about the patient. The art of asking the right questions is an important skill. One proceeds from the current and general to more specific areas and issues. The flow of the interview should be logically progressive from less intimate to more intimate subjects. From open-ended questions to more specific close ended questions. At the end of the interview it is wise to ask the patient if there is anything further that he or she would like to discuss or share.

The patient interview is usually the principal source of data, but it is not the only source. Information can be gathered from friends, family, physical examinations, laboratory tests, psychological studies, staff observations, standardized interviews, and brain-imaging techniques. Patient interviews generally require 60- to 90-minute-long sessions, although for patients with impaired concentration, sessions should be shorter and more frequent. Conversely, for healthier outpatients, the initial meeting can even be performed in less than 60 minutes.

The primary objective of these initial interviews is to obtain information that will determine the patient's diagnosis, prognosis, formulation, and treatment. These interviews should also make the patient feel comfortable, foster trust, and develop the expectation that psychiatric treatment will help. With these ingredients for establishing rapport, a therapeutic alliance can begin to form.

How a clinician seeks, selects, and organizes all the facts, figures, and fears that patients present is no easy task. A standard format is essential for mastering this task. Flexibility and following patients' leads are fine but chaos is not. As when learning to play the piano or to dance, students learn the basic formal aspects before improvising. Psychiatric assessment typically consists of eight steps, although the sequence for *conducting* and *reporting* these steps varies to some extent. The steps are (1) obtaining a *history*, (2) evaluating the patient's *mental status*, (3) collecting *auxiliary data*, (4) summarizing *principal findings*, (5) rendering a *diagnosis*, (6) making a *prognosis*, (7) providing a *biopsychosocial formulation*, and (8) determining a *treatment plan*. Table 2-1 outlines these steps and presents a method for reporting the formal assessment.

> Whether oral or written, the report given to the patient should be clear, succinct, and systematic. Although the exhaustively detailed history, or *anamnesis*, is still used in psychoanalysis, most patients will benefit more from a briefer history, since it is more likely to be read. A major challenge in reporting a patient's evaluation is to convey the germane data in the fewest words. Chapter 9 illustrates a recorded assessment.

THE HISTORY

Taking the patient's history begins with eliciting *identifying information* about the patient, followed immediately by his or her *chief complaint* (CC). The identification data include the patient's age, sex, marital status, occupa-

TABLE 2-1
An Outline of the Psychiatric Assessment

I.   HISTORY
   A. Identifying information
   B. Chief complaint
   C. History of present illness
   D. Past psychiatric and developmental history (Table 2-2)
   E. Family psychiatric and medical history
   F. Medical history and physical examination (Figure 2-1)
II. MENTAL STATUS EXAMINATION (Table 2-4)
   A. Behavior (Behaving)
   B. Sensorium—basic cognition, awareness (Sensing)
   C. Emotion (Feeling)
   D. Thought (Thinking)
   E. Perception (Perceiving)
III. AUXILIARY DATA
   A. Interviews with relatives and friends
   B. Complete medical history and physical examination
   C. Laboratory tests (Table 2-3)
   D. Standardized interviews
   E. Psychological tests (Table 2-6)
   F. Brain-imaging studies
IV. SUMMARY OF PRINCIPAL FINDINGS
V.   DIAGNOSES (although *DSM-IV* axes are no longer utilized in the latest nosologies they do assist with organizing the clinician's holistic assessment of the patient)
   A. Axis I: Mental disorder (acute state)
   B. Axis II: Personality disorder (enduring trait)
   C. Axis III: General medical conditions (non-psychiatric)
   D. Axis IV: Psychosocial and environmental problems (stressors)
   E. Axis V: Global Assessment of Functioning (GAF)
VI. PROGNOSIS
VII. BIOPSYCHOSOCIAL FORMULATION (**p**redisposing, **p**recipitating, **p**rovoking, **p**erpetuating, and **p**rotecting factors that provide an understanding of the patient and present illness)
VIII. PLAN
   A. Additional data gathering (e.g., interviews, tests, consultations)
   B. Treatment goals (immediate, short-term, long-range)
   C. Treatment plan (biological, psychological, social, and spiritual treatments)
      1. Immediate management
      2. Short-term interventions
      3. Long-term therapies

tion, religion, race, and if pertinent, nationality, ethnic group, and sexual orientation. The CC is a sentence or two describing the *patient's*, not the therapist's, view of the main problem, preferably in the patient's exact words. If the patient's CC is senseless (e.g., "I need a new dress"), the therapist can add his or her own version of the CC (e.g., the patient hears voices telling her to buy new clothes).

It is generally a good approach to begin your interview by asking some easy direct and non-threatening questions to help put the patient at ease and in some sort of context (name, birthdate, living arrangement, spouse, children, employment, etc.). These are followed by more open-ended, intimate, probing, and personal questions. Perhaps the next question is "so why did you come to the clinic or hospital today?" If the patient is extremely verbose or incoherent it may be necessary to resume more direct and specific questions, but this is not preferable. Of course suggestive or leading questions should be avoided and evasive tactics by the patient when covering certain topics should be noted.

History of Present Illness

The history of the present illness (HPI) consists of the major symptoms, issues, and events that brought the patient to treatment. For each major problem, the HPI chronicles when it began, what initiated or exacerbated it, what escalated or diminished its severity, what problems concurrently existed, what effect it had on the patient's functioning, how the patient tried to resolve it, when it ended, why it ended, and the patient's subjective view of it. When a problem emerged gradually, estimate the time of onset. If the patient has had the same disorder repeatedly, the history should start with the most recent episode. The depth and intensity and persistence of symptoms are elicited.

Any and all "entrances" and "exits"—that is, people or events entering a patient's life (e.g., a newborn) or exiting from it (e.g., a child leaving for college)—are noted. Changes are always important to identify, even ostensibly good ones. For instance, after obtaining a long-desired promotion to vice president of a major corporation, a man became severely depressed—now he bossed his former peers, traveled in a faster social crowd, and faced a wife demanding fur coats.

The therapist should ask why the patient has come for help *now*. A 37-year-old single designer sought treatment for, as she said, "an inferiority complex." When asked why she had come for treatment at this particular time, she answered that a friend suggested it. By pursuing the "Why now?" question, the therapist discovered that the day after the patient's mother had married her fifth husband, the patient had wondered, "What's wrong with me?" That is when the patient had followed the friend's advice to seek help.

The clinician should never assume that the patient's use of a technical term is the same as his or her own: Patients will say *anxiety* but mean *depression, paranoia* but mean *embarrassment, nervousness* but mean *hallucinations*. If a clinician is at all unsure of what a patient means by a word, the patient should be asked to describe it more fully or to give an example.

During intake interviews, clinicians notoriously avoid asking about three immediate and critical issues: (1) drug and alcohol use, (2) suicidal tendencies, and (3) violent or homicidal tendencies. The reasons for this avoidance vary. Without realizing it, a therapist may avoid inquiring about these problems because, if they do exist, the therapist might not know how to intervene—it's "safer" not to ask in the first place! A therapist may also fear that such questions would embarrass the patient. This embarrassment, however, is the therapist's more than the patient's. Most patients expect clinicians to ask "embarrassing" questions—it's the clinician's job—and if the clinician doesn't, some patients will feel that the clinician is being slipshod or not taking their case seriously. In any event, tactfully posed questions rarely offend patients.

Be sure to ask about present and past use/abuse of alcohol, drugs, and prescription medications. Don't assume that the middle-class suburban homemaker in front of you would never use all those terrible substances. Anyone can. Regarding prescription drugs, an easy question is, "Have you ever used more than the amount prescribed?" Obtain drug names, amount, duration used, and frequency, ask about use of IV drugs, whether needles were shared, and finally, complications and problems related to drug/alcohol use, such as periods of abstinence/sobriety, withdrawal symptoms, lost jobs, and so on. Many patients with alcohol problems, when asked if they are alcoholic, respond with "No, I only drink beer," or "No, I only get drunk on weekends." A careful, compassionate approach works best.

Suicide must be evaluated, or at least considered, with *every* patient. Suicide is the 11th leading cause of death in the United States, but among youth it has become tied with cancer as the 2nd most frequent cause of death. More people die from suicide than from homicide. Officially, about 30,000 Americans kill themselves each year, but suicide is underreported. If there is any question of suicide, the clinician *must* ask. The questions can be posed in a progressive manner, starting with passive suicidal ideation: "Have you ever felt that you would be better off dead, that if you died tomorrow, it wouldn't matter?" If the answer is yes, then active suicidal ideation can be determined by inquiring, "Have you thought about harming or perhaps killing yourself?" Questioning patients about committing suicide does *not* make people commit suicide or "introduce suicidal thoughts into their head." A patient who has been depressed, miserable, anxious, and without sleep, when asked, "Have you considered suicide?" will not respond, "Gosh, doctor, that's a good idea, I never thought of that. Thanks for the suggestion." Most potentially suicidal patients are relieved when a therapist raises the subject. Contrary to myth, people who talk about suicide *do* commit suicide. Because 80% of those who killed themselves previously mentioned their problem to somebody, clinicians should take these patients seriously.

The risk of suicide escalates as the patient's suicidal *thoughts* intensify and become more frequent. Almost everyone has had fleeting suicidal thoughts; only the suicidal ruminate about it. More dangerous is when the patient has a *plan*, especially if he or she has settled on one plan, can detail it, and has begun implementing it. People who *attempt* suicide are more likely to commit suicide; the more serious the past attempt, the greater the risk of eventual suicide. A patient is at greater risk of suicide if a past attempt involved a more lethal (in the patient's, not the clinician's, mind) method, occurred after long planning rather than impulsively, did not allow much chance of discovery afterward, and was not prefaced by a signal for help.

Almost 95% of patients who attempt or commit suicide suffer from a mental disorder: 80% of them have depression, 10% have schizophrenia, and 5% have delirium. Alcohol, especially in conjunction with depression, increases the rate of death; 15% of alcoholics commit suicide. Patients abusing drugs also kill themselves; the frequency depends on the specific drug, with IV use being especially high. Hopelessness is an experience common to many with mental disorders. Significant hopelessness is a strong predictor of ultimate suicide (Beck, Brown, Berchick, Stewart, & Steer, 1990). Asking about whether the patient has any future plans may be helpful in assessing the degree of hopelessness.

The suicide rate is greatest for men over 45 and for those between the ages of 15 and 24. Although females engage in three times more suicide attempts, men are four times more likely to complete suicide. Gun availability certainly helps; firearms kill 66% of U.S. teens versus 6% in Great Britain. The major risk factors for suicide are being male, older, unemployed, unmarried, living alone, having a chronic illness, substance abuse, and at least one major psychiatric diagnosis. Additional risk factors include a threatened financial loss, an absence of any religious affiliation, a recent loss or death (a particularly high risk factor for alcoholics), a family history of suicide, and suddenly giving away prized possessions (Motto, Heilbron, & Juster, 1985). One can remember the risk factors for suicide with the mnemonic "**SAD PERSONS**." The letters stand for **S**ex (male gender), **A**ge (older), **D**epression, **P**revious suicide attempt, **E**thanol abuse, **R**ational thinking loss (psychotic), **S**ocial supports (lacking), **O**rganized plan, **N**o spouse, and **S**ickness (chronic medical illness).

Menninger (1938) observed that patients who commit suicide do so from three, not one, possible wishes: the wish to die, the wish to kill, and the wish to be killed. Many people might want to die, yet few are prepared to kill, and even fewer, to be killed; the latter two require a degree of violence, anger, and physical pain that only the "truly" suicidal could endure. Impulsive and angry people who are depressed have a higher risk for suicide and homicide.

Knowing all of these risk factors only tells you the statistical risk of suicide in the future. They can help predict the chances of suicide in the next year or two, but won't necessarily tell you what this particular patient will do in the next few days or week. Two more personal questions can help. Assuming that the patient hasn't recently made an attempt, ask, "You have been feeling suicidal, but you haven't acted on it—what stopped you?" Answers that suggest low risk include, "I'm a mother, and I would never leave my children with a legacy of suicide. I could never do that," or "My religious beliefs [or values] would never let me commit suicide. I don't believe in it." A high-risk answer would be something to the effect of, "So far, I've been chicken, but I'm working up the courage." A second helpful question to ask is, "Why do you want to live?" Patients who are trying to conceal their suicidal feelings often can deny feeling suicidal but have a harder time making up believable reasons for living. They might say, "Because my parents don't want me to kill myself" (a high-risk answer) instead of, "I'm smart and kind. I want to see what I can do to help people" (a lower-risk answer).

The presence of violent tendencies in a patient must always be evaluated. Never assume that the mild-mannered "Clark Kent" patient in front of you would not hurt a fly. Asking, "How do you handle your anger?" is a benign introductory probe that then can be followed with, "Have you ever broken things or hurt others when you were angry?" Violent tendencies tend to be expressed via two broad patterns: ongoing suppression or repression punctuated by sudden eruptions; and routine, regular outbursts of anger and destructive behavior. Some individuals are regularly violent toward a certain person or persons (such as a spouse), but to no one else and are probably safe on voluntary inpatient units.

The history of the present illness often ends with ascertaining "significant negatives"—those symptoms, issues, experiences, or events that have *not* occurred, even though they frequently accompany problems like those of the patient. For example, significant negatives for a severely depressed patient might include a denial of suicidal thoughts, the absence of recent losses, an unchanged libido, and no family history of bipolar disorder. When significant negatives are omitted from the report, other professionals cannot tell whether these negatives are truly absent or the interviewer simply forgot to ask about them.

Past Psychiatric History

The developmental history can be integrated with past psychiatric history (PH) or social history or presented separately (whichever is clearer.) The PH describes previous episodes in the patient's life that resemble or differ from the current episode, including each episode's duration, treatment, and outcome. The PH presents the patient's longstanding personality traits and characteristic ways of dealing with problems. In setting treatment goals, it helps to determine the patient's highest level of functioning during his or her life *and* during the past year. The patient's level of functioning prior to the onset of the current episode is sometimes called *baseline functioning* and is an important reference point in deciding if the patient is better (i.e., back to normal for him or her).

Social and Developmental History

The social history can begin with the present by elaborating on "identifying information." It should include information on the present family situation, residential setting, occupation, and financial status. Although an exhaustive developmental history is usually unnecessary, it is valuable to cover the highlights, especially when they illuminate the present illness. Table 2-2 lists possible topics in the developmental history, though it is not a comprehensive outline. Two quick ways to elicit critical information are to ask the patient (1) to name the three or four crucial turning points in his or her life, and (2) to describe the most significant or memorable event during each developmental period.

It is also important to ask if there is a history of physical, sexual, or emotional *abuse*. If there is, do not assume that the patient is devastated. A majority of people who have been abused function normally as adults. Also do not assume that questions about abuse will somehow damage the patient. The questioner's level of comfort with these questions is often the key to establishing rapport. Ask the patient in a gentle, accepting way. For example, "Many people with emotional problems were abused as children and as adults. Has that happened to you?" If the patient becomes very hesitant, she or he can be told, "Does talking about this right now make you too uncomfortable? You don't have to talk about it right now. You can wait until you feel ready."

TABLE 2-2
The Developmental History

I. PRENATAL
—Pregnancy: Planned? Desired?
—Health of mother
—Complications during pregnancy and birth
—Full-term?

II. INFANCY to ADOLESCENCE
—Physical illnesses
—Temperament (especially compared to siblings and social attachments): Shy? Friends? Family Relations?
—Developmental milestones: Walking, talking, toilet training, reading, grades, menstruation, puberty?
—Education: Furthest grade level completed? Learning problems? Skipped or repeated a grade?
—Family: Stable? Abusive? Neglectful?
—Physical, emotional, or physical abuse? Bullying?
—Earliest and most vivid memories?
—Symptoms or phobias: Enuresis? Nightmares? Cruelty to animals? Fire-setting? Oppositional behavior?
—Drug or alcohol misuse? Identity problems?
—Sexuality and gender identity: Orientation? Development?

III. EARLY and MIDDLE ADULTHOOD
—Occupations: First job? Dates of each job? Repeated performance patterns? Likes and dislikes? Work
disabilities? Discrepancies between ability, education, and present work? Ambitious? Current job and
economic circumstances?
—Military service: Combat experience? Type of discharge? Disability benefits?
—Social: Dating? Recreation? Activities?
—Family of origin: Separated from? If so, when and how? If not, why not? Feelings toward them?
—Marriage: When? Why? How many? Quality of relationship? Quality of sex life? Money—who manages it?
Disputes over? "Faithfulness"? Divorce?
—Children: Dates of miscarriages, including abortions; names, dates of birth, personalities of, and feelings
toward, children?
—Religion: Its effect, if any, on the patient? Conversion? Exacerbates or alleviates psychiatric problems?
Spiritual beliefs?
—Legal problems: Previous arrests, current charges, felonies, prison term?
—Standards: Moral, political, social, atheistic, ethical?

IV. LATE ADULTHOOD
—The "seven losses": How the person prepares for, adapts to, or surmounts each of them:
(a) loss of work (unemployment)
(b) loss of financial security (insecurity)
(c) loss of familiar surroundings, including home and community (dislocation)
(d) loss of physical health and ability to function (incapacitation)
(e) loss of mental abilities (incompetence)
(f) loss of people, especially spouse (isolation)
(g) loss of life (death)

Note. This table suggests topics for inquiry; it is not a comprehensive outline of development.

Family History

Some clinicians prefer to put information about family functioning in the social developmental history and reserve the category of family history (FH) for family psychiatric problems.

In modern psychopathology all data regarding a family history of mental disorders is of great importance. Special emphasis should be placed on first-degree relatives. Ask about the past presence of alcoholism, drug abuse, antisocial behavior, depression, schizophrenia, "nervous breakdowns," suicide, and psychiatric treatment. Because diagnoses by professionals (especially before 1980) were based on different criteria from those in our current nosology, and because laypeople do not employ diagnostic terms in the way professionals do, therapists should place little weight on diagnoses ascribed to family members and rely more on the ill relative's objective characteristics (such as speaking incoherently or being hospitalized). In general, patients underreport psychiatric diagnoses in family members (Andreasen et al., 1986). A family member with major depressive disorder or generalized anxiety disorder is more likely to report the same disorder in relatives than a member who does not have this diagnosis (Kendler et al., 1991). Since response to medication is genetically transmitted, to some extent, if a mentally ill relative received medication, the clinician should inquire about the type, duration, and results.

Through a *genogram* (McGoldrick & Gerson, 1985) or a traditional narrative, the clinician indicates the "dramatis personae" and how they are related, employed, and involved with the patient. A full genogram can be quite time-consuming and may not be completed on the initial interview. The FH specifies with whom in the family the patient lives (if anyone), who the patient sees the most, trusts the most, and depends on the most in a crisis. A description of routine family functioning may include information about who plays which roles in the family, who manages the money, who sets the day-to-day rules, and who makes decisions. Family snapshots are valuable as much for how they are selected and discussed as for what they portray. Then, considering the family as a system—that is, as a totality in which each member's actions affect all others—how does the patient normally perpetuate or try to alter the family patterns, and how does the family as a whole contend with crises?

The FH documents how the patient's family members have influenced and been influenced by the patient's illness. The clinician's opinion about these influences is reported in the biopsychosocial formulation; only the opinions of relatives, whether "correct" or not, are reported here. How relatives (or friends) have tried to solve the patient's difficulties should also be mentioned.

In gathering the FH, the clinician should note if information from family members varies depending on whether the patient is present. Although the clinician should never assume that one family member speaks for all, many families will present a united front, unless the therapist explicitly asks each member to state his or her own view of the problem. Finally, psychiatric crises are highly traumatic for family members; avoid drawing derogatory conclusions about family members' typical behavior based on how they act during a crisis.

The Medical Assessment

The medical assessment consists of the patient's medical history, a physical examination, and laboratory tests (Table 2-3). The chief goals of this stage of psychiatric evaluation are (1) to detect medical causes for psychiatric symptoms, (2) to identify physical states that may alter how psychiatric medications are prescribed, (3) to discover previously undiagnosed medical diseases (which are disproportionately high among psychiatric patients), (4) to alert therapists to substance abuse, and (5) to monitor blood levels of various psychotropic agents.

Most internists agree that there is no such thing as a "routine" lab test. Too often they are ordered on a "you never know what might be wrong and anyway the patient has a good lawyer" basis. Clinical judgment, not a standard checklist, should determine which tests are ordered. The only consistently underutilized tests in psychiatry are urine drug screens (which need to be obtained within 48 hours of ingestion of most drugs in order to be effective). High blood levels in patients who are mildly intoxicated indicate drug tolerance. In a young, well-nourished adult who has no health complaints or risk factors, none of the other lab tests should be regarded as routine. The gamma-glutamyl transferase (GGT) is the most sensitive of liver function tests and can detect early signs of alcoholism. However, it is often *too* sensitive, detecting something abnormal when nothing is wrong. Careful interviewing about alcoholism has been shown to detect this disease more efficiently than any lab test. Furthermore, lab tests should be ordered on the basis of presumed diagnosis. For example, a patient with significant unexplained anxiety may need to be evaluated for hyperthyroidism; an elderly depressed patient who is eating poorly might be evaluated for malnutrition.

Whether the medical assessment should be done by the patient's psychiatrist or family physician depends on several factors, one being who is the

TABLE 2-3
Laboratory Tests for Psychiatric Assessment

A. Frequently ordered screening tests:
1. Complete blood count
2. Urinalysis (protein, glucose, microscopic exam for bacteria, blood cells)
3. Electrolytes (sodium, potassium, bicarbonate, chloride, phosphate, calcium, and glucose)
4. Hepatic and renal function tests
5. Lipid Profile (cholesterol and triglycerides)
6. Serum albumin, total protein (nutritional status)
7. Thyroid function tests (T-4 and TSH)
8. Hemoglobin A1C
9. Glucose Tolerance Testing
10. B-12 and folate levels (geriatric patients)
11. Vitamin D levels
12. Toxicology screens of urine, blood, or saliva (drugs, heavy metals, or toxins)
13. Urine pregnancy test (beta HCG)
14. Estrogen and Testosterone levels

B. Relatively inexpensive, low-yield tests:
1. Sedimentation rate (Westergren)
2. Skin testing (for infectious diseases)
3. Stools for occult blood
4. Electrocardiograms (EKG)
5. Chest and skull x-rays
6. FTA-ABS (98% sensitivity) or MHA-TP (95% sensitivity) for neurosyphilis

C. With evidence of cognitive or neurological disorders:
1. Electroencephalogram (EEG)
2. Head Magnetic Resonance Imaging (MRI) or Computerized Tomography (CT) scans
3. Lumbar puncture for cerebrospinal fluid (CSF) evaluation
4. HIV testing

D. Serum levels of psychotropic drugs (e.g., lithium and valproic acid)

most qualified to perform it. In most cases, the family practitioner or internist is the first choice. All psychiatric inpatients are required to receive a complete medical assessment, but whether all outpatients should receive one remains controversial. Commonly used guidelines for requesting a medical assessment are: any patient with signs of cognitive impairment (see Chapter 10), psychosis, or incapacitation; all patients over the age of 50 should have a medical examination once a year; those under 50, every 3–5 years. Clinicians of mental- and medical-health disciplines may wish to have all new patients fill out a questionnaire, such as the "Medical–Psychiatric History Form" (Figure 2-1).

FIGURE 2-1
Medical–Psychiatric History Form

Instructions: Please complete this form and return it to your therapist at your next appointment. By doing so, you will provide important diagnostic information while freeing up time with your therapist for other matters. If you are unsure about a question or are unable to answer it, don't worry about it: Simply place a question mark ("?") next to it and move on. Everything you indicate will be held in the strictest confidence.

PATIENT DATA

Name _____ Today's date _____

Street address _____

City _____ State _____ Zip _____

Telephone <home> _____ <work> _____

Business street address _____

City _____ State _____ Zip _____

Occupation _____ Age _____ Birth date _____

Person to contact in case of emergency: Name _____

Relation _____ Telephone _____

City _____ State _____ Zip _____

MEDICAL HISTORY

Your physician's name _____

Street address _____ City _____

State _____ Zip _____ Telephone (   ) _____

Are you allergic to any drugs? Yes (   ) No (   ). If so, to which ones:

_____

Do you have any other allergies? Yes (   ) No (   ). If so, to what:

_____

Are you pregnant? Yes (   ) No (   ). Do you smoke? Yes (   ) No (   ).

When was your last EKG? _____ Was it normal? Yes (   ) No (   ).

When did your physician last examine you?_____

Have you been treated for any of the following:

AIDS, or acquired immune deficiency syndrome, or HIV positive (   )

Alcohol abuse (   ), alcoholism (   )

Anemia (   )

Asthma (   ), hay fever (   )

Cancer (   )

Diabetes (   )

Drug abuse or addiction (   )

Epilepsy, seizures, or convulsions (   )

Fainting spells, lightheadedness, or dizziness (   )

Gastrointestinal problems (   )

Glaucoma (   )

Heart murmur or disease (   )

Hepatitis, liver disease, or jaundice (   )

High blood pressure [hypertension] (   )

Kidney disease (   )

Lung disease, pneumonia (   )

Migraine (   )

Rheumatic fever (   )

Serious injury or accident (   )

Stroke (   )

Thyroid problems (   )

Tuberculosis (TB) (   )

Ulcer (   )

Uncontrolled bleeding (   )

Venereal disease (   )

Other (   ) If so, what?

FIGURE 2-1
Medical–Psychiatric History Form (continued)

Please list any (prescription or over-the-counter) medication that you are currently taking and reason.

_____

_____

Please list any street drugs that you have taken in the past.

_____

_____

Have you ever been treated for a psychiatric illness such as anxiety, depression, insomnia, mania, psychosis? Yes ( ) No ( )

If yes, what were you treated for? _____ Who treated you (name and address)?

_____

Have you ever taken any psychiatric medication? Yes ( ) No ( ) If yes, please list them.

_____

Hospitalization: List all your hospitalizations both medical and psychiatric.

Type of Illness/Operation	Hospital	Year

Alcohol use? _____ How many days per month? _____ Average amount in a day? _____

Have people ever annoyed you by criticizing your drinking? _____

Have you ever felt bad or guilty about your drinking? _____

Have you ever tried to cut down on your drinking? _____

Have you ever had a drink first thing in the morning to steady your nerves or get rid of a hangover?

_____

Smoking? _____ How much per day? _____

Age began smoking? _____ Age stopped smoking? _____

Usual weight? _____ lbs. Recent loss or gain? _____ Weight at age 20 _____

Average hours of sleep at night?_____

SYMPTOM LIST

PLACE A CHECK (✓) in front of any of the following that are, or have been, a problem for you. DOUBLE CHECK (✓✓) the main problems for you.

_____ Rashes, color change

_____ Itching

_____ Warts, moles

_____ Eczema, lumps, hives

_____ Very dry skin

_____ Excessive sweating

_____ Excessive Bleeding or bruising

_____ Anemia

_____ Lymph node or gland swelling

_____ Ear trouble, infection

_____ Hearing loss, ringing in your ears

_____ Eye problems

_____ Nosebleeds

_____ Stuffy nose, sinus trouble, hay fever

_____ Sore throats

_____ Hoarseness

_____ Dental or gum problems

FIGURE 2-1

Medical–Psychiatric History Form (continued)

_____ Enlarged or painful breasts
_____ Breast lumps
_____ Discharge from nipples
_____ Shortness of breath
_____ Cough, chest colds
_____ Bringing up sputum or blood
_____ Wheezing, asthma
_____ Chest pain, pleurisy
_____ TB or exposure to TB
_____ Fever, sweats, chills
_____ Pneumonia
_____ Chest pain, tightness, pressure
_____ Fast or irregular heartbeat
_____ Trouble breathing when lying down
_____ Waking short of breath
_____ Swelling of feet or ankles
_____ Previous heart trouble
_____ Murmurs or rheumatic fever
_____ High blood pressure
_____ Poor circulation, varicose veins
_____ Blood clots
_____ Pain or burning on urinating
_____ Trouble starting or stopping urine
_____ Blood or pus in urine
_____ Frequent urinating
_____ Waking to urinate (# times/night___)
_____ Sores or discharge
_____ Gonorrhea or syphilis
_____ Trouble swallowing
_____ Poor appetite

_____ Gas, cramps, pains
_____ Heartburn, indigestion
_____ Nausea, vomiting
_____ Constipation, diarrhea
_____ Blood in stool or black stool
_____ Yellow jaundice, hepatitis
_____ Hemorrhoids
_____ Gall bladder problems
_____ Hernia
_____ Pains in joints, arthritis
_____ Swollen joints
_____ Back pain, neck pain
_____ Head injury, concussion
_____ Headaches
_____ Dizziness, fainting
_____ Convulsions, seizures, fits
_____ Shaking, tremor
_____ Weakness, paralysis
_____ Numbness, tingling
_____ Difficulty walking, coordination
_____ Depression, anxiety
_____ Poor sleeping
_____ Nervousness, tension
_____ Trouble thinking, remembering
_____ Crying, upset, worrying
_____ Sexual problems
_____ Cancer
_____ Diabetes
_____ Goiter, thyroid problem

FOR WOMEN ONLY:
_____ Irregular or frequent periods
_____ Very heavy periods
_____ Spotting between periods
Age your first period started _____
Number of days between periods _____
Number of pregnancies _____
Living children _____
Number of miscarriages _____ abortions _____

_____ Painful periods
_____ Vaginal discharge or itching

Date of last period_____
Date of last cancer smear (PAP)_____
Did your mother take any hormones while she
     was pregnant with you? Yes ( ) No ( )
Don't know ( )

THE MENTAL STATUS EXAMINATION

The mental status examination (MSE) describes the patient's behavior, sensorium, emotions, thought, and perception. Perhaps the term *psychological status* would more aptly describe this part of the evaluation. Whereas the psychiatric history is a *subjective* account given by the *patient* about *past* events that *have not been witnessed* by the therapist, the MSE is an *objective* report of the patient's *current* mental state as *observed* by the therapist. Although history of the patient can usually be reconstituted at future times, the MSE provides a profile of the patient that can be obtained only in the present moment. Because it is collected firsthand, the MSE is the most reliable part of the assessment; consequently, *every* patient's mental status must be ascertained.

The mental status exam (Figure 2-2) is a relatively standardized approach and set of inquiries to assess psychological status. There is not a single perfect method and different approaches can be taken at different times and situations. The mental status exam outline (Table 2-4) is primarily a way of organizing the cross-sectional data and suggests areas to investigate. It does not represent the exact order in which the examiner elicits the information. Table 2-5 provides sample documentation of the Mental Status Exam.

There are two elements of the MSE: *informal* and *formal*. Clinicians gather the informal MSE while taking a history; for most patients, these observations may be sufficient to get an accurate picture of the psychological status. It is difficult and even undesirable to separate the medical and psychiatric history in strict fashion from the mental status. To his or her informal observations, the clinician adds a series of standardized questions that assess memory, thought processes, attention span, and so on. These are part of the *formal* MSE and are particularly important for those patients with suspected cognitive or perceptual abnormalities as found in neurocognitive, psychotic, and substance use disorders.

In reporting a MSE the clinician should present concrete illustrations to justify every conclusion. It is not sufficient to state that a patient is delusional; report the content of the delusions: "The patient is convinced that penguins read his mind." Saying that a patient has a depressed mood is a conclusion and, as such, requires experienced substantiation: "The patient moved slowly, cried throughout the interview, and never laughed. The patient also said that he felt sad most of the time." The description of this forlorn patient involves several of the MSE categories including "Appearance," "Activity," "Speech," "Affect," "Mood," and "Thought Content." These observations provide evidence of psychiatric signs and symptoms to support

FIGURE 2-2
Mental Status Exam Form

Patient Name: _____ Age: _____
Clinic Location: _____
Living and Employment Situation: _____

BEHAVIOR	**A**ppearance	☐ Well-groomed ☐ Unkempt or Disheveled ☐ Appears Older/Younger ☐ Obese/Thin ☐ Bizarre Dress ☐ Excessive Makeup ☐ Other (describe):
	Activity	☐ Normal ☐ Psychomotor slowing ☐ Agitated or Restless ☐ Abnormal Movements ☐ Abnormal Posture ☐ Odd Mannerisms ☐ Hyperactive or Impulsive ☐ Other (describe):
	Attitude	☐ Cooperative ☐ Friendly ☐ Candid or Frank ☐ Defensive or Guarded ☐ Eye Contact ☐ Negative or Hostile ☐ Withdrawn or Evasive ☐ Dramatic or Seductive ☐ Other (describe):
	Articulation (Speech)	☐ Normal rate, rhythm, volume ☐ Spontaneous/Impoverished ☐ Slow or Deliberate ☐ Loud/Soft ☐ Pressured ☐ Poorly Articulated ☐ Response Latency ☐ Stilted ☐ Monotonous or Without Prosody ☐ Other (describe):
SENSORIUM	**C**onsciousness	☐ Alert ☐ Drowsy ☐ Lethargic ☐ Obtunded ☐ Fluctuating ☐ Other:
	Orientation	☐ Person ☐ Place ☐ Date and Time ☐ Situation
	Memory	☐ Registration ☐ Immediate ☐ Recent ☐ Remote
	Attention/Concentration	☐ Adequate ☐ Impaired ☐ Other (describe):
EMOTION	Affect	☐ Comfortable and Reactive ☐ Normal Range (broad) ☐ Flat/Blunted/Constricted ☐ Bright ☐ Smiling ☐ Angry ☐ Anxious or worried ☐ Tearful ☐ Pained ☐ Labile ☐ Other (describe):
	Mood	☐ Euthymic ☐ Elevated ☐ Euphoric ☐ Expansive ☐ Dysphoric ☐ Other (describe):
	Congruency	☐ Congruent ☐ Incongruent ☐ Inappropriate
	Suicidal ideation	☐ None ☐ Passive ☐ Active ☐ Active with Plan ☐ Active with Plan and Intent ☐ Hopeless ☐ Future Plans
	Homicidal ideation	☐ None ☐ Passive ☐ Active ☐ Active with Plan ☐ Active with Plan and Intent
THOUGHT	Thought Process	☐ Goal-directed ☐ Logical and Relevant ☐ Neologisms ☐ Paucity of Ideas ☐ Blocking ☐ Racing Thoughts ☐ Circumstantial/Tangential ☐ Flight of Ideas ☐ Loosened Associations ☐ Disorganized ☐ Incoherent ☐ Other (describe):
	Thought Content	☐ No unusual or disturbing thoughts ☐ Delusional Ideas of Reference ☐ Fearful ☐ Obsessive ☐ Autistic or Idiosyncratic ☐ Other:
	Intelligence	☐ Average ☐ Above Average ☐ Below Average
	Insight	☐ Full ☐ Intellectual Recognition ☐ Some Awareness ☐ Minimal ☐ Denial
	Judgment	☐ Intact ☐ Questionable ☐ Compromised
PERCEPTION		☐ Normal, not responding to internal stimuli ☐ Hallucinations: ☐ Auditory ☐ Visual ☐ Tactile ☐ Olfactory ☐ Gustatory ☐ Illusions ☐ Depersonalization ☐ Derealization ☐ Déjà vu / Jamais vu

Clinician: _____ Date: _____

TABLE 2-4
Mental Status Examination

A. Behavior (**Behaving**)
   1. Appearance
   2. Activity (including impulse control, psychomotor activity)
   3. Attitude (relating to the examiner, eye contact)
   4. Articulation (Speech)
B. Sensorium—basic cognition, awareness (**Sensing**)
   1. Consciousness
   2. Orientation (person, place, time, situation)
   3. Memory (registration, immediate, recent, remote)
   4. Attention/Concentration
C. Emotion (**Feeling**)
   1. Affect (type and lability)
   2. Mood (including suicidal/homicidal ideation, plan, or intent)
   3. Congruency (appropriateness to expressed thought content and/or mood)
D. Thought (**Thinking**)
   1. Thought process/form
      a. Word usage/language
      b. Stream of thought (production and quantity of thoughts)
      c. Continuity (association of thoughts)
   2. Thought Content
      a. Relationship to reality (delusions)
      b. Concept Formation (abstractability)
   3. Intelligence and information
      a. Simple calculation
      b. Fund of knowledge (current events, geography)
   4. Insight and Judgment
E. Perception (**Perceiving**)
   1. Hallucinations
   2. Illusions
   3. Depersonalization/Derealization

the clinician's impression for the existence and kind of psychopathology. It is important that they are recorded in a well-organized, coherent, and clear manner. The MSE records only observed behavior, sensorium, emotions, cognitions, and perceptions expressed during the interview (not collateral information). It is written in the present tense.

This chapter presents much of the language of psychopathology. Although technical terms do give professionals a shorthand for communication, they can also be abused. Jargon can mislead one into a false sense of knowledge and expertise. To know the definition of catatonia does not mean

TABLE 2-5
Sample Mental Status Exam Documentation

The patient is well-groomed with appropriate and casual dress. Body habit is thin and without dysmorphic features or abnormal movements. The patient **appearance** is consistent with stated age. There is no psychomotor agitation (**activity**). Patient is cooperative with the interview, is forthcoming with responses, and establishes good eye contact (**attitude**). Speech is clearly **articulated** with a regular rate, rhythm and volume. Patient is alert (**consciousness)** and fully **oriented** to person, place, situation, and date/time, with intact **memory** and adequate **attention** throughout the session. Patient registers and recalls 3/3 objects at 5 minutes. Patient is able to spell name forward and backward without difficulty. **Affect** is comfortable and consistent (**congruent**) with both thought content and a reported stable **mood** of 5/10, without **suicidal or homicidal ideation**, plan, or intent. **Thought process** is without flight of ideas, racing thoughts, or loosening of associations. **Thought content** is without obvious delusions or obsessions. Patient correctly identifies the last three presidents and performs simple change exactly to $3.68. Patient is able to provide an abstract proverb interpretation. Three wishes expressed are (***). **Intelligence** is considered normal based upon fund of knowledge, comprehension, and vocabulary. **Insight** is minimal and **judgment** is grossly intact to real life and hypothetical situations. No hallucinations or other **perceptual** abnormalities are evident.

Note: The MSE summary paragraph is always written in the present tense. It is useful to collect the data and report it using the same outline for organizing the mental status exam.

that the clinician knows anything else about catatonia. In reporting the assessment, descriptions in easily understood and common language are often more informative and less ambiguous than professional terminology.

At the same time, technical terms are not mere words; they also represent concepts, and so when terms are used carelessly, concepts get muddled. For instance, when clinicians interchange the terms "shame" and "guilt," they're missing an important conceptual distinction: Shame is an *interpersonal* phenomenon involving embarrassment; guilt is an *intrapsychic* phenomenon involving the violation of one's conscience or superego. Given this different focus, when clinicians overlook this distinction, assessment and treatment suffer. As Wittgenstein (1958) observed, "Philosophical problems arise when language goes on a holiday" (p. 3).

Once acquired, a professional vocabulary can shape how a professional thinks. That is to be expected—and cautioned against as well. Terms become mental categories, and being human, clinicians will fit their observations into these categories and tend to adjust their observations when they don't quite fit. With a clinical vocabulary, one is more likely to see the world *solely* through the lens of psychopathology. People no longer forget things, they "repress" them; shy persons are now "schizoid"; people aren't even people—

they're "objects." The dangers far exceed the rudeness of "psychobabble" and "psychoanalyzing" everybody: To view people only in terms of their psychopathology is to ignore all their other qualities—and that is not only bad manners, it's bad psychiatry. Clinicians do not treat psychopathology, but *people* with psychopathology.

Behavior

Appearance

This section of the MSE reports how the patient looks: physical characteristics (stigmata), apparent age, posture, bearing, peculiarity of dress (attire), grooming, cleanliness (hygiene), use of cosmetics. Clothes are a type of language; what people wear is a form of communication. "Palm reading" may reveal if the patient is frail, a hard laborer, or a nail-biter. Shaking hands with the patient at the outset of the interview does more than convey respect: It provides data. Is the patient's handshake crushing, firm, or weak? Are the palms sweaty? Are the hands rough or smooth?

Activity

This category on behavior refers to the patient's motor activity: gait, gestures, mannerisms, impulse control, stereotypies, and other muscular movements such as tremors, twitches, or tics. Psychomotor agitation and retardation, including extreme manifestations such as catatonia, are described here. Problems with impulse control refer to how the patient handles immediate aggressive, sexual, and suicidal wishes. If difficulties with impulse control arise during the interview (as opposed to only being reported in the history), they also should be reported here. Examples: A patient smashes the clinician's desktop with a fist when the interview is interrupted by a telephone call; a patient dashes from the office on hearing a distressing comment.

> *Psychomotor agitation*, or simply "agitation," is repetitive, nonproductive motor activity usually associated with feelings of tension (e.g., pacing, fidgeting, constantly standing and sitting).
> *Psychomotor retardation* describes slowed movements, reactions, or speech.
> *Catatonia* is not responding to environmental stimuli either with or without associated activity
> - *Catatonic excitement* is extreme overactivity seemingly unrelated to environmental stimuli.

- *Catatonic negativism* is an apparently motiveless and extreme resistance to all instructions or attempts to be moved. Three manifestations of this negativism are (a) *catatonic posturing*, in which a bizarre position is rigidly held for long periods; (b) *catatonic rigidity*, in which the patient resists all efforts to be moved; and (c) *waxy flexibility*, in which the patient resists having his body moved, but ends up with parts of his body being "molded" into odd positions, as if they were pliable wax.

Echopraxia is the repetitive imitation of another person's movements.

Stereotypy is an isolated, repetitive, and purposeless movement. It appears most often in catatonic and drug-induced states.

Tardive dyskinesia is delayed choreoathetoid movements related to schizophrenia (chorea is dancing movements like fingers playing the piano and athetoid movements are writhing).

Attitude

This category describes how the patient relates to the examiner. Is eye contact established? Is communication reciprocal? Descriptors include indifferent, frank, friendly, embarrassed, help seeking, evasive, afraid, resentful, sullen, angry, irritable, assaultive, erotic, negativistic, denudative, exhibitionistic, dramatic, transparent, cooperative, hostile, withdrawn, open, guarded, suspicious, angry, evasive, sneering, interactive, averted gaze, fleeting eye contact, sarcastic, and so on.

Articulation (Manner of Speech)

This category describes the manner (volume, flow, rate, quality, coherence) but not the content of speech. Speech can be rapid or slowed, hesitant, soft or loud, pressured or casual, spontaneous or hesitant, clear or slurred (i.e., dysarthria), monotonous, staccato, and pedantic or stilted (formal). Latency is a delay in responding and initiating speech that most often occurs in depressed patients. Pressured or rapid speech that cannot be interrupted is a cardinal sign of mania. Slightly pressured speech can occur with anxiety. Reporting of foreign or regional accents also occurs here. Tests for enunciation include "Methodist Episcopal," "liquid linoleum," "third red royal riding artillery brigade."

> *Poverty of speech* is a striking lack of speech, so that replies to questions are brief or monosyllabic; some questions are not answered at all. Poverty of speech refers to an inadequate *quantity*.

Mutism is not speaking; it is a frequent feature of catatonia. With mutism there is a tendency to substitute the use of related words approximating the definitive term for example "I have menu three times a day" when meals would be the definitive term.

Pressured speech is rapid, virtually nonstop, often loud and emphatic, seemingly driven, and usually hard to interrupt. It typically occurs in mania and in some drug-induced states and in severe anxiety states.

Sensorium

Sensorium refers to basic cognition and awareness. Other aspects of cognition, namely thought and perception, are addressed later. Here the clinician assesses consciousness, orientation, memory, and attention/concentration.

Consciousness

Both the level and stability (i.e., awareness of the environment and fluctuations) of consciousness are evaluated. The patient's degree of alertness should be described (is the patient in a coma, a stupor with clouded consciousness, or alert?). Descriptors of consciousness in declining order include hyper alert, alert, lethargic, confused, stuporous, and comatose. Confusion, bewilderment, and obtunded consciousness may be related to toxic or physical (organic) factors much more frequently than to psychological (functional) factors.

Clouding of consciousness is when the patient is awake and functioning, but has an incomplete or distorted awareness of the environment. It is a higher level of awareness than stupor in which an awake patient is unaware and unresponsive to the environment.

Stupor is a state of foggy consciousness and nonalertness in which the patient may respond to noxious stimuli, but otherwise be oblivious to her environment.

Coma is the most impaired end on a continuum of consciousness. Patients may be totally unresponsive to a (painful) stimulus, such as a pinprick, or may twitch, but not display any further evidence of awareness.

Orientation

As patients become progressively disoriented, they are unable to indicate the current time (and situation), then their current location (place), and last, their own name. To test for orientation to time, the clinician ascertains if patients can identify the date, the day of the week, the time of day, or how long they have been hospitalized. Failing these questions, patients are asked to identify the season and part of the day (e.g., morning, afternoon, evening). Clinicians may be astonished to discover a seemingly normal patient who, when asked directly, says the current year is 1953. Asking the patient to estimate when 60 seconds have elapsed may pick up more subtle impairment.

Memory

In the MSE, memory is categorized as *remote, recent,* or *immediate.* Remote memory refers to many years ago, recent memory to the past several days to months, and immediate memory to the past several minutes. When people begin to lose their memories, immediate memory usually goes first, remote memory, last. The ability to recall past experiences and defects may be related to lack of attention, retention difficulties, problems with registration or a combination of these three factors. The examiner should determine whether the defect in memory is variable (dissociative) or constant, circumscribed for a particular time (amnesia) or more extensive.

> Remote and recent memory can be assessed by how well patients recall historical and current events (what they ate for breakfast). Immediate memory is best evaluated by formal testing: For example, clinicians name three single-word objects (e.g., *book, umbrella, elephant*), and then have patients immediately repeat the words to ensure they registered. Clinicians then tell patients that in 5 minutes, they will be asked to repeat the three objects. Most patients can recall two out of three; one or zero suggests organic factors. One can also test registration with numbers (6 or 7 digits) delivered at one per second without rhythmic spacing or vocal inflection.

Sensing their failing memory and disorientation, many patients with neurological dysfunction feel embarrassed and try to conceal the loss by *confabulating.* One example: A 63-year-old professor with a slow-growing brain tumor had become adept at bluffing by using his charm to hide his inability to remember simple facts. When asked to name the year, he replied, "The year, well, it is the year of our discontent. Who cares about the year? It's but time, and time is relative."

Amnesia is a pathological loss of memory. There are two types:
- *Anterograde* amnesia is for events occurring after a significant point in time.
- *Retrograde* amnesia is for events occurring before a significant point in time.

Confabulation is when a patient invents responses, facts, and events to mask an organic impairment.

Attention and Concentration

Attention is the ability to sustain a focus on one task or activity. Impaired attention—distractibility—can usually be detected during a routine interview by observing if a patient's focus is frequently directed to unimportant or irrelevant external stimuli. If attention seems impaired and its immediate cause is unclear (e.g., due to anxiety, hallucinations, or to other psychotic preoccupations), formal clinical testing should be performed.

> In the most widely used test, referred to as the "serial 7's," the patient is asked to subtract 7 from 100 without stopping as far as possible. The patient's educational background or infrequent use of mathematics, however, may interfere with performance. A more informative test is the "serial 1's," in which the patient is asked to "count backward by 1's from 57 and stop at 22." Because it requires no math skills, this is a purer test of concentration, and by noting if the patient stops at 22, the clinician also tests immediate memory. As an alternative you may ask the patient to count to 27 ("until you hear 'stop'"), then resume to 42. Spelling "world" or one's name backward is a concentration test option outside of the math realm. Providing the months of the year backward is also a test of concentration.
>
> Perhaps 35% of college students use prescription stimulants to improve focus and concentration. The actual use may be higher because many of the survey questions and study methods ask about "misuse" or abuse.

Impairment of consciousness, orientation, memory, and attention (COMA) suggests the presence of cognitive dysfunction due to an organic (physical) condition versus a functional (psychological) one. Disturbances in COMA may arise from substance abuse or from medication toxicity (especially possible with tricyclic antidepressants and phenothiazine antipsychotics that have anticholinergic side effects, or the hypnoanxiolytics that have sedative side effects). Impaired orientation very rarely occurs in schizophrenic, paranoid, psychotic, or mood disorders, but more commonly in dissociative disorders and dementing illnesses. Impaired memory and attention may occur in any of these disorders. Confusion and associated agitation may become more prominent as one becomes less alert or if environmental cues to orientation are diminished (e.g., sundowners syndrome).

Delirium is a clouding of consciousness with disorientation and recent memory loss (e.g., a concussion caused by physical injury to the brain may result in a delirium).

Dementia is characterized by a loss of intellectual abilities, especially memory.

Disorientation is the inability to correctly identify the current time, situation, place, and person (familiar and self).

Distractibility is when a patient's attention is frequently drawn to unimportant or irrelevant external stimuli.

Emotion

The phenomenology of emotion is discussed psychiatrically in terms of *mood* and *affect*. *Mood* is a pervasive and subjectively experienced feeling state, whereas *affect* refers to instantaneous, observable expressions of emotion. In psychopathology, affects are overt and moods are covert. *Moods are what people tell you they feel, and affects are what you see them feeling.* Moods influence how people feel about themselves and their world; affects do not. People complain about their moods, but not about their affects. Moods persist, affects don't.

In reality, distinguishing moods from affects can be difficult. For example, is anger a mood or an affect? It could be either, and which it is doesn't matter all that much unless there is incongruence. *What does matter is that the clinician provides clear, specific descriptions of the patient's emotions.* "He states that he feels angry while smiling and appearing calm" (incongruent or inappropriate). "She cries one moment and laughs the next" (labile). "His expression never varies" (flat). "She says she feels 'like an emotional robot . . . the living dead.'" "When first mentioning his wife, he pounded the table." As in this last example, what is occurring or being discussed during an emotional display may be worth reporting.

A normal range of affect is labeled "broad," "spontaneous," "reactive" or "full." Other affective presentations include "flat," "blunt," "constricted," "labile," and "inappropriate." Shallowness or flattening of affect is indicated by an insufficiently intense emotional display in association with ideas or situations which ordinarily would call for a more adequate response. Disharmony between affect and thought content is inappropriate or incongruent. Patients who are trying to cover up symptoms and signs may feign cheerfulness and good spirits. Emotional reactions may be constant or fluctuate during the examination. Degree or intensity of affective responses would be specified using the following terms: composed, comfortable, complacent, frank, smiling, friendly, laughing, playful, teasing, silly, happy, cheerful, optimistic, boastful, elated, grandiose, ecstatic, tense, worried, anxious, pessimistic, sad, pained, perplexed, bewildered, gloomy, humiliated, shameful, melancholic, depressed, frightened, aloof, dreamy, superior, disdainful, sneering, distant defensive, suspicious, irritable, resentful, hostile, sarcastic, angry, furious, indifferent, resigned, apathetic, dull, affectionless.

Affect is the instantaneous, observable expression of emotion. It differs from mood, which is a pervasive, subjectively experienced emotion. As the saying goes, "Affect is to mood as weather is to climate." Moods are symptoms; affects are signs. Commonly described affects are:
- *Broad affect* is a normal range of affect.
- *Flat, blunted, and constricted affects* describe (in decreasing order of severity) patients who show almost no emotional lability, appear expressionless (shallow, inadequate), or look dulled. The term *restrictive affect* is sometimes used when someone seems to be deliberately attenuating emotional expression.
- *Inappropriate affect* is clearly discordant with the expressed emotional state or discordant with the content of the patient's speech, e.g., a patient giggles while talking about his father's death.
- *Labile* affect shows a range of expression in excess of cultural norms, with repeated, rapid, and abrupt shifts of emotion, as when a patient cries one moment and laughs the next.

A normal mood is called "euthymia." Moods can also be high or low. On the up side, as one gets higher, moods go from "elevated," to "euphoric," to "expansive." On the down side, "dysphoria" is any mood the patient finds unpleasant, including anxiety, apprehensiveness, dysthymia, and irritability. "Dysthymia" is used throughout this text to mean the *symptom* of depression, as distinguished from the various *syndromes* of depression. It is useful to ask patients to characterize their mood on a scale from 1 to 10 (from saddest to happiest). Associated suicidal or homicidal ideation, plan, or intent must be included. "Do you have any thoughts about wanting to harm yourself or others? Have you ever?"

Mood is a pervasive and subjectively experienced feeling state, as opposed to affect which is transitory and apparent to others. Unlike affect, mood colors the person's view of the world. Mood states include:

- *Apprehensive* mood involves worried expectation or anticipation.
- *Dysphoria* is any unpleasant mood, including irritable, apprehensive, and dysthymic moods.
- *Dysthymia* is the mood of depression or pervasive sadness, including a subjective sense of heaviness or feeling "weighted-down," blue, or down-in-the dumps. Dysthymia implies a mood that is more serious than "run-of-the-mill" unhappiness.
- *Elevated* mood is more cheerful than normal for the person, but is not necessarily psychopathological.
- *Euphoric* mood is an exaggerated sense of well-being and contentment; it implies psychopathology when elevated or expansive. (Elevated moods are "vertical"; expansive moods are "horizontal.") An elevated mood: "I feel wonderful, things are great!" An expansive mood: "I can do anything, bat .400, win every game single-handedly, and have all the fans worship me." A euphoric mood may be elevated and ex-pansive: "I'm flying, I'm on cloud 9, I feel like a god, I'm invincible."
- *Euthymia* is a normal range of mood without dysphoria or elation.
- *Expansive* mood refers to a lack of restraint in expressing feelings and an overvaluation of one's importance; it is often accompanied by an elevated or euphoric mood.
- *Irritable* mood is a feeling of tension or nervousness; one feels prickly, easily annoyed, provoked to anger, or frustrated.

Relatedness and *reciprocity* refers to the ability to express warmth, interact, and connect with the interviewer. *Mood-congruency* refers to whether a patient's behavior, affect, delusions, and hallucinations are consistent with the stated mood. If she constantly smiles while talking about her sadness and losses, her affect is incongruent with her stated mood. A depressed person who believes that she is evil and that Satan has destroyed her soul has a mood-congruent delusion. If she believes that extraterrestrials have programmed her to infiltrate the FBI, she has a mood-incongruent delusion.

Anxiety can refer to a symptom or a syndrome. As a symptom, anxiety is an emotional state of inner tension, restlessness, uneasiness, or apprehension. As a syndrome, anxiety combines this (internal) emotional state with (external) physiologic signs, such as tremor, heart-pounding, hypervigilance, dilated pupils, and agitation. Anxiety is pathological only when it chronically interferes with a person's functioning. Whereas anxiety implies the absence of a consciously recognized, external threat, fear implies that such a threat exists. Anxiety focused on an upcoming event is called *anticipatory anxiety*; unfocused anxiety is called *free-floating anxiety*.

Alexithymia is a trait in which the patient has a constricted emotional life, diminished ability to fantasize, and a virtual inability to articulate emotions. Like anhedonia, alexithymia describes the absence of emotion, but in anhedonia, positive emotion seems blocked or stymied, whereas in alexithymia, it's as if no emotion exists. Patients will complain about anhedonia, but not about alexithymia.

Anhedonia exists when there is a pervasive inability to perceive and experience pleasure in actions and events that are normally pleasurable or satisfying for the individual or most individuals. Anhedonia often begins with the person trying to carry out the activity, hoping the anticipated pleasure will materialize. Eventually, when it doesn't, the person loses all interest in the activity and tends to avoid it: A football fanatic ignores the Super Bowl; a devoted father is totally bored by his children; a civil rights activist no longer cares.

Neurosis is a mental state in which the person is experiencing a nonpsychotic anxiety or mood disturbance

Thought

Psychiatrists traditionally used the term *thought disorder* to describe any communication arising from pathological thought processes. However, because the term is so nonspecific it is best to use more descriptive categories such as word usage, stream of thought, continuity, and content.

Thought Process (Form of Thought)

Since no one can directly know another's thought processes, clinicians must infer them from patient's language and expressed ideas through speech and behavior. However, a patient may *say* that he is God, which doesn't necessarily mean he *thinks* so; the style and context of delivery will determine if the assertion is deceptive or delusional. So the physician is concerned with content but also observes the manner in which it is presented. Whenever pathological thought is reported, the clinician should also include examples.

Word Usage/Language. Word usage/language includes abnormalities such as neologisms and word approximations. *Neologisms* are self-invented words or phrases (e.g., "I need a flame to binkle my bed") that are most often seen in schizophrenia. They may also be standard words given idiosyncratic meanings by the patient. A new or misused word is not a neologism when it arises for cultural or educational reasons (e.g., malapropisms). Word approximations (e.g., "I know the time by the thing that goes around") may be a sign of brain disease. *Verbigeration* is the constant repetition of syllables and sounds. *Word salad* is a random and illogical mixture of words.

Whereas in poverty of speech the patient utters only a few words or syllables, in poverty of *content* of speech the patient's words are sufficient and individual sentences may even make sense, but the total communication remains meaningless. (Although usually pathological, this phenomenon may also be observed in political speeches and bureaucratic reports!) For example, when asked what religion meant to him, a patient replied: "All that church stuff. Amazing Grace, Amazing Grace. 'I know that my redeemer liveth, and that he shall stand at the latter day upon the earth' (Job 19:25). It is personal, very personal. I understand what you mean, you who live in God's grace." Overly metaphorical or philosophical speech may indicate brain dysfunction associated with temporal lobe epilepsy.

> *Poverty of content of speech*, sometimes called "poverty of content," "paucity of ideas," or "communication deviance" is speech which conveys little information because it is vague, barren, or filled with empty repetitions or obscure phrases. Poverty of content refers to the inadequate *quality* of speech.

Incoherence is a general, but often useful, term to describe incomprehensible speech in which the specific type of disturbed thinking is difficult to identify, or in which there is a mixture of thought pathology. Incoherent or incomprehensible speech is often referred to as verbigeration and word salad. Incoherence describes the response of a patient who was asked, "Do you fear anything specific?":

> That's just it. A doctor told me not to put a stamp on me. The Secretary of the Treasury is not part of it. People say to you, "Isn't it too bad that you're sick." It feels like I was very obstreperous. I couldn't communicate at any level. My inside couldn't make sense of my outside. All the anxieties, and all the (*pause*), and all the rococo themes of psychiatric uh, uh, uh (*pause*) illness played back upon me again and again.

Stream of Thought. Stream of thought refers to the production and quantity of thoughts (e.g., overabundant, slowed). Interruption of a train of speech before a thought has been completed is called "thought blocking."

These blockages can last seconds to minutes and may or may not be patho-logical, depending on the degree. The sudden stoppage in the stream of talk occurs for no apparent external reason or influence and without the patient being able to account for the block. It is usually due to the sudden appear-ance of affectively charged topics of preoccupation or interference by delu-sional thoughts or hallucinations.

Flight of ideas (the ideas are associated but rapidly generated) is over-productivity of ideas which is continuous but the connections between the parts of speech are often determined by chance associations between the fragments. A certain coherence is retained but the direction of talk is influ-enced by chance stimuli from internal or external sources.

Speech may be accelerated with many rapid changes in subject that derive from understandable associations, distracting stimuli, or play on words. In flight of ideas (FOI) the connections linking thoughts are under-standable, whereas in looseness of associations (LOA) they are not. Never-theless, extremely rapid FOI may be indistinguishable from LOA, and when there is a marked cultural gap between patient and interviewer, FOI is often misidentified as LOA.

Continuity of Thought. Continuity of thought refers to the associa-tions among ideas. Descriptors include circumstantiality (over-elaborative answers and the opposite of goal directed), tangential (never gets back to the point), rambling, evasive, perseverative, coherent, logical, organized. Thought derailment (getting off track) may be considered a loss of associa-tion. Some of the disturbances in this category are always pathological, such as clanging, echolalia, and perseveration. When a patient has improved moderately, the loose association of ideas will make much better sense. For example, a psychotic patient who was with a group of other patients talking about being abandoned by their families, said, "I've slept in trees before. Sleeping in trees is uncomfortable. Family trees are the worst."

> *Looseness of associations* are speech patterns characterized by leaps from subject to subject without the connections being clear or the patient being aware of his rapid shifts. "School is nice. I adore earlobes."
> *Tangentiality* is a disturbance of communication in which the person "goes off on a tangent," but unlike circumstantiality, does not return to the point. Tangentiality may be viewed as repeated derailments, which continually evade a central theme. It may, or may not be, pathological.
> *Circumstantiality* is a pattern of speech, which although filled with detours, irrelevant details, and parenthetical remarks, eventually reaches its point; tangentiality is when the point isn't reached. Cir-

cumstantiality may, or may not be, pathological. With circumstantiality the person is voluble, speech lacks incisiveness, but the goal is ultimately reached. With tangentiality the original goal and answer to the question is lost sight of and not attained.

Clanging is a type of language in which the sound of a word, instead of its meaning, dictates the course of subsequent associations (e.g., "ding, dong, dell . . .").

Echolalia is a meaningless, persistent, verbal, repetition of words or sounds heard by the patient—often with a mocking, mumbling, staccato, or parrot-like tone. (Greek *echo* = "an echo," and *lalia* = "to babble.")

Perseveration is a persistent repetition of speech or movement to varied, usually internal, stimuli. It does not include repeated use of stock phrases, such as "you know" or "like." Echolalia and perseveration are often, but not always, found in dementia and delirium. Echolalia is in response to the same stimulus, whereas perseveration is repeated responses to varied stimuli.

Derailment is a gradual or sudden deviation in a patient's train of behavior, speech, or thought onto a very different track. It may be hard to distinguish from flight of ideas and looseness of associations.

Thought Content

Content of thought, when disturbed, can result in delusions or illogical, magical, oneiric (dream-like), and autistic thinking. *Autistic thinking* is a term used to refer to thinking not in accordance with consensus reality and emphasizes preoccupation with inner experience (being alone with your thoughts to the exclusion of the outside).

If thoughts seem to have little or no basis in reality they are referred to as delusions or overvalued ideas (if less severe). Illogical thinking is another disturbance in thought content. One patient wrote: "People's bodies conform to the shape of their clothes so that my mother's body must be a rectangle because she's wearing a chemise and when my brother wears bell-bottoms, his legs become large, double-edge razors." This patient also said that by getting dressed, he could induce his father, via telepathy, to take a shower (delusional and magical thinking.) A psychology student who says, "I put a textbook by my pillow and learn by osmosis" is also demonstrating magical thinking; however, this conviction is probably not delusional, but instead an overvalued idea or a joke.

Obsessions, which are persistent, unwanted *thoughts*, are another type of disturbed content. Preoccupations are a less severe form of persistent and undesired thoughts. Because compulsions are "senseless" repeated *deeds*, they are behaviors, but since they arise from obsessions, the two can be reported together. In regard to obsessions the clinician can ask "do you have any thoughts you cannot get rid of?" or "have you ever been bothered by thoughts that don't seem to make any sense and keep coming back even when you try to stop them?" For compulsions one could ask "do you feel compelled to do certain acts or perform certain rituals?" or "do you ever have to do the same thing over and over in a certain way like checking your door or washing your hands?" and "does this interfere with your normal daily routine?" Compulsions include repetitive hand washing, rituals for dressing in a certain order, locking and checking doors repeatedly, tapping on all wooden objects a certain number of times, etc.

Illogical fears of special objects leading to strict avoidance of them are phobias and include the fear of trains, subways, elevators, close spaces, crowds, or open spaces. Certain maladaptive thoughts may lead to phobias, unnecessary worries, and other negative emotional states. Some attempt should be made to evaluate whether an emotional reaction is secondary to the thoughts or whether the thoughts are secondary to the affective state (Are the symptoms primarily the result of a thought or an emotional disorder?).

Illogical thinking involves conclusions that contain clear, internal contradictions or are blatantly erroneous given the initial premises. A patient refuses to go to the movies because the tickets are green. Illogical thinking may, or may not, lead to a delusion, or result from one. "I am a virgin, and therefore, I am the Virgin Mary."

Autistic thinking is thought derived from fantasy: The person defines his environment based on internal fantasies instead of on external realities. Autistic thinking also refers to an individual being preoccupied with his own private world; social withdrawal into one's inner world usually results.

Magical thinking is when a person is convinced that her words, thoughts, feelings, or actions will produce or prevent a specific outcome that defies all laws of cause and effect. Depending on how firmly the magical thinking is held, it may be a delusion or an overvalued idea, as in this example: "I know this seems odd, but when I move my third finger forward, I can make people walk faster; when I move my finger backward, they walk slower." Children, people in primitive cultures, and patients with obsessive-compulsive and schizophrenic-like disorders use magical thinking.

Obsessions are unwanted and uncomfortable ideas, thoughts, images, or impulses that persistently invade one's consciousness. Unlike people with delusions or overvalued ideas, those with obsessions know their beliefs are absurd and find them ego-dystonic.

Compulsions are repeated, stereotyped, overtly senseless actions or rituals, which are performed to prevent anxiety. Compulsions are obsessions expressed in behavior. Obsessions are thoughts, compulsions are deeds. Lady Macbeth's hand-washing is a compulsion to wipe clean her obsession with Duncan's blood.

Relationship to Reality

Psychosis is a mental state in which the person is unable to distinguish reality from fantasy. The examiner must appreciate normal development and cultural beliefs, such as imaginary friends in children; glossolalia or speaking in tongues is the fluid vocalizing (or, less commonly, the writing) of speech-like syllables, often as part of religious practice. Though some consider these utterances to be meaningless, those that use them consider them to be part of a holy language.

Reality testing is the ability to distinguish reality from fantasy. The failure to test reality—what Lily Tomlin calls "man's collective hunches"—is the hallmark of psychosis.

Overvalued ideas are unreasonable and persistent beliefs, held with less than delusional intensity, which are not generally held in the patient's subculture. "The mob is tapping my phone—well, I think it is." Patients are more likely to act on delusions than on overvalued ideas. When patients recover from psychosis, they often go from delusions to overvalued ideas to "normality." Overvalued ideas may have a basis in reality, and some are not pathological, such as preoccupations that one's nose is too big, that only diet can cure cancer, or that "having a baby is the only way I will ever be happy." Ideas of reference are one type of overvalued idea.

Paranoid ideation is an overvalued idea that one is being persecuted.

Ideas of reference are overvalued ideas in which the patient is virtually, but not totally, convinced that objects, people, or events in his immediate environment have personal significance for him. A man felt whenever a red car parked in front of his home, it probably was a well-disguised message from the FBI that he should be on the alert for dope addicts. With a delusion of reference, all doubt would cease. When they occur in a hypervigilant state, ideas of reference are not necessarily pathological: For instance, a man at a "swinger's bar" says, "All the chicks can't keep their eyes off me."

Ideas of influence are overvalued ideas that one's thoughts or behaviors are being controlled by someone or something else.

Delusions are fixed, blatantly false convictions deduced from incorrect inferences about external reality; they are maintained despite enormous, obvious, incontrovertible proof to the contrary, and they are not widely believed in the person's culture or subculture. Thus one's education and surroundings helps distinguish delusions from superstition. A false belief that involves an extreme value judgment is a delusion only when it defies credibility. Delusions differ from overvalued ideas, which are unreasonable and persistent beliefs. To various degrees, delusions are systematized or unsystematized. In comparison to *unsystematized* delusions, *systematized* delusions are united by a common theme or event and belong to a complete and relatively well-organized network of beliefs; they develop more insidiously, cause less confusion and impairment, and last longer. Types of delusions:

Bizarre delusions are patently absurd and weird.

Grandiose delusions involve an exaggerated sense of one's own importance, power, ability, or identity. "I am the Messiah."

Jealousy delusions involve suspicions about a rival (e.g., business rival) or about one's sex partner being unfaithful Othello.

Nihilistic delusions involve themes of non-existence (not "negativity"), either of the patient, others, or the world. "My insides are gone." "At 1:30 p.m., the world will evaporate."

Persecutory delusions are those in which the person is convinced others are trying to harm, cheat, attack, or conspire against him or her.

Somatic delusions pertain to the patient's body and are not consistent with cultural with physiology or medicine. "My intestines are rotting." "My brain is turning black."

Reference delusions are beliefs that external events or people are sending messages or commands of great personal importance to the patient. These delusions are self-referential. A woman insists that a man on TV was speaking to her specifically and instructing her to buy Ajax. (And she did—1,280 cans!) For delusions of reference or persecution one might ask "how have others been treating you?" For delusions of alien control one might ask "do you ever feel your thoughts or actions are under any outside influences or control?"

Folie à deux, or "madness for two," is when two closely related persons, usually in the same family, share the same delusions.

Paranoia is not a symptom but a mental disorder characterized by delusions of grandeur and persecution, suspiciousness, jealousy, and resentment.

Mood-congruent delusions or hallucinations are consistent with the patient's dominant mood. A mood-congruent delusion in depression might be, "My body's rotting with cancer"; in mania, "I'm the Second Coming of Christ."

Mood-incongruent delusions and hallucinations are those that are inconsistent with the patient's dominant mood. Mood-incongruent delusions may be persecutory (e.g., "The Rainbow Coalition is poisoning my tulips") or may involve Schneiderian symptoms.

Delusions in which the patient experiences his actions, thoughts, feelings, and perceptions as not her own or somehow imposed on her are called Schneiderian first-rank symptoms (FRS), after Kurt Schneider, who first identified the phenomenon. Common examples include experiencing thought insertion or broadcasting, thought removal, and getting special messages from the TV or radio. Although no longer considered pathognomonic of schizophrenia, FRS are often found in schizophrenia and are sometimes observed in mania. A sign or symptom is *pathognomonic* if it exists in only one disorder.

Thought broadcasting is the belief that one's inner thoughts are no longer private, have escaped from one's mind, and have become known to everyone. "Everyone in the hospital knows what I'm thinking." Telepathy is not thought broadcasting, since it is culturally sanctioned and, therefore, not delusional.

Thought insertions are ego-alien convictions that thoughts have been placed into one's mind, with the person believing his thoughts are not his own.

Thought withdrawal is a patient's ego-dystonic belief that thoughts are being taken, or stolen from her mind or brain, and that she has fewer thoughts than before. "I was discussing Rome when suddenly my whole brain was sucked empty by the Pope's vacuum cleaner."

A patient may be reluctant or embarrassed to reveal certain content. Some screening questions that might elicit disturbed thought content include: "How would you change yourself or the world or both if you could?" "Is there anything you think a lot about that really bothers you?" "Have you had any unusual or troublesome experiences?"

The patient's main preoccupation or content of thought often reveals significant dynamic factors either directly or in the form of projections that enable the clinician to gain some understanding of the development of the illness. The responses to projective questions provide a window into intrapsychic processing and its basis in reality. For example, the clinician may ask, "If you could have any 3 wishes come true, what would you wish for?" To be rid of the worms that are eating my brain gives you a different clinical impression from a new sports car, seeing a deceased relative, or getting out of this black hole (lifting of my depression).

Concept Formation (Abstractibility)

The ability to abstract—to think symbolically, to generalize, and to conceptualize is frequently absent with a functioning IQ under 90 or with schizophrenia. A patients' behavior during the interview usually provides enough data to determine the ability to abstract. If there is any reason to question this ability, especially with evidence of psychosis or organicity, formal testing should be performed. A cautionary note: Too much stock should not be placed in any single answer or on clinical tests in general, since at best they are only rough measures of patients' abilities. They do, however, provide some relatively objective data. Whenever formal clinical testing is done, clinicians should record not only their conclusion—for example, "the patient's similarities were concrete"—but also what the patient actually said.

> One test of abstractive ability determines whether patients can recognize *similarities*. Questions are asked such as, "What is the similarity between a poem, novel, and sculpture?," or "How are truth and beauty alike?," or "What is the similarity between a table, desk, and chair?" To the latter question, a properly abstracted answer would be, "They are all furniture." A concrete answer would be, "All are made of wood"; even more concrete would be, "I don't see any similarity." A bizarre answer would be, "They're all more human than humans."
>
> Another test involves patients' abilities to interpret *proverbs*. Ideally, the proverbs given to patients should contain words and ideas within the parameters of their educational and cultural backgrounds, and *not* be ones that

have been heard many times before. If patients already know the proverb, asking what it means may test prior learning but not the capacity to abstract. The responses may be literal, concrete, personalized, idiosyncratic, or bizarre. An example: "The opera's not over till the fat lady sings." An abstract response would be, "Nothing is resolved until everybody does their thing." A concrete response would be, "An opera is never finished until a fat woman sings." A bizarre response would be, "Fatso opera singers like death." A personalized response would be, "I'm not fat!" Other proverbs to ascertain the ability to abstract include "Don't cry over spilled milk," "When the cat's away the mice will play," "Stitch in time saves nine," "He who lives in a glass house should not throw stones."

Concrete thinking is the inability to think abstractly, metaphorically, or hypothetically. Ideas and words are usually limited to a single meaning. Figures of speech are taken literally and nuances of language are missed and not used. Sometimes the person may have the ability to abstract but prefers a concrete cognitive style.

Intelligence and Information

The only precise measure of intelligence comes from an IQ test, such as the Wechsler Adult Intelligence Scale (WAIS). IQ tests were originally developed to predict school performance, and they do this fairly well. However, they *don't* do as well when used for other purposes, such as to predict a person's ability to fix a car, run a company, or win a Nobel Prize. Because there are different forms of intelligence and no one global entity, IQ intelligence can be thought of as "scholastic potential." By definition, IQ is whatever an IQ test measures, the average IQ being 100. Most people reading this book will not know anyone in their personal lives with an IQ below 90. The diagnosis of mental retardation requires a tested IQ of below 70. High IQ scores may reflect the cultural enrichment of a person's inborn biological potential. Intelligence is related to vocabulary, fund of knowledge, and calculation. It is strongly influenced by early and cultural deprivation.

The assessment of intelligence includes examining the patient's general fund of information, which is why intelligence and information are usually linked in the MSE. Both are affected by culture, education, performance anxiety, and psychopathology, especially the presence of delirium or dementia. Because the initial interview can only reveal gaping deficits, intelligence can be tested clinically by having patients perform simple math (e.g., "multiply 7 × 12) or by having them read something and then tell the examiner what it meant. Performing simple calculations involving money is correlated with intelligence (e.g., How much change would you get back if you purchased an item for $6.32 with a $10 bill?). Evaluating patients' information resources involves questioning their general knowledge and awareness of current events. Such questions should be geared to the patient's background: Who wrote Hamlet? Who won last week's election for governor? Tell me something that's going in the news. Name a continent, large state, large city.

Insight

In the MSE *insight* refers to patients' awareness and understanding of their chief problem. Does the patient understand and realize the significance of his symptoms and of the situation in which he finds himself? Does the patient offer possible explanations of his symptoms and provide spontaneous suggestions for his own treatment? A delusional patient who claims she came for treatment to get the telephone company to stop the ringing in her ears lacks insight. The insight continuum ranges from (1) a complete denial of illness, to (2) a dim and fleeting admission of illness, to (3) an awareness of illness but with accusations that others are causing it, to (4) an intellectual recognition of problems and their origin within, to (5) a convincing awareness of the disorder and its internal sources. The patient's level of insight is a rough predictor of how much he will cooperate with treatment and benefit from insight-oriented psychotherapy; the latter can be predicted further by offering the patient several interpretations during the assessment, not for therapeutic purposes, but to see how she reacts to an interpretation.

Judgment

This category evaluates patients' abilities to exercise judgment in dealing with social situations, which includes acting appropriately during the interview and understanding the consequences of their actions. Although judgment is largely assessed by observing patients during the interview, if the clinician remains uncertain about the evaluation, patients can be asked what they would do in hypothetical situations: "What would you do if you found a stamped, addressed envelope lying on the street?" or, "What would you do if you were the first one in a theater to see a fire?" Asking a patient to provide three wishes may also help assess judgment in addition to revealing projected information that improves the clinician's understanding and provides further support for the diagnosis.

For judgment, does the patient understand the likely outcome of his behaviors and is he influenced by that understanding or unable to apply knowledge acquired? Is the patient logical and practical in handling activities of daily living? Is judgment impaired in personal matters versus neutral or nonpersonal? "How do you know if something really happened or you just imagined it?" "What do you do when you are walking down the street and you hear someone call your name but turn around and no one is there?" Sometimes judgment is intact for hypothetical situations but not real-life situations. Asking about the differences between a lie and a mistake or between a dwarf and a child, or asking what the person would do with a gift of $10,000 will give an idea of the patient's reasoning ability and judgment.

Perception

This category describes fundamental abnormalities in the five senses: hearing, seeing, touching, tasting, and smelling. These abnormalities, which include hallucinations, illusions, depersonalization, derealization, and déjà vu, are often, but not always, psychopathological. Technically, dreams are hallucinations, but they are not reported as perceptual disturbances. Most people have brief experiences with derealization, depersonalization, and déjà vu. Hallucinations are false sensory impressions without any external basis in fact.

Although some patients will readily admit when they are hallucinating, many will not. Patients may be hallucinating when their eyes dart from side to side, when they stare at nothing, or when they seem preoccupied, as if they were listening to voices. Ask, "Do you see or hear things that other people do not?" Because some patients will refer to their own thoughts as voices, the clinician should ask if the voices come from inside or from outside their head. If from the inside, ask if the voice is the patient's or someone else's. Other questions you could ask include: If you heard voices what would they be saying? Do you ever think you see something out of the corner of your eye but when you turn and look at it directly it is gone? What is it that you think you saw? Do you ever see that object at other times?

In general, only auditory and visual hallucinations occur in psychiatric disorders, whereas these and olfactory, tactile, and other hallucinatory phenomena occur in disorders caused by drug use or medical conditions. The hallucinations of patients with mood disorders tend to be mood-congruent; those of people with schizophrenia, mood-incongruent.

Illusions are misperceptions of real external stimuli. During delirium tremens, alcoholics will misperceive the hair on their arms as bugs: These are illusions, not hallucinations, since they are based on a real stimulus.

Hallucinations are false perceptions in the senses—hearing, seeing, touching, tasting, and smelling—based on no external reality. They differ from illusions which are false perceptions based on real stimuli. Hallucinations are disorders of perception; delusions are disorders of thinking. Delusions are always psychotic, hallucinations only sometimes. Some patients know their hallucinations are unreal (e.g., "My mind is playing tricks on me"); those who don't are described as giving a "delusional interpretation" to their hallucinations. *Hallucinosis* is a state in which the patient realizes his hallucinations are false. Except for dreams, hallucinations are pathological. *Hypnogogic* and *Hypnopompic* hallucinations are dreams which occur on falling asleep or on waking up, respectively; if unaccompanied by other symptoms, they are merely variants of normal. Pathological hallucinations include:

- *Auditory* hallucinations are false perceptions of sound, usually of a voice or voices.
- *Gustatory* hallucinations are false, usually unpleasant, perceptions of taste. (Metallic tastes may be a side effect of medications or physical illnesses.)
- *Olfactory* hallucinations are false perceptions of smell, such as the patient who kept smelling rotting flesh, as she viewed her "happily dead husband."
- *Somatic* hallucinations are false perceptions of a physical experience inside the body. "I feel an orgasm running in my spleen."
- *Tactile* hallucinations are false perceptions of touch. *Formication* is a tactile hallucination in which the patient feels that things, often insects, are crawling under his skin; it occurs most during withdrawal from alcohol, cocaine, or hypnosedatives.
- *Visual* hallucinations are false perceptions of sight; they may consist of actual people or flashes of light.

Hallucinosis is when patients hallucinate following cessation or reduction of a substance, usually in a clear (or mildly clouded) consciousness. Most, but not all, hallucinosis is very unpleasant. Knowing these hallucinations are not real, the patient is less likely to act on them than on hallucinations he believes to be genuine.

Depersonalization is when a person perceives her body as unreal, floating, dead, or changing in size. A person's arm may feel like wood or seem detached from her body.

Derealization is when a person perceives his environment as unreal. The individual feels removed from the world, as if he is viewing it on a movie screen. Both depersonalization and derealization often occur in nonpathological situations, with or without stress.

Déjà vu literally "already seen" is a sense of familiarity when confronted by a situation or event that has not been experienced previously. Although it usually occurs in nonpathological states, it may be pathological.

Jamais vu literally "never seen" is when a recognized or familiar situation is experienced as unfamiliar.

AUXILIARY DATA

Information gathered outside the patient interview is considered auxiliary data; typically, this auxiliary data constitute a tenth to a third of the information needed to determine the patient's diagnosis and treatment. Sometimes with uncooperative or very disorganized patients, outside information is central. As discussed already, two major sources of auxiliary data are interviews with friends or relatives and results from the medical assessment. In addition there are specialized tests and procedures.

Psychological and Neuropsychological Tests

Psychological tests are most often used to quantify personality, intelligence, and the presence, degree, and type of neuropsychological brain dysfunction. Psychological tests can add valuable information that complements the interview. The best tests are *objective* measurements that are structured and utilize standardized questions, scoring, and interpretation. The reliability and validity of psychological tests vary. These tests, like laboratory tests, should not be used routinely but to address *specific* questions, the answers to which may alter the patient's treatment. Patients must not be intoxicated or going through drug withdrawal at the time of testing. Specific clinical questions might be: "What is the patient's intellectual aptitude?" "How tenuous is the patient's contact with reality?" "Which conflicts most trouble the patient?" "How much control does the patient have over aggressive impulses?" "Does the patient have problems with executive functioning (e.g., frontal lobe impairment)? If so, which functions are affected and to what extent?" Table 2-6 outlines the most commonly used psychological tests.

Most psychological tests were developed before *DSM-5*, and some still reflect a psychological, rather than descriptive, diagnostic approach. As a result, patients are more likely to be diagnosed with schizophrenia or border-

TABLE 2-6
Psychological Tests/Instruments

I. **Achievement tests:** Also known as "proficiency tests," measure the outcomes of systematic education and training. The *Wide Range Achievement Test* is an example.

II. **Aptitude tests:** Attempt to measure potential ability in specific areas, such as music, medicine, and accounting. NEPSY-II (SAT) and *Medical College Admissions Test* (MCAT) are examples.

III. **Intelligence tests:** Types of aptitude testing that predict academic performance. They include the *Wechsler Adult Intelligence Scale* (WAIS-IV), commonly used for adults, and the *Wechler Intelligence Scale for Children* (WISC-V). The Stanford–Binet is sometimes used. In addition to measuring IQ, the tests can detect psychotic and organic (physical) impairments. The WAIS and WISC yield verbal comprehension (which also includes arithmetic), spatial abilities, reasoning, working memory, processing speed, and full-scale IQ scores. Education tends to affect the verbal more than the other performance scores; in dementia, performance often declines more than verbal. Learning disabilities exist when there is a discrepancy between one's aptitude and achievement.

IV. **Personality tests:** These assess personality **traits** (the more enduring aspects of personality) and psychological **states** (acute psychopathology). There are two general types:

    A. *Objective.* In these largely quantitative tests, the patient's response is compared to a "right" or "normal" response, based on answers from a sample of subjects on which the test was standardized. The *Minnesota Multiphasic Personality Inventory* (MMPI) is the most widely used objective personality test. It has 567 true–false questions covering a wide range of subject matter (e.g., "I like parties and socials"; "I'm afraid of the germs on doorknobs"). It also has validity scales, which measure tendencies to portray oneself in a favorable or pathological manner, and measures of defensiveness. The *Personality Assessment Inventory* (PAI) and *Millon Clinical Multiaxial Inventory-III* are other examples of structured assessment instruments based upon self-report. Structured clinical diagnostic assessments based upon DSM or ICD also belong in this category and include the *Diagnostic Interview Schedule* (DIS) and the *Structured Clinical Interview for DSM* (SCID).

    B. *Projective.* In these largely clinician-administered qualitative tests, there are no "correct" answers, only the patient's projections. Projective tests include the *Rorschach* ("Inkblot Test"), the *Thematic Apperception Test* (TAT), *Sentence Completion Test*, and *House-Tree-Person*. The responses provide a window into intrapsychic processing and its basis in reality.

V. **Neuropsychological tests:** These tests (and batteries of tests), such as the *Halstead–Reitan Battery*, *Luria-Nebraska*, the more flexible *Developmental NEuroPSYchological Assessment* (NEPSY-II), and a variety of scales from the WAIS and WISC (when used according to the *Boston Process Approach*), specifically evaluate brain impairment, determining if cerebral damage exists and whether it is diffuse or localized. Often the goal of the testing may be to determine the patient's capacity to function in the real world. Many tests can be used to assess specific types of brain functioning:

    A. Executive functioning—higher order cognition for planning, abstract reasoning, and problem-solving located in the prefrontal cortex of the brain (*Wisconsin Card Sorting Test*; *Delis-Kaplan Executive Functioning System*)

    B. Memory—immediate, recent, remote (*Wechsler Memory Scale-IV*)

    C. Orientation (cf. the Brief Cognitive Screening subtest from the *Wechsler Memory Scale IV*)

    D. Perception—auditory, visual, tactile, motor, tactile, visual-motor and visual-spatial constructional tasks (*Bender Visual Motor Gestalt Test*)

    E. Language—both receptive and expressive language (*Boston Naming Test*)

    F. Flexibility of thinking and speed of response (*Trail-Making Test A; Stroop Color-Word Test*)

    G. Attention and concentration—*Continuous Performance Test* (sustaining), *Digit Span* (capacity) *Trail-Making A* (visual information scanning speed), *Trail-Making B* (alternating/shifting sets) line personality by psychological tests than by more recent *ICD* or *DSM* criteria. With these reservations in mind, the clinician should formulate specific questions and then ask the testing psychologist whether they can be answered. The choice of specific tests then would fall upon the testing psychologist and not the referring clinician.

Projective testing is unstructured and labor-intensive because it requires the clinician to ask the questions, record the individualized responses, and score the items. Instruments based upon behavioral observation such as the *Childhood Autism Rating Scale* (CARS) are highly dependent upon the objectivity of the rating clinician. Semi-structured interviews use both open-ended and closed questions. Examples of structured clinical diagnostic assessments based upon *DSM* criteria are the *Diagnostic Interview Schedule* (DIS) and the *Structured Clinical Interview for DSM* (SCID). The more highly structured assessment instruments lend themselves to self- and computer administration.

Evidence for psychopathology may be picked up from certain abbreviated tools and rating scales that screen for specific disorders or clinical conditions. Examples of these abound and include the *SNAPV-IV* rating scale (for ADHD), *Mini Mental State Exam* (for dementia), *Center for Epidemiological Studies Depression* (CESD), *Zung Anxiety Scale*, *Alcohol Use Disorders Identification Test* (AUDIT), and the *Generalized Anxiety Disorder* scale (GAD-7).

Amytal and Polygraph Assisted Interviews

Although popularly known as "truth serum," amytal does not make people tell the truth; some patients even confabulate while receiving it, and malingerers can continue to malinger. Consequently, amytal interviews have little place in the routine assessment. On occasion, they may be helpful in retrieving lost memories, in differentiating neurological from psychiatric disorders (Ward, Rowlett, & Burke, 1986), in distinguishing schizophrenic from mood disorders, and in unblocking a stuck psychotherapy. They will not help in detecting a malingerer. Polygraphy (lie detection), which relies upon continuous physiological monitoring to infer an accurate response to questioning, has some limited clinical applications (e.g., assessment of sex offenders).

SUMMARY OF PRINCIPAL FINDINGS

After the history, MSE, and auxiliary data are reported, the clinician's next task is to highlight the major findings in a paragraph or two. This summary must indicate if there is an immediate threat to life (via suicide, assaultive-ness, or homicide) and does *not* include the patient's diagnosis, prognosis, biopsychosocial formulation, or treatment plan. These are all conclusions (of sorts) based on the findings summarized in this section.

References

American Psychiatric Association. (2013). *Diagnostic and statistical manual of mental disorders*, 5th ed., Washington, DC: American Psychiatric Association.

Andreasen, N.C., Rice, J., Endicott, J., Reich, T., & Coryell, W. (1986). The family history approach to diagnosis. *Archives of General Psychiatry, 43*, 421–429.

Beck, A.T., Brown, G., Berchick, R.J., Stewart, B.L., & Steer, R.A. (1990). Relationship between hopelessness and ultimate suicide: A replication with psychiatric outpatients. *American Journal of Psychiatry, 147*, 190–195.

Centers for Disease Control and Prevention. (April 4, 2008). *National Vital Statistics Reports*, Vol. 56, number 10.

Kendler, K.S., Silberg, J.L., Neale, M.C., Kessler, R.C., Heath, A.C., & Eaves, L.J. (1991). The family history method: Whose psychiatric history is measured? *American Journal of Psychiatry, 148*, 1501–1504.

McGoldrick, M., & Gerson, R. (1985). *Genograms in family assessment*. New York: Norton.

Menninger, K. (1938). *Man against himself*. New York: Harcourt, Brace & World.

Motto, J.A., Heilbron, D.C., & Juster, R.P. (1985). Development of a clinical instrument to estimate suicide risk. *American Journal of Psychiatry, 142*, 680–686.

Ward, N.G., Rowlett, D.B., & Burke, P. (1986). Sodium amylobarbitone in the differential diagnosis of confusion. *American Journal of Psychiatry, 135*, 75–78.

Wittgenstein, L. (1958). *Philosophical investigations*, 2nd ed. Translated by G.E.M. Anscomb. New York: Macmillan.

3

Diagnosis and Prognosis

Di-agnostic? . . . Lessee . . . agnostic means "one what don't know."
. . . an' di is a Greek prefix denotin' two-fold—so the di-agnostic
team don't know twice as much as an ordinary agnostic . . . right?
—Pogo, *New York Post*, August 11, 1966

Diagnostic labels may imply more knowledge than actually exists. Despite increased reliability and validity, the diagnostic categories of *ICD-10 or DSM-5* are not eternal truths, but they are state-of-the-science hypotheses. The multiple and ongoing revisions are proof that these diagnostic categories are not immutable. They are to be used with caution, but used nonetheless, for unless the clinician makes a correct diagnosis, effective treatment cannot be launched and accurate prognosis cannot be estimated.

Considering that *DSM-5* entails over 157 disorders, making a diagnosis has become an increasingly complex task, if only because the number of diagnoses has skyrocketed. In 1840 there was but one psychiatric diagnosis: idiocy (or insanity). In 1880 there were seven: mania, melancholia, monomania, paresis (syphilis of the brain), dementia, dipsomania, and epilepsy. Over the next 100 years, the number of psychiatric disorders rose at an average rate of two per year. The term "disorder," while not exact, describes a group of clinically recognizable signs and symptoms that are associated with personal dysfunction or distress. It avoids some of the inherent problems with using such terms as "illness" or "disease."

DEFINITIONS

Differential diagnosis is the process of choosing the correct diagnosis from conditions with similar features. Traditionally, differential diagnosis began with two general questions: (1) Was the patient's condition caused by a known medical condition or a drug? (2) Was it a psychosis, nonpsychosis, or personality disorder? In large measure, the first question addresses an *etiological* distinction; the second, a *descriptive* distinction.

Disorders caused by other medical conditions were originally called *organic mental disorders*. This term was eventually dropped because it implies that other psychiatric disorders do not have a biological basis. The remaining disorders were called *functional disorders* because no organic cause was known, and the prime etiology was assumed to be psychosocial. Because research on schizophrenia, manic depression, and other so-called functional disorders has revealed a strong biological component, the term *functional* has been eliminated. The term *primary mental disorder* is used to separate these from mental disorders that are the result of another medical condition or substance use.

Psychosis exists when reality testing is grossly impaired; *reality testing* is the ability to evaluate the external world objectively and to distinguish it from inner experience. Delusions, hallucinations, and massive denial are indicative of impaired reality testing and, therefore, of psychosis. Minor distortions of reality—such as a person who experiences transitory derealization or a man overestimating his attractiveness to women—are not considered psychotic. Psychosis is usually inferred when a patient's behavior is grossly disorganized as characterized by incoherent speech, "senseless" violence, and total inattentiveness to the environment. Psychosis may be experienced as distressful and alien (i.e., ego-dystonic) or as an acceptable and integral part of the self (i.e., ego-syntonic).

Neurosis, a nonpsychotic and ego-dystonic syndrome, can be very disabling but in general does not paralyze the individual's functioning or violate social norms. Reality testing and personality organization remain intact. It is purely a descriptive term, without etiological or theoretical associations. *Neurotic process* is primarily driven by anxiety and expressed through unconscious defense mechanisms that are believed to produce neurotic symptoms (e.g., dysphoria, obsessions, compulsions, sexual dysfunction, panic, phobias). This terminology is no longer featured in the latest nosologies but is still used by some health care professionals.

Personality disorders are longstanding conditions, beginning in adolescence or early adulthood, and characterized by inflexible and maladaptive patterns of sufficient severity to cause either clinically significant functional impairment or subjective distress. Unlike psychoses and neuroses, personality disorders are *always* chronic, even though their intensity may fluctuate. As a rule, they are nonpsychotic and ego-syntonic, but exceptions exist.

Exemplifying the rule is antisocial personality disorder, a nonpsychotic state in which the patient doesn't mind his thievery, but his victims do. Two exceptions are the painful shyness seen with avoidant personality disorder and the transient psychosis of the borderline personality disorder. The rages of borderline personalities may be distressing to themselves and others but are usually ego-syntonic because they are considered acceptable and integral parts of the individuals.

TWO BASIC DIAGNOSTIC PRINCIPLES

Diagnostic classification stresses two fundamental principles: *parsimony* and *hierarchy*. The principle of parsimony recommends that clinicians seek the single most elegant, economical, and efficient diagnosis that accounts for *all* the available data; when a single diagnosis is insufficient, the fewest number of diagnoses is sought. The principle of hierarchy is that mental disorders generally exist on a hierarchy of syndromes, which tend to decline in severity: Medical or pharmacological > psychotic > mood > anxiety > somatic > sexual > personality > adjustment > no mental disorder. Thus, when a patients symptoms could be attributed to several disorders, but are entirely explainable by the most severe disorder, the most parsimonious diagnosis belongs to the disorder in that more severe category. The Overview of Differential Diagnosis in Figure 3-1 illustrates how these two principles guide differential diagnosis.

Without the use of these principles, the diagnosis of a patient with auditory hallucinations, persecutory delusions, apprehensiveness, and somatic preoccupations could range from schizophrenia to a paranoid personality, generalized anxiety, or somatoform disorder. With these principles, there is but one diagnosis—schizophrenia—because it is the highest ranking disorder on the hierarchy that accounts for *all* the symptoms. However, more than one diagnosis is sometimes justified. If this person has other clusters of symptoms that are not completely explained by the diagnosis of schizophrenia, then the clinician would proceed down the left column in Figure 3-1. For example, if this person also has panic attacks during remission from psychosis, then panic disorder might be added to the diagnosis. The figure also serves as a guide to understanding the organizational structure for the *ICD* and *DSM* classification of disorders and to establishing hierarchical treatment priorities. A patient with substance abuse, a mood disorder independent of substance abuse, and an avoidant personality disorder is likely to be treated in a hierarchical fashion, with the substance abuse being the first priority of treatment.

SEVEN STEPS FOR PSYCHIATRIC DIAGNOSIS

The following procedure involving seven somewhat overlapping steps is one among several perfectly good ways of reaching a diagnosis:

1. *Collecting data*: Performed during the assessment (Chapter 2).

2. *Identifying psychopathology*: Performed during the assessment (Chapter 2).

3. *Evaluating the reliability of data*: Not all information is equally reliable, and not all informants are equally reliable. Present information is more reliable than past information, since memories fade and current moods often color past recollections. Information garnered during a crisis must be evaluated cautiously. Signs are more reliable than symptoms, because signs can be observed. Objective findings are more reliable than intuitive, interpretive, and introspective findings. Observations such as "The patient seems to be concealing a depression" or "I'm feeling manipulated by the patient" may be true and worth pursuing, but they are far less useful in making a reliable diagnosis than more readily verifiable observations, such as crying, slow gait, and incoherence.

4. *Determining the overall distinctive feature*: The clinician should try to identify the patient's most prominent symptom cluster, such as those listed in the left-hand column of Figure 3-1. If one general category of distinctive features does not stand out, pick two; the next two steps will resolve uncertainty.

5. *Arriving at a diagnosis*: Following the principles of parsimony and hierarchy, the clinician systematically considers every mental disorder that exhibits the patient's overall distinctive feature. The *ICD* and *DSM* diagnostic categories of mental disorders are summarized in Table 3-1.

6. *Checking diagnostic criteria*: The clinician should confirm the diagnosis by verifying if the patient's characteristics meet the diagnostic criteria for the disorder. To demonstrate: Table 3-2 lists criteria for generalized anxiety disorder. Note how criteria E and F illustrate the principle of hierarchy of other disorders above GAD. Criterion F illustrates that generalized anxiety disorder (GAD) is at the bottom of the anxiety disorder hierarchy (some have even referred to GAD as a "wastebasket diagnosis"). It is not a rigid hierarchy; a person with alcohol abuse and/or a mood disorder can have a diagno-

FIGURE 3-1
An Overview of Differential Diagnosis

PRIMARY DISTINCTIVE FEATURE	SYNDROMES	REPRESENTATIVE DISORDERS
Physiological condition or psychoactive substance use	Mental problems due to another medical condition or substance/addiction	Epilepsy, hyperthyroidism Medication induced movements Drug intoxication and withdrawal
Abnormal cognitive and behavioral functioning in early development	Neurodevelopmental	Disorders of intellectual development Autistic spectrum disorder Developmental learning disorder Attention deficit disorder
Acquired abnormalities in cognitive functioning	Neurocognitive	Delirium Dementia
Thinking departs from reality	Psychosis	Delusional disorder Brief transient psychotic disorder Schizophrenia
Episodic changes in mood	Mood	Bipolar and related disorders Depressive disorders
Excessive fear or anxiety and related behavioral disturbances	Anxiety	Generalized anxiety disorder Panic disorder, agoraphobia Specific phobia Social anxiety disorder Separation anxiety disorder
Repetitive thoughts and behaviors	Obsessive-compulsive	Obsessive-compulsive disorder Body dysmorphic disorder Hoarding, trichotillomania
The primary and causal factor for symptoms is severe stress or trauma	Trauma and stress	Reactive attachment disorder Posttraumatic stress disorder Adjustment disorder
Disrupted integration of memories, awareness of identity, immediate sensations, and bodily control	Dissociative	Dissociative amnesia Depersonalization-derealization disorder Trance and possession disorder Dissociative identity disorder
Bodily concerns	Psychosomatic	Somatic symptom disorder Illness anxiety (hypochondriasis) Conversion disorder
Intentionally produced symptoms/signs	Münschhausen	Factitious disorder Malingering (external incentive)

FIGURE 3-1
An Overview of Differential Diagnosis (Continued)

PRIMARY DISTINCTIVE FEATURE	SYNDROMES	REPRESENTATIVE DISORDERS
Abnormal eating, feeding, voiding urine, or passing stool	Feeding, eating, and elimination	Pica, rumination disorder Anorexia nervosa, bulimia nervosa Binge eating disorder Enuresis, encopresis
Sleep disturbance	Sleep-wake	Insomnia, hypersomnolence, narcolepsy, sleep apnea, sleep walking, sleep terrors Circadian rhythm disorder
Unsatisfying sexual activities Atypical sexual arousal Gender identity problems	Sexual dysfunction Paraphilias Gender incongruence	Anorgasmia, dyspareunia pedophilia, fetishism Gender dysphoria
Inability to resist impulse, drive, or urge	Impulse control	Pyromania, kleptomania
Behavior that ranges from defiant to violating rights, social norms, or laws	Disruptive behaviors	Intermittent explosive disorder, oppositional defiant disorder, conduct-dissocial disorder
Enduring behavior problems	Personality	Paranoid, borderline, avoidant
Problems in living	Relational and social Abuse or neglect Educational or occupational Housing or financial Legal or criminal	No mental disorder Issues that may be a focus of clinical attention

Note. In placing the differential diagnosis of *DSM* and *ICD* categories into a manageable perspective, this overview contains some simplifications. The right column presents sample diagnoses. The middle column lists general syndromes, which are clusters of signs and symptoms. The left column indicates the most distinctive overall feature of each syndrome. In general, the clinician moves down the left column of the table from top to bottom until finding the primary clinical feature and then from left to right in order to identify its associated syndrome and the specific disorder that best accounts for all the signs and symptoms.

sis of GAD if the symptoms are present after the person has been abstinent for a few months and not in the midst of the mood disorder.

These criteria are guides, not laws. A patient, for instance, might well have a genuine generalized anxiety disorder even if her condition does not quite match the definition. The symptoms listed under criterion C do not include "an exaggerated startle response" or "nausea and diarrhea," and yet

TABLE 3-1
ICD and DSM *Diagnostic Categories of Mental Disorders*

1. ***Mental Disorders Due to Another Medical Condition***
   Signs and symptoms typical of mental disorders may be due to the direct physiological consequences of another medical condition. As such the diagnosis would not be a primary mental disorder. This category underscores the importance of a thorough medical examination as part of the diagnostic process.

2. ***Substance Use Disorders*** are mental and behavioral disorders that develop as a direct result of the use of predominantly psychoactive substances, including medications. Disorders due to substance use include intoxication, harmful use, dependence, and withdrawal. The term "substance" can refer to drugs of abuse or medications or toxins.

3. ***Neurodevelopmental Disorders*** are behavioral and cognitive disorders that are present from birth or that arise during the developmental period that involve impaired or aberrant development of intellectual, motor, or social functions. Although cognitive deficits are present in many mental disorders that may arise during the developmental period (e.g., schizophrenia, bipolar disorders), only disorders whose core features are neurodevelopmental are included in this grouping. These disorders, although present early, may be an attenuated form and consequently sometimes are not diagnosed until adulthood.

4. ***Neurocognitive Disorders*** are characterized by primary clinical deficits in cognitive functioning that are acquired rather than developmental. These dysfunctions may be temporary or permanent. Neurocognitive disorders represent a decline from a previously attained level of functioning. Although cognitive deficits are present in many mental disorders (e.g., schizophrenia, bipolar disorders), only disorders whose core features involve changes in cognition are included in the neurocognitive category. In cases where the underlying pathology and etiology for neurocognitive disorders can be determined, the identified etiology constitutes a separate classification.

5. ***Schizophrenia Spectrum and Other Primary Psychotic Disorders*** are characterized by substantial departures from reality testing and symptoms such as delusions, hallucinations, formal thought disorder, disorganized behavior, avolition, psychomotor disturbances, and blunted or flat affect, which occur with sufficient frequency and intensity to deviate from expected cultural or subcultural norms. These symptoms are the primary features of these disorders; they do not arise as secondary to or as an associated feature of another disorder (e.g., a mood disorder).

6. ***Mood Disorders*** refers to a superordinate grouping of Bipolar and Depressive Disorders. Mood disorders are defined according to particular types of mood episodes and their pattern over time. The primary types of mood episodes are Depressive episode, Manic episode, Mixed episode, and Hypomanic episode. Mood episodes are not independently diagnosable entities, and therefore do not have their own diagnostic codes. Rather, mood episodes make up the primary components of Depressive and Bipolar Disorders. Patients may or may not have psychotic symptoms; when they do, delusions and hallucinations are usually mood-congruent.

7. ***Anxiety and Fear-Related Disorders*** are characterized by excessive fear and anxiety and related behavioral disturbances. These disorders are characterized by physiological signs of anxiety (e.g., palpitations) and subjective feelings of tension, apprehension, or fear. Anxiety may be acute and focused (panic disorder) or continual and diffuse (generalized anxiety disorder). This category also includes specific phobias.

TABLE 3-1
Continued

8. **Obsessive-Compulsive and Related Disorders** is a group of disorders characterized by repetitive thoughts and behaviors that are believed to share etiologic similarities. Cognitive phenomena such as obsessions, intrusive thoughts, and preoccupations are central to a subset of these conditions (e.g., Obsessive-compulsive disorder, Body dysmorphic disorder, Hoarding) and are accompanied by related repetitive behaviors. Also included in the grouping are Body-focused repetitive behavior disorders, including Trichotillomania and Excoriation disorder, which are primarily characterized by repetitive behaviors and lack of a prominent cognitive aspect.

9. **Stress- or Trauma-Related Disorders** are thought to arise always as a direct consequence of acute severe stress or continued trauma. The stressful events or the continuing unpleasant circumstances are the primary and overriding causal factor and the disorder would not have occurred without their impact. Although not all individuals exposed to similar stressors will develop the disorder, the disorder would not have occurred without exposure to the stressor. The disorders in this section can thus be regarded as maladaptive responses to severe or continued stress, in that they interfere with successful coping mechanisms and therefore lead to problems of social functioning.

10. **Dissociative Disorders** are characterized by disruption or discontinuity in the normal integration of memories of the past, awareness of identity, immediate sensations, and control over bodily movements that are not better explained by another mental and behavioral disorder, medical condition, or substance. They include identity disorders, dissociative amnesia, and depersonalization/derealization. The disruption or discontinuity may be complete, but is more commonly partial, and can vary from day to day or even from hour to hour. These disorders may also have a gradual onset and become chronic.

11. **Psychosomatic (Somatoform) Disorders** are dominated by somatic symptoms that resemble physical illness but cannot be fully accounted for by disease or a pathophysiological mechanism. Typically the patient persistently requests medical investigations, in spite of repeated negative findings and reassurances by doctors that the symptoms have an insufficient physical basis. The patient usually resists attempts to discuss the possibility of psychological causation. The symptoms are not produced intentionally, and there must be strong evidence that psychological factors have an important role in their genesis. This category includes Somatic symptom disorder (formerly called Somatization disorder, hypochondriasis, conversion, and pain disorder). Body dysmorphic disorder is now considered more related to Obsessive-compulsive disorders.

12. **Factitious Disorders** are characterized by the individual repeatedly and consistently feigning, falsifying, or inducing medical or psychological signs and symptoms or injury. The symptoms are produced voluntarily for no apparent (or ulterior) motive other than being ill. These disorders are distinguished from malingering by the absence of obvious external rewards, stressors, or incentives. The focus of these disorders (i.e., the person that is presented as ill, injured, or impaired) may be the self or another person such as a child or spouse.

(continued)

TABLE 3-1
Continued

13. **Feeding, Eating, and Elimination Disorders** involve abnormal eating or feeding behaviors whereas elimination disorders involve the inappropriate voiding of urine or passing of stools. They are not better explained by another mental and behavioral disorder or medical condition and are not developmentally appropriate or culturally sanctioned.

14. **Sleep Disorders** covers problems with sleep regulation and the dyssomnias, including primary insomnia, primary hypersomnia, narcolepsy, breathing-related sleep disorder, and circadian rhythm sleep disorder. Also included are problems that occur during sleep (the parasomnias): nightmares, sleep terrors, and sleep walking disorders.

15. **Sexual and Gender Identity Disorders** includes sexual dysfunctions, atypical sexual arousal (paraphilias), and problems with gender identity. Sexual dysfunctions comprise the various ways in which adult men and women may be unable to experience satisfying, non-coercive sexual activities. Gender incongruence is characterized by a marked and persistent incongruence between an individual's experienced gender and the assigned sex.

16. **Impulse-Control Disorders** are characterized by the repeated failure to resist an impulse, drive, or urge to perform an act that is rewarding to the person, at least in the short-term, despite longer-term harm either to the individual or to others. These disorders of impulse control include kleptomania, pyromania, intermittent explosive disorder, and pathological gambling. Pathological gambling is considered as an addictive disorder in *DSM-5*.

17. **Disruptive Behavior and Dissocial Disorders** are characterized by persistent behavior problems that range from markedly and persistently defiant, disobedient, provocative, or spiteful (i.e., disruptive) behaviors to those that persistently violate the basic rights of others or major age-appropriate societal norms, rules, or laws (i.e., dissocial). Onset of disruptive and dissocial disorders is commonly, though not always, during childhood.

18. **Personality Disorders** are characterized by a relatively enduring and pervasive disturbance in how an individual experiences and interprets himself or herself, others, and the world that results in maladaptive patterns of emotional experience, emotional expression, and behavior. These maladaptive patterns of personality traits are long-standing and inflexible leading to significant problems in functioning that are particularly evident in interpersonal relationships, manifested across a range of personal and social situations.

19. **Problems in Living** may be a focus of clinical attention and include categories of abuse/neglect, relational/social, educational/occupational, housing/financial, and legal/criminal problems.

---

these commonly occur in generalized anxiety disorder. If a patient's condition only approximates the criteria, the clinician can write: "The patient meets *DSM-5* criteria for generalized anxiety disorder, but has had only 5 months of excessive anxiety and worry and only two symptoms in criterion C." By using existing classification systems as a reference point, clinicians speak the diagnostic language of their colleagues, while not being locked into its use. If clinicians have reason not to use *ICD-10* or *DSM-5*, they should specify which criteria are being used (e.g., Feighner, RDC).

TABLE 3-2
Diagnostic Criteria for Generalized Anxiety Disorder

A. Primary **symptoms of anxiety are present most days for at least several weeks at a time**, and usually for several months. *DSM-5 specifies 6 month duration of symptoms.*

B. **Anxiety is generalized and persistent but not restricted to, or even strongly predominating in, any particular environmental circumstances** (i.e., it is "free-floating"). *DSM-5 specifies that the individual finds it difficult to control the worry.*

C. The dominant **symptoms are variable but should usually involve elements of apprehension, motor tension, and autonomic overactivity**.

Apprehension
    (1) Worries about a variety of future misfortunes
    *(2) Nervousness or feeling on edge
    *(3) Concentration difficulty
    *(4) Irritability

Motor Tension
    (5) Fidgeting
    *(6) Muscle tension and related headaches
    *(7) Fatigue
    (8) Inability to relax
    (9) Trembling

Autonomic Overactivity
    *(10) Sleep Disturbance
    (11) Lightheadedness or dizziness
    (12) Sweating
    (13) Tachycardia, palpitations, or tachypnea
    (14) Epigastric discomfort

In children, frequent need for reassurance and recurrent somatic complaints may be prominent.

DSM-5 requires 3 of the 6 symptoms indicated by asterisks for adults and a single symptom for children.

D. The above symptoms result **in significant distress or significant impairment** in personal, family, social, educational, occupational, or other important areas of functioning.

E. The disturbance **is not due to the direct physiological effects of a substance or another medical condition**.

F. The above signs and symptoms must not meet the full criteria for depressive episode, phobic anxiety disorder, panic disorder, or obsessive-compulsive disorder and are **not better explained by another mental disorder**. The transient appearance (for a few days at a time) of other symptoms, particularly depression, does not rule out generalized anxiety disorder as a main diagnosis. *In addition to these disorders DSM-5 specifically mentions that the patient's anxiety is not better explained by psychotic disorders, Separation Anxiety Disorder, Anorexia Nervosa, Somatic Symptom Disorder, Hypochondriasis, or Posttraumatic Stress Disorder.*

This disorder is more common in women, and often related to chronic environmental stress. Its course is variable but tends to be fluctuating and chronic.

Note: Adapted from *ICD-10* (p. 115) and *DSM-5* (p. 222)

7. *Resolving diagnostic uncertainty*: If at this stage, one diagnosis does not suffice, or if some evidence is inconsistent with other data, or if the diagnosis remains unclear for any reason, the most likely culprits are (a) inadequate data, (b) premature closure, (c) atypical presentations, or (d) multiple disorders.

Inadequate data may reflect missing information that clarifies the diagnosis, once obtained. For instance, brief psychotic disorder must be "at least 1 day and no more than 1 month" in duration, but the patient, previously normal, manifested psychotic symptoms every 3 or 4 days and then returned to normal. Additional data solved the puzzle of this intermittent psychosis: When the patient's urine tested positive for amphetamines, his diagnosis was changed to substance-induced psychotic disorder. Sometimes data are inadequate because the therapist has not talked to the right people. After conducting 2 months of stalemated couples treatment, the therapist insisted on seeing the couple's 5-year-old daughter as part of a family assessment. Until then, Mother and Father had colluded in a secret, which in pure childhood innocence, their daughter revealed when she asked, "How come Daddy stumbles around every night after he comes home?"

Premature closure amounts to "to jumping the diagnostic gun," without proper differential diagnosis. A common trap is the "5-minute diagnosis": After interviewing a patient for 5 minutes, the therapist "unconsciously" reaches a diagnosis and then inadvertently distorts, converts, and selectively seeks information that confirms this initial diagnosis. Call it human nature, but *every* clinician is prone to see what he or she wants to see. What distinguishes the skilled professional is the willingness to double-check a diagnosis by repeating the previous six steps.

> A clinician in training diagnosed a patient in the emergency room as having a major depression. The diagnosis seemed obvious: The patient's face was blank, his gait slow, his movements agitated; he felt sad and lonely. He even *said* he was depressed. Yet soon after the patient was admitted, the trainee was called by a supervisor who said that the patient's diagnosis was Parkinson's disease, not depression. The clinical error was that he saw a depressed-looking person and stopped thinking: he assumed that the patient was depressed, did not perform a systematic differential diagnosis, and only saw what he expected to find.

Although *atypical presentations* cause diagnostic confusion, some patients simply do not conform to classic textbook descriptions. For instance, patients with major depression usually feel sad, yet some don't feel sad at all and complain primarily of bodily aches and pains. Another advantage of systematically moving down the classification hierarchy is that clinicians often detect these atypical cases.

Multiple diagnoses—that is, more than one diagnosis per axis—may be indicated after first attempting to ascribe a patient's symptoms to a single diagnosis. Just as medical patients can have more than one disorder, so can psychiatric patients.

If a diagnostic uncertainty persists, the clinician should use the most applicable diagnostic label: "diagnosis deferred," or specific diagnosis ("provisional"), or "other specified" class of mental disorder, or "unspecified" class of mental disorder, Finally, the patient may have "no mental disorder," a most under-utilized diagnosis.

MULTIAXIAL DIAGNOSIS

Multiaxial diagnosis was first proposed in Sweden in 1947, but not adopted. Five years later, Danish psychiatrists officially adopted a biaxial system that separated symptoms from etiology. After two decades of promotion by the World Health Organization, the concept surfaced in United States in 1975, when John Strauss suggested a multiaxial approach with an axis for social functioning. In 1980, *DSM-III* incorporated multiaxial diagnosis in order to clarify the complexities and relationships of biopsychosocial difficulties and thereby facilitate treatment planning. *DSM-5* no longer uses the 5 axes format so that all diagnoses are listed together. However it is still being used as a convenient way to organize diagnoses and therefore included in this text.

Axis I: Clinical syndromes (e.g., mental disorders); developmental disorders; other conditions that may be a focus of clinical attention
Axis II: Personality disorders/traits; mental retardation
Axis III: Other medical conditions
Axis IV: Psychosocial and environmental problems (stressors)
Axis V: Assessment of Functioning (GAF)

The main advantage of separating Axes I and II is to prevent the typically more florid presentations of Axis I mental disorders from overshadowing, or becoming confused with, the more chronic and subtle Axis II personality disorders. Distinguishing between these axes may clarify what therapy can reasonably accomplish, given that treatment is more likely to alleviate Axis I than Axis II disorders. Therapists (and clients) who fail to separate mental from personality disorders are frequently disappointed, however unjustifiably, when only the former remits with brief treatment. Where uncertainty exists, clinicians may choose to add "provisional" after the diagnosis on any axis.

Axis III lists only medical conditions that are "potentially relevant to the understanding or management of the case." It is unfortunate that some non-physicians are reluctant, or believe it is inappropriate, to list an Axis III diagnosis, since a patient's diagnosis should be complete. When writing an Axis III diagnosis, many nonphysicians like to add the source of this diag-nostic information parenthetically (e.g., the patient's doctor, the patient, the chart).

In its dry way, Axis IV attempts to include all of Shakespeare's "slings and arrows of outrageous fortune." It lists the psychosocial and environmental problems that may affect prognosis of mental disorders on Axes I and II. Stressors may involve jobs, finances, living situations, health, social support, family conflicts, and negative life events. Even "positive" stressors should be listed, if they are problematic. For example, a job promotion brings higher financial reward (good news!) but longer hours at the office, more travel, and increased responsibility (bad, stressful news!). All relevant problems should be listed, including those that *contributed to* the disorder(s) and those that *resulted from* the disorder(s). In general, this list is confined to problems in the past year. However, earlier problems should be listed if they clearly con-tribute to the present diagnosis or have become a focus of treatment; for example, post–traumatic stress disorder, rape, childhood sexual and physical abuse, or combat experience could all be listed. Problems that have become the primary focus of treatment should be recorded not only in Axis IV but also in Axis I. For example, if the therapy only focuses on "bad hair" and it really is bad, it might be listed in Axis I. However, the astute clinician in this situation might consider body dysmorphic disorder instead. The *DSM-5* includes the former Axis IV stressors as V, Z, or T codes in "other conditions that may be a focus of clinical attention." The categories for these problems are relational, other social enironment, abuse or neglect, emotional or occu-pational, housing or financial, and legal or criminal.

Other Conditions That May Be a Focus of Clinical Attention

Mental- and medical-health professionals see many people with emotional or behavioral difficulties that are not mental disorders but problems in living. Though mainly a classification of mental disorders, the DSM also catalogues these problems in living as relational and social, abuse or neglect, educational or occupational, housing or financial problems, and legal or criminal difficulties. For some problems in living, such as uncomplicated bereavement or occupational problems, patients themselves seek help; for other problems in living, such as malingering or adolescent antisocial behavior, people other than patients request professional consultation. An individual can have a mental disorder and a problem in living yet only want assistance for the latter. The problem in living may be a manifestation or consequence of the mental disorder. Problems in living may become a focus of clinical attention if they affect the development, course, prognosis, or treatment of an identified mental disorder.

Axis V indicates the patient's current overall level of social, psychological, and occupational functioning. Physical functioning and limitations are not included here but may be listed in Axis IV. The Global Assessment of Functioning (GAF) was used for rating Axis V on a 100-point scale. Usually this rating is done to ascertain the patient's level of functioning in the present. The new recommended alternative to assess functioning is the World Health Organization Disability Assessment Schedule 2.0 (WHODAS 2.0). This 36-item measure assesses disability in adults across the six domains of understanding and communicating, getting around, self-care, getting along with people, life activities, and participation in society (see Table 3-3). There is also a child version of the WHODAS.

This current rating of disability or dysfunction, together with the Axis I diagnosis, helps clinicians decide if patients should be hospitalized immediately or live in a group home. Clinicians may also want a rating of patients' highest level of functioning in the past year, which helps to determine prognosis and treatment (since patients who previously functioned at a higher level usually recover at a higher level). To illustrate: With everything else being the same, and with Tom and Jerry being equally delusional—one's certain he's a cat, the other, a mouse—if before becoming ill Tom had a solid marriage, good job, and satisfying hobbies, whereas Jerry did not, then after recovery Tom would probably function better than Jerry. Treatment goals should reflect these different expectations.

PROGNOSIS

A patient's prognosis or outcome is a product of several factors: (1) the natural course of the particular disorder; (2) the patient's highest prior level of functioning ; (3) the duration of the present illness (the longer the duration, the

TABLE 3-3
WHODAS 2.0—World Health Organization Disability Assessment Schedule

In the past 30 days how much difficulty did you have in the following activities because of physical, mental, or other health conditions?	None	Mild	Moderate	Severe	Extreme
	1	2	3	4	5

Understanding and communicating
1. Concentrating on doing something for ten minutes?
2. Remembering to do important things?
3. Analyzing and finding solutions to problems in day-to-day life?
4. Learning a new task, for example, learning how to get to a new place?
5. Generally understanding what people say?
6. Starting and maintaining a conversation?

Getting around
7. Standing for long periods such as 30 minutes?
8. Standing up from sitting down?
9. Moving around inside your home?
10. Getting out of your home?
11. Walking a long distance, such as a kilometer (or equivalent)?

Self-care
12. Washing your whole body?
13. Getting dressed?
14. Eating?
15. Staying by yourself for a few days?

Getting along with people
16. Dealing with people you do not know?
17. Maintaining a friendship?
18. Getting along with people who are close to you?
19. Making new friends?
20. Sexual activities?

Life activities—Household
21. Taking care of your household responsibilities?
22. Doing most important household tasks well?
23. Getting all the household work done that you needed to do?
24. Getting your household work done as quickly as needed?

Life activities—School/Work
25. Your day-to-day work/school?
26. Doing your most important work/school tasks well?
27. Getting all of the work done that you need to do?
28. Getting your work done as quickly as needed?

TABLE 3-3
WHODAS 2.0 Continued

Because of your health condition, in the past 30 days how much of a problem did you have:	None	Mild	Moderate	Severe	Extreme
Participation in society	1	2	3	4	5
29. Joining in community activities (for example, festivities, religious, or other activities) in the same way as anyone else can?					
30. With barriers or hindrances around you?					
31. Living with dignity because of the attitudes and actions of others?					
32. Spending a lot of time on your health condition or its consequences?					
33. Being emotionally affected by your health condition?					
34. With your health being a drain on the financial resources of you or your family?					
35. With your health affecting your family?					
36. Doing things by yourself for relaxation or pleasure?					

WHODAS 2.0 Scoring Instructions

Scores are assigned to each of the items as indicated above "None" (1), "Mild" (2), "Moderate" (3), "Severe" (4), and "Extreme" (5). A simple sum of all the scores across the seven domains constitutes a statistic that is sufficient to describe the degree of overall functional limitations. It can be converted to a percentage score by dividing the simple sum by the maximum number of points (180).

Another scoring paradigm is to calculate the average scores for each domain by dividing the raw domain score by the number of items in that domain. As an example, if all the scores for the self-care domain were rated as severe then the average score is 16/4 = 4, indicating severe disability. The average general disability score would simply be the sum of all the scores for all domains divided by the total number of 36 items.

bleaker the outlook); (4) the abruptness of onset (the more acute the onset, the better the prognosis); (5) the age of onset (the earlier in life, the poorer the outcome); (6) the availability of effective treatments; (7) the patient's compliance or adherence with treatment; and (8) the presence of a supportive social network.

It is worth noting that how disturbed a patient is during an acute episode is *not* always a good predictor of long-term outcome. A 20-year-old patient who has deteriorated over a period of 6 years from schizophrenia and who now displays social withdrawal and flat affect has a far worse long-term prognosis than a 50-year-old patient who functioned well until a month ago, when she became acutely manic, insisted she was the reincarnation of Queen Victoria, threw $100 bills out the window, and spoke nonstop. Clinicians should be clear about *which* prognosis they are determining: is it for a short-term (e.g., posthospitalization) or a long-term (e.g., a year after discharge) outcome? Is it for an acute versus a more chronic disorder? Is it a forecast of something more specific, such as relapse, suicide, assault, social functioning? When clinicians dispense prognostic information to patients and their families, they should describe these various types of outcomes instead of indicating a single, and less meaningful, prognosis.

Warnings about *DSM* and *ICD*

Rote memorization of diagnostic criteria is a long and pointless endeavor; the learning of specific criteria occurs most effectively through clinical experience. However, when this text presents a disorder, students should still examine its criteria in order to (1) obtain an overall picture of the disorder, (2) learn its defining characteristics, (3) become familiar with its common symptoms, (4) understand the meanings of the technical terms that describe it, and (5) learn which features differentiate it from other disorders.

For decades the classification of mental disorders has been based on a categorical approach to diagnosis. As in medicine, this type of approach works best for disorders that have homogeneous characteristics and clear boundaries differentiating them from other disorders. A stroke and a myocardial infarction are examples of such discrete medical categories. This categorical approach does not work as well for disorders that exist on a continuum—those that can be better described by dimensions and have great variability within the diagnostic category. Anemia and vitamin deficiency are medical examples of dimensional-continuum types of disorders. Because the diagnosis of anemia depends on a hematocrit (a red blood cell count), what count constitutes anemia is always open to debate. Some people function normally with "low" hematocrits, whereas others with "low-normal" do not. Diagnosing psychopathology presents the same problems, since every disorder has both categorical and dimensional aspects. Autistic disorder is an example of a diagnosis that seemed to fit a pure categorical approach relatively easily (language impairment). However, with the increased recognition of higher-functioning forms of autism and Asperger's disorder, the dimensional approach seems better suited to the spectrum of pervasive developmental disorders that share some degree of impairment in social relatedness. The *DSM-5* now includes these separate diagnoses on the continuum of a single Autistic Spectrum Disorder. Many other disorders have continuous dimensional qualities. For example, antisocial personality traits might range from a persistent breaking of parking laws (a not uncommon quality in the general populace) to killing with no remorse (a much rarer characteristic). How to establish hyperactivity in attention-deficit/hyperactivity disorder is equally difficult. Where do you set the bar? In response to the reality of dimensional complexities within a categorical approach, the clinician should not assume that every mental disorder is a completely discrete entity with absolute boundaries.

Also, individuals sharing the same diagnosis may differ in important ways.

References

American Psychiatric Association. (2013). *Diagnostic and statistical manual of mental disorders*, 5th ed. Washington, DC: American Psychiatric Association.

Endicott, J., Spitzer, R.L., Fleiss, J.L., & Cohen, J. (1976). The Global Assessment Scale: A procedure for measuring overall severity of psychiatric disturbance. *Archives of General Psychiatry*, 33, 766–771.

Feighner, J.P., Robins, E., Guze, S.B., Woodruff, R.A., Winokur, G., & Munoz, R. (1972). Diagnostic criteria for use in psychiatric research. *Archives of General Psychiatry*, 26, 57–63.

Luborsky, L. (1962). Clinicians' judgments of mental health. *Archives of General Psychiatry*, 7, 407–417.

Spitzer, R.L., Williams, J.B.W., & Skodal, A.E. (1980). *DSM-III*: The major achievements and an overview. *American Journal of Psychiatry*, 137, 151–164.

World Health Organization. (1992). *The ICD–10 Classification of mental and behavioural disorders: Clinical descriptions and diagnostic guidelines*. Geneva: World Health Organization (WHO).

World Health Organization. (2010). *Measuring health and disability: Manual for WHO Disability Assessment Schedule*. Geneva, World Health Organization (WHODAS 2.0 36-item version self-administered or interview administered www.who.int/classifications/icf/whodasii/en).

4

Etiology

In general, *etiology* refers to the *origins* of a disorder, whereas *pathogenesis* refers to *all the mechanisms* that ultimately produce it. In this chapter, the term *etiology* encompasses pathogenesis and includes everything that has caused the patient's presenting difficulties. At the turn of the 20th century, the most prevalent mental illness was general paresis (i.e., syphilis of the brain). Other common psychiatric disorders were "myxedema madness" (a type of hypothyroidism), the epilepsies, and psychoses due to vitamin deficiencies and brain infections. As soon as the cause for each of these conditions was discovered, the job of treatment shifted to physicians *other* than psychiatrists, such as internists and neurologists.

Indeed, a major reason *DSM-III* and *DSM-IV* switched to a nosology based on descriptive instead of on etiological criteria was that the etiology of most mental disorders was considered idiopathic. (*Idiopathic* refers to unknown causation, whereas *iatrogenic* refers to physician-induced illness such as drug side effects). Exceptions existed, as when a disorder's etiology was both obvious and inherent to its definition, such as the role of amphetamines in amphetamine intoxication, or the role of psychosocial stressors in producing a posttraumatic stress disorder. Unlike its predecessor and because of advances in neuroscience, *DSM-5* now considers etiological hypotheses—biological as well as psychosocial.

Although the precise etiologies of most mental disorders are still largely unknown, more is understood about etiology today than ever. Most dramatic have been advances in psychobiology and epidemiology; less heralded (but equally important) has been the growing appreciation of how intrapsychic, familial, and social influences interact with biology to produce mental disorders. Etiology can be attributed to either genetic influences or environmental influences or the interaction of genetic and environmental influences.

A complete psychiatric assessment, or "workup," includes the detailed history, composed of personal history, family history, physical examination, a medical review of systems, and mental status examination, culminating in a case formulation, and finally the *DSM* or *ICD* diagnosis, with prognosis included if possible. Thus through the formulation the clinician has an opportunity to explain his or her thinking process and rationale for the conclusions represented succinctly in diagnoses, even if provisional. The case formulation should discuss predisposing, precipitating, provoking, perpetuating, and even protecting factors in relation to the etiology and pathogenesis of the disorder. One approach to organizing the formulation is to use the *biopsychosocial model* wherein the patient's present illness is discussed in terms of biological, psychodynamic, cognitive, emotional, and behavioral aspects, as well as familial, interpersonal, cultural, and spiritual etiologies (see Engel, 1977). A full understanding the person will lead to the etiology and pathogenesis of the disease in that person.

Etiology is generally sought not only to explain the origin of illness or disease in a particular patient but also to generalize to all patients who present similarly. This allows for development of more reliable diagnostic criteria and invites the study of mechanisms of illness that then pave the way to rational design of therapeutic interventions. Although etiology of many psychiatric disorders and their symptoms may be uncertain, the clinician strives for a reliable diagnosis and formulation that fits the history and examination data and then supports and guides individualized treatment planning. The initial assessment requires a complete history to catalogue the precise sequence of facts particular to the individual case—facts about the individual from prenatal to the present time as well as facts about the individual's environment, all of which must be placed in the context of the patient's chief complaint and his or her personal narrative or interpretation of such facts. Throughout the process it is prudent to keep separate these many facts from the patient's interpretations of them (and the clinician's, for that matter). Determination of etiology must therefore be based on reliable sources and observations; it cannot otherwise be satisfactorily ascertained. Since reliable evidence is not always available, the establishment of more precise etiology in many cases may need to be suspended or presumed until such facts can be discovered. In the meantime, available evidence is used to support what is called a presumptive, or working, diagnosis. After available data sources have been surveyed and data have been organized according to reliability and apparent relevance to the individual, the diagnostician engages in a process known as differential diagnosis that involves comparing and contrasting several possible diagnoses to determine which of them most closely fits all the available detail and time course of the evidence.

McHugh and Slavney (1998) offer some categories to help organize common perspectives on etiology. They present the characteristics and unique properties of the *disease perspective* (e.g., dementia syndromes or manic–depressive disorder), the *dimensional perspective* (e.g., autism, intellectual development, and personality disorders), the *behavioral perspective* (e.g., pathological gambling, alcoholism), or the *life story perspective* (e.g., adjustment disorder with depression, conversion disorder). Appropriate discussions of etiology will follow naturally once the clinician identifies the type of disorder.

THE DIMENSIONS OF "CAUSATION"

To speak of "*the*" cause of a mental disorder is naive; it is akin to patients who enter treatment and say, "I want to get to the *root* of my problem." This "root myth" assumes that a single factor has caused the problem and that unearthing it will result in cure. Unfortunately, there is no such thing as *the* root to a problem; at most, there are roots, with many sprouting, variegated phenomena. Formulations, therefore, should consider diverse etiological influences. For example, a teenager begins drinking alcohol to feel grown up. But what *initiates* a disorder usually differs from what *perpetuates* it. So, if the individual is still drinking at age 30, the reason is no longer to feel like an adult; at this point, they are drinking from habit or dependence. What originates and maintains a problem may also differ from what *exacerbates* it; for example, stress may rekindle drinking in somebody who previously had stopped.

Another factor in causation is *predisposition* (or risk). At the present time this concept is generally cast in terms of a susceptibility gene or set of genes that becomes activated under certain stressors or conditions, such as exposure to a microbe, toxin, antigen, emotional trauma, irradiation, or an injurious physical environment.

Many mechanisms might lead to a pathological cascade of gene expression or biological transformation that leads to a complex and highly pleiotropic phenotype such as the phenomenon we observe clinically as "schizophrenia." While we observe from clinical histories that schizophrenia takes place over time, there are data to support the idea that the disease process may be initiated as early in development as prenatally or within the first trimester of development. Several lines of evidence point to and support this hypothesis, which is aptly called the *neurodevelopmental hypothesis*. Many experimental animal models have shown that insults of many types during this early period of neurodevelopment can lead to aberrant gene expression and subsequently abnormal brain development and brain function later in life. In an epidemiological study of children born in Denmark from 1973 to 1995 (Khashan et al., 2008), a higher incidence of schizophrenia was found in those born to mothers who had lost a first-degree relative in their first trimester. It is not known whether an emotional trauma in itself leads to other pathological events that start the cascade toward schizophrenia. It seems likely that such a pathological insult acts through known mechanisms such as hypoxia, hypoglycemia or hyperglycemia, hypercortisolemia, alcohol or drug-induced brain injury, malnutrition, infection, or hippocampal maldevelopment.

A predisposition may be "disorder-*specific*" (e.g., a gene producing a vulnerability to a particular disorder) or "disorder-*nonspecific*" (e.g., broken families during childhood produce a vulnerability to many mental disorders). When determining causation, clinicians should be careful to delineate these four levels (the 4 **P**s): **p**redisposition, **p**recipitation (initiation), **p**rovocation (exacerbation), and **p**erpetuation. Many theories of mental illness are originally proposed as initial causes of a disorder, whereas subsequent data indicate that these theories are more relevant to what maintains (perpetuates) or aggravates (provokes) a disorder. The 5th P would be protective factors, including the strengths, internal resources, or environmental advantage that mitigate the condition and contribute to the individual's resiliency.

> For instance, the hypothesis that "double-bind communication" causes schizophrenia has been largely refuted, yet growing evidence shows that double-bind communication and high-expressed emotion in the environment can trigger a relapse to psychotic symptoms with about the same likelihood as discontinuing medication (Hogarty et al., 1974). An example of double-bind communication would be "for a fat kid, you are pretty good looking."

Clinicians should also distinguish between what is *inherent* to a disorder and what is a *consequence* of it. Both factors feed into one another and may profoundly affect the patient. The importance of this distinction becomes apparent by carefully examining the sequence of events. For example, one may presume that a job loss caused a severe depression, whereas a careful history demonstrates that the patient's depressive symptoms of low energy, indecisiveness, and poor concentration caused the job loss. Causes can be categorized as (1) necessary and sufficient, (2) necessary but not sufficient, or (3) facilitating or predisposing, but neither necessary nor sufficient.

Few diseases have causes that are necessary and sufficient; one example is Huntington's chorea, a progressive and fatal dementia, in which having the autosomal dominant genetic mutation of the *huntingtin* gene on chromosome 4 is all that is needed to produce the illness. Alcoholism illustrates the second type; although alcohol is necessary for the disorder, other factors are required to produce it, since not everyone who drinks becomes an alcoholic. These other factors may include stressful environments and comorbid predisposing genes, such as the short-form allele of the serotonin transporter promotor gene, which also predisposes to anxiety (Herman et al., 2003). Many causes fall into the third category; for example, loss of parents during childhood or physical or sexual abuse in childhood may contribute to psychopathology later in life. Such events are neither necessary nor sufficient, however, to produce the psychopathology we may observe in clinical settings. Conversely, the harmful effects of a disorder may be reduced or prevented by rectifying the facilitating or predisposing causes (e.g., poverty, stress), even when they are not necessary or sufficient causes. And it must be remembered that there are very likely protective factors that lend remarkable resilience or even relative immunity from some disorders in some individuals in spite of traumatic events or harsh environments.

> Resilience is the capacity to adapt to various adversities. Psychopathology is influenced positively or negatively by such resiliency factors as intelligence, insight, moptivation, locus of control, and will. "Dandelion child" is a Swedish metaphorical expression for the capacity of some children to survive and thrive under whatever conditions they encounter, similar to how dandelions seem to flourish regardless of the type or amount of soil, moisture, and light. Observations of such children have sparked an extensive developmental literature on the phenomenon of resilience. A contrasting metaphor is the "orchid child" or context-sensitive individual whose survival depends upon nearly optimal environmental conditions. In harsher or neglectful environments, the orchid promptly fades but with nurturance and greenhouse conditions it blooms brilliantly. Whereas natural selection seems to favor dandelion children who can survive under a wide range of conditions and tolerate adversities, there is a growing body of evidence suggesting that more sensitive or reactive phenotypes under specific environmental conditions may thrive and even outperform (Boyce & Ellis, 2005). Together there is maximal adaptive flexibility for the family or species. The challenge is to

determine the ideal environmental conditions for the specific child and then consistently provide them.

Because mental disorders have multiple rather than singular causes, and because some of these causes are facilitating or predisposing, *multicausality* has been misconstrued as *omnicausality*: That is, anything can cause anything, as long as there is a tenuous connection. If a passive father has a schizophrenic son, then passive fathers are deemed a cause of schizophrenia. This line of thinking is nonsense; it's like saying that milk is a cause of schizophrenia because a person with schizophrenia drank milk. Omnicausality falters because it equates a *casual* with a *causal* association between two events—a confusion that can only be clarified by studying the matter with scientific *controls* (Goodwin & Guze, 1989).

Some diagnostic categories, such as schizophrenia, consist of more than one typical presentation (symptom constellation) despite sharing the same core (cardinal) features. The specific subtype may be defined by the most prominent symptom, as in the various *subtypes* of schizophrenia (paranoid, catatonic, etc.). Each subtype may involve different etiological factors. Conversely, entities that present with the same clinical picture may have arisen via different etiological routes. For instance, genetics clearly produces some depressions, but not others; some antihypertensive medications induce some major depressions, bereavement triggers others, and "learned helplessness" causes others. The reason these depressions may present with the same symptoms is because, no matter what their origins, at some point a specific series of changes was launched within the brain—that is, a "final common pathway" that produced the characteristic symptoms of major depression.

Symptoms and *issues*, although related, are of a different order. Symptoms may be reported, such as hallucinations or insomnia, whereas issues contain the meaning of symptoms and reflect how patients cope, how they feel toward authorities, and so on (see Chapter 1).

> For 15 years a middle-aged man occasionally had the delusion that people were sneaking itching powder into his food. Since his divorce of 20 years ago, homosexual urges had frightened him. When he felt close to another man— or to use his words, "got the itch for somebody"—his delusion would arise. The man's symptom was a delusion; many patients have delusions. The man's issues about itching powder and homosexuals were idiosyncratic; they derived from his life experience, were symbolically meaningful to him, and erupted in circumstances stressful for him.

Symptoms have *form* whereas issues have *content.* For instance, two patients may present with major depression; both complain of severe guilt, hopelessness, and insomnia. Their symptoms are the same, yet their issues vary. The first patient, a young, successful TV executive, insists that her sleeplessness stems from her being "a total failure," while the second, a retired Baptist postal clerk, is sure his sleeplessness is a punishment from God. Both patients suffer from the biologically induced insomnia of major depression. Yet the issues the patients bring to their insomnia—that is, what it means to them and how they deal with it—differ according to their life experiences.

In general, biology determines symptoms and psychosocial influences shape issues. How a particular patient expresses signs and symptoms of a mental disorder greatly depends on his or her personality traits and biological constitution. When drunk or "stoned," some people may giggle, some babble, some dance, some cry, some withdraw, some get the munchies, and others become violent. They all have a drug-induced mental state, yet how it manifests varies according to the individual's constitutional traits. The same holds for medical illness. For example, coronary patients cope with heart attacks in many different ways depending on their personality. Arthur Kleinman (1988) makes a similar distinction for all medical disorders: There is a *disease* that may be caused by a virus, bacteria, etc., with *symptoms*, such as fever and abdominal pain; and there is the *illness* and with it, *illness behavior*—going to a doctor, having a shaman exorcise the demon, or trying to make spiritual sense out of the fever-induced hallucinations.

Like intoxication, mental disorders tend to amplify personality traits. During a major depression, a lifelong worry-wart frets nonstop, a chronically suspicious man becomes paranoid, and a mild hypochondriac becomes a severe one. Consequently, the cause of a patient's behavior can never be fully attributed to either psychology *or* biology. Both are responsible for behavior, albeit in different ways—a truism recognized long ago by Hughlings Jackson, the Father of English neurology: "There is no physiology of the mind anymore than there is a psychology of the nervous system." As long as people have minds *and* brains, it is hard to imagine how one could function without the other!

Given that mental disorders neither overpower personality nor make it disappear, being mentally ill or taking LSD, PCP, or alcohol neither explains nor justifies committing antisocial acts. Mental illness is no excuse for bad manners. Statements such as "Peter beat up Sally because he was drunk" or "Darlene's schizophrenia caused her to drown her child" imply that the patient/ criminal is not responsible for the act, as if the drug or the mental illness *made* him or her commit the crime. Being schizophrenic *per se* does not make one violent. Being acutely psychotic may diminish normal social restraints or magnify preexisting violent tendencies, but that's quite different from dissociating the person from his or her crime by totally blaming the illness. It is akin to the old defense, "The devil made me do it."

VOLITION

"Volition" refers to the act of willing. How much a patient is able to willfully influence or determine his behavior during a mental disorder may be difficult to discern. The first question is "Can people fake mental illness?" The answer is "Yes, but not for long." If there are any doubts, try it! Actors can fake madness for 3 hours a night and twice on Wednesdays and Saturdays, but not much longer. Only those with mental disorders can pace for hours, shadowbox for days, and dwell on rotting bladders and stinking bowels. It's too exhausting to sustain. Nor can one hallucinate at will, except with the help of certain chemicals or a sensory-isolation chamber.

Nevertheless, the question of people faking mental illness stubbornly persists, partly because some patients seem to respond to the environment according to what's "convenient" or "necessary." When clinicians must decide whether to permit a floridly psychotic inpatient to attend the funeral of a loved one, they find that most patients pull themselves together, go to the funeral, and do just fine. How come? Because, like the intoxicated, the mentally ill can still modify their behavior depending on the situation and the severity of their illnesses. When an inebriated student receives a telephone call from his parents, he can "get his act together," as long as the call is not too long and he is not too drunk. Likewise, if they are not too ill and not required to act "properly" for too long, people with mental illness are often able to "normalize" their behavior. Therefore, highly disturbed psychiatric patients are not helpless automatons, for they can exert some control over their disorder.

Conversely, just as being intoxicated makes it extremely difficult to perform routine tasks, so does being mentally ill. Like everyone else, people with mental illness must contend with problems in living, but unlike everyone else, they must do so with the added burdens of psychiatric symptoms. Interviewing for a job is hard enough; feeling certain that the interviewer is Satan doesn't help. Writing a term paper can be stressful, but imagine trying to do so with racing thoughts and taunting hallucinations. Mental illness makes everything harder. Simple chit-chat isn't easy when you're sure a bomb is going to explode in your stomach. Given all their symptoms, what amazes many clinicians is not how poorly people with mental illness do, but how well.

EXPLAINING VERSUS UNDERSTANDING

In the formulation the clinician should seek to understand as well as to explain the patient's difficulties. Unfortunately, many clinicians are unaware of the difference between "explaining" and "understanding." In this context, *understanding* is not being used in the *explanatory* sense of "I understand *why* Jim hates his mother," but rather in the *descriptive* sense of "I understand *how* Jim hates his mother."

To explain something is to view it from the outside; to understand it is to view from within. Explaining relies on logic and intellect, understanding on experience and empathy. Explanations should be objective, whereas understandings can only be subjective. Explanations address the "why" of behavior, understanding, the "what." For different reasons, both explaining and understanding are crucial for clinical care. One is not better than the other; they are simply different.

Clinicians often say they are understanding (*verstehen*) when actually they are explaining (*erklaren*). Consider Karen, a psychiatric inpatient who was convinced she had no legs. When her psychiatrist went on vacation, she walked up to the staff and complained, more intensely than ever, of having no legs. Every time this occurred, her substitute therapist replied, "You're walking, so that proves that you have legs. But even so, you're obviously worried about having no legs because your doctor is on vacation." Karen was infuriated; she claimed that the staff "doesn't understand me." The staff responded, "But we do understand: Your psychiatrist has gone away, and you're understandably upset." Patient and staff were talking past each other. The patient accurately felt that she was being "explained away." The staff mistakenly believed that they were showing understanding, when they were actually giving a correct explanation. Another psychiatrist demonstrated empathic understanding when he said to Karen, "You must feel like a paraplegic. It's frightening to feel you have no control over your legs, or that they don't work properly, or that they don't belong to you. No wonder you're upset!" Feeling that somebody was finally on her "wavelength," Karen was ready to consider the explanation about her therapist's absence.

It's not that clinicians never understand their patients; to various degrees, they all do. Yet to the degree that clinicians do understand, it's more a product of their being *people* than of their being *professionals*. Therapists are inherently no better or worse than anyone else at understanding people. Indeed, a good novelist reveals a thorough understanding of a character's psychology without using a single psychological term. The ability to understand can be improved with experience and training, but it doesn't originate in the reading of books or articles.

In contrast, by learning etiological theory, clinicians are far more adept at explaining behavior. They can learn how the unconscious does this and how the id does that; they can learn how the brain's chemicals affect this and how the person's environment affects that. Both explanation and understanding are important, and both belong in the formulation. The following sections introduce explanatory theories, since they, unlike understandings, lend themselves to didactic presentations.

NEURONS AND NEUROTRANSMITTERS

The fundamental unit of biologically derived behavior is the nerve cell or *neuron*. The brain has at least 100 billion neurons; each neuron consists of a microscopic *cell body* (or "head") that trails off into an *axon* (or "tail") with an extremely narrow width but a length of up to several inches or feet. By definition, axons transmit electrical impulses *away* from the cell body, whereas *dendrites* transmit them *toward* it. Electrical impulses originate in cell bodies and run through these axons, until they are conveyed to hundreds, or even thousands, of other nerve cells.

Although in very close proximity, neurons are anatomically separate from one another. Therefore, to reach a nearby neuron, electrical impulses do not travel over continuous tissue, but flow across the spaces between neurons. As illustrated in Figure 4-1, this passage is accomplished by chemicals called *neurotransmitters*, which transmit messages over these tiny spaces called *synaptic clefts*.

Neurotransmitters are synthesized inside the neuron and actively transported to the axon's end or *presynaptic terminal*; from here, neurotransmitters "swim" (diffuse) across the synaptic cleft and bind onto *receptors* that are

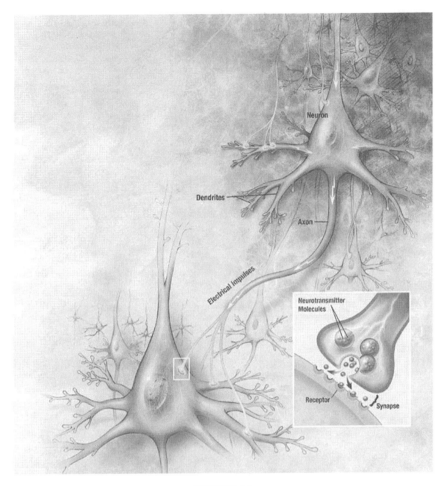

FIGURE 4-1
The Neuron, Synapse, and Neurotransmitters
National Institutes of Health

located on the surface (membrane) of adjacent dendrites or cell bodies. By doing so, neurotransmitters can trigger or inhibit the receptor's ability to fire. The nerve cell acts like a wet sponge: When it fires, it releases its fluids of neurotransmitters; when not firing, it expands and reabsorbs them. Learning is related to establishing synaptic connections and networks. It is estimated that the brain may have up to 500 trillion of these synapses. The mature adult brain has many more synapses than the younger brain but the ability to form connections (plasticity) is optimal in childhood. Stress seems to be associated with less connectivity, perhaps mediated by cortisol, a stress hormone.

Whether a nerve cell fires mainly depends on the quantity and arrangement of neurotransmitters reaching its receptors at any instant. Other determining factors include (1) variations in the rate of synthesis and release of a neurotransmitters from the first cell; (2) increases and decreases in the sensitivity and numbers of the receptors on the second cell; and (3) inhibition of the first cell's ability to reabsorb neurotransmitters, thereby increasing their concentration at the second cell's receptors. Drugs also exert effects. In pharmacology, *agonists* are substances that enhance or potentiate the firing of a neuron, whereas *antagonists* are drugs that block or reduce the effects of an agonist.

Many types of receptors have been discovered, including some for benzodiazepines, marijuana, and opiates. Endorphins, opiate-like peptides synthesized in the brain, bind to opiate receptors to mediate the perception of pain. The jogger's "high" has been attributed to a buildup of these endorphins. Endorphins are released in response to any tissue damage and this helps explain the behaviors of certain suffering individuals who repetitively cut on themselves to feel better. Most receptors are affected by one type (or subtype) of neurotransmitter. Symptoms of mental disorders appear to arise from changes in these receptor–neurotransmitter systems. The most influential neurotransmitters and their receptor properties are discussed further in Chapter 6 and include dopamine, norepinephrine, serotonin, acetylcholine, glutamate, gamma-aminobutyric acid, and endorphins. Dopamine and norepinephrine are *catecholamines*; serotonin is an *indoleamine*. Table 4-1 lists the major neurotransmitters and their primary precursors (major chemical antecedents), primary metabolites (major breakdown products), and brain source.

Although a great deal more research is needed before it is clear how neurotransmitters contribute to mental disorders, there are several widely touted hypotheses: Schizophrenia seems to involve excessive activity in the dopamine receptor systems. The "catecholamine hypothesis" of depression holds that a functional underactivity of norepinephrine causes severe depression, whereas a functional overactivity of this neurotransmitter causes mania. Other theories contend that depression stems from a high ratio of acetylcholine to catecholamine (e.g., dopamine or norepinephrine), whereas mania erupts with the ratio reversed. Sleep and perhaps mood are affected by changes in the serotonin receptor system. When stimulated, GABA receptors inhibit neurons and induce calm; thus, anxiety increases when this system becomes less active. Abrupt opiate (and sometimes tobacco) withdrawal apparently accelerates the firing of norepinephrine from the *locus coeruleus*—a densely populated area of neurons that produces most of this neu-

TABLE 4-1

Neurotransmitters: Precursors, Metabolites, and Origins

NEUROTRANSMITTER	PRIMARY PRECURSORS	PRIMARY METABOLITES	PRIMARY ORIGINS
Dopamine (DA)	Tyrosine → L-DOPA → DA	Homovanillic acid (HVA)	Nucleus accumbens, ventral tegmental area, hypothalamus, substantia nigra
Norepinephrine (NE)	Tyrosine → L-DOPA → DA → NE	Methoxyhydroxy-phenyl-glycol (MHPG)	Locus coeruleus, lateral tegmental field
Serotonin (5-HT)	Tryptophan → 5 hydroxy L tryptophan (5-HTP) → 5-HT	5-Hydroxyindole-acetic acid (5-HIAA)	Raphe nuclei
Acetylcholine (Ach)	Choline + Acetyl-CoA → Ach	Choline, acetate	Pontomesencephaloteg-mental complex, basal optic nucleus of Meynert, and medial septal nucleus
Gamma aminobutyric acid (GABA)	Glutamate → GABA	Succinate	All levels of CNS, including hypothalamus, hippocampus, cerebral cortex, and cerebellar cortex
Glutamate (Glu)	Glutamine → Glu	α-Ketoglutarate	Cortex, thalamus, basal ganglia, amygdala, hippocampus
Histamine (H)	Histidine → H	Histidine	Posterior hypothalamus, various tuberomammillary nuclei
Endorphins	Pro-opiomelanocortin (POMC) → endorphin + ACTH	Inactive peptides	Pituitary, hypothalamus

rotransmitter. Theories are many, and continually growing as to basis of mental disorders.

PSYCHONEUROENDOCRINOLOGY

The field of *psychoneuroendocrinology* studies the influence of hormones in the central nervous system and, as such, seeks to explain their interrelationships with receptors, neurotransmitters, and the resultant functioning (thoughts, motivations, emotions, and behaviors). Unlike neurotransmitters, which act close to their locus of origin, *hormones* are produced by glands, secreted into the bloodstream, and often act at a distance from their locus of origin. Until recently, psychoneuroendocrinology focused on hormonal actions outside the brain. Now, more sophisticated technologies have made it possible to study the *pituitary*, a "window" into the brain, by examining how neurotransmitters, hormones, and the brain interact to produce mental disorders.

The *hypothalamus* is located directly above the pituitary gland, and considerable psychoendocrine activity transpires along this "hypothalamic–pituitary axis." For example, the biological or vegetative signs of depression (e.g., disturbances in sleep, appetite, sex) are partially mediated in the hypothalamus, the chief connecting station where neurotransmitters and hormones affect each other. An underactive thyroid gland can cause depression, and too much thyroid hormone can induce depression, mania, or psychosis. Conversely, during cases of major depression and anxiety disorders, the adrenal glands may release excessive amounts of cortisol. The amygdala, which plays an important role in mediating emotional states (anxiety, fear) and emotional aspects of memory, is also intimately connected with the hypothalamus. Figure 4-2 traces the hypothalamic–pituitary–adrenal pathway.

TECHNOLOGY AND ETIOLOGY

Throughout history, etiological knowledge has been only as advanced as the methods available to study it. For example, psychodynamic etiologies have always reflected the patients and the society that were investigated. Freud revealed the pathogenic power of repressed sexuality in a sexually repressive society; Jung's patients were not sexually inhibited but religiously troubled, and his theories focused on philosophical, cosmic, and religious themes. Adler, not surprisingly, uncovered the inferiority complex when dealing with ambitious, middle-class patients (Wender & Klein, 1981).

More recently, an explosion in biomedical technology has uncovered alterations in the brain's anatomy, chemistry, and physiology that were previously undetectable. Introduced in 1973, *computerized tomography* (CT) provides a two-dimensional anatomical image by contrasting the specific gravities of various brain tissue. Newer is *magnetic resonance imaging* (MRI), in which images reflect the chemical properties of tissues by measuring the resonances of a particular atom (e.g., phosphorus) within those tissues. At

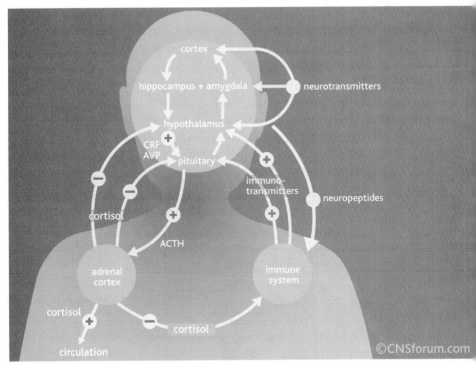

FIGURE 4-2
Hypothalamic–Pituitary–Adrenal Axis

present, functional MRI (fMRI) can help to correlate metabolic defects with behavior, and unlike the CT scan, it can more accurately distinguish brain tissues (e.g., white matter vs. gray matter, a tumor vs. normal brain tissue, a multiple sclerosis plaque vs. white matter). *Positron emission tomography* (PET) measures the metabolic activity of a compound (e.g., glucose) at various sites in the brain. By labeling a psychotropic drug, such as haloperidol, PET can measure the number and alterations of dopamine receptors. Magnetic resonance spectroscopy (MRS) can measure local variations in molecular species important to metabolism of neurotransmitters. Magnetic encephalography (MEG) can map magnetic field variations. Electroencephalography (EEG) mapping is also useful.

This new technology is helping to invalidate the traditional distinction between *organic* and *functional* disorders by demonstrating that many "functional" disorders involve fine (versus gross) changes in neuronal tissues and in cerebral ventricles; altered glucose metabolism and neurochemical changes are also being elucidated. Because the organic–functional distinction has little basis in fact, the current diagnostic nosologies have dropped this distinction.

ENVIRONMENTAL BIOLOGY

"Environmental biology" might be described as the study of the two-way relationship between environment and biology in the production of mental disorders. Three of these relationships deserve comment: (1) biological effects from the environment, (2) psychosocial trauma-induced biological changes, and (3) genotypes and phenotypes.

Biological Effects from the Environment

Environmental stress and psychosocial stress are *not* synonymous, since the environment can also generate biological stress. Conditions during pregnancy and afterward, including viruses, drugs, malnourishment, physical abuse, or premature birth, may produce mental disorders in children or, at least, predispose them to one. For example, in comparison to normals, people with schizophrenia have a higher rate of birth complications.

Light—both natural and artificial—appears to be another biological (or physical) force, the absence of which contributes to mental disorders. Patients with seasonal mood disorders may become depressed every fall and winter and recover every spring and summer. These patients' depressions improve with prolonged exposure to bright artificial light. The antidepressant effect of light is given further credence by the finding that people are more likely to have depressions the farther they live from the equator (Rosenthal et al., 1984).

Psychosocial Trauma-Induced Biological Changes

Biological changes do not necessarily have biological origins; they may be generated psychosocially. Kandel (1983) demonstrated how environmental stress can alter the brain's anatomy and biochemistry to produce avoidance behavior (a model of anxiety). He used the marine snail *Aplysia* in his research, because it has a relatively simple nervous system with large and easy-to-visualize brain cells. The *Aplysia* weighs up to 4 pounds, consists of only 20,000 cells, and has the largest neurons in the animal kingdom—up to 1 mm in diameter. Whereas a simple human behavior typically involves hundreds of thousands of brain cells, simple behaviors of an *Aplysia* involve fewer than 50. By conditioning the *Aplysia* and then photographing its neurons, Kandel recorded the actual anatomical changes in a brain cell caused by a specific stressful environment.

> The brain matures in interaction with the environment, and, once developed, it continues to be influenced by the environment. Being continually unable to cope—"learned helplessness"—can induce biological changes resulting in depression. As another example, patients with advanced Parkinson's disease who can hardly walk will nonetheless race to the exit if they are in a movie theater that catches on fire. They *do* have brain disease, yet how their diseased brains functions depends on the environment.

Genotypes and Phenotypes

Having a gene, and having it produce visible effects, are two different things. The gene structure itself is the *genotype*; how this gene is expressed—that is, if it becomes manifest—is the *phenotype*. If there is a gene (or genotype) for an ulcer, whether it develops into an ulcer (the phenotype) depends on environmental factors such as diet, stress, infection, and smoking. Because of this interrelationship, to ask whether a mental disorder is caused by genes *or* environment is naive. When a person inherits the genotype for a mental disorder, how the person's environment affects that gene determines the degree, form, and existence of the disorder. Genetic theory is not equivalent with behavioral predestination. If a person inherits the genotype for a mental disorder, other "protective" genes or biological and psychosocial interventions can still alleviate or prevent it.

> Epigenetics is the study of changes in gene expression caused by mechanisms other than the underlying DNA base sequence. So even though the underlying nucleotide sequence is unaltered, the other modifications (methylation and histone) produced by environmental influence will affect the degree to which the gene is turned on or off. These minor changes to DNA are called epimarks and may persist for multiple cell divisions. Thus the regulation of certain gene expression may even be passed to the progeny and future generations.

THE GENETICS OF MENTAL DISORDERS

Genetic factors are prerequisites for most, but certainly not all, cases of schizophrenia and manic–depression, and somewhat less frequently, for major depression. Heredity partly contributes to panic and obsessive–compulsive disorders, but appears to be less implicated in generalized anxiety disorders. Historically these conclusions derived mainly from research on twins and adoptees. However, the same techniques that completed the sequencing of the entire human genome have led to the use of DNA microarrays to identify specific genes and their variations that may contribute to psychopathology.

Twin Studies

By comparing identical or *monozygotic* (MZ) twins with fraternal or *dizygotic* (DZ) twins, investigators attempt to assess the relative contributions of nature and nurture in causing certain mental disorders. Identical twins have identical genes; the genes of fraternal twins are like those of any other pair of siblings. A *concordance rate* for a phenotype is the percentage of twins who both exhibit the same phenotype. Because MZ and DZ twins usually share a similar environment, the difference in concordance rates between MZ and DZ twins largely reflects genetic influences.

For example, on average the concordance rate for schizophrenia among MZ twins averages 45%; this means that when one twin of an MZ pair has schizophrenia, 45% of the time the other twin does also. In contrast, DZ twin pairs have a concordance rate of about 10% for schizophrenia. (If one sibling has schizophrenia, other siblings have a 10% chance of developing schizophrenia.) The statistically significant difference between 45% and 10% suggests that genes transmit schizophrenia. At the same time, these figures also demonstrate an important role for nongenetic factors. If genes alone were involved, one would expect a 100% concordance rate; that is, if one member of an MZ pair had schizophrenia, then the twin would also have schizophrenia. But it's not; it's only about 45%.

Geneticists attribute this 55% difference to *penetrance*, a term used to account for why the genotype does not become the phenotype 100% of the time. Penetrance may occur because the abnormal genes were too weak to express or were impeded by other genes; spontaneous genetic mutations, viral infections, and in utero difficulties may also explain penetrance.

Concordance rates of identical twins might be altered if they were treated differently from fraternal twins. However, two findings do not support this contention. First, MZ twins who were physically dissimilar showed the same concordance rates as those who looked the same. Second, identical twins who grew up with everybody (themselves included) assuming that they were fraternal twins showed concordance rates of identical twins.

Adoption Studies

To further clarify the nature–nurture question, various studies of adoptions have been conducted. The first major adoption studies of mental disorders occurred in 1963. They were conducted in Denmark, because the government had a register of every adoption, including those infants who were separated from their biological parents when less than 3 months old and then legally adopted.

One method of using these records for research purposes is to compare the biological and adoptive parents of adult adoptees with schizophrenia. Because biological parents gave away the child so early in life, their psychosocial influence on the adoptee with schizophrenia was probably nil; only genetic influences would persist. Therefore, if schizophrenia were genetically transmitted, the biological parents should have a much higher incidence of schizophrenia than the adoptive parents. On the other hand, if schizophrenia were produced psychosocially, just the opposite should occur. The results were striking: Repeatedly, the adoptee's biological parents were schizophrenic, whereas the adoptive parents were "normal."

In another adoption analysis the children of biological parents with schizophrenia who were reared by adoptive parents were contrasted to a matched control group of adoptees whose biological parents had no family history of mental disorders. Once again, genetic interpretations prevailed, since schizophrenia-like disorders were far more common among the offspring of parents with schizophrenia than among those of "normal" parents. These and similar findings have provided overwhelming evidence that genetic factors play a major role in the etiology of schizophrenia.

Subsequent research has suggested that what is genetically transmitted may not be a single gene for schizophrenia, but a gene, or genes, for "schizophrenia-spectrum disorders." Besides schizophrenia, this spectrum may include several disorders that are similar, but not identical to, schizophrenia, such as the schizotypal personality and schizoaffective disorders. Similarly, the concept of *genetic spectrum disorders* also may apply to other syndromes. For example, investigators are pursuing genes for "depressive-spectrum disorders," which may contribute to the etiology of major depression, bipolar disorder, substance dependence, and anxiety disorders.

Finally, even when genes are implicated, this concept of spectrum disorders underscores the need to specify *what* is being inherited. Is it a predisposition to one disorder or to a number of possible disorders? Is it a particular trait, such as shyness or the inability to synthesize information? Or is it a vulnerability to certain psychosocial stressors, such as a chaotic family life, loss, or intense emotions? Some of these answers probably involve psychosocial influences.

PSYCHOSOCIAL THEORIES

Numerous psychological and social factors influence the course of a mental disorder, and the many ways in which they do so can be divided into seven general models: developmental, defense mechanisms, intrapsychic conflict, stress, behavioral, family systems, and sociocultural.

> Some important models are not mentioned partly because their direct application to diagnostic psychopathology has (as yet) been limited. These include (1) the *existential* model, which focuses on the purpose and meaning of life, (2) the *humanistic* model, which concentrates on fulfilling or actualizing one's potential, (3) Piaget's *cognitive* model, which portrays the stages of development of a child's thought processes, and (4) Kohlberg's *moral* development model, which applies the stages of cognitive development to moral reasoning.

Developmental Models

Three developmental models are of particular etiological significance: Freud's *psychosexual*, Erikson's *psychosocial*, and Bowlby's *attachment* models. Each model presents a series of overlapping stages (or "passages") and claims that an "arrest" or "crisis" at any stage may induce associated psychopathology. A developmental *crisis* is not a catastrophe or an emergency; it is the normal developmental challenge posed by each psychosocial stage, which becomes a "necessary turning point, a crucial moment, when development must move one way or another, marshalling resources of growth, recovery, and further differentiation" (Erikson, 1968, p. 16). One stage builds upon the previous ("epigenesis"), and regressions to an earlier stage of functioning may occur. Since each stage provides a new perspective that is foundational for the next, it is not possible to skip ahead. It is not expected that one would function at the highest achieved stage at all times. Sometimes psychopathology represents completely aberrant development versus delays or arrest of normal developmental stages. Successful interventions assist the patient in getting "unstuck" or onto the normal developmental trajectory. Tables 4-2 and 4-3 outline the psychosexual and psychosocial models of development, respectively.

TABLE 4-2
Freudian Psychosexual Development

AGE (YEARS)	STAGE	RESOLUTION SUCCESSFUL	PATHOLOGICAL
0–1	ORAL Primary gratification from mouth, lips, and tongue	Self-reliance; self-trust; trust in others; capacity to give and receive without dependence and envy	Needy; demanding; dependent on others for self-esteem; pathological optimism or pessimism; jealousy; immature and image distorting
1–3	ANAL Primary gratification from sphincter control; aggressive, sadistic, and libidinal impulses	Autonomy; independence; capacity to cooperate	
3–6	PHALLIC Primary gratification from genital area; oedipal issues	Basis for sexual identity; drives constructively redirected; superego established	Castration fear in boys, penis envy in girls; failure to identify with same-sexed parent; neurotic disorders
6–12	LATENCY Relative quiescent sexual drives	Integration and consolidation of prior psychosexual gains; basis for love, work, and play	Lack of, or excessive, inner controls; poor sublimation; precociousness; premature closure of personality; neurotic disorders
12–18	GENITAL Reawakening of libidinal drives; sexual maturation	Full and satisfying genital potency; consolidation of prior accomplishments	Any of the above problems; impaired ability to love and work; neurotic disorders

TABLE 4-3
Eriksonian Psychosocial Development

AGE (YEARS)	PERIOD	TASKS	VALUES
0–1	Infancy	Trust vs. mistrust	Hope
1–3	Toddler	Autonomy vs. shame	Will and doubt
3–6	Preschool	Initiative vs. guilt	Purpose
6–12	School-age	Industry vs. inferiority	Skill and competence
12–20	Adolescence	Identity vs. identity diffusion/confusion	Fidelity
20–30	Young adulthood	Intimacy vs. isolation	Love
30–65	Adulthood	Generativity vs. stagnation	Care
65+	Late adulthood	Integrity vs. despair/disgust	Wisdom

Bowlby considered "attachment behaviors" to be those observable actions of a child that facilitate closeness to the primary caregiver, usually the biological mother. In theory, this attachment behavior serves the evolutionary purpose of protecting the child from predators. "Maternal bonding" refers to the mother's attachment to the child. Disturbances in attachment and bonding may produce insecurity, anxiety, dysthymia, distrust, fear of loneliness, and so on. A significant loss during childhood, usually of a parent, may be of special etiological significance, especially in depression (Gardner et al., 2005).

Development does not stop with adolescence; it continues through life. The patient's presenting problems may result not only from an immediate precipitant, but also from a phase-of-life, or developmental, crisis. A 40-year-old man may be fired and develop acute, overwhelming anxiety. Losing his job is clearly the primary precipitant, yet why he was fired and why he is *that* devastated may be secondary to a "midlife (psychosocial) crisis."

Intrapsychic Conflict

Freud divided the *topography* of the mind into three levels: the *unconscious*, whose mental content is rarely in awareness; the *preconscious*, the mental content of which is not immediately in awareness, but can be readily recalled by conscious effort; and the *conscious*, the mental content of which is in awareness. Freud also proposed three psychic *structures*: the *id*, which harbors instinctual sexual and aggressive drives; the *superego* or conscience; and the *ego*, which mediates between these psychic structures and between the person's inner needs and the environment. Defense mechanisms (see below) are ego functions that keep conflicting ideas out of consciousness. Intrapsychic conflict involves struggles between these various levels and structures of the mind. Although the Freudian structural model is an attempt to "understand" complex inner workings of mental life, as shared by a particular patient, it falls short of objectively "explaining" those workings. Despite being rather vague and abstract, when carefully employed, it can assist patients in understanding and managing their suffering.

Defense Mechanisms

Sometimes called "coping mechanisms," defense mechanisms are relatively involuntary patterns of feelings, thoughts, or behaviors that arise in response to a perceived internal or external psychic danger in order to reduce or avoid conscious or unconscious stress, anxiety, or conflict. Whether a defense mechanism is adaptive depends on the defense and the circumstance. For example, projection is generally not adaptive, whereas sublimation is generally adaptive; denial is usually maladaptive, but when the person is dealing with an overwhelming, acute stress, denial may help to maintain psychic equilibrium. Table 4-4 describes the major defense mechanisms in alphabetical order and categorizes them from the least to the most mature: "image-distorting (narcissistic)," "immature," "neurotic (intermediate)," and "mature." The more immature and image-distorting defenses are primitive (used early

---

TABLE 4-4
Defense Mechanisms

Acting-out is the direct expression of impulses without any apparent reflection, guilt, or regard for negative consequences. Whereas "acting-*up*" is a lay term for misbehavior, acting-*out* is a misbehavior that is a response to, and a way of coping with, stress or conflict. After breaking up with his girlfriend, a teenager acts-out by impulsively overdosing. [Immature]

Altruism is demonstrated when people dedicate themselves to the needs of others, partly to fulfill their own needs. [Mature]

Denial is the lack of awareness of *external* realities that would be too painful to acknowledge. It differs from repression (see below), which is a denial of *internal* reality. Denial operates when a woman says, "I'm sure this lump in my breast doesn't mean anything." [Immature] Denial may be temporarily adaptive or more extreme and pathological. For example, the same woman says, "I don't really have a lump in my breast." [Image-distorting]

Devaluation is the demeaning of another or oneself by the attribution of exaggerated negative qualities. By constantly ridiculing his competence, a patient devalues a therapist to avoid facing her sexual feelings toward him. [Image-distorting]

Displacement is the discharge of pent-up emotions, usually anger, onto objects, animals, or people perceived as less dangerous than those that originally induced the emotions. A man comes home after a bad day at work and kicks the dog. [Neurotic]

Distortion is a major reshaping of external reality to suit internal needs [image distorting].

Fantasy is the excessive retreat into daydreams and imagination to escape problems or to avoid conflicts (also called "autistic fantasy" or "schizoid fantasy"). [Immature]

Humor is the use of irony or amusing, incongruous, or absurd associations to reduce what otherwise might be unbearable tension or fear. An example: the character of Hawkeye Pierce in *M*A*S*H*, or *Seinfeld*. [Mature]

Idealization is the unwarranted praise of another or oneself by exaggerating virtues. "Better" to idealize a spouse than to see the jerk for what he is and be a very lonely divorcée. [Image-distorting]

Identification is the unconscious modeling of another's attributes. It differs from role modeling and imitation, which are conscious processes. Identification is used to increase one's sense of self-worth, to cope with (possible) separation or loss, or to minimize helplessness, as with "identification with the aggressor," as seen in prisoners who may assume the mannerisms of their guards. [Immature]

TABLE 4-4
Continued

Intellectualization is the overuse of abstract thinking, which, unlike rationalization (see below), is self-serving only in its aim to reduce psychic discomfort. Alcoholics use intellectualization when they quibble over the definition of alcoholism as a way of avoiding their drinking problem. [Neurotic]

Introjection is the incorporation of other people's values, standards, or traits to prevent conflicts with, or threats from, these people. Introjection may also help a person retain a sense of connection to a lost loved one, as when people adopted John Kennedy's accent after his death. [Immature]

Isolation of affect is the compartmentalization of painful emotions from the events associated with them, thus allowing the experience or recollection of an emotionally traumatic situation, without the anxiety customarily or originally experienced. A soldier may kill without experiencing the terror or guilt he would otherwise feel. [Neurotic]

Projection is the unconscious rejection of unacceptable thoughts, traits, or wishes by ascribing them to others. [Image-distorting when delusional; immature otherwise]

Rationalization is the self-serving use of plausible reasons to justify actions caused by repressed, unacceptable emotions or ideas. Psychotherapist: "I charge a high fee so that therapy will be meaningful to the patient." [Neurotic]

Reaction formation prevents the expression or experience of unacceptable desires by developing or exaggerating opposite attitudes and behaviors. "The lady doth protest too much." [Neurotic]

Regression is retreat under stress to earlier or more immature patterns of behavior and gratification. On hearing terrible news, an adult begins sucking his thumb. [Immature]

Repression is the exclusion from awareness of distressing feelings, impulses, ideas, or wishes. Repression is unconscious, suppression (see below) is conscious. A man is unaware that he resents his more successful wife. [Neurotic]

Somatization (hypochondriasis) is an excessive preoccupation with physical symptoms in response to psychologically stressful situations. [Immature]

Splitting is the viewing of oneself or others as all good or all bad, as opposed to being a mixture of positive and negative attributes. In splitting, the person frequently alternates between idealization and devaluation. [Image-distorting]

Sublimation is the gratification of a repressed instinct or unacceptable feeling by socially acceptable means. Better a surgeon than a sadist. Better a therapist than a voyeur. [Mature]

Suppression is the conscious and deliberate avoidance of disturbing matters: A basketball player is penalized for a foul but he suppresses his anger and soon scores a goal. [Mature]

Turning against the self occurs when the person takes a hostile thought or impulse aimed at another and inappropriately redirects it inward. Less distress is experienced by blaming, hurting, or even mutilating the self than by feeling guilty for being furious at the other person. [Immature]

Undoing is the use of behavior or thoughts to cancel or eradicate the effect of a previous act or thought associated with a painful idea, event, or emotion. After arranging a murder, Lady Macbeth washed her hands, which had no blood on them, and said, "Out, out damn spot." [Image-distorting when delusional; otherwise neurotic or mature, depending on circumstances] in development) and are usually maladaptive and therefore pathological in adults.

Stress

The body's response to any demand for adaptation is called *stress*, and the demand, a *stressor*. By itself, stress is neither good nor bad: Without stress, people stagnate or atrophy; with too much stress, however, they become overwhelmed. A stressor can be acute or chronic. When it is acute and severe, people react in a series of steps, as depicted in Figure 4-3; these reactions may

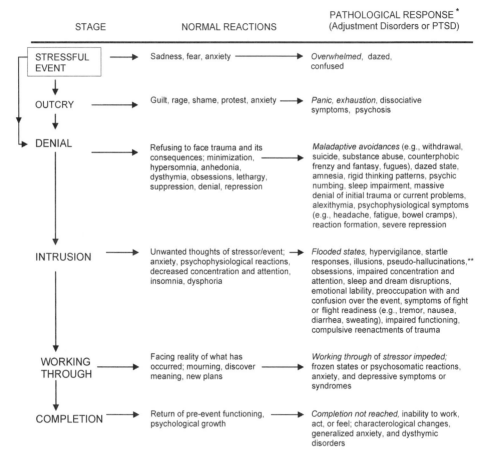

STAGE	NORMAL REACTIONS	PATHOLOGICAL RESPONSE * (Adjustment Disorders or PTSD)
STRESSFUL EVENT	Sadness, fear, anxiety	*Overwhelmed*, dazed, confused
OUTCRY	Guilt, rage, shame, protest, anxiety	*Panic, exhaustion*, dissociative symptoms, psychosis
DENIAL	Refusing to face trauma and its consequences; minimization, hypersomnia, anhedonia, dysthymia, obsessions, lethargy, suppression, denial, repression	*Maladaptive avoidances* (e.g., withdrawal, suicide, substance abuse, counterphobic frenzy and fantasy, fugues), dazed state, amnesia, rigid thinking patterns, psychic numbing, sleep impairment, massive denial of initial trauma or current problems, alexithymia, psychophysiological symptoms (e.g., headache, fatigue, bowel cramps), reaction formation, severe repression
INTRUSION	Unwanted thoughts of stressor/event; anxiety, psychophysiological reactions, decreased concentration and attention, insomnia, dysphoria	*Flooded states,* hypervigilance, startle responses, illusions, pseudo-hallucinations,** obsessions, impaired concentration and attention, sleep and dream disruptions, emotional lability, preoccupation with and confusion over the event, symptoms of fight or flight readiness (e.g., tremor, nausea, diarrhea, sweating), impaired functioning, compulsive reenactments of trauma
WORKING THROUGH	Facing reality of what has occurred; mourning, discover meaning, new plans	*Working through* of *stressor impeded;* frozen states or psychosomatic reactions, anxiety, and depressive symptoms or syndromes
COMPLETION	Return of pre-event functioning, psychological growth	*Completion not reached,* inability to work, act, or feel; characterological changes, generalized anxiety, and dysthymic disorders

FIGURE 4-3
Sequential Responses to Trauma

Modified from Horowitz (1985). *Pathological variations also include unusually intense or prolonged "normal" reactions. *Main features are italicized.* **Pseudo-hallucinations are fantasized reactions in which people intensely experience something as real, despite intellectually knowing otherwise. These may be the "felt presence" of a dead grandfather or an "out-of-body" experience.

be normal or pathological, but even when normal, they may temporarily impair functioning. One need only recall the morning the *Challenger* exploded or 9/11 to remember how most people immediately reacted with either "outcry" or "denial." Chronic stressors, such as a failing marriage, though less severe at any one moment, may eventually "wear a person down" and lead to a deteriorating mental state.

Behavioral

Traditionally, the behavioral (or learning) model focused exclusively on how identifiable environmental forces influence the production of observable behaviors. This model has expanded to include "inner behaviors" that are environmentally induced, yet nonobservable, such as thoughts and feelings. Cognitive–behavioral and rational–emotive therapy approaches use this expanded model, and some behaviorists attempt to integrate psychodynamic with behavioral principles. Still, behaviorism focuses on how the environment creates, shapes, changes, or alters the frequency of a behavior. A behavioral formulation would indicate whether the patient's difficulties are encouraged (through *positive or negative reinforcement*) or punished by the environment. Often the internal (intrapsychic) environment of the person's thoughts provides its own reinforcement and punishment.

Family Systems

In this model the family is viewed as a *system*, which is a complex of interacting elements. Systems theory holds that one cannot fully understand a system (e.g., organization, family, person) by examining only its parts. What happens in one part of a system eventually reverberates and affects the others; no person is an island. In the family systems model, the patient's behavior is viewed less as the product of an intrapsychically induced mental disorder and more the result of intrafamilial disturbances. This approach does not necessarily deny the existence of mental illness but suggests that the confluence of forces within the family maintains, exacerbates, and perhaps even initiates it.

Sociocultural

The pathogenic role of social, cultural, political, economic, religious, racial, and gender aspects are often given short shrift, partly because ideology tends to overwhelm the few facts that exist. Sociologists examine these matters, but usually lack training in psychopathology to place them in context, whereas mental-health professionals usually lack sociological sophistication. Therefore, clinicians should be especially careful when attributing mental pathology to social pathology (or even social normality). On the other hand, when specific social factors are responsible, their influence (for good or ill) should be recorded in the patient's biopsychosocial formulation.

References

Boyce, W.T., & Ellis, B.J. (2005). Biological sensitivity to context: I. An evolutionary-developmental theory of the origins and functions of stress reactivity. *Development & Psychopathology, 17*, 271–301.

Crain, W.C. (1985). *Theories of development: Concepts and applications*, 2nd rev ed. Englewood Cliffs, NJ: Prentice-Hall.

Engel, G.L. (1977). The need for a new medical model: A challenge for biomedicine. *Science, 196*(4286), 129–136.

Erikson, E.H. (1968). *Identity: Youth and crisis*. New York: Norton.

Gardner, K.L., Thrivikanan, K.V., Lightman, S.L., Plotsky, P.M., & Lowry, C.A. (2005). Early life experience alters behavior during social defeat: Focus on serotonergic systems. *Neuroscience, 136*(1), 181–191.

Goodwin, D.W. (1985). Alcoholism and genetics: The sins of the father. *Archives of General Psychiatry, 42*, 171–174.

Goodwin, D.W., & Guze, S.B. (1996). *Psychiatric diagnosis*. Oxford: Oxford University Press.

Herman, A.I., Philbeck, J.W., Vasilopoulos, N.L., & Depetrillo, P.B. (2003). Serotonin transporter promoter differences in alcohol consumption behavior in a college student population. *Alcohol, 38*(5), 446–449.

Hogarty, G.E., Goldberg, S.C., Schooler, N.R., & Ulrich, R.P. (1974). Drugs and sociotherapy in the aftercare of schizophrenic patients: II. Two-year relapse rates. *Archives of General Psychiatry, 31*, 603–608.

Horowitz, M.J. (1985). Disasters and psychological responses to stress. *Psychiatric Annals, 15*, 161–167.

Kandel, E.R. (1983). From metapsychology to molecular biology: Explorations into the nature of anxiety. *American Journal of Psychiatry, 140*, 1277–1293.

Khashan, A.S., Abel, A.M., McNamee, R., Pedersen, M.G., Webb, R.T., Baker, P.N., Kenny, L.C., & Mortensen, P.B. (2008). Higher Risk of Offspring Schizophrenia Following Antenatal Maternal Exposure to Severe Adverse Life Events. Archives of General Psychiatry, 65(2), 146–152.

Kleinman, A. (1988). *The illness narratives: Suffering, healing, and the human condition*. New York: Basic Books.

Kohlberg, L., Levine, C., & Hewer, A. (1983). *Moral stages: A current formulation and a response to critics*. Basel, NY: Karger.

Masten, A.S. (2007). Resilience in developing systems: Progress and promise as the fourth wave rises. *Development and Psychopathology, 19*, 921–930.

McHugh, P.R., & Slavney, P.R. (1998). *The perspectives of psychiatry*, 2nd ed. Baltimore: Johns Hopkins University Press.

Perry, J.C., & Cooper, S.H. (1989). An empirical study of defense mechanisms. *Archives of General Psychiatry, 46*, 444–452.

Rosenthal, N.E., Sack, D.A., Gillin, J.C., Lewy, A.J., Goodwin, F.K., Davenport, Y., et al. (1984). Seasonal affective disorder. *Archives of General Psychiatry, 41*, 72–80.

Vaillant, G.E., Bond, M., & Vaillant, C.O. (1986). An empirically validated hierarchy of defense mechanisms. *Archives of General Psychiatry, 43*, 786–794.

Weiner, H. (1985). Schizophrenia: Etiology. In H.I. Kaplan & B.J. Sadock (Eds.), *Comprehensive textbook of psychiatry*, 4th ed. (pp. 651–680). Baltimore: Williams & Wilkins.

Wender, P.H., & Klein, D.F. (1981). *Mind, mood, and medicine: A guide to the new biopsychiatry*. New York: Meridan.

5

Treatment

The most important factor in deciding treatment is the patient's diagnosis. Other factors—psychological, medical, sociocultural, ethical, intellectual, financial—influence the choice and conduct of treatment, but except for emergency interventions, no treatment should begin without a diagnosis. Conversely, although diagnosis may serve other ends, its chief purpose is to help determine treatment. Therefore, when clinicians debate a patient's diagnosis, it is important to know how a change in diagnosis will alter the patient's treatment.

WHAT DO TREATMENT PLANS INCLUDE?

Every patient should have a *treatment plan*—that is, an organized program of one or more treatments designed to help him or her achieve specified objectives. The clinician should indicate the type, amount, focus, goals, and timing of each treatment.

1. The *types* are numerous and varied according to the model of the provider and the needs of the patient. The variants include, but are not limited to, individual, couple, family, or group psychotherapy, and medication. Each of these modalities has a number of options based on psychodynamic, cognitive, and/or behavioral principles. Furthermore, in acute situations, the type of treatment may be very short-term and straightforward, such as "rapid tranquilization," "suicide precautions," "continuous observation," "physical restraint," and so on. The specific interventions should be specified in the treatment plan.

2. The *amount* of treatment refers to its frequency and duration. Will psychotherapy sessions occur once or twice a week? Will therapy continue for 6 weeks or 6 months? The dose, frequency, and duration of medication should also be indicated.

3. The *focus* refers to the specific problem(s) that treatment will address.

Treatment does not, and cannot, concentrate on everything; choices and priorities must be set. Is it better to focus on a patient's depression or attention-deficits? Should the etiological focus be on childhood trauma, ongoing familial problems, or precipitating stressors?

4. The *goals* (or objectives) of each treatment should be specified; otherwise, clinicians and patients cannot know *where treatment is going, when it should end*, and *whether it has succeeded*. A goal of "helping the patient function better" is too vague, because it does not specify the areas in which the patient should function better. To report that risperidone is being prescribed to "treat the patient's schizophrenia" borders on poverty of content. Is the goal to eliminate hallucinations or to stop the patient from telling everyone about his hallucinations? Is it to stop delusions, elevate mood, diminish agitation, increase social interactions, make it possible to leave the hospital, or function at work? No medication should be prescribed without first specifying its target symptoms and functions.

At times, the objectives are clear but unrealistic: "To help the patient enjoy her (thoroughly obnoxious) mother." In establishing goals, two generalizations should apply: (a) the briefer the treatment, the less ambitious the goals; and (b) the more recent the problem, the fuller and faster it will improve with treatment.

> Outlining treatment goals *on paper* helps clinicians sharpen their awareness; if they can't articulate the goals clearly, they don't really know what the goals are. Discussing goals with patients before treatment begins helps patients make a more informed judgment about entering treatment and reduces unrealistic expectations of therapy. Furthermore, having agreed upon goals up front helps develop the therapeutic relationship, a critical piece of the therapeutic process. Expecting too much of therapy may be the greatest preventable cause of malpractice suits. When patients and therapists explicitly agree on the goals of treatment, both are also more likely to be on the same "wavelength" during treatment. Clearly delineating goals also minimizes the possibility of other providers working at cross purposes, as when an individual psychotherapist tells a teenager "to liberate himself from parental domination," while the family therapist tells his parents "to set limits on their kid." This may also mean contacting (with an appropriate release of information) other professionals involved in the patient's care, such as a physician or counselor.

5. The *timing* of therapies—that is, when and in what sequence—generally follows these guidelines: Treatment should rectify biological changes

before psychosocial influences, symptoms before issues, acute crises before chronic problems, and psychoses before neuroses. Psychotic patients should receive supportive psychotherapy; only later, when nonpsychotic, can they benefit from other forms of psychotherapy. The hierarchy of diagnoses listed in Figure 3-1 can also be used as a guide to determine which diagnosis/problem should be treated first.

> Treatments cannot happen all at once, nor should they. For instance, patients with severe major depression view all information in the worst possible light; they use insights not for self-improvement but for self-punishment. During insight-oriented psychotherapy, a very proper 55-year-old woman recalled a long-forgotten affair from 30 years earlier. But instead of using this insight to unburden herself of a long-repressed guilt (as would "normal" people), she berated herself: "This proves I'm a whore and deserve to die." Like most severely depressed patients, she could benefit from insight only *after* antidepressant medications had alleviated her symptoms.

One model that has helped inform clinicians on how to match their approach to their patients' timing is the transtheoretical model or stages of change model (Prochaska, Diclemente, & Norcross, 1992). This model (Figure 5-1) argues that patients vary in how ready, willing, and able they are to engage in treatment. For example, one person may have recently been told that she has a drinking problem and needs help, but she is not con-

Stage of Change	Characteristics
Precontemplation	Not currently considering change: "Ignorance is bliss"
Contemplation	Ambivalent about change: "Sitting on the fence"; not considering change within the next month
Preparation	Some experience with change and are trying to change; "testing the waters," planning to act within 1 month
Action	Practicing new behavior for 3–6 months
Maintenance	Continued commitment to sustaining new behavior post 6 months to 5 years
Relapse	Resumption of old behaviors: "Fall from grace"

FIGURE 5-1
Prochaska's Stages of Change

vinced there is a problem (precontemplation stage). Another may have just gotten his third DUI and lost his job because he failed a drug test at work—this individual, hopefully, sees he has a significant problem and is ready to engage actively in a treatment plan (action stage). This approach argues that clinicians need to recognize these different stages and adjust *their* approach to help patients advance through the stages toward lasting behavior change. One such approach to engage patients toward change is motivational interviewing (Miller & Rollnick, 2002). Motivational interviewing is an empathic counseling style that employs Open-ended questions, Affirmations, Reflective Listening, and Summarizing (OARS). It seeks to work with the patient's intrinsic motivation and adjusts to patient resistance rather than aggressively confronting it.

Achieving high quality and cost-effective health care will require the participation of informed and activated patients. There are now standardized ways to assess patient activation (Hibbard et. al., 2004)

> The inpatient treatment of anorexia nervosa further illustrates the importance of timing and the tailoring of interventions. These self-starving young females (see Chapter 20) are admitted when their weight has become medically precarious. Since 10–15% of these patients who are hospitalized die prematurely, regaining weight is a medical necessity and the first goal of treatment. Yet, on first meeting these patients, clinicians are often struck by their "goodie two-shoes" personae that belie significant levels of distress and self-doubt. Furthermore, the disorder often appears during or following a time of stress, such as going away to college. Clinicians are tempted to explore those areas right away, but when immediately addressed, patients usually become so distressed, they actually lose weight. Only after their weight is stabilized can patients benefit from examining these issues.

THREE LEVELS OF TREATMENT

Psychiatric treatment occurs in three levels: biological, psychosocial, and moral–existential. First, if needed, the psychiatrist prescribes medication to rectify *biological* abnormalities. Second, the therapist facilitates psychotherapies to address *psychosocial* problems. Third, the therapist uses the clinician–patient relationship to demonstrate that he or she values the patient as a person, moving into the *moral–existential* dimension of therapy (Abroms, 1983).

This three-level model holds that biological and psychosocial treatments are both valuable, albeit in *different* ways. To argue that talk therapy is better than drug therapy (or vice versa) is pointless; they serve different functions. Group therapy frequently helps diabetics cope with their illness, yet nobody would suggest that such groups regulate blood sugar; conversely, insulin regulates blood sugar, yet nobody would suggest it helps diabetics cope with their illness. Just as group therapy and insulin help patients with diabetes in different ways, so do psychotherapies and biotherapies help patients with mental disorders. Excellent therapists can have very different interests (e.g., psychoanalysis, medications), but still appreciate that each treatment serves a distinct purpose.

In general, biological therapies eliminate or alleviate *symptoms*, such as the insomnia of a person with depression, the delusions of a person with schizophrenia, or the spending sprees of a person in a manic state. In contrast, psychosocial therapies usually address *issues*, such as coping with a job loss, a failed marriage, a medical condition, or a psychiatric disorder. When used properly, biological and psychosocial therapies do not impede but *facilitate* one another. Repeated evidence has shown that medications do not increase patient's passivity, decrease motivation, or diminish involvement in psychotherapy. Correctly medicated patients gain more from psychotherapy. Wildly hallucinating people with schizophrenia feel so bombarded by stimuli that they cannot focus sufficiently to benefit from psychotherapy; once medicated, they can.

Conversely, psychotherapies can accomplish what drugs cannot. They can teach patients about their mental disorders—their symptoms, dangers, causes, and precipitants. Psychotherapies can alert patients to situations that are likely to trigger another episode of illness, help patients understand what their conditions mean to them, and improve patients' willingness to adhere to the psychiatric treatment plan, such as taking medication. They can also facilitate social adjustment, interpersonal relationships, and leisure-time pleasures and occupational skills, as well as heighten self-esteem, guide ambition, and promote well-being. Finally, psychotherapeutic investigation can reveal how previous experiences affect current difficulties. A patient who cannot figure out why terrible things keep happening to her—why people are rude to her, why men avoid her, why nobody will hire her—can be shown why these events happen, what she can do about them, and how she can regain control over her life.

The moral–existential aspects of therapy do not involve particular treatments or occur during specified periods. Instead, they prevail throughout therapy, pervading both biological and psychosocial treatments. To quote Abroms (1983), moral–existential interventions involve the "realm of pure value, where the ultimate aim is integrity of the person. . . . [They entail] moral qualities of trust and gratitude, of loyalty and devotion, and above all, of respect . . . the therapist becomes firm in the resolve to stand by the patient, even to tolerate a measure of moral failure" (p. 744). While therapists may not condone their patients' behaviors and choices, they accept patients for who they are. Once patients fully understand what their choices are, they must make an existential decision. Sometimes they may decide not to change, or at least not at this time. Therapists must learn to accept such decisions.

OVERALL GUIDELINES FOR SELECTING TREATMENTS

Treatment selection is most often based primarily on pragmatic, rather than on etiological, considerations. Some of the major difficulties of linking treatment with an etiological theory are as follows: (1) The definitive cause of most mental disorders is unknown. (2) The treatment must then be consistent with the theory, which may determine what can and cannot be treated. For example, Freud's early feelings about schizophrenia excluded this illness from the scope of psychoanalytic therapy. (3) A total commitment to any single etiological theory and its accompanying treatments limits the therapist's range of interventions. (4) The goals of therapy may become the fulfillment of a theory rather than what the patient actually needs or desires. (5) Even if the etiology of a disorder were known, therapies addressing it are unlikely to rectify the patient's current disorder. For example, a man who is chronically depressed because he was deprived as a child might find that further insight into his childhood cannot alter the many self-destructive patterns that he has developed over the years. When theory prevails over pragmatism, a therapist may insist that a patient who feels and functions substantially better has not "really" improved because the patient has not accepted the origins of his problem and that, as long as he continues to "resist," he will never improve. In other words, the patient can't get better unless he "buys" the therapist's theory.

To serve up pragmatically based treatments, one should follow (Bill) *Tilden's Law*: "Never change a winning game." If a treatment works, don't change it; if a treatment doesn't work, do change it. This does not mean that clinicians should alter treatments every time patients have setbacks, but it does mean that if patients fail to improve following an ample trial with a particular treatment, another treatment should be tried. For example, even if a patient "should" respond to antidepressant medications, if she doesn't, she doesn't, and a different treatment should be attempted. Or, if a patient has failed to improve after three trials of insight-oriented psychotherapy with three different therapists, chances are that a fourth trial of insight-oriented therapy won't help; however, another treatment, such as behavioral, cognitive, or drug therapy, might help.

When pragmatically chosen treatments are based on *scientific evidence* instead of on intuition or theory, they have the greatest chance of being effective. For instance, studies show that if a patient's biological relative has improved with a particular drug, so will the patient. "Scientific," however, is not synonymous with "biological"; although medications are more amenable to scientific investigation, hundreds of well-controlled, quantified studies have evaluated psychotherapy. Furthermore, meta-analytic studies, such as the seminal work of Smith, Glass, and Miller (1980), have shown a robust effect for psychotherapeutic interventions (more recently, Anderson & Lambert, 1995; McDermut, Miller, & Brown, 2001; Shadish et al., 2000).

> Scientific studies of social relations can also guide the treatment of patients. For example, before discharging inpatients, staff must decide how much patients should change their lives during the immediate posthospital stage. One investigation (Breier & Strauss, 1984) indicated that the answer was "very little." This research reported that discharged psychotic patients go through two stages: First, a period of *convalescence*, in which they mainly see themselves as "ex-patients" and maintain contacts with hospital staff and former patients. During the second stage of *rebuilding*, these patients view themselves more as members of society and less as "ex-patients"; key relationships are formed with people in the community instead of with former hospital associations. In general, patients fare much better when therapy fosters stability during the convalescence stage and does not encourage patients to make changes until they enter the rebuilding stage.

As the mental health field has continued to expand, and as health care costs have skyrocketed, pressure has increased to provide evidence-based treatments. These are interventions that, first, have demonstrated "efficacy," meaning that they work under relatively ideal conditions. Second, the treatments are judged "effective" because they work in real-life settings where people's lives are more complicated. Clinicians and patients need these solutions—that is, ones that generalize to daily practice. A number of resources exist to aid practitioners in determining *which* treatments to use *when* (e.g., Barlow, 2001). Furthermore, major professional organizations, as well as some governmental agencies, have published evidence-based practice guidelines that are available on the Internet—examples include the American Psychiatric Association (www.psych.org), the American Psychological Association (www.apa.org), the American Academy of Child and Adolescent Psychiatry (www. aacap.org), and the National Institute on Drug Abuse (www.nida.nih.gov).

Acutely psychotic patients benefit most from psychotherapeutic contacts that are relatively simple, clear, and brief. These patients are frequently overwhelmed by external stimuli, have trouble distinguishing reality from fantasy, often confuse their outer with their inner world, and have short attention spans. Thus, insight-oriented therapies rarely help, but frequently harm, the acutely psychotic person; emphasizing reality testing is more beneficial. If a patient says, "I'm the worst sinner on Earth," the therapist can empathize with the patient's emotional state but still test (or clarify) reality: "I understand that you feel miserable, but what evidence do you have that your sins are worse than others' sins?" Sessions should be shorter and more frequent: A patient in an extremely psychotic state, with a short attention span, may profit more from five, 10-minute contacts a day than from the classical, once-a-day, 50-minute hour.

Acutely ill patients should also be discouraged from making any important life decisions, especially if the decisions are irreversible. This does not mean that therapists should run their patients' lives, nor that *all* patients in therapy should place major decisions on hold. Therapists should intervene only when a patient's judgment is severely impaired by a mental disorder.

> Each axis highlights a key issue for planning treatment. In setting treatment goals, clinicians distinguish between Axes I and II, since diagnoses on Axis I usually respond more readily to treatment than those on Axis II. Treatment plans address the stressors in Axis IV and use the level of functioning on Axis V for determining treatment goals. Axis III disorders should not be overlooked. Many people with physical illnesses also suffer from psychiatric disorders. For example, the lifetime prevalence of depression for persons with diabetes is approximately 25%, for coronary heart disease 26%, while the current prevalence for cancer has been estimated as high as 42% (Popkin & Tucker, 1994).

PSYCHOPATHOLOGICAL CLUES

During assessment, clinicians should sprout antennae for seven psychopathological clues that facilitate both biological and psychosocial treatments.

1. *Locus of responsibility*: Patients who always view others as responsible for their difficulties—so-called "externalizers"—do poorly in psychotherapy and are less cooperative in taking medication. Patients can change themselves much more readily than they can change others.

2. *Habitual view of "helping" figures*: How patients feel about other helping figures—doctors, nurses, teachers, parents—may predict how they will behave toward the therapist. Some patients are highly suspicious of helping figures. The paranoid wonders, "What's the *real* reason this therapist claims he likes me and wants to help?" With suspicious patients, therapists should keep a safe psychological distance to prevent what patients might experience as phony intimacy. These patients are also allergic to interpretations that are too frequent or probing, viewing them as too intrusive and the therapist as "playing with my head." Conversely, for patients who view helping figures as omnipotent, unending sources of gratification and dependency, therapists should avoid becoming swamped by their needs by limiting phone calls and not scheduling too many sessions at the outset of treatment (sessions can always be added). The objective is to provide a structure for the therapeutic relationship that is experienced as safe enough for making changes in thoughts, feelings, and behaviors.

3. *Defense mechanisms and coping patterns*: Patients who rely on more immature defense mechanisms, such as projection and massive denial, are more likely to *not* benefit from, and to even be harmed by, insight-oriented psychotherapy. Because past behavior is the best predictor of future behavior, therapists should ask, "How have you handled major problems and stresses in the past?" Therapists can then decide if patients have used avoidance, denial, overcompensation (i.e., reaction formation), or intellectualization. These responses often predict "flights into health," in which patients dramatically improve after several sessions and want to stop therapy; this first blush of relief quickly pales as they discover that their old problems remain.

4. *Therapist-patient relationship*: Treatment is not just about the medication, or the treatment technique, or even the specific disorder being treated. There are a number of "common" or "nonspecific" factors that cut across treatments that influence outcomes. One important variable is the ability of the patient and provider to form a supportive and respectful working relationship. Some patients will be unable to form a productive therapeutic relationship, such as those with severe personality disorders. Based on where they fall using the stages of change model, others may not yet be ready to engage in the therapeutic process. Either way, therapists need to be aware of and evaluate the ability of the therapist and patient to form a good working relationship.

If the patient or therapist is unsure if psychotherapy holds promise, the clinician may recommend an initial *trial period* of (roughly) six weekly sessions. Each party can see if the "chemistry" between them is likely to be therapeutic. A formal trial period allows both parties to begin therapy without feeling committed to ongoing treatment. As long as therapists do not make patients feel as if they are "on trial," a trial period allows each person a graceful way to terminate treatment. This approach is particularly helpful with certain male patients who are fearful of establishing a dependency relationship such as therapy and are quite uncomfortable talking about their feelings. Furthermore, given that the average number of therapy sessions is five (Hanson et al., 2002), a six-week trial is likely to provide enough time to agree upon what to do next.

5. *Following the affect*: By noting what is being discussed when the patient's affect changes abruptly, the therapist can discern, from among many issues, the ones of prime import to the patient. For instance, a man claims he's gotten over a divorce yet breaks down and weeps when mentioning his former wife. Usually nonverbal, these telltale affective signals may be subtle—a tear is shed, a gaze averted, a leg moved, a body tensed. Therapists can gain considerable information by sensitively pursuing any topic that suddenly triggers an intense affect.

6. *Listening for the associations*: When patients jump to apparently unrelated topics, or when they keep returning to the same topic, that topic deserves attention. To illustrate: While continually harping about his daughter's failure to apply to medical school, a 65-year-old man kept raising the topic of his own retirement. Initially, the connection between these two concerns was unclear; but exploring the association revealed the man's rage at his daughter for "giving up." Realizing this, he stopped being angry at his daughter and could more objectively consider retirement.

7. *The therapist as "emotional barometer"*: How a therapist feels toward a patient is often, though not always, a reliable indication of how most people feel about the patient. If the therapist is constantly irritated by a patient, even if the therapist doesn't know precisely how or why, the patient is probably irritating. (If the therapist is irritated by *all* her patients, then the problem lies with the therapist, not the patient. In psychoanalytic terms, this is called *countertransference* and it means the therapist might need therapy.) The therapist's reactions to a patient are not irrelevant feelings but germane clinical data. For instance, when a paranoid patient emotionally attacks a therapist, the patient may be conveying, however unconsciously, how he always feels under attack in the "real" world. In many cases, the therapist picks up

the patient's feelings. The task is to use these feelings as data about what the patient is experiencing, what the world looks like through his eyes. It may also help the therapist deal with her irritation to recognize that being irritating is the best strategy the patient has come up with to manage his distress/fears in interpersonal situations.

A SUMMARY OF PSYCHIATRIC TREATMENTS

Despite the ever-increasing number of therapies—in reality, the commonly used treatments of any enduring importance have not changed very much over the years. These treatments are listed in Table 5-1 and briefly described below.

Biological Therapies

Biological therapies are the subject of Chapter 6.

Psychosocial Therapies

This text defines psychosocial therapies as the informed and systematic application of techniques based on established psychological principles by professionals who are trained and experienced to understand these principles and to apply these techniques to modify maladaptive feelings, thoughts, and behaviors. With so many psychosocial treatments (and so many defended passionately), one can easily overlook their similarities. Both explicitly and implicitly, psychosocial treatments all involve a contract and a degree of rapport and trust between a supposed expert and a patient or client with emotional or behavioral problems. Whether or not the patient has symptoms, all treatments seek to combat demoralization by restoring the patient's sense of mastery. Furthermore, they all derive from a particular theory or set of principles in which both parties have some faith; the commonality across therapies is that they all work to change a person's thoughts, feelings, and behaviors to improve functioning. Most therapists are not exclusive practitioners of one particular school of therapy, but instead combine approaches depending on the patient's needs.

In preparing patients for psychotherapy—whichever particular treatments are utilized—two questions should be answered before therapy is formally begun: (1) Are there realistic goals that can be reached? (2) What is this therapy all about; how should I act and how will you act? The activity of

TABLE 5-1
Modern Psychiatric Treatments

I. BIOLOGICAL THERAPIES
  A. Medication
    1. Antipsychotics (e.g., chlorpromazine, haloperidol, risperidone)
    2. Antidepressants
      a. Selective serotonin reuptake inhibitors (SSRIs; e.g., fluoxetine, sertraline, paroxetine, fluvoxamine)
      b. Serotonin and norepinephrine reuptake inhibitors (SNRIs; e.g., venlafaxine)
      c. Tricyclics (TCAs) and multicyclics (e.g., imiprimine, amitriptyline)
      d. Monoamine oxidase inhibitors (MAOIs; e.g., phenelzine)
      e. Atypical (e.g., trazodone, bupropion, venlafaxine)
    3. Mood stabilizers (e.g., lithium, carbamazepine, valproic acid, and calcium channel blockers)
    4. Hypnoanxiolytics (e.g., benzodiazepines)
      a. Antianxiety agents (e.g., diazepam, alprazolam)
      b. Hypnotics (e.g., flurazepam, temazepam)
      c. Atypical anxiolytics—azapirones (e.g., buspirone)
      d. Atypical hypnotics (e.g., zolpidem)
    5. Stimulants to improve attention (e.g., methyphenidate, amphetamine salts)
    6. Cholinesterase inhibitors for dementia (e.g., tacrine, rivastigmine, donepezil)
  B. Electroconvulsive therapy (ECT), transcranial magnetic stimulation (TCMS), and vagal nerve stimulation (VNS) primarily used for severe depression. (ECT is also used for refractory mania and schizophrenia.)
  C. Phototherapy
II. PSYCHOSOCIAL THERAPIES
  A. Individual treatments
    1. Insight-oriented therapy (psychodynamic/psychoanalytic)
    2. Cognitive therapy
    3. Behavioral therapy
    4. Supportive therapy/counseling
  B. Group treatments
    1. Psychotherapy
    2. Psychoeducational
    3. Self-help (e.g., Alcoholics Anonymous, Recovery)
  C. Couple and family treatments
    1. Couple therapy
    2. Family therapy
III. Specialized treatment techniques
    1. Hypnosis
    2. Biofeedback
    3. Relaxation

agreeing on realistic goals can be therapeutic in itself. The patient may feel better now that this "great blob of bad feeling" is being sorted out with somebody who seems to understand and has information and tools to help. Almost all patients have unspoken misconceptions about therapy that can be corrected. At this stage, unrealistic expectations such as "I really want to learn how to change my mother" or "You are wise, just tell me what to do" can be dealt with before they undermine the therapy. A patient may come to agree on a preliminary framework such as "I can only change myself" or "I am not here to attain enlightenment but rather to control my negative thoughts." Later, more specific goals can be established. Preparing patients for what to expect in therapy has been shown to reduce the duration of therapy and result in better outcomes (Yalom, 2005). Too often patients are told to say whatever comes to mind, only to find that talking about the weather and baseball scores wasn't the idea. Patients need to be educated on how they can get the most out of treatment and what they can expect from the therapist.

Individual Psychotherapies

There are four basic types of psychotherapies that involve a single patient: insight-oriented psychotherapy, cognitive-behavioral, behavioral, and supportive therapy. (For clarity, the distinctions between these therapies drawn below are somewhat overstated.)

• *Insight-oriented psychotherapy*. There are two primary forms of insight oriented psychotherapy: *psychoanalysis* and *psychodynamic psychotherapy*. For psychoanalysis "free association" is the cardinal rule—that is, without self-censorship, the patient should say whatever comes to mind, including dreams, fantasies, early memories, current experiences, or feelings about the analyst (i.e., transference). Psychoanalysis aims to heal by uncovering as much as possible about how the patient's mind functions. The approach is physically and verbally structured to foster an environment untainted by the analyst—she adopts a position of nondisclosure and is emotionally and behaviorally neutral toward anything offered by the patient. Consequently, the patient reclines on a couch; the analyst sits behind the patient so that no nonverbal signals influence the patient's free associations. By deliberately acting as a "blank screen" and not as a "real person," the analyst assumes that everything the patient attributes to her are projections of the patient rather than qualities of the analyst.

Psychoanalysis requires three to five meetings a week. It is prescribed for "problems in living," and for mild to moderate depression, anxiety, and obsessiveness, which do not interfere with more than one of the three main areas of functioning: familial, occupational, and recreational. The patient must be bright, introspective, usually under the age of 50, a good abstract thinker, nonpsychotic, and able to pay out-of-pocket for four sessions per week for a period of at least two or three years. For most, this treatment is an expensive luxury. It is like having a car that isn't running quite right over-hauled, when a tune-up might have been enough.

In *psychodynamic psychotherapy*, clinicians also address the patient's dif-ficulties by relying on insight—bringing unconscious or unclear material into sharp awareness. In comparison to psychoanalysis, the patient sits face-to-face with the therapist, has one or two sessions a week, does not free asso-ciate, and pays more attention to the realities of current life than to dreams and childhood recollections. The patient should be nonpsychotic, intro-spective, intelligent, and capable of abstract thought. Psychodynamic psy-chotherapy is therefore best used for problems in living, neurotic symptoms, and ego-dystonic character traits. Interpretation is the hallmark of this form of treatment, but the therapist is more active and directive in gathering infor-mation and offering interpretations (Malan, 1995). In Malan's model, the clinician makes an interpretation by articulating the coping strategy (or defense) that the person is currently using, the anxiety it tries to prevent, and the underlying hidden feeling (or unconscious impulse). This intrapsychic conflict or pattern manifests itself often in the relationship with the therapist, as well as past and present significant others. Once the patient understands, that is, has insight into his feared emotions, the fear is reduced and he is able to cope more effectively.

Like psychoanalysis, successful psychodynamic therapy does not elimi-nate every problem or bestow "perfect mental health." Problems are inher-ent to the human condition, and perfect mental health does not exist. By therapy's end, however, the patient should have developed more realistic and flexible ways of dealing with and reconciling personal needs and envi-ronmental demands; psychic pain, especially when the patient produces it "unnecessarily," should be reduced; the patient should leave with an under-standing of why "bad things" were happening and how to avoid similar pit-falls in the future; and lastly, the patient should have acquired a framework for continued self-reflection and problem solving.

Humanistic psychotherapy is a focused form of treatment that is based on the belief that human beings are naturally predisposed toward growth and self-actualization. However, this natural path has been altered and/or blocked by the person making choices based on obtaining recognition/approval from others rather than their own values. The most widely recognized form of humanistic psychotherapy is client-centered therapy, developed by Carl Rogers. This approach emphasizes the client-therapist relationship as the key to improvement. The therapist views the client with unconditional positive regard, and uses reflection as a means to demonstrate empathy. This process ultimately allows the client to experience and integrate his/her underlying emotions, resulting in an increased ability to take responsibility for one's life, including finding meaning in it. This approach to psychotherapy is mentioned here because it seems to best fit with the insight-oriented category.

• *Cognitive therapy.* "Cognition" means "the process of knowing or perceiving." Cognitive theory assumes that patients' faulty evaluations of the data they take in through their senses produce pathological moods—anxiety, depression, worry, guilt, and so on. In cognitive therapy, whether a glass is half empty or half full all depends on the mind's eyeglasses (rose-tinted or gray?).

The cognitive therapist identifies the habitual ways in which patients distort information (Beck, Rush, Shaw, & Emery, 1979). They make mountains out of molehills, project their own fears onto others, or see things in the worst possible light. These patterns, which are called "automatic thoughts," are accompanied by "automatic emotions" such as dread, worry, and tension. The cognitive therapist teaches patients to recognize their distressing emotions, the situations that produce them, and their usual patterns of automatic thoughts. The work is then to generate "disputing beliefs" that view the information in a more rational and accurate way (Ellis, 1975, 1984).

> As an example, a student social worker entered cognitive therapy for a moderate depression that intensified when she started her placement on a psychiatric inpatient service. A typical exchange between her and the therapist:
>
> PATIENT: [Situation] On my very first day on the ward, a patient asked me if his medication should be changed. I freaked.
>
> THERAPIST: When you were freaking, what did you think about?
>
> PATIENT: [Automatic thoughts] I felt like an idiot. That I can't even answer a simple question, and if I can't do that, then maybe I shouldn't be a therapist. [automatic emotions] I felt terrible, filled with shame and guilt.
>
> THERAPIST: [Pointing out a more rational thought] But you're a social work student, not a trained physician. Why should you know about this medication?
>
> PATIENT: [Automatic thought] Maybe, but then the patient asked me when he'd be discharged and I felt like a fool for not knowing the answer.
>
> THERAPIST: In retrospect, do you believe your feeling was justified?

PATIENT: [Rational thought] No. That's silly! Why should I know when he'd be discharged—I had just arrived on the ward 2 hours earlier. He's not even my patient!!

[Note: Behind this is a more global thought that will resurface in other situations and needs to be disputed: "I should know everything. If I don't, that means I'm stupid and everybody will think I'm stupid."]

For example, a combat veteran feels guilty because "I should have prevented Jack from jumping up to return fire. If I had, he wouldn't have been killed." The "irrational belief" is the vet's expectation that he "should" have been able to apply the knowledge he gained only after the death of his buddy to save him. A rational, disputing belief might be "Given the circumstances and what I knew at the time, I did the best I could, and Jack's death was a tragedy, but not my fault." Incorporating these new beliefs decreases distress and increases self-confidence, thereby allowing a person to try new behaviors; they are frequently and effectively combined with behavioral techniques such as relaxation training or exposure treatments (*cognitive-behavioral therapy*). Cognitive therapy is used most often to treat mild to moderately severe depressions, anxiety, panic attacks, and phobias (e.g., Beck et al., 1979; Chambless & Ollendick, 2001). Throughout the typical 10–25 weekly sessions, patients record episodes at home that led to troublesome feelings and thoughts, and at the following session, the cognitive distortions creating them are examined.

Dialectical behavior therapy is an evidence-based cognitive-behavioral treatment developed to help people diagnosed with borderline personality disorder, particularly those individuals who were chronically suicidal (Linehan, 1993). It employs skills training, individual therapy, and coaching by telephone. There are four sets of skills included in the therapy: mindfulness practice, interpersonal skills, tolerating distress, and regulating emotion. More recently, this approach has been used successfully to treat individuals with other disorders, such as substance dependence and PTSD.

• *Behavior therapy.* Any treatment that attempts to alter quantifiable behavior by systematically changing the environment that produces the behavior is behavior therapy. Generally speaking, changed behaviors are believed to lead to changed feelings and beliefs.

There are two primary schools of behavior therapy, one based on classical conditioning (Pavlovian) and one based on operant conditioning (Skinnerian). In Pavlov's original experiments, meat powder (the unconditioned stimulus, or UCS) was placed in a dog's mouth, thereby causing the dog to salivate (the unconditioned response, or UCR). Then Pavlov rang a bell when the meat powder was applied. After a number of trials, the bell *alone* (now a conditioned stimulus, or CS) was able to elicit the salivation (a conditioned response, or CR). Classical conditioning spawned the anxiety-reducing therapies of systematic desensitization and prolonged exposure, or flooding. The concept is that the brain sees something in the environment as a threat that in reality is not as dangerous as is feared (or not dangerous at all—either way, it's a CS). The brain reacts with fear, a CR, to prepare the person to respond to the perceived danger (e.g., the fight/flight response). As the exposure continues, the brain recognizes that there is no actual threat present, the CS loses its power to generate anxiety, and the fear extinguishes.

Exposure and Response Prevention (Abramowitz, Deacon, & Whiteside, 2011) is an evidence-based desensitization treatment that focuses on exposure to a fear hierarchy coupled with preventing the use of safety behaviors that would typically occur in response to the anxiety generated by the stimulus.

In *systematic desensitization*, treatment proceeds from the least to the most anxiety-producing stimuli. The patient is first taught muscle relaxation skills. Then a hierarchy of fears is constructed; as a simplified example, a person with a fear of snakes might find a color picture of snakes mildly distressing, a rubber snake more so, and a live snake terrifying. The therapist has the patient create a relaxed state and then presents the picture. Once the patient can view the picture with little anxiety, the therapist moves up the hierarchy. Consequently, over time the fear, in this case of snakes, lessens (Wolpe, 1958).

> If the patient is phobic about cats, the therapist might say after the patient relaxes, "Picture a cat 100 yards away—that is, the full length of a football field." Once the patient can do this without becoming tense, the therapist might say, "Now imagine this cat 75 yards away." This progressive desensitization process is continued so that, after the patient is able to imagine touching a cat, she may be exposed to cats in photos, and then to cats in real life (in vivo). It is this in vivo step that is critical for success. In fact, some patients can skip the progressive relaxation step and go straight to the in vivo part when accompanied by a trusted person.

Flooding, by contrast, does not gradually expose the patient to the fear-provoking stimulus, but instead presents the feared object or situation "all at once" for a prolonged period of time. In using flooding, a child with a school phobia would be taken to school (often kicking and screaming) and be maintained in that environment against his will. After a couple of days the child realizes that he has no option but to attend school and that he has survived being at school. The result is desensitization to his fear and restoration of daily functioning. While this process is the "opposite" of systematic desensitization, the result is the same in that exposure to the feared situation leads to decreased anxiety.

Operant conditioning is a process of systematically rewarding and reinforcing positive behaviors. An *operant* is a behavior shaped by its consequence. *Positive reinforcement* is a procedure that uses consequences for increasing operant behaviors. For example, by repeating a routine, a stand-up comic learns which jokes elicit laughs and which do not: The audience's laughter, which is a consequence, positively reinforces certain jokes, which become operants.

> With her behavior therapist, a person with bulimia may discover that binge-ing and vomiting reduce anxiety or boredom, thus reinforcing the harmful behaviors. The behavior therapist helps the patient find other activities that reduce anxiety or boredom (e.g., taking a warm shower, going for a walk, calling a friend). Substitution of the benign activities helps reduce the frequency of binges.
>
> Token economies are programs that systematically apply operant conditioning. They are used most often to prepare chronically hospitalized patients with schizophrenia or mental retardation for living in the community. When these patients display adaptive behaviors, they receive tokens, which they can exchange for desired goods (e.g., candy) and privileges (e.g., watching TV). This positive reinforcement supposedly conditions patients to perform adaptive behaviors (operants) in response to society's natural rewards (e.g., praise) without needing tokens.
>
> The distinctions between behavior therapies and psychotherapies are more semantic than real, more professional than clinical. Psychotherapies emerged from a medical (and thus, psychiatric) tradition, whereas behavior therapies have their origins in experimental psychology. In any effective therapy new behavior always changes feelings, and vice versa. To varying extents, all psychotherapies address behavior, and all behavior therapies address feelings. As the fields of behaviorism, psychoanalysis, and even psychobiology increasingly influence each other, techniques are often called "behavioral" more from tradition than from anything else.

• *Supportive psychotherapy/counseling*. Whereas psychodynamic psychotherapy stresses insight, supportive psychotherapy emphasizes advice, education, persuasion, reason, and other appeals to conscious processes to alleviate current and practical life difficulties. This is generally what is meant by the term *counseling*. The therapist supports the patient's more mature defenses and adaptive capacities and discourages immature defenses and maladaptive behaviors. To benefit, patients need not be particularly introspective, intelligent, or able to think abstractly, but they do need to have a willingness to change, to examine themselves, and to show up for usually one to four sessions a month.

During an acute psychosis, supportive psychotherapy is the verbal therapy of choice; it provides reality testing, emotional comfort, and help in distinguishing between sensible and senseless ideas, feelings, and actions. After an acute episode, supportive psychotherapy can show patients how to prevent a relapse by avoiding situations that are likely to precipitate symptoms. For instance, after enduring several bouts of major depression, many patients become so adept at identifying the earliest symptoms that they can avert a full-fledged (9–12 months) relapse by calling their psychiatrist, resuming medication, and examining their concerns with the help of professional perspective.

> *Short-term therapy.* This is a time-limited treatment (usually 8–20 sessions) that focuses on a clearly delineated problem that has erupted recently (within the past 2 months) and the goals of which are specified and agreed upon from the outset. There are numerous models of short-term therapy, including behavioral, cognitive, interpersonal, and insight-oriented. These therapies often focus on the same goals and problem areas but differ in the type and timing of interventions (Bloom, 1992; Ursano & Hales, 1986).
>
> Depending on whether it suppresses or provokes anxiety, short-term psychotherapy may stress support or insight. When supportive, short-term psychotherapy helps people get over acute problems and maintain the psychological status quo. When educational, patients may learn about thoughts and behaviors that interfere with their functioning and how to replace them with more adaptive ones. An example: A patient puts off responding to a complaint, and the complainer gets increasingly angry. In educational therapy, the patient learns how to respond to the complaint, which makes her less anxious and less likely to delay responding. When combined with other biological or psychosocial treatments, this therapy becomes part of a crisis intervention program. Insight-oriented short-term psychotherapy typically examines a "focal conflict"—a recent and well-defined wish that conflicts with the person's enduring traits. Marty suddenly faces a focal conflict when he meets a woman and must choose between Mom and marriage. Anxiety-provoking short-term psychotherapy would focus on this choice, but not on

other related yet more peripheral issues in Marty's life, such as his painfully low self-esteem. The brevity of this therapy helps keep the patient more intensively focused.

Group Treatments

Homo sapiens are one of the most social creatures on the planet, and therefore relationships are the source of much of the joy of human existence. However, the opposite is also true—stress, distress, and unhappiness often result from interpersonal problems. Over the years, multi-person interventions, such as group psychotherapy and psychoeducational groups, have been created as modalities to treat these interpersonal problems effectively.

• *Group psychotherapy.* More than any other treatment, group therapy is ideally suited to address *interpersonal* difficulties. Methods vary, but generally patients learn how they affect others and practice better ways of relating to people. Irvin Yalom (2005), perhaps the most well-known pioneer of group psychotherapy, has described 11 therapeutic factors in group treatment (Table 5-2). The group offers a safe environment in which to try new behaviors. Once confident enough, patients can try out the new behaviors in the "real" world, and then go over the results in the group to further refine

---

TABLE 5-2
Yalom's Curative Factors of Group Treatment

- *Instillation of hope*—faith that the treatment mode can and will be effective
- *Universality*—demonstration that we are not alone in our misery or our "problems"
- *Imparting of information*—didactic instruction about mental health, mental illness, psychodynamics, or whatever else might be the focal problem of the group
- *Altruism*—opportunity to rise out of oneself and help somebody else; the feeling of usefulness
- *Corrective recapitulation of primary family group*—experiencing transference relationships growing out of primary family experiences, providing the opportunity to relearn and clarify distortions
- *Development of socializing techniques*—social learning and development of interpersonal skills
- *Imitative behavior*—taking on the manner of group members who function more adequately
- *Catharsis*—opportunity for expression of strong affect
- *Existential factors*—recognition of the basic features of existence through sharing with others (e.g., ultimate aloneness, ultimate death, ultimate responsibility for our own actions)
- *Direct advice*—receiving and giving suggestions for problem-solving strategies
- *Interpersonal learning*—receiving feedback from others and experimenting with new ways of relating

Note: Adapted from Yalom, 2005.

---

their skills. A typical group session lasts 60–90 minutes, occurs once a week for outpatients (three to five times a week for inpatients), has 6–10 members, and is led by one or two therapists.

Group psychotherapy differs from (1) *encounter groups*, which help "normal" people engage in consciousness raising and self-actualization, and (2) *T-groups* (the *T* stands for *training*), which teach normal people how groups function (group process) by having them participate in a group.

Surveyed patients claim that groups help most by giving them a sense of belonging and by showing them they are not the only ones in the world facing difficulties. However, patients with psychosis and people who are extremely sensitive to personal slights or to feelings of persecution are likely to panic or become further disorganized if the group becomes too intense. Narcissistic, paranoid, or rigidly moralistic patients generally do poorly in therapy groups and are quickly ostracized by other patients.

• *Psychoeducational groups.* These groups provide patients with specific information and/or skills to improve their ability to function in their various life roles. An assertiveness training group, for example, would teach members about different styles of behavior—passive, assertive, and aggressive. Group members would then pick problematic situations and practice using assertive skills in the group. Between sessions, members apply the lessons learned in their real lives. They then review their experiences in the group and continue to refine their skills via this feedback loop.

• *Self-help groups.* Self-help groups provide a vehicle for people with a common problem to come together to receive support, share information, and get feedback. These groups are very popular and can be found for a wide range of medical, psychological, and social problems. They are not led by professionals. Interestingly, the advent of the Internet has spawned a new generation of cyberspace self-help groups.

The most recognized self-help groups are probably those for drug and alcohol recovery. Alcoholics Anonymous, Narcotics Anonymous, and Ala-non are well established in many parts of the world as a method to promote recovery. Some providers criticize these groups for their dubious efficacy, evangelistic nature, lack of trained leadership, and avoidance of scientific scrutiny. Nonetheless, many self-help groups assist patients who are alcoholics and drug addicts, whom many therapists don't like or can't help.

Couple and Family Treatment

In many instances the interpersonal issues reside within the family. When the difficulties are between spouses, meeting with both partners for couple therapy may provide an effective intervention. If the family includes children

or there are others who are part of the family, then treatment may be expanded
to work with the additional members. Such an approach usually views the
family as a system, meaning that by changing any part (the relationship
between two people, or even one person's behavior), the larger system can be
changed. Further adding to the treatment arsenal, group and family therapies may be combined to create a multiple family group therapy.

• *Couple therapy.* Couple therapy focuses on improving the relationship
between two partners. Neither party is therefore considered the patient. The
goal is to improve each person's satisfaction with the relationship. There are
typically two focal points in this work: communication and conflict resolution. Enhancing communication requires paying specific attention to the
intent and the impact of the communication (Gottman, 1999). This requires
partners to ask one another their perception of a communication, and to
attend to both verbal and nonverbal messages. Each partner then has the
opportunity to clarify. This technique is sometimes referred to as "active listening." For example, when the wife says "You never listen to me!," the husband may conclude that he's not doing a good enough job (e.g., fixing the
sink, watching the children). If he asks if she means he's not doing enough
tasks, the husband may learn that his wife is actually seeking emotional support and not a new sink in the kitchen. He can then specifically provide what
she wants. Thus increased skill in transmitting and receiving messages accurately can lead to increased satisfaction in the relationship.

The other primary focus is conflict resolution, sometimes called negotiation. Many people are uncomfortable in managing disagreements and resort
to short-term coping strategies to reduce their immediate discomfort. As an
illustration, imagine a husband and wife disagreeing over whether to have
joint or separate bank accounts. The husband wants separate, but the wife
thinks that's unfair because she is only working part-time. As the debate heats
up, both people become more rigid in their positions, and soon the husband
starts yelling over the top of his wife's voice. She responds by walking out and
slamming the door. What began as a problem for the couple to solve soon
became an exercise in each person fighting to reduce his or her immediate
distress—he bellowed, and she walked out. These coping methods may well
reduce discomfort temporarily; however, they not only don't solve the original problem, they also can create additional dissatisfaction in the overall
relationship. Therapy teaches partners how to identify (1) guidelines for
interacting during a disagreement (e.g., not yelling or walking out), (2) the
goals of their interaction (e.g., solving the bank account question), and (3)
the tools they need, such as problem-solving skills, to address the problem
(Emery, 1994).

• *Family therapy.* Like couple work, family therapy seeks to improve communication and conflict resolution skills to reduce stress and increase adaptive functioning. There are many models of family therapy (Nichols, 1984) in which the focus is on the family as a dysfunctional system. Thus there is no single patient and the unit of treatment is the family itself. One of the more common approaches is structural family therapy (Minuchen, 1974). This model focuses on family members' alliances and boundaries. For example, suppose the mother confides in her daughter that "Your dad isn't that interested in me" instead of dealing directly with her husband to improve the marriage. The husband/father resents this arrangement and pulls further away from both, thereby reinforcing the dysfunctional structure. Treatment would focus on moving the parents closer together as partners and removing the daughter from the marriage and into the role of their child.

Every family, like every relationship, has a structure or set of rules. Not surprisingly, major life changes in the family can require an adjustment or recalibration of how people interact. Times of transition, such as a child moving into adolescence and pushing for more independence, create potential issues that families sometimes need help in navigating. Family therapy, using tools such as role-playing inside and homework outside the sessions, can help family members get (back) in synch with one another.

• *Multiple family group therapy.* This format of group therapy generally consists of four to seven families meeting with two or more therapists for 60–90 minutes. These families typically have a hospitalized relative on the same unit. The meetings occur once or twice a week and usually include the hospitalized patients. In many respects, multiple family group therapy offers something other treatments cannot: It affords relatives a chance to see that they are not alone in the world, to share mutual problems with a uniquely sympathetic audience, to learn how other families cope with similar problems, and to feel more hopeful by observing other patients' improvement. Conversely, this group format enables inpatients to see what other patients' families are like; as a result, when patients talk to one another outside of the multiple family group—informally or in group therapy—they can speak with firsthand knowledge of their families.

With the above treatments, a convenient distinction is made between "counseling" and "therapy." Couple and family *counseling* is used if the psychopathology mainly resides within the patient, or if the couple or family had been functioning normally but now is doing poorly as a result of a crisis. If the psychopathology is enduring and resides within the couple or family, couple or family *therapy* should be used. Changes in behaviors and interpersonal interactions are the goal.

Whether or not the family has played a major role in producing the disorder, counseling is based on the assumptions that there is a patient with a mental disorder who disrupts the family members, and who, in turn, may act "neurotically," unwisely, or harmfully. Family members are not viewed as victimizers. In a sense, everybody is a victim. Counseling usually helps family members to solve problems, to minimize psychological trauma to other family members, and to deal more constructively with the patient's disorder. Family members, for example, might learn to stop telling a depressed member to "pick yourself up by your bootstraps," but that it *is* okay to ask her to do a few chores or join the family on an outing.

In family therapy, clinicians consider the real patient to be the entire family even though the family may implicate a single member (usually the most vulnerable) as the *identified patient*. In this view, the family is as much an unwitting victimizer as a victim. Therapy tries to rectify distorted communications and relationships within a couple or a family as a means of helping the entire family, including the identified patient.

Specialized Treatments

In addition to the psychological treatments that rely on talking with the patient to change thoughts, feelings, and/or behavior, therapists sometimes augment their treatment by incorporating specialized techniques that can help improve symptoms. Three of the more common tools include hypnosis, biofeedback, and relaxation training.

• *Hypnosis.* Hypnosis is a state of hypersuggestibility in which the patient is relatively oblivious to everything except the hypnotist's voice. Hypnosis is *not* sleep but a form of intense, restricted alertness. The "power" of hypnosis lies within the subject, not the hypnotist. When a person says "You can't hypnotize me," he is correct. Psychological (and probably neurological) variables affect patients' ability to enter a trance (Pettinati et al., 1990). The hypnotist cannot "control" the patient. Most people have experienced hypnosis without realizing it. In driving long distances at night on a highway, the driver will "glaze over" and then suddenly jerk awake to attention. When "glazed over," the driver is in a light hypnotic trance, focused on the road and oblivious to everything else.

Although the public may view hypnosis as a magic potion that, without any time or effort, will remedy every human affliction, its clinical efficacy is far more limited. Mental-health professionals also have become enamored with hypnosis, particularly since the attention the work of Milton H. Erickson received in the 1980s. Nonetheless, hypnosis can be helpful in treating habits such as overeating and smoking. When psychotherapy with a patient becomes "stuck," hypnosis can be used to accelerate information-giving. Hypnosis is generally ill-advised for patients who are currently or potentially psychotic.

• *Biofeedback.* An electronic instrument informs the patient about changes in one or more physiological variables that she does not normally perceive, such as brain-wave activity and blood pressure. A patient with tension headaches, for example, can identify tension in her facial muscles by the sound of beeps from a biofeedback machine, which reflect the degree of this tension. She then experiments with different mental activities (e.g., fantasizing lying on a beach, deep breathing, humming "Ooooooooommmm") to see which decreases the frequency of beeps, indicating diminished facial tension and headaches. Biofeedback is mainly used to treat psychophysiological disorders such as tension headaches and hypertension.

• *Relaxation training.* Relaxation techniques such as "progressive muscle relaxation" allow a patient to systematically contract each muscle group in his body and then fully relax it. These exercises, which resemble meditation techniques, can reduce anxiety and induce sleep. They are also used in conjunction with behavioral techniques such as systematic desensitization. Relaxation training can also engage the imagination through the addition of guided imagery. In this version of the exercise, the therapist verbally guides the patient through a pleasant and relaxing experience while the patient uses his imagination to visualize it.

No Treatment

"All that's therapy isn't therapeutic." This dictum of Thomas Detre's receives too little attention. All treatments, including psychosocial treatments, have side effects. Abraham Kardiner (1977) wrote, "Freud was always infuriated whenever I would say to him that you could not do harm with psychoanalysis. He said, 'When you say that, you also say that it cannot do any good. Because if you cannot do any harm, how can you do good?'" (p. 69). Clinical experience confirms Freud's observation: An upsurge of repressed thoughts or primitive feelings can exacerbate psychotic, neurotic, and affective symptoms. Patients can become overly dependent on therapists or "addicted" to therapy; they may substitute therapists for friends and therapy for living. For some patients, insight becomes an excuse to avoid change, while others misuse it as punishment, not learning. Thus, in devising treatment plans, clinicians should weigh a therapy's potential hazards and benefits, and for certain patients conclude that "no treatment" is the prescription of choice.

Sometimes no treatment is the best treatment, not because therapy would harm, but because it would most likely fail. Many patients with psychosomatic problems are not helped by therapy, nor are many of those with personality disorders (especially antisocial personality disorder). Too often, somaticizing patients emerge from therapy "psychologizing" their problems—and newly equipped with a whole new list of symptoms and issues. The same often applies to the "unmotivated" and to those seeking compensation, disability, or a lawsuit. (Clinicians should think twice when explaining a failed treatment as due to the patient, who was "unmotivated." The patient may be unmotivated, but after all, it is at least part of the therapist's job to motivate—that's what makes a treatment successful!) Some people, such as those seen during bereavement or an acute crisis, will improve without therapy if they have supportive friends. Thus, don't assume that every patient needs, or will benefit from, treatment, and don't forget that a failed treatment hurts more than no treatment.

DOES THERAPY WORK?

Strange how people say "I don't believe in psychiatry." No one says, "I don't believe in surgery." That's because everyone knows that surgery helps sometimes, but not at other times: It depends on the patient, the illness, the goals of surgery, and the surgeon. The same holds true for psychiatric treatment: Whether it helps depends on the patient, the disorder, the goals of treatment, and the therapist.

Also strange is asserting "I don't believe in psychiatry" as if it were a matter of theology, as in "I don't believe in God." Patients should evaluate their therapy by trusting their own judgment, not as a question of faith. They can ask themselves if, given reasonable expectations and sufficient time, treatment seems to be helping or not.

What is meant by the assertion "I don't believe in psychiatry"? Surely people do believe that psychoactive drugs can treat some problems, and surely they believe that talking to a relatively neutral, objective, and skilled professional who's uninvolved in the patient's personal life can affect how the patient views herself and the world.

To ask "Does psychotherapy work?" is akin to asking "Does a restaurant work?" No one would compare McDonald's with Chez Andre's Exclusive French Cuisine. Each is splendid at what it does. The same is true for psychotherapy. It does what it does, as long as what's expected of it is appropriate, and as long as the therapist, like the restaurateur, knows her stuff. And just as whether a restaurant "works" depends on who's making the judgment, so too with therapy. In evaluating if a patient has improved, who's the best judge? The patient? The therapist? A researcher? A family member? A friend? There is an abundance of research on the effects of psychotherapy, and the overall conclusion is that approximately two-thirds of people improve in the short term from psychotherapy (Shadish et al., 2000; Smith et al., 1980).

Therefore, the proper question is not "Does psychiatry work" but "Which treatments work for which disorders, in which patients, with which goals, under which conditions, and according to whom?" In evaluating if a particular therapy is effective, valid research now compares the effects of an active treatment (e.g., cognitive therapy, fluoxetine) with an inactive or placebo treatment (e.g., supportive contact, placebo pill). The patients, and when possible the clinicians, are "blind" to (uninformed about) which treatment is active or, if it's medication, which treatment the patient is receiving. When only patients are blind, it is called a single-blind study; when both clinicians and patients are kept uninformed, it is a double-blind study. In the pages that follow, as we consider specific psychopathologies and clinical syndromes, results from this type of experimental research are presented. Nevertheless, as mentioned previously, although our scientific evidence in psychiatry is growing, it is also still just emerging.

Evidence-based treatment is where scientific findings, clinical experience, and patient preferences overlap. It is an approach to clinical-decision-making that incorporates these three elements simultaneously and with balance (see Figure 5-2). The intersection of these three elements is most likely to accomplish the goal of effective care. It becomes necessary to evaluate the latest scientific evidence to determine its quality and relevance to the specific patient's condition. Randomized placebo-controlled double-blinded and cross-over studies are considered to be the highest quality research design (see Riegleman, 2013). It is common for a study to control for as many variables as possible and consequently exclude more typical patients. Consequently the results of the study may be specific to this cohort of outliers and generalizations of the finding to other persons may not be valid. Also, research may demonstrate the statistical significance of a proposed treatment but with such a small effect size that it is not worth doing. For example, the treatment may be so labor intensive and costly that it is not practical for the real world. The treatment may be resisted because of time involved or undesirable side effects. So a treatment approach may have evidence of being efficacious but not be effective. Effectiveness includes safety, tolerability, adherence, practicality, and the degree of improvement (effect size).

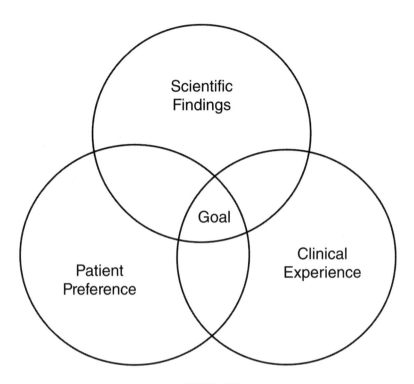

FIGURE 5-2
Evidence-Based Treatment

References

Abramowitz, J.S., Deacon, B.J., & Whiteside, P.H. (2011). *Exposure therapy for anxiety.* New York: Guilford.

Abroms, E.M. (1983). Beyond eclectism. *American Journal of Psychiatry, 140,* 740–745.

Anderson, E.M., & Lambert, M.J. (1995). Short-term dynamically oriented psychotherapy: A review and meta-analysis. *Clinical Psychology Review, 15,* 503–514.

Barlow, D.H. (Ed.). (2001). *Clinical handbook of psychological disorders.* New York: Guilford.

Beck, A.T., Rush, A.J., Shaw, B.F., & Emery, G. (1979). *Cognitive therapy of depression: A treatment manual.* New York: Guilford.

Bloom, B.L. (1992). *Planned short-term psychotherapy.* Boston: Allyn & Bacon.

Breier, A., & Strauss, J.S. (1984). The role of social relationships in the recovery from psychotic disorders. *American Journal of Psychiatry, 141,* 949–955.

Chambless, D.L., & Ollendick, T.H. (2001). Empirically supported psychological interventions: Controversies and evidence. *Annual Review of Psychology, 52,* 685–716.

Ellis, A. (1984). Rational–emotive therapy. In R.J. Corsini (Ed.), *Current psychotherapies,* 3rd ed. Itacsa, IL: Peacock Press.

Emery, R.E. (1994). *Renegotiating family relationship: Divorce, child custody, and mediation.* New York: Guilford.

Gottman, J.M. (1999). *The marriage clinic: A scientifically-based marital therapy.* New York: Norton.

Hanson, N.B., Lambert, M.J., & Forman, E.M. (2002). The psychotherapy dose: Response effect and its implications for treatment service delivery. *Clinical Psychology: Science and Practice, 9,* 329–343.

Hibbard, J.H., Stockard, J., Mahoney, E.R., & Tusler, M. (2004). Development of the Patient Activation Measure (PAM): Conceptualizing and measuring activation in patients and consumers. *Health Services Research, 39,* 1005–1026.

Kardiner, A. (1977). *My analysis with Freud.* New York: Norton.

Linehan, M.M. (1993). *Cognitive behavioral treatment of borderline personality disorder.* New York: Guilford.

Luborsky, L. (1984). *Principles of psychoanalytic psychotherapy.* New York: Basic Books.

Malan, D.H. (1995). *Individual psychotherapy and the science of psychodynamics,* 2nd ed. London: Hodder Education.

McDermut, W., Miller, I.W., & Brown, R.A. (2001). The efficacy of group psychotherapy for depression: A meta-analysis and review of the empirical research. *Clinical Psychology: Science and Practice, 8,* 98–116.

Miller, W.R., & Rollnick, S. (2002). *Motivational interviewing: Preparing people to change.* New York: Guilford Press.

Minuchen, S. (1974). *Families and family therapy.* Cambridge, MA: Harvard University Press.

Nichols, M.P. (1984). *Family therapy: Concepts and methods.* New York: Gardner Press.

Pettinati, H.M., Kogan, L.G., Evans, F.J., Wade, J.H., Horne, R.L., & Staas, J.M. (1990). Hypnotizability of psychiatric inpatients according to two different scales. *American Journal of Psychiatry, 147,* 69–75.

Popkin, M.K., & Tucker, G.J. (1994). Mental disorders due to a general medical condition and substance induced disorders. *DSM-IV Sourcebook,* 243–276.

Prochaska, J.O., DiClemente, C.C., & Norcross, J.C. (1992). In search of how people change: Applications to addictive behaviors. *American Psychologist, 47,* 1102–1114.

Riegelman, R.K. (2013). *Studying a study and testing a test: Reading evidence-based health research.* Philadelphia: Lippincott Williams & Wilkins.

Rogers, C.R. (1951). *Client-centered therapy: Its current practice, implications, and theory.* Boston: Houghton Mifflin.

Safran, J.D., & Moran, J.C. (2000). *Negotiating the therapeutic alliance: A relational treatment guide.* New York: Guilford.

Shadish, W.R., Matt, G.E., Navarro, A.N., & Phillips, G. (2000). The effects of psychological therapies under clinically representative conditions: A meta-analysis. *Psychological Bulletin, 126,* 512–529.

Smith, M.L., Glass, G.V., & Miller, T.I. (1980). *The benefits of psychotherapy*. Baltimore: Johns Hopkins University Press.

Ursano, R.J., & Hales, R.E. (1986). A review of brief individual psychotherapies. *American Journal of Psychiatry, 143*, 1507–1517.

Wilkins, W. (1973a). Client's expectancy of therapeutic gain: Evidence for the active role of the therapist. *Psychiatry, 36*, 184–190.

Wilkins, W. (1973b). Expectancy of therapeutic gain: An empirical and conceptual critique. *Journal of Consulting Psychology, 40*, 69–77.

Wolpe, J. (1958). *Psychotherapy by reciprocal inhibition*. Palo Alto, CA: Stanford University Press.

Yalom, I.D. (2005). *The theory and practice of group psychotherapy*, 5th ed. New York: Basic Books.

www.psych.org for American Psychiatric Association treatment guidelines

www.aacap.org for American Academy of Child and Adolescent Psychiatry treatment guidelines

www.nida.nih.gov for National Institute on Drug Abuse treatment guidelines

To obtain information about any self-help group, contact the National Self-Help Clearinghouse, Graduate School and University Center of the City University of New York, 365 5th Avenue, Suite 3300, New York, NY 10016, or on the Web at www.selfhelpweb.org.

6

Psychopharmacology

How does the brain, through physical and neurochemical processes, give rise to perception, memory, emotion, and thought? With the right tools one can examine the chemical changes in the brain when a person smiles, or remembers the first day of school, or is sad. How hard could it be to map the physical processes associated with individual experiences of memory, perception, emotion, and thought and then to determine how these processes might go awry? Perhaps then it would be possible to have a simple medication that would discretely "fix" problems with each of those core brain functions. However, these functions are not independent but influence each other. When a person is transiently anxious he or she may be unable to recall a fact that easily pops to mind when the anxiety passes. Another time it is the smell of a perfume or the taste of a cookie that revives a vivid memory, complete with its attendant emotions. Perception, memory, thought, and emotion are too deeply intertwined to explain simply.

An example will illustrate the interdependence of neurotransmitter function in a pathological state. James, an active and engaging 70-year-old man, dies unexpectedly in his sleep, leaving behind his 68-year-old wife Luna. Luna is shocked and bereft; her daughters rally around her and handle the funeral arrangements. Over the next few months Luna's grief evolves into a pervasive and incapacitating depression. She no longer socializes. She rarely showers and sleeps much of each day. Although she had always ably managed the couple's finances, she now neglects to pay some bills and underpays others to the point that foreclosure on her home is being threatened. Her daughters find her forgetful, inattentive, and disinterested, at times even unable to recall the name of her only granddaughter. She becomes fixated on the idea that she is penniless and will be forced to a homeless shelter, saying she would rather be dead. Her daughters repeatedly reassure her that she is financially comfortable but her delusion is unshakeable.

Luna's primary problem is depression. However, not just her mood is affected; she is forgetful, inattentive, and socially unaware to the extent that she appears to have a dementia. Her depression is so bad it has affected her concentration and attention and hence her cognition and memory. Cognitively she looks slower and duller. Her anxiety level is elevated. Finally, the depression has become sufficiently severe that Luna has developed a psychosis in the form of falsely believing that she is financially destitute.

In this case, the neurotransmitters most affected by grief and depression are norepinephrine and serotonin, as will be described later. However Luna's extreme loss has compromised not only the functioning of norepinephrine and serotonin but also of those neurotransmitters that regulate cognition, attention, anxiety, and reality testing. The transmitters in the brain are connected like a chain or an interwoven net, where a failure in one part of the system causes problems in many parts (Figure 6-1).

In explaining the functional systems of the brain it becomes important to keep these complex interactions in mind. To understand psychopharmacol-

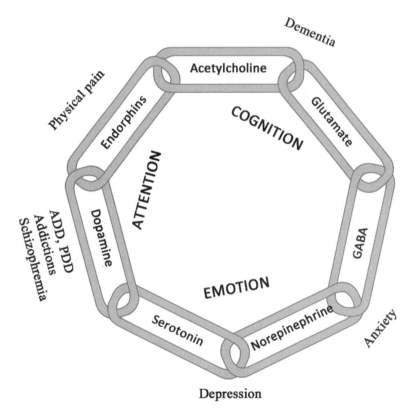

FIGURE 6-1
Neurotransmitters Chain (with associated functions and disorders)

ogy it is necessary to understand the basics of neurochemical transmission; the primary functional neurotransmitters, their pathways, and their semi-hierarchical function; how psychopathology is associated with neurotransmitter changes; and how influencing these neurotransmitters can affect psychopathology.

In other chapters of this book there will be greater detail of the mechanisms of action for specific categories of medication for specific disorders. For example, with respect to depression the strategies behind the use of medication to affect serotonin and norepinephrine will be considered.

NEUROCHEMICAL TRANSMISSION

As introduced in Chapter 4, the brain is composed of neurons that communicate with each other across short gaps called *synapses* (see Figures 4-1 and 6-2). Neurons with cell bodies in one part of the brain may stretch their axons into an adjoining or distant part of the brain to affect neurons there. Neurons make chemicals that allow themselves to communicate with one another and thereby control body movements, thoughts, feelings, and actions. When the neuron activates, it releases chemicals called *neurotransmitters* into the synapse. These, and other chemicals with similar molecular structures, bind to receptors on the receiving neuron (like a key into a lock) and stimulate or modulate its electrical activity. The chemical key can unlock the receptor completely (agonist) or lock it completely (antagonist) or partially lock or unlock it. The transmitted chemical message then results in an electrical charge (depolarization) that travels down the entire length of the receiving neuron, influencing further neurons across other synapses. It is through this electric flow down an axon that information is conducted.

As the brain matures, the axon becomes coated with a fatty substance (myelin) that serves as insulation to improve the efficiency of the signal. This process of myelination (which continues from birth into the 20s) explains how we become more thoughtful and less impulsive as we age. One can imagine the harm at the cellular level that huffing gasoline (or other organic solvents) can have in the developing brain—it literally dissolves the myelin sheath and contributes to a short-circuiting of the electric impulses (an "irritable brain"). At birth a person has the largest number of neurons he will ever possess, and then careful pruning occurs especially in the first two decades. Incorrect pruning and altered neuron migration in the course of development are suspected mechanisms in schizophrenia.

Activation of a single neuron of the billions in the brain would be

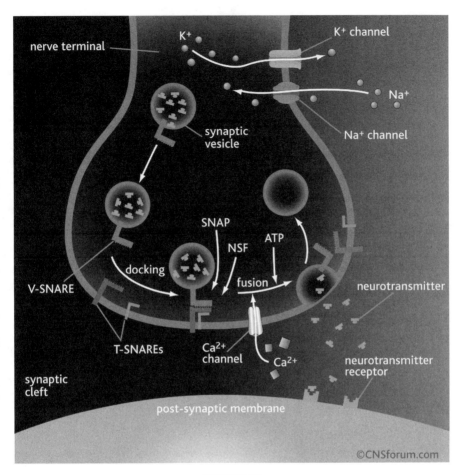

FIGURE 6-2
The Synapse and Neurotransmission

expected to have little effect. However, activation of whole tracts of neurons leads to phenomena such as motor activity, sensation, or even thought. Neurons are usually dedicated to producing one primary neurotransmitter. A collection of nerve cell bodies of the same neurotransmitter type (e.g., dopamine) performing the same function is referred to as a *nucleus* (e.g., nucleus accumbens). After the neurotransmitter has been released into synapses, it is inactivated either by enzymatic breakdown or a reuptake process in which it is "vacuumed" up by the releasing neuron (specifically, reuptake inactivation through presynaptic receptors). In this chapter the idea of a neurotransmitter "chain" or net will be expanded. This chain when stressed may fail at a certain link and cause dysfunction.

Some parts of the brain are more prominently featured in psychopathology than others. These include the reticular activating system, the limbic system, the prefrontal cortex, the amygdala, the basal ganglia, and the thalamus. The limbic system, a series of deep brain structures encircling the middle brain, is responsible for regulating emotion (Figure 6-3). Disturbance in limbic system function underlies many psychiatric disorders. The sections that follow will intentionally simplify some aspects of psychopharmacology in order to establish a solid foundation for the beginning or nonmedical student, and to share useful metaphors for the purpose of providing education to our patients on this topic. Understanding improves a person's ability to commit to and adhere to treatment.

The seven neurotransmitters currently known to have an effect on perception, motor activity, sensation, emotion, attention, and cognition are acetylcholine, glutamate, gamma-aminobutyric acid (GABA), dopamine, serotonin, norepinephrine, and endorphins. All of these transmitters are necessary for the smooth functioning of the brain, interacting in complex ways. For example, endorphin-releasing neurons modulate GABA neurons, which in turn modulate dopamine-releasing neurons in the main reward pathway in the brain. In another example, serotonin down-regulates dopamine; this is the pathway by which some antidepressants may actually worsen ADHD symptoms. A similar result occurs when the release of glutamate through action at the NMDA receptors, causes reduced levels of dopamine. Figure 6-4, illustrates the interactions of three monoamine transmitters. If a person is at dinner with a new romantic interest, brain levels of dopamine and serotonin rise, leading to pleasurable feelings. If a waiter drops a tray, startling the individual, norepinephrine might suddenly spike so that anxiety decreases the immediate pleasure.

Each neurotransmitter seems to have a different major function. Several modulate the function of other neurotransmitters. All of the neurotransmitters are necessary in exact proportions for optimal functioning of the central nervous system. These neurochemical interactions must balance for normal functioning. Another environmental factor is the availability of the raw materials in the diet to manufacture the neurotransmitters. The building block for serotonin is the essential amino acid tryptophan that may be lacking in the diets of strict vegetarians. Abnormalities in function can be associated with problems that are either inborn or are acquired. In the course of daily living, demands are made on these neurochemical pathways; if these demands are persistent or excessive they may exhaust the pathways' capabilities and alter or shut down functioning (i.e., mental breakdown).

Stressors, in essence, pull on the chain of neurochemicals and cause it to break at the weakest link. Certain individuals may have been born with rela-

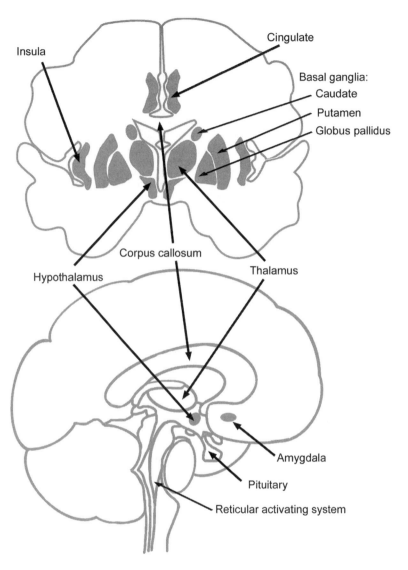

FIGURE 6-3
Deep Brain Structures

tive deficiencies in neurotransmitters or receptors (weak links) that predispose them to breaking under stress—in certain individuals even under the minimal stressors of everyday life. In such cases, treatment involves increasing the chemical suspected to be deficient (fortifying the link) and relieving the stress on the chain through various types of psychosocial therapies (as previously discussed). Someday we may be able to scan the brain and determine the exact cause of the imbalance, but for now we surmise which neu-

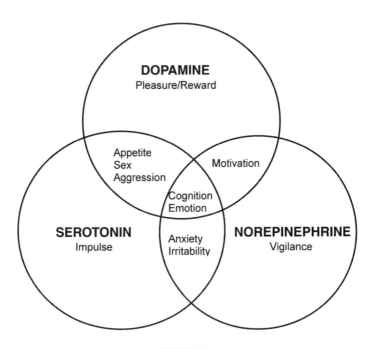

FIGURE 6-4
Overlapping Functions of Monoamine Neurotransmitters

rochemical to address based upon the clinical presentation (again refer to Figure 6-1).

An important consideration in treatment is that neurochemistry (and response to medications designed to restore balance) varies across the life-cycle by age and ethnic group. For example, many medications that are pre-scribed to restore balance are metabolized in the liver by an enzyme system called cytochrome P450. This system has over two hundred variants of enzymes. Because people of Asian descent have lower levels of cytochrome P450 enzymes than do people of northern European extraction, they metab-olize many psychotropic medications more slowly and lower doses may be needed for the same clinical effect. The same applies to older adults, who generally are less able to metabolize drugs.

The body tends to maintain itself in a stable state of neurotransmitters, a state called *homeostasis*. This tendency toward stability applies to both healthy and pathological neurotransmitter states. The brain, once depressed, will maintain the neurotransmitters and receptors in the depressed state. Waiting for neurotransmitters to reset on their own may take years; histori-cally, people were placed in asylums (meaning "sanctuary" or "refuge") where the cares of the world were removed with the hope that under less-stressful conditions (removing tension from the chain), the neurophysiology would be rebalanced.

MAJOR NEUROTRANSMITTERS

As mentioned earlier, seven major neurotransmitters are of particular interest in psychiatry: acetylcholine, glutamate, gamma-aminobutyric acid, dopamine, serotonin, norepinephrine, and endorphin. As each is considered, it is important to remember that they influence each other.

Acetylcholine

Acetylcholine is present in both the peripheral and the central nervous systems. In the peripheral nervous system it allows motor neurons to stimulate muscle fibers to fire, causing contraction of the muscle. In the central nervous system it has a more complex role: Although it is somewhat involved in excitatory activity, it is also involved in synaptic plasticity, learning, and short-term memory. Disorders associated with acetylcholine include Alzheimer's disease and delirium, and some of the medications used to treat this problem directly affect acetylcholine function.

There are two types of acetylcholine receptors: nicotinic receptors in the peripheral nervous system, and muscarinic receptors in the peripheral as well as central nervous systems. Muscarinic receptors are *metabotropic*, meaning that they affect neuronal functioning indirectly through signal transduction on ion channels, rather than directly through the ion channels themselves. These receptors influence second messenger systems and account for synaptic plasticity.

There are relatively few cholinergic receptors in the brain. The site of greatest acetylcholine synthesis in the brain is the interpeduncular nucleus (near the substantia nigra in the midbrain). Patients with Alzheimer's disease sometimes, but not always, show reductions in cholinergic neurons in Meynert's nucleus (nucleus basalis). Acetylcholine nuclei and pathways in the brain are illustrated in Figure 6-5.

Glutamate

Glutamate is the most pervasive excitatory neurotransmitter in the brain (Figure 6-6). It could be thought of as the accelerator that drives brain func-

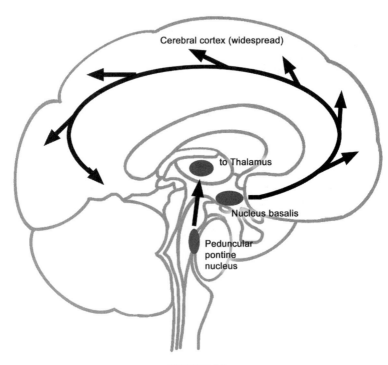

FIGURE 6-5
Acetylcholine Pathways in the Brain

tion. Glutamate is necessary for thought, learning, and motor activity. An excess of glutamate can be associated with seizures. There is some evidence that chronic use of alcohol followed by withdrawal leads to a relative excess of glutamate; one medication (acamprosate) used for alcohol dependence is a glutamate receptor modulator.

The primary brain glutamatergic pathways are those that connect the thalamus and the cortex, those going from one part of the cortex to another, and the extrapyramidal pathway (i.e., connections between the cortex and striatum). Other glutamate connections exist between the cortex, substantia nigra, subthalmic nucleus, and pallidum. Glutamate-containing neuronal terminals are very common in the brain, accounting for almost 50% of all neurons.

Gamma-aminobutyric Acid

GABA is the primary inhibitory neurotransmitter in vertebrates. If glutamate is the accelerator, GABA can be thought of as the brake that decelerates cerebral function. GABA receptors are *ionotropic*, meaning that their activation

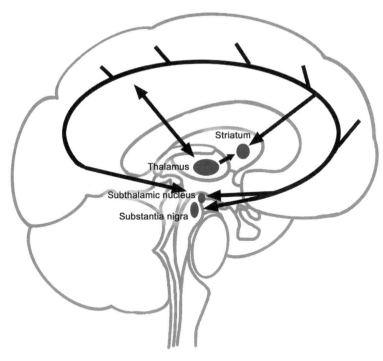

FIGURE 6-6
Glutamate Pathways in the Brain

directly affects potassium or chloride ion channels in the neuron. Relative lack of this inhibitory neurotransmitter can result in seizures. Many drugs of abuse substitute for natural GABA. Alcohol, benzodiazepines, and barbiturates all fall into this category. At low doses, these drugs suppress anxiety and lead to euphoria. In higher doses they are central nervous system depressants. When a person uses these substances for a long period of time, the brain down-regulates production of GABA. If the person abruptly stops ingesting the external drug, the relative lack of GABA activity compared to glutamate can lead to severe overactivity of excitatory brain neurons, causing a withdrawal seizure. GABA is also profoundly involved in anxiety regulation.

GABAergic inhibition is seen throughout brain structures, including in the hippocampus, hypothalamus, and cerebral and cerebellar cortices (Figure 6-7).

Dopamine

Dopamine is involved in goal-directed activity and reasoning, as well as in distinguishing imagination from reality. Although there are five types of

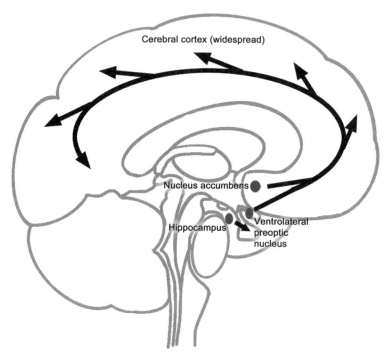

FIGURE 6-7
GABA Pathways in the Brain

dopamine receptors in the brain, with important roles in cognition, motor activity, reward, muscle tone, sleep, mood, attention, and learning, most of the higher-level effects of dopamine are governed by the D1 or D2 receptors. Insufficient dopamine in the basal ganglia leads to Parkinson's disease; insufficient dopamine in the frontal cortex can contribute to attention-deficit disorder. Dopamine is the major neurotransmitter involved in the primary reward system of the brain. This system is deeply engaged in the reinforcement of motivated behavior, including pursuit of food, pleasure, and sex. It is this part of the brain that is "hijacked" by drugs such as cocaine and amphetamines, which substitute for dopamine. A major category of drugs, most commonly used to treat schizophrenia, and psychosis in general, are the antipsychotics. Most of these seem to have some effect on the dopaminergic system.

There are three major dopamine pathways in the brain. The first extends from the ventral tegmentum to the mesolimbic forebrain (Figure 6-8) and is responsible for cognition, reward systems, and emotional behavior. The second extends from the substantia nigra to the caudate nucleus putamen (neo-

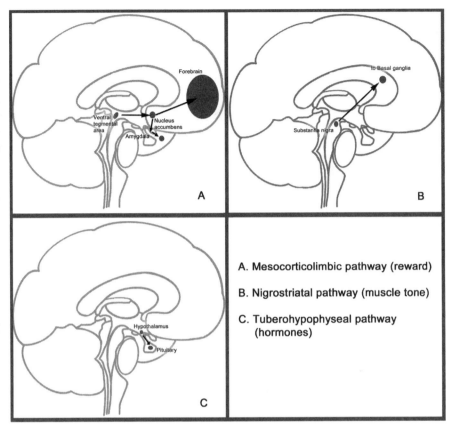

FIGURE 6-8
Dopamine Pathways in the Brain

striatum) and is associated with movement and sensory stimuli. The final pathway extends from the hypothalamus to the pituitary and is concerned with neuronal/hormonal control of the hypothalmic–pituitary endocrine system.

Serotonin

Serotonin (5-HT) is a neurotransmitter involved in the regulation of mood, anxiety, aggression, sleep, appetite, and sexuality. There are several types of serotonin receptors; all except one work via a secondary messenger system in the neuron. Diminished levels of serotonin have been associated with violent behavior. Many medications used in the treatment of anxiety and mood disorders modulate serotonin levels.

The principal nuclei for serotonin are the rostral and caudal raphe nuclei. Axons from the rostral raphe nuclei project to the cerebral cortex, limbic regions, and the basal ganglia and profoundly influence anxiety and mood (Figure 6-9). Serotonergic nuclei in the brainstem give rise to descending axons, some of which terminate in the medulla, while others descend the spinal cord.

Norepinephrine

Norepinephrine is a chemical that functions locally within the brain as a neurotransmitter, and can also function as a hormone in the blood stream. Like dopamine, norepinephrine seems to be involved in reward, arousal, and mood regulation. Deficiencies in norepinephrine function in the brain can lead to depression and to attention-deficit disorder.

The primary noradrenergic nuclei are the locus coeruleus and the caudal raphe nuclei. The ascending axons from the locus coeruleus project to the frontal cortex, thalamus, hypothalamus, and limbic system. The locus

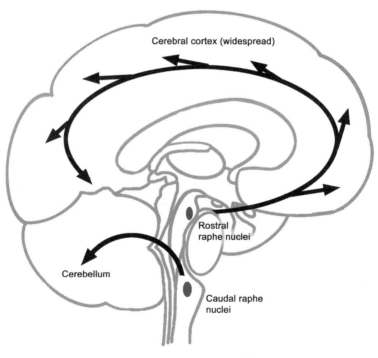

FIGURE 6-9
Serotonin Pathways in the Brain

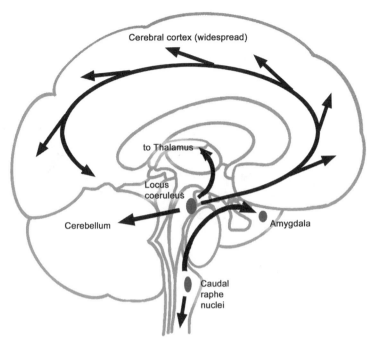

FIGURE 6-10
Norepinephrine Pathways in the Brain

coeruleus is very actively involved in symptoms of withdrawal from drugs of abuse. Nerves projecting from the caudal raphe nuclei rise to the amygdala and descend to the midbrain (Figure 6-10).

Endorphin

Endorphins are peptide neurotransmitters that work as natural painkillers and as antianxiety transmitters. Endorphin receptors on GABA neurons diminish their inhibition of dopamine neurons, causing opioids to activate the reward system, leading to addiction. The primary use of opioid agonists is for control of pain. Excessive use leads to substance use disorders. Treatment is primarily focused on the use of an opioid antagonist, naltrexone, to diminish the risk of relapse to both alcohol and opioid abuse. Use of naltrexone can diminish cravings to the point of actually giving a person in early recovery a chance to establish healthy patterns of living. Notice how closely the endorphin pathways (Figure 6-11) parallel the dopamine reward pathways in the mesocorticolimbic system (Figure 6-8A).

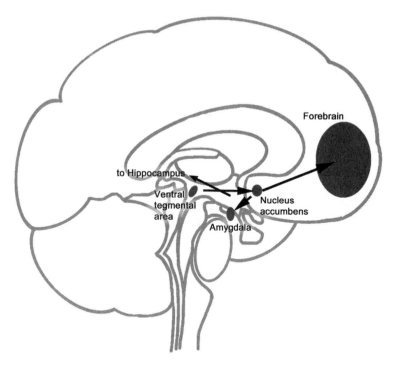

FIGURE 6-11
Endorphin Pathways in the Brain

Pharmacodynamics and Pharmacokinetics

Much of the action of drugs used in psychiatry and neurology can be explained by their effects on neurotransmitter systems. Some medications— for example, some of the selective serotonin reuptake inhibitors—are highly preferential to which type of receptor they affect. These are sometimes called "clean" medications. Other medications—for example, the tricyclic antide- pressants—affect multiple receptors and are sometimes called "dirty" medi- cations. Although both types of medications may have side effects that could be intolerable to a given person, there are a broader range of possible side effects in a given individual with dirty medications.

It is important to realize that multiple neurotransmitter systems can be involved in a psychiatric illness. For example, dopamine, serotonin, and nor- epinephrine are all involved in the modulation of mood and anxiety. As a result many medications that are originally developed for treatment of a particular illness (e.g., antidepressants for depression) are applied in the treatment of other illnesses (e.g., antidepressants for anxiety disorders and obsessive– compulsive disorder). Before describing how various categories of drugs affect various neurotransmitter systems, it is helpful to understand two subfields of study: pharmacodynamics and pharmacokinetics.

Pharmacodynamics is the study of what a drug does to the body, whereas *pharmacokinetics* is the study of what the body does to a drug. Pharmacodynamics is discussed under each section of psychiatric medication. Pharmacokinetics, however, can be discussed in more general terms. (In this text the terms "drug" and "medication" are used interchangeably.)

A drug must have some means of getting into the body to be effective. Most commonly used drugs are given orally; once entering the bloodstream through the gut these drugs are directed to the liver ("first pass metabolism") where they may be partly inactivated or absorbed for slower release. Some drugs given by injection, transdermal patch, or inhalation initially bypass the liver to deliver more of the parent drug to the target receptors. Yet other drugs are actually inactive themselves ("prodrugs") before they are transformed into active compounds by the body.

Because of the first-pass metabolism by the liver, higher concentrations of medications are required orally than intravenously to achieve the same pharmacological effect. Some drugs have very poor oral bioavailability. For example, buprenorphine has little absorption if you swallow it in pill form. However it is rapidly and effectively absorbed if nebulized in a nasal spray or if the pill is given sublingually. Ingesting food may interfere with or improve absorption, depending on the medication. Various preparations of medications are developed for the purpose of improving pharmacodynamics for an intended therapeutic effect or to improve side effects by either increasing or delaying absorption. For example, a medication may be mixed with a waxy substance and delivered in a pill so that the coating slowly erodes in the gut and the drug is absorbed over many hours instead of all at once (sustained or extended release). This may improve compliance by allowing a single daily dose instead of several. Other drugs can be given in an injectable form that is released slowly over a period of weeks. These so-called depot drugs are especially useful in psychiatric conditions such as schizophrenia for which compliance with taking drugs consistently each day is poor.

The FDA allows generic drugs (i.e., drugs that go by the chemical name of their active ingredient) to have 80–120% of the bioavailability of the brand-named medication. Brand names are given to medications by the company that initially developed the drug. Although the patent is for 17 years, the extended time utilized to develop the drug and obtain approval means that the patent (and exclusive rights to market) lasts an average of 7 years from initial marketing until other companies can make the generic equivalents.

Once a drug is absorbed, it is distributed throughout the body. In part this distribution depends on factors such as the medication's solubility in water versus in lipids, its ability to cross the blood–brain barrier, and whether it binds to protein in the bloodstream. For example, valproate is entirely protein-bound within the vascular space and unavailable to the brain unless its blood level exceeds 50 mg/ml. Because older adults typically have a greater proportion of body fat (and less water), the distribution of the drug in the body may change with weight and with percentage of body fat.

Once the drug has been distributed throughout the body, it exerts both therapeutic and nontherapeutic effects. The therapeutic effects, of course, are the reason to prescribe the drug. The nontherapeutic effects are side effects and may range from trivial to life-threatening. All medications—even placebos—have side effects. Fortunately, the FDA must approve all pharmaceuticals prior to their marketing; the results of this agency's extensive testing for safety and efficacy on approved medications are summarized in the *Physician's Desk Reference* (PDR). These include potentially adverse effects in a "black box warning" (so-called because of the surrounding black border in the PDR). A frequently reported measure of relative medication safety is the therapeutic index. This is the ratio of the lowest concentration of a medicine that causes toxicity to the lowest concentration that produces the desired therapeutic effect. Tricyclic antidepressants, lithium, and opiates are examples of medications with low therapeutic indices (i.e., they are more dangerous).

The actual effects of drugs occur on the cellular level at receptor sites. The major neurotransmitters mentioned above bind to these receptors, which are located on neurons and other cells in the body. The therapeutic effect for psychotropic medications most commonly occurs in neurons, whereas side effects can occur on any cell (including neurons) that has a receptor to which the medicine can bind. For example, some of the gastrointestinal side effects of SSRIs result from action on serotonin receptors in the gut and not the brain. When drugs attach to receptors in the central nervous system, they may stimulate an electric impulse, partially stimulate, or inhibit activity (agonists, partial agonists, and antagonists, respectively). In general, agonism at a postsynaptic receptor will increase neuronal activity, and agonism at a presynaptic receptor will decrease it by negative feedback.

The body begins metabolizing drugs as soon as they are absorbed. Some drugs are broken down enzymatically in the synapse or other extracellular space, some in the liver, and some excreted via the kidneys. It is important to know whether a drug has metabolites (breakdown products) that themselves have either therapeutic or nontherapeutic effects.

Most psychotropic drugs undergo two phases of metabolism mediated by enzymes. In the first phase, drugs are oxidized, reduced, and hydrolyzed into intermediate metabolites. The second phase further breaks down these intermediate products, through glucouronidation and acetylation, into water-soluble metabolites that can be excreted by the kidneys. Some medication is already very water-soluble (e.g., lithium and gabapentin) and can be directly excreted renally, especially if the molecule is a small one. A few medications (equivalent to intermediate metabolites) undergo only phase II metabolism (e.g., lorazepam and oxazepam) and require less enzymatic work prior to excretion. This is important to understand when treating patients with compromised liver function (e.g., the patient with a cirrhotic liver needing alcohol detoxification with benzodiazepines).

As mentioned above, a major oxidative enzyme system involved in breaking down many psychotropic drugs is the cytochrome P450 system, located in the endoplasmic reticulum of hepatocytes. The system comprises well over 200 isozymes and varies remarkably from individual to individual. Many psychiatric drugs are not only substrates broken down by this system but also inhibit certain of the isozymes. For example, cimetidine, fluvoxamine, and grapefruit juice all inhibit certain cytochrome enzymes (3A3/4) and cause elevated blood levels of the drugs these enzymes break down. Medications can work in the other direction by inducing these same isoenzymes; for example, phenytoin, carbamazepine, and rifampin, prescribed over time, lead to increased enzyme levels (3A3/4) with consequent decrease in the blood levels of the drugs (autoinduction). The clinician must be aware of potential and known drug–drug interactions.

The half-life of a drug is the time needed for the drug concentration in the body to fall by 50%. Clinically the term refers to the time required for half of the active ingredient to be metabolized to an inactive form or eliminated from the body. After five or six half-lives the amount of active drug remaining in the body is negligible (<5%). It is important to note that many intermediate metabolites are active, in that they may attach to receptors and have clinical effects. The half-life of active metabolites often exceeds (and is rarely shorter than) the half-life of the original drug. *Prodrugs* are medications that do not have any therapeutic activity until they are metabolized — that is, the metabolites are the active drug.

The absorption, action, and metabolism of drugs change throughout the life cycle. Generally children and adolescents are more sensitive to medications than adults and metabolize them faster per body weight. As we grow older, especially over the age of 60, our ability to break down drugs begins to deteriorate. Some drugs show markedly elevated blood levels in older adults at doses commonly given to younger people.

PSYCHOTROPIC MEDICATIONS

At first glance, the use of psychotropic medications may appear confusing because a medication that is labeled for one condition is used in multiple conditions. For example, the tricyclic antidepressant imipramine is used as a treatment not only for depression but also for generalized anxiety disorder, panic disorder, social phobia, and bedwetting.

Psychiatrists often choose medications on the basis of a drug's therapeutic receptor action rather than the category of drug. When several medications are likely to be equally effective, medication choice is often based upon side effect profiles. A medication that is initially approved by the FDA for a particular category, say, valproate for epilepsy, may become established through common use as effective for other illnesses, such as bipolar disorder or migraine.

In the remainder of this chapter it may help to look at Tables 6-1 and 6-2 that show, respectively, where particular categories of drugs have their effects (either activation or inhibition) and the effects of receptor activation or blockade. One is able to predict likely side effects and therapeutic benefits based on the receptor-binding profiles of any medication. Many psychotropics affect more than one type of receptor either directly, by binding, or indirectly, by modulating other neurons ("dirty drugs," as described above). Because patients may present with multiple symptoms associated with different neurotransmitter systems, some manufacturers combine two different medications (e.g., Symbyax, a combination of olanzapine [an antipsychotic] and fluoxetine [an antidepressant]) with different receptor targets into one preparation in order to restore balance—essentially creating a dirtier drug. The second-generation antipsychotics hit several receptors in addition to dopamine and yet are better tolerated—so cleaner may not be better in every case. Another example: By influencing serotonin *and* norepinephrine, serotonin norepinephrine reuptake inhibitors (SNRIs) may be more versatile antidepressants.

Antidepressants

There are multiple categories of antidepressants. Most of them seem to exert their benefit either by inhibiting monoamine oxidase, the enzyme that breaks down serotonin, dopamine, and norepinephrine, or by inhibiting reuptake inactivation by the releasing neuron. These medications will be separated into classes based on which neurotransmitters they affect.

Although antidepressants begin to raise the levels of the neurotransmit-

TABLE 6-1
Receptor Effects of Psychotropic Drugs

	DOPAMINE	NOREPINEPHRINE	SEROTONIN (5-HT)	GABA-AMINO-BUTYRIC ACID	GLUTAMATE	ENDORPHIN MU	HISTAMINE	ALPHA-ADRENERGIC	BETA-ADRENERGIC	ACETYLCHOLINE
Tricyclic antidepressants		+ to +++	+ to +++				———	———		———
MAOIs	++	+++	+++				——	———		——
SSRIs	+/—		+++							
SNRIs	+/—	++	+++							
DNRIs	+ to ++	++	+++							
Stimulants	++ to +++	++ to +++			+					
Typical antipsychotics—high potency	———									
Typical antipsychotics—low potency	———						——	———		——
Atypical antipsychotics—high potency	———		+ to ++				——	———		
Atypical antipsychotics—low potency	———		+ to ++				——	——		——
Hypnoanxiolytics (sedative/hypnotics)				+++						
Opioid antagonists						——				
Lithium			+ to ++				——			
Anticonvulsant mood stabilizers								—		
Clonidine, guanfacine									++	

+ (weak agonist), ++ (medium agonist), +++ (strong agonist), — (weak antagonist), —— (medium antagonist), ——— (strong antagonist)

TABLE 6-2
Clinical Effects with the Associated Neurotransmitters/Receptor Conditions

	DOPAMINE	NOREPINEPHRINE	SEROTONIN (5HT)	GABA-AMINO-BUTYRIC ACID	GLUTAMATE	ENDORPHIN MU	HISTAMINE	ALPHA-ADRENERGIC	BETA-ADRENERGIC	ACETYLCHOLINE
Antidepressant	++	+++	+++							
Antianxiety	—	—	+++	+++						
Obsessive-Compulsive		—	— — —							
Antipsychotic—(reduction in positive symptoms)	— —									
Antipsychotic—(improvement in negative symptoms)			++							
ADHD—improved attention	++									
Reduction in cravings	+++			+		—			++	
Sedation			++				—			—
Weight gain	—		++				—			
Lightheadedness							—	— —		— —
Cognitive slowing				++		+				—
Constipation, blurred vision, dry mouth										— —
Nausea	— —		+++	—						
Irritability	++	++	—	—	++		— to +			
Hypotension								—	+	
Tachycardia								—	—	

+ (weak agonist), ++ (medium agonist), +++ (strong agonist), — (weak antagonist), — — (medium antagonist), — — — (strong antagonist) ters in the synapse within several hours of administration, it may take anywhere from 2 to 8 weeks to see their full benefit. Ultimately there are changes in the number of receptors and second-messenger systems that seem to coincide with therapeutic effect. Generally the recommendation is to continue treatment with antidepressants for at least a year following remission of the depression because stopping it earlier carries increased risk of relapse. Sudden discontinuation of short-acting serotonin reuptake inhibitors may cause flu-like symptoms. This phenomenon is referred to as a "discontinuation syndrome." There are many serotonin receptors in the gastrointestinal tract, which explains the initial nausea and at least some of these effects.

Just as too little serotonin can cause symptoms, so can too much. "Serotonin syndrome," in which the body must cope with excessive amounts of serotonin both in the central nervous system and peripherally, is a potentially life-threatening condition with symptoms of tachycardia, diaphoresis, mydriasis, hypertension, rhabdomyolysis, and hyperthermia. Not all drugs that increase serotonin are psychiatric ones. For example, tramadol, an analgesic, also raises serotonin, as do the herbs St. John's wort, yohimbine, and boswellia. Ecstasy (or MDMA), a so-called club drug, acts as a hallucinogen and stimulant but also increases serotonin levels. Ecstasy abusers sometimes take fluoxetine prior to ingesting the ecstasy because fluoxetine inhibits the cytochrome enzyme that breaks down the abused drug. By using these two drugs together, users increase the risk of serotonin syndrome.

Tricyclic Antidepressants

Tricyclic antidepressants (TCAs), beginning with amitriptyline and imipramine, revolutionized the treatment of depression. These "dirty" medications are serotonin and norepinephrine reuptake inhibitors. They delay or prevent the releasing nerve cell from reuptake inactivation of the neurotransmitter. As a result, the serotonin or norepinephrine has a greater effect on the target neuron. Tricyclic antidepressants generally work in approximately two-thirds of depressed people.

There are three problems with this category of medication. First, as "dirty" medicines they have effects not only on serotonin and norepinephrine receptors, but also on histamine (H-1), cholinergic, and alpha-adrenergic receptors; these multiple receptor actions increase side effects that reduce tolerability. Side effects include weight gain, sedation, constipation, blurred vision, and mild cognitive slowing. Remembering that depressed patients are advised to continue the medication for a year, it is understandable that the side effects could be poorly tolerated over time.

Second, TCAs interact in complex ways with other commonly prescribed medications. These drug–drug interactions can raise severe problems that can be difficult to anticipate. Many TCAs are metabolized by cytochrome P450-2D6 enzymes.

Tricyclics affect sodium channel transmission in the heart. This is the mechanism that allows the heart muscle to recover after each beat. An overdose on as little as a week's worth of a tricyclic medication can result in a fatal cardiac arrhythmia. Given that a substantial number of depressed people experience suicidal thoughts and the fact that it takes a few weeks for a full antidepressant response, the practitioner must exercise caution to *not* provide patients with an instrument for suicide by overdose.

Tricyclic antidepressants are also used for anxiety disorders, panic disorder, and obsessive–compulsive disorder. In nonpsychiatric illnesses they are used in enuresis, sleep disorders, and pain medicine. They are used in pain medicine because they bolster serotonin and norepinephrine. There are two types of pain transmission in humans: Acute sharp pain is mediated by endorphin neurons ("fast pain tracts"), and chronic, nagging pain is mediated by serotonin neurons ("slow pain tracts").

All antidepressants work in approximately two-thirds of depressed individuals. Head-to-head comparisons have largely been unconvincing. However, among individuals with "melancholic depression," clomipramine may have an advantage. A melancholic depression is one in which the individual simply cannot experience pleasure and often suffers extreme neurovegetative signs of depression.

Heterocyclic antidepressants such as trazodone, nefazodone, and maprotiline are similar to the TCAs for all practical purposes. Nefazodone is rarely used because of hepatic toxicity. Trazodone is now used most commonly as a sleep aid because of its combined serotonergic and antihistaminic actions.

Selective Serotonin Reuptake Inhibitors

The introduction of fluoxetine under the brand name of Prozac in 1986 revolutionized the treatment of depression. Generally selective serotonin reuptake inhibitors (SSRIs) like fluoxetine are much safer in overdose than are the TCAs. Previously primary-care physicians with concerns about the risks of TCAs referred depressed patients to psychiatrists for treatment. Because of the stigma of mental illness, many people simply did not go.

With fluoxetine and the other SSRIs, the front line of treatment for depression was moved from the psychiatrist's office to that of the primary-care doctor. Fluoxetine and its successors have become among the most

widely prescribed medications in the history of the world. All the medications in this category work by inhibiting the brain's removal of serotonin by
reuptake inactivation. Drugs in this category share more similarities than
differences. The primary differences involve whether the drug affects enzymes
in the liver that break down other drugs. These enzymes of the cytochrome
P450 system, have many slight variations and are highly variable from person
to person. Roughly speaking, the SSRIs may be divided into two groups: one
with little cytochrome interaction and one with more. The group with little
cytochrome interaction includes sertraline, citalopram, and escitalopram.
The group with more cytochrome interactions includes fluoxetine, paroxetine, and fluvoxamine. Other drugs, ranging from something as simple as
the over-the-counter cough medicine dextromethorphan to asthma drugs,
antibiotics, and cardiac drugs, may be broken down by the cytochrome system. As a result caution must be exercised to not prescribe an SSRI that
might cause problematic elevation of blood levels of other drugs. Most SSRIs
are highly protein-bound in the range of about 46% (escitalopram) to 98%
(sertraline).

Roughly speaking, each SSRI leads to improvement in about two-thirds
of depressed people, similar to tricyclic response rates but with much less
risk. Further study has shown their utility in the treatment of generalized
anxiety disorder, panic disorder, obsessive–compulsive disorder, social phobia, and bulimia.

In a small subgroup of children and young adults, use of the SSRIs may
lead to an increase in suicidality. However, this slight possibility must be balanced against the significant risk of suicide in untreated depression. Since
the FDA required that all SSRIs be labeled with a caution of possible severe
complication (the "black-box warning") in 2004, the number of prescriptions for this category of drugs for children and adolescents has markedly
dropped. Regrettably, this decline has led to an increase in the number of
completed suicides. In prescribing any medication, the risks and benefits of
NOT treating must be balanced with those of treating the illness. More
recent epidemiologic studies have suggested that withholding effective
depression treatment from children and adolescents may have unfortunate
consequences. Bad as depression is in adults, in children and adolescents it
has a more pervasive effect because it can derail the child's ability to achieve
normal psychological growth.

Mirtazapine, which acts indirectly on both serotonin and norepinephrine, is effective in treating depression but has a very high incidence of
weight gain (also because of antihistaminic receptor activity). About 17% of
patients on this medication gain more than 10 kilograms. Mirtazapine in

low doses is fairly sedating and has found a useful niche in inducing sleep while augmenting antidepressant response with another medication.

Vilazodone is a newer antidepressant that also functions as an SSRI.

Selective Serotonin Norepinephrine Reuptake Inhibitors

Some drugs slow reuptake inactivation of more than one neurotransmitter. For example, *venlafaxine* and *duloxetine,* as selective serotonin norepinephrine reuptake inhibitors (SNRIs) both inhibit reuptake inhibition of serotonin and norepinephrine. Both affect serotonin at any dose. Venlafaxine affects norepinephrine only at doses of 150 mg or above. Duloxetine affects both serotonin and norepinephrine throughout its dosage range. However, tolerability of the two drugs may differ. Both drugs cause nausea in the immediate release form in roughly a third of patients because of serotonin receptors in the gut. Venlafaxine is available in an extended release form that significantly reduces the incidence of nausea. Duloxetine is not. On the other hand, duloxetine has been demonstrated to be of value in certain types of neuropathy, specifically when caused by diabetes. Venlafaxine has the lowest protein binding of any antidepressant and has few cytochrome interactions.

Newer antidepressants include levomilnacipran which, unlike other SNRIs, has a greater effect on norepinephrine than serotonin. Vortioxetine is a serotonin modulator and stimulator which also affects norepinephrine receptors. Although it is similar in side effects and efficacy to other SNRIs, its unique structure may lead to improvement in some individuals who have not responded to other medications in this category.

Selective Dopamine Norepinephrine Reuptake Inhibitors

Bupropion is the prototypical member of this class. It inhibits reuptake of both dopamine and norepinephrine. It is an effective antidepressant. However, in some vulnerable individuals, boosting norepinephrine seems to increase anxiety—a not uncommon side effect of this drug. Interestingly, because the final reward pathway for addiction seems to involve dopamine, bupropion has been demonstrated to be helpful in alleviating nicotine and stimulant addiction. Unfortunately, bupropion may lower the seizure threshold more than other antidepressants. Most antidepressants have an incidence of seizures of about 1 in 3,000, but bupropion has an incidence of 1 in 1,000. One confounding variable is that this medication was field-tested at higher than currently recommended doses in a cohort of females with bulimia who undoubtedly had some electrolyte abnormalities that may have lowered the seizure threshold. In addition, patients with bulimia may show cerebral dysrhythmias in up to 15% of people with the disorder. Nonetheless, bupropion is contraindicated in patients who have a preexisting seizure disorder or who have an active eating disorder.

Reboxetine is an antidepressant similar to bupropion without the increased risk of seizures, but it is not available in the United States. Atomoxetine, an approved antidepressant in Europe, is approved for use in the United States for attention-deficit disorder because of its ability to increase norepinephrine.

Monoamine Oxidase Inhibitors

This category of drugs acts by inhibiting monoamine oxidase (MAO), the second catabolic pathway for dopamine, norepinephrine, and serotonin. Monoamine oxidase is also important in metabolizing stimulants and a toxic nonessential amino acid called tyramine. If a person on a monoamine oxidase inhibitor (MAOI) eats tyramine-containing food, tyramine is not metabolized and can cause extremely high blood pressure, with the possibility of stroke or myocardial infarction as a result. Tyramine is a product of bacterial degradation of protein and is present in many aged or fermented foods, including some cheeses and soy sauce. Patients on MAOIs must very carefully exclude such foods from their diet.

There are two types of MAO in the body, type A and type B. Type A is found both intracerebrally and extracerebrally and is responsible for breaking down tyramine. Type B is found in the brain only and is the one that affects mood.

Currently three MAOIs are available in the United States. Two of them, tranylcypromine and phenelzine, are irreversible, nonselective inhibitors of both MAO A and B. Once they bind to MAO, the enzyme molecule is permanently inactivated. New MAO molecules are inactivated if the drug is in the body and the effect diminishes only as new MAO is produced after the drug leaves the system. Because these inhibitors bind to both A and B, dietary precautions are necessary.

A third MAOI, selegiline, is a reversible type B inhibitor. It works to help with depression and no dietary precautions are necessary in the lower doses. However, drug-drug interactions must still be avoided. Selegiline has been used in treating Parkinson's disease and is now available in a transdermal patch.

When a depressive episode has not responded to two adequate trials of different antidepressants, it is considered to be *treatment refractory*. Techniques used in this situation include electroconvulsive therapy or other pharmacological options. For example, two antidepressants might be used at the same time, or a potentiator added. A *potentiator* is a drug that, by itself, may have no antidepressant action but which, when added to an antidepressant, improves the efficacy. Examples include low-dose thyroid hormone, lithium, buspirone, and atypical antipsychotics.

Antipsychotics (also called Neuroleptics)

Ancient literature from India refers to the use of Indian snake root (*Rauwolfia serpentina*) as an antipsychotic. In fact, one of the active chemicals in it, reserpine, has some weak antipsychotic properties.

Typical Antipsychotics

Chlorpromazine was the first modern drug synthesized in 1950 specifically for treatment of psychosis. It was the prototype of a class of antipsychotics that are now called *typical* antipsychotics. All antipsychotics tend to block D2 receptors in the dopamine pathways in the brain. Excessive dopaminergic activity in the mesolimbic system has been associated with psychosis; too little results in poor attention, little pleasure, parkinsonism (poverty of movement), tardive dyskinesia, and neuroleptic malignant syndrome. The typical antipsychotics are nonspecific in their dopamine blockade and are associated with a fair amount of side effects, decreasing their tolerability. Side effects may include extrapyramidal or parkinsonian side effects (imbalance between dopamine and acetylcholine) such as restlessness, increased muscle tension, or muscle spasm (dystonic reaction). Long-term use can also lead to a potentially permanent movement disorder called *tardive dyskinesia*. In this disorder an individual has ongoing involuntary movements, often of the mouth and tongue, of which he or she is not aware. These movements can be socially disabling. In some cases, when the involuntary movements spread to the trunk, they can interfere with walking, balance, and even breathing. Tardive dyskinesia occurs much more with typical antipsychotics than with the newer atypical ones. Acute extrapyramidal side effects (EPS) can be alleviated with the use of anticholinergic medication. However, this treatment is ineffective with tardive dyskinesia.

Older, so-called typical antipsychotics are commonly divided into low-potency and high-potency classes. The potency does not refer to the effectiveness of the medication but rather to the number of milligrams necessary to achieve therapeutic effect. Chlorpromazine, thioridazine, and prochlorperazine are low-potency medications with doses usually in the several-hundred-milligram range. The low-potency medications typically have anti-histaminic, alpha-adrenergic, and anticholinergic side effects and are fairly sedating.

High-potency typical (or traditional) antipsychotics include haloperidol, fluphenazine, trifluoperazine, and perphenazine; dosing is typically in the 5–60 mg range daily. These medications have less sedation but are more likely to cause EPS. This effect is partly due to the fact that low-potency antipsychotics often carry their own anticholinergic actions that would tend to alleviate acute EPS. Two of the high-potency typical antipsychotics, halo-peridol and fluphenazine, are available in a long-acting intramuscular depot form. These depot medications are especially useful to stabilize people with psychosis who have had a history of poor or erratic compliance. As we will see below, an increasing number of the newer "atypical" antipsychotics are also available in depot form.

Atypical Antipsychotics

The category of atypical (second-generation) antipsychotics was led by the prototype clozapine. Approved by the FDA in 1989, clozapine, like many other members of this class, inhibits serotonin reuptake as well as blocks dopamine receptors. However, each of the atypicals has a somewhat differ-ent spectrum of effect on receptor subtypes, leading to different side effect profiles. As noted in Chapter 12, schizophrenia carries both positive symp-toms such as hallucinations or delusions and negative symptoms such as apathy, poor social awareness, abulia (paralysis of will), and anhedonia (absence of pleasure). In many ways these negative symptoms can be more incapacitating over the long run than positive symptoms. The atypical anti-psychotics, led by clozapine, show remarkable improvements in alleviating the negative symptoms of schizophrenia, which are not shown by the typical antipsychotics.

Clozapine was very helpful in allowing many patients with chronic schizophrenia to leave long-term hospitals and be treated in the community. Unfortunately, it has significant side effects. The most serious is agranulocy-tosis, a potentially fatal lack of infection-fighting white blood cells. In a per-son with agranulocytosis a strep throat may be fatal. Agranulocytosis occurs in about 1% of patients on the drug in the first 3 months. Thereafter, the incidence falls over time to less than 0.01% after a year. For this reason patients on clozapine have their white blood cell counts monitored fre-quently. Clozapine is also associated with weight gain and development of metabolic syndrome or diabetes mellitus (which tend to be class effects of the atypicals).

During the 1990s several other atypical antipsychotics were introduced. Olanzapine and quetiapine have similar effects to clozapine but without the risk of agranulocytosis. However, they are also associated with significant chances of weight gain and development of metabolic syndrome. Risperidone has a less sedating effect but is more likely to raise prolactin levels; elevated prolactin levels may be associated with galactorrhea.

Relatively new atypical antipsychotics are aripiprazole, paliperidone, and asenapine. Aripiprazole has a partial agonist binding pattern to the dopamine receptors, which seems to help prevent some extrapyramidal symptoms. Paliperidone is the primary active metabolite of the older antipsychotic risperidone. Asenapine blocks more subtypes of dopamine receptors than do most antipsychotics; it is primarily given as a sublingually dissolving tablet.

Ziprasidone is an effective antipsychotic that does not have weight gain as one of its side effects. However, it does have a side effect of slightly affecting repolarization of the heart muscle and prolongation of the QTc interval on the electrocardiogram (EKG). This is usually not clinically significant but can become so if the patient has natural conditions that prolong this interval or is on other drugs that do so. Iloperidone had some difficulty passing FDA trials and has some QTc prolongation as well. Like ziprasidone it requires twice-daily dosing.

Some of the newer atypical antipsychotics have received FDA indications for conditions other than psychosis. For example, olanzapine and quetiapine have some benefit in the stabilization of bipolar disorder. Because they have serotonergic and other receptor binding activity rather than just dopamine, it is not surprising there is growing evidence that in addition to antipsychotic properties, this category of drugs also has some anxiolytic and antidepressant properties.

In older patients with dementia-related psychosis, the drugs in this category increase the risk of cerebrovascular accident.

Hypnoanxiolytics

Benzodiazepines are the prototypical drugs in this class and have their effect as agonists on the GABA system, duplicating the calming, sedating, and muscle-relaxing effects of GABA. With chronic use of benzodiazepines the brain down-regulates production of GABA and benzodiazepine use tends to increase gradually. Remembering that GABA is the major inhibitory neurochemical balancing glutamate, if the benzodiazepine is abruptly discontinued, there is insufficient GABA to balance the glutamate. The patient then experiences anxiety, tremor, and perhaps even seizures. Because of the abuse potential and the life-threatening withdrawal associated with benzodiazepines, they should be used with caution and over as short a period of time as possible. Benzodiazepines are ideally suited for the very short-term treatment of anxiety. For example, a patient just diagnosed with cancer and facing major surgery within a few days would be an ideal candidate.

Individual members of the class of benzodiazepines have more in common than they differ. All of the members of the class have strong antianxiety action. However, they differ in how rapidly absorbed and metabolized they are. Alprazolam, one of the shortest-acting members of this class, reaches a peak blood level very quickly and for that reason is useful for treating an acute panic attack. However, its abuse potential is among the highest for that very reason of the rapid peak and fast decline. The rapidity with which a benzodiazepine reaches its peak blood level is highly correlated with its abuse potential. A benzodiazepine such as alprazolam or triazolam is highly abusable because, as its blood level rapidly climbs, the person gets a noticeable "buzz." The fast decline causes withdrawal symptoms, and the discomfort provides the negative reinforcement to "take another pill."

Some of the benzodiazepines (diazepam, chlordiazepoxide, clorazepate) have short half-lives (2–6 hours) and rapid absorption but are broken down into a metabolite (nordiazepam) that has a very long half-life of 96 hours. These benzodiazepines carry a risk of a very gradual buildup of sedation, incoordination, and cognitive problems because of increasing levels of nordiazepam. Some of the benzodiazepines are metabolized by cytochrome P450-3A4 enzymes. Table 6-3 provides dosage equivalents and half-lives of various benzodiazepines.

TABLE 6-3
Benzodiazepines

DRUG	EQUIVALENT DOSAGE (MG)	HALF-LIFE (HOURS)	ACTIVE METABOLITE HALF-LIFE (HOURS)
Alprazolam*	0.5	6–12	N/A
Chlordiazepoxide	10.0	5–30	36–200
Clorazepate	2.5	1–2	36–200
Diazepam	5.0	4–12	36–200
Flurazepam	15.0	2.3	30–100
Loprazolam	0.5	6–12	6–12
Lorazepam*	0.5	12	N/A
Clonazepam*	0.5	19–50	N/A
Oxazepam*	15.0	5–15	N/A
Temazepam*	10.0	8–15	N/A
Triazolam*	0.25	1.5–5	N/A

*No active metabolites

Other Antianxiety Medications (Anxiolytics)

As indicated above, antidepressants, acting through different receptors, are used successfully to treat most anxiety disorders over the long term. Unlike the hypnoanxiolytics, which have an immediate effect, the antidepressants take a couple of weeks for a therapeutic effect (right about the time that tolerance would start to be a problem with benzodiazepines). Sometime anti-histamines, such as hydroxyzine, are prescribed because antihistamine action helps anxiety. Buspirone is a nonaddictive antianxiety agent that works as a partial agonist at the 5-HT1A presynaptic serotonin receptor. In addition, buspirone acts as a partial agonist on postsynaptic dopamine receptors. Although it has been shown to be more effective than placebo in treating generalized anxiety disorder, it may take six weeks to see a result; when effective, it is typically prescribed at doses higher than 40 mg per day. Because of the long lag time to act, it is less commonly used in treatment of anxiety disorder than the SSRIs. One area in which buspirone may have a niche is in the augmentation of the other antidepressants, including SSRIs.

There are other categories of hypnotics (sleep agents) that, although they work on the GABA system, have somewhat less abuse potential than the benzodiazepines or barbiturates. These include zolpidem, zaleplon, and eszopiclone. Because melatonin rises during the nighttime and induction of sleep, a novel medication (ramelteon) has been developed that is a melatonin agonist and has no abuse potential. However, ramelteon is broken down by cytochrome P450-1A2 and therefore must be used with caution or not at all when a person is taking fluvoxamine, a potent inhibitor of this enzyme.

Lithium

In the 19th century lithium was used to treat gout. Lithium carbonate, a naturally occurring mineral salt, is an unusual medication because of its chemical simplicity. After absorption into the body the lithium ion can readily displace sodium or potassium at some receptors. The exact mechanism of lithium's action in psychiatric disorders is still being elucidated. The mechanism probably involves working postsynaptically at G-proteins and other secondary messenger systems to change intracellular homeostasis, perhaps by inhibiting inositol function. Since the late 1940s lithium has been used as a well-documented treatment for bipolar disorder because it is effective in not only depression but also mania. Most importantly, it is used for maintenance treatment of bipolar disorder because it is effective in preventing relapse to depression or mania. Lithium is the only medication that has been consistently shown to decrease the risk of suicide in people taking it.

Lithium is excreted unchanged via the proximal tubule of the kidneys. The usual blood level targeted for lithium is 0.6–1.1 mEq/liter. It often becomes toxic at blood levels above 1.5 mEq/liter. In the toxic range it can cause acute renal, thyroid, or cerebellar damage. Over time even therapeutic doses of lithium can be nephrotoxic in a small proportion of people. Because lithium may be used for years in maintenance treatment of people with bipolar disorder, it is important to follow their renal function, with creatinine clearance tests, over time. Other drugs that affect renal function may elevate blood levels of lithium. Another potential long-term side effect to lithium is thyroid suppression, with about 5% of people on lithium developing iatrogenic hypothyroidism.

Mood Stabilizers/Anticonvulsants

Multiple anticonvulsants have been shown to be effective in treatment of bipolar disorder, especially the rapid-cycling variant. Some of them, such as valproate, topiramate, gabapentin, and tiagabine, enhance GABA function via various mechanisms. Valproate may be more effective than lithium in mixed bipolar states and rapid cycling. It is metabolized by the liver with no active metabolites. It does have serious and potentially fatal side effects which fortunately are rare; these include toxic hepatitis, hemorrhagic pancreatitis, aplastic anemia, and thrombocytopenia. Carbamazepine inhibits voltage-dependent sodium channels. It also has the possibility of causing aplastic anemia and idiosyncratic hepatitis. Oxcarbazepine is an analogue of carbamazepine with somewhat less risk of aplastic anemia. Tiagabine and gabapentin are less potentially toxic than the prior mentioned medications; however, so far studies have been more equivocal at demonstrating their effectiveness in bipolar disorder.

Another anticonvulsant, lamotrigine, works by inhibiting glutamate and voltage-gated sodium channels. It has FDA approval for treatment of bipolar depression. An unfortunate but rare side effect of the medication is development of Stevens–Johnson syndrome, a potentially fatal allergic reaction involving gross inflammation of the skin and mucous membranes. A person with this syndrome in its more severe forms can look like someone with second-degree burns all over the skin and in the mouth and throat. The risk of Stevens–Johnson syndrome with lamotrigine is markedly elevated if the person is already on either carbamazepine or valproate. Despite this risk, lamotrigine is a valuable tool in the treatment of bipolar disorder.

Stimulants

Stimulants are drugs that function as agonists at dopamine and/or norepinephrine receptors, usually through the transporter system. They increase alertness, decrease fatigue, and sharpen attention and concentration. All of the members of this class have significant abuse potential. Amphetamine, the prototype of this class, was first synthesized in 1887 but not used medically until 1929, when a pharmacologist named Gordon Alles tried it on himself. It was sold as an inhaler under the brand name Benzedrine as a decongestant from the mid-1930s and was widely used by soldiers during the Second World War to increase alertness. From the late 1930s it was marketed in oral form as the first antidepressant.

Other similar members of the stimulant class include methylphenidate and dextro-amphetamine. Stimulants are used to treat narcolepsy, but their most common use is in treating attention-deficit disorder in children, adolescents, and adults alike. While in normal individuals the psychostimulants may cause anxiety and difficulty focusing attention as a dose-dependent side effect, in people with attention-deficit disorder the stimulants have a paradoxical anti-anxiety and calming effect. Amphetamine is excreted unchanged in urine over a period of several days. Normally about 30% is excreted within 1 day. Acidifying the urine increases this to 75%, and alkalinizing it reduces it to 1%.

In addition to significant abuse potential (the chemical structure is similar to cocaine) there are other significant potential problems with stimulants. For example, they generally increase heart rate and pulse, decrease appetite, interfere with sleep, and may lower the seizure threshold.

There are multiple stimulants available on the market today. Some of them are mixtures of various amphetamine salts (e.g., Adderall) with different absorption profiles leading to extended benefit. Concerta and Metadate are sustained-release forms of methylphenidate. An interesting drug is lisdexamfetamine. The compound is not itself psychoactive but is converted on absorption through the intestine into an active amphetamine drug. Use of this prodrug helps prevent inappropriate abuse of the stimulant because snorting or injecting it is completely ineffective.

Anti-Alzheimer Drugs

Accessing memory and the higher executive functions of the mind such as reasoning and social judgment requires the functioning of all neurochemicals. For example, depression in older adults due to a serotonin deficit can cause a clinical presentation that is difficult to distinguish from senile dementia of the Alzheimer's type. This pseudodementia of depression, unlike Alzheimer's disease, is completely reversible with treatment of the mood disorder. Even in people with true Alzheimer's, cognition can be partly improved by treating any coexisting mood disorder.

The main neurotransmitters involved in Alzheimer's disease are acetylcholine and, to a lesser extent, glutamate. Part of the primary pathology in Alzheimer's dementia is deterioration of acetylcholine pathways important for memory, which with progression of the disease gradually show decreasing amounts of the neurotransmitter. At the same time glutamate pathways show some abnormalities of neuronal function. These two facts have led to separate treatments for this type of dementia.

Acetylcholine is primarily broken down by a synaptic enzyme called *cholinesterase*. The primary category of anti-Alzheimer medication is that of *cholinesterase inhibitors*. By incapacitating cholinesterase, these drugs— donepezil, tacrine, and rivastigmine—allow brain levels of acetylcholine to rise. All three drugs are approved for use in moderate to severe Alzheimer's disease. Donepezil and rivastigmine are also approved for milder versions of the illness. None of these medications reverses disease progression, but for at least the first several months of treatment, cognitive decline is slowed. There are some data suggesting that these drugs delay the need for placement of afflicted patients in nursing homes.

Treatment of Alzheimer's dementia via the glutamate pathway is exemplified by use of memantine. In Alzheimer's disease excessive accumulation of calcium in glutamate neurons leads to neuronal damage over time. This mechanism is called *excitatory amino acid neurotoxicity*. Memantine modulates a particular glutamate subreceptor, N-methyl-D-aspartate (NMDA). Memantine is an NMDA antagonist with a low to moderate affinity for the receptor. Blocking NMDA receptors with memantine slows intracellular calcium accumulation and thereby diminishes progressive nerve damage. Memantine has been shown to have an efficacy similar to the cholinesterase inhibitors in moderate to severe Alzheimer's dementia but has failed to distinguish itself from placebo in treatment of the milder stages of the illness.

One symptom of Alzheimer's disease is an increase in aggressive and even violent behavior by sufferers. This aggression, more than cognitive decline, forces families to place relatives in nursing homes or dementia units because the patients cannot be maintained at home. Memantine has more of an antiaggressive effect than the cholinesterase inhibitors and delays the point at which the patient must be institutionalized for his or her own safety as well as that of the caregivers.

Memantine and donepezil together have been shown to be more effective than either alone, probably because of their independent but complementary modes of action.

Many people with dementia become more paranoid and even psychotic as the illness progresses. The initial approach to this condition is reassurance, reinforcement of reality testing, and reorientation. In those patients with more severe forms of psychosis, treatment with an antipsychotic becomes necessary. As a class atypical antipsychotics have been effective in treating dementia-related psychosis but significantly raise the risk of stroke. Research shows a similar risk from the typical antipsychotics. This risk must be balanced against the risks of not treating the psychosis.

Herbals and Nonpharmaceuticals (Food Supplements)

Herbals and other food supplements are not to be confused with over-the-counter medications like acetaminophen that similarly do not require a physician's prescription. Over-the-counter medications are pharmaceuticals closely monitored by the FDA. Herbal and nutritional supplements do not go through rigorous field testing any more than would the produce in grocery stores. There are few double-blind or placebo-controlled studies supporting their effectiveness, and even where those studies exist with the purported active ingredient, there is no way to be certain that the product being purchased has the ingredient in the advertised concentration. They are not consistently assayed for potency, nor are they studied for harmful contaminants. What is being purchased may not be pure and may have thousands of chemicals mixed in that, at best, do nothing and, at worst, are toxic. For example, years ago some batches of the amino acid supplement tryptophan were apparently contaminated and associated with eosinophilia myalgia syndrome. This is not to say that these herbals might not have some beneficial effect (in fact, a substantial percentage of today's pharmaceuticals are derived from plants and most of the others that are synthesized are based on variations from chemicals extracted from herbals). It is the unregulated preparations that pose potential danger to the unsuspecting consumer. Also, herbals and the many compounds contained within may interact unfavorably with other medications.

Reference

Physicians' Desk Reference. (2014). Montvale, NJ: Thomson PDR. Available online at www
.pdrhealth.com.

7

Systems-Based Practice

Systems-based practice is defined as awareness of, and responsiveness to, the larger context and system of health care, as well as the ability to call effectively on other resources in the system to provide optimal health care. Systems-based practice includes the abilities to (1) work effectively in various health care delivery settings and systems relevant to clinical specialty; (2) coordinate patient care within the health care system relevant to clinical specialty; (3) incorporate considerations of cost awareness and risk–benefit analysis in patient care and/or population-based care, as appropriate; (4) advocate for quality patient care and optimal patient care systems; (5) work in interprofessional teams to enhance patient safety and improve patient care quality; and (6) participate in identifying systems-based errors and in implementing potential systems-based solutions.

> Systems-based practice has been defined as a core competency in medicine through a joint initiative of the Accreditation Council for Graduate Medical Education and the American Board of Medical Specialties. This initiative defined core competencies that cut across all specialties in medicine. These include patient care, medical/clinical knowledge, practice-based learning and improvement, interpersonal and communication skills, professionalism, and systems-based practice. These core competencies are now a major focus for residency training and board certification, and have also been adopted by the Joint Commission for the Accreditation of Health Care Organizations for the evaluation of physician competency for hospital credentialing.

DELIVERY OF CLINICAL SERVICES

There are aspects of clinical service delivery within systems-based practice that are unique to psychiatry and to the needs of people with mental illness.

These include clinical needs, provision of support, normalization of care environment, and recovery and resiliency needs.

Clinical needs include diagnostic services, pharmacotherapy, psychotherapy of different modalities, case management, and different levels of care and intensity (ambulatory, intensive outpatient, day treatment, mobile crisis, intensive community-based services, group homes, residential programs, acute inpatient services, dual-disorder treatment for people with mental illness and substance abuse or developmental disorders).

Support needs for patients and families include care management, housing, finances, education/vocation, respite, family support, consumer and family education, recreation/socialization, and assistance with independent living skills.

Needs for normalization of the care environment include using the least restrictive environment of care, community integration, teaching daily living skills to achieve independence and self-sufficiency, freedom from discrimination and stigma, and facilitation of family and peer connections/relationships.

Recovery and resiliency needs include promotion of strengths while addressing needs, instilling hope for a meaningful life and assisting the individual in achieving it, and identifying natural resources and coping skills in dealing with adversity.

COST AND FUNDING OF SERVICES

There is generally a lack of insurance parity for psychiatric and mental health services, with much more restricted coverage for psychiatric disorders. A disproportionate share of funding for mental-health services has been traditionally borne by government, which had funded long-term state hospitals for the seriously mentally ill and more recently funded public mental-health services through Medicaid and Medicare. With the advent of effective pharmacotherapy, more people were released from long-term institutions, but the infrastructure for support in communities was not adequately provided, leading to homelessness and high rates of rehospitalization as well as of incarceration and placement in state custody. During a time in the 1970s and 1980s private insurance coverage for mental-health services was liberal, but this led to major overuse of high-cost institutional (inpatient and residential) services. These developments culminated in concerns both by advocates that people with mental illnesses were being reinstitutionalized, and by insurers that the cost of care was skyrocketing.

In the late 1980s behavioral managed care "carveouts" (separate companies to manage mental health benefits) became an approach used by insurers to control costs, mainly through tightly restricting the use of hospitalization and extended outpatient psychotherapy, leading to increased fragmentation of care as a result. Managed care was first adopted by private health plans but then spread to Medicaid- and even Medicare-funded programs. At the same time, public mental-health programs began to experiment with different approaches to the delivery of intensive community-based services for more seriously ill individuals as a way to maintain them in their communities and prevent rehospitalization, institutionalization, or homelessness. More recently, these community-based services have incorporated increased roles for patients (now termed *consumers*) and for family members, as these parties have advocated both for greater funding for care and for a greater role in the self-determination of their or their family member's care.

ORGANIZATION OF MENTAL HEALTH SERVICES

Mental-health and psychiatric services are organized across various service sectors that, at times, overlap. These include the private, academic, state hospital, and community mental-health sectors. The private sector includes not-for-profit and for-profit institutions, which can be freestanding (i.e., solely psychiatric or mental health), or part of broader medical institutions. These institutions serve patients covered by private or public insurance plans, with only a few being exclusively private. They can either focus solely on inpatient, residential, or outpatient care, or they can comprise continuums of care that include different levels of care intensity and restrictiveness (e.g., acute inpatient units, longer-term residential programs, partial hospital programs, intensive outpatient clinics, and outpatient clinics). Some institutions are operated by, or closely affiliated with, medical schools and/or are part of academic medical centers. There are still remnants of the large state hospitals for the severely mentally ill that dominated state-funded systems, but these are mostly downsizing or being closed as more and more patients are "deinstitutionalized" into community-based services.

There has always been, and continues to be, a strong community-based sector of independent private practitioners, including psychiatrists, psychologists, and other licensed mental-health professionals, delivering outpatient services for people with mild to moderate mental health needs who have insurance or the ability to pay out of pocket. In the 1960s, as part of federal enabling and funding legislation, hundreds of community mental-health centers were developed in the United States to provide care for people with mental illnesses closer to their own communities, both for the poor and in underserved regions. These were largely modeled after child guidance clinics, which developed in the 1920s to care for children and youth with behavioral problems coming to the attention of juvenile courts or child welfare agencies. Community mental-health centers enjoyed much support during the 1960s through 1980s, but suffered from federal budget cuts. As the funding system shifted to Medicaid and Medicare funding of public mental-health services, many of these community mental-health centers evolved into not-for-profit entities, providing outpatient and intensive community-based services. Many of these programs now include more comprehensive community outreach services or are co-located in schools, welfare offices, detention centers or jails, and developmental disorders programs.

The mental-health system interacts with a number of other service systems to comprise the overall system of care for people with mental illnesses or emotional disturbances. These include medical, educational/vocational, criminal/juvenile justice, and welfare services.

Medical Service System (Primary Care, Community Hospitals, Tertiary Medical Centers)

Medical illness is often comorbid with psychiatric disorders, with high rates of depression and anxiety disorders particularly seen in people with chronic medical illnesses such as diabetes, cancer, and heart disease. Psychiatric consultation services are commonly found in tertiary medical centers and in many community hospitals, particularly those with integrated psychiatric services. However, the primary-care sector and ambulatory specialty medical sectors are largely cut off from psychiatric or mental-health services. Many barriers exist in obtaining mental-health service referrals for ambulatory primary-care patients, including separate physical locations, different insurance systems (medical and behavioral), lack of referral relations between sectors, and poor communication of critical information. Another component of the medical service sector where there is a high prevalence of need but significant shortages and barriers, is composed of facilities serving older adults (nursing home and assisted-living facilities). Older adults not only face high rates of dementia but also high-prevalence levels of depressive and anxiety disorders. There is an increasing interest in, and practice models for, the provision of integrated as well as consultative mental-health services in primary-care clinics, health maintenance organizations, nursing homes, and assisted living facilities to serve these increasing needs.

More recently, health care reform has promoted the establishment of Medical Homes and Accountable Care Organizations (ACOs), where individuals receive primary care services and coordination of specialty care. This has facilitated a movement to integrate specialty services within ACOs, especially psychiatric and behavioral health services, to enhance collaboration with primary care physicians in ACOs. For psychiatric services, this enhances access to entry level services and promotes prevention of higher end and higher cost services. The full implementation of these models calls for systematic screening for behavioral health needs in ACOs and a stepped model of care, where (a) the primary care physician directly delivers psychiatric care in collaboration with a care manager-therapist, (b) the primary care physician refers the patient for stabilization by the psychiatric service and receives him/ her back for maintenance followup once stabilized, or (c) the primary care physician and psychiatrist collaborate longitudinally in the patient's care. There is both ready access to psychiatric consultation (direct and indirect) as well as case management support to enable the primary care physician to deliver these services within the ACO or Medical Home and assist with specialty referrals. In fully integrated models within ACOs, the primary care physician is trained and supported by psychiatric and mental health consultation in screening, assessment, and often follows treatment algorithms or protocols for common psychiatric disorders (such as depressive or anxiety disorders). There is embedded case management and therapist support, access to regular psychiatric consultation on the panel of patients served, and continuity tracking of the patient's course of treatment and outcomes, typically using systematic rescreening and patient registries. There have been a number of formal model demonstration trials of collaborative and integrated models, particularly in depression care in adults and child psychiatric disorders. These have demonstrated superior outcomes in treatment response to treatment as usual, superior adherence, and reductions in cost of care not only for psychiatric but also the care of comorbid chronic medical conditions.

Educational/Vocational Service System

The educational and vocational systems face the impact of increased educational demands for average students or workers, due to the increased technological and informational demands on our society. In addition, the increasing needs of people with learning disorders and serious emotional disturbances are placing added burdens on schools and vocational agencies. These challenges occur in the context of underfunding of service, and this lack of funding is especially felt in the area of special education services. Many school districts and state vocational programs actively avoid the mandates of federal laws such as the Individuals with Disabilities Education Act (IDEA) and Section 504 of the Americans with Disabilities Act, which outlines requirements for accommodations of mentally ill/emotionally disturbed children and adults in schools and workplaces. The avoidance of these laws results in an underidentification of people with covered disabilities. A recent salutary development in the area of interagency systems of care for children is a renewed interest in school-based services, coordinated services for people with developmental disabilities, and integrated vocational services in intensive community treatment programs.

Criminal/Juvenile Justice Service System

Studies have documented high rates of psychopathology among youth in the juvenile justice system, with estimates of approximately 50–70%, and among adults in the criminal justice system, with rates of 20–40%. Mentally ill individuals are often arrested due to their propensity to abuse substances and display aggressive or disruptive behaviors. There is also disproportionate representation of poor and minority populations, especially of African-Americans and Latinos, among people referred into juvenile or criminal justice. This lopsided representation reflects the adversity faced by these populations as well as the lack of culturally competent services in mental health and other agencies. Individuals going into juvenile and criminal justice underutilize mental-health services over their lifetime when compared to cohorts in other systems. The poor level of services within juvenile justice facilities also deprives inmates of adequate services, with racial bias further preventing access to services. In spite of similarities in their populations, the justice and mental-health systems have significant differences in their orientations and philosophies (with the former having more of a community safety and punishment orientation, except for some rehabilitation focus in juvenile justice). Areas of natural collaboration between these systems occur in the diversion of mentally ill or emotionally disturbed individuals and their treatment after entering these systems. Multisystemic therapy (MST) and community-based systems-of-care programs for youth, assertive community treatment (ACT) for adults, mental-health courts, and drug courts have all resulted in significant reductions in detention or jail, rates of arrest and incarceration, and treatment costs.

Welfare and Child Welfare

Children and adults served in the welfare system have extremely high mental-health needs, with prevalence rates estimated at about 50% for both children and for their mothers, yet they are significantly underserved with respect to mental-health services. Already traumatized by the conditions of abuse and neglect that led to removal from their homes, children placed in foster care and women in welfare programs are confronted with the additional traumas of the loss of relationships, multiple relocations, uncertainty about their future, and the difficult task of establishing new positive attachments and embarking on new lives. A high percentage of these individuals are also of racial/ethnic minority backgrounds, in need of culturally competent services. In addition to having trauma-related disorders, these individuals are also at high risk for disruptive behaviors and substance abuse, and have greater difficulties in functioning at home, work, school, and their communities—placing them at high risk for additional failed placements and services. The welfare system also faces significant challenges posed by the legal system, lack of resources, and legislation. These challenges include an increasing orientation toward family reunification (over 90% of abused children are returned to their families), under-enforcement of protective orders for battered women, lack of adequate numbers and quality of foster homes, and increasing welfare-to-work requirements for poor women with children. Several models have effectively addressed the needs of children and parents served in the welfare system, including in-home intervention for abused or at-risk infants/toddlers and their families, visiting nurse programs for abused infants, family preservation and intensive in-home mental-health programs, and co-located mental-health services in welfare to work. The implementation of trauma-focused therapies in schools and community programs also addresses the needs of these populations.

PHILOSOPHIES OF CARE

Two predominant philosophies underlying systems-based practice have evolved, one addressing services for children and the other addressing services for adults.

Community Systems of Care Principles

The systems-of-care model for children's mental health is guided by a core set of principles. These principles were first outlined under the Child and Adolescent Service Systems Program (CASSP) initiative that set up the state-level offices for child mental health across the United States in the 1980s. The key principles include access to a comprehensive array of services, treatment individualized to the child's needs, treatment in the least restrictive environment possible (with full utilization of the resources of the family and the community), full participation of families as partners in service planning and delivery, interagency coordination, the use of case management for coordination of services, no ejection or rejection from services due to lack of "treatability" or "cooperation" with interventions, early identification and intervention, smooth transition of youth into the adult service system, effective advocacy efforts, and the provision of nondiscriminating, culturally sensitive services.

Recovery Principles

Under these principles, mental-health recovery is seen as a journey of healing and transformation that enables a person with a mental-health problem to live a meaningful life in a community of his or her choice while striving to achieve his or her full potential. The 10 fundamental values of recovery-oriented services are (1) self-direction, (2) individualized and person-centered care, (3) empowerment (presenting a range of care options and participating in all care decisions), (4) holistic perspective (services address an individual's whole life, including mind, body, spirit, and community), (5) nonlinear perspective (recovery not seen as a step-by-step process but one based on continual growth, occasional setbacks, and learning from experience), (6) strengths-based approach (focuses on valuing and building on the multiple capacities, resiliencies, talents, coping abilities, and inherent worth of individuals), (7) peer support (by other consumers, sharing effective coping strategies), (8) respect, (9) responsibility, and (10) hope (providing essential and motivating message of a better future).

Models and Evidence-Based Practices

A number of models for organized interagency systems of care have been developed in the United States through the Comprehensive Community Mental Health Services for Children and Their Families Program, funded by the Center for Mental Health Services. This center has funded over 80 model sites serving over 80,000 children since 1994. These programs involve the multiple child-serving agencies in addition to mental health, as well as family and youth participation. Children and youth in these systems-of-care programs have shown significant results in improved child behavior and functioning, fewer contacts with law enforcement, increased stability in living situation, improvements in child and family strengths and resources, reduced caregiver strain, and improved family function. Preliminary results demonstrate reduced cost of care within these programs when indirect cost offsets are considered, such as child welfare, juvenile justice, educational, and general health costs.

A number of community-based interventions for children and youth that have shown promise include school-based interventions, mentoring programs, family support and education programs, wilderness programs, crisis mobile outreach teams, time-limited hospitalization with coordinated community services, and family support services. Studies involving these modalities have demonstrated significantly better outcomes than traditional outpatient or residential services. These include reduced levels of externalizing and internalizing symptoms, improved family functioning, reduced utilization of more restrictive services, and improved cost-effectiveness. Additionally, a number of in-home preventive parent–child interventions with infants and young children have demonstrated long-term effectiveness in reducing child abuse as well as adverse behavioral and academic outcomes. Multisystemic therapy is one model that combines home-based, wraparound, and cognitive–behavioral interventions within a systemic context. It has been evaluated with youth at risk of detention/incarceration and at risk of psychiatric or substance abuse hospitalization, with significant results in reducing out-of-home placement, externalizing problem behaviors, rates of recidivism, and costs of treatment.

The model that has emerged that exemplifies the community-based system approach for adult services is the assertive community treatment team model. This model serves a group of people with serious mental illnesses at high risk for recidivism, using an integrated team of mental health, substance abuse, and vocational therapists, a psychiatrist, nurses, and peer counselor. The team takes responsibility for the patient's care and delivers whatever care is needed (e.g., psychotherapy, support services) in the community to ensure that the patient is able to function in the community and live a meaningful life. The ACT programs have been successful in reducing hospitalizations, homelessness, incarceration, and in improving function in the community. Also available are various evidence-based community practices

—for example, intensive case management, family psychoeducation, integrated dual-disorders treatment (mental health and substance abuse), supported employment, and disease management—that involve community systems-of-care approaches and have demonstrated outcomes in improving function for people with serious mental illnesses in the community.

CLINICAL PRACTICE

In addition to the clinical skills of diagnostic assessment, medical assessment, treatment planning, pharmacotherapy, different forms of psychotherapy, and implementation of specialized treatments (e.g., as electroconvulsive therapy, biofeedback, hypnosis, behavioral therapy), mental-health professionals working in broader systems of care must master a number of additional skills, including consultation, advocacy, cultural competence, interdisciplinary systems coordination, and quality improvement.

Consultation

Mental-health consultation is the process of interaction between two professionals: one who is a specialist (consultant) and one who invokes the consultant's help (consultee) in a current work problem that is believed to be within the realm of the specialist's competency. It may include management of one or more clients of a counselor or planning of a program for these clients (Caplan, 1999). Successful consultative work requires several ingredients: (1) a clarity of roles and responsibilities for the consultant, (2) clear expectations for the consultation, (3) clarity of communication (and attunement to lines of communication/hierarchy), (4) clarity of roles and priorities among all players in the system, (5) attunement to the priorities and mandates of the organization, and (6) respect and utilization of the skills of other professionals in the system. The three A's of *ability, affability,* and *availability* are also important in being a successful consultant. There are different types of consultative relationships:

• *Case-based consultation* includes both client-centered consultation, where the focus is on the client and/or provider in order to serve the need of a specific patient(s), and consultee-centered consultation, where the focus is on the skills/knowledge of the consultee as opposed to the client (analogous to supervision).

• *Administrative-based consultation* is consultee-centered, where the focus is the professional and his or her skills, or program-centered, where the focus of the evaluation and recommendations is the program, often regarding administrative issues.

• *Internal consultation* (often called *mental-health collaboration*) involves shared responsibility for the case, and the consultee agrees to respect the advice of the consultant because of the sharing of responsibility and expertise.

• *Liaison-based consultation* is an ongoing relationship developed with a consultee and/or specialty team. The liaison clinician is still seen as external to the team but approximates becoming a team member, while bringing in objective perspectives and external resources on either cases or programmatic issues. The liaison clinician uses his or her knowledge of the relations and interactions in the team to leverage ongoing improvement and change in team members' function.

Advocacy

The Institute of Medicine (2001) endorsed the empowerment of patients and their families in the "new rules" for a 21st-century health care system. These rules emphasize the points that (1) care is based on continuous healing relationships (most notably, family relationships), (2) care is customized according to the patient's and family's needs and values, (3) the patient (or family, in the case of minors) is the source of control, (4) knowledge is shared with patients and families and information flows freely, and (5) transparency in the care process is necessary. The president's New Freedom Commission on Mental Health (2003) also endorsed family-driven care.

Patient-centered, family-driven care implies that families must take a central role in defining their care. They have a primary decision-making role in the care of themselves (or with parents, their children), as well as the policies and procedures governing care for all children in their community. This role includes choosing supports, services, and providers; setting treatment goals; designing and implementing programs; monitoring outcomes; partnering in funding decisions; and determining the effectiveness of all efforts to promote the mental health and well-being of children and youth. In patient-centered and family-driven care, patients and families are given accurate, understandable, and complete information, which is necessary to set goals and to make choices for service planning. Patients, families, providers, and administrators embrace the concept of sharing decision making and responsibility for outcomes. Families, consumers, and their organizations engage in peer support activities to reduce isolation, gather and disseminate accurate information, strengthen their voices, and provide direction for decisions that impact funding for services, treatments, and supports. Efforts to change community attitudes focus on removing barriers and discrimination created by the stigma associated with mental illness. Experiential expertise coming from the lived experience of the patient and his and her family is seen as equally valid as professional expertise (from formal education, training, practice-based learning, and scientific literature).

Clinicians have a responsibility to advocate on behalf of, and with patients and their families at both the clinical level and at the systems level. They also have an advocacy responsibility toward their patients and families regarding both their psychiatric care as well as their education about the broader system. Furthermore, they have a responsibility to empower the patient and family in the development of the services plan and in making the critical choices on treatment selection—with the rare exception being when the patient's life is endangered by the direction proposed by the patient and family. Clinicians should advocate for patient and family support services, which are formal and informal supports that enable patients and their families to make use of treatment. These may include some financial supports, respite care, peer counseling, referral information, and other nontraditional services.

At the systems level, clinicians should advocate for sufficient resources for safe and effective service delivery in their communities, but also to have patients and family members sit on oversight, policy-making, and quality improvement bodies for mental-health care organizations. Clinicians should also collaborate with consumer and family organizations, which often promote and sustain patient and family supports and advocacy at the local, state, and national levels, and serve as sources of considerable information for both professionals and family members. Major family/consumer organizations include the National Alliance for the Mentally Ill, Mental Health America, the Federation of Families for Children's Mental Health, and many disorder-specific organizations. Such organizations have played instrumental roles in preserving federal research and services funding in the face of threatened funding cuts, and are pushing for legislation that establishes parity in insurance coverage of mental disorders with physical illnesses.

Cultural Competence

The United States is becoming an increasingly diverse nation, especially with the growth of minority groups with non-European origins. By the year 2050, the United States will no longer have a numerical "majority" racial/ethnic population, and this will happen by 2030 for those under 18 years of age. Increasing immigration into the United States means that currently over 40 million Americans were not born in this country. This demographic and cultural shift has significant implications for mental-health services. Cultural values and beliefs influence normal human development (at the physical, psychological, cognitive, and social levels), family development, and the development of protective factors/strengths. Culture also impacts on mental illness at various levels: biologically (e.g., genetic polymorphisms and variations in medication metabolism found in different populations); in terms of the explanatory models used for understanding illness, disease, and psychopathology (based on science, religion, spiritual beliefs, or even interpersonal factors, including stigma of mental illness); and in relation to help-seeking expectations and service-utilization patterns.

The principle of cultural competence is an integral aspect of the philosophy of community-based systems of care (Cross et al., 1989). It proposes that practitioners in systems of care develop the necessary attitudes, skills, and knowledge base to serve minority and culturally diverse children and families in their communities. It also proposes that practitioners develop policies and procedures within these systems to remove any barriers to the accessing of services and to make these services more responsive to the values of diverse communities. The systems-of-care approach is congruent with the cultural values of ethnic minority populations, which first emphasize strong extended family involvement in the life of the individual and the use of natural community resources in dealing with emotional and physical problems.

Guidelines for evaluating cultural competence skills, published by the Center for Mental Health Services and more recently the American Academy of Child and Adolescent Psychiatry (Pumariega, et al., 2013), operationalize elements of cultural competence at both the clinical and systems levels. Important applications of cultural competence include linguistic competence and support for linguistic minorities; special approaches to engagement, assessment, and diagnosis (particularly taking into account culturally specific symptom expressions, the cultural context of symptoms, and special stressors such as immigration trauma, acculturation stress, and community violence); treatment planning that involves the family and minority community; and treatment approaches that are adapted to the cultural values and beliefs of the patient and have an evidence base with that specific population. It also involves systems-wide applications of cultural competence, including cultural competence planning for the system (i.e., identifying the population distribution for an area being served and the special cultural needs); governance that reflects the diversity of the area served; services that are culturally appropriate; quality assurance and improvement and information systems oriented to examining disparities and cultural needs; and staff training and development oriented to developing cultural competence in practitioners.

Interagency/Interdisciplinary Care Planning and Systems Coordination Skills

Given the complexity of these systems of care, the skills and roles that clinicians and particularly psychiatrists must display go far beyond their circumscribed clinical roles. Beyond serving as a front-line clinician, these roles include serving as a clinical consultant and collaborator to other professionals, clinical team leader, administrative leader in delivery organization/system, quality assurance/improvement consultant, consultant to interagency teams, and outcome evaluator/researcher in systems of care. Psychiatrists, given their broad biopsychosocial and developmental perspectives, should be best able to integrate and coordinate community-based treatment delivered by multiple professionals with diverse skills.

Clinicians need knowledge and skills in a number of areas to promote inter-agency and interdisciplinary coordination of care. Most of these skills are deployed in interdisciplinary and interagency teams that assemble to coordinate care for multi-need patients receiving services from multiple professionals and agencies. The knowledge and skills needed include *knowledge* of community resources, agencies and their legal and operational mandates, the skills and strengths provided by different human services professionals, *skills* in leadership, communication, collaboration, and systemic assessment and intervention. The latter often involve carefully outlining the structure and lines of authority and relations in an organization, and evaluating how clinicians can most effectively advocate and consult for their patients or population of patients.

Given the emphasis on tertiary care models in the training of many psychiatrists, they often have not developed all the skills needed to serve as effective members and leaders of these new systems. Three publications from the American Academy of Child and Adolescent Psychiatry, *Guidelines for Training Child and Adolescent Psychiatrists in Community-Based Systems of Care*, the "Practice Parameters for Child Mental Health in Systems of Care," and *Best Principles for Integration of Child Psychiatry into the Pediatric Health Home* provide guidance on the skills, knowledge, attitudes, training experiences, and practices that psychiatrists need to function effectively within community-based systems of care.

Wraparound Model

One established model for interdisciplinary and interagency planning is the wraparound process involving a care-planning team. This type of approach is most often seen in children's systems-of-care programs, and in treatment or care planning programs for youth with complex needs and their families. The wraparound model prioritizes family voice in the process of developing a team of people with complementary strengths committed to improving the mental health of the child or youth. The team is facilitated by a care coordinator, who may also have had experience with raising a child with complex needs. This complementary approach to the usual medical model involves the following stages:

Pre-meeting preparation of the family establishes the initial engagement and provides mutual orientation as well as safety planning and developing a shared vision for services and outcomes by the family with a care coordinator and, when available, a family partner (a peer counselor with personal experience with a child with emotional disturbance/mental illness).

Pre-meeting preparation of all team members is necessary to discuss provider hopes and concerns for their work with the family, to review a summary of history and other information on the child's status ahead of time, with family informed consent, and for preliminary conversations between professionals to help them sort out their own interface issues without further burdening the family when the team meeting occurs.

In the actual *team meeting*, (1) family members identify the domains to be addressed (e.g., housing, employment, transportation, school, or legal, emotional, or behavioral concerns); (2) needs and strengths in the youth, family, and community for the domain chosen are identified; (3) options are generated to meet the needs, ideally building on strengths; and (4) a plan of care is developed, settling on the best options and identifying *who* will do *what* by *when*.

Weekly to monthly *followup meetings* continue for the youth and family team until the family's vision is achieved or the family chooses to withdraw, and the team follows the youth through different levels of care to provide continuity. A care coordinator is responsible for tracking outcomes from the plan of care and supporting accountability; if progress is not made, the assumption is that the plan of care was flawed, not that the youth or family or provider is to blame.

Quality Improvement

As systems of care move toward greater accountability and a stronger evidence-base, quality improvement becomes an integral function. Quality improvement should not only evaluate and improve effectiveness and efficiency of services, but assure consumer (youth and family) satisfaction and, foremost, promote and assure safety in care delivery.

Skills

An ongoing orientation toward improvement implies that clinicians are never satisfied with the quality of their care and its outcomes (clinical and functional), and that they always seek to improve not only the effectiveness of their practices but also the process of care in terms of efficiency (cost and time) and effectiveness (improving access and reducing errors). Important skills in participating in and implementing quality improvement approaches include planning skills, analytic skills (especially the use of tools for analyzing processes of care, e.g., "wish-boning" and flow diagrams), outcome evaluation skills (some of these border on clinical research skills), data management and analysis skills, communication and collaboration skills, and financial analysis skills. Clinicians need to balance cost and quality considerations in pursuing quality improvement projects or programs, keeping in mind the classic triangle of *cost, quality,* and *access* and how these interact in care delivery. Staff and patient involvement in problem identification, analysis, solution identification, and policy and procedure development is critical to the success of any safety or quality improvement program.

Patient Safety

Patient safety is an important component of quality improvement and self-analysis by mental-health-care organizations on issues involving significant risk (e.g., medication interactions; identification of, and intervention in, cases involving suicidal and aggressive risk; management of substance detoxification and co-morbid medical conditions; side effects from procedures such as seclusion and restraint and electroconvulsive treatment). Rule 6 of Recommendation 4 in the Institute of Medicine's (2001) *Crossing the Quality Chasm* is that "safety is a systems property" (p. 8). The Hippocratic Oath ("Above all else, do no harm") belongs not just to the individual physician, but to the system of care as a whole.

Patients and families often interact with multiple individuals and agencies concurrently and are therefore key to addressing safety issues and concerns. Coordinated, respectful, and collaborative communication between system partners can promote safe and effective care. Systems that do not communicate adequately, that communicate in a conflicted manner, and/or that give patients and families contradictory requirements can augment distress in the family, causing harm. Clinicians have a leadership responsibility to model collaborative, respectful interactions with system partners to help reduce the harm that "system stress" causes to families. Patients and families, as experts in their life experience, also provide invaluable information on the physiological and psychological responses to interventions used with their children. Failure to listen to families in this regard can, in itself, become a safety issue.

The first rule of *Crossing the Quality Chasm* is "Care is based on continuous healing relationships." Supporting the capacity of families to promote healing and continuous support for patients maximizes the impact of continuous healing relationships. Disrupted attachments, when occasioned by multiple placements in out-of-home settings, can be harmful to the health of patients and to family function. Short-term emergency response (e.g., repeated hospitalizations or acute residential treatment), although necessary for safety, must be balanced against long-term harm caused by disrupted attachments. Also, the episodic nature of much of mental-health care in fragmented systems of care contributes to a discontinuity of providers that can create safety issues. Care can be enhanced and harm reduced by promoting engagement with needed clinical and support services in systems of care on a continuous basis.

References

American Academy of Child and Adolescent Psychiatry, Work Group on Community-Based Systems of Care. (2007). *System-based practice: Modules for teaching systems-based practice*. Washington, DC: American Academy of Child and Adolescent Psychiatry.

Caplan, G. (1970). *The theory and practice of mental health consultation*. London: Tavistock.

Caplan, G. (1999). *Mental health consultation and collaboration*. Long Grove, IL: Waveland Press.

Cross, T., Bazron, B., Dennis, K., & Isaacs, M. (1989). *Towards a culturally competent system of care*. Washington, DC: CASSP Technical Assistance Center, Georgetown University Child Development Center.

Elpers, J. (2000). Public psychiatry. In B. Sadock & V. Sadock (Eds.), *Comprehensive textbook of psychiatry* (Vol. II, pp. 3185–3199). Philadelphia: Lippincott, Williams & Wilkins.

Four Racial Ethnic Panels. (1999). *Cultural competence standards for managed mental health services for four underserved/underrepresented racial/ethnic groups.* Rockville, MD: Center for Mental Health Services, Substance Abuse and Mental Health Services Administration, U.S. Department of Health and Human Services.

Huffine, C., & Anderson, D. (2003). Family advocacy development in systems of care. In A.J. Pumariega & N.C. Winters (Eds.), *Handbook of community systems of care; The new child and adolescent community psychiatry* (pp. 35–65). San Francisco: Jossey Bass.

Institute of Medicine. (2001). Formulating new rules to redesign and improve care. In Institute of Medicine Committee on Quality of Health Care in America (Ed.), *Crossing the quality chasm: A new health system for the 21st century* (pp. 61–89). Washington, DC: National Academy Press.

Institute of Medicine. (2002). *Unequal treatment: Confronting racial and ethnic disparities in health care.* Washington, DC: National Academies Press.

Kolko, D., Campo, J., Kilbourne, A., Hart, J., Sakolsky, D., & Wisniewski, D. (2014) Collaborative care outcomes for pediatric behavioral health problems: A cluster randomized trial. *Pediatrics, 133,* 2013–2516.

Lieberman, R., Kopelowicz, A., & Smith, T. (2000). Psychiatric rehabilitation. In B. Sadock & V. Sadock (Eds.), *Comprehensive textbook of psychiatry* (Vol. II, pp. 3218–3245). Philadelphia: Lippincott, Williams & Wilkins.

Martini, R., Hilt, R., Marx, L., Chenven, M., Naylor, M., & Sarvet, B. (2012). *Best principles for integration of child psychiatry into the pediatric health home.* Washington, DC: American Academy of Child and Adolescent Psychiatry. http://www.aacap.org/App_Themes/AACAP/docs/clinical_practice_center/systems_of_care/best_principles_for_integration_of_child_psychiatry_into_the_pediatric_health_home_2012.pdf. Last accessed on December 28th, 2014.

New Freedom Commission on Mental Health. (2003). *Achieving the promise: Transforming mental health care in America.* Final Report. Rockville, MD: U.S. Dept. of Health and Human Services, No. SMA-03-3832.

Osher, T.A., & Osher, D. (2002). The paradigm shift to true collaboration with families. *Journal of Child and Family Studies, 11,* 47–60.

Pumariega, A.J., Diamond, J., England, M., Fallon, T., Hanson, G., Lourie, I., et al. (1996). *Guidelines for training towards community-based systems of care for children with serious emotional disturbances.* Washington, DC: American Academy of Child and Adolescent Psychiatry.

Pumariega, A.J., Nace, D., England, M.J., Diamond, J., Mattson, A., Fallon, T., et al. (1997). Community-based systems approach to children's managed mental health services. *Journal of Child and Family Studies, 6*(2), 149–164.

Pumariega, A.J., Rogers, K., & Rothe, E. (2005). Culturally competent systems of care for children's mental health: Advances and challenges. *Community Mental Health Journal, 41*(5), 539–556.

Pumariega A.J. (2006). Residential treatment for youth: Introduction and a cautionary tale. *American Journal of Orthopsychiatry*, 76, 281.

Pumariega, A.J., Rothe, E., Mian, A., Carlisle, L., Toppelberg, C., Harris, T., Gogineni, R., Webb, S., Smith, J., & the Committee on Quality Issues. (2013). Practice parameter for cultural competence in child and adolescent psychiatric practice. *Journal of the American Academy of Child and Adolescent Psychiatry*, 52(10), 1101–1115.

Raney, L. (2015). *Integrated Care: Working at the interface of primary care and behavioral health*. Arlington, VA: American Psychiatric Publishing.

Ruiz, P. (2003). Systems-based practice core competencies. In S. Scheiber, T. Kramer, & S. Adamowski (Eds.), *Core competencies for psychiatric practice* (pp. 109–118). Washington, DC: American Psychiatric Press.

Stein, L., & Santos, A. (1998). *Assertive community treatment of persons with severe mental illness*. New York: Norton.

Steinberg, D.S., & Yule, E. (1985). Consultative work. In M. Rutter & H. Lionel (Eds.), *Child and adolescent psychiatry: Modern approaches*, 2nd ed. (pp. 914–926). Boston: Blackwell Scientific.

U.S. Office of the Surgeon General. (2001). *Mental health: Culture, race, and ethnicity. A supplement to mental health: A report of the surgeon general*. Rockville, MD.: U.S. Department of Health and Human Services, Substance Abuse and Mental Health Services Administration, Center for Mental Health Services, National Institutes of Health, National Institute of Mental Health.

Walker, J.S., & Bruns, E.J. (2006). Building on practice-based evidence: Using expert perspectives to define the wraparound process. *Psychiatric Services*, 57, 1579–1585.

Winters, N.C., & Terrell, E. (2003). Case management: The linchpin of community-based systems of care. In A.J. Pumariega & N.C. Winters (Eds.), *Handbook of community systems of care: The new child and adolescent community psychiatry* (pp. 171–200). San Francisco: Jossey Bass.

Winters, N.C., & Pumariega, A.J. (2007). Work group on community-based systems of care, committee on community psychiatry, and work group on quality issues practice parameters for child mental health in systems of care. *Journal of the American Academy of Child and Adolescent Psychiatry*, 46(2), 284–299.

8

Legal, Ethical, and Multicultural Issues

Ethics and law are not the same, but they often interrelate. In managing their professional work with patients, health care providers' primary focus should be patients' well-being and best interest. However, it may be difficult at times for professionals to ascertain what action or decision will best benefit the patient. In addition, practitioners also must consider what is in the best interest of society or persons directly involved with the patient.

LEGAL ISSUES

The law regulates specific aspects of psychiatric practice in a manner distinct from other forms of medical practice, because of the issues surrounding autonomy and safety that are often encountered. Importantly, such laws often vary considerably between jurisdictions. It is essential that all clinicians seeking to work with individuals suffering from psychiatric disorders familiarize themselves with the relevant laws. Some specific areas of psychiatric practice that are regulated by the legal system, either in the form of specific state or federal laws or through judicial case rulings, include involuntary hospitalization and involuntary treatment. Other areas similarly regulated include informed consent, confidentiality, duty to warn and/or protect a potential victim who might be in danger, capacity to provide informed consent for psychiatric treatment and surrogate decision making, admission and treatment of minors, reporting of abuse and/or neglect, and standards of care.

Mr. Smith is a 35-year-old unmarried Caucasian male who was diagnosed with schizophrenia, paranoid type, at the age of 22. At the time, he was in college and doing well academically but had started to become increasingly withdrawn from his friends and family. Those close to him began noticing that he appeared increasingly suspicious, making remarks about being followed and recorded by members of the Secret Service. He gradually stopped attending hockey practice and a book club, and his grades started to slip. One evening, his college roommate Adam arrived home to find Mr. Smith attempting to disassemble the microwave oven while it was still plugged into the wall outlet. When his roommate attempted to intervene, Mr. Smith became acutely agitated, started making angry remarks about hidden transponders, and threw a chair across the room. His roommate called the police, and Mr. Smith was escorted to the emergency room of the university hospital, where he remained extremely agitated and continued to make paranoid statements. He was admitted to the inpatient psychiatric service on an involuntary commitment status. During the hospitalization, a diagnosis of schizophrenia, paranoid type, was confirmed based on history obtained from multiple sources. He was stabilized on an antipsychotic medication, which almost completely dissipated his delusional thinking, and he was discharged in stable condition.

Mr. Smith did well for about a month after his discharge, but then stopped taking his medication and started to become paranoid again. He also developed auditory command hallucinations telling him to kill his college principal, because he was the leader of the secret conspiracy to kill Mr. Smith. Mr. Smith described these hallucinations to his roommate Adam and told Adam that he would likely kill his principal "before he gets me killed." Adam again contacted the police, and Mr. Smith was escorted back to the hospital emergency room and readmitted to the inpatient psychiatric service. Upon admission, he denied any urges to harm himself or others but did present as agitated and refused to accept any medication. He was again admitted on an involuntarily committed status and a request for authorization of medications by force was submitted to the court. At a judicial hearing, it was determined that Mr. Smith lacked capacity to make his own treatment decisions because he did not appreciate the fact that he suffered from a mental illness, and hence involuntary treatment was authorized. Treatment with antipsychotics was instituted and Mr. Smith appeared to improve. However, he remained somewhat suspicious and did appear somewhat preoccupied with internal stimuli, even though he consistently denied hallucinations and any urges to harm himself or anyone. Meanwhile, Adam, who had been unable to visit Mr. Smith in the hospital due to his college schedule, left two messages for Mr. Smith's attending physician requesting a call back to discuss Mr. Smith's status prior to admission. Five days after admission, Mr. Smith's attending physician deemed that Mr. Smith no longer met criteria for continued involuntary hospitalization, even though he remained mildly psychotic, and Mr. Smith was discharged per his own insistence.

Three days after discharge, Mr. Smith shot and killed his college princi-pal, Mr. Jones. He was arrested and charged with second-degree murder. At the time of arrest, he was noted to be muttering to himself about having "done God's will," but was unable to receive any antipsychotic medication for the first 48 hours of his incarceration due to lack of availability and the absence of a psychiatrist on the medical unit of the jail. He continued to make psychotic remarks when he first met with his court-appointed attorney, Mr. Black. Mr. Black had much concern about Mr. Smith's mental state and petitioned the court to have Mr. Smith evaluated for competency to stand trial. Mr. Smith was found incompetent to stand trial and was committed to a forensic psychiatric hospital for restoration to competency. Following resto-ration of competency to stand trial after 3 weeks of inpatient treatment, he collaborated with his attorney and successfully mounted an insanity defense. This led to his incarceration in the state forensic psychiatric hospital for 5 years, followed by continued hospitalization in the state civil forensic hospi-tal for another 2 years. He was eventually released to the community.

In the year following the murder, Mr. Smith's family filed a malpractice lawsuit against the attending physician and the hospital where Mr. Smith had been admitted. The suit alleged that the attending physician failed to follow the standard of care by not obtaining appropriate collateral informa-tion when making a decision about Mr. Smith's readiness for discharge and not having conducted an adequate risk assessment. During initial deposi-tions, the attending physician testified that he had indeed contacted Adam and had not been able to elicit any additional information of concern. How-ever, he acknowledged that there were no entries in the medical record to substantiate his testimony. Adam testified that he never heard back from the attending physician. The family of Mr. Jones also filed suit, alleging that the attending physician failed to take reasonable steps to warn or protect Mr. Jones from a potentially dangerous patient. Both suits were settled out of court for an undisclosed amount.

Following his release from the state civil hospital, Mr. Smith has been stable and relatively free of psychiatric symptoms. He has, however, been unable to procure work because of his past criminal and psychiatric history. He has applied for Social Security disability benefits, but his application has been denied.

The case above illustrates some of the various ways in which the law interfaces with the practice of psychiatry. This interface can be conceptual-ized as consisting of at least three separate elements: (1) the legal regulation of the practice of clinical psychiatry, (2) the specialized application of psychiatric expertise to answer legal questions in legal contexts (both civil and criminal), and (3) the diagnosis and treatment of psychiatric disorders in the correctional system.

Involuntary Hospitalization

Individuals known to suffer from, or suspected to suffer from, psychiatric disorders may be admitted to inpatient psychiatric units against their will if certain conditions are met. The state's ability to detain psychiatric patients involuntarily stems from two primary legal principles: *parens patriae* (i.e., the state's obligation to protect individuals from the consequences of their own limitations) and "police powers" (i.e., the state's right to protect society from the acts of potentially dangerous persons). Historically, psychiatric patients were confined to institutions for indefinite periods while receiving little treatment. Over the past several decades, there has been considerable evolution in society's views on the balance between protecting the civil rights of psychiatric patients and protecting the community from potential harmful acts that such individuals might commit.

State laws now vary considerably with regard to (1) the criteria that must be met before involuntary hospitalization can be considered, (2) the process that must be followed in order to involuntarily hospitalize an individual, and (3) the duration of time the individual can be held without judicial review. As a general matter, most states require that individuals be deemed to suffer from a psychiatric disorder that renders them at high risk of harm to themselves or others, and/or their ability to provide for their basic needs is significantly compromised. The precise language used in the relevant legal statutes may significantly influence whether or not an individual meets the criteria for involuntary hospitalization; for example, a requirement that an individual pose an "imminent danger" to self or others is a much higher threshold relative to the requirement that the individual simply be at risk for significant deterioration in psychiatric status. Most states allow clinicians to place a time-limited hold on a patient (typically a matter of days), during which a judicial proceeding can be scheduled. At such a proceeding, a trier of fact (i.e., a judge or magistrate) determines whether the initial commitment and/ or continued hospitalization is legally justifiable. Germane to such a legal determination is testimony by a treating psychiatrist or other mental-health professional relating to the individual's psychiatric disorder, current mental status, degree of risk for harmful behavior in the near term, and ability to provide for basic daily needs in a safe manner. Most states allow such individuals to retain independent psychiatrists (typically at their own expense) to testify at such hearings. Testimony by significant others is also permitted in most instances.

A generally accepted principle is that psychiatric patients must be treated in the "least restrictive alternative" available; that is, involuntary commitment is the last resort after patients have refused the opportunity to voluntarily agree to be hospitalized. An additional issue that arises in some states is the patient's capacity to consent to voluntary hospitalization. That is, individuals who are willing to be hospitalized must have a rational understanding of the reasons for hospitalization and the implications of that hospitalization. If the individual lacks such an understanding, involuntary hospitalization may need to be considered, even though the patient is agreeable to hospitalization, in order to allow for judicial review and ensure that the patient's legal rights are being protected to the appropriate degree. It is important to note that involuntary hospitalization does not, in most instances, automatically provide legal authorization for involuntary treatment (e.g., administration of scheduled medications).

Involuntary Treatment

Most jurisdictions allow for emergency use of medications or physical restraints to manage situations involving physical aggression or imminently dangerous behavior by patients, without the need to obtain judicial authorization. However, ongoing scheduled treatment with psychotropic medication over a patient's objection requires that the treating clinician obtain advance judicial authorization by following a legal protocol prescribed by a jurisdiction or agency. Historically, commitment to a psychiatric institution was deemed to authorize involuntary treatment. Recent shifts in the criteria for civil commitment toward a "dangerousness" standard led to the recognition of the distinction between the goals and rationale for hospitalization versus forced treatment. Furthermore, the law has come to recognize that committed patients are not necessarily incompetent in a broad sense.

Currently, jurisdictions adopt one of two approaches to involuntary psychiatric treatment. Some courts afford wider authority to mental-health professionals to force treatment in psychiatric settings based upon professional judgment, with relatively little oversight by the legal system. Such a model reduces delays inherent in the legal process and allows for more timely treatment. This model is often opposed by legal professionals and some patient advocates for not offering enough protection to patient rights. Other jurisdictions require a court to make a decision about a patient's decisional capacity with regard to consenting to (or refusing) psychiatric treatment. A legal finding of incompetence results in the court's application of the *substituted judgment* principle, that is, an opinion that includes prescription of those treatments that the patient would have elected to accept if competent. From a practical perspective, treatment refusal in an inpatient psychiatric setting must first be approached clinically by addressing issues such as the therapeutic relationship and reasons for the refusal. Common reasons for treatment refusal include adverse effects from medications or denial of illness (Hoge et al., 1990; Guthiel & Appelbaum, 2000). Negotiation may be appropriate in some situations, and recruiting significant others to assist may be helpful. If such measures are unsuccessful, or if there are concerns about the patient's capacity to make an informed choice to accept or refuse psychiatric treatment, then the process prescribed by applicable law must be followed. Discharge from inpatient care is appropriate only if treatment refusal cannot be overcome through clinical and legal means, and if the patient is deemed not to meet criteria for commitment. Certain states have legal provisions that allow for forced outpatient treatment ("outpatient commitment"). The success of such programs varies considerably.

Informed Consent

The doctrine of informed consent, well recognized in law, has evolved considerably in recent decades, shaped by historical, social, and cultural forces (Appelbaum et al., 1987; Schwartz & Roth, 1989). It is essential that informed consent be obtained from the patient before any treatment is initiated. Essential elements of such consent include *disclosure, voluntariness,* and *competency.* At a minimum, *disclosure of information* that is essential for the patient to make a reasoned and informed choice includes the indication for the treatment proposed, the potential risks and benefits of such treatment, alternatives to the proposed treatment, and potential consequences if the proposed treatment is not administered. *Voluntariness* refers to a consent that is free from coercion or threat. While this issue may often be straightforward, certain treatment situations (e.g., patients admitted involuntarily to locked psychiatric units) may unintentionally but inherently involve an element of coercion. Attempts must be made to minimize such effects. As a matter of law, adults are presumed competent unless adjudicated otherwise, whereas minors are presumed to lack decisional capacity.

When consent is being obtained from patients suffering from active psychiatric disorders, it is particularly important to assess the elements of *competency.* These include an understanding and appreciation of the necessary information, an adequate reasoning process, and the evidencing of a choice.

It is important to note that suffering from a psychiatric disorder does not, per se, render a patient incompetent to make treatment decisions. Individuals may retain the capacity to make certain treatment decisions but not others, and any evaluation of competency must be decision specific rather than global. A related principle of the "sliding scale" requires higher levels of competency to make decisions about treatments that carry a higher risk–benefit ratio.

Some situations do not require clinicians to obtain informed consent. *Psychiatric emergencies*—situations wherein there is an imminent danger of serious harm to the patient or to others—permit the administration of treatment that is essential only to prevent such harm. With *incompetent patients*, relevant law must guide the process of obtaining consent from surrogate decision makers, and attempts must be made to involve the patient in the decision-making process to the degree possible. A patient may choose to *waive the right* to make his or her own decision. Such a scenario warrants careful exploration and discussion with the patient. A clinician may wish to withhold information about a treatment option on the grounds that provision of certain information to the patient in the process of obtaining informed consent may be harmful to the patient. This so-called *therapeutic privilege* is no longer recommended except under very specific and limited circumstances (e.g., if the disclosed information would prompt suicidal behavior).

Special considerations apply when informed consent is to be obtained for certain types of mental health treatment (e.g., electroconvulsive therapy or psychotherapy), certain patient populations (e.g., older adults), or certain contexts (e.g., participation in clinical research) (Schwartz & Mack, 2003). Finally, it is important to recognize that obtaining informed consent is an ongoing process that is engaged in, with the patient, during the course of treatment, rather than a single event in time.

Confidentiality

Without first obtaining appropriate authorization from the patient, clinicians are ethically bound to hold confidential (not disclose to most third parties) information obtained in the course of evaluating or treating him or her. This principle is the cornerstone of the psychotherapeutic relationship. Such disclosure may occur without prior authorization, in most instances, to other care providers within the same system of care, to consultants, or to other staff members intimately involved in the care of the patient. Most jurisdictions allow for exceptions to confidentiality in any circumstance where a typical patient–clinician relationship is not established (e.g., forensic or independent evaluations). Also, emergency situations usually allow for disclosure of the minimum amount of confidential information necessary to conduct an assessment and provide immediate management. There are laws mandating that abuse or neglect be reported and that the safety of third parties, the public, or the patient takes precedence over confidentiality. Group and marriage/family therapies present special challenges with regard to confidentiality, as information is disclosed with multiple parties present. Practitioners who work with minors should have specialized training with their patient population and related state laws regarding parental or guardian rights to information.

Privilege refers to the patient's right to prevent the professional information from being presented as testimony in a legal proceeding. In many states, the patient or the patient's legal guardian holds the privilege in patient–practitioner communication. Privileged communication is not subject to disclosure except under conditions prescribed by law or regulation; in other words, practitioners should not disclose patient information unless the right to confidentiality is waived by the patient or where mandated or permitted by law, as discussed above. Practitioners should be aware of their state's specific laws regarding provider–patient privilege. Ethical practitioners should discuss the limits of confidentiality with patients, describing any specific applicable exceptions, at the outset of a professional relationship.

When child, elder, or dependent-adult abuse is suspected, most states require reporting to a government agency, which necessitates breaking confidentiality. Practitioners should stay current in their detailed knowledge of their state's current laws regarding reporting of abuse. For example, some states require that a practitioner report suspected abuse of an individual even if the practitioner knows that another professional has already made a report on that patient. In addition, mental-health professionals are typically required by law to break confidentiality, if necessary, in order to intervene when there is clear and imminent danger posed by patients to themselves or others. Furthermore, health care providers may be required by a court order to disclose certain patient information.

Most states permit or require health care providers to breach confidentiality in order to protect patients from harming themselves and to warn or protect other persons threatened by them; these practices are required to implement the moral principle of compassion toward the suicidal patient and to implement the principles of compassion and fairness to persons threatened by a patient. With regard to suicidal patients specifically, it is standard to consider the least intrusive protective measures necessary to ensure patient safety. Protective measures may include contacting a patient's family members, even if the patient does not agree, or arranging for the potential involuntary psychiatric hospitalization of a patient for a period of stabilization and treatment. As indicated above, arranging for involuntary psychiatric hospitalization should be done judiciously and within the purview of state law. With regard to threatened dangerous behavior toward others, a practitioner may have the duty to notify law enforcement authorities and warn identified potential victims. Predicting future dangerousness is not an exact science, and health care providers cannot be expected to perfectly predict violence. However, in such situations, providers should be able to show that they exercised reasonable professional judgment in comparison with their peers. Thus, timely consultation with other professionals can be a highly valuable risk-management strategy. Obviously, direct threats of violence should be taken very seriously and should likely trigger a warning. It is also very important to promptly create a written clinical record with careful documentation of any reasoning behind clinical decisions and related actions, including written documentation of the content of conversations with colleagues.

Health Insurance Portability and Accountability Act

The Health Insurance Portability and Accountability Act (HIPAA) was passed by Congress in 1996 to promote standardization and efficiency in the health care industry. This promotion involves the electronic transmission of health information for facilitating communication. In addition, the act was intended to give patients more rights and control over their health information by limiting its use and requiring providers to establish policies and procedures to protect the security of health information. All health care providers are ethically and legally obliged to be familiar with the specific requirements of HIPAA, which are typically taught at specific training sessions that providers are required to attend by their health care institution employers.

The Duty to Warn and/or Protect

The case of *Tarasoff v. Regents of the University of California* brought into sharp focus the issue of warning a potential victim of one's patient of threats made by the patient against the individual, or taking steps to prevent such threats from being carried out (Ewing & McCann, 2006). Jurisdictions vary considerably in whether or not they impose a "Tarasoff Duty" on clinicians, and if so, precisely under what circumstances such a duty attaches, or how it might be satisfied. From a practical perspective, a thorough clinical risk assessment is vital. For outpatients deemed to be at imminent risk of harm to others, hospitalization is usually necessary and also sufficient to satisfy such requirements in most instances. Inpatients should be stabilized to the point that they no longer pose a threat to identified others prior to discharge. A written or verbal warning may be indicated in circumstances where an outpatient is deemed imminently dangerous to another individual but cannot be restrained in a timely fashion. All warnings must involve disclosure of the minimal amount of confidential information necessary to convey the concern and must be carefully documented in the patient's medical record, including a clear rationale for having issued the warning.

Malpractice

Malpractice suits against mental-health professionals were considered rare historically but have become increasingly frequent. Some common reasons for malpractice lawsuits against psychiatrists include allegations of failure to adequately evaluate and manage risk of suicidal behavior or violence, to adequately monitor and manage adverse effects from psychopharmacological agents, to appropriately diagnose or treat a psychiatric disorder, and to appropriately supervise trainees (e.g., residents or medical students). In order for an individual to successfully bring a suit of malpractice against a clinician, all the following elements must be established: (1) There must have been a *duty* to provide care to the plaintiff. Such duty may sometimes be deemed to have been established by the giving of advice in informal settings. (2) There must have been a *dereliction* of such duty by failure to follow the established standard of care, that is, providing care less than that expected from ordinary practitioners in the specialty. Some jurisdictions are now requiring that a physician provide that level of care that is expected from a competent (rather than average) practitioner in the community, thereby raising the standard of care. (3) The plaintiff must have developed *damage*, or an adverse event or outcome. (4) There must be a *direct* relationship between the alleged negligence and the occurrence of harm to the plaintiff. This fourth point is often the most difficult element of malpractice to establish due to the potential contribution of other factors.

All health care providers are at risk for being accused of, and/or sued for, malpractice and should carry adequate professional liability insurance. Measures that may reduce the risk of malpractice suits include engaging patients in the decision-making process to the extent possible; obtaining second opinions and consultations when dealing with complex issues or those that involve subspecialty expertise; maintaining a positive therapeutic relationship with patients and their families and attempting to address negative outcomes within the therapeutic relationship when appropriate; and documenting patient encounters completely, precisely, and in a timely fashion. Fostering positive therapeutic relationships, of which open communication and attention and sensitivity to patients and their behavior are characteristic, generally reduces risk of being sued by recipients of services. Patients are generally hesitant to fault the practitioner who consistently communicates well and applies the moral principles of fairness, integrity, and compassion in mental-health care. Practicing ethically and responsibly is basic to more specific risk-management strategies. Professional organizations can provide information regarding risk-management strategies; continuing education courses can be taken in risk management and are required by some state licensing boards as a condition of license renewal.

Expert Witness (Consultation to the Court)

Distinct from the legal regulation of clinical practice is an area of practice involving the application of psychopathological knowledge in legal contexts, either criminal or civil, to answer specific legal questions. This constitutes "forensic psychiatry" or "forensic psychology" defined in its strictest sense. Questions requiring expertise in psychopathology frequently arise in both the criminal and civil arenas of law. Attorneys, judges, insurance companies and other administrative bodies frequently solicit expert opinions, in the form of a written report and/or oral testimony, to resolve legal conflicts. Clinicians who participate in such proceedings do so at their own discretion, based on interest, training, and certification.

> Participation in such activities involves adherence to certain principles that are distinct from clinical practice. For example, the opinions that result from such examinations are not typically confidential to the same degree as other clinical records are, since they are generated for the purpose of informing a specified individual or agency. It is essential for the "examinee" to understand this limitation to confidentiality in advance. The examinee must also understand that participation in such examinations will not result in the creation of a typical clinician–patient relationship, i.e., the clinician performing the examination functions as an agent of the individual or organization that is retaining his or her services rather than an advocate for the examinee, as would be expected in a typical diagnostic or therapeutic rela-

tionship. It stems from this arrangement that examinees must understand that the opinions generated may not necessarily be "helpful" to their case, and may result in punishment, denial of benefits, or a finding of liability. In order to avoid ethical dilemmas and conflict of interest issues, it is essential that a treating clinician not render forensic opinions with regard to his or her own patient. It is of paramount importance that clinicians seeking to undertake forensic examinations always strive for objectivity to the extent possible and not fall prey to the biases and coercive forces that are inherent in working in an adversarial system of justice.

An important starting point in conducting any forensic examination involving mental illness is to fully understand and delineate the question(s) that the clinician is being asked to answer. It is important that the clinicians have expertise and experience in the issue that is being addressed, and resist the tendency to address issues that fall beyond their area of clinical expertise, or to answer questions that are primarily legal rather than clinical. Commonly requested forensic evaluations in criminal court include evaluations of *competency to stand trial*, of a defendant's mental state at the time of the offense to assist in determining whether the defendant should be held *criminally responsible* for the alleged offense, and of other competencies, such as competency to confess or competency to be sentenced or executed. Commonly requested forensic evaluations in civil contexts include evaluations of psychiatric disability in a variety of contexts (e.g., worker's compensation benefits, Social Security Disability or private insurance), of a plaintiff in a personal injury lawsuit where emotional harm or psychic damages have been alleged, and of civil competencies such as testamentary capacity, ability to manage funds, or need for a guardian of person.

Competency to Stand Trial

Competency to stand trial (CST) evaluations are among the most commonly requested forensic psychiatric and psychological evaluations in criminal court. The case of *Dusky v. United States* (1960) first provided criteria for competency to stand trial, describing them as "whether he [the defendant] has sufficient present ability to consult with his lawyer with a reasonable degree of rational understanding and whether he has a rational as well as factual understanding of the proceedings against him." Miller (2003) has described the necessary capacities as including a cognitive element (i.e., the capacity to comprehend relevant legal concepts and procedures) and a volitional element (i.e., the capacity to utilize information appropriately in one's own defense and to function effectively in the legal environment). To try an individual who does not have such capabilities deprives the defendant of "due process of law" and casts doubt on the fairness of the criminal justice system. Mental illnesses such as psychotic disorders or intellectual disability may interfere with such capacities, rendering the defendant incompetent to stand trial. Clinicians (usually a psychiatrist or psychologist), in addition to evaluating such competencies, may be required to opine on whether the condition underlying such incompetency is treatable, i.e., whether the individual can be "restored" to competency. Evaluations of CST are "here and now" functional evaluations, based on the defendant's current abilities. It follows that CST may change with time.

Criminal Responsibility/Insanity Defense

In most states criminal defendants may mount a defense to the effect that they were mentally ill at the time of an alleged crime and hence should not be held accountable for their actions. The concept of excusing criminal behavior on the basis of mental illness has a long historical tradition in English case law, with a variety of definitions or "tests of legal insanity" having applied over the centuries. The current definition of legal insanity in most U.S. jurisdictions stems, in part or in whole, from the famous *McNaughten* case. Broadly speaking, most insanity tests require the individual to have suffered from a serious mental disorder or intellectual disability that results in the satisfaction of one or both of two "prongs" of insanity: (1) a *cognitive* element—i.e., inability to understand or appreciate the nature of the act committed, or an inability to recognize that the act was wrong, either from a legal or a moral viewpoint; and (2) a *volitional* element—i.e., an inability to control one's behavior or conform one's behavior to what is legally or morally correct. The outcome of the evaluation will depend in large part on the specific definition of legal insanity that is applicable in the jurisdiction where the crime occurred. Unlike an evaluation of CST, an evaluation of criminal responsibility is a retrospective evaluation. The evaluator must utilize multiple sources of data (e.g., defendant interview, review of witness accounts and transcripts, police reports, medical and mental-health records) to reconstruct the defendant's mental state at the time of the crime and then reach conclusions relevant to the applicable legal criteria. An actual finding of whether or not the defendant was sane at the time of the crime is a legal determination that is made by the trier of fact (judge or jury), based in part upon a written report or oral testimony provided by the mental-health expert.

Evaluation of Psychiatric Disability

Individuals with psychiatric disorders may, in some instances, be rendered unable to perform one or more work-related functions that may impair their ability to work. In this regard it is important to recognize the difference between the concepts of impairment (i.e., the loss of a certain body part or bodily function) and disability (i.e., the inability of an impaired individual to meet certain social or occupational demands). For example, a depressed individual may suffer from low motivation and concentration and is hence impaired—unable to adequately focus on complicated graphics—which in turn disables him from his usual occupation that requires such ability.

The definition of disability varies considerably depending upon the agency granting disability benefits. The Social Security Administration requires that the individual be unable to engage in any "substantial gainful occupation," whereas a private insurance company may require only that the individual be unable to perform his or her usual occupation. Exclusions may exist with regard to conditions that are eligible for consideration; for example, worker's compensation carriers typically require that the disabling condition have developed in the course of work.

The role of a forensic psychiatrist or psychologist is to understand the relevant definition of disability and then perform a detailed evaluation focusing not only on symptoms and diagnostic issues but also on the specific functions that the individual is, or is not, able to perform. Such requests often include questions about recommended treatment, prognosis for recovery, and whether or not the individual has reached the point of "maximum medical improvement" (MMI)—that is, the point at which the impairment is well stabilized such that no further improvement can be expected over the next year, even with additional treatment.

Evaluation of Emotional Harm in Personal Injury Litigation

Forensic psychiatrists and psychologists are often called upon to render expert opinions in the course of personal injury litigation in cases where emotional or psychological harm is alleged. Questions posed for the examining clinician include whether or not the plaintiff suffers from a mental disorder or condition, the causal link of such a disorder to the alleged act or negligence that is the focus of the suit, and the degree of impairment that has resulted (used in the evaluation of damages or monetary compensation that the plaintiff will be awarded).

Documentation

Thorough and timely documentation of patient encounters is an essential practice in medicine and important for purposes of clinical care as well as risk reduction. The actual format utilized for documentation may vary depending upon institutional requirements (e.g., availability of electronic medical records) and personal style. However, attention to *timeliness, completeness, clarity, brevity,* and *professionalism* is sure to improve documentation across practice settings.

Timeliness. A record of an encounter should be created as soon as is reasonably possible following the patient contact or other clinical event. Records of high-risk situations must be created immediately after adequate interventions have been made. Progress notes and other documentation may be required by law, by managed-care companies, and by other third parties. Ethically, it is standard practice to keep accurate and timely records of all mental-health assessment, treatment interventions, and patient contacts.

Completeness. The components of a medical note will vary depending upon the nature of the encounter. For office visits, date and time of visit, duration of visit, encounter code and diagnostic code (if applicable), a description of relevant history, objective findings, investigational results (if appropriate), current medications, comorbid conditions, a summary impression, and proposed plan should all be included. Emergency visits or inpatient encounters may also need to include an expanded section on risk assessment. If collateral contacts are made, these should be described.

> The minimum information typically described by law to be contained in mental-health records includes the following: patient identifying information, signed informed consent for treatment, releases of information obtained, types of services provided, precise times and dates of appointments made and kept, chief complaints and pertinent history, intake sheet, objective findings from the most recent physical examination, documentation of referrals for health care, reports of diagnostic procedures and tests, determined diagnosis, prognosis and significant continuing problems or conditions, treatment plans with specific target problems and goals, signed and dated progress notes, and termination and discharge summaries (Corey, Corey, & Callahan 2007, p. 172). Progress notes typically address categories of information such as current symptoms and changes in symptom patterns, patient functional status, social support resources and utilization of social support, response to treatment, treatment recommendations, medication changes with clear justifica-

tion, homework or assignments, use of alternative or complementary treatments, referral information, diagnosis, and treatment plan.

Clarity. It is essential to clearly describe the basis of diagnoses and conclusions and the reasons that certain interventions were made. In many instances, it is equally important to include which other interventions were considered and why they were not deemed to be necessary. When documenting assessment and treatment, it is important that written records be legible, descriptive, and objective. The *Clinician's Thesaurus* (2010) by Edward Zuckerman is a helpful resource for finding appropriate language for use in mental health care documentation.

Brevity. While describing one's thinking and reasoning is of paramount importance, it is equally important to keep the narrative succinct. It is reasonable to acknowledge uncertainty when this exists, while avoiding undue conjecture.

Professionalism. Describe clinical impressions based upon historical or objective facts, without resorting to the use of pejorative labels, expressing provider frustration, or blaming the patient. It is prudent to remember that the created record is permanent and assume that it will eventually be available to the patient for review. The information in health care records is legally accessible by patients in most, if not all, states and it is good practice to assist patients in understanding any record that they will review. Explaining diagnostic classifications as representing clusters of behaviors or symptoms may be especially helpful in decreasing confusion and errors in patient interpretation of recorded information. Records may also be introduced as evidence in criminal and civil legal proceedings, including malpractice litigation. Other professionals involved with the patient currently or in the future may read the clinical record. Keeping accurate records assists practitioners in organizing clinical information, monitoring progress, and communicating treatment.

Some third-party payers allow for an accessible record of essential clinical information, while permitting a second set of psychotherapy process notes kept in a separate file that is kept confidential from the third party. But it is the health care provider's responsibility to be aware of all legal and third-party policies (which can change frequently) regarding psychotherapy process notes. Some providers elect to omit any specific reference to especially sensitive or potentially damaging clinical information from all of their written records and write notes in more general diagnostic terms. This approach to documentation is guided by the fear of discovery by other parties (confidentiality concerns with the potential for misuse) or by the patient who accesses the record (potential misinterpretation and therapeutic harm).

Practitioners should consult their specialty's code of ethics and relevant law regarding the time periods required for retention of records and when it is permissible to destroy old health care records. Practitioners must also consult ethical code and law when planning for the safekeeping and handling of health care records in the event of provider incapacitation or death.

Emergency Medical Treatment and Labor Act

In 1986 Congress enacted the Emergency Medical Treatment and Labor Act (EMTALA). This act requires most hospital emergency departments and ambulance services (all that accept payment from the U.S. Department of Health and Human Services Centers for Medicare and Medicaid Services under the Medicare program) to provide emergency treatment, as needed, to any and all persons regardless of insurance coverage, ability to pay, citizenship, or legal status. Thus, EMTALA essentially enforces the moral principle of compassion. Such hospitals must perform a medical screening examination to determine whether an emergency medical condition is present for all individuals requesting emergency care. Examination and treatment cannot be delayed because of any insurance or payment issues. In addition, those for whom emergency care is provided must be treated until the condition is resolved or stabilized. Furthermore, if the hospital cannot treat the condition, the hospital must transfer the patient to another hospital that has the ability to treat the condition. According to the nondiscrimination clause in EMTALA, this second hospital is required to accept the patient if it has the specialized capability and capacity.

The greatest impact of EMTALA is that everyone in need of urgent medical care is now legally guaranteed to receive it. Therefore, all mental-health care providers should recognize that any patient in need of urgent evaluation for immediate psychiatric hospitalization can be transported by their family members or ambulance to the nearest hospital emergency room where they will receive such an evaluation and care, if necessary, regardless of ability to pay for that service. However, there are criticisms (generally based on the moral principle of fairness) ranging from arguments that EMTALA is incomplete to complaints regarding cost pressures on hospitals and related financial ramifications.

ETHICAL AND CULTURAL ISSUES

Ethics refers to moral principles that are embraced and used to guide behavior. In Western societies there is a general consensus that a decision or action is ethical if it simultaneously implements the universal moral principles of *integrity, compassion,* and *fairness.* These principles underlie the core ethics of the mental-health professional: *nonmaleficence* ("do no harm"), *beneficence* ("best interest" of the patient), *justice* (equal treatment), and *autonomy* (self-determination). Ultimately based on these moral principles and core values, codes of ethics delineating required ideal standards for the conduct of practitioners are adopted by organizations that regulate health care professions. Most of these codes and other resources on this subject can be accessed through the website www.centerforethicalpractice.org.

Managed Care

With the expectation of improving their incomes, unlicensed mental-health professionals in the mid-1970s strongly lobbied to obtain state licensure in order to become eligible for third-party reimbursement. However, mental-health practitioners were surprised when third-party payment sources began closely regulating mental-health care practices through managed care in order to control rising costs. The benefit of managed care has been that more people have access to mental-health care benefits. In addition, having strict standards for practicing mental-health treatment protects the public. The disadvantage is that practitioners have less control over decision-making in the provision of services. Treatment decisions may be more related to financial concerns than to the actual quality of care.

Having a third party involved in the therapeutic relationship obviously raises ethical questions. For example, diagnoses must "qualify" for third-party payment, and the payer may even impose requirements regarding the nature and amount of treatment that fits the given diagnosis. Thus, practitioners may find themselves in the position of trying to fit presenting problems into a diagnosis that will elicit reimbursement and then develop a treatment plan that fits, according to the managed-care company, with this diagnosis. Of course, this third-party control over treatment factors leads to specific concerns regarding the termination of treatment. In short, providers are ethically bound not to abandon their patients (the principle of compassion) and are responsible for providing competent care (the principle of integrity), yet practitioners may be working under the treatment limitations imposed by managed care (often a violation of the principle of fairness).

Additional concerns that extend from third-party involvement in the therapeutic relationship pertain to confidentiality and informed consent. As discussed previously, there are important limitations to confidentiality that involve ensuring the safety of the patient and others with whom the patient is involved. In addition, patients are able to consent to the release of their confidential clinical information in specific ways for the purpose of coordination of treatment between providers. However, the managed-care environment has greatly impacted the confidentiality rights of consumers of health care, sometimes without consumers' full realization, requiring providers to release patient information in order for mental-health services to be authorized and reimbursed. With the advent of managed care, informed consent, which involves fully informing patients about pertinent clinical issues to enable them to make informed decisions about their treatment choice, must now also include information regarding the complicating role of the third party in the therapeutic relationship. And, because managed care requires that a diagnosis be assigned, patients should be informed that a diagnosis can become a permanent part of their medical history, possibly impacting future health and life insurance costs and eligibility and even employment opportunities. Obtaining fully informed consent from patients at the outset of mental-health services demonstrates respect for patient rights and acknowledges patients' autonomy in making health care decisions. When informed of the risks to confidentiality that accompany third-party reimbursement, some patients will elect to forfeit third-party payment benefits and pay for mental-health services themselves to maintain greater confidentiality; therefore, mental-health care providers do well in applying the moral principles of compassion and fairness by informing patients of this option and letting them consider the risk–benefit ratio of using their health insurance for a mental-health condition.

The managed-care environment of mental-health care creates challenges that must be appropriately managed by practitioners. In addition, this environment begs reflection regarding how to best educate mental-health consumers regarding their role in their own treatment and payment for mental-health care, because their choice of practitioner and the nature of the treatment received are strongly influenced by third-party payment sources. Providers may be burdened with the need to actively seek authorizations for their clinical services and for potential further treatment options necessitating referrals for their patients, often with no billable reimbursement for the professional time required by these duties.

At times, especially during occasions of patient crisis, practitioners acting ethically may choose to provide low- or no-cost services. Pro bono services, however, are not cost-free for the provider. Practitioners may also bear the burden of obtaining additional training in time-limited or brief treatment models. Federal regulations, laws, and insurance companies can create a dilemma for providers who are required by their profession's ethical code to provide pro bono services when needed, but simultaneously prohibited by law from charging patients differently (e.g., charging the indigent nothing, but others a fee) for the same mental-health service. In such a case, the law must be followed, while creatively and compassionately working out a way for the patient to receive the needed mental-health services. In serving indigent patients, providers need to be aware of federal third parties and insurance company policies that may make it illegal or impermissible to tell patients that they will waive deductible or co-pays that third parties require be billed to them. In such cases, providers may maintain integrity in following the law together with their compassion for their patients by choosing not to send indigent patients' unpaid accounts to collection. However, to stay within the law, providers cannot tell the patients in such cases that they do not enforce payment of billed co-payments.

Dual/Multiple Relationships

The concept of dual or multiple relationships refers to simultaneously serving two masters. Such double agency exists when having more than one role with a person, such as when someone serves as both psychotherapist and professor for a graduate student. The concept may also refer to having a relationship or role with an individual who is close to a patient, such as a parent, or having a patient's spouse as a business partner, or dating a patient's relative. Generally, avoiding dual or multiple relationships is necessary for maintaining the integrity of the professional mental-health care relationship.

Small rural communities tend to be especially challenging with regard to preventing multiple relationships and handling them when they inevitably occur. When practicing in small communities, it is important to address concerns up front and on an ongoing basis with patients. It is likely to be helpful to directly acknowledge and discuss with patients in advance any known contacts that might occur outside the health care relationship. Indeed, it may be helpful when working in any practice environment to discuss with patients general guidelines for handling spontaneous contacts, should they occur. For example, a practitioner and patient might decide that if an unplanned contact occurs, the practitioner will not acknowledge the patient unless first approached by the patient. This agreement respects the privacy of the patient and the patient's social boundaries. A patient may want to introduce his or her spouse, but choose not to acknowledge the presence of a therapy relationship when in the company of a friend or business partner.

Of course, it is important to realize that the acceptability and even therapeutic value of multiple relationships may vary between cultures and situations. Thus, practitioners are urged to learn about the unique cultures and individuals with whom they work in order to provide the most ethical and therapeutic care possible. In addition, community counseling, which emphasizes the use of various community resources to assist patients, may require helpers to balance multiple professional roles.

Mental-health care providers should be aware that social contact of any kind with a patient may impact the therapeutic relationship. Thus, the practitioner must be open to exploring this impact and must be responsible for initiating such discussion, when appropriate, during the treatment process. Of course, social contact with a patient can vary from running into a patient at the grocery store to interacting for business purposes to attending social functions in common to having a romantic relationship.

Pursuing a business partner relationship of any kind with a current or former patient is not considered ethical by codes of ethics and by many states' professional regulations, and could result in disciplinary action by the professional licensing board. Sexual relationships with either current or former patients are clearly unethical and also illegal in most states. Although less clear than with regard to sexual relationships, developing friendships with patients or taking friends on as patients also raises ethical and clinical concerns, threatening the integrity of the therapeutic relationship. For this reason, many practitioners wisely avoid mixing friendship with mental-health care provision. In addition, complications are likely to occur when bartering for services takes place. Ethical practitioners rarely accept bartering agreements and only under certain extraordinary circumstances and with much forethought. Remember, it is the responsibility of the provider of mental-health care services to maintain appropriate professional boundaries regardless of patient behavior. Situations such as those noted above have the potential to create problems for both patient and provider, and mental-health care providers are generally wise to avoid them when possible. Keeping professional boundaries in health care relationships helps practitioners maintain objectivity and good judgment. This stance protects patients and keeps the proper focus of the relationship on treatment issues.

When avoidance of a dual role is not possible or the professional finds that a dual role has arisen unexpectedly, it is important to manage the situation and relationships with great care, attempting to protect the patient from harm. There is an inherent power differential in the health care relationship, and the patient's well-being must be of primary importance to ensure that exploitation does not occur. It is wise to seek peer consultation or supervision when grappling with ethical concerns, especially those involving dual/multiple relationships.

Conflicts of interest ("dual agency") arise when the practitioner's other relationships create a situation where his or her allegiance is divided and may conflict with the patient's best care. For example, as discussed above, a clinician may work for a managed-care company whose policies are designed to reduce services. Another example might be a clinician initiating involuntary commitment to a psychiatric unit in a hospital for which she works. Many such conflicts present themselves on a regular basis in clinical practice. The onus is upon clinicians to ensure that patient care is not compromised and to avoid relationships that would jeopardize their integrity in this regard.

Although it is often necessary to individualize treatment, professional boundaries should be carefully maintained. For instance, *boundary crossings* may occur when personal information is disclosed after carefully weighing the risks, benefits, and alternatives to achieve the desired therapeutic goal. The motivation for such a disclosure must be effective treatment versus any personal gain for the clinician. At no time should the patient–therapist relationship serve as a means for meeting the psychological, social, or physical needs or desires of the clinician. These are clearly *boundary violations* that exploit patients and are never appropriate.

Multiculturalism and Spirituality in Ethical Care

Rooted in the moral principles of fairness and compassion, professional codes of ethics require mental-health providers to be sensitive to cultural, religious, and spiritual issues important to their patients (Sperry, 2007). The multicultural world in which we live adds complexity for health care professionals who are trying to practice in an ethical manner. Applying the commonly known basic ethical dictums in health care fields, "First, do no harm" (nonmaleficence), "Promote good" (beneficence), and "equal treatment" (justice), is not as simple as it might initially seem. An intervention that would "do no harm" and "promote good" for an individual from one cultural background might harm or create the possibility for harm for a person from another culture. For example, encouraging an Anglo person from middle-class America to stop worrying so much about what others think of him or her might be helpful within the context of treatment. However, this "encouragement" might have a much different impact on an Asian-American individual who values community more highly than independence. To take this example a step further, should the Asian-American patient really take this suggestion to heart and begin to make changes based on it, persons in his or her social support system may not respond very positively to these changes. Because social support is widely known to be a cornerstone of good mental health, this intervention might not be as helpful as intended. This brief example is but one illustration of the complexity of health care intervention in a pluralistic world. Practitioners must be knowledgeable regarding the general cultural characteristics of the populations with which they work, while closely attending to their patients in order to understand them as unique individuals.

> Culture comprises the patterns and practices of human behavior which reflect the values, standards, customs, and roles within a societal grouping. The culture pervades family life, academics, politics, economics, and religion. Ethnicity is a person's basic identity in relation to other human groups. It is associated with the culture of origin (often the minority culture) as opposed to the cultural context (majority culture). Individuals carry the values, traditions, assumptions, and worldview transmitted over generations within their ethnic group along with the concurrent and often competing perspective of the dominant cultural context. Acculturation is the process by which a cultural subgroup adopts new behaviors and attitudes because of exposure to practices of a different dominant group.
>
> An investigation of a person's culture will help make the behavior understandable and will explain relationships. The competent clinician investigates a patient's culture in order to accurately diagnose and formulate the present illness and choose effective treatment. Formulation should include an overall cultural assessment that includes the patient's cultural identity, a cultural explanation of the signs and symptoms, and cultural factors related to the psychosocial environment. The clinician may use Kluckhohn's Value Orientation Theory to define a patient's culture according to how it solves the dimensions of time, space, activity, relationships among people, man–nature relationships, and the basic nature of humans (Kluckholn & Strodbeck, 1961).

As required by the principles of fairness and compassion, ethical healthcare professionals will honor and protect patients' civil rights to make their own decisions regarding their therapeutic goals; and patients' goals will differ according to culture, subculture, or value system. As long as patients' treatment goals are within the law, do not threaten harm to self or others, and are both clinically reasonable and achievable, the health care professional must work in accordance with patients' goals.

Science and religion both strongly influence worldview (*Weltanschauung*) and have been intertwined throughout history. Prior to the 1800s, Judeo-Christian doctrine provided the most common framework for interpreting and perceiving reality in Western culture. As the scientific method gained prominence as the standard for study even outside the natural sciences, science and religion were increasingly viewed as separate entities. Religion was relegated to the private lives of individuals. Modern psychology seemed to bring about a parallel internal split within the Western individual between the psychological and spiritual aspects of the self. Paradoxically, as public and private life with regard to science and religion became increasingly separate, 20th-century technological advances placed diverse peoples with diverse worldviews increasingly in contact. Perhaps this increased exposure to different others moved the evolution of thought toward the postmodern realization that an individual's perspective impacts his or her perception of reality. Indeed, the lenses through which individuals view and understand themselves and their worlds became center-stage.

Related to these changes came an increased focus on multicultural concerns and contextual factors in the application of psychology. Science realized that healing and illness occur and are perceived through the internal and external contexts of the individual. One such context is religious/spiritual experience. Sperry (2007) noted the recent new practice of incorporating spirituality into the therapeutic realm as adjunctive therapy or as a strengths-based resource. Clinicians and patients may share meaningful spiritual dialogue despite differences in their personal spiritual choices. Common elements for connection include such concepts as meaning, mindfulness, morality, and community. There are therapists who consider spirituality as the foundation for clinical practice and expand their understanding through a biopsychosociospiritual perspective (e.g., Pargament, 2007).

Along with these advances, modern medicine employed new technologies that have vastly increased knowledge in neuropsychiatry. There had always been debate regarding the relationship between body and mind, and this new knowledge seemed to "weigh in" on the monistic belief that all reality is material. The other side of this debate, dualism, purports that mind and matter substantively differ. But, even if the mental-health care provider is a monist, believing that mind emerges out of matter, one cannot ignore the importance of the patient's perception regarding spirituality or religion. For example, in the United States, empirical studies indicate that a minority of mental-health care providers report theistic beliefs, whereas the majority of the nation's population affirms belief in God (94%), in the deity of Jesus Christ, and in answered prayer (Steere, 1997). Ethical clinical practice respects the spiritual convictions of the patient and refrains from denigrating or undermining the patient's spiritual commitments. Sperry (2007) makes the case that the ethically required process of incorporating sensitivity to the significance of a patient's spirituality in mental-health care needs to involve a spiritual assessment. While not a standardized protocol, the following four questions are quite useful in eliciting key information (Koenig & Pritchett, 1998): (1) Is religion or spirituality important to you? (2) Do your religious or spiritual beliefs influence the way you look at your problems and the way you think about your health? (3) Are you part of a religious or spiritual community? (4) Would you like me to address your religious or spiritual beliefs and practices with you? When patients express reluctance or opposition to receiving mental health services from a clinician who does not share their cultural identity and/or religious beliefs, the ethical clinician will attempt referral to a provider who shares the patient's worldview and/or cultural perspective.

It is incumbent upon treatment professionals to explore and clarify their own values, as it is now widely accepted that these will impact the therapeutic relationship and work. Sue and Sue outline the moral and professional responsibility of mental-health care professionals to develop (1) increased awareness and handling of the biases, stereotypes, and assumptions that are elemental in their work; (2) increased awareness of cultural differences in values and world-view; and (3) appropriate, diversity-sensitive intervention strategies (as cited in Corey et al., 2007).

Any one professional cannot be expected to work well with all patients. Yet, it seems important that practitioners view persons holistically and understand mental illness in a multidimensional and contextual fashion. Multiple components, including psychological, social, biological, and spiritual factors, influence the definition of, development of, maintenance of, and recovery from mental illness. Influencing these factors are key elements of diversity such as gender, age, socioeconomic status, and sexual, cultural, race/ethnic, and religious/spiritual identities. Because mental illness does not occur in a vacuum, interventions that are insensitive to diversity issues may be unhelpful, toxic, or oppressive. Corey et al. (2007) implore counselors not to impose their own personal value system on mental-health care consumers "as the criteria for how all patients should think and act." They later distinguish between having strong convictions and imposing those convictions on others.

Though the prevalence of mental illness around the world suggests that all cultures, races, and societies are vulnerable, mental-health care services have not been equally accessible to all in need. Persons from minority groups tend to underutilize mental-health care services and often terminate services early. In many of these cases the barrier is not access but rather educational and cultural factors. Regardless, justice—a basic ethical value—may not be served in the allocation of scarce or limited resources in such situations.

Ethics of Nontraditional Treatment

In general, the principle of integrity, the professional codes of ethics, and even governmental regulations require that clinical interventions offered by the practitioner be within the standards of care for the profession, conforming to conventional clinical procedures. Public interest in nonconventional treatments in mental-health care has been increasing since the 1990s. The integration of conventional and nonconventional mental-health care is not simple, yet it seems to be increasingly in demand as consumers of mental-health care become aware of and seek more treatment options and may have preferences and perspectives that differ from those of the health care providers. Nonconventional mental-health treatments themselves—arising from non-Western and native healing traditions—are diverse, ranging from self-healing prayer, meditation, yoga, and other "centering" exercises, to the use of herbs for the treatment of anxiety or depressed mood to treatments based in Chinese medicine. Perhaps the increasingly global nature of our world (discussed above) is related to this rise in interest level, as people learn about practices common or known in other cultures. Lake et al. (2007) propose that this rise in interest is fueled by constraints that are placed on conventional treatments by biotechnological advances. The biomedical model of mental illness focused attention so greatly on the brain and nervous system as explaining all behavioral problems that other aspects of persons and mental illness were neglected. For example, compared to the shorter sessions with mental-health professionals approved by the managed-care environment, nonconventional practitioners tend to spend longer periods of time with their patients. Perhaps people are responding to the therapeutic nature of the practitioner–patient relationship itself.

Because current consumers of health care may seek treatments other than conventional methods based in Western health care or may obtain conventional *and* non-conventional treatments simultaneously, health care providers do well to become more familiar with nonconventional treatments. Today, health care practitioners are likely to encounter patients from diverse spiritual and ethnic traditions. It seems that relevant treatment would have to consider diversity factors that have been identified above as important in culturally sensitive mental-health care. Community workers need to be aware of cultural factors that may be instrumental in contributing to patients' problems or resources that might help alleviate or solve patients' problems; in many cultures individuals with problems are more likely to put their trust in traditional healers. For these reasons, counselors need to be aware of indigenous healing systems and be willing to work collaboratively with them when it is to the benefit of the patient. In addition, people often come together around spiritual and other diversity-related practices and activities; and social support is generally encouraged, as it widely accepted as a cornerstone of mental health. However, with the legitimate emphasis upon evidence-based practice, mental-health professionals have an ethical obligation to engage in the clinical research necessary to establish that they are doing no harm and, indeed, truly providing benefit with any nontraditional treatments. Also, there are times when clinicians must understand cultural factors and practices in order to effectively change them for patients' benefit.

The guidelines of the Federation of State Medical Boards (FSMB; 2002) recognize that persons seeking treatment have a right to explore any methods of their choosing. Yet, nonconventional treatments vary in cost and availability and the quality and quantity of research and clinical and anecdotal evidence backing them. Admittedly, some current conventional treatments were once considered nonconventional but later supported as efficacious by new evidence revealed through inquiry and well-designed investigations. FSMB guidelines recognize that a comprehensive discussion of the risks and benefits of all treatments is in the best interest of patients. Detailed documentation of such conversation is necessary and further guidelines regarding documentation related to integrative treatment are provided by the FSMB. Shared decision-making is one way of reducing liability. The FSMB has passed guidelines for practitioners who provide nonconventional treatments and for those who provide conventional treatments.

The Professional Person

Ethical professional judgment must simultaneously incorporate the universal moral principles of and *compassion, integrity,* and *fairness*; an ethical violation is likely if the mental-health practitioner leaves out any one of these three principles in making a decision about his or her professional conduct in any specific situation. However, it must be acknowledged that in trying to provide quality care that is in the best interest of the patient, no matter how much forethought and planning has taken place, mental-health care professionals will inevitably come across situations in which the appropriate ethical course of action is ambiguous at best. Consulting with colleagues during such times is invaluable. Thus, it is important to nurture ongoing connections with other mental-health care professionals.

In addition, practicing mental-health care can be emotionally taxing. Personal self-care and stress management skills are extremely important for practitioners. Furthermore, ethical professional helpers face the mixed emotional bag of ongoing self-exploration and personal development, in that being with patients triggers reactions, and working well with them requires self-awareness. For this reason, pursuing counseling or psychotherapy can be immensely helpful, both personally and professionally, for mental-health care providers. Change and growth are certainly challenging and can even be experienced as painful at times. Mental-health care professionals usually find their work to be both rewarding and stressful. Perhaps these are truly two sides of the same coin, as taking responsibility in relationships with others and with the self is the path leading to both.

References

Appelbaum, P.S., Lidz, C.W., & Meisel, A. (1987). *Informed consent: Legal theory and clinical practice*. New York: Oxford University Press.

Corey, G., Corey, M.S., & Callahan, P. (2007). *Issues and ethics in the helping professions*, 7th ed. Belmont, CA: Thomson Brooks/Cole.

Dusky v. United States. (1960). 362 US 402.

Ewing, C.P., & McCann, J.T. (Eds.). (2006). Prosenjit Poddar and Tatiana Tarasoff: Where the public peril begins. *Minds on trial: Great cases in law and psychology* (pp. 57–67). New York: Oxford University Press.

Federation of State Medical Boards. (2002). *Model guidelines for physician use of complementary and alternative therapies in medical practice*. Available at www.fsmb.org/pdf/2002 _grpol_ Complementary_Alternative_Therapies.pdf.

Gutheil, T.G., & Appelbaum, P.S. (2000). *Clinical handbook of psychiatry and the law*, 3rd ed. Philadelphia: Lippincott, Williams & Wilkins.

Hoge, S.K., Appelbaum, P.S., Lawlor, T., Beck, J.C., Litman, R., Greer, A., Gatheil, T.G., & Kaplan, E. (1990). A prospective, multicenter study of patients' refusal of antipsychotic medication. *Archives of General Psychiatry, 47*, 949–956.

Josephson, A.M., & Peteet, J.R. (2004). *Handbook of spirituality and worldview in clinical practice.* Washington, DC: American Psychiatric Publishing.

Kilgus, M.D., Pumariega, A.J., & Cuffe, S.P. (1995). Influence of race on diagnosis in adolescent psychiatric inpatients. *Journal of the American Academy of Child and Adolescent Psychiatry,* 34(1), 67–72.

Kluckhohn, F.R., & Strodtbeck, F.L. (1961). *Variations in value orientations.* Evanston, IL: Row, Peterson.

Koenig, H., & Pritchett, J. (1998). Religion and psychotherapy. In H. Koenig (Ed.), *Handbook of religion and mental health* (pp. 323–336). San Diego, CA: Academic Press.

Lake, J.H., & Spiegel, D. (2007). *Complementary and alternative treatments in mental health care.* Arlington, VA: American Psychiatric Association.

Miller, R.D. (2003). Criminal competence. In R. Rosner (Ed.), *Principles and practice of forensic psychiatry,* 2nd ed. (pp. 186–212). New York: Wiley.

Pargament, K.I. (2007). *Spiritually integrated psychotherapy: Understanding and addressing the sacred.* New York: Guilford.

Schwartz, H.I., & Mack, D.M. (2003). Informed consent and competency. In R. Rosner (Ed.), *Principles and practice of forensic psychiatry,* 2nd ed. (pp. 97–106). New York: Wiley.

Schwartz, H.I., & Roth, L.H. (1989). Informed consent and competency in psychiatric practice. In A. Tasman, R.E. Hales, & A.J. Frances (Eds.), *Review of psychiatry* (Vol. 8, pp. 409–431). Washington, DC: American Psychiatric Association.

Sperry, L. (2007). *The ethical and professional practice of counseling and psychotherapy.* Boston: Pearson Education.

Sperry, L., & Shafranske, E.P. (2005). *Spiritually oriented psychotherapy.* Washington DC: American Psychological Association

Steere, D. (1997). *Spiritual presence in psychotherapy: A guide for caregivers.* New York: Brunner/Mazel.

Swinton, J. (2001). *Spirituality and mental health care: Rediscovering a 'forgotten' dimension.* London: Jessica Kingsley Publishers

United Kingdom House of Lords Decisions. "Daniel M'Naghten's Case. May 26, June 19, 1843." British and Irish Legal Information Institute.

Zuckerman, E.L. (2010). *Clinician's thesaurus: The guidebook to conducting psychological interviews and psychological reports,* 7th ed. New York: Guilford.

9

Sample Case History:
Sherlock Holmes

In *The Seven-Per-Cent Solution*, Nicholas Meyer (1993) revealed that Sigmund Freud had evaluated Sherlock Holmes, yet not until now has Freud's initial writeup of the case come to light. Quite remarkably, Freud's presentation illustrated the standard approach used 100 years later!

IDENTIFYING INFORMATION

2 June 1891

The patient, Mr. Sherlock Holmes, is a 41-year-old, white, single, Protestant private detective, referred for cocaine misuse, depression, and bizarre behavior by his friend and colleague, Dr. John H. Watson. (*Informant*: Quotations are from the patient, while all other information, unless specified to the contrary, is from Dr. Watson, a reliable historian.)

CHIEF COMPLAINT

"I have applied all my will to banishing this [cocaine] habit and I have not been able to do so. . . . Once a man takes the first false step, his feet are set forever on the path to his destruction."

HISTORY OF PRESENT ILLNESS

The patient was apparently well until 24 April 1891, when late at night he snuck through the back door of Watson's home, appearing agitated, perspiring, gaunt, and pale. His eyes roved restlessly, but nothing seemed to register.

He started to close and bolt every shutter in the room, but suddenly stopped and began to pace until Watson persuaded him to sit. Holmes then launched into a rambling story that people with air guns were after him because he had penetrated the defenses of a Professor Moriarty, an ex–university professor of mathematics with "incredible mental prowess and hereditary diabolic tendencies." He insisted that Moriarty is the "Napoleon of crime, the organizer of half the evil in the world, and the center of a web of malefactors."

After an hour of standing, sitting, and pacing, Holmes's excited speech slowed into inarticulate mutterings, followed by whisperings. He slept for 2 hours and awoke with a blank stare. He did not recognize the name Moriarty when it was mentioned, but insisted that before he slept he was discussing an entirely different subject. Although earlier Watson had mentioned that his wife was away, Holmes requested that she be thanked for an excellent dinner (which had never been eaten).

The next day, Holmes would not admit Watson to his room, fearing he was Moriarty in disguise. Holmes questioned Watson about items that only Watson would have known. Once inside, Watson noted that there were new shutters of heavy iron and new locks on the doors. Holmes rambled on about Moriarty.

Later that day, Watson was approached by Professor Moriarty, who taught math at a small school but had privately tutored Holmes and his older brother Mycroft when both were children. Moriarty claimed that for the previous 5 weeks, Holmes had been harassing him by standing outside his house all night, dogging his footsteps, telling his superior that he was a master criminal, and sending him telegrams with warnings such as, "Your days are numbered." The professor was contemplating legal action to prevent this harassment, but was dissuaded from doing so by Watson's reassurances.

Mrs. Hudson, Holmes's landlady of many years, told Watson that around the end of February, Holmes began spending his days locked in his study-bedroom; he would barricade the doors, bolt the shutters, see no one, and refuse all meals. Late at night, he'd sneak out to spy on the professor.

Watson believes that Holmes has episodically snuffed cocaine for at least 5 years, but that only recently has this use escalated to where it totally impairs occupational and social functioning. He now intravenously injects himself with unknown (but increasing) amounts of a 7% solution of cocaine three to four times a day. Holmes only makes wild accusations about Moriarty during cocaine intoxication; at other times on cocaine Holmes becomes grandiose, saying such things as, "It is very dangerous for me to leave London for any length of time. It generates in the criminal classes an unhealthy excitement when my absence is discovered." He denies and conceals his cocaine use, but without his usual meticulousness and caution—syringes are left in open drawers, his shirt sleeves are rolled up, thereby exposing puncture marks, etc.

Two weeks ago, at Watson's insistence, Holmes stopped taking cocaine, and within a day, felt extreme despair, gloom, and boredom—extreme even for Holmes. He has stopped working on any other case, believing that no other criminal in Europe is clever enough to bother with. He has lost all interest in his usual activities, has no appetite, has shed 10 pounds, looks pale, and stays in bed most of the day. Watson has never heard Holmes speak of suicide. Being concerned about his worsening state, Dr. Watson, in collusion with Mycroft Holmes and Professor Moriarty, tricked the patient into leaving London for treatment here in Vienna.

DEVELOPMENTAL, PSYCHIATRIC, DRUG AND ALCOHOL, AND FAMILY HISTORY

Little is known about the patient's early childhood. His mother was involved in an illicit love affair, which Holmes's father discovered. He then shot her to death. Moriarty, then Holmes's tutor, was the one who told the patient the news. There is no information as to his behavior prior to, or immediately after, this catastrophe. Sherlock was an intelligent child and went through college with high grades. His income derives from family landholdings and a thriving detective practice.

Watson thinks that the patient's father died years ago, but knows nothing of the circumstances. The patient's sole living relative is his older brother Mycroft, who is also a bachelor. Watson claims that Mycroft is even more intelligent, reclusive, and eccentric than he, living in London's highly traditional Diogenes Club, the main qualifications for membership of which are shyness and misanthropy, and whose main distinction is that members' chairs are positioned back-to-back so that nobody speaks with another. Watson is unaware of any mental illness in the family.

Watson describes the patient as a "deeply private person, whose reclusivity reaches major proportions" at times and who behaves "as a 'thinking machine,' impassive, aloof, and austere and not in direct contact with the sordid realities of physical existence." Holmes once observed, "Watson, I am a brain." Nonetheless, Watson contends that underneath this bravado, Holmes is a deeply compassionate man who regards his emotions as interfering with his mental processes. He tries, Watson maintains, to suppress his emotions by indulging in intellectual pursuits, such as chemical experiments and violin improvisation for hours on end, or by practicing shooting at the walls of his room. Except for a brief attraction to Irene Adler, women have been conspicuously absent in the patient's life.

Watson considers Holmes to be an ill-mannered eccentric, who is easily bored when not confronted with an interesting problem to solve. Holmes confirmed this by saying, "I abhor the dull routine of existence, I loathe stagnation." On occasion, he becomes demoralized, sad, and hopeless; he lacks energy, sleeps 10–12 hours a day (normally he sleeps under 5 hours a day), socially isolates himself, and has lost interest in everything. These depressive periods occur once or twice a year, lasting from several days to weeks, but no longer than 2–3 months. Some of these periods end when Holmes gets a new and challenging case, some end for no apparent reason, and some because Holmes binges on cocaine for a week or two. When confronted with an interesting problem, he would stop using cocaine, but return to it when bored or depressed. Except for some prior experimentation with morphine injections, Holmes has not used any drug except cocaine.

MEDICAL HISTORY AND PHYSICAL EXAMINATION

Although a physical exam was not performed, the patient was observed to be malnourished, had dilated pupils, puncture marks on both arms, and a weak pulse.

MENTAL STATUS EXAMINATION

[Formal testing not performed.]
A. Behavior
  Appearance: Gaunt, sallow, malnourished, tired-looking, and appears to have lost weight. He continues to wear his only double-visored hat indoors.
  Activity: Enters office slowly, weak handshake, dry palms, and sits throughout the 80-minute consultation. His movements are a bit slow, although when speaking of Moriarty, he becomes fidgety and speaks with more animation.
  Attitude: Cooperative but generally lacking enthusiasm, averted gaze.
  Speech: Non-elaborative, i.e., says very little and only speaks when asked a direct question. His speech is hushed, moderately slow, but not slurred.

B. Sensorium

Consciousness: Alert.

Orientation: Knows the date, time, place, his name, Watson's name, and my name.

Memory: Excellent immediate, recent, and remote memory.

Attention: His mind seems to wander on occasion, but not while speaking.

C. *Emotion*: Patient says that he is despondent, has no interest in things, and that nothing brings him pleasure. His facies is glum, his general look, bored. His affect and mood are appropriate to what is said. There are no signs of anxiety. He denies suicidal or homicidal ideation, plan, or intent.

D. *Thought processes and content*: During the middle of the interview, he says that he thinks I am Moriarty in disguise, and that his brother and Watson have concocted a sinister plot to deliver him into the clutches of his enemies. Yet, when confronted, Holmes abandons this idea and apologizes. When asked if he still believes that Moriarty is a master criminal, he says he would rather not discuss the matter. Despite these apparently overvalued ideas, there is no evidence of actual delusions, ideas of reference, incoherence, phobias, obsessions, or compulsions. His thinking is goal-directed. He denies suicidal ideation.

Intelligence, information, and abstraction: Extremely high.

Insight: On confrontation, he admits to cocaine addiction and acknowledges that it is a serious problem.

Judgment: No apparent functional disturbance.

E. *Perception*: Although not specifically tested, there are no indications of a perceptual disturbance.

DIAGNOSIS

Axis I:	292.84	Cocaine abuse; substance-induced mood disorder
	292.0	Cocaine withdrawal (Provisional)
	296.30	Major depression (Provisional)
	296.80	Bipolar disorder (Provisional)
Axis II:	301.40	Obsessive–compulsive personality disorder (Provisional)
		Schizotypal personality disorder (Provisional)
		Paranoid personality disorder (Provisional)
Axis III:	None	
Axis IV:	Psychosocial and environmental problems: None elicited	
Axis V:	Global Assessment of Functioning (GAF)	

Current: GAF 35; impairment in reality testing and impairment in mood, judgment

Highest in past year: GAF 70; excellent work functioning, but few relationships

PROGNOSIS

Guarded prognosis for cocaine abuse, especially in view of (1) the disorder's natural course and the patient's (2) history of depressive symptoms, (3) current reluctance to abandon cocaine, and (4) characteristic unwillingness to place himself under the care of others.

BIOPSYCHOSOCIAL FORMULATION

The patient's heavy cocaine abuse produces grandiose, persecutory, and overvalued ideas and agitation. Holmes's particular choice of cocaine may partly serve to self-medicate an underlying depression (especially given his unusual intolerance of boredom), and partly due to his attraction to the sense of sharpened intellect cocaine affords. Stopping cocaine brings on, and/or aggravates, depressive symptoms, especially dysthymia, anhedonia, hypersomnia, psycho-motor retardation, and social isolation. Why the patient's use of cocaine sharply increased late last February remains unclear, since no precipitant has been identified.

The diagnosis of cocaine abuse is firm. In addition, in light of current information, the patient's symptoms strongly suggest a mood disorder, even though they fall short of meeting *DSM-5* or *ICD-10* diagnostic criteria. The episodes lasting 2 weeks after cocaine use strongly suggest a substance-induced mood disorder. Because his depressive symptoms are episodic, a dysthymic disorder is highly unlikely, whereas a major depression is a distinct possibility. Slightly more probable would be bipolar disorder, since his periods of enormous energy, even when not on cocaine, resemble hypomania, and his hypersomniac depressive intervals suggest bipolar depression. Because we lack information, a family history of mood disorder or substance abuse is impossible to make. In view of his longstanding meticulousness, perfectionism, excessive use of logic and intellect at the expense of emotion, and mild self-righteousness and suspiciousness, an obsessive–compulsive personality disorder should be considered. A schizotypal or paranoid personality disorder should also be considered. The patient's belief in having a "sixth sense" for criminals, his odd appearance, always wearing his special hat, and his frequent social anxiety support a schizotypal diagnosis. His brother Mycroft probably has a schizotypal personality disorder—a disorder that has strong genetic components. The patient's paranoid ideas and the social anxiety that tends toward paranoia support a paranoid diagnosis. However, the patient's ability to have close friends other than relatives, the appropriateness of being suspicious as a professional detective, and the variability of his overvalued ideas (which may fluctuate with cocaine use) argue against a diagnosis of schizotypal or paranoid personality disorder.

Psychodynamically, *repression*, supplemented by other defenses, appears to have played a major role in shaping Holmes's preoccupations and behavior. His *repressed* rage at his father for killing his mother seems to have been *displaced* onto Moriarty, the man who informed Holmes of the murder. *Introjecting* rage intended for his father may have compounded Holmes's depression. His repressed rage at his mother's unfaithfulness and her subsequent "abandonment" of young Sherlock may have contributed to his disinterest in women—his viewing them as untrustworthy, immoral, and undependable. By *sublimation*, Holmes excelled in detective work "to punish the wicked and see justice done."

PLAN

1. Withdrawal from cocaine.
2. Observation; look for hidden cocaine use.
3. Evaluation of mood and personality disorders.
4. Evaluate unconscious, or "automatic," thoughts for irrational beliefs that may trigger substance use and consider use of cognitive therapy to replace with "rational beliefs."
5. Consider use of behavioral techniques to reduce anxiety and tension, such as progressive muscle relaxation.
6. Encourage involvement with social supports—friends and family.
7. Encourage involvement in other pursuits that usually bring him pleasure, such as violin playing, attending Wagnerian opera, chasing criminals.
8. Next appointment: Tuesday, 16:00.

—Sigmund Freud, M.D.

Reference

Meyers, N. (1993). *The seven-per-cent solution*. New York: Norton.

MENTAL DISORDERS

Clinical Presentation
Cardinal Features (Diagnostic Criteria and Subtypes)
Epidemiology (Prevalence and Demographics)
Differential Diagnosis and Assessment Tools
Etiology and Pathogenesis (Causes and Correlations)
Clinical Course, Complications, and Comorbidities
Management, Treatment, and Prognosis

Information for each of the disorders is generally organized in the following chapters according to the outline above. It is intended to serve as an advance organizer for the reader. Not all of these sections are used as headings under each disorder but material is presented in this prescribed sequence.

10

Neurocognitive Disorders
(Delirium, Dementia, and Amnesia)

"Like trees, we grow old from the top," says Gore Vidal's Emperor Julian. Although most would agree, they're barking up the wrong tree: Dementia— or what is commonly called "senility"—is *not* inherent to aging, but a set of illnesses that strikes 15–20% of elderly Americans. To assume that with age certain disease states are natural and inevitable, stereotypes older adults and causes many curable dementias to go untreated. Dementia is most simply defined as "mental deterioration." While there are definite changes in cognition associated with aging, the development of serious impairment of cognitive function that results in loss of function, loss of self-care ability, emotional distress, and behavioral disturbance is not a normal result of aging alone.

Neurocognitive disorder is used in this chapter to describe what was formerly called *organic brain syndrome*. The term *organic* was dropped because it implies a false dichotomy between physical and mental disorders. The cardinal symptoms of neurocognitive disorders are memory loss, disorientation, poor judgment, confusion, and a general loss of intellectual functions. Also common are psychotic symptoms, including hallucinations, delusions (often paranoid), and illusions. Emotions such as depression, anxiety, fear, and irritability frequently occur, as do personality changes and behavioral disturbances, including agitation and aggression. The neurocognitive disorders are proven (or reasonably presumed) to be produced by medical, neurological, and/or biochemical alterations in the brain's structure or function. Overall, as our population lives longer the rates of dementia are increasing. The remaining lifetime risk of any dementia, including Alzheimer's disease (AD), for women who live to be at least age 55 is 21%. Thus more than one in five American women who live to be at least age 55 can expect to develop dementia in their remaining lifetime. Remaining lifetime risk of dementia for men is 14%, or one in seven men who live to be at least age 55. One in 5 women and 1 in 6 men who reached 65 years of age developed dementia.

This chapter examines three types of neurocognitive disorder: *delirium*, whose primary characteristic is a clouding of consciousness (a reduced awareness of the environment); *dementia*, whose chief feature is a deterioration of intellectual functions; and *amnestic disorders*, whose cardinal symptom is memory impairment.

Two other types of cognitive disorder, *intoxication* and *withdrawal*, are discussed in Chapter 11. Other disorders caused by a *medical condition* or *substance abuse*, such as psychotic disorder and anxiety and mood disorders, are discussed in related chapters.

DELIRIUM

Clinical Presentation

Delirium—from the Latin *delirare*, meaning to rave, to be crazy—is characterized by a clouding of consciousness, disorientation, and recent memory loss. These signs arise abruptly (e.g., from several hours to days), fluctuate wildly, often become worse at night or in the dark (i.e., "sundowning"), and rarely persist for more than a month. Often appearing frightened and agitated, patients with delirium frequently have illusions, hallucinations (in any of the five senses, but vision most commonly), incoherent speech, and disrupted sleep–wake cycles. The diagnostic criteria for delirium are listed in Table 10-1.

Disorientation to time usually comes first: At midnight, the patient may say it's noon or that the year is 1948. As delirium worsens, the patient becomes disoriented to place (e.g., thinks he's at a country club when he's sitting in his bedroom), and later to people (e.g., misidentifies her spouse). Immediate memory dwindles first, followed by intermediate (10-minute), and then remote memory. If either disorientation or recent memory loss is absent, the diagnosis of delirium is doubtful. Lucid intervals, with symptoms often becoming worse at night, are usually diagnostic of delirium. It is important to remember that unlike chronic dementias, delirium is sudden in onset, fluctuates with lucid intervals, and has a high frequency of visual hallucinations. Complicating this presentation, however, is the fact that anyone with limited "brain reserve capacity," such as those with dementia, is more predisposed to the occurrence of delirium.

TABLE 10-1
Diagnostic Criteria for Delirium

A. For a definite diagnosis, symptoms should be present *in each one* of the following areas:

1. **Impairment of consciousness and attention** (on a continuum from clouding to coma) with reduced ability to direct, focus, sustain, and shift attention.

2. **Global disturbance of cognition** (perceptual distortions, illusions and hallucinations—most often visual; impairment of abstract thinking and comprehension, with or without transient delusions, but typically with some degree of incoherence; impairment of immediate recall and of recent memory but with relatively intact remote memory; disorientation for time as well as, in more severe cases, for place and person);

*3. **Psychomotor disturbances** (hypo- or hyperactivity and unpredictable shifts from one to the other; increased reaction time; increased or decreased flow of speech; enhanced startle reaction);

*4. **Disturbance of the sleep-wake cycle** (insomnia or, in severe cases, total sleep loss or reversal of the sleep-wake cycle; daytime drowsiness; nocturnal worsening of symptoms; disturbing dreams or nightmares, which may continue as hallucinations after awakening);

*5. **Emotional disturbances** (e.g., depression, anxiety or fear, irritability, euphoria, apathy, or wondering perplexity).

These criteria are not required in DSM-5 for a diagnosis of delirium.

B. The **onset is usually rapid** (hours to days), the course **diurnally fluctuating**, and the total duration of the condition **less than 6 months**.

C. *In addition to impaired attention, DSM-5 specifies another cognitive disturbance such as memory deficit, perceptual distortions, disorientation, and language impairment which is already included above in A.2.*

D. The above symptoms are **not better accounted for by another mental disorder,** especially dementia or other neurocognitive syndromes, acute and transient psychotic disorders, and from acute states in schizophrenia or mood disorders in which confusional features may be present.

E. There is evidence suggesting that the symptoms are related to the **direct physiological effects of a substance or another medical condition**. Cerebral dysfunction can be demonstrated by an abnormal electroencephalogram, usually but not invariably showing a slowing of the background activity. If the above symptoms are induced by alcohol or other psychoactive substances, the diagnosis of substance intoxication or withdrawal could be more strongly considered. The above clinical picture is so characteristic that a fairly confident diagnosis of delirium can be made even if the underlying cause is not clearly established. This is a common diagnosis in older adults because frequently more than one medication, medical condition, or infection is at play.

Note: Adapted from *ICD-10* (p. 56) and *DSM-5* (p. 596)

Differential Diagnosis

Accentuated *normal personality traits* are part of patients' past history and persist in aging with minimal fluctuation, whereas personality in delirium often shows wild fluctuations between normal (during lucid intervals) and abnormal/out of character (during confused intervals). Unlike *dementia*, delirium is characterized by an abrupt onset, a fluctuating course, and clouding of consciousness. Sometimes the strokes in vascular dementia cause abrupt deterioration, but they almost always have accompanying neurological deficits. When delirium is superimposed on dementia, it appears as a sudden, unexplained worsening with much fluctuation.

When *schizophrenia* erupts, the patient's hallucinations and apparent confusion can resemble a delirium, but the patient will not show the disorientation, memory loss, and diurnal pattern seen in delirium. It is unusual for visual hallucinations to be present early in the course of schizophrenia. *Generalized anxiety disorder* and delirium may both present with agitation, yet the former is without disorientation, confusion, or memory loss.

Substance-induced delirium can usually be determined by history from the patient, family, or friends, or by direct detection of the offending agent or agents. Withdrawal-related delirium can be more difficult to detect than delirium from intoxication. A good example is delirium from alcohol withdrawal. By the time an individual in alcohol withdrawal becomes delirious, it is likely alcohol will no longer be detectable (3–5 days postdrinking). History-taking, usually from family or friends, as well as keeping this condition in the differential diagnoses, are vital.

There is a growing body of evidence supporting a relatively new form of dementia with diffuse *Lewy bodies*. Dementia with Lewy Bodies (DLB) may be the second most common form of dementia and involves a much more rapid loss of cholinergic neurons. DLB often resembles delirium. Cognitive loss is mild in early DLB, but sudden episodes of confusion, parkinsonism, disorientation, and visual hallucinations, with a return to fairly good lucidity, are common. Falls and a marked intolerance to antipsychotics are also common; the latter may help differentiate DLB from delirium and other dementias. Unlike delirium, no clear underlying medical cause is easily identified in DLB, from which patients "just recover" back to their baseline until another episode occurs.

Etiology and Pathogenesis

Most patients with delirium have an underlying medical, surgical, chemical, or neurological problem; it may be an infectious disease, drug intoxication or withdrawal, congestive heart failure, fluid and electrolyte imbalance, or stroke. Sometimes the first sign of a medical illness will be a delirium. Drug-induced delirium is most often secondary to anticholinergic toxicity. Psychotropic medications, especially tricyclic antidepressants and low-potency antipsychotics, frequently cause delirium because of their substantial anticholinergic properties. Hypnoanxiolytic agents (e.g., lorazepam, alprazolam) can also cause delirium. Older adults are especially susceptible, because they are highly sensitive to anticholinergics and hypnoanxiolytics. Fortunately, most of the newer antidepressants (SSRIs, SNRIs, and bupropion) are not anticholinergic. Unfortunately, several drugs for blood pressure, heart malfunction, ulcers, emphysema, allergies, and inflammation have significant anticholinergic effects. Other commonly prescribed and over-the-counter medications are frequently overlooked because they are thought to be benign; for example, diphenhydramine (Benadryl), which in overdoses creates the perfect example of "anticholinergic delirium." Others include antibiotics (ciprofloxacin [Cipro], levofloxacin [Levaquin], and related agents), drugs used to treat urinary incontinence, some drugs used for acid reflux, and certainly opioid pain medications. Delirium is often multifactorial!

Another cause of delirium is sensory isolation, which can occur in intensive and cardiac care units (ICU/CCU psychoses). The monotony of a strange and unfamiliar setting may cause patients to see walls quiver, mistake technological noises for human voices, hallucinate taps on their shoulders, and so on. The extent to which patients' deliria stem from sensory isolation or from the disease, medical complications, and treatment that brought them to an ICU or CCU is often unclear and varies depending on the circumstances.

The most common causes of delirium in hospitalized older adults are urinary tract infections, pneumonia, drug interactions, fever, heart failure, postoperative states, other pulmonary conditions, and environmental change. Delirium is a marker of "brain reserve capacity," and recent evidence suggests that those with recurrent delirium are at greater risk of developing Alzheimer's disease and other dementias. Close monitoring, therefore, of a patient's cognitive status following episodes of delirium is indicated.

Clinical Course and Complications

Any time there is a sudden, unexplained behavioral change or psychosis, delirium must be suspected. Early detection of delirium is extremely important because it can lead to death. Delirium usually arises quickly, from several hours to days, depending on its cause. The onset may be dramatic, as when patients begin thrashing about, tearing out IVs, or fighting. When the onset is subtle and the symptoms are exaggerations of normal personality traits, delirium may go undetected. For instance, a normally perfectionistic physician recovering from heart surgery started to cuss at nurses for not washing their hands. Initially the staff said, "Everybody knows doctors make the worst patients," and missed the delirium, until his behavior became frankly psychotic. At first, patients with delirium may simply appear a bit confused, mistake a night nurse for a relative, or not find their rooms. Nurses' and families' reports may be the first clue to a delirium when they describe a calm patient by day and a confused one by night. Frequent, around-the-clock mental-status testing is often needed to detect a delirium.

Accidents are common in delirium; the patient may fall out of bed or step in front of a truck. The longer delirium continues, the greater the chance of permanent brain damage. Delirium greatly increases both mortality and morbidity; it rarely persists for over a month—by then, the patient is either diagnosed as demented or dead. If delirium has a protracted course, a review of the diagnosis and consideration of a more permanent and chronic condition should be entertained. The one exception here is persisting delirium and cognitive impairment due to chronic alcoholism. There have been many cases where ongoing abstinence, usually through placement or in state psychiatric hospitals, over the course of 12 months or more, has allowed the slow but often full recovery of brain function, even in older adults.

Management and Treatment

The first priority is to keep the patient alive and to medically stabilize him or her; a close second is to prevent brain damage; third is to prevent the patient from inflicting self-harm. A thorough history from family, friends, past caregivers, and charts may reveal similar confusional periods with a known cause (e.g., hypoglycemia in diabetes or drug overdose) that immediately suggests a present cause and possible treatment. Quick identification of a delirium and then referral to a physician to determine its cause are critical to these goals. Careful nursing care is also essential and often lifesaving. Because medically hospitalized patients with delirium may fall out of bed, wander off, trip, break bones, develop concussions, rip out IVs, hurl IV bags, and so on, these patients often need constant observation and sometimes physical restraints. Restraint use is somewhat paradoxical. Restraints frequently cause problems, including injury; however, there is often no alternative to provide for patient safety and, equally important, maintenance of interventions such as IVs and airways essential for treatment. Foley catheters should be viewed as a restraint, as they are well proven to act as such. Clearly, a patient-specific and thoughtful assessment for the use of any restraint must be made and then performed correctly. The proper use of restraining devices and techniques is important and a staff-training issue.

> Patients with delirium should be frequently oriented. Health care professionals' contacts with the patients should be brief and numerous (e.g., 3 minutes four times an hour), always telling the patient the date, the place, the staff member's name, and what he or she is doing. The patient should be reassured as to her safety and repeatedly oriented. Pictures of family members, a clock, and a calendar showing the date should be visible to the patient. The best treatment for an ICU psychosis is removal from the ICU. If that is medically unsafe, all the above measures should be taken.

Before the underlying cause of the delirium is rectified, the patient may be helped initially by small doses of antipsychotic medications (e.g., haloperidol 0.5–2 mg or ziprasidone 10–20 mg IM). Some (Wells & McEvoy, 1982) claim that antianxiety agents (e.g., lorazepam 1–2 mg IM) are as helpful and safe as antipsychotics. Other authors (Goodwin & Guze, 1989) opine that many patients with delirium become even more agitated and disorganized on antianxiety medication; they therefore recommend antipsychotics. Often, both are given together. If one is managing an alcohol withdrawal delirium, there is an evidence-based protocol available (Mayo-Smith, 1997) but doses need to be reduced for the elderly. The most important aspect of this treatment is to keep the patient safe while not further complicating the delirium. Antipsychotics can cause dystonia and/or neuroleptic malignant syndrome, but their benefits and risks in treating delirium are well established. The newer second-generation or "atypical" antipsychotics (including ziprasidone, olanzepine, aripiprazole, quetiapine, and risperidone) are less likely to manifest side effects but are not available in an intravenous delivery form. Anxiolytics can cause disinhibition or excess sedation; older adults should receive one-half to one-third of these hypnoanxiolytic doses. They may benefit most from benzodiazepines (e.g., oxazepam or lorazepam) that are not conjugated into other medically active compounds, have a relatively short half-life and accumulate less. If it is clearly an anticholinergic delirium (e.g., diphenhydramine overdose), physostigmine is sometimes used to achieve an immediate though occasionally short-lived lucid period in someone experiencing severe and frightening visual hallucinations and subsequent agitation (Stern, 1983). Case reports have suggested that symptoms of delirium and frequency of recurrence of delirium can be improved by cholinesterase inhibitors (e.g., donepezil, rivostigmine, galantanine) (Wengel et al., 1998).

More important than the choice of medication is the dose: Too little, and the delirium worsens and becomes more dangerous; too much, and more delirium, coma, and respiratory depression may follow. Errors on either side of this delicate balance can lead to death, but it is probably better to err on the side of too little. More of a medication can always be given, but not *less!* If the initial doses mentioned above are insufficient or wear off, they may be repeated hourly, as long as the patient is checked before each new dose is administered.

In summary, a thorough evaluation of each patient with delirium is necessary, and treatment should be individualized according to the specific situation and unique needs. Treatment is closely monitored and well-coordinated with all involved professionals.

DEMENTIA

Clinical Presentation

Dementia—from the Latin *demens*, meaning "out of one's mind"—is characterized by a loss of intellectual abilities, especially memory, judgment, abstract thinking, and language skills, together with marked changes in personality and impulse control. Most dementias begin gradually (months to years). Unlike delirium, dementia occurs without a clouding of consciousness. Table 10-2 lists diagnostic criteria for dementia. *DSM-5* employs the broader category of Major Neurocognitive Disorder to include the dementia syndrome and the growing number of subtypes based upon a wide range of etiological factors according to the latest findings.

Initially, there is *memory loss* for recent events: Ovens are left on, keys misplaced, conversations forgotten. Later, episodes of getting lost while driving in once-familiar locations begin; questions are repeated because the question and the answer are quickly forgotten. Retained, and often dwelled on, are details from childhood and other long-term memories. *Personality changes* are often intensifications or exact opposites of preexisting character traits. A gregarious grandfather retreats to a corner and daydreams. A mildly suspicious and self-righteous woman begins calling the police every night, accusing her neighbors of performing abortions in their basements. *Impaired judgment* and *poor impulse control* are common: Patients may start speaking crudely, exhibit genitals, or shoplift. A normally cautious businessman has three car accidents in 6 months because he impulsively passes cars on hills and swerves back and forth between lanes "to get ahead of the traffic."

TABLE 10-2
Diagnostic Criteria for Dementia Syndrome (Major Neurocognitive Disorders*)

A. Dementia is a syndrome due to disease of the brain, usually of a chronic or progressive nature, in which there is **disturbance of multiple higher cortical functions,** including memory, thinking, orientation, comprehension, calculation, learning capacity, language, and judgment.

1. Dementia produces an **appreciable [*significant*] decline** in both memory and thinking.

2. *DSM-5 specifies that the substantial impairment in cognitive performance be quantified in a standardized assessment (e.g., neuropsychological testing).*

B. The decline in higher cortical functions **interferes with personal activities of daily living,** such as washing, dressing, eating, personal hygiene, excretory and toilet activities. How such a decline manifests itself will depend largely on the social and cultural setting in which the patient lives.

The impairments of cognitive function are commonly accompanied, and occasionally preceded, by deterioration in emotional control, social behavior, or motivation.

C. If dementia is the sole diagnosis, **evidence of clear consciousness** is required. However, a double diagnosis of delirium superimposed upon dementia is common.

D. The cognitive disturbance is **not better explained by another mental disorder** such as schizophrenia, amnestic disorder, or a depressive disorder, which may exhibit many of the features of an early dementia, especially memory impairment, slowed thinking, and lack of spontaneity; delirium; mild or moderate mental retardation; states of subnormal cognitive functioning attributable to a severely impoverished social environment and limited education; mental disorders due to medication or other substance.

E. The above symptoms and impairments should have been evident **for at least 6 months** for a confident clinical diagnosis of dementia to be made.

According to DSM-5 Mild Neurocognitive Disorder differs from Major Neurocognitive Disorder in that the cognitive decline and deficits in one or more cognitive domains are modest and do not sufficiently interfere with personal activities of life so as to lose the capacity for independence.

F. Dementia syndrome is typically attributable to an underlying neurological condition, trauma, or disease process affecting the brain, or to chronic use of specific substances or medications. The appropriate etiological diagnosis should also be assigned as a dementia subtype.

1. **Dementia in Alzheimer disease** usually has an insidious onset and develops slowly but steadily over a period of several years. Onset before the age of 65 has a relatively rapid deteriorating course and marked decline of multiple higher cortical functions.

2. **Vascular dementia** (multi-infarct, lacunar) usually has an abrupt onset usually later in life with stepwise progression and is the result of infarction of the brain due to vascular disease. The infarcts are usually small but cumulative in effect. Binswanger's Disease (subcortical infarcts)

3. **Dementia in substance use** (alcohol most common)

4. **Dementia due to other medical conditions**

   a. **Dementia in human immunodeficiency virus [HIV] disease** develops in the course of HIV disease, in the absence of a concurrent illness or condition other than HIV infection that could explain the clinical features.

(continued)

TABLE 10-2
Continued

b. **Dementia in Parkinson disease** has its onset about one year after the appearance of the extrapyramidal motor symptoms. Anosmia is common.

c. **Dementia in Prion Disease, e.g., Creutzfeldt-Jakob disease** is a very rapidly progressive dementia with extensive neurological signs, caused by a transmissible proteinaceous infective agent, and leading to death within one to two years.

d. **Dementia in Huntington disease** occurs as part of a widespread degeneration of the brain. The disorder is transmitted by a single autosomal dominant gene with symptoms typically emerging in the third and fourth decade. Progression is slow, leading to death usually within 10 to 15 years.

e. **Dementia in Pick Disease and other frontotemporal disease** usually commences in middle age and is characterized by early, slowly progressing changes of personality and social deterioration, followed by impairment of executive functioning, and emotions.

f. **Dementia in Lewy body disease** presents as Alzheimer's and Parkinson subtypes but can have a more sudden onset with the additional symptom of visual hallucinations

g. **Dementia in Traumatic Brain Injury (Dementia Pugilistica)** is characterized by emotional lability and personality changes

h. **Multiple etiologies**, e.g., Alzheimer's and vascular dementias often occur together

i. **Reversible** (sometimes called "Treatable") **dementias**

Note: Adapted from *ICD-10* (p. 54) and *DSM-5* (p. 602)

Intellectual abilities deteriorate. Patients may have trouble naming objects (anomia) and may have difficulties understanding language (aphasia); speech becomes stereotyped, slow, vague, and filled with irrelevant detail as these patients increasingly are unable to concentrate, to follow conversations, or to distinguish the germane from the trivial; words are misused, chosen more by sound than by sense. Patients cannot perform simple motor tasks (apraxia); driving, cooking, handling money, and using tools become too complicated. They find it hard to draw a simple house, copy the placement of four match-sticks, or assemble blocks. Recognizing sensory input of any kind may be impaired (agnosia). The patients themselves lack insight into their condition (*anosognosia*—reduced awareness of symptoms; *anosodiaphora*—lack of concern about the consequences of symptoms). Often the severity of these symptoms is not recognized by others until the patient is observed in a new place (where inability to learn new information is a tip-off), or until the spouse dies and family members become aware, for the first time, of how sick their parent is. Initially they blame this deterioration on grief but then realize it has been going on much longer.

In response to these impairments, patients most commonly use denial and seem not to notice these major problems; less commonly, they become ashamed, anxious, demoralized, irritable, and dysthymic; hypochondriasis increases; energy and enthusiasm decline. Some patients display "catastrophic reactions" or "emotional incontinence"—they respond to stimuli by excessive laughing, hostility, or weeping, or by suddenly becoming dazed, evasive, or immobile. Also common is *confabulation* (the fabrication of stories to conceal memory loss); so, too, are suspiciousness and paranoid ideation, especially when the patient has trouble hearing or seeing. Fear invades the memory vacuum: Forgetting where he left his wallet, the patient assumes it was stolen and may accuse others, including loved ones, of the crimes.

Whereas memory loss is an early symptom and the hallmark of Alzheimer's disease, it is often behavioral problems that precipitate referral to a physician. Difficult behaviors occur in up to 70% of patients with AD, usually isolated to the middle stages of the chronic, deteriorating illness.

Delusional syndromes commonly present include delusions of theft, *Capgras syndrome* (misidentifying familiar people, often believing they are someone else or strangers), *Charles Bonnett's syndrome* (visual hallucinations of little people often dressed in uniforms, coming and going), *one's house is not one's home* (belief they are in an unfamiliar place despite being at home), *phantom boarder syndrome* (a stranger is living in the house, often the one accused of leaving the oven on, etc.) and many more. Often delusions and behavior do not require medication, but rather environmental manipulations and an understanding on the part of the family.

The patient's deterioration may go unrecognized for months or even years because intellectual decline is usually insidious. Memory loss is dismissed as the natural result of normal aging or of not paying attention. The patient's impaired judgment and poor impulse control are explained by stereotyping (e.g., "Old folks naturally get crusty and cantankerous with age"). If Granddad starts making lewd gestures to teeny-boppers, he's a fun-loving "dirty old man." Inappropriate jocularity, which arises from impairments of the brain's frontal lobe, is dismissed as "simply being in good spirits." The patient's loss of intellectual sharpness or wit may be too subtle or gradual to be noticed. It is important to have some knowledge of the patient's premorbid levels of intellectual and cognitive function, given the usually slow and frequently insidious onset and progression of symptoms, along with the usual self-denial and denial to others that occur. In most cases a person of high intellectual ability, significant education, and application of both is not going to demonstrate clearly recognizable signs or symptoms until the dementia has been present for a long time. On average, dementia is diagnosed at least 2 years into the disease process. Persons with lower levels of premorbid function will usually demonstrate these symptoms "sooner." Any form of memory loss, especially progressive loss, must be evaluated and should not be chalked up to "normal aging" or "senility."

When presenting clinically, patients with dementia may move slowly or fidget. They may look glum, bored, or tense. On a formal mental-status examination, they show recent memory loss and disorientation and usually have difficulties subtracting serial 1s or 7s and performing abstractions. However, it is possible they will present without any identified abnormality at all!

The Mini-Mental State Examination (MMSE) is a widely used screening test for dementia (see Figure 10-1). It does not detect very early, mild dementias but is effective at detecting dementias that are mild to moderate or worse. (A score of 24 or below indicates probable dementia.) Although of value, the practitioner should remember the above-discussed issues and account for them. It is likely that an individual with a fourth-grade education and relatively low premorbid function will not score well on this test, even if no dementia is present. At the same time, a highly educated and highly functioning patient is likely to "ace" this test, even though serious deterioration has already happened. Patients should never be diagnosed with dementia or Alzheimer's disease while in the hospital where complicating medical (e.g., delirium) and environmental conditions are present. Unless history is very evident or the patient is in the moderate to severe stages of AD, it may take several outpatient appointments and several MMSE scores before a diagnosis is comfortably made. The diagnosis of Alzheimer's disease can have a high probability, is never definite, and involves ruling out several other conditions.

Subtypes

There are four major subtypes of dementia: (1) *Alzheimer's disease* is the most common type and accounts for over 60% of all dementias. (2) *Vascular dementia* (formerly called "multi-infarct dementia") accounts for 9–15% of dementias and is mainly caused by hypertension or emboli. Emboli are small blood clots that break off from the heart or a carotid artery in the neck, flow to the brain, block part of the blood supply, and cause the death, or infarct, of those brain cells. Contrary to popular belief, vascular dementia is not directly caused by arteriosclerosis ("hardening of the arteries"). Many experienced clinicians believe that vascular dementia is often overdiagnosed and is frequently comorbid with Alzheimer's disease (AD). (3) *Substance use demen-*

FIGURE 10-1
Mini Mental State Examination (MMSE)

Date _____

Patient's Name _____

Examiner's Name _____

Maximum   Score
Score

ORIENTATION

5   (   ) What is the (year) (season) (date) (day) (month)?

5   (   ) Where are we: (state)(county)(town or city)(hospital)(floor)?

REGISTRATION

3   (   ) Name three common objects (e.g., "apple, table, penny"):
                    Take 1 second to say each. Then ask the patient to repeat all three after
                    you have said them. Give 1 point for each correct answer. Then repeat
                    them until he/she learns all three. Count trials and record:

ATTENTION AND CALCULATION

5   (   ) Serial 7's backward. Give 1 point for each correct answer. Stop after five
                    answers. Alternatively, spell *WORLD* backward. One point for each correct
                    letter.

RECALL

3   (   ) Ask for the three objects repeated above. Give 1 point for each correct
                    answer. (Note: Recall cannot be tested if all three objects were not
                    remembered during registration.)

LANGUAGE

2   (   ) Name a "pencil" and "watch."

1   (   ) Repeat the following: "No ifs, ands, or buts."

3   (   ) Follow a three-stage command:
                       "Take a paper in your right hand, fold it in half, and put it on the floor."

1   (   ) Read and obey the following: Close your eyes.

1   (   )   Write a sentence.

1   (   )   Copy the following design:

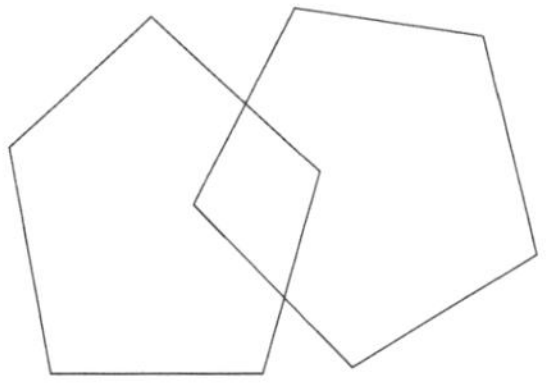

Total Score _____

Adapted from Folstein et al. (1975).

tias produce 7–9% of the dementias, with alcoholic dementia accounting for most cases. (4) *Dementia due to other medical conditions* accounts for 20% of the dementias. This category includes dementias that are primarily caused by neurological diseases or by systemic illnesses. Parkinson's disease is included because 20–30% of patients with this disease develop dementia. Two rare dementias, the rapidly progressive Creutzfeldt–Jakob disease (prion infections) and the slowly progressive Huntington's disease ("Woody Guthrie" disease), are also included here. Human immunodeficiency virus (HIV) dementia is more complicated because it can include dementia from HIV itself or treatable dementias from secondary infections. Toxoplasmosis, a protozoan infection, has been identified as a cause of dementia in HIV-positive patients. Pick's disease is the prototype of the frontotemporal dementias with other, less defined entities such as dementia associated with amyotrophic lateral sclerosis. Onsets of these dementias occur earlier than in other types and are believed to account for between 2.5 and 10% of all dementias. Interestingly but not unexpectedly, given the neuroanatomy involved, other cognitive domains than memory are generally more affected. The triad of cognitive impairment, Parkinson-type symptoms, and visual hallucinations classically defines Dementia with Lewy Bodies (DLB). The presence of histologically distinct Lewy bodies in the brain, which are different from the classical amyloid plaques and neurofibrillary tangles associated with Alzheimer's disease, argue for a distinct etiology of DLB. The above dementias are considered to be incurable. Table 10-3 provides some diagnostic clues to distinguish among the growing number of dementia subtypes.

Unlike Alzheimer's Disease and vascular dementia, many secondary dementias may be reversible. Patients who present with dementias *must* receive thorough medical and neurological examinations to determine if they are among the roughly 20% of patients with dementia who can be treated and sometimes cured, either medically or surgically. Excluding depression, less than 5% of dementias are considered reversible, partially reversible, or able to be halted from further progression. Table 10-4 presents diagnostic modalities for the evaluation of dementia.

First, a thorough history and corroboration are vital. Neuropsychological evaluation can be important, and the Halstead–Reitan and Nebraska-Luria are both sensitive tools. Positron emission tomography (PET) scanning with the necessary software can be diagnostic by measuring regional cerebral blood flow and neuroreceptor density. Single-photon emission computed tomography (SPECT) can also be valuable and has cost advantages over

TABLE 10-3
Dementias with Specific Diagnostic Clues

DISEASE	PATHOGENESIS	DIAGNOSTIC CLUES
Alzheimer's dementia	Neurofibrillary tangles, Amyloid plaques, Apolipoprotein E4	Cortical impairment: aphasia, agnosia, apraxia
Vascular dementia	Multiple infarctions (strokes) from emboli, thrombosis, or ruptured small vessels; hypertension most common cause	Focal neurological signs, abnormal reflexes, specific weak muscles
Parkinson's disease	Destruction of dopamine-containing cells	Slow, shuffling gait, bradykinesia, "pill-rolling" hand tremor, lack of facial expression, anosmia
Creutzfeldt–Jakob disease	Prions (smaller than viruses), contagious	Rigidity and myoclonic jerks, abnormal EEG, fatal in months
Huntington's chorea	Genetic	Writhing, choreiform movements
Frontotemporal dementia	Tau accumulation and silver-staining inclusions (Pick's bodies)	Early personality change, disinhibition
Dementia with Lewy Bodies	Rapid loss of cholinergic neurons	Visual hallucinations, hypersensitivity to antipsychotics
Wernicke-Korsakoff syndrome	Thiamine (B_1) deficiency from alcoholism and poor nutrition	Diplopia, ataxia
Normal pressure hydrocephalus	Increased fluid in lateral ventricles	Incontinence, "magnetic" gait disturbance, abulia

PET. Functional magnetic resonance imaging (fMRI) and magnetic resonance spectroscopy (MRS) scanning measure regional cerebral blood flow and brain chemistry. Some cerebrospinal fluid tests, such as a combined measurement of alpha, beta, peptide 42, and tau protein, may be of value. Coordination of the primary-care physician and other pertinent specialists is essential.

The "big four" reversible dementias—each accounting for about 6% of all reversible dementias—are *normal pressure hydrocephalus, chronic drug toxicity, resectable brain masses,* and *major depression.* About 50% of patients with normal pressure hydrocephalus improve with the help of a brain shunt that diverts cerebrospinal fluid. During the first year of abstinence, alcoholic dementia improves some but seldom completely. By preventing further strokes, low-dose aspirin therapy may arrest or slow the progress of vascular dementias. There are also many less common but reversible dementias (see

TABLE 10-4
Useful Studies in the Clinical Evaluation of Patients with Dementia

Initial Studies Performed on All Patients

—Detailed history and physical examination (MOST IMPORTANT—including history of onset from collateral source).
—Chest x-ray
—Electrocardiogram (EKG)
—Complete blood count with red cell indices and erythrocyte sedimentation rate (ESR) and/or C-reactive protein
—Urinalysis
—Urine and serum drug levels, as indicated
—Electrolytes, blood urea nitrogen (BUN), calcium
—Hepatic enzymes, bilirubin
—Thyroid function tests
—Serum B$_{12}$ level
—Serum VDRL
—CAT or MRI (only as indicated by history, quick onset, review of systems, and physical exam)

Additional Studies Tailored to Individual Patients

If a metabolic cause is suspected
—Serum ammonia level
—Urine heavy metal screen—rarely needed
—Urine porphyrins

If an infectious cause is suspected
—Lumbar puncture with thorough cerebrospinal fluid (CSF) evaluation, including glucose, protein, cell count, India ink, VDRL, cultures (bacterial, TB, fungal, viral), protein electrophoresis
—Evaluation of possible systemic infection

If a structural or neoplastic cause is suspected
—CAT scan or MRI
—Vascular studies (cerebral arteriogram, carotid Doppler ultrasound)
—CSF cytology

Other Helpful Studies in Some Patients

—Electroencephalogram (metabolic, degenerative, or structural processes)
—Intrathecal cisternogram (normal pressure hydrocephalus)
—Antinuclear factor (vasculitis)
—Serum copper and ceruloplasmin (Wilson's disease)
—Measurement of alpha, beta, peptide 42, and tau protein
—PET, fMRI, SPECT
—APOE4 genetic testing

Table 10-4). Other somewhat common reversible dementias or cognitive disorders that can be stabilized include hypothyroidism and anemia/B12 deficiencies.

> On her 70th birthday, widowed, modest Mrs. Kass moved to Miami. Quite unlike her "normal self," she launched her first of many sexual flings "for the hell of it." As she informed relatives, "life is short." Hotly debated was whether Mrs. Kass belonged in a motel or a mental hospital. While the family was paralyzed by worry, Mrs. Kass was thrilled and active. She'd laugh at anything, so much so that one night a policeman noticed her on a fishing pier, lost, confused, and giggling. When he asked her where she was, she burst into "Swanee River," until she forgot a lyric and began weeping all the way to the hospital. Her dementia, initially attributed to Alzheimer's disease, was due to a benign (frontal lobe) brain tumor, which was surgically removed. After a full recovery, she regained her normal temperament and settled down with a retired businessman. This case illustrates a cluster of symptoms common to the frontal lobes (impulsivity, hypersexuality, personality change) and a reversible dementia.

Epidemiology

Currently there are 35 million Americans over the age of 65 with dementia. The incidence of dementia increases with age, arising most often in people between the ages of 70 and 80 years. The prevalence of dementia is 15% for people over 65 years; 10% in all persons between 65 and 74 years; 25% in persons 75–84 years; 45% for those over 80 years old. Over half of all hospitalized elderly mental patients have dementia, and over half of those with dementia have AD—the fourth leading cause of death in the United States. With more people surviving to old age, the number of individuals with dementia is expected to at least triple in the next 20 years. The direct and indirect costs (both financial and emotional) associated with dementia are substantial and incalculable to families and society.

Differential Diagnosis

As discussed earlier, dementia must be distinguished from *delirium*. Because delirium presents with disorientation and memory loss, dementia cannot be diagnosed until *after* a delirium clears. Agnosia, apraxia, and aphasia are much more common in Alzheimer's dementia than in delirium. In *normal aging* there is a 10–15% loss in neuropsychological functioning. This decline includes some memory loss (names and dates are forgotten and papers misplaced), new learning becomes harder, thinking becomes slower, and problem-solving is more difficult. Much of the loss in function is due to slowed performance speed. (Give the seniors enough time, and they come much closer to their abilities.) These changes do not substantially interfere with occupational or social functioning, whereas the changes from AD and other dementias do. In AD the decline in neuropsychological functioning is typically over 85%. Some intellectual deterioration may occur in *chronic schizophrenia* ("dementia praecox"), but it is milder than in dementia, specific neurological abnormalities are not usually found, and there usually is a clear history of schizophrenic symptoms.

Another important fact about dementia is that it may be confused with "pseudodementia" or dementia syndrome of depression (DSD), a sign of *major depression* that is a true cognitive impairment but highly reversible with treatment.

> *Pseudodementia* is somewhat of a misnomer and has gone out of favor with most geriatricians. In fact, there is nothing "pseudo" about late-life depression that presents with quicker onset, multiple somatic and cognitive complaints, poor sleep, poor appetite and energy, and anxiety, while "tired all the time." It may take twice as long to complete an MMSE in a depressed patient, who discusses and highlights every question with correct or near-miss answers, than in a patient with dementia who quickly answers the question but gets it wrong. Asking whether one has memory difficulties can be very telling: Answers such as "Oh, I'm glad you asked—it's horrible" (depression); "It ain't what it used to be, but I get by" (normal), or "Oh, it's great" (dementia) are generally accurate rules of thumb.

From 10 to 33% of older adults with major depressive disorder are misdiagnosed as having dementia, because both disorders may present initially with the same symptoms of memory loss, confusion, disorientation, apathy, and hypochondriasis. To further complicate matters, as indicated above, 20–40% of patients with dementia also have a major depressive disorder. For patients with pseudodementia (more appropriately termed *late-life depression*), antidepressants may completely improve the "dementia" and, in depressed patients with dementia, antidepressants may improve the dementia.

Interestingly, patients with depression are more likely to complain about memory problems than patients with *real* memory problems. Patients with dementia are often brought in by their families. For example, Aunt Maude, who has AD, was brought in by her family after burning the pots on the stove three nights in a row. She wonders what the fuss is all about and doesn't complain about memory problems. In contrast, the patient with depression paces the floor, complaining that he can't remember all the stocks he owns and that he has forgotten his friend's phone number.

Another symptom, the *anhedonia* seen in depression, differs from the normal *narrowing of interest in activities* seen in dementia. When a patient with depression is asked what she enjoys doing, she might say, "Nothing." The patient with dementia might say, "I like picking up the mail, reading large-print books, and watching my TV shows." A typical interviewer who has a wide range of interests might mistakenly conclude that the dementia patient is depressed, because *she* (the interviewer) would feel depressed with so few activities. The patient with dementia can't do the more complex ones, such as cooking, gardening, or handicrafts, but still likes to do the few that she is still able to do. Patients with depression frequently respond to questions with silence or by saying, "I don't know"; patients with dementia answer with near misses. In depression, the cognitive problems develop relatively abruptly within days to 2 months. True dementia usually evolves much more slowly. Unlike dementia, pseudodementia does not have accompanying neurological symptoms such as aphasia, apraxia, or agnosia. Disorientation to time, getting lost easily, and difficulties with dressing are also much more common in dementia (Reynolds et al., 1988). In the patient who has both depression and dementia, dementia symptoms are present before depression symptoms. Pervasive sadness, feelings of guilt, and genuine suicidal ideation are primarily associated with depression.

Patients with cognitive decline associated with depression or dementia syndrome of depression (DSD) often have a prior, or family history of mood disorder. Although the CT or MRI scan is more likely to show cortical atrophy and enlarged ventricles in dementia than in depression, 20% of the time the CT or MRI scan may be misdiagnosed (Charatan, 1985). Up to 70–80% of older adults with depression have abnormal MRI scans; a significant number of normal older adults have abnormal imaging studies. The diagnosis is therefore clinical, not radiological, the key test being whether the patient improves with biological treatments such as antidepressants or electroconvulsive therapy. (That ECT *increases* instead of diminishes the memory of patients with DSD suggests that it does not harm brain cells.) Van Gorp and Cummings (1996) highlighted the importance of multiple neuropsychiatric (test-retest) evaluations in differentiating DSD from dementia syndromes. However, many of these patients develop true dementia several years later (Emery & Oxman, 1992). Unfortunately, between one-third and one-half of people with first onset of major depressive disorder after age 65 years will go on to develop a diagnosable dementia. In these cases, major depressive disorder can be viewed as a physiological stressor that brings out a nascent dementia that later manifests on its own. Fortunately, many patients with DSD do not develop true dementia.

> Subsyndromal or apathetic late-life depression is somewhat different from the typical late-life depression wherein patients present with multiple somatic/physical complaints. In apathetic depression, patients are less of a "squeaky wheel," don't complain, and are content not participating. Many feel this apathy is due to executive cognitive dysfunction. This type of memory involves sequencing and planning, and is impaired early in cognitive disorders and in these depressive states. With executive cognitive impairment, patients are not able to plan multistep activities such as gardening, social conversations, and grocery shopping so they quit doing these things. This presents as apathy and whether with depression or early cognitive loss, apathy is a "red flag" for further cognitive problems to come. These patients should be closely monitored and treated with stimulants, stimulating antidepressants, and memory enhancers. Fortunately, many patients with late-life depression, especially nonapathetic, although at risk, do not develop true dementia.

Etiology and Pathogenesis

In general, the biological factors that produce a dementia vary according to the subtype. For example, Huntington's chorea is caused by an autosomal dominant gene. In contrast, vascular dementia has numerous biological causes that are not so directly related genetically. Psychosocial influences depend more on the individual's personality and circumstances.

> As noted, during the early stages of most dementias, patients respond with either exaggerations of their normal personality traits or their exact opposite. As discussed later, those close to the patient may also influence the patient's experience and quality of life. During the later stages, most dementias "take over" personalities, irrespective of psychosocial influences.
>
> *Genetic.* First-degree relatives (e.g., brother, mother, daughter) of patients with AD demonstrate three to four times the prevalence of this disease as the general population. The incidence is even higher among relatives of those few who develop AD before age 60. Some researchers believe that an autosomal dominant gene is *a* (not *the*) culprit. In some families, if one parent has

the gene, the child has a 50% chance of having AD; this likelihood increases to 75% if both parents have the gene. Children in these families tend to manifest the disease at the same age their parents did. In other cases, genetic vulnerability to AD is less clear. In some cases, a dominant gene may express itself late in life so that only some live long enough to show the disease. Estimates vary from 30 to 80% of the disease as being genetically induced. In many of these cases, a sporadic or polygenetic transmission is the cause. Most think AD represents a variety of diseases that will become clearer with future research. While there is a small subset of familial AD (usually clearly genetic or with early onset) the majority of cases appear to be sporadic and multifactorial with fewer genetic and familial contributions the later the onset. Down's syndrome is also a predisposition, with most Down's patients developing a pattern of AD in their 20s. An autosomal dominant gene definitely causes Huntington's chorea. There are some racial differences, with those of African, Spanish, and Asian descent having increased to high risk. Although still unclear, studies have linked the allele APOE4 as a major risk factor for the development of late-onset of AD (>65 y.o.). Gene-expression patterns of the hippocampus show substantial risk in patients with APOE3/4 and APOE4/4 types. Demonstrated associations with APOE4 alleles include activation of multiple tumor suppressors, tumor inducers, negative regulators of cell growth or repressors possibly leading to cell arrest, senescence, or apoptosis reduction of neurotransmitter receptors and decreased expression of large gene clusters associated with synoptic plasticity, fusing, and axonal/ neuronal outgrowth.

Medical. In addition to the etiologies of reversible dementias listed in Table 10-5, some irreversible dementias are probably due to "slow" viruses or prions (infectious particles that lack nucleic acid) and immunological deficiencies. Alcohol aggravates all dementias. High-risk factors for vascular dementia include hypertension, cigarette smoking, obesity, hyperlipidemia, family history of stroke, and heart disease.

Physiological. In normal aging, although the blood supply to the brain decreases, the brain extracts oxygen more efficiently. In AD, however, the brain's blood supply is also diminished, but the brain extracts both *less* oxygen and glucose. Additionally, AD patients show a distinctly different pattern of reduced cerebral blood flow with decreases bilaterally in the temporoparietal areas. Moreover, the enzymes that both synthesize and metabolize acetylcholine are deficient. Ultimately, most neurotransmitters are affected. On autopsy, inside the neurons of patients with AD are twisted clumps of tau protein called "neurofibrillary tangles," which are probably microtubules

TABLE 10-5
The "Reversible" Dementias

A. INFECTIONS
  1. Abscesses
  2. Encephalitis
  3. Meningitis, chronic
  4. Syphilis of the brain
  5. AIDS with secondary fungal, bacterial, viral, or protozoal infection
B. AUTOIMMUNE DISEASES
  1. Lupus Erythematosis
  2. Multiple sclerosis
C. MECHANICAL DISORDERS
  1. Normal pressure hydrocephalus
  2. Chronic subdural hematoma
  3. Vascular (cerebral aneurysm, AV malformation, vasculitis)
D. METABOLIC DISORDERS
  1. Porphyria
  2. Hypothyroidism (myxedema)
  3. Hyponatremia (low sodium)
  4. Hypo- or hypercalcemia (low or high calcium)
  5. Hyperadrenalism
  6. Wilson's disease
  7. Uremia (kidney failure with toxicity)
  8. Hepatic encephalopathy (liver failure with toxicity)

E. NEOPLASMS (Benign tumors)
  1. Gliomas, meningitis
  2. Other brain tumors (Primary and metastatic)
F. CHRONIC INTOXICATION AND POISONS
  1. Alcohol
  2. Barbiturates
  3. Anticholinergics
  4. Bromides
  5. Carbon monoxide
  6. Metals (e.g., mercury, lead, arsenic, manganese)
  7. Organic phosphates
  8. L-dopa
G. COGNITIVE DISORDERS RESEMBLING DEMENTIA ("PSEUDODEMENTIAS")
  1. Major depressive disorder
  2. Psychoses
H. VITAMIN DEFICIENCIES
  1. B_1 (Wernicke's encephalopathy)
  2. B_{12} (pernicious anemia)
  3. Folic acid
  4. Niacin (pellagra)

that normally maintain the shape of the cell (a cytoskeleton) and assist in the internal transport of molecules. Coating the outside of blood vessels are remnants of nerve-cell endings, called "neuritic plaques" (not neurotic!), around a core of beta-amyloid protein. These occur in the normal aging process, but in AD there are usually more than 10 times as many. There is a high correlation between the number of these plaques and tangles and the severity of the dementia. Beta-amyloid precursor protein (BAPP) is ubiquitous in the normal brain. Some think that in AD this amyloid protein is not broken down normally and leaves behind neurotoxic or nonsoluable amyloid fragments that interfere with the brain's functioning and cause dementia. Others believe that the hyperphosphorylation of tau, creating tangles, is the primary cause of AD.

Clinical Course

Although it usually appears after age 65, early-onset AD can emerge during the 40s, rarely even younger, as it did in the case first described by the German neuropsychiatrist Alois Alzheimer in 1906. Its stealthy onset typically manifests with memory loss and intellectual decline. In about 15–20% of these cases, the initial complaints are personality change with "negative" symptoms—apathy or withdrawal—or "positive" symptoms—agitation, irritability, suspiciousness, or moodiness. Most accept the staging of AD as "mild," "moderate," or "severe." In general, patients with AD in the milder stages deteriorate gradually and do not have marked diurnal changes. Difficulties with speech (finding the right words) and getting lost in familiar places are early signs. Aphasia, apraxia, or agnosia typically appear after several years in the moderate stage. Hallucinations and delusions become more common as the disease progresses, again in the moderate stage. Patients with severe AD are often mute, bed-bound, and malnourished.

During the end stage of AD, memory is almost totally gone. Patients cannot recognize their closest relatives; everyone becomes a stranger. Speech is reduced to a phrase or two; they cannot dress or feed themselves; bladder and bowel control fail; muscles deteriorate and insomnia plagues. At the very end, full nursing care is required, as patients are bedridden, disoriented, oblivious, and incoherent. They may become mute, stop eating, and lose the ability to swallow. They frequently aspirate food into their lungs and get pneumonia. Patients with AD may survive up to 15 years, but they usually expire in 7–10 years, dying most often from malnutrition, dehydration, infections, pneumonia, or heart failure.

Vascular dementia usually occurs in patients with histories of strokes and cardiovascular disease, causing "patchy" focal neurological signs such as inarticulate speech, small-stepped gait, abnormal reflexes, and specific weak muscles. These neurological signs are rarely seen in mild to moderate AD and are reliable clues for vascular dementia. In contrast to the slow, generalized deterioration of AD, vascular dementia may begin abruptly and progress in a stepwise, individual fashion. In people with many micro-infarcts, this disease may appear to progress gradually, as in AD. For unknown reasons, this stepwise worsening is also occasionally seen in other dementias and is therefore not a completely reliable symptom in diagnosing vascular dementia. To further complicate the differential between vascular dementia and AD, recent evidence suggests that microvascular disease may be the second leading risk factor for AD (second to advancing age as the primary risk factor).

Although many dementias look alike in their early stages, several develop very specific symptoms that can be used to make a differential diagnosis. These include vascular dementia, Parkinson's disease, normal pressure hydrocephalus, Huntington's chorea, Wernicke–Korsakoff, and the very rare, contagious (only if you eat or handle brains or body fluids) Creutzfeldt–Jakob disease. Table 10-6 lists the causes and symptoms of these quite recognizable dementias.

In the late stages of dementia, reflexes last seen in infancy reappear. When touched on the mouth or cheek, the patient shows a *rooting reflex* in which the mouth, face, or head moves toward the touch. This is an adaptive reflex in breast- and bottle-feeding babies. When an object is put in the patient's mouth or on the lips, a *sucking reflex* is often seen. Passively moving the patient's limbs elicits a semipurposeful resistance called *paratonia* or *gegenhalten*. The very demented patient may show *perseveration*, the continued repetition of a verbal or motor response that is no longer required (e.g., "Good morning! Oh boy! Oh boy! Oh boy!"). The same answer may be given to a series of different questions. A variation is perseveratory groping, in which the patient constantly and aimlessly picks at bed sheets or clothing. The apparent opposite of this is *motor impersistence*, the inability to continue a simple action such as extending a hand; within seconds, the patient drops her hands into her lap.

TABLE 10-6
Diagnostic Criteria for Amnestic Disorder

A. A **defect of recent memory** with preserved immediate recall but impaired ability to learn new material resulting in anterograde amnesia and disorientation in time, retrograde amnesia, and a reduced ability to recall past experience in reverse order of their occurrence.

B. The memory disturbance results in significant **impairment** in personal, family, social, educational, occupational or other important areas of functioning and represents a **significant decline** from a previous level of functioning.

C. The memory disturbance is **not better accounted for** by delirium or dementia, dissociative amnesia, impaired memory function in depressive disorders, attention deficits, substance use disorders, other medical conditions in which memory impairment is prominent, global intellectual impairment, or malingering presenting with a complaint of memory loss.

D. There is **evidence of an insult to, or a disease of, the brain** (especially with bilateral involvement of the hypothalamus-diencephalic and medial temporal structures). Additional signs of confabulations, lack of insight, and emotional changes (apathy, lack of initiative) although not necessary in every case, point to this diagnosis.

Note: Adapted from *ICD-10* (p. 55)

Complications

Dementia is a life-shortening illness. Demented patients are susceptible to medical illness and delirium. Their work and social functioning gradually decline. As their condition worsens, they may evidence life-threatening behavior such as wandering away from home, falling off a ladder, or tripping on a curb.

> If a patient smashes his head and loses consciousness, he may suffer a potentially fatal subdural hematoma—a sudden or gradual bleeding under the outer lining (or dura) of the brain. The patient may lose consciousness immediately, yet more often there is a fluctuating course of drowsiness, headache, and confusion that persists for weeks to months, until the patient finally loses consciousness.

Although dementia often induces severe despair and depression, it rarely leads to suicide. Major depression occurs in 20–40% of patients with AD; it is more common in the early milder stages because insight about what is lost is still intact.

Management and Treatment

AD is a chronic, terminal illness. The goal of currently available treatments is palliative in nature. Treatment can improve cognitive function, self-care, behavior, and quality of life but not stop overall decline. Part of treatment, as with any terminal illness, is to support the family's educational and emotional needs to minimize caregiver burden and depression. Many patients qualify for hospice in the final stages of the illness.

Biomedical Interventions

After the reversible dementia is treated, there may be residual dementia. In AD there is a deficiency of acetylcholine along with other neurotransmitters. Cholinesterase inhibitors (e.g., tacrine, rivastigmine, donepezil) increase brain acetylcholine by preventing its breakdown and are sometimes used to help these patients. A few improve significantly, but most patients improve minimally or not at all with these drugs. Memantine is a NMDA antagonist that is sometimes beneficial by reducing glutamate. It has been shown to be beneficial when prescribed with one of the cholinesterase inhibitors. There is a widespread belief that these drugs can slow the deterioration caused by AD. This is very unlikely and unproven. It is more plausible that these drugs may enhance the function that remains as the disease progresses. The most likely future focus is the development of drugs that block the deposition of amyloid into the brain cells or normalize the phosphorylation of tau proteins so as to arrest or delay the terrible decline in AD. No successful agent has yet been developed.

Management with a palliative approach is the main goal. A majority of people with AD develop at least one psychotic symptom. Not infrequently, the psychosis does not cause the patient any discomfort, further loss of function, or disruptive behavior. If it does, treatment is indicated. Although not FDA approved for this purpose, very low doses of typical and atypical antipsychotics (e.g., haloperidol 0.5–3 mg or quetiapine 25–100 mg) are usually effective for this, as well as for the agitation that may accompany the psychosis. Cholinesterase inhibitors and SSRIs may be the only tolerated and effective medications in diffuse DLB. Antidepressants should also be used as a first-line intervention for anxiety, restlessness, lability of mood, and nonaggressive agitation. Common clinical mistakes include using higher doses, more anticholinergic antipsychotics, or using hypnoanxiolytics, all of which can worsen the dementia. Parkinson's-related dementia is also not really treatable, but adequate treatment of the disease itself can improve cognition.

Depression is a common complication developing in up to 40% of patients with dementia. Antidepressants must be used with caution because these patients are more prone to delirium. Those with strong anticholinergic side effects (e.g., TCAs) are not the first choice. Antidepressants that are low in cognitive side effects, such as SSRIs and SNRIs, are preferred. As with all medications in older patients, the adage "Start low and go slow" is good to keep in mind. However, older patients frequently require the same antidepressant doses as younger patients. The biggest treatment mistakes made by physicians with this population involve prescribing too low a dose of antidepressant and for too short a time.

For calming agitation and alleviating insomnia, psychoactive drugs should be used cautiously, because they can also aggravate the patient's confusion and generate intolerable side effects. The patient, and especially his family, should be questioned about other drugs used medically or surreptitiously that might compound (or produce) symptoms. Anticholinergic agents, including those sold over the counter or prescribed for glaucoma, are common culprits. Drugs that show some promise of calming agitation in dementia without increasing confusion include SSRIs, atypical antipsychotics, SNRIs, buspirone, and propranolol. Benzodiazepines must be used cautiously, if at all, as they can be disinhibiting. Shorter-acting agents should be used first to prevent the serious side effects often seen with long-acting drugs in older adults. The use of several anticonvulsants utilized in bipolar disorder, most commonly valproic acid, lamotrigine, and carbamazepine, can also be safe and effective.

If the patient has a vascular dementia, then removing the risk factors of hypertension (e.g., cigarette smoking) is the starting point. Low-dose aspirin may reduce the risk of new infarcts.

Psychosocial Interventions

Because the care of patients with dementia falls mainly to loved ones and custodians, they must become partners in the patient's treatment plan. For family members, being a caretaker is usually a novel but highly stressful experience; it is difficult and draining, demoralizing and devastating. Relatives need support and practical instruction, and a major task of the physician or therapist is to provide both.

Patient care. The primary goal is to make the patient with dementia as comfortable as possible. The environment should be kept simple and helpful. Clocks, calendars, labels, lists, familiar routines, short-term tasks, brief walks, and simple physical exercises (to prevent muscle atrophy) are the elements that improve the patient's quality of life and foster self-respect. In a majority of patients with AD, memory for facts is much worse than memory for how to do things; they may still enjoy activities such as golf as long as someone else keeps score.

Patients should be allowed and encouraged to do what they can, but *only* what they can. Pressing too hard—for example, trying to preserve memory by exercising it—only leads to frustration and resentment. Patients with dementia dislike abdicating familiar tasks such as handling money, driving, cooking, and later on, the self-care of bathing, dressing, using the toilet, and living alone. Attempts should be made to include the patient in these tasks however minor the input. It is helpful to break tasks down into small steps and keep possessions simple and organized. Attempts to help may be greeted with insults, complaints, annoying questions, tears, or rage. Responding with hostility is pointless and harmful; distracting and calming patients works better. When these patients lose things and then blame others for stealing them, instead of refuting the accusation, which is pointless, offer to look for the lost items. Reassurance repeated several times each hour is never too much. Later, as words fail, touch may still reassure. Music, television, and other distractors may help calm the individual. Sleeping areas should be made safe, since patients are likely to become more confused at night, wander about, and hurt themselves.

Moving patients to a senior citizen's apartment, sheltered housing, or a nursing home is usually necessary when they become dangerous to themselves, hallucinate, lose bowel or bladder control, or otherwise make life impossible for their caretakers. The reasons for such a move should be calmly reiterated; patients will forget the content of the explanations, but the *repeated reassurance* is what counts. Caretakers often feel guilty for "putting Mom away." However, caretakers need to recognize that many facilities today provide very positive environments. After successful placement, most caretakers state, "I waited too long to do this. I now see I should have done this much sooner."

Family counseling. When dementia is first diagnosed, some relatives deny the patient's illness (e.g., "Everybody grows old"), others blame the patient for being "deliberately difficult" (e.g., "She remembers when she wants to!"), while others are relieved to have an explanation for the patient's difficult behavior. In time, the family members feel overwhelmed and helpless. They may become angry at professionals for "not doing enough"; they may vent their frustrations on each other, and latent family tensions may surface under the strain of caring for a relative with dementia. A son or daughter may feel guilty about resenting the ill mother or father; the children may be ashamed of the parent or think he or she would be better off dead. A spouse may regret the "loss" of the golden years. The clinician must care for the caretakers, who must be told that caring for a loved one with dementia is an enormously difficult task, over which the family members must not destroy themselves. Thorough education about dementia and how to manage it is critical in order to prevent the many destructive approaches families may use. Loved ones often benefit from a self-help group and the kind of literature often provided through the national Alzheimer's Association or local chapters. The "caregiver bill of rights" should be given to families. Families should be told to lower expectations, understand why psychosis occurs with memory loss, try to live with it rather than react, and use humor whenever and wherever possible. Of course, to be a good caregiver, the caregiver must remain healthy, which requires trusting others to help and giving him- or herself clear and scheduled breaks, among other things. Caregivers should be encouraged to take advantage of private sitters, bath aides, daycare facilities, and respite beds, so that they can have several hours to a couple of days off from their responsibilities. Addressing legal issues soon after a diagnosis of dementia is made is an extremely important action. Having a legal, durable power of attorney, including medical decision-making, assigned to a person who is chosen and trusted by the patient, while he or she remains competent to do so, will greatly ease the stressful and extremely difficult course and problems that come with dementia. Matter-of-factly and calmly addressing legal issues, including monies and driving, will help the patient and family. Driving is often a volatile issue and one the physician should not avoid.

In summary, there are four treatable aspects of dementia: memory loss, depression, psychosis and agitation, and the caregiver/family. By diagnosing and treating depression and reversible dementias, by removing risk factors, by helping families help the patient, and by monitoring the treatment of the memory symptoms, today's clinicians can offer enormous assistance to these patients and their families. Treatment of AD and dementias can be very rewarding and is a great example of the virtues of palliative medicine, where all interventions are aimed at improving quality of life and slowing disease progression while not creating additional discomfort or symptoms.

AMNESTIC DISORDERS

Clinical Presentation

Amnesia, Latin for "forgetfulness," may occur by itself. The patient with an amnestic disorder may have profound difficulty remembering anything from yesterday or from 1 hour ago, but can converse sensibly with clear awareness and reasonable judgment. Immediate recall is preserved but there is a severe deficit in acquiring memories of new experiences or learning new information (anterograde amnesia). Very commonly there is also a retrograde memory deficit, involving loss of memories for episodes, experiences, and information acquired before the onset of the disorder (retrograde amnesia). In amnestic disorder only memory is affected and other cognitive functions are intact. The diagnostic criteria for amnestic disorders are listed in Table 10-6. Amnestic disorders are typically attributed to an underlying neurological condition such as infection, trauma, tumors, or other disease affecting the hypothalamic-diencephalic system or the hippocampal regions. Prognosis depends upon whether the underlying lesion or pathological process has a tendency to improve.

Clinical Course and Complications

If the memory loss resulted from a single event, such as a stroke in the hippocampus, all events after that date will be vaguely or never remembered.

Events prior to the stroke have been stored and still can be recalled. Toxins, including alcohol, can more insidiously cause pure memory loss. Social, intelligent patients may attempt to mask the problem with confabulation ("Didn't I see you at Harry's Bar last week?") or punting questions back to the examiner ("What do you usually call this place?"). Those who have had no memory for years will be perplexed each day at how old people around them look, because they only remember how they looked many years ago. In some, remote memory may also deteriorate, but unlike in dementia, other areas of function remain intact.

Management and Treatment

Removal of risk conditions such as alcohol use, poor nutrition, exposure to toxins, and hypertension can prevent further deterioration. Patients should be kept in familiar environments as long as possible, because new ones may be difficult or impossible for them to learn. As in dementia, memory devices such as clocks, calendars, labels, lists, and familiar routines help. If patients have completely lost the ability to establish new memories, the deficit can be used to their advantage, as the following case illustrates.

> A 72-year-old woman with no recent memory had always liked her lifelong work as a cherry picker. She was brought into the hospital after hitting an attendant at a nursing home. When she had asked "When can I go back to cherry picking?," the attendant had told her "Never." The attendant later regretted this choice of words. The woman was not usually violent and, in the hospital, continued to ask when she could work. She got increasingly agitated as staff stalled, trying to avoid confrontations. Then one day she sat by a window smiling; this continued for several days. When her nurse was asked what had caused this pleasant transformation, the nurse said she realized that the patient never remembered yesterday, so each day she told the patient that she could go cherry picking tomorrow. From then on, she happily anticipated the coming day.

OTHER NEUROCOGNITIVE DISORDERS

As would be expected, there are patients who present with cognitive deficits or frank impairment who do not "fit" into the categories previously discussed. As new scientific evidence comes to light, our diagnostic categories may expand and become increasingly precise. For the present time, this category is for those people with cognitive dysfunction that is not easily explained.

The *DSM-5* has added a new diagnostic category, Mild Neurocognitive Disorder, characterized by *modest* impairment in cognitive functioning as evidenced by neuropsychological testing or quantified clinical assessment, accompanied by objective evidence of a systemic medical condition or central nervous system dysfunction. This disorder bears some relationship to what was called benign senescent forgetfulness, or mild cognitive impairment (MCI). Since this condition can develop into a full dementia, there is considerable interest and controversy concerning its diagnosis, etiology, and mechanisms.

Postconcussional disorder follows head trauma. Usually, specific areas of the brain suffering injury correlate with the impairment seen, but not always. This condition again represents our "edge of knowledge" and has various presentations that do not always make sense with our current understanding of the brain and its function. Prevention of head trauma is the prudent course of action—parents may want to look into headgear for their aspiring soccer stars. Boxers, such as Mohammed Ali, provide testimonials to the dementing effects of repeated head trauma (*dementia pugilistica*).

References

Advancing Excellence in America's Nursing Homes. (2008). Available at http://www.nhqual itycam paign.org.

Alzheimer's Association National Office, 225 N. Michigan Ave., Fl. 17, Chicago, IL 60601. 24/7 Helpline: 1.800.272.3900 Online: http://www.alz.org.

American Psychiatric Association, (2013). *Diagnostic and statistical manual of mental disorders*, 5th ed. Arlington. VA: American Psychiatric Association.

Burggraf, V., Kye, Y., Kim, K.Y., & Knight, A.L. (2014). *Healthy aging: Principles and clinical practice for clinicians*. Philadelphia: Wolters Kluwer Health

Changing Aging in America. (2008). Available at http://www.almosthomedoc.org.

Charatan, F. (1985). Depression and the elderly: Diagnosis and treatment. *Psychiatric Annals*, 15, 313–316.

Emery, V.L., & Oxman, T.E. (1992). Update on the dementia spectrum of depression. *American Journal of Psychiatry*, 149, 305–317.

Folstein, M.F., Folstein, S.E., & McHugh, P.R. (1975). "Mini-Mental State": A practical method for grading the cognitive state of patients for the clinician. *Journal of Psychiatry Research*, 12, 196–198.

Goodwin, D.W. (1985). Alcoholism and genetics: The sins of the father. *Archives of General Psychiatry*, 42, 171–174.

Institute for Healthcare Improvement. (2008). Available at http://www.ihi.org.

Mayo-Smith, M.F. (1997). Pharmacological management of alcohol withdrawal: A meta-analysis and evidence-based practice guideline. *JAMA*, 278, 144–151.

Reynolds, C.F., Hoch, C.C., Kupfer, D.J., Buysse, D.J., Houck, P.R., Stack, J.A., et al. (1988). Bedside differentiation of depressive pseudodementia from dementia. *American Journal of Psychiatry, 145,* 1099–1103.

Stern, T. (1983). Continuous infusion of physostigmine in anticholinergic delirium: A case report. *Journal of Clinical Psychiatry, 44,* 463–464.

Tune, L., Carr, S., Hoag, E., & Cooper, T. (1992). Anticholinergic effects of drugs commonly prescribed for the elderly: Potential means for assessing risk of delirium. *American Journal of Psychiatry, 149,* 1393–1394.

van Gorp, W.G., & Cummings, J.L. (1996). Depression and reversible dementia in an HIV-1 seropositive individual: Implications for the dementia syndrome of depression. *Neurocase, 2,* 455–459.

Wells, C.E., & McEvoy, J.P. (1982). Organic mental disorders. In J.H. Greist, J.W. Jefferson, & R.L. Spitzer (Eds.), *Treatment of mental disorders* (pp. 3–43). New York: Oxford University Press.

Wengel, S.P., Roccaforte, W.H., & Burke, W.J. (1998). Donepezil improves symptoms of delirium in dementia: Implications for future research. *Journal of Geriatric Psychiatry and Neurology, 11,* 159–161.

World Health Organization. (1992). *The ICD–10 classification of mental and behavioural disorders: Clinical descriptions and diagnostic guidelines.* Geneva: World Health Organization.

11

Substance-Related Disorders

Substance abuse is as old as the substances abused. Rock carvings in caves from the fourth millennium BC display workmen making beer from barley. In 2285 BC a gentleman in China was allegedly banished for getting soused on a rice beverage. Individuals and religions of every era have sought to suspend reality and alter moods by the simplest and quickest way possible—"better living through chemistry."

> *Substance* is a general term encompassing alcohol, recreational drugs, and medications. *Substance, chemical,* and *drugs* are employed interchangeably. Nonpsychoactive drugs (e.g., insulin) are also abused, but this book solely discusses *psychoactive* substances. Unless otherwise specified, *this* text uses *misuse* and *abuse* synonymously.

The current frequency of this "better living" is hard to assess epidemiologically: The drug scene constantly changes, users are reluctant to mention their drug-taking, antidrug/alcohol groups have vested interests in exaggerating dangers, definitions of drug misuse vary considerably, and it is unclear which substances are deemed problematic—tobacco? caffeine? alcohol? Having said this, seven facts are worth noting: (1) The National Epidemiologic Survey on Alcohol and Related Conditions (NESARC) by adult Americans revealed yearly prevalence rates of 8.5% for alcohol abuse and alcoholism and 9.4% for any other substance of abuse. (2) These figures do not include the most frequent substance disorder among Americans, tobacco use disorder, which has a lifetime prevalence of 36%. (3) Substance abuse varies across the life cycle, with changes over time in the prevalence of various drug use. During middle age, alcoholism is more of a problem. As the perceived risk of using a drug increases, the actual use of that drug decreases (and vice versa). (4) After age 44, substance misuse declines for both sexes. (5) Substances are abused more by men than women, more by inner-city residents than country dwellers, more by nongraduates than college graduates. (6) European-Americans and African-Americans have the same overall rate of substance abuse. (7) People with psychiatric disorders, including anxiety, antisocial personality, and mood disorders, have greatly increased rates of substance abuse. The NESARC results show substantial comorbidity between substance use disorders and independent mood and anxiety disorders: About 20% of persons with a substance use disorder within the past year experience a mood or anxiety disorder within the same time period. Similarly, about 20% of persons with a current mood or anxiety disorder experience a current substance use disorder. Seventy-eight percent of people with drug and alcohol problems experience a psychiatric disorder in their lifetime, and 65% at any point in time. The most common disorders are antisocial personality disorder, anxiety disorders, psychosexual dysfunctions, major depression, and dysthymia. Alcohol and other substance abusers have a higher rate of mood and anxiety disorders than the general population (e.g., Comsay et al., 2006).

DEFINITIONS

Intoxication and withdrawal are the most prevalent substance-related disorders. *Intoxication* is a reversible substance-specific syndrome that arises during or shortly after ingesting a substance and often disturbs perceptions, wakefulness, sleep, attention, judgment, emotionality, and movement. Intoxication becomes a disorder when clinically significant maladaptive behavioral changes (e.g., picking fights with everyone, driving into a ditch) or psychological changes (e.g., alternatively laughing and crying, inability to compute the restaurant bill) occur during or soon after ingestion. All drugs of abuse have an intoxication syndrome. *Withdrawal* is a substance-specific syndrome that follows when a chronic intake of a substance has been abruptly stopped or greatly diminished and usually manifests as restlessness, apprehension, anxiety, irritability, insomnia, and impaired concentration. It becomes a disorder when clinically significant distress or impaired function occur. Not all drugs have a withdrawal syndrome (e.g., hallucinogens and inhalants). Table 11-1 lists criteria for substance intoxication and withdrawal.

Intoxication and withdrawal involve two pharmacological phenomena: *tolerance*, which is the need to markedly increase a drug's intake to attain its original effects, or experiencing a markedly diminished effect with continued use of the same amount of the drug; and *cross-tolerance*, which occurs when a drug exhibits tolerance to other drugs, usually in the same class. For

TABLE 11-1
Diagnostic Criteria for Substance Intoxication and Withdrawal
Substance Intoxication

A. A **transient condition following the administration of alcohol or other psychoactive substance**. Acute intoxication is usually closely related to dose levels. Intensity of intoxication lessens with time, and effects eventually disappear in the absence of further use of the substance.

B. The administration of the psychoactive substance results in **clinically significant disturbances in level of consciousness, cognition, perception, affect or behavior, or other psychophysiological functions and responses**.

C. **Signs and symptoms characteristic for the psychoactive substance** develop during or shortly after administration. Symptoms of intoxication need not always reflect primary actions of the substance: for instance, depressant drugs may lead to symptoms of agitation or hyperactivity, and stimulant drugs may lead to socially withdrawn and introverted behavior. Effects of substances such as cannabis and hallucinogens may be particularly unpredictable. Moreover, many psychoactive substances are capable of producing different types of effect at different dose levels. For example, alcohol may have apparently stimulant effects on behavior at lower dose levels, lead to agitation and aggression with increasing dose levels, and produce clear sedation at very high levels.

D. The disturbance is **not better explained by another mental disorder, medical condition, or psychoactive substance.** This should be a main diagnosis only in cases where intoxication occurs without more persistent alcohol- or drug-related problems being concomitantly present.

Substance Withdrawal

A. A **transient physiological state when substance use has ceased or been reduced.** Onset and course of the withdrawal state are time-limited and are related to the type of substance and the dose being used immediately before abstinence. The withdrawal state may have associated medical complications.

B. **Characteristic signs and symptoms for the psychoactive substance** develop closely following cessation or reduction of its administration, usually after prolonged and/or high-dose use of that substance. Physical symptoms vary according to the substance being used. Psychological disturbances (e.g., anxiety, depression, and sleep disorders) are also common features of withdrawal. It should be remembered that withdrawal symptoms can be induced byconditioned/learned stimuli in the absence of immediately precedingsubstance use. In such cases a diagnosis of withdrawal state should bemade only if it is warranted in terms of severity.

C. The signs and symptoms result in **significant distress or significant impairment** in personal, family, social, educational, occupational, or other important area of functioning.Typically, the patient is likely to report that withdrawal symptoms are relieved by further substance use of the same (or a closely related) substance with the intention of relieving or avoiding withdrawal symptoms.

D. The disturbance is **not better explained by another mental disorder, medical condition, or psychoactive substance**.

Many symptoms present in drug withdrawal state may also becaused by other psychiatric conditions, e.g., anxiety states and depressive disorders. Simple "hangover" or tremor due to other conditions should not be confused with the symptoms of a withdrawal state. The withdrawal state is one of the indicators of dependence syndrome and this latter diagnosis should also be considered. Withdrawal state should be coded as the main diagnosis if it is the reason for referral and sufficiently severe to require medical attention in its own right.

Note: ICD-10 (pp. 68–72) and DSM-5 (pp. 581–583)

example, patients tolerant to diazepam are tolerant to barbiturates, but not to heroin. In general, the greater the tolerance to a drug, the worse the withdrawal and the greater the amount needed to become intoxicated.

DSM-5 no longer subdivides *substance use disorders* into substance *dependence* and substance *abuse*. The *consequences* of the substance use was what defined these illnesses. *Addiction* is the common name for the more severe substance use disorders and is equivalent to the former term substance dependence. *Psychological dependence* is characterized by the compulsive misuse of a substance; taking it longer than planned, intense craving (urges and anticipation); unsuccessful efforts to cut down (loss of control); a preoccupation with obtaining it; the sacrifice of social, occupational, and recreational activities; and often physical or psychological consequences. *Physiological dependence* is the repeated use of a drug to avert physical withdrawal reactions or taking larger amounts to get the same effects (tolerance). Psychological and physical dependencies often coexist. Table 11-2 lists diagnostic criteria for substance use disorders.

Problems caused by substances include car accidents, demotions or job terminations, divorce, loss of child custody, arrests, and loss of friends. The addicted (dependent) person typically minimizes the extent of his substance use disorder: "Yeah, sure I've had a few DWIs (driving while intoxicated), paid a few visits to the emergency room for stitches after bar fights, and spent the night in jail once—but I'm no alcoholic. I can stop anytime I want. I always drink the same amount and I never have withdrawal."

ASSESSMENT OF SUBSTANCE MISUSE

Many factors complicate the diagnosis and treatment of substance abusers. For starters, many potential patients are unreliable informants. Unlike most patients, their objectives differ from their therapists': Many abusers *want* their habit—or as a heroin addict put it, "If I had to choose between heroin and food and sex, I'd take heroin." Denial and lying are often their norms; at times, even addicts don't know which they are doing. Outright lying is common to avoid detection and to hasten discharge. On admission, however, already-discovered addicts may exaggerate their intake to garner more of the drug during detoxification. For all these reasons, clinicians should favor objective signs and social behaviors over subjective reports, and corroborate and supplement this information by interviewing family and friends and obtaining a urine drug screen. Because these patients frequently lie, deny, manipulate, and relapse, they habitually frustrate and infuriate clinicians.

TABLE 11-2
Diagnostic Criteria for Substance-Use Disorders

A. A maladaptive pattern where more than one of the following have been present together at some time during the previous year and caused significant distress or impairment:

(1) **difficulties in controlling substance-taking** behavior in terms of its onset, termination, or levels of use;

(2) **desire or inability to cut down** on substance use;

(3) **increased amount of time** necessary to obtain or take the substance or to recover from its effects;

(4) a **strong desire or sense of compulsion [craving]** to take the substance; the subjective awareness of compulsion to use drugs is most commonly seen during attempts to stop or control substance use;

*(5) *recurrent use leads to failure in fulfilling major role obligations at home, school, or work;*

*(6) *continued use despite having persistent or recurrent interpersonal problems;*

(7) progressive **neglect of alternative pleasures or interests** because of psychoactive substance use;

*(8) *recurrent use in situations where it is physically hazardous;*

(9) persisting with **substance use despite clear evidence of overtly harmful consequences (physical or psychological)**, such as harm to the liver through excessive drinking, depressive mood states consequent to periods of heavy substance use, or drug-related impairment of cognitive functioning; efforts should be made to determine that the user was actually, or could be expected to be, aware of the nature and extent of the harm;

(10) **evidence of tolerance**, such that increased doses of the psychoactive substance are required in order to achieve effects originally produced by lower doses (clear examples of this are found in alcohol- and opiate-dependent individuals who may take daily doses sufficient to incapacitate or kill nontolerant users);

(11) a **physiological withdrawal state** when substance use has ceased or been reduced, as evidenced by the characteristic withdrawal syndrome for the substance or use of the same (or aclosely related) substance with the intention of relieving oravoiding withdrawal symptoms.

DSM-5 adds the three criteria indicated by asterisks.

The greater the number of met criteria increases the likelihood of addiction (dependence). The dependence syndrome may be present for a specific substance (e.g., tobacco or diazepam), for a class of substances (e.g., opioid drugs), or for a wider range of different substances (as for those individuals who feel a sense of compulsion regularly to use whatever drugs are available and who show distress, agitation, and/or physical signs of a withdrawal state upon abstinence).

Note: From ICD-10 (p. 69) and DSM-5 (p. 577)

Therefore, therapists should constantly monitor their own angry and moralistic feelings. Moreover, therapists should not take these patients' provocations and relapses personally: They are a "natural" part of the course of substance abuse.

There are many screening instruments for alcoholism. The CAGE questionnaire (Ewing, 1984) is so called because the name is an acronym for the four areas probed (Cut Down, Annoyed, Guilty, and Eye Opener) and because one is prisoner to an addiction. The following questions are used:

Cut Down   1. Have you ever felt you should cut down on your drinking?
Annoyed   2. Have other people annoyed you by criticizing your drinking?
Guilty   3. Have you ever felt guilty about drinking?
Eye Opener   4. Have you ever taken a drink in the morning to steady your nerves or get rid of a hangover?

Two or more positive answers indicate alcohol dependence and predicts ≥8 drinks per day. This questionnaire accurately determines the presence or absence of alcoholism over 85% of the time (Beresford, Blow, Hill, Singer, & Lucey, 1990); however, it misses more cases of alcohol dependence in women than it does in men, and is relatively insensitive on picking up alcoholism early in the illness. Substituting question 3 with "How many drinks does it take to make you high?" may improve sensitivity (more than two drinks suggests tolerance). Some clinicians use the CAGE questions with slight modification (substitute drug use for drinking) to screen for other drugs of abuse. For adolescents and young adults who have not yet experienced negative consequences from their drug use, a positive response to "Have you used street drugs more than five times in your life?" suggests the need for further assessment.

One drink is defined as equivalent volume amounts having 0.6 oz of ethanol (12 oz beer = 5 oz wine = 1.5 oz liquor). One drink (8–12 grams of ethanol) is metabolized in one hour and raises the blood alcohol level about 150–200 mg/100ml. You can smell alcohol on breath down to about 30 mg/100 ml.

A more sensitive instrument is the Alcohol Use Disorders Identification Test (AUDIT), a 10-item questionnaire. With a maximum score of 40, a score of 8 or above indicates problematic drinking. A very simple screening tool derived from the diagnostic criteria is to ask two questions: (1) "Has use of the substance caused psychological or physical harm to the patient or other people?" (2) "If so, has the patient continued to use the substance?" After screening patients for substance misuse, Table 11-3 can be used to assess substance intoxication by applying its extensive evaluation guidelines to those who are suspected of having substance-related disorders.

As soon as clinicians identify and treat one drug problem, another typi-

---

TABLE 11-3
The Assessment of Suspected Substance Misuse

I. HISTORY
  A. Substance(s)
      1. Name(s) (e.g., diazepam, cocaine)
      2. Polydrug use: Indicates names and preferred combinations
      3. Special preparations (e.g., freebasing)
  B. Route (e.g., ingestion, inhalation, injection)
  C. Amount
      1. Typical dose, frequency, and duration of drug use
      2. Dose and duration of drug use during past 10 days
      3. The time and amount of the most recent drug use
  D. Patterns of use
      1. Self-medication: Is it for physical, psychiatric, or emotional problems, or "just for fun"?
      2. Identifiable events or stressors that increase or decrease the use of a substance (e.g., drinking before sex, "chipping" heroin before job interviews, smoking after meals)
      3. History: How did substance abuse begin? Why does it continue? Are there conditioned relapses? What began and ended the patient's longest drug-free period?
      4. Timing: How early in the day does the patient first use the substance?
      5. Style (e.g., sneaking drugs, hiding bottles, boasting, running away, using substances with others or alone)
  E. Acquisition
      1. Sources: legal, illegal, prescription, theft, "mobsters," friends
      2. Time and money spent obtaining substances (e.g., illegal activities such as theft, prostitution, and drug dealing)
  F. Network
      1. Family and friends: Who exerts beneficial and harmful influences on the patient?
      2. Family history of antisocial personality, substance misuse, or mood disorders?
  G. Functioning
      1. Interference with social, occupational, recreational, academic, and familial functioning
      2. Adverse influence on physical health, appearance, finances, and self-image
      3 Legal problems
      4. How does the patient feel *without* the drug?
      5. Impaired organic functioning such as forgetting location of "stash," poor concentration, impaired judgment
      6. Does patient become suicidal or assaultive on the drug?

(continued)

TABLE 11-3
Continued

H. Medical and psychiatric history

1. Drug-related medical illnesses: hepatitis, infections, insomnia, allergies, cirrhosis, TB, AIDS, epilepsy

2. All recently taken prescribed and over-the-counter drugs. Does the patient use these medications differently from what they were prescribed or intended to treat? Does the patient take or sneak other family member's or people's medications? Does the patient use multiple doctors and pharmacies to avoid detection? (Have family bring all medications from the patient's home.)

3. History of psychiatric symptoms or mental illness prior to substance misuse

4. History of substance-related syndromes: flashbacks, delirium, idiosyncratic intoxication, hallucinosis

I. Prior treatment

1. Type, duration, degree of participation, including experiences with community agencies and self-help groups

2. Results as seen by (a) the patient, (b) his or her relatives, and (c) his or her therapist

J. Current motivations to change

1. Why is the patient seeking treatment now?

2. Current threat of jail, divorce, etc.

II. COMMON SYMPTOMS AND SIGNS [With special signs of abuse by adolescents and teenagers in brackets]

A. Prodromal phase

1. Increased tolerance

2. Sneaking chemicals [frequenting odd places during school, such as closets or storage rooms, to take drugs]

3. Temporary amnesia

4. Preoccupation with chemical use

5. Avoids talking about personal use

6. More frequent loss of memory

B. Crucial or basic phase

1. Time lost from work [or changes in school attendance, grades, or discipline]

2. Loss of control (unusual or apparently unmotivated temper outbursts)

3. Alibis [especially about not doing homework]

4. Increased extravagance—time, money, advice; being a "know-it-all"

5. Aggressive or abusive behavior

6. Persistent remorse

7. Periodic abstinence

8. Losing or changing friends

9. Losing clients or position

10. Persistent resentments

11. Diminished self-care and unhealthy appearance

12. Slovenly dress, sunglasses at inappropriate times (to hide dilated or constricted pupils and to diminish glare) and long-sleeved shirts (to hide needle marks)

TABLE 11-3
Continued

13. Borrowing money [and theft of small items from school] to buy drugs
14. Escape—geographical, psychological, social
15. Protecting supply [furtive looks to avoid stash being detected]
16. Morning use of chemical(s)

C. Chronic phase
   1. More-or-less continuous use over 10-hour period
   2. Ethical deterioration
   3 Decreased tolerance
   4. Sleeping at inappropriate times
   5. Indefinable fears
   6. Tangential or incoherent speech; inappropriate remarks
   7. Tremors

III. PHYSICAL EXAMINATION
   A. Rectal and pelvic examinations
      1. Should be considered since substance abusers have a higher incidence of unprotected sexual activity with resulting increased risk of sexually transmitted diseases.
   B. Physical signs
      1. Marks: Scarring along a vein, tattooing over a vein, abscesses, ulcers, and needle tracks. The quantity and age of needle marks can serve as a rough check on the validity of the patient's history.
      2. Nose: Is it dripping? Are nasal membranes infected, swollen, or septum eroded from snorting cocaine?
      3. Pupils: Constricted (miosis) as with opiates or PCP use? Dilated (mydriasis) as with the use of amphetamines, anticholinergics, and hallucinogens?
      4. Signs of intoxication or withdrawal

IV. LABORATORY EXAMINATIONS
   A. Urine screens
      1. Thin layer chemistry (TLC): Sometimes inaccurate; used only for screening
      2. Enzyme immunoassay (EIA) and radio immunoassay (RIA): These two tests have relatively high degrees of sensitivity and specificity; the EIA is a qualitative test, the RIA, quantitative. Detects people who eat poppy seed cake as opiate positive.
      3. Gas chromatography mass spectrometry (GC/MS): The most reliable and informative of tests; expensive but the "gold standard."
   B. Serum levels
      1. Abused substances (primarily to establish quantity when urine tests are positive or abused substances are already known)
      2. Other psychotropic drugs (e.g., antidepressants)
   C. Liver and renal function tests
      1. GGT: This liver enzyme (gamma glutamyltranserase) is often the first to rise in alcoholism.
      2. Carbohydrate deficient transferrin (CDT) is a liver enzyme that rises only in heavy drinking over a long period of time.

cally pops up, resulting in a constant information lag about drug abuse. More serious is that *polydrug abuse* has increased sharply. In comparison to single-drug abusers, polydrug abusers have more severe and complicated withdrawals and bleaker prognoses. They are harder to diagnose and treat, especially in emergencies, since they present a more confounding mix of signs and symptoms than single-substance abusers. Not uncommonly, an inpatient being successfully treated for an opiate intoxication suddenly convulses from benzodiazepine withdrawal 4 days later. The lesson is that polydrug abuse must be evaluated for every substance abuser. Use may be confirmed through testing body fluids (see Table 11-4 for typical length of detection times in urine or blood).

In general, withdrawal, intoxication, and dependence are addressed in this sequence. The most dangerous acute problem is *hypnoanxiolytic* (including alcohol) withdrawal, since this can be lethal, whereas opiate or stimulant (cocaine, amphetamine) withdrawal is uncomfortable but not likely to cause serious morbidity unless the patient has pre-existing serious medical conditions. When it is unclear whether patients are intoxicated or

TABLE 11-4
Typical Length of Detection Times after Substance Use

SUBSTANCE	URINE	BLOOD
Alcohol	6–24 hours	12–24 hours
Amphetamine	1–3 days	12 hours
Methamphetamine	3–5 days	1–3 days
Cocaine	2–5 days	2–10 days
	(7–10 days with heavy use)	
Cotinine (product of nicotine)	2–4 days	2–4 days
MDMA (Ecstasy)	3–4 days	3–4 days
PCP	3–8 days	1–3 days
	(30 days with heavy use)	
LSD	2–24 hours	2–4 days
Barbiturates	24 hours	1–2 days
Phenobarbital	2–3 weeks	4–7 days
Benzodiazepines	7 days	6–48 hours
	(4–6 weeks if heavy use)	
Cannabis	7–10 days	2–3 days
	(30 days if heavy use)	(two weeks if heavy use)
Morphine or Heroin	2–4 days	1–3 days
Methadone	7–10 days	24 hours
Codeine	2–3 days	1–4 days
Steroids	3–30 days	—

withdrawing from a hypnoanxiolytic (sedative) by itself, the clinician usually errs on the side of treating withdrawal, since that poses a greater threat than intoxication. However, opiate intoxication can certainly be lethal especially when in combination with hypnoanxiolytics. So whenever in doubt, the possibility of opiate intoxication must be considered and appropriately treated (often with the opioid antagonist naloxone). Table 11-5 lists the major pharmacological effects of psychoactive substances.

ETIOLOGY AND COMORBIDITY

The underlying neurobiological mechanisms for substance intoxication are still being elucidated. Drugs of abuse seemed to have a final common reward pathway in the brain, leading from the ventral tegmental area and the nucleus accumbens to the frontal and prefrontal cortex, where dopaminergic pathways complete the reward process.

> According to the "self-medication hypothesis," the original choice of an abused drug is not random, but is partly made to alleviate a specific distressing symptom or affect. At first, narcotics are used to mask pain, hypnotics to induce sleep, cocaine to eliminate depression, amphetamines to "get up," marijuana to join the crowd, or bourbon to rid boredom. No matter how substance abuse begins, however, once it becomes habitual and stopping it causes severe distress, drug dependence has occurred. At this juncture the habit is sustained less from original motives and more to quell a drug-induced biological imperative. Therefore, treating only the initial cause is less effective: Drug dependence must be directly treated, along with the original problems. An example: When hospitalized, a chronic alcoholic was very suspicious. After 3 weeks of "drying out," his "head cleared" and his suspiciousness disappeared. Only then did it become apparent that marital problems greatly affected his alcoholism.
>
> Although the comorbidity between substance abuse and other psychiatric illnesses is high, use of many substances mimic psychiatric illnesses. Many problems, including conditions likely to prompt relapse, cannot be evaluated properly until the substance abuser has been drug-free for 10 days. (Some experts suggest 1–3 months.) In general, the substances that have no withdrawal syndromes (e.g., hallucinogens) are likely to elicit only psychological dependence. Hallucinogens can also induce "reverse tolerance" in the user: The *more* the drug is used, the less is needed to obtain the original effects. Alcohol, barbiturates, opiates, phencyclidine, solvents, and inhalants

TABLE 11-5

Quick Recognition of Substance Intoxication (X) and Withdrawal (0)

SIGNS AND SYMPTOMS	ALCOHOL	HYPNO-ANXIOLYTICS	STIMULANTS			CANNABIS	PCP	HALLUCINOGEN	INHALANTS	OPIOIDS
			CAFFEINE	NICOTINE	COCAINE					
Dysarthria/slurred speech	X	X					X		X	X
Ataxia /incoordination	X	X					X	X	X	X
Unsteady gait	X	X							X	
Inattention or confusion	X	X	O		X	X			X	X
Concentration problems	X	X		O		X			X	X
Drowsiness or lethargy	X	X	O						X	X
Stupor or coma	X	X			X				X	X
Restlessness			X	O		O				
Inexhaustibility			X							
Agitation or aggression	O	O	X		X O	X O				
Motor slowing					X O				X	
Nervousness or anxiety	O	O	X	O		X				
Excitement or euphoria			X			X			X	
Dysphoria			O	O	O	O				O
Nystagmus	X	X					X		X	
Dilated pupils					X			X		O
Constricted pupils							X			X
Blurred vision								X	X	
Injected conjunctiva						X				
Diaphoresis		O			X	O		X		O
Flushed			X							
Fever or chills					X	O				O

Symptom	1	2	3	4	5	6
Tachycardia	o	x	x		x	o
Palpitations	o	x	x		x	o
Hypertension			x	x	x	
Appetite increase			o	o		o
Anorexia or weight loss			x	o		
Dry mouth			x	x		
Nausea, vomiting, diarrhea	o	x	x	x	x	o
Lacrimation or rhinorrhea						o
Diuresis	o					o
Insomnia	o	x	o	o		o
Hypersomnia			o	o		
Twitching or tremor	o	x	o	o	x	
Seizures	o		x		x	
Muscle rigidity			x		x	
Muscle aches or pain						o
Reflexes decreased		x			x	
Numbness to pain			x	x		
Weakness or fatigue		x	x o	x	x	
Hyperacusis					x	
Hallucinations or illusions	o		x	x		
Vivid dreams			o	o		
Dizziness		x				
Headache	o					
Rambling speech	x					
Irritability or anger			o			

TABLE 11-6
Major Substance-Related Diagnoses

SUBSTANCE	MISUSE (ABUSE AND DEPENDENCE)	INTOXICATION	WITHDRAWAL
Alcohol	X	X	X
Caffeine		X	X
Xanthine derivative, stimulant and performance enhancers, coffee, tea, soft drinks			
Cannabis	x	X	X
Hashish from resin, marijuana from leaves, stems, and buds			
Cocaine	X	X	X
Hydrochloride powder, freebase (ether/ammonia extract), crack (sodium bicarbonate extract)			
Hallucinogens		X	X
LSD, mescaline from cactus, psilocybin from mushrooms, myristicin from nutmeg			
Inhalants	X	X	
Organic solvents such as gasoline, toluene, ether; nitrous oxide, amyl nitrite			
Nicotine	X	X*	X
Stimulant in cigarettes and chewing tobacco			
Opioids	X	X	X
Pain-killers including fentanyl, morphine, heroin, oxycodone, methadone, codeine			
Phencyclidine	X	X	
Animal tranquilizer, anesthetic			
Sedatives	X	X	X
Hypnotics and anxiolytics including barbiturates, chloral hydrate, and benzodiazepines			
Stimulants including amphetamine salts	X	X	X
Other:	X	X	X
MDMA (3,4-methylene-dioxy-methamphetamine)			
Anticholinergics including atropine, belladona, and diphenhydramine			
Steroids			

*Not classified in *DSM-5* but does exist.

are most likely to kill in overdose. Table 11-6 lists possible diagnoses for frequently misused substances.

ALCOHOL

There are more English synonyms for *drunk* than for any other word. Benjamin Franklin was the first to publish them—228; recently Flexner listed 353 synonyms and said that he had just scratched the surface. *Alcohol* comes from the Arabic *alkuhl*, because Arabs distilled it in AD 600. The practice spread and so did the problems. Ghengis Khan counseled his troops, "A soldier must not get drunk oftener than once a week. It would, of course, be better if he did not get drunk at all, but one should not expect the impossible" (Goodwin & Guze, 1984, p. 148).

Annual per capita alcohol consumption in 2010 in the United States was estimated at 2.29 gallons of pure ethanol. Today, alcoholism, along with nicotine dependence, is America's most serious substance abuse problem, as it is for every other industrialized nation (it costs New York City alone well over $1 billion a year). Alcoholism is an illness of "normal" people, not bums. The typical person with alcoholism is in his or her mid-30s and has a good job, home, and family; less than 5% of this population lives on Skid Row.

A practical definition of alcoholism is "when a person's alcohol consumption repeatedly interferes with occupational or social functioning, emotional state, or physical health." This definition stresses impairment of the individual rather than an arbitrary consumption figure, such as whether the person downs 1 or 5 or 50 drinks a week. People with a condition called "idiosyncratic intoxication" often become violent on a single drink; for them, one drink constitutes alcoholism. In the service of denial, patients and relatives will nitpick over the definition of alcoholism. By stating that alcoholism exists whenever problems with alcohol arise repeatedly, the clinician circumvents semantic quibbling. Part of the clinician's job is to teach patients how the diagnosis is made so that they can make it for themselves. Many patients believe the term *alcoholic* only applies to Skid Row bums. For many, it is initially easier to agree to having "problems with alcohol."

Clinical Presentation

Although people with alcoholism vary considerably, in general they suffer from apprehension, agitation, dysphoria, guilt, remorse, despair, hopelessness, futility, self-deprecation, and insomnia. Their symptoms are usually worse in the morning, after not drinking for hours. *The Lost Weekend*—an instructive movie for every clinician—portrays with bone-chilling accuracy the "typical" life of a person with alcoholism: obsessed with drink, continually lying about it, hiding bottles, sneaking drinks, and disappearing repeatedly. After "going on the wagon," people with alcoholism typically reexperience anxiety or depression and start drinking again; a vicious spiral of abstinence–dysphoria–drinking escalates until the individual reaches "rock bottom."

The generic diagnostic criteria for substance use disorder in Table 11-2 apply exactly to alcohol. So do the diagnostic criteria for intoxication and withdrawal enumerated in Table 11-1. Other mental disorders related to alcohol are delirium, persisting amnestic disorder, psychotic disorder (with delusions or hallucinations), mood disorder, anxiety disorder, sexual dysfunction, and sleep disorder.

Withdrawal is most critical, since 15% of alcoholics who develop delirium tremens ("DTs") die. The first and most common withdrawal symptom is tremulousness, which begins a few hours after stopping, or greatly reducing, alcohol intake. The others are the same for all hypnoanxiolytics (see Table 11-5).

> Alcohol is one of the few drugs to cause "*blackouts*," a temporary (anterograde) amnesia in which short-term (but not long-term) memory is lost, while other intellectual and motor functions remain intact. To illustrate: The day after a "bender" (remaining drunk for several days), a surgeon with alcoholism became angry at a nurse for allowing a tracheostomy to be done on one of his patients without notifying him. She reminded the surgeon that he himself had performed the procedure the day before. He apparently had a blackout, since he had no recollection of doing it. As in this case, people with alcoholism may appear to function normally and even perform complex tasks during a blackout. Research suggests that the forgotten material does not hold special psychological significance, but results from a neurological deficit in retrieving new information. Blackouts scare people with alcoholism, who are often terrified of having committed violence they can't remember; blackouts are also frightening because they appear to be dramatic proof that alcohol is destroying their brains. In truth, however, blackouts have little prognostic significance.

Epidemiology

In the United States the National Institute on Drug Abuse (NIDA) estimates that approximately 8.5% of adults are alcoholic, for a total of perhaps 14 million people with alcoholism in the country. One-quarter of these individuals have an onset prior to the age of 20, and 85% have become alcoholic by the age of 40; onset is earlier for African-Americans and Native-Americans than for European-Americans. Many times (3:1 or greater) more men than women are alcoholic. Women develop alcoholism later but more rapidly than men; in women, an average of approximately 13 years elapses prior to treatment; in men, it is 21 years.

Etiology and Pathogenesis

About half of all hospitalized males with alcoholism have a family history of alcoholism. In contrast to people with nonfamilial alcoholism, these individuals develop alcoholism earlier in life, have greater dependency, bleaker prognoses, fewer nonalcoholic psychiatric problems, and are less able to maintain "controlled drinking" (Bohman et al., 1987). The best predictor of future alcoholism among adolescents is a family history of alcoholism (Goodwin, 1985).

Twin studies generally support this division by showing that heredity plays a major role in some, but not all, cases of alcoholism. Whether reared by biological parents with alcoholism or by nonalcoholic adopted parents, the sons of fathers with alcoholism have three to four times the normal rate of alcoholism, whereas daughters have only a slightly higher rate than the general population. Cloninger (Bohman et al., 1987) described "type 1 alcoholism" as milder, starts after age 25, hits men and women equally, needs environmental factors (e.g., social drinking in bars) as well as genetics, and is 20% heritable. "Type 2 alcoholism" is often severe, starts in the teens, hits men only, and is 90% heritable for male offspring of type 2 fathers. Twenty to 35% of sons of fathers with alcoholism develop alcoholism; 5–10% of daughters do so. Mood disorders may run in families with alcoholism, but this remains controversial. There may also be a relationship between anxiety disorders and alcohol problems: Alcohol problems are more likely to follow the onset of agoraphobia and social phobia; alcohol misuse is more likely to precede and perhaps cause panic disorder and generalized anxiety disorder (Kushner, Sher, & Bertman, 1990).

Clinical Course

A large number of males with alcoholism begin heavy drinking during their late teens or 20s, but only in their 30s, after a long and insidious course, do they fully acknowledge their problem. Jellinek's (1952) three phases of alcoholism—prodromal, crucial, and chronic—are still relevant today and are outlined in Table 11-7. In addition to recognized phases there are familiar patterns to problematic drinking. Several types of alcoholism have been described:

1. The *alcohol-dependent drinker* relies on alcohol for relief of stress. There is no loss of control or gross intoxication and little progression in the

TABLE 11-7
Jellinek's Three Phases of Alcoholism
PRODOMAL PHASE

Avid drinking (gulping)	Preoccupation with drinking
Avoiding reference to drinking	Surreptitious drinking
Guilt	
Palimpsests (blackouts, amnesia not associated with loss of consciousness)	

CRUCIAL PHASE (Heralded by the onset of increased palimpsests)

Loss of control	Changes in interpersonal relationships
Rationalization	Geographic escape
Social pressures to quit drinking	Changed family habits
Grandiosity	Unreasonable resentments
Aggressiveness	Protecting the supply
Persistent remorse	Poor nutrition
Remaining abstinent for periods of time	Decreased libido
Setting rules as to when to drink	Morbid jealousy
Dropping friends	Regular morning drinking
First hospitalization for alcoholism	Quitting jobs
Alcohol-centered behavior	Loss of interests

CHRONIC PHASE

Benders (remaining drunk for several days)	Loss of tolerance for alcohol
Ethical deterioration	Undefinable fears
Impaired thinking	Tremors
Psychosis (10%)	Psychomotor inhibition
Decline in social level	Obsessive drinking
Drinking nonpotables	Religious desires
Rationalization fails and the patient becomes accessible to treatment	

Note: Information from Jellinek, 1952.

course of the illness. Gradually there is loss of physical health. These individuals are rarely recognized as having a problem.

2. The *wine drinker* is unable to abstain without withdrawal symptoms and is in a constant state of mild intoxication (especially prevalent in France and Italy).

3. The *compulsive person with alcoholism* exhibits extreme loss of control and will drink until unconscious (especially prevalent in the United States and Canada).

4. The person with *secondary alcoholism* drinks secondary to one or more

psychiatric disorders (mood disorder, phobic or anxiety states, cognitive disorders, or psychoses).

5. The *person who drinks periodically* has long periods of sobriety interspersed with binges ("the weekend drunk").

6. The person with *chronic alcoholism* displays the final common path of many alcohol abusers. This type of alcoholism is associated with decreased tolerance, physical complications, and social deterioration.

Mortality rates of people with alcoholism are approximately twice normal in males, three times normal in females, and especially high in younger age groups. The predominant causes of death in this population are accidents, suicides, cancer of the upper digestive and respiratory organs, arteriosclerotic heart disease, pneumonia, cirrhosis, and ulcers. Selzer (1969) found that of 96 drivers responsible for fatal accidents, 88 were people with chronic alcoholism. In almost half of fatal auto accidents, the culpable drivers were drunk. In France, a 1999 law requires any driver involved in a fatal crash to undergo alcohol and possibly drug testing. In France the legal level is 0.05 g/mL, as opposed to the United States where the usual legal level is 0.08. Twenty-one percent of drivers involved in severe accidents had a blood alcohol level above the French legal limit (Biecheler et al., 2008). Following liver transplantation for alcoholic liver disease, a surprising 15% of people resumed drinking within 6 months (De-Martini et al., 2006).

Because "spontaneous" improvement is more common than generally realized, if people with alcoholism can keep functioning when they reach midlife, their long-term prognosis improves considerably. In other words, alcoholism is *not* a hopeless condition!

Complications

Alcoholism is a major factor in 20% of divorces and 40% of problems brought to family court. Half of all police work, hospital admissions, homicides, and automobile fatalities are alcohol-related. One-fourth of all suicides involve alcohol, especially in men over 35 who have suffered a loss in the last 6 months. In addition, many people who are depressed and have suicidal thoughts do not act on them until they are intoxicated.

Alcoholism assaults every organ; it causes anemia, muscle weakness, gastritis, diarrhea, ulcers, pancreatitis, "fetal alcohol syndrome," and other birth defects. Pregnant women who drink put their unborn children at risk of low birth weight and fetal alcohol syndrome. Combined with poor nutrition, alcoholism may produce a fatty liver and cirrhosis. Three or four beers a day over 15 years results in cirrhosis in 18% of people (Sorensen et al., 1984). Poor nutrition and alcoholism also cause the rapidly erupting *Wernicke–Korsakoff syndrome* of eye movement disturbances (nystagmus and inability to look laterally in one or both eyes), ataxia, and mental disturbances (confusion, impaired recent memory). If this syndrome is not promptly treated with massive doses of thiamine, in several days the patient may develop *Korsakoff psychosis*—which is not really a psychosis but a potentially permanent dementia characterized by impaired recent memory with lowered ability to think, disorientation, and confabulation (confabulation is not necessary to make the diagnosis). In the less severe cases, complete recovery may occur slowly over a period of months. Severe cases may be left with serious memory deficits. Of patients who have both alcoholic and metabolic or nutritional problems, Wernicke's encephalopathy is seen in 65%, Korsakoff's psychosis in 53%, and alcoholic polyneuropathy in 70%.

Alcohol withdrawal can cause seizures (rum fits), *delirium tremens* (DTs, "alcohol delirium with onset during withdrawal" in *DSM* terms), and alcoholic hallucinosis ("alcohol psychotic disorder with hallucinations" in the *DSM*). *Alcoholic grand mal seizures* usually occur within the first 3 days after stopping drinking. In about a third of the cases, they are associated with DTs, the seizures preceding the delirium. The best treatment is prophylaxis with phenytoin in patients who are known to be predisposed to seizures as well as aggressive use of benzodiazepines to ameliorate withdrawal. DTs usually occur within 1 week (3–4 days average) after stopping drinking and usually last 3 days or less, although more severe DTs may occur with more prolonged drinking. Symptoms of DTs include disorientation, visual hallucinations, wakefulness, tremulous picking motions, and frequently mild temperature elevations. People with long-term (5–20 years) alcoholism are most likely to get DTs. In the past, 6–15% of patients with DTs died, usually of head trauma, seizures, or pneumonia, but rapid diagnosis and treatment have lowered the death rate. Patients with DTs should be hospitalized and given oral fluids and sedation. Keeping someone with the patient and the lights on can help reduce terror and visual hallucinations.

Alcoholic hallucinosis (usually auditory) is a syndrome (somewhat rarer than DTs) in which patients complain of vivid, usually identifiable voices in a clear sensorium. The voices are frequently unpleasant, and patients' behavior is usually consistent with the content of the voices, including fearful attempts to escape and, occasionally, attempted suicide. This syndrome occurs as a withdrawal phenomenon, usually within the first 3 days after cessation of drinking in alcoholism of long standing. In some cases, hallucinations may persist for up to 6 months (Tsuang et al., 1994). Treatment should consist of supportive therapy, prevention of convulsions, and antipsychotics, when indicated.

Treatment and Management

Thirty years ago, the primary measure and goal of treatment was complete abstinence and sobriety. Partial gains in treatment were at times glossed over. For example, an addict who had been injecting heroin went into treatment for this but later relapsed to swallowing opioid pain medication. Although this is a clearly less than optimal outcome, even temporarily, clinicians sometimes failed to reinforce the positive aspects of the change, in that oral abuse of opioids carries less risk than intravenous abuse.

Prochaska and DiClemente developed a model of change that applies very well to addiction (see Chapter 5). This model recognizes that simply warning people of the ill effects of their behavior will usually not result in a substantive change in that behavior. This model, sometimes called the transtheoretical model of change, characterizes six stages of change. First is *precontemplation*, wherein the individual is not even aware that there is a problem and is not considering change. Next is *contemplation*, in which the individual is ambivalent about change and is not considering change within the next month. This stage is followed by the *preparation* stage, wherein the individual has identified the wish to change and is experimenting with it and planning to act within the next month. Next comes the *action* stage, in which the individual is actively working on change and dealing with obstacles until the new behavior (e.g., sobriety) becomes habitual. This is followed by the *maintenance* stage, during which the change is sustained over a long period of time with less effort. The *relapse* stage exists when a trigger (often the dysphoric emotional state) precipitates resumption of the undesirable behavior. Approaching a patient in a hopeful manner to catalyze and effect change requires different techniques depending on which stage of change the individual occupies (e.g., motivational interviewing for precontemplation and Antabuse or Alcoholics Anonymous for the action stage).

The treatment for alcohol dependence is abstinence and Alcoholics Anonymous (or an equivalent recovery program). Since clinicians can't reliably predict the 5–15% of people with alcoholism who eventually will be able to drink moderately, abstinence should be urged, especially for the first 6–12 months after hospitalization, when 70–90% of patients relapse. The longer patients remain dry, the sharper their thinking and the better their occupational, social, and sexual functioning. Some patients are very tentative about their diagnosis and hence their treatment. It may be useful to elicit their agreement not to drink at all for 3–6 months, "just to see what abstinence feels like and how it affects them." In advance, patients are told that inability to follow through on this temporary abstinence is proof of alcoholism.

Supervised (but *not* unsupervised) Antabuse (disulfiram) treatment for alcoholism works better than placebo (Brewer, 1992). For the subgroup of people with alcoholism who sincerely believe in and desire this as an *adjunct* to treatment, Antabuse may be helpful. Cravings are countered by the knowledge that drinking within 3–5 days of taking the drug will produce severe nausea, flushing, tachycardia, and hypotension. The standard dose is 250 mg/day; higher doses offer no more deterrence and, if mixed with alcohol, are potentially lethal. Antabuse usually should not be the sole treatment. Lithium has been reported to help both depressed and nondepressed people with alcoholism stay abstinent (Fawcett et al., 1987). Acamprosate and naltrexone both show improvement in the sobriety rates of active alcoholics. Three months after an acute treatment episode, only about 15% of individuals are still sober. With these two agents, the sobriety rates doubled or tripled. There is some controversy about these drug approaches because the ability to stay *compliant* with any medication or placebo regime predicts abstinence.

Alcoholics Anonymous (AA) greatly benefits a majority of people with alcoholism. AA doesn't go into *why* people drink, just that they *do*, and shouldn't; it stresses a "one-day-at-a-time" philosophy, which allows people with alcoholism to deal with manageable units of time and end a "dry day" with a sense of accomplishment. On a trial basis at least, all people with alcoholism should attend AA meetings. Clinicians can help their patients by finding a socially appropriate AA chapter for them, by not giving into rationalizations for why they can't attend this or that AA meeting, and by getting patients linked up with an AA member who is on the same "wavelength." Finding sponsors can help patients begin the AA process and find the right meetings. Some meetings are open to drop-ins and beginners, whereas others are closed so that group members can focus on a certain aspect of their recovery. If there are several choices, patients should explore to see which location(s) is the best fit for them. If patients are on medication for a psychiatric problem such as depression, it is important to find AA groups that are supportive of pharmacological treatments. AA also welcomes people with other drug problems, especially hypnoanxiolytic, marijuana, and cocaine dependence. Polysubstance abusers can also go to more specialized meetings such as Narcotics Anonymous (NA). Some patients never feel comfortable with the AA philosophy of a "higher power" and do better with alternatives such as Rational or SMART Recovery groups that have a cognitive–behavioral emphasis. Women often feel more comfortable at "women only" groups.

The clinician must also attend to the needs of the family of the affected person. If one member drinks, the others needn't drown. Growing up with a parent with alcoholism can be devastating; so is living with a spouse who has alcoholism. The clinician should assure family members that they are not responsible for the individual's harmful drinking, nor do they have any ethical obligation to "reform" him or her. Whether or not the person with alcoholism goes to AA, the patient's relatives should attend Alanon, a support group for family members, or Alateen, which offers information and assistance to teenagers with alcoholism and their teenage relatives. For people with alcoholism who are resistant to diagnosis and treatment, the family can become an invaluable ally in penetrating the denial and rationalizations. In these cases, an "intervention" might be arranged: Significant people in the individual's life get together and, in a very firm, direct, and compassionate manner, confront the person regarding the alcoholism. Interventions are best done with the help of an experienced professional. Many people who have recovered from alcoholism look back on these dramatic confrontations as the turning points in their lives.

HYPNOANXIOLYTICS

Hypnoanxiolytics quell anxiety, induce sleep, or both. They are classified into three groups: barbiturates, barbiturate-like drugs, and benzodiazepines. *Barbiturates* are the prototypic hypnoanxiolytic. The first barbiturate, Veronal—named after the tranquil city of Verona in Italy—was introduced in 1902 as a "safe" replacement for alcohol. *Benzodiazepines* are now the most widely prescribed hypnoanxiolytics in the world.

When taken as an overdose, barbiturates are frequently lethal, but benzodiazepines only rarely. Relative to barbiturates, less tolerance develops to benzodiazepines, withdrawal is less frequent, and potentiation by alcohol is less (Goodwin & Guze, 1984). With benzodiazepines, tolerance tends to develop more often to the sedative than to the anxiolytic effects. Benzodiazepines, however, are not innocuous: Older adults are highly sensitive to them, and they are associated with birth defects (e.g., midline hypoplasia as in cleft palate). Longer-acting benzodiazepines may accumulate to toxic levels and insidiously retard cognition and movement. Psychological and physical dependence may arise from ongoing use; in one survey, 58% of long-term users admitted they would have "difficulty" without them (Salzman, 1985). Four to six years after being hospitalized for hypnoanxiolytic dependence, 84% of patients were using hypnoanxiolytics, 52% were abusing them, 42% had been rehospitalized for drug misuse, and 12% had withdrawal convulsions (Allgulander, Borg, &Vikander, 1984). Although benzodiazepine withdrawal is usually mild, it can be severe. Withdrawal symptoms are the same as with alcohol (see Table 11-6). Benzodiazepines that reach the brain the fastest and produce a "buzz" are most likely to be abused. For example, diazepam (Valium) and chlordiazepoxide (Librium) have similar characteristics, except that diazepam is a highly lipid soluble and quickly penetrates the blood–brain barrier, producing a rapid onset of action. Alprazolam (Xanax) is also lipophyllic but has a much shorter half-life than diazepam and reaches higher blood levels much faster. These medications, if crushed and injected or snorted, will have a faster onset of action because they bypass the gut.

In most clinic studies fewer than 5% of patients on benzodiazepines meet criteria for a substance use disorder. Many people are so worried about this happening that they underuse these drugs. People with a history of alcohol abuse or a family history of alcohol or hypnoanxiolytic abuse are more likely to abuse benzodiazepines (Ciraulo et al., 1989). Several patterns in the development of misuse and addiction have been noted. One prototype — the "prescription pill popper" — is that of the middle-class, middle-aged woman who obtains a prescription because of anxiety or insomnia. Later she increases the dose and frequency of use on her own, using the drug to cope with even minor problems. Another pattern involves males in their teens or early 20s who obtain these drugs from illicit sources and use them for their euphorigenic effects. It is common for patients on methadone programs, who have discontinued opiate abuse, to continue to use benzodiazepines sporadically. Cognitive–behavioral approaches, SSRIs, or buspirone (a non–habit-forming anxiolytic) are recommended as the first treatment in these high-risk groups.

> When first prescribing any psychoactive agent, but especially a hypnoanxiolytic, physicians should warn patients that, for a week or so, their reflexes might be a tad slow and they should be extra careful around machines, crossing streets, and cooking. Daytime sedation might last a week. In older adult patients, when they must be used, the patients should be warned of unsteadiness and possible fall risk. As far as is known, the anxiolytic effect continues indefinitely in most patients. Patients without alcoholism can drink alcohol

while taking hypnoanxiolytics (and other psychotropic drugs), but they should be told that one drink will probably feel like two to three drinks.

Benzodiazepines are classified as "short-acting," "intermediate-acting," or "long-acting," with half-lives of 2–6 hours, 8–12 hours, and over 24 hours, respectively. A drug's "half-life" is when 50% of it has become pharmacologically inactive. Complicating the picture is the fact that a parent drug may have a short-acting half-life, but its major breakdown product may be long-acting (e.g., chlordiazepoxide's half-life is 4 hours, but its metabolite, nordiazepam, has a half-life of 96 hours). The chances of withdrawal increase with increased dosage and duration of use. More cases of benzodiazepine withdrawal have been reported with long-term, low-dose use than with short-term, high-dose use. For example, 15 mg of daily diazepam for 2 years apparently causes more physical dependence than 50 mg of daily diazepam for 6 weeks.

Longer-acting benzodiazepines are less likely to be abused than short-acting ones. The longer-acting benzodiazepines are eliminated more slowly and gradually, causing less and more delayed withdrawal than the shorter-acting ones. In a sense, they taper themselves. In some people, alprazolam may last only 6 hours. If their prescription specifies usage every 8 hours, this gap may result in three mini-withdrawals a day.

High-potency benzodiazepines may actually have higher withdrawal risks because they are often used in higher dosage equivalents than the older, low-potency benzodiazepines. For panic disorder, alprazolam is commonly used in doses over 3 mg a day, which would be equivalent to over 30 mg a day of diazepam, a dosage almost never used. A majority of patients with panic disorder who have taken alprazolam for over 1 year report withdrawal symptoms, even when gradually tapered off of it, that are worse than the original panic symptoms. Too often, physicians' decisions in treating patients can increase the chance of addiction. *Fast, frequent,* and *forceful* reinforcements are most likely to cause addiction. They often follow many of the principles of what we could title "How to Create an Addict":

1. Choose a fast and powerful reinforcer. Pick a substance that has a rapid onset of action and therefore gives a "buzz" or "rush."
2. Make sure the drug has to be used often to get the reinforcement and, better yet, use a drug that has nasty withdrawal symptoms. This will increase the craving to use the drug again to eradicate the withdrawal symptoms and to get the buzz. The wider the gulf between withdrawal

symptoms and the buzz, the stronger the reinforcement provided. Short-acting drugs work best for this. Secobarbital meets all of these criteria.
3. Prescribe the drug prn (as needed) or schedule with a frequency that precipitates withdrawal before the next dose is taken. For example, if it is prn, tell the patient to take the drug "only when you feel very anxious"; and if it's scheduled, prescribe a drug to be taken every 6 hours that lasts only 4 hours.

Unfortunately, the steps that create addiction are too often used in pain and anxiety treatment. For patients who seek help for benzodiazepine dependence, a very gradual withdrawal extending over 2–3 months is often recommended. High-potency benzodiazepines probably should be replaced with low-potency benzodiazepines. For a gradual, gentler withdrawal, the longer-acting benzodiazepines such as chlordiazepoxide, clorazepate, and clonazepam can be substituted for the shorter-acting ones on which the patient has become dependent. For a comfortable withdrawal in under 7 days, divalproex sodium or carbamazepine (both anticonvulsants) can be used for dependent patients who have taken benzodiazepines in high doses or for a long period of time (Covington, 1998).

STIMULANTS

Cocaine

Sigmund Freud introduced cocaine into mainstream medicine as a safe, non–habit-forming treatment for opium addiction. He frequently used it himself. According to the National Survey on Drug Use and Health (NSDUH), the rate of past-year use for cocaine (powder and crack combined) among individuals age 12 and older (2.4%) has remained stable since 2002. Ten percent of Americans have taken "even one sniff" of cocaine, as Cole Porter's (1934) lyric goes. Chic in Porter's day, cocaine was snorted and was relatively expensive. Now cocaine powder for snorting has dropped in price and the availability of cheap "crack" cocaine has led to abuse in all social classes.

With growing use, there is a growing awareness of its hazards. Reflecting Porter's "Some get a kick from cocaine," its use has dropped in high school and among college students and professionals, but is unchanged among lower-class street users. The diagnostic criteria for substance use disorders, intoxication, and withdrawal apply to the stimulants (see Tables 11-1 and 11-5). Also, the signs and symptoms for amphetamine and cocaine intoxication and withdrawal are identical. Other disorders related to stimulant use are also listed: delirium, psychotic disorder (with delusions or halluci-nations), mood disorder, anxiety disorder, sexual dysfunction, and sleep dis-order.

A typical story of cocaine addiction in the 1980s started when the curious person paid $75–$150 a gram for a white powder, which is usually 30% cocaine and 70% adulterants (inactive sugars). After making a thin, 2-inch line of the powder, the user snorted it with a straw or rolled-up dollar bill. This launched a 30-minute high, which tapered off in 60–90 minutes. The user feels energetic, creative, talkative, attractive, excited, euphoric, moti-vated, grandiose, and "connected." Initial negative reactions include restless-ness, agitation, anxiety, hyperexcitability, and hostility.

More recently, "crack" cocaine has been available, especially in inner-city areas, for $5–$15 a "rock." The rock is pure cocaine alkaloid extracted from the powder using heat with sodium bicarbonate. "Freebasing" is another method that has been used to separate the adulterants with ether (highly flammable solvent) or ammonia. The pure cocaine is vaporized and inhaled in a pipe (that may be homemade from a soda can), launching an intense high that peaks in 5 minutes and tapers off in 15, followed by extreme dysphoria, craving, and often by marathon "coke" binges of 24–96 hours, or until supplies run out. Because of its lower price, this form of cocaine is affordable even by middle- and high-school students.

Habitual cocaine abusers gradually become obsessed with the drug and securing its supply. Not uncommonly, the user blows over $3,000 a week on the drug. A week, and then a day, cannot pass without that "extra boost." When high, users are unable to sleep, and once asleep, cannot awaken. Among people snorting cocaine powder, an average of 2 years elapses before they seek help. Among crack users, this period is shortened to 6 months. Fifty to 70% of heavy cocaine users report paranoid episodes, which happen almost exclusively during the high (Satel & Edell, 1991). On crashing (with-drawing), users feel depressed, anergic, and unmotivated. Appetite disap-pears and weight drops, often to medically precarious levels. Snorters' noses drip and bleed continuously, exhausting endless supplies of gauze. Crack smokers cough up blood-tinged sputum with black flecks (carbonized cocaine and necrotic lung tissue). Work is missed, jobs are lost, friends lose patience, and marriages end.

Despite these serious consequences, of those who have called a cocaine hotline, most still preferred to continue their habit because it produced euphoria (82%), diminished boredom (57%), increased energy and self-confidence (48%), and stimulated sexuality (21%). Callers said that cocaine was more important than food (71%), sex (50%), family activities (72%), and friends (64%). Among all the callers, 61% snorted the drug, 21% smoked, and 18% injected it. Half used the drug daily. On average, users spent $637 a week on cocaine (Gold, 1984).

Although no definitive therapy for cocaine dependence yet exists, recent research into drugs acting on GABA, glutamate, or dopamine systems show promise (Karila et al., 2008). There has been some evidence suggesting that tricyclic antidepressants may help some cocaine-dependent patients (Gawin et al., 1989) and that bromocriptine (a dopamine agonist dosed at 0.625 mg four times daily) exerts an anticraving effect in 1–2 minutes. Early successes with these pharmacological treatments, used alone without other treatments, have been tempered by relapse rates 6 months later that are as high as when no treatment is received. However, by helping patients get off and stay off cocaine for some period of time, these drugs might enable abusers to participate more effectively in rehabilitative treatments such as Cocaine Anonymous or AA. As Sherlock Holmes's case illustrates (Chapter 9), cocaine's many "advantages" offer former abusers little incentive to remain drug-free. Therefore, therapy must help patients find or rediscover interests that will "replace" cocaine. One of the best things cocaine addicts can do is replace cocaine-using friends with abstinent friends (Kandel & Raveis, 1989). A multi-component behavioral treatment—using money payments for negative urine specimens, significant others to reinforce abstinence, training in recognizing antecedents and consequences of cocaine, and help in developing new alternative activities to cocaine use—has been shown to be superior to traditional drug counseling (Higgens et al., 1993). Less specific weekly psychosocial therapy does not improve abstinence (Kang et al., 1991).

Amphetamines

Intoxication and withdrawal from cocaine and amphetamine are similar. NIDA reports methamphetamine use has generally decreased over the last decade. Overdoses are potentially fatal. Acute usage of amphetamines causes tachycardia, and with increased dosage, ventricular fibrillation and respiratory arrest may occur. Hyperpyrexia (increased body temperature) is frequent; seizures may occur, and deaths have resulted from status epilepticus (continuous seizures). The depression following use may lead to suicide. After a high-dose binge, some users develop a transient psychosis with a mixture of paranoid and manic-like symptoms. Visual and tactile hallucinations may also be present. At other times, a confused toxic psychosis may develop.

Anorexia and weight loss are common in regular users. Long-term use of amphetamines is associated with increased morbidity, mortality, criminality, as well as ongoing, diffuse suspiciousness and a chronic delusional syndrome.

Noteworthy differences between cocaine and amphetamines exist. Because of cocaine's short half-life, tolerance may not develop as rapidly as it does to amphetamines: In just 3 days, "speed freaks" can go from ingesting 15 mg to 2,000 mg a day to obtain the original effects. Whereas the acute effects of a single amphetamine dose lasts 4–6 hours, those from cocaine rarely extend beyond 2 hours. Cocaine is typically used in binges, whereas amphetamines are used more continuously. More often than cocaine, amphetamines trigger a toxic psychosis resembling paranoid schizophrenia.

Seven days before taking the Medical College Admissions Test (MCAT), Brittany was frantic. Night and day she crammed, hourly popping a 5 mg "black beauty" (dextroamphetamine). Brittany was not only awake, she was flying. Never did she feel more alert and focused. After 2 days of nonstop studying, she began pacing "because I could concentrate better." By day 3, she repeatedly told her roommate that the MCATs were "dumb"—an insight that Brittany alone considered brilliant—and by day 4, she began shouting this indictment out her apartment window. By nightfall, she was convinced the MCAT people had hired mobsters to break her arms and legs. Already they were playing tricks on her eyes: One moment beetles were crawling in her hair, the next moment they disappeared. The telephone rang, wrong number, surely the MCAT mobsters. To protect herself, she bolted the door. Believing strangers in front of her apartment were also MCAT mobsters, she hurled darts and dishes at them. As typically occurs, Brittany became psychotic on 60 mg a day, remained psychotic for 2 weeks, and recovered fully. (Six months later she got high scores on the MCATs, but had trouble getting her driver's license renewed because she had been hospitalized for psychosis.)

The mainstay of acute treatment of stimulant abusers is observation, rest, and nutritious food. During the intoxication phase, benzodiazepines may be used to treat significant anxiety and agitation. Propranolol or clonidine are used for sympathetic overactivity. During an acute stimulant intoxication, safety should be ensured and patients should be observed continuously. Physical restraints may be needed. If paranoid, patients' environment should be simplified, as few people as possible should care for them, and anything they deem dangerous should be removed. An increasing body temperature indicates an increasingly dangerous toxicity. Antipsychotic drugs (e.g., haloperidol 2–5 mg orally or IM) are effective in treating intoxication.

Amphetamines have no safe role in dieting and a limited one in depression. They do have three legitimate medical indications: treating narcoleptic sleep attacks, childhood attention-deficit/hyperactivity disorder, and (occasionally) resistant depression. Even here they must be used cautiously—or, as rock star Frank Zappa warned, "Speed will turn you into your parents."

Nicotine

There are two "minor stimulants": caffeine and nicotine. Caffeine's intoxicating effects are presented in Chapter 11 on anxiety disorders. Caffeine withdrawal is often accompanied by headache, lethargy, and dysphoria. It begins within 2 to 24 hours and lasts about 1 week (Hughes et al., 1992). This reaction occurs even when consumption is limited to two or three cups of coffee a day.

Nicotine has always been controversial. The Turkish and German governments once considered smoking in public an offense punishable by death; the Russians preferred castration. Americans, however, have subsidized its growth so that tobacco use disorder and withdrawal are classified as mental disorders.

Historically, men smoke more than women, but women have almost reached parity. Men have been more successful in stopping. The most effective treatment programs combine education, group support, and behavior modification, yet even here, within a year, 80% of patients relapse. People who have had a history of major depression are most likely to fail attempts at permanent abstinence. Hypnosis, nicotine gum, and gradual substitution with lower nicotine–containing cigarettes help only some smokers. Nicotine patches are more widely accepted and provide a continuous release of nicotine into the blood. The patch increases abstinence, decreases withdrawal symptoms and depressive symptoms associated with withdrawal, and reduces the rewarding effects of smoking (Levin et al., 1994). Bupropion in a sustained-release preparation (Zyban) is a proven aid to smoking cessation. Varenicline (Chantix), a nicotine receptor partial agonist, is the most recent medication approved by the FDA for treatment of nicotine dependence. Behavioral treatment approaches have become increasing effective over time (LeFoll & George, 2007).

HALLUCINOGENS

In 1938, while investigating ergot preparations for a pharmaceutical firm in Basel, Switzerland, Albert Hofmann first synthesized LSD-25 (lysergic acid diethylamide) from ergotomine produced by a fungus that infects rye and other grains (the Salem witch trials may have been the result of hallucinations caused by ingesting such contaminated grain). The number 25 may refer to its potency with just 25 micrograms being the threshold dose). Five years later, he unwittingly absorbed it through his fingers and experienced a "not unpleasant delirium." Several days later he swallowed 250 micrograms, and in 40 minutes he felt a "mild dizziness, restlessness, inability to concentrate, visual disturbance and uncontrollable laughter." His diary continues to describe "the bicycle trip heard round the world":

> on the way home (a four-mile trip by bicycle), the symptoms developed with a much greater intensity than the first time. I had the greatest difficulty speaking coherently and my field of vision fluctuated and was distorted like the reflections in an amusement park mirror. I also had the impression that I was hardly moving, yet later my assistant told me that I was pedaling at a fast pace. So far as I can recollect, the height of the crisis was characterized by these symptoms; dizziness, visual distortions, the faces of those present appeared like grotesque colored masks, strong agitation alternating with paresis [partial paralysis], the head, body and extremities sometimes cold and numb; a metallic taste on the tongue; throat dry and shriveled; a feeling of suffocation; confusion alternating with a clear appreciation of the situation; at times standing outside myself as a neutral observer and hearing myself muttering jargon or screaming half madly.
>
> Six hours after taking the drug, my condition had improved. The perceptual distortions were still present. Everything seemed to undulate and their proportions were distorted like the reflections on a choppy water surface. Everything was changing with unpleasant, predominately poisonous green and blue color tones. With closed eyes multi-hued, metamorphizing fantastic images overwhelmed me. Especially noteworthy was the fact that sounds were transposed into visual sensations ["synesthesias"] so that from each tone or noise a comparable colored picture was evoked, changing in form and color kaleidoscopically. (Coles, Brenner, & Meagher, 1970, pp. 44–45)

Hofmann apparently slept well and the next day felt "completely well, but tired."

Despite some differences most *pure* hallucinogens (or "psychedelics") produce experiences like Hofmann's. "Street acid," however, is rarely pure, usually consisting of anticholinergics (which are hallucinogens in toxic doses), quinine, sugar, and PCP (discussed later); it might even contain LSD. As a result, clinicians cannot assume that patients on a "bad trip" know what drug they've taken. Therefore, it is safest to "talk patients down" by reassuring them that the trip will end in a few hours, that they are safe, and that they are not going mad, shrinking, or becoming a zombie. Patients should not fight the experience, but "flow with it"; they should be encouraged to become curious about it, and if they wish, to talk about it. If clinicians do not have the time to offer this reassurance, or if patients remain terrified despite it, diazepam 5 mg or alprazolam 0.5 mg can be given orally every hour until patients are reasonably comfortable or asleep; either drug causes less hypotension and fewer bad drug interactions than antipsychotics. Because some antipsychotics increase anticholinergic activity, these drugs can worsen the condition of someone who already has anticholinergic toxicity. A person with an anticholinergic psychosis has been described as "dry as a bone, red as a beet and mad as a hatter." It's quite recognizable, if you know what to look for.

> Less than 5% of Americans have ever tried a psychedelic, and if these drugs were legal, only 1% claimed they would take them. Traditionally, hallucinogens have been used more frequently by high school and college students, the affluent, artistic, and philosophically minded, rather than by the poor or antisocial. Chronic use is uncommon. Hallucinogens can trigger "flashbacks," in which a person off drugs re-experiences an LSD trip days to months and sometimes years after taking it. Hallucinogen abuse among teens and young adults increased from 1992 to 1995 but has remained stable since then.
>
> What causes flashbacks (Hallucinogen Persisting Perception Disorder) is unknown. Psychedelics rarely, if ever, cause psychosis *de novo*, but they, as well as PCP and *high* doses of marijuana, can easily rekindle a preexisting psychosis. High-risk patients include those with borderline or schizotypal personality disorder, and those with a personal or family history of drug-or nondrug-induced psychoses. Clinicians should inform these patients about their increased risk.

Cannabis

The hemp plant, *Cannabis sativa*, grows anywhere it doesn't freeze; marijuana comes from its stems and leaves, while hashish derives from the resin of female plants. (George Washington smoked hemp at a time when it was believed to be a treatment for "catarrh.") The main psychoactive substance in cannabis is THC (delta-9-tetrahydrocannabinol), which does not typically exceed 1%. However, through genetic selection, marijuana leaves have reached 24% THC in "prize" crops. Hashish can be in the 15–20% range, and hashish oil contains up to 70% THC. Smoking is the primary mode of use in a joint (≈0.75 gram cigarette), a blunt (≈1 gram cigar), or a bowl (≈0.5 gram pipe). With normal recreational use, marijuana intoxication peaks in 30 minutes, persists for 3 hours, and sometimes impairs driving for up to 6 hours. It stimulates appetite ("the munchies"), causes dry mouth, produces bloodshot eyes, elevates mood, intensifies experiences and perceptions, and heightens relaxation and apathy. Dronabinol (Marinol), a synthetic THC, is an FDA-approved medication for anorexia and nausea. Refer to Tables 11-1 and 11-2 for the diagnostic criteria shared by cannabis with other substance use disorders, intoxication, and withdrawal.

Over 60% of American adults and adolescents have smoked "weed" at least once, and relatively few have experienced severe reactions after 24 hours of using the drug. Panic attacks, which account for 75% of all severe *acute* side effects, can last 2–6 hours. Severe cases can be treated with benzodiazepines. Otherwise, heavier cannabis use can cause toxic delirium represented by the "4 Ds": depersonalization, derealization, déjà vu, and dysphoria. Another effect is a cognitive disorder with impairment in goal-directed, memory-dependent behavior and in carrying out multiple-step tasks. The "short attention span theater" becomes a favored form of entertainment. Marijuana can also exacerbate a preexisting psychosis. Its effects are greatly influenced by "set and setting"—that is, by the user's "mind set" or attitudes toward the drug, and the degree of receptivity and safety in the environment. Adverse reactions occur more often among those who smoke because of peer pressure or who have negative expectations of the drug. In the 1980s less than 1% of university students at campuses with high marijuana use developed panic attacks, whereas 25% did so at rural Southern colleges where use of the drug is discouraged.

Longer-term psychological problems associated with marijuana use are fewer than with some other drugs. Only 9% of marijuana users meet criteria for a cannabis use disorder. Marijuana hallucinosis, flashbacks, or transient delusional syndrome may occur. Although an "amotivational syndrome" of laziness, apathy, and a lack of ambition has been attributed to marijuana, this finding derived from biased samples of largely lower-class patients and has not been supported by more recent surveys in countries where marijuana use is extensive (Jamaica, Costa Rica, and Greece). Passive, unmotivated people may choose marijuana for chronic use. Medically, cannabis diminishes respiratory capacity, produces bronchial and pulmonary irritation (more than equal amounts of nicotine, and like tobacco, may result in constrictive pulmonary disease), causes tachycardia, temporarily impairs cognition and recent memory, reduces fertility, harms the fetus, reduces immune response, and impairs driving and school performance.

Two main types of marijuana dependence have been described. In the more severe type users smoke marijuana many times a day and finally seek treatment on their own. In the second type, users smoke it every day or two and end up in treatment only after involuntary drug testing (Tennant, 1986). Both types may produce a withdrawal syndrome days later and have high relapse rates (Tennant, 1986).

Ever since *Reefer Madness* obtained cult-film status, the dominant question has been whether marijuana leads to the abuse of "heavier" illegal substances. Repeated studies have strongly suggested that the best predictor of illegal drug use is *legal* drug use. In other words, the chief "gateway" drug is not marijuana but tobacco or alcohol (Rittenhouse, 1982). Nevertheless, patients are not statistics, and the hazards of marijuana use must be evaluated in the light of each person's history. Marijuana is the most used illicit drug in the United States and its use is rising with an average of 7% of Americans using marijuana each month, including 8.5% of 8th graders, 19.2% of 10th graders, and 25.5% of 12th graders by recent NIDA statistics (2013 Monitoring the Future).

Phencyclidine

Originally an animal tranquilizer, "hog" or phencyclidine (PCP) became a battlefield anesthetic in Vietnam. It resurfaced as a recreational drug in California during the late 1960s, ironically rechristened as "angel dust." PCP produces a euphoric, floating, energized, invincible, other-worldly, and dreamlike state in which time is slowed, thinking is quickened, fantasies are dramatic, life is intensified, and reality goes on holiday.

But PCP is *not* the dust of angels. Users may be immobilized and stare blankly. Myoclonic (leg) jerks and confusion are common. On large doses, patients may become stuporous, enter a coma, and convulse with their eyes wide open. If they recover from the coma, they exhibit an agitated delirium marked by persecutory delusions, hallucinations, illusions, disorientation, agitation, and episodic assaultiveness: asleep or calm one moment, without warning they may become fanatically violent the next. For no apparent reason, users fight with police, wreck cars, commit suicide, kill strangers. This violence may stem from the extreme suspiciousness and persecutory delusions produced by PCP. Being a "dissociative" anesthetic, PCP makes users feel as if they are outside their bodies; users do not perceive pain and are unaware and amnestic for such experiences. This delirium can last a week.

Some patients die, usually due to respiratory depression; others are killed in accidents—drowning, automobile crashes, falls, and fires. Medically, PCP intoxication causes ataxia, nystagmus, and muscle rigidity. Whereas hallucinogens produce dilated pupils, PCP produces normal or small pupils. Again, Tables 11-1 and 11-2 present the criteria for substance use disorders and intoxication that apply to PCP and other psychoactive substances. The one difference is that PCP and the hallucinogens do not have an identified withdrawal syndrome.

PCP is often sprinkled on top of marijuana or parsley. When smoked, its effects arise in 1–5 minutes, peak after 5–30 minutes, remain high for 4–6 hours, and dwindle over the next 18 hours. Snorting PCP hastens its effects. Intravenous use is uncommon. NIDA reports that at least 225,000 Americans between age 12 and 17 years and 777,000 between age 18 and 25 years have used PCP at least once. Most users are polydrug abusers. They often drink alcohol while on PCP, even though the combination usually makes them dreadfully sick. Despite the drug's horrifying effects, PCP users typically say they take it because "it's the perfect escape." It is frequently—and misleadingly—sold as cannabinol, mescaline, LSD, amphetamine, or cocaine.

> The treatment of acute PCP overdose includes cardiopulmonary resuscitation, treatment for seizures, acidification of the urine (to hasten the drug's elimination) with 500–1,000 mg ammonium chloride orally every 3–5 hours, until the urine pH is below 5. Since patients are unpredictably violent and frequently combative, a low sensory environment should be used; physical restraints may be needed until patients have been calm for several hours. Some clinicians recommend (as needed) hourly haloperidol 5 mg IM; others suggest diazepam 10–30 mg orally or IM. Response to aggressive treatment is generally slow. Most experts agree that phenothiazines should be avoided, since they may compound PCP's anticholinergic and hypotensive effects. After the acute psychosis, PCP users often do not remain in drug treatment programs.

MDMA

Also known as "ecstasy" or "XTC," 3,4-methylene-dioxy-methamphetamine (MDMA) was synthesized in 1914, but it wasn't until the early 1970s that it quietly became a recreational and psychotherapeutic drug. In 1985 the popularity of this then-legal drug was featured in *Time* and *Newsweek* magazines; by June of that year, the Drug Enforcement Agency had "temporarily" made it illegal. Many opposed this decision, claiming that MDMA had been confused with the psychedelic MDA (3,4-methylene-dioxy-amphetamine or "speed for lovers"), that harm allegedly due to MDMA was really from adulterants (e.g., Borax), and that research into a potentially therapeutic drug was being stymied. Human recreational doses have been reported to be neurotoxic in primates (Barnes, 1988); memantine, a glutamate receptor modulator protects against this damage in rats (Chipara et al., 2008).

In recreational doses of 75–175 mg, MDMA produces a tranquil, floating, introspective, talkative, 2- to 4-hour "trip." Grinspoon and Bakalar (1985) claim that it "invites rather than compels intensification of feelings and self-exploration." Chemically related to amphetamines and mescaline (a psychedelic), ecstasy exerts some stimulant effects. It induces a sense of well-being without alterations of consciousness, perception, movement, or coordination. Unlike with psychedelics, information revealed during MDMA usage is more readily remembered and applied afterward. The person does not feel "stoned."

The usage pattern of MDMA is unlike that of any other drug. Users tend to wait several weeks between doses, because taking it too soon increases negative effects and decreases positive effects. Because the positive effects seem to decrease over subsequent doses, MDMA probably is not addictive. The mean number of doses taken by users is only 5.4 (Peroutka, 1987, 1989). NIDA reports that in 2006 2.1 million Americans over the age of 11 used MDMA during the past year.

> Physical side effects, which are dose-related, include dry mouth, increased blood pressure and pulse rate, anorexia, nystagmus, urinary urgency, blurred vision, loss of balance, and jaw-clenching. Fatigue may persist for a day or two. Fatal overdoses have been reported. Bad trips, flashbacks, and psychotic reactions are rare; weekly use is also rare. At present, there have been no reports of MDMA-induced craving or withdrawal. However, animal studies have shown that relapse to MDMA use can be triggered by drug-related cues (Ball et al., 2007).

OPIOIDS

> Junk is the ideal product . . . the ultimate merchandise. No sales talk necessary. The client will crawl through a sewer and beg to buy. . . . The junk merchant does not sell his product to the consumer, he sells the consumer to this product.
> —William S. Burroughs, *Evergreen Review*, Jan./Feb. 1960

Opioids (also called *opiates*) are compounds with morphine-like properties. *Opium* is derived from the Turkish word for juice—juice of the poppy— because opium, the original opioid, derives from the head of the opium poppy *Papaver somniferum*, cultivated mainly in the Middle East, Southeast Asia, China, India, and Mexico. Although growing it in the United States has always been illegal, throughout the 1840s it was the most popular sleep aid in Kansas. Heroin is the only illicit opioid, and morphine is the prototypic opioid.

Clinical Presentation

In therapeutic amounts, morphine produces analgesia, induces tranquility, constricts pupils, and elevates mood (although some get dysphoria). Anorexia, nausea, and vomiting may occur, as may reduction in sex, aggression, and hunger drives. As Taylor Mead once quipped, "Opium is very cheap considering you don't feel like eating for the next six days." Skin itches, constipation develops, and respiratory rate and other vital signs decline. Except for meperidine (whose metabolite normeperidine is a cerebral irritant), opioids do not cause seizures.

Most opioid intoxication comes from shooting morphine or heroin intravenously, which produces a "rush"—a strong, flushing sensation coupled with an orgastic feeling in the belly. However, the purity of street heroin seized by federal agents in the United States has risen from 3.8% in 1970 to 38% in 2012. As a result, snorting heroin has become much more addictive than it had been. Waves of pleasant, floating drowsiness ("the nod") and dreams follow. Tolerance to opioids develops quickly. Table 11-2 lists the diagnostic criteria that apply to opioid intoxication and withdrawal. Specific signs and symptoms are listed in Table 11-6. Morphine withdrawal peaks up to 72 hours after the last dose and subsides slowly. Most opioid withdrawal symptoms disappear within 7–10 days, although some craving, restlessness, weakness, and fitful sleep may persist. Serious medical consequences of withdrawal are rare. Insomnia and dysphoria usually occur throughout the withdrawal. Lacrimation, rhinorrhea, and sweating are early signs. Later, gooseflesh (piloerection, hence "cold turkey"), muscle twitches (hence "kick the habit"), and lack of appetite are experienced. Finally, muscle aches, severe nausea, vomiting, and diarrhea can develop. Opioid withdrawal is usually not dangerous unless dehydration from vomiting and diarrhea becomes severe. As can be seen in Table 11-8, the speed of the withdrawal syndrome depends on which opioid is being used.

TABLE 11-8
Opioid Onset and Withdrawal

DRUG	EQUIV DOSE TO 10 MG MORPHINE (IM/Oral)	ONSET/PEAK (minutes)	HALF-LIFE (hours)	WITHDRAWAL ONSET/ DURATION (days)
Codeine	130/200	10–30/30–90	3	1–5
Fentanyl	0.1/NA	7–15/30–120	0.5–2	1–5
Heroin	5/30–60	2–15/10–90	2	1–5
Hydrocodone	20/25–30	10–30/30–60	4	1–5
Meperidine	75/100	15/60–90	3–5	1–5
Methadone	10/20	10–60/60–450	24	2–30
Morphine	10–30/60	10–20/20–90	2	1–5
Oxycodone	60–80/150–250	15/80	3	1–5

Epidemiology

Although accurate epidemiological data on opioid misuse are especially elusive, household surveys during the 1970s revealed that under 1% of adults over age 25 had used an opioid at least once for nonmedical reasons. It is now much higher with extensive abuse of prescription pain medications. Among high school seniors in 2007, the lifetime prevalence of heroin is 1.5% and other opioids over 13% (Johnston, 2007).

The "demographic" heroin addict is male (four males to one female), from the inner cities of both coasts, nonwhite, and with a teenage history of truancy, poor school performance, and delinquency. Immediate availability of opioids greatly increases the number of *new* cases of heroin misuse, whereas *chronic* misuse depends less on neighborhood access. All the sorrows of social blight and community disorganization—poor housing, lack of sanitation, malnutrition, unemployment, low educational levels, lack of family cohesiveness, and low cultural morale—correlate with opioid misuse. However, over the past several years there has been rapid growth of a population of nonheroin opioid abusers. These people use prescription opioids obtained from diversion or theft. The incidence has been high in poor rural areas, especially of oxycontin, a slow release form of oxycodone that is extremely potent (and often lethal) when crushed and then snorted or injected.

In addition to personality disorders (particularly antisocial), depression and anxiety disorders commonly accompany opioid dependence. Many opioid addicts are polydrug abusers, especially with "downers" such as alcohol and hypnoanxiolytics. Polydrug abuse is a bad prognostic indicator for heroin addicts.

Clinical Course

Although infrequently seen by professionals, many "chippers" use heroin in a controlled fashion. Otherwise, about half of all opioid abusers become opioid dependent. Whether this opioid dependency becomes chronic depends on the setting. For example, statistics on relapse and survival rates of heroin addicts were studied at the Washington University in St. Louis on two cohorts of individuals from 1972 through 1996. The first cohort were civilians; the second were individuals who had become addicted to heroin while serving in the military in the Vietnam War. This war, more than any other except possibly Afghanistan, was characterized by easy availability of heroin.

While 20% of veterans returned from Vietnam with heroin dependence, within a year only 0.7% continued to use and these were most likely veterans who had abused drugs prior to Vietnam (Price et al., 2001). This compares with a relapse rate of nearly 98% in nonveteran heroin addicts (Vaillant, 1966). The differences were attributed partly to baseline psychological stability of the veterans, but more so to the change in setting. One principle of addiction treatment is that the recovering addict must change "people, places, and things" that were associated with his or her active addiction. One non-Vietnam patient completing addiction treatment returned to opioid use within one year of discharge. Danny returned to his old New York neighborhood after 6 months of abstinence. As soon as he passed a street corner where he once had shot heroin, he immediately developed goose bumps, diarrhea, and hot flashes. As with Danny, such *conditioned withdrawal symptoms* often trigger a relapse. A month later, when Danny was asked why he used heroin, he explained, "If I had to be castrated to keep getting heroin, have me castrated."

The annual death rate of heroin addicts under age 30 is 1.6%; for those over age 30, 3%. Addicts usually die from accidental or intentional overdoses, allergic and acute toxic reactions (including pulmonary edema), infections and foreign material from shared unclean needles (hepatitis; AIDS; abscesses in liver, lung, and brain; tetanus; septic pulmonary emboli), a lowered immunological resistance, and from murder. Many addicts, if asked if they "share" needles, will say no, but if asked, "Do you ever *use* other people's needles?," will say yes.

Treatment and Management

No single program works for a majority of opiate abusers, and considerable controversy remains over the preferred approach. In general, there are two schools of thought: The "soft" pro-methadone school and the "tough" anti-methadone school. Methadone can be used for withdrawal and later for maintenance.

Methadone is an opioid with a long (12-hour) half-life that exerts pleasant effects when ingested. Because methadone is cross-tolerant with other opioids, once signs of opioid withdrawal begin, clinicians can initiate *methadone substitution* by giving patients roughly 10 mg three times daily, and then withdrawing them by gradually diminishing the dose by no more than 20% each day. However, federal law prohibits titrating outpatients (except in methadone clinics) with tapering doses of *any* opioid, or of detoxing an addict in an inpatient setting using an opioid for more than 72 hours. An exception is made for doctors who have been trained to use *buprenorphine* (a partial opioid antagonist) for maintenance or withdrawal of opioid addicts.

In addition, the alpha-2 adrenergic agonist clonidine has also been used for detoxification. Both drugs appear to be equally efficacious, if the level of tolerance is not greater than the equivalent of 30 mg of methadone per day. At higher levels methadone appears to more effectively suppress the abstinence syndrome. For those patients who have achieved considerable rehabilitation with methadone maintenance treatment, detoxification on an outpatient basis over a period of 2–6 months is reasonably effective. In any given year, less than 10% of chronic opioid abusers participate in community-based treatment programs. Giving up opioid use is a very slow process, and most users who have not achieved abstinence by their late 30s probably never will (Hser et al., 1993).

During opiate withdrawal, patients should be encouraged to participate in therapy. Small doses of a benzodiazepine may be given temporarily for insomnia. If patients convulse, they are probably also withdrawing from alcohol or hypnoanxiolytics and should be started on benzodiazepine withdrawal.

The loudest argument against methadone substitution is that using it makes withdrawal too easy and therefore fails to "teach the patient a lesson." No scientific evidence indicates that having this "lesson" prevents relapse. As one patient stated, "I've learned to never let myself run out of heroin again."

The rationale for *methadone maintenance* (MM), which begins following opiate withdrawal, is that ingested methadone usually blocks the euphoria of injected opiates. A high enough dose of heroin can override methadone blockade and, therefore, to achieve the objective, high doses of methadone may be required. Because methadone is taken orally and daily, it diminishes addicts' daily search for heroin and their commission of crimes to pay for it; the users become better workers and family members. Without needles, there are far fewer medical complications and deaths.

Although studies repeatedly support these findings and show that MM produces the best overall results, critics charge that one narcotic is merely being replaced for another, that many addicts sell methadone illicitly, that many studies favorable to MM included only patients with initially good prognoses, that some addicts get a high from shooting up on methadone, and that many patients on methadone can overcome the blockade by taking high doses of heroin. These objections are significant, yet studies have indicated that after 4 years of MM, a majority of ex-addicts live productively, with 94% no longer committing crimes to obtain "smack."

Whereas buprenorphine maintenance seems to be a better approach, MM continues to be a reasonable treatment for some opioid addicts. The FDA has set very stringent criteria for admission and continued treatment in these programs. Most programs include group and individual counseling as well as vocational rehabilitation and educational guidance.

With or without buprenorphine or MM maintenance, the usefulness of psychosocial treatments—including self-help groups, therapeutic communities, and drug treatment centers—remains unknown. More people quit restrictive "tough love" programs; less than 10% of addicts are suitable for these programs. Those who do best are highly motivated, have good ego strength, and are legally committed to the programs. The effectiveness of any therapy for opioid dependence varies largely in relation to the characteristics of various subgroups.

Sometimes *antagonist therapy* is used as an adjunct to opioid treatments. It is based on the idea that if a person continues to use opioids without pleasurable effects, the opioid craving will subside over time. The most commonly used opioid antagonist, naltrexone, has been most effective for recently detoxified methadone patients who have made substantial recovery, professional people, and addicts who are court-referred.

Tables 11.9 and 11.10 provide treatment and detoxification summaries for various addictions.

The *DSM-5* classifies gambling as a non–substance-related addiction as opposed to an impulse control disorder which is where it will be addressed in this textbook.

TABLE 11-9
Treatment of Addictions in Relation to Stages of Change Model

STAGE OF ADDICTION	CHARACTERISTICS	TREATMENT GOAL	INTERVENTION	PHARMACOTHERAPY
Precontemplation Pretreatment	•Denial of problem/diagnosis •Disinterest in behavioral change	•Make accurate diagnosis •Engage the patient	•Pretreatment education (premotivational engagement groups) •Motivational counseling	**Acute treatment and stabilization** Detoxification •Alcohol (clonazepam) •Benzodiazepines (valproate)
Contemplation Transition	•Considering change •Recognition of problem	•Interrupt denial and resistance	•Symptom management •Encouragement/advice •Structured living	•Stimulants •Opioids (clonidine) •Nicotine (buproprion)
Determination Stabilization, preparation, decision-making	•Decision to change behavior	•Reduce or discontinue drug use	•Recovery groups (e.g., AA/NA, Double Trouble, Steps 1–3) •Sponsor—support, structure, accountability •Cognitive–behavioral therapy •Support system (e.g., church groups, volunteer organizations)	**Maintenance and rehabilitation** •Aversive therapy (disulfiram) •Reduce craving (naltrexone, acamprosate) •Block reinforcing effects of opiates (naltrexone) •Treat underlying or drug-induced psychopathology (various psychotropics) •Opioid maintenance (methadone, LAAM, buprenorphine)
Action Early recovery	•Positive change in drug use	•Identify irrational thoughts, resulting negative emotions, and self-destructive behaviors		
Maintenance Sustained recovery	•Greater than 1 year of no drug use	•Maintain ongoing support for sobriety •Identify and manage relapse warning signs •Maintain relationship and lifestyle changes	•Psychotherapy groups •Relapse prevention groups •AA/NA Steps 4–12	
Relapse	•Return to drug use	•Return to recovery as soon as possible		

TABLE 11-10
Detoxification Protocols for Various Addictions

ALCOHOL	BENZODIAZEPINES	COCAINE/STIMULANTS	OPIOIDS	NICOTINE
Clonazepam 0.5 mg po tid for 2 days, bid for 2 days, then DC (adjust according to severity of withdrawal symptoms, liver functions, repeat blood alcohol level)	Switch to equivalent dose of long-acting BZDP (e.g., clonazepam)	Support	Grade 1: Yawning, sweating, lacrimation, rhinorrhea	Assess for history of seizures, eating disorders, cardiac disease
	Slowly taper to the lowest tolerated dose	Rest	Grade 2: Mydriasis, muscle twitching, piloerection, anorexia	Begin bupropion 150 mg SR po q am for 7 days, then increase to bid (breakfast and supper)
Thiamine 100 mg po or IM for 30 days	Begin valproate 250 mg po bid and increase as tolerated to 1000 mg po qd	Food	Grade 3: Insomnia, increased pulse, increased respirations, hypertension, abdominal cramps, vomiting	Patient instructed to reduce smoking by one half each week for 2 weeks
Multivitamin/mineral qd for 90 days	Discontinue BZDP	Psychotherapy	Taper down opioid if possible	Begin nicotine patch when patient is down to <½ pack per day
Insomnia:	Continue valproate for at least 30 days, then gradually DC	Pharmacological treatment for depression	Increase clonidine: Begin with 0.1 mg test dose then 0.1–0.2 mg po q 4–6 hours as tolerated	Patient has not had cigarette for 12 hours prior to first nicotine patch
Trazodone 100 mg i-iii po qhs prn sleep	**Maintenance Medications:**		Various prn medications:	Begin transdermal nicotine patch at 21 mg qd for 4 weeks, then 14 mg for 2 weeks, then DC (with significant cardiac disease reduce to 14 mg qd × 4 weeks, then 7 mg qd × 2 weeks)
Seizures:	Disulfiram 250–500 mg po qhs	Naltrexone 50 mg ½ tab po q am with meal for 7 days, then increase to 1 tab (50 mg) po q am with meal	•loperamide or kaolin/pectin	
Phenytoin 100 mg iii po qhs for 7 days, ii po qhs for 3 days, i po qhs for 3 days, DC	•Careful education and consent		•trazodone or amitriptyline	
Psychosis/delirium:	•Significant other involved	•No opiates for 2 weeks	•antihistamines (hydroxyzine or diphenhydramine)	
Olanzapine 10 mg po qhs	•No alcohol within 7 days	Buprenorphine	•promethazine	
	•Exam q 4 months with liver enzymes		•NSAIDs	

DC = discontinue; BZDP = benzodiazepine; NSAIDs = nonsteroid anti-inflammatory drugs.

References

Allgulander, C., Borg, S., & Vikander, B. (1984). A 4–6 year follow-up of 50 patients with primary dependence on sedative and hypnotic drugs. *American Journal of Psychiatry*, *141*, 1580–1582.

American Psychiatric Association. (2013). *Diagnostic and statistical manual of mental disorders*, 5th ed. Arlington, VA: American Psychiatric Association.

Ball, K.T., Walsh, K.M., & Rebec, C.-V. (2007). Reinstatement of MDMA (ecstasy) seeking by exposure to discrete drug-conditioned cues. *Pharmacology and Biochemistry of Behavior*, *87*(4), 420–425.

Barnes, D.M. (1988). New data intensify the agony over ecstasy. *Science*, *239*, 864–866.

Beresford, T.P., Blow, F.C., Hill, E., Singer, K., & Lucey, M.R. (1990). Clinical practice: Comparison of CAGE questionnaire and computer-assisted laboratory profiles in screening for covert alcoholism. *Lancet*, *336*, 482–485.

Biecheler, M.D., Peytavin, J.F., SAM Group, Facy, F., & Martineau, H. (2008). SAM survey on "drugs and fatal accidents": Search of substances consumed and comparison between drivers involved under the influence of alcohol or cannabis. *Traffic Injury Prevention*, *9*(1), 11–21.

Bohman, M., Cloninger, R., Sigvaardson, S., & von Knorring, A.L. (1987). The genetics of alcoholisms and related disorders. *Journal of Psychiatric Research*, *21*(4), 447–452.

Brewer, C. (1992). Controlled trials of Antabuse in alcoholism: The importance of supervision and adequate dosage. *Acta Psychiatry Scandinavia Supplement*, *369*, 51–58.

Chipana, C., Torres, I., Camarasa, J., Pubill, D., & Escubedo, E. (2008). Memantine protects against amphetamine derivatives induced neurotoxic damage in rats. *Neuropharmacology*, *54*(8), 1254–1263.

Ciraulo, D.A., Barnhill, J.G., Ciraulo, A.M., Greenblatt, D.J., & Shader, R.I. (1989). Parental alcoholism as a risk factor in benzodiazepine abuse: A pilot study. *American Journal of Psychiatry*, *146*(10), 1333–1335.

Coles, R., Brenner, J.H., & Meagher, D. (1970). *Drugs and youth: Medical, psychiatric, and legal facts*. New York: Liveright.

Comsay, K.P., Compton, W., Stinson, F.S., & Grant, B.F. (2006). Lifetime co-morbidity of DSM-IV mood and anxiety disorders: Results from the National Epidemiologic Survey on Alcohol and Related Conditions. *Journal of Clinical Psychiatry*, *67*(2), 247–257.

Covington, E.C. (1998). Anticonvulsants for neuropathic pain and detoxification. *Cleveland Clinic Journal of Medicine*, *65*, Suppl 1, S121–S129.

DiMartini, A., Day, N., Deco, M., Javid, L., Fitzgerald, M.G., Jain, A., et al. (2006). Alcohol consumption patterns and predictors of use following liver transplantation for alcoholic liver disease. *Liver Transplantation*, *12*(5), 813–820.

Ewing, J.A. (1984). Detecting alcoholism: The CAGE questionnaire. *Journal of the American Medical Association*, *252*, 1905–1907.

Fawcett, J., Clark, D.C., Aagesen, C.A., Pisani, V.D., Tilkin, J.M., Sellers, D., et al. (1987). A double-blind, placebo-controlled trial of lithium carbonate therapy for alcoholism. *Archives of General Psychiatry, 44,* 248–256.

Gawin, F.H., Kleber, H.D., Byck, R., Rounsaville, B.J., Kosten, T.R., Jatlow, P.I., et al. (1989). Desipramine facilitation of initial cocaine abstinence. *Archives of General Psychiatry, 46,* 117–121.

Gold, M.S. (1984). *800-Cocaine.* New York: Bantam.

Goodwin, D.W. (1985). Alcoholism and genetics: The sins of the father. *Archives of General Psychiatry, 42,* 171–174.

Goodwin, D.W., & Guze, S.B. (1984). *Psychiatric diagnosis,* 3rd ed. New York: Oxford University Press.

Grinspoon, L., & Bakalar, J. (1985). What is MDMA? *Harvard Medical School Mental Health Letter, 2*(2), 8.

Higgens, S.T., Budney, A.J., Bickel, W.K., Hughes, J.R., Foerg, F., & Badger, G. (1993). Achieving cocaine abstinence with a behavioral approach. *American Journal of Psychiatry, 150*(5), 763–769.

Hser, Y.I., Anglin, M.D., & Powers, K. (1993). A 24-year follow-up of California narcotics addicts. *Archives of General Psychiatry, 50,* 577–584.

Hughes, J.R., Oliveto, A.H., Helzer, J.E., Higgens, S.T., & Bickel, W.K. (1992). Should caffeine abuse, dependence, or withdrawal be added to *DSM-IV* and *ICD-10*? *American Journal of Psychiatry, 149,* 33–40.

Jellinek, E.M. (1952). Phases of alcohol addiction. *Quarterly Journal of Studies on Alcohol, 13,* 673–684.

Johnston, L.D., O'Malley, P.M., Bachman, J.G. & Schulenberg, J.E. (2007). *Overall, illicit drug use by American teens continues gradual decline in 2007.* University of Michigan News Service: Ann Arbor, MI.

Kandel, D.B., & Raveis, V.H. (1989). Cessation of illicit drug use in young adulthood. *Archives of General Psychiatry, 46,* 109–116.

Kang, S.Y., Kleinman, P.H., Woody, G.E., Millman, R.B., Todd, T.C., Kemp, J., et al. (1991). Outcomes for cocaine abusers after once-a-week psychosocial therapy. *American Journal of Psychiatry, 148*(5), 630–635.

Karila, L., Weinstein, A., Benjaminn, A., Coscass, L.C., Noble, F., Lowenstein, W., et al. (2008). Current pharmacotherapies and immunotherapy in cocaine addiction. *Presse Medicine, 37*(4), 689–698.

Kushner, M.G., Sher, K.J., & Bertman, B.D. (1990). The relation between alcohol problems and the anxiety disorders. *American Journal of Psychiatry, 147*(6), 685–695.

LeFoll, B., & George, T.P. (2007). Treatment of tobacco dependence: Integrating recent progress into practice. *Canadian Medical Association Journal, 177*(11), 1373–1380.

Levin, E.D., Westman, E.R., Stein, R.M., Carnahan, E., Sanchez, M., Herman, S., et al.

(1994). Nicotine skin patch treatment increases abstinence, decreases withdrawal symptoms, and attenuates rewarding effects of smoking. *Journal of Clinical Psychopharmacology, 14*, 41–49.

Peroutka, S.J. (1987). Incidence of recreational use of 3,4-methylenedioxymethamphetamine (MDMA, "Ecstasy") on an undergraduate campus. *New England Journal of Medicine, 817*, 1542–1543.

Price, R.K., Risk, N.K., Murray, K.S., Virgo, K.S., & Spitznagel, E.L. (2001). Twenty-five year mortality of US servicemen deployed in Vietnam: Predictive utility of early drug use. *Drug and Alcohol Dependence, 64*(3), 309–318.

Prochaska, J.O., DiClemente, C.C., & Norcross, J.C. (1992). In search of how people change: Applications to addictive behaviors. *American Psychologist, 47*, 1102–1114.

Rankin, J.G., Winkenson, P., & Santamaria, J.N. (1970). Factors influencing the prognosis of the alcoholic patient. *Australian Annals of Medicine, 19*, 232–239.

Rittenhouse, J.D. (1982). Drugs in the school: The shape of drug abuse among American youth in the seventies. In G.G. Nahas & H.C. Frick (Eds.), *Drug abuse in the modern world: A perspective for the eighties* (pp. 99–105). New York: Pergamon.

Salzman, C. (1985). Benzodiazepine dependence. *Harvard Medical School Mental Health Letter, 1*(10), 8.

Satel, S.L., & Edell, W.S. (1991). Cocaine-induced paranoia and psychosis proneness. *American Journal of Psychiatry, 148*, 1708–1711.

Selzer, M.L. (1969). Alcoholics at fault in fatal accidents and hospitalized alcoholics: A comparison. *Quarterly Journal of Studies on Alcohol, 30*(4), 883–887.

Sorensen, T.I.A., Bentsen, K.D., Eghoje, K., Orholm, M., Haybye, G., & Christoffersen, P. (1984). Prospective evaluation of alcohol abuse and alcoholic liver injury in men as predictors of development of cirrhosis. *Lancet, 2*(8397), 241–244.

Tennant, F.S., Jr. (1986). The clinical syndrome of marijuana dependence. *Psychiatric Annals, 16*(4), 225–234.

Treatment Improvement Protocols (TIPS). Printed copies of these useful publications and materials are available from SAMHSA's National Clearinghouse for Alcohol and Drug Information NCADI. Publications may be ordered online, http://ncadistore.samhsa.gov /catalog/or by phone, at (800) 729–6686.

Tsuang, J.W., Iruin, M.R., Smith, T.L., & Schuckit, M.A. (1994). Characteristics of men with alcoholic hallucinations. *Addiction, 90*(2), 289–290.

Vaillant, G.E. (1966). A 12-year follow-up of New York narcotic addicts. *Archives of General Psychiatry, 15*, 599.

Victor, M., & Hope, J.M. (1958). The phenomenon of auditory hallucinations in chronic alcoholism. *Journal of Nervous and Mental Disorders, 126*, 451.

World Health Organization. (1992). *The ICD–10 classification of mental and behavioural disorders: Clinical descriptions and diagnostic guidelines*. Geneva: World Health Organization.

12

Schizophrenia and Other
Thought Disorders

Of all psychiatric illness, thought disorders arguably devastate as no others, for no other disorders cause more pervasive or profound an impact—socially, economically, and personally. Patients with thought disorders occupy a disproportionately large number of American hospital beds and, excluding geriatric patients with cognitive disorders, two-thirds of all psychiatric beds. In 2002, the overall U.S. cost of schizophrenia alone was estimated to be $62.7 billion: $7.0 billion for direct outpatient services, $5.0 billion for pharmaceuticals, $2.8 billion for hospitalization, $8.0 billion for long-term care, $7.6 billion for total direct non-health care costs, including living cost offsets, and $32.4 billion for total indirect costs. On any given day, there are over 2 million patients with schizophrenia needing care in the United States, and over 2 million new cases arising each year worldwide.

SCHIZOPHRENIA

Schizophrenia is the most common of the thought (psychotic) disorders. In schizophrenia the disturbance of thinking is characterized by a focus on information that is irrelevant and peripheral to the situation at hand so that cognitive processing seems obtuse, vague, obscure, and sometimes incomprehensible to others. Consequently the individual suffering from this illness is perplexed and has difficulty making sense of the world. He often ascribes idiosyncratic and non–reality-based meaning (often with sinister attributions) to everyday common situations and responds accordingly with unusual or otherwise inexplicable behaviors.

Parents and siblings of individuals with schizophrenia may endure years of uncertainty, guilt, dashed hopes, rage (at, and from, the patient), financial burdens, self-doubt, and futility. Siblings may resent their ill brother or sister getting "all" the attention, may berate themselves for feeling resentful, and may worry they too will develop an uncontrollable psychotic illness. Yet it is not difficult to imagine that the individual who has schizophrenia suffers even more. When Bleuler (see Chapter 1) invented the term *schizophrenia*, he did not mean a "split personality" (i.e., multiple personality), but rather a *shattered* or fragmented personality. Whereas patients with other severe mental disorders may share certain symptoms of schizophrenia, the curse of the person with schizophrenia is to be plagued by so many of them. While reading the following case vignette, try to imagine being that person and having to negotiate your most challenging everyday activities.

David Sebastian, a 24-year-old single, Roman Catholic ex-divinity student, was hospitalized for "episodes of inappropriate behavior and being out of touch with reality." For 16 hours nonstop, his inappropriate behavior consisted of masturbatory movements accompanied by groans, prayers, flailing limbs, and head-banging. During these episodes, he was totally self-absorbed: If asked questions, he wouldn't respond; all attempts to restrain him (for his own physical safety) were fiercely resisted. Eventually, he slept.

On awakening, he stared and smiled at a nurse, who described him as "Rasputin imitating the Mona Lisa." He accused the pope of "fornicating nuns," "spreading diarrhea and gonorrhea," and "plotting to assassinate me [David]." He was convinced that St. Christopher, the Roman Catholic patron saint of travel, was removed from the Catholic Church calendar because he [David] was having sexual thoughts while traveling. His thoughts seemed disorganized as he jumped incoherently from topic to topic. When asked if he feared anything, he replied with a flat affect: "Nothing, but the pope wants slivers up his ass or my ass or he's an ass; you know, this is not me talking but a taped recording of how you are today that couldn't communicate at any level as a dialectical incongruence of spiritual sexuality."

About a year ago, David began to exhibit changes in his behavior. He had previously been an outstanding biology student, a jogger, a bit of a loner prone to lengthy philosophical and religious discourses, and as his neighbors would remark, "such a sweet boy to live with his parents." At age 23, however, David's grades began to slip and he became more reclusive. Seven or so months later, and several weeks before his sister's wedding, he spent days and nights making his sister's wedding gift: a stained-glass penis. Two days before the wedding, his father accidentally knocked the gift off a table, and as it smashed into a million pieces, David did too. For the next month he attacked his family for destroying him, turning him into a robot, and sapping his vital fluids.

God's voice accused him of being too preoccupied with sex and pro-claimed that becoming a priest was his only salvation. This instruction gave renewed purpose to his life while permitting a rapprochement with his fam-ily. He enrolled in divinity school, but a month later he could no longer concentrate. New and unfamiliar voices began discussing his plight, with one saying that "David's prick doesn't work," and the other saying, "If you were a *real* man, you'd go out and use your prick." He met a co-ed, went to her apartment, they went to bed, but when David was about to enter her, he began praying out loud and banging his head. Horrified, she fled from the room, called the police, and David was taken to a hospital for evaluation.

Repeated neurological exams and tests revealed no physical disorder. He was placed on antipsychotic medication and over the next 10 days, his episodes (catatonic excitement alternating with negativism), delusions, hal-lucinations, incoherence, paranoia, and self-referential ideas gradually dis-appeared. Three days after admission he joined group therapy, but within minutes he pointed to the nine people in the room and exclaimed, "Eigh-teen eyes haunting my head, changing its size, televising my mind, eating it, bleeding it, feeding it. You gyrating Judases, how dare. . . ." Suddenly silent, he left the room. Days later he said he had felt besieged by the other mem-bers and that he left the room to escape this bombardment and to stop "embarrassing myself further." Once his psychotic symptoms abated, David actively participated in group and supportive individual psychotherapy. In meetings with the entire family, his parents vented their frustration, were told "the facts" about catatonic schizophrenia (David's diagnosis), and dis-cussed how they could all live more peaceably together. After 3 weeks of inpatient care, he was discharged on medication and was to receive weekly psychotherapy.

For 3 months David worked at his father's grocery store, visited daily with a neighborhood priest, lived at home, read theology, painted a little, and saw friends. Then, when his father suggested that maybe he should live away from home, David stormed out of the house, wandered the streets, and stopped his medication because "it was digesting my sex organ." Within weeks he looked like a rag picker. He kept to himself. Voices (hallucinations) were mocking his "scrawny figure and sexual inadequacies" and insisted he "go out with prostitutes." With considerable guilt he succumbed, but upon entering the prostitute's room he quickly extricated himself, praying loudly and striking himself in the head. The prostitute called the police, and David's second hospital admission ensued. Later he told a therapist that he was in a "no-win" situation: If he did have intercourse, he was committing a sin; if he didn't, his voices were right and he wasn't a man.

David passed through the proverbial "revolving door" for three more hospitalizations; each occurred after a fight at home or a sexual confrontation. When his parents visited, at first he'd accuse them of "warping" his penis; these meetings, however, would eventually calm him down. Whenever the staff tried to separate David from his parents, he would vegetate in a corner, stop talking, and starve himself; one time, he had to be physically restrained from jumping out the window. After 6 tumultuous months, David returned home: He worked regularly in a bookstore, remained on moderate doses of antipsychotic drugs, and participated in weekly group therapy. He began a theology class, where he befriended a shy young woman who felt nobody would ever like her. David did. Three years later they are still seeing each other ("We'll marry when *he* can afford me!" she laughs). He works at the bookstore and lives at home. He remains on medication ("I go bonkers without it"), and although he stopped the group ("I outgrew it"), he continues to receive individual psychotherapy ("so my crazy ideas don't overwhelm me").

Students of psychopathology will appreciate the writings of Emil Kraepelin, which include rich and comprehensive descriptions of schizophrenia in its many forms, depressive disorders, and manic-depressive disorders in vivid clinical detail from an era decades before modern mood stabilizers, antidepressants, and antipsychotics were available.

Clinical Presentation

The essential features of schizophrenia are (1) a history of acute psychosis with delusions, hallucinations, disorganized speech, catatonia, grossly disorganized behavior, or flat affect; (2) chronic deterioration of functioning; (3) duration that exceeds 6 months (with one month of continuous positive symptoms), and (4) the absence of a concurrent mood disorder, substance abuse, or another medical condition that would explain the clinical presentation.

The prognosis for a person who meets criteria for schizophrenia generally is such that he or she will have great difficulty achieving full developmental potential. The usual course of the illness is chronic and episodically downhill. However, with timely and adequate treatment and support, this person may nevertheless become moderately independent and productive, and in some instances achieve extraordinary successes in their lives. Nobel laureate John Nash (economics) is an example of one who succeeded in spite of schizophrenia. Table 12-1 lists diagnostic criteria for schizophrenia.

Criterion A indicates that at least one very clear "positive symptom" (numbers 1–3) of schizophrenia, must be present for a significant portion of

TABLE 12-1
Diagnostic Criteria for Schizophrenia

A. *Active phase*: A minimum of one very clear positive symptom belonging to the criteria listed in (1), (2), or (3) and if less clear-cut usually two or more, including the possibility of another one from (4) and (5), have been clearly present for most of the time during a period of **1 month or more**.

(1) **Delusions**
   a. delusions of control, influence, or passivity, clearly referred to body or limb movements or specific thoughts, actions, or sensations; delusional perception; or
   *b. persistent [*bizarre*] delusions of other kinds that are culturally inappropriate and completely impossible, such as religious or political identity, or superhuman powers and abilities (e.g., being able to control the weather, or being in communication with aliens from another world);

(2) **Hallucinations**
   *a. hallucinatory **voices giving a running commentary** on the patient's behavior, or discussing the patient among themselves, or other types of hallucinatory voices coming from some part of the body; or
   b. persistent hallucinations in any modality, when accompanied either by fleeting or half-formed delusions without clear affective content, or by persistent over-valued ideas, or when occurring every day for weeks or months on end;

(3) **Formal thought disturbance** as expressed through speech as
   a. breaks or interpolations in the train of thought, resulting in incoherent or irrelevant speech, or neologisms; or
   b. thought echo, thought insertion or withdrawal, and thought broadcasting;

(4) **Catatonic** [*or disorganized*] **behavior**, such as excitement, posturing, or waxy flexibility, negativism, mutism, and stupor;

(5) **"Negative" symptoms** such as
   a. marked apathy, paucity of speech, and blunting or incongruity of emotional responses, usually resulting in social withdrawal and lowering of social performance; it must be clear that these are not due to depression or to neuroleptic medication; or
   b. a significant and consistent change in the overall quality of some aspects of personal behavior, manifest as loss of interest, aimlessness, idleness, a self-absorbed attitude, and social withdrawal. These "residual" symptoms should be present for one year.

B. *Social/occupational dysfunction*: The signs and symptoms result in **significant distress, decrement/decline, or developmental arrest** in personal, family, social, educational, occupational, or other important areas of functioning.

C. *Duration*: Conditions meeting symptomatic requirements but of **duration less than 1 month** (whether treated or not) should be diagnosed in the first instance as **acute schizophrenia-like psychotic disorder** [*Brief Psychotic Disorder*] and reclassified as schizophrenia if the symptoms persist for longer periods.

(continued)

TABLE 12-1
Continued

Because of the difficulty in timing onset, the 1-month duration criterion applies only to the specific symptoms listed above and not to any "prodromal" nonpsychotic phase. Viewed retrospectively, it may be clear that a prodromal phase in which symptoms and behavior, such as loss of interest in work, social activities, and personal appearance and hygiene, together with generalized anxiety and mild degrees of depression and preoccupation, preceded the onset of psychotic symptoms by weeks or even months.

DSM-5 requires that continuous signs of the disturbance persist for at least 6 months. This 6-month period must include at least 1 continuous month of symptoms (or shorter in duration if successfully treated in that time period) that met Criterion A (i.e., active-phase symptoms) and may include periods of prodromal or residual symptoms. During these prodromal or residual periods, the signs of the disturbance may be manifested by attenuated positive symptoms (e.g., odd beliefs, unusual perceptual experiences) or only negative symptoms. If continuous signs of the disturbance last for at least one month but less than 6 months Schizophreniform Disorder is diagnosed using DSM-5 criteria.

D. Schizoaffective and Mood Disorder exclusion: The diagnosis of schizophrenia should not be made in the presence of extensive depressive or manic symptoms unless it is clear that schizophrenic symptoms antedated the affective disturbance. If both schizophrenic and affective symptoms develop together and are evenly balanced, the diagnosis of **schizoaffective disorder** should be made, even if the schizophrenic symptoms by themselves would have justified the diagnosis of schizophrenia.

E. Substance/general medical condition exclusion: The disturbance is **not better explained by the direct physiological effects of a substance or another medical condition**. Schizophrenia should not be diagnosed in the presence of overt brain disease or during states of drug intoxication or withdrawal. Similar disorders developing in the presence of epilepsy, other brain disease, or induced by drugs are separately coded.

F. The disturbance is **not better explained by another mental disorder, particularly autistic spectrum or communication disorders.**

Note: Adapted from *ICD-10* (p. 78) and *DSM-5* (p. 99)

*There is often added weight given to these symptoms (bizarre delusions and running commentary auditory hallucinations) due to the widely accepted notion that they are indicative of the most serious and most reproducible of presentations of schizophrenia (Schneiderian "first-rank" symptoms, named after psychiatrist Kurt Schneider). In fact, they are seen not only in schizophrenia but also in bipolar disorder and other psychotic disorders, so the careful clinician does not diagnose on the basis of these Criterion A components alone).

**Since mood disorders, substance-induced disorders, brain-injured states, dementias, and delirium states are so often accompanied by severe hallucinations, delusions, and thought disorder, one must be very careful to assess mood and general medical signs and symptoms and their detailed time courses in the History of Present Illness. Remember "All that hallucinates is not schizophrenia."

time during a 1-month period. Commonly observed acute symptoms are delusions of persecution, delusions of control (bodily control or thought control), delusional perceptions, and particular forms of auditory hallucinations (especially voices commenting about the patient's actions or arguing back and forth). Less frequent, but no less important to note, are incoherence of speech (and thoughts), disturbed (or incongruent) affect, and catatonia (with decreased motor activity or excited motor activity).

Schizophrenic *delusions* are often bizarre and mood-incongruent. One can readily empathize with the delusions of the person with depression, but not those of the person with schizophrenia. His or hers are weird, from a different world or dimension. They may be of Schneiderian first-rank form (see Chapter 2), such as delusions of bodily control in which the person with schizophrenia announces, "Martians have taken over my body," or thought control delusions (thought insertion, thought withdrawal, and thought broadcasting). In thought insertion, one's thoughts are not his own but have been somehow put there; in thought withdrawal one's thoughts have somehow been removed; in thought broadcasting one's thoughts have somehow been made known to all. Persecutory delusions are also common, but unlike when they appear in organic or mood disorders, in schizophrenia the source of the menace is often an ill-defined and remote source—a vague "they."

Hallucinations are reported by roughly 75% of newly admitted patients with schizophrenia; they are usually in one sensory modality, with about 90% being auditory but cases with all five are not uncommon. Fifteen percent of hallucinations are of the Schneiderian first-rank type (Ludwig, 1985) namely, in the third person, conversing or arguing about the patient, or commenting on his or her actions, or hearing his or her thoughts out loud. Voices may whisper or shout, comment on the patient's actions, or demand morally offensive acts ("command hallucinations"). The voices may be from known people (e.g., a dead grandmother) or strangers; they may be verbose or just one or two words repeated constantly. Because some people refer to their own thoughts as "voices," be sure to ask, "Do the voices come from inside or outside your head?" and "Is it your own voice or someone else's?" Visual hallucinations are often bizarre, frightening, and/or threatening (snakes crawling out of skulls, blood dripping from dead relatives) and when present usually occur in conjunction with the auditory hallucinations. Olfactory hallucinations are rare and should prompt an investigation into a seizure disorder; frequently cited are disgusting smells from the patient's body, smoke from burning substances, and toxic drugs or chemicals. Tactile (haptic) hallucinations are not as uncommon; the patient may report, for example, electric sensations along the spine, a needle puncturing the ear drum, or bones being broken; they may be in conjunction with delusions that so and so is beating me, hitting me, stabbing me, or causing the pain. Delusional perceptions were also among Kurt Schneider's first-rank phenomena. These occur when a patient falsely attributes a bizarre meaning to a common perception, such as hearing a bird chirping and suddenly believing the patient will now be the savior of the world.

> Initially, many of those with schizophrenia present with an unshakable belief in their delusions and hallucinations. After months of consternation, patients may suddenly come up with another delusion that "explains" everything to their way of understanding; this "insight" may have enormous personal meaning to patients, while it mystifies everyone else. In normal recovery occurring over several weeks, patients typically gain increasing distance from their psychosis. They will go from assertions that "The telephone company is poisoning my food," to "*It seems like* the telephone company is poisoning my food." As the psychosis resolves further, the statement may become, "I'm not so sure about that telephone-company stuff." And later, "Every so often I think the phone company is poisoning my food. Isn't that crazy!" This process may be referred to as "softening" of the delusions. Frequently, however, delusions only partially soften, such as "I've learned not to pay attention to those ideas about the telephone company. They just get me in trouble."

Speech abnormalities in schizophrenia are caused by defects in cognitive processes and are the best evidence of a *thought disorder*. *Irrelevant* and *disorganized speech* is the third possible symptom of group-A criteria and manifests as incoherence, frequent derailment, loose associations, tangentiality, circumstantiality, and/or illogical thinking. Poverty of content, perplexity, or severe thought blocking may occur, but more often, patients seem flooded with ideas and are unable to separate or filter the relevant from the immaterial. Such an example unexpectedly occurred when Dr. Maxmen received a telephone call from a total stranger speaking in a monotonously pert voice (the author's responses are in brackets):

> "Hello. I'm paranoid schizophrenic from Tampa. Are you the Dr. Maxim [*sic*] who wrote *The New Psychiatry?* [Yes.] Well, I'm 75 years old, but I grew up in the home of the very famous Dr. Zuckerman who graduated from P&S, your school. He was the Dr. Obsessive–Compulsive Neurosis psychiatrist, who was a brilliant cardiologist, and I was his only psychiatric patient, and he never said he was my father, but my mother was a borderline butch-

lesbian personality, and Dr. Zuckerman was the first to take me to the Metropolitan Museum of Art because I have a tooth on the right side that's too big, just as in that Picasso painting, and I have a malformed skull, and a right leg also much longer than my left, and my daughter Infanta Marguarita Pequina lives in Chicago, but Dr. Zuckerman didn't rescue me from a terrible marriage from 1948, to 1966 in which a man beat and raped me in the Jewish community—are you Jewish? [Yes] Dr. Zuckerman didn't end the marriage, but I got out of it in 1962 and have been on Mellaril ever since. [What happens if you stop the Mellaril?] My brain waves flash too fast, just as you said in your book, which I'm taking to my clinical psychologist, where I go three times a week, although Dr. Zuckerman studied with A. A. Brill and Dr. Freud and belonged in psychoanalysis, but that couldn't help my skull, which was genetically deformed and made worse by my sadist husband in the Jewish community. Do you see patients?"

When incoherence is milder or first appears, many listeners will "read into" the patient's speech. Consider this example from a term paper written by an acutely disturbed college student with schizophrenia:

we see the stately dimension of godly bliss that marlowe's *dOctOr fAUstUs* dies and lives. lucifer—oh lucy, luck, lackluster, lazy lucifer—devilishly adorns all sanctifarious, all beauty, all evil. Our world dissolves into *SACRED* nihilism.

Individually, the sentences might make sense, but collectively, they're nonsense. Punning without intentional humor, as around "lucifer," is typical of schizophrenic speech; so too is the neologism "sanctifarious." The strange punctuation would seem to have a private meaning, a hunch later confirmed by the patient, who explained, "It's all about Christ. Don't you see? Marlowe's first name is Christopher. Christ. Get it?"

With *catatonia*, patients have impaired interaction with, or responsiveness to, the environment. Characterized by disorganized motor and speech behavior, catatonia presents alternatively in a retarded or stuporous form or as an excited, activated form, like the case of David Sebastian, above. Signs include echolalia, echopraxia, posturing, catalepsy, mutism, negativism, akinesia, waxy flexibility, and automatic obedience.

Negative symptoms are the final criterion in group A; they are distinguished more by what is missing than what is present. A certain group of people with schizophrenia become *avolitional* and *unmotivated*. In the hospital, our nurses call it "bed flopping." The untrained mistake this behavior for laziness, but it's not. Many behaviors are diminished, including verbal behavior, resulting in fewer or no words spoken ("alogia" or "mutism"). These symptoms may be the consequence of giving all attention to internal stimuli, or they may be experienced as the complete absence of stimuli. One patient with schizophrenia described it as, "The light's not on and nobody's home."

Affects, flat and/or inappropriate, typically develop insidiously and persist chronically. At times they arise acutely. However, the pathological affects discussed below are not diagnostically specific: Depressed mood, drug-induced states, and akinesia (a frequent side effect of antipsychotic drugs) can appear as flat affect; brain-injury syndromes also may produce inappropriate affects. Flat affect is one of the common negative symptoms of schizophrenia. Inappropriate affect is a manifestation of disorganized behavior. A reasonable inference is that inappropriate affects emerge because patients are attending and responding to internal more than to external stimuli. They may cry when talking about the weather or laugh when hearing about a massive airplane crash. When a person with schizophrenia giggles for no obvious reason, the listener's skin crawls due to the bizarre nature of such behavior. The "humor" is not funny; it is, in fact, tragically pathetic.

Subtypes

Because the latest evidence does not as strongly support the predictive validity for clinical course and treatment response of the previously identified schizophrenia subtypes, they are no longer listed in *DSM-5*. Each of these five subtypes of schizophrenia was based upon the patient's most prominent presenting features. The *disorganized* type was characterized by marked incoherence along with a flat, silly, perplexed, or inappropriate affect. Formerly called "hebephrenic," these patients have an early and insidious onset, poor premorbid functioning, severe social impairment, and a chronic course.

The *catatonic* type primarily displayed psychomotor disturbances. Patients with catatonia tend to have a more sudden onset, a better prognosis, a greater prevalence of mood disorders among first-degree relatives, and respond to electroconvulsive therapy—four features commonly associated with mood disorders. Pointing out that catatonic excitement and stupor may be due to severe psychomotor agitation and retardation, respectively, Ries (1985) and others claim that *catatonia occurs more often in bipolar disorders than in schizophrenia*. Other studies have suggested that in some patients who present with catatonia, a mood disorder will be the most common diagnosis, and both *catatonia due to another medical condition* and *schizophrenia* will tie for second place.

The *paranoid* type of schizophrenia was characterized by prominent persecutory or grandiose delusions or hallucinations with similar content. These patients are often unfocused, angry, argumentative, violent, and anxious. Stiff and mistrustful, they assume people can't be trusted and that anybody who likes them must be up to no good. Unsure of their own identity, they may project these fears onto others and be terrified of other races or ethnic groups. These patients live a "contained," highly structured existence. Relative to the other schizophrenic types, the paranoid type manifests later, interferes less with social functioning, and has a more stable course. The lucky ones have highly encapsulated delusions. For example, a patient might believe that everybody at a certain shopping center is a satanic murderer, but all other locations are safe. This person can live a relatively happy life simply by avoiding that shopping center.

Patients with schizophrenia who do not fit one of the above three types were diagnosed as *undifferentiated type* if they are actively psychotic, and as *residual type* if, after an active phase, chronic symptoms predominate.

Epidemiology

The prevalence and incidence of schizophrenia tend to be the same regardless of political system, nationality, or historical time period. The lifetime prevalence of schizophrenia varies between 0.8% and 1%. With an incidence of 0.3 to 0.6 per thousand, about 100,000 new cases of schizophrenia arise annually in the United States. For perspective, the prevalence of schizophrenia is about twice that of Alzheimer's disease and about six times that of insulin-dependent diabetes. The disorder afflicts men just slightly more frequently than women with later onset in women (Hofner & Meiden, 1997; Lewine, Burbach, & Meltzer, 1984), European-Americans and African-Americans about the same, and urbanites more than rural folk. Less stressful rural settings may result in fewer and less severe episodes, while affording a low-stress environment for the patient with chronic schizophrenia to function at maximum, but still likely diminished, potential. For example, a Wisconsin dairy farmer brought in one of his bachelor hired hands for evaluation because the man had stopped milking the cows. When the farmer was asked if this man heard voices, the farmer said, "Yes, for 20 years, but we didn't mind until he stopped milking the cows."

Lower socioeconomic classes have a disproportionate number of people with schizophrenia. To explain why, two theories are usually advanced: "social causation" and "drift." The former asserts that poverty causes stress, which in turn causes schizophrenia. The drift theory holds that because schizophrenia devastates social and occupational functioning, people with schizophrenia migrate to society's lower echelons. Most evidence points to the drift theory. For example, studies in four nations revealed that, whereas the fathers of sons with schizophrenia were equally distributed among social classes, their sons had drifted downward (Goodwin & Guze, 1989; Hafner & Heiden, 1997).

Differential Diagnosis

Schizophrenia needs to be differentiated from other psychotic disorders such as schizophreniform disorder, schizoaffective disorder, bipolar disorder, delusional disorder, brief psychotic disorder, shared psychotic disorder (*folie à deux*), substance-induced psychotic disorder, and psychotic disorder due to another medical condition such as a traumatic lesion, neoplasm, or epilepsy. Details on differential diagnosis are presented later in this chapter, when each disorder is examined individually. In general, patients with these potential imitators of schizophrenia do not display all the symptoms needed for a schizophrenia diagnosis or they have not had them long enough. The most important clue in distinguishing schizophrenia from a *mood disorder* or a *psychotic state* that is caused by substances or a medical condition is this: *Between psychotic episodes, people with schizophrenia most often do not completely resolve their symptoms or maintain completely normal behavior, whereas with these other conditions, patients usually do return to normal function with proper clinical management and treatment adherence.*

Patients appearing to have schizophrenia, *catatonic type*, are more likely to have a *mood disorder*, but may also have *catatonia due to another medical condition*. Those with a mood disorder usually have normal baseline function, report previous episodes of depression or mania, and often have relatives with mood disorder, typically bipolar disorder. A sodium amytal interview or a brief trial of benzodiazepine can sometimes be of help to temporarily "unfreeze" a catatonic stupor and help clinicians elicit more information about the actual diagnosis of these patients. Profoundly elevated or depressed mood states are suggestive of mood disorder and may be accompanied by mood-congruent delusions without a formal thought disorder (e.g., disorganized speech, loose associations) and prominent psychomotor retardation or agitation. Patients with mania may temporarily have all the positive symptoms of schizophrenia, but also have very expansive moods. Remember well the clinical rule-of-thumb triad seen with mood disorders: prominent mood abnormality, altered sense of self and self-worth, and altered vital sense (or sense of well-being). Disorientation and a worsening with amytal may be clues to a medically caused catatonia. Medical causes of catatonia to consider include neurological conditions (e.g., cerebrovascular disease, encephalitis) and metabolic conditions (e.g., hypercalcemia, hepatic encephalopathy, homocystinuria, diabetic ketoacidosis). A careful history, physical exam, and laboratory investigation are essential in assessing catatonia. Occasionally, neuroleptic medication can cause dystonias: acute spasms of particular muscle groups that may closely resemble the posturing of catatonia. This side effect is usually seen in proximity to antipsychotic medication dosing and administration schedules.

Anxiety and somatoform disorders may resemble schizophrenia intermittently, but not for long. Patients with obsessive–compulsive disorder or hypochondriasis may become preoccupied with their concerns to a near-delusional intensity. Yet, unlike patients with schizophrenia, the patients with obsessive–compulsive disorder know that their obsessions are "silly," and patients with hypochondriasis know, to some degree, that their fears are unfounded or excessive.

Schizotypal, schizoid, paranoid, and *borderline personality disorders* may intermittently present with psychotic symptoms and resemble the prodromal or acute phase of schizophrenia. But unlike schizophrenia, the unstable phase, perhaps including "mini"-psychotic symptoms, remits in hours or days and does not leave lasting changes of any profound nature. Severe *schizoid personality disorder* may produce a schizophrenic-like social withdrawal with odd affect and behavior; these patients, however, rarely become psychotic. Schizotypal personality disorder seems to be on the schizophrenia spectrum as a long-standing condition of subthreshold criteria with some degree of social or occupational functioning preserved (see Table 12-2).

Etiology and Pathogenesis

The causes of schizophrenia and the mechanisms of symptom production are not yet known, but evidence is strong for both genetic as well as environmental influences on its etiology and pathophysiology. Cases of schizophrenia involve abnormalities of the brain's anatomical structure and function, which in turn are associated with perceptual, cognitive, physiological, and behavioral abnormalities.

Biological Theories

Genetic. It is clear that schizophrenia is sometimes familial, conferring additional risk to relatives of those afflicted (see Table 12-3). First-degree

---

TABLE 12-2
Diagnostic Criteria for Schizotypal Personality Disorder

Schizotypal disorder possesses many of the characteristic features of schizophrenic disorders and is probably genetically related to them; however, the hallucinations, delusions, and gross behavioral disturbances of schizophrenia itself are absent and so this disorder does not always come to medical attention. It is also discussed in the chapter on personality disorders.

A. A **pattern of eccentric behavior and anomalies of thinking and affect which resemble those seen in schizophrenia**. There is no dominant or typical disturbance, but **at least three of the following** (*DSM-5 specifies five or more*) have been present, continuously or episodically, for at least 2 years:

   (1) occasional transient quasi-psychotic episodes with intense illusions, auditory or other hallucinations, and delusion-like ideas, usually occurring without external provocation;

   (2) odd beliefs or magical thinking, influencing behavior and inconsistent with subcultural norms;

   (3) unusual perceptual experiences including somatosensory (bodily) or other illusions, depersonalization or derealization;

   (4) vague, circumstantial, metaphorical, overelaborate, or stereotyped thinking, manifested by odd speech or in other ways, without gross incoherence;

   (5) suspiciousness or paranoid ideas; (*and associated social anxiety as per* DSM-5);

   (6) inappropriate or constricted affect (the individual appears cold and aloof);

   (7) behavior or appearance that is odd, eccentric, or peculiar;

   (8) poor rapport with others and a tendency to social withdrawal;

   (9) obsessive ruminations without inner resistance, often with dysmorphophobic, sexual or aggressive contents;

B. **No definite and characteristic features of schizophrenia, affective disorder with psychotic features, other thought (psychotic) disorder, or another mental disorder, particularly autistic spectrum or communications disorder**, have occurred at any stage of the illness.

A history of schizophrenia in a first-degree relative gives additional weight to the diagnosis but is not a prerequisite. It is more common in individuals related to schizophrenics and is believed to be part of the genetic "spectrum" of schizophrenia.

The disorder runs a chronic course with fluctuations of intensity. Occasionally it evolves into overt schizophrenia. There is no definite onset and its evolution and course are usually those of a personality disorder.

Note: Adapted from *ICD-10* (p. 83) and *DSM-5* (p. 655)

---

relatives (parent or sibling) of individuals with schizophrenia have a 10% risk, whereas second-degree relatives (e.g., cousin, aunt, grandson) run a 3% chance of developing schizophrenia. Monozygotic twins have several times the concordance rate of dizygotic twins (Torrey, 1992). Adopted-away studies (Chapter 4) provide strong evidence for a genetic transmission of schizophrenia and "schizophrenia spectrum disorders" (SSD), variably inclusive of schizophrenia, schizotypal personality disorder, and sometimes borderline and paranoid personality disorders. These studies reveal that SSD is five

TABLE 12-3
Risk for Relatives of a Patient with Schizophrenia

PATIENT WITH SCHIZOPHRENIA	PERSON AT RISK	RISK (%)
General population	Everybody	0.8–1.0
Father	Each Child	10–18
Mother	Each Child	10–16
Both Parents	Each Child	25–46
Child	Each Parent	5
One sibling	Each Sibling	8–10
Second-degree relative	Another second-degree relative	2–3
Monozygotic twin	Other MZ twin	40–50
Dizygotic twin	Other DZ twin	12–15
Adoptive parents with schizophrenia	Adoptee with "normal" biological parents	4.8
Biological parents with schizophrenia	Adoptee reared by "normal" parents	19.7

to six times more common among biological than among adoptive parents of adults with schizophrenia. Furthermore, if an adoptive parent with schizophrenia rears an adoptee from biologically "normal" parents, the adoptee's risk of becoming schizophrenic is four times less than if the adoptee had a biological parent with schizophrenia and was reared by "normal" adoptive parents. The more severe the schizophrenia, the greater its likelihood of inheritability. Genetic studies have yielded many potential "candidate genes" for further study, including BDNF, COMT, uregulin (NRGI), Reelin, and DISC1 (OMIM, 2008; Ross et al., 2006). Still, about 7 of every 10 cases of schizophrenia arise spontaneously without a family history.

Biochemical. The longest-standing and most widely regarded theory, the dopamine hypothesis, states that the symptoms of schizophrenia arise from a relative excess of dopamine (DA) in the brain and an overstimulation of DA receptors. This theory does not necessarily contend that excessive DA is the "cause" of schizophrenia, but merely that it plays a role in producing the signs and symptoms of schizophrenia. Snyder (1981) demonstrated a positive correlation between how much an antipsychotic drug blocks DA receptors (in a receptor-binding assay) and how much it reduces schizophrenic symptoms. The antipsychotic drugs also indirectly inhibit DA receptors by increasing the neurotransmitter glutamate leading some to suggest a primary role for glutamate dysregulation in schizophrenia.

Amphetamines, which can produce a paranoid, psychotic state, stimulate the release of DA into synaptic clefts; they also inhibit the uptake of DA. L-dopa, a direct precursor of DA useful in the treatment of Parkinson's disease, can also trigger paranoid, psychotic symptoms. Both high levels of dopamine and its metabolite, HVA, as well as high levels of dopamine receptors have been found in subcortical regions of schizophrenic brains. However, the negative symptom cluster in schizophrenia may be associated with low dopamine activity in the prefrontal cortex (Davis et al., 1991). High activation of the dopamine system may be a nonspecific marker of psychosis. It also occurs in mania and psychotic depression.

Anatomic and physiological. The recent advances in biomedical technology (see Chapter 4) have uncovered changes in schizophrenia that were previously undetectable. For example, computed tomography (CT) scans reveal that a subgroup of patients with chronic schizophrenia, predominantly male, have enlarged lateral, and perhaps third, ventricles. These have been seen in patients undergoing their first episode of schizophrenia and are therefore unlikely to be a consequence of the illness or its treatment. What is clear is that cerebral atrophy produces these enlarged ventricles, a finding confirmed by magnetic resonance imaging (MRI). Positron emission tomography (PET) scan studies have indicated that the frontal lobes of patients with schizophrenia metabolize more slowly, and neuropsychological tests show that these individuals have impaired frontal-lobe performance. The frontal lobes are necessary for planning, organizing, and executing plans. Frontal-lobe dysfunction is thought to be responsible for the cognitive and psychosocial impairments associated with schizophrenia.

Psychosocial Theories

With an unusual consistency for scientific investigations of psychosocial influences, one finding stands out: *The amount of tension to which patients are exposed within their families is the most critical psychosocial variable affecting the course of schizophrenia.* American and British studies compared families with "high-expressed emotion" (HEE) to those with "low-expressed emotion" (LEE). The high emotion expressed is not positive; HEE families are more openly critical of the patient, display greater hostility and dissatisfaction, convey little warmth or encouragement, and form overprotective and symbiotic relationships. Typical comments from HEE relatives toward the patient are: "You do nothing but bitch"; "I wish you'd just get out of my hair!"; "I worry so much about you, I don't think you should go out tonight."

Nine months after their initial discharge, patients with schizophrenia living with HEE and LEE families relapsed at rates averaging 56% and 21%, respectively (Caton, 1984; Hogarty et al., 1974). Similar results occurred 2 years following discharge. Those in HEE families who took, or didn't take, their medication had relapse rates of 66% and 46%, respectively. Patients exposed to HEE families for more or less than 35 hours a week had relapse rates of 69% and 28%, respectively. In LEE families, relapse rates were uniformly low and unaffected by use of medication and duration of contact. Vaughn and Leff (1976) report that patients with the highest 9-month relapse rate (92%) had high exposure to HEE families and did not take their medications, whereas patients with the lowest relapse rate (12%) took their meds and lived with LEE families. Hogarty et al. (2004) successfully used cognitive restructuring to lower the impact of EE, which in turn correlated with clinical improvements.

Clinical Course

In most cases, schizophrenia first manifests during adolescence or early adulthood. Schizophrenia in childhood is extremely rare. It may present either abruptly or slowly. One-fourth of patients have an abrupt (acute) onset with active, positive, group-A symptoms (numbers 1–3). The majority have an acute episode only after a slow, insidious onset of chronic or negative symptoms—social withdrawal, markedly impaired functioning, poor hygiene, flat or inappropriate affect, and the beginnings of positive symptoms—vague, rambling speech, odd or magical thinking, ideas of reference, overvalued ideas, persecutory thoughts, social isolation, and unusual perceptions such as illusions, derealization, or depersonalization. When these chronic symptoms occur before the initial full-blown flare-up, which we call an *acute phase*, they constitute schizophrenia's *prodromal phase*; when they occur following an acute phase, they constitute its *residual phase*, manifested by chronic signs and symptoms, including psychosocial and cognitive deficits. During these prodromal and residual phases, patients often seem unmotivated and burned out; in society at large, they are often labeled as "oddballs," "eccentrics," and "weirdos."

In order to support a diagnosis of schizophrenia the patient's social or occupational functioning must also be impaired (criterion B). Active symptoms must be present for at least 1 month and with chronic symptoms must be present for at least 6 months (criterion C). Criterion C rules out shorter and potentially better-prognosis psychoses, such as schizophreniform disorder and brief reactive psychotic disorders.

For most patients schizophrenia is a chronic illness characterized by exacerbations (relapses) and remissions. Women tend to have fewer rehospitalizations and shorter stays then men (Goldstein, 1988). Whereas the first several years of the disease are dominated by active symptoms and frequent hospitalizations, the condition eventually evolves into a nonpsychotic state with chronic symptoms of apathy, low energy levels, social withdrawal, and increased vulnerability to stress. At the worst end of the spectrum are patients who become completely isolated from families, chronically symptomatic even on antipsychotic medications, socially unable to function or care for themselves, perhaps requiring a guardian or power of attorney to give substituted consent for important medical care and other life decisions. Most people with schizophrenia, however, function to some degree in the community. They can marry and work, usually at jobs involving moderate to low levels of stress. As with patients who have other chronic disorders, such as diabetes or congestive heart failure, these patients generally require many hospitalizations over the course of their lifetime. Figure 12-1 graphs the four patterns of clinical course in schizophrenia.

Roughly half of all patients with schizophrenia report depressive symptoms at some point during their illness. They'll complain of feeling depressed or of an affectless state in which they don't feel anything ("I'm empty, numb"). These depressive episodes, which occur most often after an acute psychotic episode ("postpsychotic depression"), are associated with an increased risk of suicide and relapse, poor social functioning, longer hospitalizations, and bleaker outcomes. This is a particularly dangerous period in the life of a person with schizophrenia, for she's apt to feel hopeless, abandon treatment, and kill herself. The first indications of a pending psychotic relapse are often mood disorder symptoms such as decreased sleep, energy, and mood. Whether these depressive symptoms are inherent to schizophrenia or a reac-

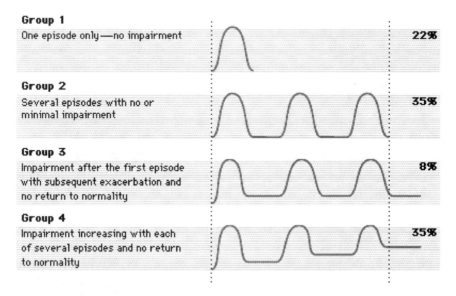

FIGURE 12-1
Patterns of Clinical Course in Schizophrenia

tion to it is unclear. In either case, criterion D points out that to qualify as schizophrenia, symptoms of depression (or mania) must not occur concurrently with the active-phase symptoms or, if they do, they are very brief.

How completely patients recover from an acute episode is not necessarily related to the severity of the psychosis. Instead, better prognoses are associated with (1) an abrupt acute onset, (2) a clear precipitant, (3) prominent confusion and disorganization that later completely resolve, (4) highly systematized and focused delusions whose symbolism is clear and often related to the precipitating event, (5) being married, (6) good premorbid functioning, (7) a family history of depression or mania, (8) no family history of schizophrenia, (9) a cohesive, supportive family, and (10) minimal negative symptoms.

Complications

As if the symptoms of schizophrenia weren't already bad enough, its timing in life couldn't be worse. It strikes at a stage of development when individuals are trying to establish themselves in the world as stable, self-sufficient, independent identities. Schizophrenia interferes with a person's ability to navigate the tasks of breaking away from home, stepping up performance and responsibility levels at school or in the workplace, planning and launching a career, and participating in ever more complex and demanding relationships. Patients with schizophrenia will have, on average, fewer children, will marry less often (the men far less than the women), will divorce and separate more frequently, and will have greater difficulties with intimacy and higher rates of celibacy.

The most life-threatening complication of schizophrenia is *suicide*. At least 1 of 10 will die by suicide; about 20% will attempt it, and some of these will attempt it many times. Fifty percent of those who do make an attempt will eventually succeed. In general, the most vulnerable time for completed suicide is not during a psychosis, but rather in its immediate aftermath. Thirty percent of outpatient suicides occur within 3 months of hospital discharge, and 50% occur within 6 months of discharge. Typically, suicides occur after a patient acquires a certain degree of insight into his or her illness, becomes discouraged, and may suddenly feel depressed and hopeless. In contrast to those with schizophrenia who do not commit suicide, the ones most likely to complete a suicide attempt tend to be those with better premorbid functioning and higher levels of education. These patients may have greater expectations of themselves, view schizophrenia as a greater obstacle to achieving their goals, and be less tolerant of a marginal existence. Patients on relatively low doses of medication, those who have abruptly stopped their medication, and those from relatively nonsupportive families are also at greater risk of completed suicide. Roughly 75% of these patients are male and usually unemployed, unmarried, isolated, and paranoid (Drake, Gates, Whitaker, & Cotton, 1985).

> Most people with schizophrenia do not commit violent crimes. When they are arrested, it's most often related to vagrancy, disturbing the peace, urinating in public, or other misdemeanors. However, individuals with schizophrenia, when compared to those with no psychiatric history, more often report using a weapon in a fight (4.2 times more). Unlike virtually any other group, women with schizophrenia commit violent crimes as often as the men. The meaning of these data in relation to the disease is complicated by the fact that one-third of people with schizophrenia also have alcohol or drug abuse or dependence—which greatly increases the risk of violence and homelessness. Despite sensational headlines, the insanity defense is used in only 1% of violent crimes that go to court, and most of these are not upheld. As *victims* of crime this population suffers a higher rate than the general populace.
>
> *Homelessness* is another frequent complication of schizophrenia. Compared to the general populace, schizophrenics have a 15–20 times higher risk of becoming "street people." However, they comprise a minority of the total number of homeless today. Socioeconomically there is a "downward drift" of those with chronic and persistent mental illness. Nationally, about 30% of the homeless have a severe psychiatric disturbance and at least 40% have substance abuse, especially if mentally ill (Mowbray, 1985; Gonzalez & Rosenheck, 2002).

Management and Treatment

The goal of treatment for schizophrenia is usually not to *cure* but to improve *quality of life* by minimizing symptoms, preventing suicide, averting relapses, enhancing self-esteem, improving social and occupational functioning, and generally supporting the patients and their families and caregivers. These are similar to the goals of treating patients with heart disease, diabetes, arthritis, and other chronic nonpsychiatric ailments that affect the quality of everyday life.

Treatments vary in type and intensity depending on the stage of the disorder and the target symptoms under consideration. This section focuses primarily on *acute care*, which involves management of risks to the safety of the patient and others, stabilization of behaviors, and treatment of florid psychotic symptoms; *transition care*, which is focused on maintaining stability of the patient as he or she moves from one level of care to another; and *chronic care*, which is generally the posthospitalization, community-based outpatient treatment of relatively stable, albeit impaired, patients.

Biological Treatments

With each of these three stages of treatment, overwhelming evidence demonstrates that the vast majority of patients with schizophrenia benefit from antipsychotic medications. Traditional antipsychotics are most effective in eliminating the active positive symptoms, but they also diminish the negative symptoms. Newer antipsychotics, such as clozapine and risperidone, which block both dopamine and serotonin-2 receptors more effectively, treat negative symptoms and are also effective in about one-third of patients who exhibit resistance to traditional antipsychotics. When first prescribed, antipsychotics may take days or weeks to produce significant effects. *Some* neuroleptics also have a *sedative* effect, which manifests in 15–45 minutes following an oral dose, peaks around 2 hours, and subsides by 6 hours. Antipsychotic actions generally continue as long as patients are on the drug; sedative effects tend to diminish in 7–10 days as tolerance improves.

> *Acute care.* Clinicians' first priority is to prevent patients from harming themselves or others. If this danger is imminent, observation, medication, and sometimes physical restraints are needed temporarily. Symptoms of aggression and agitation can be reduced most quickly by "rapid tranquilization," during which patients receive a small dose of an antipsychotic (e.g., 20 mg IM ziprasidone, 5 mg haloperidol, po or IM), every 30–90 minutes until symptoms subside. Caution must be observed in order to prevent or treat immediately any serious side effect such as dystonia, orthostatic hypotension, or neuroleptic malignant syndrome. As an initial safeguard, a reasonable target dose (such as 15 mg haloperidol) is established in advance. Benzodiazepines are often used to control aggression and agitation in patients who remain severely agitated or aggressive after receiving their target neuroleptic dose. To avert a hypotensive crisis or a fall, (1) blood pressure should be taken lying and standing before each dose, and (2) antipsychotics should be withheld if patients are ataxic, dizzy, or lightheaded on standing.
>
> When immediate safety is not at issue, antipsychotic medication should not be given until diagnoses other than schizophrenia have been ruled out. Since all antipsychotic drugs have D-2 blockade in common as their primary mechanism of efficacy against hallucinations and delusions, the clini-

cian's choice of antipsychotic agent and its dose will depend greatly on the side effect profile, the patient's history of treatment responses, and the clinician's experience with particular medications (see Chapter 6). In general, there is an inverse relation between parkinsonian side effects and anticholinergic (e.g., dry mouth) and sedative side effects. For example, the highly sedating thioridazine is among the most anticholinergic and sedating and yet the least parkinsonian of antipsychotics. Thus, if sedation is desired or if patients are at high risk for parkinsonian side effects, thioridazine could be used. On the other hand, the anticholinergic effect might be prohibitive in an elderly patient prone to delirium. Benzodiazepines also provide an alternative for sedating patients without anticholinergic side effects. Then when the psychotic symptoms that are driving the agitated and aggressive behaviors decrease, patients may no longer need sedation, and the benzodiazepines can be stopped while the less sedating antipsychotic is continued. Patients should receive only as much sedation as required to ensure their safety and to reduce their anguish. If patients are catatonic, a modest dose of a benzodiazepine can sometimes temporarily mobilize them enough to allow a better assessment of the underlying psychopathology—which may prove to be a mood disorder or some other disorder. Dosage is always tailored to the specific needs of an individual patient, taking into consideration age, hepatic and renal functions, medical comorbidities, allergies, history of treatment response, and concurrent medications, whether prescription or nonprescription.

Transition care. The general consensus in psychiatric practice is that patients should be discharged on the same regimen (i.e., dose and type of medication) on which they became stable when they were inpatients; prematurely decreasing medication opens up a grave risk of resurgence of acute-phase symptoms and behaviors and often leads to rehospitalization. After living in the relative security of a hospital, discharged patients may suddenly have to contend with all the environmental stressors that prompted their admission. To face these stressors, patients need a great deal of assistance, which means psychosocial support as well as medication. Since transition involves so many psychosocial changes, if medications are also changing, it is harder to pinpoint which changes account for any behavior problems or symptoms that might arise. Our patients often inquire about, or request, discontinuation of medications and do so for many understandable reasons, including weight gain, drowsiness, stigma of mental illness, they "feel fine," it is costly. Educating the patient and family members about early signs of relapse, advising them to develop plans for action should these signs appear, and encouraging the patient to attend outpatient visits on a regular basis are warranted and necessary in every case to ensure against relapse. Second-generation antipsychotics (SGAs) may help to reduce severe complications, such as tardive dyskinesia, while careful selection from among SGAs is necessary to avoid pathological weight gains.

At no time should caregivers or providers imply that taking medication is a crutch. That would be akin to telling a diabetic that using insulin is a crutch. In reviewing all well-controlled studies, Davis (1975) found that of 3,609 patients sampled over 4–6 months, 20% relapsed on drug and 53% relapsed on placebo. Davis determined that the probability of this difference being due to chance is quite low. Thus, every effort should be made to ensure that patients receive their medication, which includes educating patients and their families about the medication and ways to acquire the needed supply. There may be transportation issues, communication gaps, financial constraints, physical inabilities involved that were not foreseen or were not planned for, lack of oversight and supervision, and incompetent or impaired caregivers—all requiring psychosocial interventions.

When patients do not improve sufficiently on antipsychotic medication, the first consideration is whether the drug is being taken and properly absorbed. These questions can be answered by obtaining serum levels. If noncompliance (likely in two-thirds of patients with schizophrenia) is an issue, the physician may consider using injectable fluphenazine or haloperidol in the decanoate form (which persists for 2–4 weeks) as an alternative to oral doses, having parents or guardians monitor the daily/nightly intake of antipsychotic in liquid form, or having patients receive their once-a-day dose in front of a nurse or other responsible party. Of the SGAs, risperidone, paliperidone, olanzapine, and aripiprazole are available in a long-acting (2–4 week) injection form. Paliperidone is even available in an every 3-month injectable. Also, patients may not be improving because of misdiagnosis or because they have developed affective symptoms that might be better treated with antidepressants or lithium.

Chronic care. How long patients should remain on antipsychotic medications following *subsequent* hospitalizations depends on the duration and severity of the illness. Although the beneficial effects of antipsychotic drugs are greatest during the acute stage, they control symptoms for at least a year and decrease relapses for many years. Indefinite maintenance on antipsychotic medication is recommended for patients who have had multiple prior episodes or two episodes within 5 years. In patients for whom antipsychotic medications have been prescribed, monitoring for signs and symptoms of impending or actual relapse is recommended.

Unfortunately, this long-term use of antipsychotics creates one of the most difficult problems in psychopharmacology: *tardive dyskinesia* (TD).

From 10 to 40% of patients who take antipsychotic medication for over 2 continuous years (though it can be as little as 6 months) develop involuntary, bizarre (choreoathetoid) movements of the mouth, limbs, and hips. Although 80–90% of cases are mild, severe impairment occurs in 3–5% of all patients. Most often TD appears as "tobacco-chewing," lip-smacking," and "fly-catching" movements of the mouth and tongue; less often, as hip jerks or slow, undulating motions of the hands or feet. When TD is present, these grotesque movements typically erupt within a few days of decreasing or stopping antipsychotics; they subside only when patients sleep or are put back on D2-blocking medication.

The precise causes and mechanisms of TD remain unknown. One prevalent theory, the dopamine supersensitivity hypothesis, maintains that when dopamine (DA) receptors are blocked for long periods of time, they develop what has been called "supersensitivity" to DA. Thus, when the antipsychotic medication is stopped or decreased, the now "supersensitive" receptors allow the uncontrolled jerking and writhing (choreoathetoid) movements of TD to occur. This hypothesis, however, does not explain why the receptors do not return to their normal functional level after the antipsychotic medications are stopped. There appears to be enduring pathological change of the synaptic function in the dopamine neuron system. This apparent change poses quite an intriguing problem for neuropathologists, who are also aware that pathology such as TD was also observed in some patients with schizophrenia prior to the age of the so-called neuroleptic (i.e., literally nerve paralyzing) drugs, which points to the possibility of additional causative factors or to the possibility that TD is another manifestation of the same disease process.

TD may be most successfully avoided by treating schizophrenia with clozapine. Since this is not always an option because of adverse reactions (may dangerously lower white blood cell count) or intolerance, the next best alternative appears to be another SGA medication. SGAs currently approved for use in the United States are aripiprazole, olanzapine, quetiapine, paliperidone, risperidone, ziprasidone, and lurazidone. These seem to have a much lower risk of TD and are better tolerated in general. Curiously the widespread use of these agents has not improved compliance (adherence), despite equal efficacy to traditional antipsychotics in treating positive symptoms (Lieberman et al., 2005).

In some cases TD can be reversed if it is detected early enough and is not too severe by removing gradually the offending medications (generally first-generation antipsychotic drugs). Worsening of the condition may also be averted by changing to clozapine, if possible. Although other drugs may occasionally counteract it, once TD occurs, there is usually *no* easy way to eliminate it. The risk and severity of TD may be reduced by maintaining patients on the lowest possible dose and by periodically testing if the drug might feasibly be discontinued. The only way to avoid TD is to avoid the use of, or minimize exposure to, FGAs. For unknown reasons, when TD appears, it reaches a plateau in most patients, beyond which there is no further worsening, and in some cases, there may be spontaneous improvement. Doctor and patient (or responsible substituted consent giver) must decide, as with any medication, if the side effects of treatment are worse than the disease.

Psychosocial Treatments

Acute care. When hospitalized, most actively psychotic patients with schizophrenia have a short attention span, are overwhelmed by stimuli, and cannot easily discern reality; they often feel lost, alone, and frightened. Therefore, contacts with these patients should be no longer than they can tolerate; in one day most acute patients will benefit more from several 5-minute contacts than from one 40-minute contact. These frequent contacts should stress reality testing and reassurance, while avoiding psychologically sensitive material. Patients with schizophrenia may not think they need help for their hallucinations or delusions, but they may have problems upon which both they and staff can agree. Treating poor sleep, "worrying" too much (paranoia), or disorganized thinking can become the cornerstones of a treatment alliance. Arguing with patients about their delusions not only won't work but may worsen their condition and the treatment alliance. Contacts should be performed by as few staff as possible. As the patient's psychosis diminishes, the role of psychosocial treatments increases. At some point, individual supportive therapy should identify the stressors (e.g., as high-expressed emotion) that led to hospitalization and prepare patients to contend with similar stressors following discharge, for example, cognitive restructuring (Hogarty et al., 2004).

> Hospitalization is also a major crisis for the patient's family. Prior to hospitalization, most relatives deny or "explain away" the person's symptoms (e.g., "It's normal for teenagers to lock themselves in a room"; "Kids often fly off the handle"). When the patient is psychotic and finally admitted, the family is shell-shocked: Members might insist "nothing is wrong," telephone the ward 15 times a day, not leave the unit, etc. These are typical responses to an acute and severe stress (see Figure 4-5); they are not indicative of the "craziest family on earth." Only *after* the immediate crisis is it possible to assess the family's normal behavior.

Because schizophrenia is a chronic disorder, the family's long-term involvement as an extension of the treatment team is essential. On admission, most families already feel guilty about "creating a schizophrenic"; this guilt is only compounded if therapists blame them, either directly or euphemistically (e.g., "The family has problems communicating"). Not only do attempts to rectify a family's "communication problems" and "pathological relations" reinforce the family's guilt, but they don't work—at least not during short-term hospitalizations. Similarly, separating patients with schizophrenia from their families is usually not necessary or advisable.

Near the outset of hospitalization, several members of the staff should begin forming a *collaborative* relationship with the family. Nurses should monitor visits to gather information. A new family should be introduced to relatives of other patients with schizophrenia so that the family members feel less alone, embarrassed, and guilty. Since research demonstrates that most acutely psychotic patients with schizophrenia do as well, if not better, during 3 weeks, rather than 3 months, of hospitalization, discharge planning that *includes* the family should begin the day the patient is admitted. This is even more critical now in this era of "managed care." In many cases, even 3 weeks has become a luxury; 7 days has become a more typical length of stay. The goal is to begin treatment and stabilize patients enough to allow treatment to continue in less restrictive settings such as (partial) hospital intensive outpatient, or outpatient care.

Transitional care. Chance of relapse and suicide is greatest within the first 6 months, and especially within the first 14 weeks, following discharge. In general, the patients who fare best during these 14 weeks are those who have the most stability in their lives. This transitional phase is *not* the time to introduce major alterations in the patient's living arrangements, social life, medications, therapists, and so on. Some changes may be necessary but should be kept to a minimum. Considerable research and experience show that discharge planning should focus on preventing the conditions most likely to produce relapse:

1. *The failure to take medication* is the most frequent cause of readmission—and a common prelude to suicide. Because two-thirds of outpatients with schizophrenia discontinue or take less than the prescribed dose, *all* patients and their families should be educated regarding the purpose and importance of medication (Lieberman et al., 2005).
2. *The failure to continue aftercare* stems less from a lack of resources than from patients' refusal to participate in available programs. Dropout rates

from aftercare programs are as high as 75%. Effective discharge planning ensures that patients have visited the aftercare facility, know how to travel there, understand the nature and purpose of aftercare treatment, feel comfortable with the outpatient staff, and know the time of their first aftercare appointment.

3. *Inadequate life support*, especially in housing and income, but also in money-management skills, hygiene, and medical care, should be addressed in occupational therapy.

4. *Inadequate socialization and recreation* often prompt rehospitalization. If a bowler stops bowling, the bowling skills atrophy; so too with the leisure-time and social skills of the patient with schizophrenia. Recreational and group therapy should prevent further deterioration of these skills.

5. *The effects of high expressed emotion families* can be reduced by using a "psychoeducational approach," whose effectiveness has been repeatedly demonstrated (Anderson, Hogarty, & Reiss, 1980; Cozolino et al., 1988). This approach aims to reduce the guilt, overresponsibility, confusion, and helplessness of families, and although its implementation varies in different settings, it generally involves five steps: (1) The patient and family are given "the facts" about schizophrenia, including information about its symptoms, natural course, genetics, etc. (2) The family and patient are encouraged to express pent-up concerns about the illness and each other, preferably with other families. (3) The family is taught about the psychonoxious effects of HEE environments. (4) Next, family members are trained to contain emotional outbursts, to avoid (or at least delay and mute) criticisms, to praise positive activities, to reduce unrealistic guilt and overresponsibility, and to be less judgmental. (5) If the family is, for whatever reason, an immutably HEE family, than the patient's amount of contact with the family should be reduced. Community-based self-help groups for the families of schizophrenics often provide a kind of psychoeducational approach over the long haul. (6) The patient can benefit from cognitive enhancement therapy to learn better stress management.

The greatest danger during the transitional period is suicide, which mostly occurs when patients (1) have a postpsychotic depression, (2) are discouraged about their treatment, (3) believe their future is hopeless, (4) misconstrue a drug-induced akinesia for depression and futility, or (5) stop taking medication. Therapists should be alert to these specific warning signs, tell family members also to be aware of them, and meet frequently with patients to check on them.

Inpatient treatment plans should include the following goals for discharge planning to ensure continued stabilization and momentum toward recovery:

1. Arrangements made for psychiatrist follow-up appointment(s); or,
2. Alternative to outpatient care for the more vulnerable or symptomatic hospitalized patients include day hospital or intensive outpatient services to more gradually transition to the level of outpatient care; or, referring to physicians who can provide the patient with weekly or twice-weekly appointments until more stability is observed;
3. Prescription amounts necessary to assure continuity until the next opportunity for the physician to identify tolerability, adherence, side effects, and, of course, efficacy and continued indications for prescribing, and renew or make necessary adjustments to the regimen;
4. Involve family and orchestrate ancillary support network to enable a supportive, LEE recovery-promoting environment that minimizes stressors and other contributors to relapse as presented above.

Chronic care. Contrary to many long-held assumptions, more therapy is not always better therapy. Hogarty, Goldberg, Schooler, and Ulrich (1974) found that supportive psychotherapy is more beneficial with patients who take medication, more likely to hasten relapse in nonmedicated patients, and more effective the longer the patients have not been actively psychotic. However, even at the best facilities, long-term intensive psychotherapy is ineffective in treating schizophrenia. A 15-year follow-up at Chestnut Lodge showed that only 14% of these patients were functioning "good" or better (McGlashan, 1984). More recently, it is being discovered that certain programmatic applications of cognitive therapy, called *cognitive remediation*, can be significantly beneficial to patients with schizophrenia (Lindenmeyer et al., 2008; Hogarty et al., 2004). Chronically hospitalized patients function better in the community when they are *gradually* released from the hospital, often to day hospital care, halfway houses, or to group settings with patients they knew in the hospital. Assertive community treatment (ACT) teams provide more intensive out-patient services, such as weekly home visits with medication delivery. Clubhouses and compensated work–therapy programs offer opportunities for social integration and gainful activity that promote self-worth and full recovery.

Despite the severity and chronicity of schizophrenia, modern treatments can enable patients to live more satisfying lives. We know many patients who, after 5–15 years of institutionalization, went on to become independent and productive with persistent, appropriate forms of treatment. These cases are not rare; patients and families should be made aware of these successes, if for no other reason than to combat demoralization with a vision of hope.

SCHIZOAFFECTIVE DISORDER

In 1933 the term "schizoaffective disorder" was introduced to describe a psychosis with prominent schizophrenic *and* affective symptoms; since then, the term's use has been equally "schizophrenic" and "affective." Experts disagree whether schizoaffective disorder is an actual disorder. Some claim it is nothing more than a mere label, a fudge-factor, or a provisional diagnosis to be used until the patient's *real* diagnosis—schizophrenia or affective disorder—becomes apparent. Others contend that schizoaffective disorder is a genuine entity that includes features of both disorders. It may be on the continuum of a schizophrenia spectrum or mood spectrum disorder (see Table 12-4).

By these criteria, Fred, a 24-year-old librarian, would seem to have a schizoaffective disorder. At first, over a period of 7 months, he developed typical signs of schizophrenia: He believed a nearby hospital was zapping his brain

---

TABLE 12-4
Diagnostic Criteria for Schizoaffective Disorder

A. A diagnosis of schizoaffective disorder should be made only when both definite schizophrenic and definite affective (mood) symptoms are prominent simultaneously, or within a few days of each other, within the same episode of illness. As a consequence of this, the episode of illness does not meet full criteria for either schizophrenia or a depressive, manic, or mixed episode.

B. *DSM-5 specifies that delusions or hallucinations are present for two or more weeks during the lifetime of the illness.*

C. *DSM-5 specifies affective symptoms meeting the criteria for a major mood disorder are present for the majority of the total illness duration. The term should not be applied to patients who exhibit schizophrenic symptoms and affective symptoms only in different episodes of illness.*

For example, It is common for a patient with schizophrenia to present with depressive symptoms in the aftermath of a psychotic episode (post-schizophrenic depression).

D. The disturbance is not better explained by the direct physiological effects of a substance or another medical condition.

Schizoaffective episodes are classified as either being of a bipolar or depressive type.

Patients who suffer from recurrent schizoaffective episodes, particularly those whose symptoms are of the manic rather than the depressive type, usually make a full recovery and only rarely develop a defect state.

Note: Adapted from *ICD-10* (p. 89) and *DSM-5* (p. 105)

with x-rays, thereby controlling his actions. By stringing together the first letter of each book title returned to the library, Fred uncovered a secret code, which auditory hallucinations later informed him was part of a plot to destroy Dartmouth College. After a 3-week period of hospitalization, including treatment with antipsychotics, Fred recovered, returned to work, and then secretly stopped his medication. Within a week his delusions reappeared, but this time accompanied by symptoms of major depression: insomnia, anorexia, anhedonia, psychomotor retardation, and severe dysthymia. The delusions and syndrome of major depression continued for 6 more weeks. Did Fred have a postpsychotic depression? Probably not, because in postpsychotic depression the patient feels hopeless, or anergic, or depressed—in other words, a *symptom*, instead of a *syndrome*, of depression. Fred had the syndrome and met criteria for a schizoaffective disorder.

When schizoaffective disorder is used as a temporary diagnosis awaiting further clarification, appending the term *provisional* clarifies the clinician's intention. In Fred's case, however, schizoaffective disorder was diagnosed as a disorder. Little is known about this "true" disorder. It may be a heterogeneous entity with numerous etiologies. Some genetic studies have shown that these patients have an increased family history of alcoholism, affective, and schizophrenic disorders. It appears to occur more often in women. Age of onset, degree of recovery, natural history, and prognosis fall roughly between those for schizophrenia and affective disorders. Treatment is focused on both the mood disorder component as well as the schizophrenia component, such that schizophrenia symptoms would be treated with antipsychotics, manic symptoms with mood stabilizers (e.g., lithium), and depressive symptoms with antidepressants. Psychosocial rehabilitation should include all of the elements and considerations as for schizophrenia, including a low-stress, LEE environment, to the greatest degree possible.

A history of normal baseline functioning between each psychotic episode and a mood disorder with every psychosis indicate the possibility of an atypical psychotic mood disorder, which has a better prognosis.

DELUSIONAL DISORDER

Delusions, such as delusional jealousy, lasting over a month are the chief features of delusional disorder (Table 12-5), in which the delusions are enduring, systematized, interrelated, and internally consistent. Their themes can be single or multiple, simple or complex. Delusional disorder does not mani-

TABLE 12-5
Criteria for Delusional Disorder

A. Delusions constitute the most conspicuous or the only clinical characteristic. They must be present for at least 3 months and be clearly personal rather than subcultural [*non-bizarre*]. *DSM-5 specifies 1 month or longer duration*.

B. There must be no history of schizophrenic symptoms (delusions of control, thought broadcasting, etc.) and no or only occasional auditory hallucinations.

C. Apart from actions and attitudes directly related to the delusion or delusional system, affect, speech, and behavior are within a normal range with no significant impairment in functioning.

D. Depressive symptoms or even a full-blown depressive episode may be present intermittently, provided that the delusions persist at times when there is no disturbance of mood.

E. There must be no evidence of brain disease and the disturbance is **not better explained by the direct physiological effects of a substance, another medical condition, or another mental disorder**.

Specify type (the following types are assigned based on the predominant delusional theme):

Erotomanic Type: delusions that another person, usually of higher status, is in love with the individual

Grandiose Type: delusions of inflated worth, power, knowledge, identity, or special relationship to a deity or famous person

Jealous Type: delusions that the individual's sexual partner is unfaithful

Persecutory Type: delusions that the person (or someone to whom the person is close) is being malevolently treated in some way

Somatic Type: delusions that the person has some physical defect or general medical condition

Mixed Type: delusions characteristic of more than one of the above types but no one theme predominates

Unspecified Type

Onset is commonly in middle age but sometimes, particularly in the case of beliefs about having a misshapen body, in early adult life. The content of the delusion, and the timing of its emergence, can often be related to the individual's life situation, e.g., persecutory delusions in members of minorities.

Note: Adapted from *ICD-10* (p. 84) and *DSM-5* (p. 90).

fest the prominent hallucinations, incoherence, disorganized or catatonic behavior, or negative symptoms seen in schizophrenia. The delusions are not bizarre or Schneiderian, such as thought broadcasting or delusions of control. Delusional disorder, which is rare, is characterized by delusions involving nonbizarre real-life situations in otherwise well-functioning people. There are five types of this disorder.

In the *grandiose type*, patients may believe that they have created a wonderful secret invention, discovered a cure for AIDS, or are confidantes of the president.

With *delusional jealousy*, a spouse's "unfaithfulness" is fabricated on issues of "evidence"—a misplaced stocking, a misconstrued remark.

A patient with the *erotomanic type* may believe that she is secretly Matt Damon's lover, badgers him with phone calls or angry letters of feeling rejected, and perhaps even stalks him. About 80% with erotomanic type are women. The typical erotomanic patient leads a socially empty life, is unmarried, unattractive, and from a lower socioeconomic stratum. The object of their attention is believed to be, and usually is, of superior status, looks, intelligence, and/or has authority (Segal, 1989). Movie and entertainment stars are commonly targets of people with erotomanic delusions.

A patient with the *somatic type* of delusional disorder may believe that he has cancer and is giving it to other people, or that his head is so small that most people can't see it. *Somatic type delusional disorder* is to be distinguished from *body dysmorphic disorder*, which is classified as a somatoform disorder and is a morbid preoccupation with an imagined defect in appearance ("My nose is too big"; "My eyes are too close together"). Somatic delusions are more extreme, far exceeding the magnifications of imperfections normal to adolescence.

In the *persecutory type*, patients may think that they are being drugged, poisoned, followed, conspired against, or maligned. It may begin with a plausible suspicion or grievance against an individual, government agency, or business. As the patient becomes increasingly frustrated in trying to rectify her complaint, she may develop psychotic fantasies as she presses for justice. She may bring legal action, recruit supporters, make public appeals, or send petitions. With growing self-importance and messianic zeal, she may sometimes display a pressured form of speech similar to what is observed, to a much greater degree, in mania. Yet unlike mania or schizophrenia, *the psychopathology does not affect other areas of functioning.*

Most cases of persecutory delusions arise gradually during middle or late adult life, have chronic and stable courses with few remissions and exacerbations, and disproportionately affect those who are female, married, immigrants, and in lower socioeconomic groups. Paranoia constitutes 1–4% of all psychiatric hospital admissions, with an incidence of first admissions between 1 and 3/100,000 population per year. Its etiology is unknown. Paranoia does not run in families; social isolation and stress may foster paranoia in older adults. Projection is its chief defense mechanism.

Because the delusions are usually ego-syntonic, patients with delusional disorder seldom seek treatment. If they do—and it's usually under coercion—a trial of antipsychotic medication is indicated, even though they are unlikely to take it, as prescribed or as needed to be effective. The somatic type may respond to pimozide, an atypical-like first-generation antipsychotic if other antipsychotics fail. If the somatic or jealousy delusions are mild and it is a preoccupation that dominates, treatments for obsessive–compulsive disorder (e.g., SSRIs) can be tried. The erotomanic type of delusional disorder may lead to behaviors that require a restraining order to keep the patient from abusing the love object.

SHARED PSYCHOTIC DISORDER (*FOLIE À DEUX*)

This very rare, strange disorder looks like psychosis by contagion, in which one person "catches" another's "delusion virus." However, no virus or other detectable means of transmission is actually involved. The person who "gives" the delusions (the primary case) already has a psychotic disorder with delusions and usually dominates in a very close, long-term relationship with a socially isolated, more passive, initially healthy person who "gets" the delusions too. This person acquires the same or very similar delusions as the delusion "donor." That is, they "share" the same delusions. Table 12-6 presents criteria for shared (induced) psychotic disorder which is no longer specified in *DSM-5*.

The delusions in shared psychotic disorder are usually within the realm of possibility and may stem from common past experiences of the two people. Although most commonly involving two people (*folie à deux*), cases have been reported involving up to 12 family members. The disorder tends to be chronic, with the recipient typically less impaired because only part of the primary person's delusional system is adopted. Treatment involves either successful antipsychotic medication of the primary person or interrupting the relationship with the primary person.

TABLE 12-6
Diagnostic Criteria for Induced Delusional Disorder (folie à deux)

A. A delusional disorder shared by two or more people with close emotional links.

B. Only one of the people suffers from a genuine psychotic disorder; the delusions are induced in the other(s) and usually disappear when the people are separated.

C. The disturbance is not better explained by another Thought Disorder (e.g., Schizophrenia) or a Mood Disorder with Psychotic Features and is not due to the direct physiological effects of a substance or another medical condition.

Note: Adapted from *ICD-10* (p. 84) and *DSM-5* (p. 90)

SCHIZOPHRENIFORM DISORDER

The criteria for schizophreniform disorder and schizophrenia are identical, except that schizophreniform disorder has (1) shorter duration (between 1 and 6 months) and (2) social or occupational function need not be impaired. This 6-month cutoff point and absence of poor functioning were chosen because they appear (for now) to be the best predictors of which patients recover (schizophreniform) and which become chronic (schizophrenia).

Schizophreniform disorder is further classified in DSM-5 as having *good prognostic features* if the patient has two of the following four indicators: (1) onset of prominent psychotic symptoms within 4 weeks of first noticeable unusual behavior or functioning; (2) confusion or perplexity at the height of the psychotic episode; (3) absence of blunted or flat affect; and (4) good premorbid social and occupational functioning.

Roughly half of patients *initially* diagnosed as having schizophreniform disorder will improve or recover substantially; in general, the longer the disorder persists, the worse the prognosis. Although findings conflict, most suggest that there is no increased prevalence of schizophrenia among relatives. The ECA survey (Chapter 1) found a lifetime prevalence of 0.1% for schizophreniform disorder in the general population. The disorder's etiology is unknown. All the factors for differentiating *medical- and substance-induced syndromes* and *mood disorders* from schizophrenia also apply to schizophreniform disorder. Schizophreniform disorder is treated symptomatically, with observation, antipsychotic medication, supportive psychotherapy, suicide precautions, family involvement, and close follow-up.

Schizophreniform disorder differs from *brief psychotic disorder*, which resolves in under 1 month and does not include negative symptoms as part of the criteria. Brief psychotic disorder often occurs after a major stressor (brief reactive psychosis), and the content of the psychoses often involves the stressor. For example, an intern, after 3 weeks of substantial sleep deprivation and feeling overwhelmed by his duties, began complaining that the nurses were persecuting him by paging him all the time. The nurses told him that they hadn't paged him in hours. Then he knew there was a plot.

Mood disorders with psychotic features involve delusions and hallucinations, but they are most often mood-congruent. Delusions of poverty, sin, and disease are common in psychotic depression; those of overconfidence and grandiosity are common with mania; patently bizarre, Schneiderian, and mood-incongruent delusions are more typically schizophrenic. When asked why he is being persecuted, the person with mood disorder is likely to say "because I deserve it," whereas the patient with paranoid schizophrenia might say, "I am angry and will seek revenge." Persecutory delusions may occur in both mood and schizophrenic disorders. Indeed, distinguishing these two disorders is a frequent and difficult problem, since at some point over half of all patients with schizophrenia have depressive symptoms, and patients with mood disorders may show deterioration, isolation, thought disorder, catatonia, cognitive disturbance, and a wide variety of hallucinations and delusions. When patients exhibit symptoms of both disorders, the timing and duration of symptoms are critical to determine the best formulation consistent with available history and examination findings. Schizophrenia should be diagnosed only if (1) no major depressive or manic episodes have occurred along with the active psychosis, and (2) the schizophrenic symptoms have persisted for 6 months. In the prodromal or residual phase, these may be only negative symptoms or attenuated positive symptoms. When mood disorders with psychotic features and schizophrenia-related disorders cannot be distinguished from each other and truly occur simultaneously, *schizoaffective disorder* would be diagnosed.

BRIEF PSYCHOTIC DISORDER (ACUTE SCHIZOPHRENIA-LIKE PSYCHOTIC DISORDER)

Occasionally, a real psychotic break looks just like it does in the movies. "Brief psychotic disorder" is just what the director ordered. Typically a relatively normal person develops psychosis rapidly (the person "snaps") after a very stressful event. This is accompanied by emotional turmoil with rapid shifts of mood, perplexity, or confusion. Negative symptoms are not a usual feature. Most recover entirely. In a few cases this is an unusual, abrupt beginning of a schizophrenic disorder. A clinical rule of thumb is that the faster the onset of the disorder, the faster the offset.

> Marc, a 30-year-old hotel executive, was at work when a "moderate" earthquake toppled the hotel, killing four occupants and injuring many others. Dazed but physically unharmed, Marc wandered away from the rubble, arrived home hours later, and kept mumbling that he was responsible for the hotel's collapse. Staring into space as if listening to someone, Marc would mumble, "The devil is saying, 'You're to blame, you're to blame. You'll fry in hell.'" At times Marc would sit and sulk, rigid and mute, while at other times he would pace the floor, apparently arguing loudly with "the devil." Marc had had no previous psychiatric difficulties, and his mental state was stable prior to the earthquake.

Marc's wife took him to the emergency room for treatment. His drug screen was negative and his brief reactive psychosis was treated with 5 mg of haloperidol stat and 2 mg tid for the next 2 days. Marc's psychotic symptoms began to recede the day after the earthquake, and 3 days later, they resolved and he was able to return to work and regular activities. His treatment plan included scheduled visits to an outpatient therapist to provide additional support for him to work through the effects of the tragic experience and a psychiatrist to taper carefully the antipsychotic medication.

Because Marc's symptoms lasted for over 24 hours, his diagnosis would have been *brief psychotic disorder*; if they had persisted for 1 month, his diagnosis would have been *schizophreniform disorder*. Gradually increasing psychopathology before the florid psychosis characterizes schizophrenic and schizophreniform disorders, but not brief psychotic disorder. In contrast to *schizophrenia*, brief psychotic disorder usually has an acute precipitant, a rapid onset, delusions and hallucinations that pertain to the stressor, and a relatively quick recovery with eventual complete resolution without recurrence. However, not all cases have acute precipitants, making them look more like other disorders. If the patient meets the full criteria for *mood disorders*, brief psychotic disorder should not be diagnosed. At their worst, *adjustment disorders* and *uncomplicated bereavement* do not usually produce florid psychosis. Auditory and visual hallucinations of the deceased are commonly experienced in an otherwise normal bereavement and require only supportive therapy. *Malingering* and *factitious disorder with psychological symptoms* must be considered, as should organic conditions, especially *delirium* and *psychomotor* or *partial complex seizures* that suddenly produce delusions, hallucinations, anxiety, and repeated automatisms with fluctuating levels of consciousness; a third of these cases occur without significant confusion (McKenna, Kane, & Parrish, 1985). EEG abnormalities are found in approximately 50% of patients with partial complex seizures. *Petit mal seizures*, which present as absence attacks, may resemble catatonia, but no other psychotic symptoms are present. Finally, *substance abuse*, intoxication, or withdrawal are prime suspects and very important to diagnose and treat promptly to avoid life-threatening complications.

The priorities in treating brief psychotic disorder are the following: First, prevent suicide attempts, dangerous and destructive behaviors, or even assaultiveness. Second, hasten recovery by prescribing antipsychotics or mood-stabilizing agents or sedatives as indicated. If the patient is imminently suicidal or dangerous, rapid sedation with benzodiazepines as well as antipsychotics may be indicated. Tapering medication should begin only after the patient is clearly recovering. Third, initiate psychotherapy that emphasizes reality orientation and repeated assurances of safety and improvement to the patient. At this point, relatives and therapists should refrain from "psychologizing" the meaning of the psychosis with the patient. (For instance, probing Marc's guilt over the earthquake might have further disorganized him.) Fourth, *after* the psychosis resolves, some patients benefit from several sessions of psychotherapy that address (1) the stressor and its personal meaning, or (2) incompletely resolved issues related to the psychosis. For example, on returning to his wife's grave a year after she died, a well-functioning man developed an acute psychosis that disappeared in a week. Recognizing that his psychotic episode indicated that he was more distressed by his wife's death than he had realized, he entered brief psychotherapy to examine this concern.

The genetics and prognosis of brief psychotic disorder are not clear. Some patients have more than one brief psychotic episode. A family history of mood disorder is frequently found in those who experience stress-induced brief psychotic episodes. These patients may have a higher risk of developing a mood disorder at a later time in their life.

PSYCHOTIC DISORDER DUE TO OTHER MEDICAL CONDITIONS

This psychotic disorder presents with delusions or hallucinations often accompanied by incoherence and inappropriate or labile affects. Dementia and delirium are not considered other (nonpsychiatric) medical conditions. Therefore, psychotic symptoms with profound confusion, memory loss, fluctuating levels of consciousness, and disorientation would be diagnosed as dementia or delirium "with delusions" or "with hallucinations." Schizophrenic hallucinations are most often auditory and frequently visual. On the other hand, hallucinations seen in cases involving a primary medical condition may involve any of the senses, including olfactory, tactile, and gustatory. Patients with schizophrenia generally defend their hallucinations as reasonable and valid—in other words, these patients are delusional and lack insight into these phenomena—whereas patients with general medical causes of hallucinations more often recognize them as inexplicable, crazy, and foreign— not their "real selves." However, in either situation, patients may become terrified and act on the delusions or hallucinations, causing danger to self or others unless treated. It is crucial for clinicians to rule out general medical conditions causing psychotic symptoms before giving a patient a primary diagnosis of schizophrenia, bipolar disorder, and so on.

If there is no family history of *schizophrenia*, or if schizophrenic-like symptoms first arise in a person over 40, the diagnosis is less likely to be schizophrenia. *Complex partial seizure disorder* can simulate schizophrenia, but is usually associated with complete or nearly complete remissions and abrupt recurrences (unless the seizures are nearly constant). Many other medical conditions, including *hormone abnormalities* (hypothyroidism, hyperthyroidism), *Cushing's disease* (too much cortisol), *head injury* (traumatic brain injury), and *brain tumor* can be the culprits in causing this form of psychosis.

SUBSTANCE-INDUCED PSYCHOTIC DISORDER

Substance-induced psychotic disorder, especially intoxication from amphetamines, cocaine, hallucinogens, PCP, cannabis, and alcohol, may be indistinguishable from the active phase of schizophrenia, schizophreniform disorder, or acute psychosis. Symptoms are usually temporary and can be confirmed by urine screening. Although *alcoholic hallucinosis* typically stops within 48 hours of withdrawal, it may persist for weeks and resemble the early stages of schizophrenia. However, in alcoholic hallucinosis, the hallucinations are most commonly auditory, not visual, and the patient's response to them is appropriate to their content, for example, anxiety in response to threatening voices. Of course, patients with schizophrenia can also have a superimposed drug-induced psychosis. Amphetamine psychosis can blend into a prolonged and sometimes chronic paranoid delusional and hallucinated state. People who already have risk factors for schizophrenia are more likely to experience this prolonged result; the amphetamines may push the vulnerable person "over the brink."

Psychosis can also be induced by drug withdrawal. Here lab tests are useless in making the diagnosis, but a history of recent, usually prolonged, drug use may help. Changes in vital signs (e.g., increased blood pressure, heart rate, and temperature), sweating, and tremulousness frequently accompany serious withdrawal from alcohol or hypnoanxiolytics. Prescribed drugs can also cause psychotic symptoms: Corticosteroids, thyroid hormone, and anticholinergics are common culprits. Sleuthing through these numerous and varied substance-induced and medically induced syndromes makes most psychiatrists glad that they went to medical school!

References

American Psychiatric Association. (2013). *Diagnostic and statistical manual of mental disorders*, 5th ed. Arlington, VA: American Psychiatric Association.

Anderson, C.M., Hogarty, G., & Reiss, D.J. (1980). Family treatment of adult schizophrenic patients: A psycho-educational approach. *Schizophrenia Bulletin, 6*, 490–505.

Caton, C.L.M. (1984). *Management of chronic schizophrenia*. New York: Oxford University Press.

Cozolino, L.J., Goldstein, M.J., Nuechterlein, K.H., West, K.L., & Snyder, K.S. (1988). The impact of education about schizophrenia on relatives varying in expressed emotion. *Schizophrenia Bulletin, 14*, 675–687.

Davis, J.M. (1975). Overview: Maintenance therapy in psychiatry: I. Schizophrenia. *American Journal of Psychiatry, 132*, 1237–1245.

Davis, K.L., Kahn, R.S., Ko, G., & Davidson, M. (1991). Dopamine in schizophrenia: A review and reconceptualization. *American Journal of Psychiatry, 148*(11), 1474–1486.

Drake, R.E., Gates, C., Whitaker, A., & Cotton, P.G. (1985). Suicide among schizophrenics: A review. *Comprehensive Psychiatry, 26*, 90–100.

Goldstein, J.M. (1988). Gender differences in the course of schizophrenia. *American Journal of Psychiatry, 145*, 684–689.

Gonzalez, G., & Rosenheck, R.A. (2002). Outcomes and service use among homeless persons with serious mental illness and substance abuse. *Psychiatric Services, 53*(4), 437–446.

Goodwin, D.W., & Guze, S.B. (1989). *Psychiatric diagnosis*, 4th ed. New York: Oxford University Press.

Hafner, H., & ander Heiden, W. (1997). Epidemiology of schizophrenia. *Canadian Journal of Psychiatry*, 139–151.

Hogarty, G.E. Flasher, S., Ulrich, R., Carter, M., Greenwald, D., Pogue-Gelle, M., et al. (2004). Cognitive enhancement therapy for schizophrenia: Effects of a 2-year randomized trial on cognition and behavior. *Archives of General Psychiatry, 61*(9), 866–876.

Hogarty, G.E., Goldberg, S.C., Schooler, N.R., & Ulrich, R.P. (1974). Drugs and sociotherapy in the aftercare of schizophrenic patients: II. Two-year relapse rates. *Archives of General Psychiatry, 31*, 603–608.

Lewine, R., Burbach, D., & Meltzer, H.Y. (1984). Effect of diagnostic criteria on the ratio of male to female schizophrenic patients. *American Journal of Psychiatry, 141*, 84–87.

Lieberman, J.A., Stroup, T.S., McEvoy, J.P., Swartz, M.S., Rosenheck, R.A., Perkins, D.O., et al. (2005). Effectiveness of antipsychotic drugs in patients with chronic schizophrenia. *New England Journal of Medicine, 353*(12), 1209–1223.

Lindenmeyer, J.P., McGurk, S.R., Mueser, K.T., Khan, A., Wance, D., Hoffman, L., et al. (2008). A randomized controlled trial of cognitive remediation among inpatients with persistent mental illness. *Psychiatric Services, 59*, 241–247.

Ludwig, A.M. (1985). *Principles of clinical psychiatry*, 2nd ed. New York: Free Press.

McGlashan, T.H. (1984). The Chestnut Lodge follow-up study, II. *Archives of General Psychiatry, 41*, 586–601.

McKenna, P.J., Kane, J.M., & Parrish, K. (1985). Psychotic syndrome of epilepsy. *American Journal of Psychiatry, 142*, 895–904.

Mowbray, C.T. (1985). Homelessness in America: Myths and realities. *American Journal of Orthopsychiatry, 55*, 4–8.

Noga, J.T. (1999). Schizophrenia as a brain disease: What have we learned from neuroimaging studies of twins? *Medscape General Medicine, 1*(3). http://www.medscape.com/view article/ 430605.

OMIM, On-line Mendelian Inheritance in Man. (2008). Available at http://www.ncbi.nlm .nih.gov/ sites/entrez?db=omim

Ries, R.K. (1985). *DSM-III* implications of the diagnosis of catatonia and bipolar disorder. *American Journal of Psychiatry, 142*(12), 1471–1474.

Ross, C.A., Margolis, R.L., Reading, S.A.J., Pletnikov, M., & Coye, J.T. (2006). Neurobiology of schizophrenia. *Neuron, 52*, 139–153.

Segal, J.H. (1989). Erotomania revisited: From Kraepelin to *DSM-III-R. American Journal of Psychiatry, 146*(10), 1261–1266.

Snyder, S. (1981). Dopamine receptors, neuroleptics, and schizophrenia. *American Journal of Psychiatry, 138*, 460–464.

Sorensen, J. (2006). *Relapse prevention in schizophrenia and other psychoses.* Manual with workbooks. Hertfordshire, UK: University of Hertfordshire Press.

Torrey, E.F. (1992). Are we overestimating the genetic contribution to schizophrenia? *Schizophrenia Bulletin, 18*, 159–170.

Vaughn, C.E., & Leff, J.P. (1976). The influence of family and social factors on the course of psychiatric illness: A comparison of schizophrenic with depressed neurotic patients. *British Journal of Psychiatry, 129*, 125–137.

Weinberger, D.R., Berman, K., Suddath, R., & Torrey, E. (1992). Evidence of dysfunction of the prefrontal-limbic network in schizophrenia: A magnetic resonance imaging and regional cerebral blood flow study of discordant monozygotic twins. *American Journal of Psychiatry, 149*, 890–897.

World Health Organization. (1992). *The ICD–10 classification of mental and behavioural disorders: Clinical descriptions and diagnostic guidelines.* Geneva: World Health Organization.

Wu, E.Q., Birnbaum, H.G., Shi, L., Ball, D.E., Kessler, R.C., Moulis, M., et al. (2005). The economic burden of schizophrenia in the United States in 2002. *Journal of Clinical Psychiatry, 66*(9), 1122–1129.

https://fms-teaching.ncl.ac.uk/psy/disorders/schizophrenia/ Newcastle University Medical Student Teaching Resource Videos simulating various psychiatric diagnoses and signs/ symptoms. Authors: Faculty of Newcastle University, Director, Professor Chris Day.

13

Mood Disorders

Some people experiencing depression say they would rather have cancer. Depression is an example of a mood disorder with increasing prevalence, and suicide as its most serious complication. Morbidity from mood disorders extends to body, soul, and spirit, profoundly impacting all spheres of a person's life. Its cost to society is enormous, but its ravages are often preventable. When most people speak of depression, they usually mean dysthymia—i.e., the *emotion* of feeling sad, "blue," down in the dumps, unhappy, or demoralized. When clinicians speak of depression, they are usually referring to a *syndrome* or mental disorder consisting of many symptoms and signs, including appetite loss, anhedonia, hopelessness, insomnia, and dysthymia. Whereas the emotion of depression affects everyone to some degree, the syndrome afflicts only some—a "mere" 17% of Americans during their lives and well over a 100 million earthlings every day. So in this text *dysthymia* refers to the emotion or symptom of depression, whereas *depression* refers to the syndromes and disorders of depression. *Dysphoria* refers to any unpleasant mood, including dysthymia.

Mood disorder (also *affective* disorder) is the overall category for entities whose predominant symptom is usually a pathological mood: dysphoria, euphoria, or both. Mood disorders that consist solely of "lows" are called "major depression" and its milder version, "persistent depressive disorder (dysthymic disorder)"; those that combine "highs" and "lows" are called "bipolar disorder" and its milder form, "cyclothymic disorder." The terms "mania" and "severe depression" are used in diagnostic classification to denote the opposite ends of the affective spectrum. "Hypomania" is used to denote an intermediate state without delusions, hallucinations, or complete disruption of normal activities.

Mood disorders have also been classified according to at least four different conceptual models. First, the *endogenous versus reactive model* considers endogenous depression to be a strictly biological event unrelated to any environmental forces, whereas reactive depression must be psychosocially triggered and devoid of any biological factors. This distinction unjustifiably assumes that the etiology of depression is (1) known and (2) either biological *or* psychosocial. Indeed, many "endogenous" depressions follow environmental stressors, and many "reactive" depressions emerge without any obvious precipitant. Second, in the *primary and secondary model depressions*, secondary depressions are preceded by another physical or mental disorder (e.g., alcoholism, hypothyroidism, anxiety disorder), whereas primary depressions are not. Third, in the *unipolar versus bipolar model*, a bipolar disorder exists whenever a manic episode has occurred. Patients with bipolar depression must have a history of mania or hypomania, whereas those with unipolar depressions don't. Fourth, historically *psychotic* and *neurotic depressions* were distinguished, with psychotic depressions referring to any severe depression, even when the patients were not psychotic. Today, however, a "psychotic depression" must display psychosis. Neurotic depressions were roughly equivalent to dysthymic disorder.

CLINICAL PRESENTATION

Major Depression

The first essential feature of major depression is either a depressed mood or anhedonia—that is, a pervasive loss of interest or ability to experience pleasure in normally enjoyable activities. The mood is usually sad, but it can also be irritable or apprehensive. Patients describe this mood as "living in a black hole or in a deep pit," "feeling dead," "overwhelmed by doom," or "physically drained." However, many patients with major depression do *not* feel depressed or even dysphoric, but anhedonic. A baseball fan suddenly doesn't care about the World Series; a loving father loses interest in his child; a devoted nurse cares little for her patients. Just because individuals don't look unhappy or complain about "being in the dumps," if anhedonic, they might still have a major depression. A majority of persons with major depression look lifeless, boring, or dull, rather than sad and crying. Persons suspected of having a major depression should be asked not only if they feel depressed (or sad, blue, down, etc.), but also if they no longer enjoy things anymore. In medically ill patients, questions about enjoyment should be restricted to things they can still do. For example, a person with back pain may still enjoy reading, watching TV, or even taking walks, but it would be clinically unproductive to ask "Do you still like bowling?"

The second essential feature of major depression is the presence of at least five other symptoms. The *biological (also called vegetative) signs and symptoms of depression* generally include a lack of energy or fatigue, appetite loss, unintentional weight loss or gain, insomnia or hypersomnia, psychomotor retardation or agitation, and diminished libido. With another common biological sign, "diurnal mood variation," persons feel worse in the morning and slightly better by night; this pattern continues through weekends and is not just a result of facing work or school. These individuals typically awake in the middle of the night (middle insomnia) or in the early morning (terminal insomnia), and find it hard or impossible to return to sleep. Individuals who have improved slightly may say that their sleep and appetite are okay when both are still abnormal. Continue to probe by asking, "How does that compare to normal?" The psychological signs and symptoms of depression include a diminished ability to think or make decisions, negative thinking about the past (e.g., guilt), present (e.g., low self-esteem), and future (e.g., hopelessness), and thoughts about death and suicide.

As presented in Table 13-1, diagnostic criteria for major depression require a mood change *or* anhedonia *and* several biological signs of depression, which must exist nearly every day for at least 2 weeks. The acronym **DEPRESSING** can be used to help remember the criteria for depression. The letters represent **D**epression (sadness), **E**nergy (loss of), **P**leasure (diminished interest), **R**etardation (psychomotor slowing or agitation), **E**ating (changes in weight or appetite), **S**uicide (recurrent thoughts of death), **S**leep (insomnia or hypersomnia), **I**ndecision (poor concentration), **N**egative thinking (pessimism, hopelessness, reduced self-esteem) or inappropriate **G**uilt (unworthiness). The diagnosis of depression is based on *symptoms*, not on whether the disorder is produced by stressors in the environment.

Everything about people with psychomotor retardation is slow — walking, talking, thinking, eating, reacting. Frame-by-frame analysis of movies shows that, in walking, depressed people lift their thighs with their lower legs lagging behind, whereas most people propel their lower legs and feet forward. If asked their spouse's name or their own occupation, it may take 20–30 seconds to answer. For unknown reasons, this latency of response also occurs with psychomotor agitation. Concentration can be so impaired that they may be unable to sit through a sitcom or to read a simple paragraph. Their slowed thinking, impaired concentration, and negative worldview paralyze their decision-making abilities. Readily overwhelmed by easy tasks, depressed

TABLE 13-1
Diagnostic Criteria for Major Depressive Disorder

A. **Depressed mood, loss of interest and enjoyment, and increased fatigability** are usually regarded as the most typical symptoms of depression, and **at least 2 of these, plus at least 2 of the other symptoms** should usually be present for a definite diagnosis. **Minimum duration of the whole episode is about 2 weeks** (shorter periods may be reasonable if symptoms are unusually severe and of rapid onset).

　　1. depressed mood
　　2. loss of interest and enjoyment
　　3. reduced energy leading to increased fatigability (marked tiredness after only slight effort is common)
　　4. disturbed sleep
　　5. diminished activity or agitation
　　6. significant changes in appetite and weight
　　7. ideas of guilt and unworthiness (even in a mild type of episode)
　　8. indecision, reduced concentration, and inattention
　　9. ideas or acts of self-harm or suicide
　　10. bleak and pessimistic views of the future (*not specified in DSM-5*)
　　11. reduced self-esteem and self-confidence (*not specified in DSM-5*)

Note: DSM-5 specifies that at least 5 of the first 9 symptoms above have been present during the same 2-week period and represent a change from previous functioning; at least one of the symptoms must be either (1) depressed mood or (2) loss of interest or pleasure.

B. The symptoms result in **significant distress or significant impairment** in personal, family, social, educational, occupational, or other important area of functioning.
C. The disturbance is **not better explained by the direct physiological effects of a substance or another medical condition.**
D. The symptoms **are not better explained by another mental disorder**, particularly psychotic thought disorders such as schizophrenia, delusional disorder, and schizoaffective disorder.

The presence of dementia or mental retardation does not rule out the diagnosis of a treatable depressive episode, but communication difficulties are likely to make it necessary to rely more than usual for the diagnosis upon objectively observed somatic symptoms, such as psychomotor retardation, loss of appetite and weight, and sleep disturbance.

E. The sufferer **must not meet the criteria for a manic, hypomanic, or mixed mood episode**.

Note: Adapted from *ICD-10* (p. 99) *and DSM-5* (p. 160)

individuals no longer try to do anything. In contrast, those with psychomotor agitation may fidget, pace, wring their hands, and exhibit frenzied preoccupation with somatic concerns. In milder forms, it is important to find out if the psychomotor behavior is a change from normal. Sometimes family members can more accurately determine this than the depressed person.

Individuals with depression view the world through gray-tinted glasses.

To them, everything is bleak—their life, their world, their future, and their treatment. "I beg you to shoot me," a depressed woman pleaded, "if they'll put a sick horse out of its misery, why not a person?" They ruminate over personal failures, real or imagined, often making mountains out of mole-hills. With a nearly delusional conviction, they may feel utterly hopeless, helpless, worthless, or guilty. A self-made millionaire declared that he was a "financial flop" who had "forced his family into the poorhouse." Whereas the unhappiness of everyday life comes and goes, the dysphoria of major depression never leaves. With everyday unhappiness, one can go to a movie and temporarily enjoy it, but with major depression, individuals cannot be distracted by a movie. The suicidal preoccupations of depressed patients often arise more from a wish to escape unrelenting dysphoria than to actu-ally die. These patients frequently revise their history so that what was good, average, or at least bearable now becomes terrible and deserving of infinite guilt. In revising their life events, they can be so convincing that the inter-viewing clinician also feels dysphoric and becomes convinced that the per-son's depression was inevitable.

> Virtually diagnostic of major depression is that relatives or others have devoted hours to reassuring the depressed person, but to no avail; no matter how effective or frequent their pleas, nothing they say "sticks" for more than a minute or two. People with depression view all decisions as a choice between something awful and something terrible. Loved ones may become impatient or even furious at the person: They realize she is ill, but feel that she has spurned their advice and does nothing to help herself. Depression is also "contagious" in that the person's futility may become the family's futil-ity. People avoid depressed people—they are depressing! Although the with-drawal of others may aggravate the depression, at other times it doesn't really matter, since the depressed person is too self-absorbed to care. For these people, it feels like No Exit: They can't escape depression; they can't talk about it, and they can't *not* talk about it.

Bipolar Disorder

This disorder is characterized by episodes in which the patient's mood and activity levels are significantly disturbed. The disturbance consists of an ele-vation of mood and increased energy and activity (mania or hypomania) on some occasions, and a lowering of mood and decreased energy and activity (depression) on other occasions. Usually, recovery is complete between epi-sodes, and the incidence in the two sexes is more nearly equal than in other mood disorders. Perhaps 15% of those with major depression eventually exhibit mania or its attenuated version, hypomania. By definition, a person with bipolar disorder displays mania with or without a period of depression. Most patients, however, have both manic and depressive episodes in various sequences and frequencies.

An elevated, euphoric, expansive, or irritable mood is the cardinal feature of mania. People with mania may be hyperactive, highly distractible, and grandiose. They may experience flight of ideas, pressured speech, tangentiality, and a diminished need for sleep. They may be prickly and quick to anger. As their disorganization worsens, they may develop persecutory and grandiose ideas of reference that often become delusions. Sherlock Holmes's obsession that Professor Moriarty was interfering with his attempt to rid the world of evil was a typical manic persecutory delusion. About a quarter of people with mania develop hallucinations that are usually auditory or visual and of shorter duration than those in schizophrenia; disorganization may also occur, but more briefly than in schizophrenia. Table 13-2 lists diagnostic criteria for a manic episode under Bipolar I disorder. The mnemonic "**DIGFAST**," referring to the increased activity in mania, may assist in committing the cardinal symptoms of mania to memory. The letters represent Distractibility, Impulsiveness (pleasure seeking), Grandiosity (elevated self-esteem), Flight of ideas (or racing thoughts), Activity (increase in goal-directed activities), Sleep (decreased need for), and Talkativeness (pressured speech).

TABLE 13-2
Diagnostic Criteria for Bipolar I Disorder

A. The occurrence of **at least one distinct manic episode that lasts for at least 1 week**.

B. During the manic episode, **mood is elevated out of keeping with the individual's circumstances** and may vary from carefree joviality to almost uncontrollable excitement. The mood change is accompanied by increased energy. In some manic episodes the mood is irritable and suspicious rather than elated. Other manic symptoms include:
   1. inflated self-esteem, and **grandiose** or over-optimistic ideas are freely expressed;
   2. decreased need for **sleep;**
   3. pressured **speech;**
   4. **flight of ideas** or racing thoughts;
   5. attention cannot be sustained and there is often marked **distractability**;
   6. **overactivity;**
   7. normal social inhibitions are lost resulting in **impulsive** high-risk behaviors (e.g., the individual may embark on extravagant and impractical schemes, spend money recklessly, or become aggressive, amorous, or facetious in inappropriate circumstances).

TABLE 13-2
Continued

DSM-5 specifies that 3 of the above symptoms must be present to meet criteria for mania (4 symptoms if the mood is only irritable versus elevated or expansive).

Perceptual changes may accompany the manic mood state such as the appreciation of colors as especially vivid (and unusually beautiful), a preoccupation with fine details of surfaces or textures, and subjective hyperacusis.

C. The episode should be severe enough to disrupt ordinary work and social activities more or less completely, i.e., the symptoms result in **significant distress or significant impairment** in personal, family, social, educational, occupational, or other important area of functioning.

D. The disturbance is **not better explained by the direct physiological effects of a substance or another medical condition.**

E. The symptoms **are not better explained by another mental disorder**, particularly schizoaffective, schizophrenia, delusional disorder, or other psychotic thought disorders.

F. There must have been **at least one other affective episode** (hypomanic, manic, depressive, or mixed) in the past.

As patients who suffer only from repeated episodes of mania are comparatively rare, and resemble (in their family history, premorbid personality, age of onset, and long-term prognosis) those who also have at least occasional episodes of depression, such patients are classified as bipolar.

Mixed Episode: Although the most typical form of bipolar disorder consists of alternating manic and depressive episodes separated by periods of normal mood, it is not uncommon for depressive mood to be accompanied for days or weeks on end by overactivity and pressure of speech, or for a manic mood and grandiosity to be accompanied by agitation and loss of energy and libido.

A diagnosis of mixed bipolar affective disorder should be made only if the two sets of symptoms are both prominent for the greater part of the current episode of illness, and if that episode has lasted for at least 2 weeks.

Rapid Cycling: Depressive symptoms and symptoms of hypomania or mania may also alternate rapidly, from day to day or even from hour to hour.

Psychotic features: Inflated self-esteem and grandiose ideas may develop into delusions, and irritability and suspiciousness into delusions of persecution. In severe cases, grandiose or religious delusions of identity or role may be prominent, and flight of ideas and pressure of speech may result in the individual becoming incomprehensible. Severe and sustained physical activity and excitement may result in aggression or violence, and neglect of eating, drinking, and personal hygiene may result in dangerous states of dehydration and self-neglect.

Delusions or hallucinations can be specified as congruent or incongruent with the mood. "Incongruent" should be taken as including affectively neutral delusions and hallucinations; for example, delusions of reference with no guilty or accusatory content, or voices speaking to the individual about events that have no special emotional significance.

The term "manic-depressive disorder or psychosis" is now used mainly as a synonym for bipolar disorder.

Note: Adapted from *ICD-10* (p. 97) and *DSM-5* (p. 123)

People with mania may talk incessantly, do "20 things at once," and launch outrageous projects. These individuals often resemble fast-talking comics of the Robin Williams and Jim Carey genre. People laugh with, not at, people with mania. They have pressured speech, and it's hard to get a word in edge-wise. People with mania can be super salespeople. Caught unaware, a clinician was visited by a salesman with mania who almost sold him a set of encyclopedias for his children—the problem was that he didn't have any children.

> A person, when manic, spent $100,000 hiring city planners, attorneys, architects, and a guru to construct a 90-story building on 1 square foot of land. Another, a UCLA undergraduate, telephoned the Russian president to invite him to the Rose Bowl, and although the president didn't get the message, the student did reach a high Kremlin official (who declined).
>
> On the spur of the moment, a Dartmouth graduate who resided in California jumped on a plane and admitted himself to "the hospital of my alma mater." He arrived with four tennis rackets, three suitcases, a fishing rod, dozens of lollipops, and a swimsuit; it was winter. Five minutes after his grand entrance, he coaxed all the patients and staff into singing, "The Yellow Rose of Texas." Further demonstrating tangential thinking, he declared that everybody should wear a yellow ribbon and surrender peacefully.
>
> Many females with mania dress in bright multicolored clothing. Women may present with excessive makeup, provocative clothing, and high heels. They may become angry if asked about their clothing or flirtatious behaviors, providing further evidence of their lack of insight and judgment. Their sexual disinhibitions make it prudent to have a chaperone in the room.

But eventually, things get out of control in mania. When crossed, or when people don't go along with them, people with mania become irritable, nasty, and sometimes cruel. They may play the "manic game," in which they are constantly testing everybody's limits; they manipulate others' self-esteem, perceive and exploit people's vulnerabilities, and project responsibility. After wreaking havoc and infuriating everybody, they blame everyone but themselves. On the slightest whim, people with mania will call total strangers and amass enormous phone bills. These individuals may have no inhibitions. A well-respected "Southern gentleman" was brought into the hospital by neighbors when he was found dancing naked on a pizza in his backyard. He told the staff, "I wanted to raise my spiritual awareness and that was the best way to do it."

Patients with mania develop reputations as normally being a Dr. Jekyll—

upstanding, likeable, and productive—yet sometimes becoming a Mr. Hyde—outrageously excitable, intrusive, and demanding. *Unpredictable* is what some people call them: fine one month, profoundly depressed the next month. Because periods of high energy, creativity, and achievement are not recognized as hypomania, bipolar disorder may go undiagnosed. Clinicians find that an excellent barometer of these hypomanic periods is the patient's diminished need for sleep. The adaptiveness of moderate hypomanic behavior allows many individuals with bipolar disorder to stand with society's most accomplished members.

Bipolar disorder is more severe than major depression. Patients with bipolar depressions stay depressed longer, relapse more frequently, display more depressive symptoms, show more severe symptoms, have more delusions and hallucinations, commit more suicides, require more hospitalizations, and experience more incapacitation. Bipolar I disorder most often starts with a depression; only 10–20% experience exclusively manic episodes. Manic spells may evolve rapidly or slowly. Yet when a person first presents with a severe depression, it's usually hard to tell if it is bipolar or major (unipolar) depression. However, because prognoses and treatments differ substantially, it's desirable to distinguish these two depressions as soon as possible.

Patients with bipolar depression are more likely than patients with unipolar depression to have extremely low energy, psychomotor retardation, and the reverse vegetative symptoms: hypersomnia, hyperphagia, and mood worsening in the evening. In general, people with bipolar depression prefer to remain in bed and have what are termed "laying-down depressions." They are also more likely to have psychotic depressions and many lack insight into past manic episodes. They minimize or deny having poor judgment and acting grossly different from normal. However, they can describe episodes lasting many days or weeks in which they did not need much sleep and still had a lot of energy. Close friends, roommates, or family members are often helpful allies in making the right diagnosis of bipolar disorder. Table 13-3 lists the characteristics that tend to distinguish unipolar from bipolar depressions.

One common problem is differentiation of this disorder from schizophrenia spectrum disorders, particularly if the patient is seen only at the height of the illness when delusions, incoherent speech, and psychomotor agitation may obscure the basic disturbance of mood. Patients treated for mania with neuroleptic medication and who no longer have abnormal levels of physical or mental activity may continue to have hallucinations or delusions and therefore present a similar diagnostic problem.

The increased activity and restlessness (and often weight loss) must be

TABLE 13-3
Characteristics That Tend to Distinguish Unipolar from Bipolar Depressions

UNIPOLAR DEPRESSION	BIPOLAR DEPRESSION
PRESENTING SYMPTOMS	
Psychomotor agitation or retardation	Psychomotor retardation
Anxiety	Lethargy
Insomnia	Hypersomnia
Anorexia	Hyperphagia
Underweight	Overweight
Feel worse in the a.m. and better in the p.m. ("diurnal mood variation")	Feel worse in the p.m. and better in the a.m. ("reverse diurnal mood variation")
Psychosis less likely	Psychosis more likely
LONGITUDINAL FEATURES	
Less family history of mood disorders	More family history of depression and mania
Premorbidly obsessional, shy, moralistic, insecure	Premorbidly outgoing, active, uninhibited, successful
No prior mania or hypomania	Prior mania or hypomania
No prior hospitalizations	Prior hospitalizations

distinguished from the early states of "agitated depression," particularly in late middle age, which may bear a superficial resemblance to hypomania of the irritable variety. Patients with severe obsessional symptoms may be active part of the night completing their cleaning rituals, but there is unlikely to be a commensurate elevation in affect or mood.

Dysthymic Disorder

Formerly called "depressive neurosis," dysthymic disorder presents with a chronic dysphoria or anhedonia that is not severe enough to meet all the criteria for major depression. *DSM-5* requires that symptoms exist for at least 2 years. This dysphoria or anhedonia may be continual or episodic; euthymia may exist for several days to weeks, but no longer than several weeks. The diagnosis should not be made if an interval of normal mood lasts for more than a few months. Whereas many patients with major depression are unable to work or to socialize, those with dysthymic disorders function, though not at their peak. By definition, dysthymic disorders never present with delusions or hallucinations. When a major depression is superimposed on a dysthymic disorder, it's dubbed a "double depression." Table 13-4 lists diagnostic criteria for dysthymic disorder.

TABLE 13-4
Diagnostic Criteria for Persistent Depressive Disorder (Dysthymic Disorder)

A. The essential feature is a very **long-standing depression of mood which is never, or only very rarely, severe enough to fulfill the criteria for major depressive disorder**, mild or moderate severity.

DSM-5 specifies a duration of 2 years for adults and at least 1 year for children and adolescents who may manifest irritable mood as an equivalent to depressed mood.

B. Sufferers have **at least two other symptoms associated with depressed mood** (see Table 13-1 Criterion A).

They often brood and complain, sleep badly, and feel inadequate, but are usually able to cope with the basic demands of everyday life. Dysthymia therefore has much in common with the concepts of depressive neurosis and neurotic depression.

C. The sufferers usually have periods of days or weeks (*but not more than 2 months at a time*) when they describe themselves as well, but **most of the time (often for months at a time) they feel tired and depressed**; everything is an effort and nothing is enjoyed. The balance between individual phases of mild depression and intervening periods of comparative normality is highly variable.

D. The symptoms result in **significant distress or significant impairment** in personal, family, social, educational, occupational, or other important area of functioning.

E. Individual episodes of depressed mood do not fulfil the criteria for any of the other diagnostic categories describing mania, hypomania, or depression.

F. The symptoms **are not better explained by another mental disorder**, especially psychotic thought disorders such as schizophrenia, delusional disorder, and schizoaffective disorder.

G. The disturbance is **not better explained by the direct physiological effects of a substance or another medical condition.**

Dysthymia usually begins early in adult life and lasts for at least several years, sometimes indefinitely. When the onset is later in life, the disorder is often the aftermath of a discrete depressive episode and associated with bereavement or other obvious stress.

Note: Adapted from *ICD-10* (p. 107) *and DSM-5* (p. 168)

In contrast to major depression, dysthymic disorder is more relenting and less consuming. Patients may laugh and tell a joke and on occasion, they even enjoy themselves. Although loved ones find dysthymic disorders less infuriating and frustrating than major depressions, others become bored with the person's habitual moaning and complaining. Patients with dysthymia often become upset over matters that others take in stride. A woman whose brother had dysthymic disorder described him as having a "garlic depression—he makes everyone around him feel a little worse." Patients with dysthymic disorder have been shown to have slightly more impairment than those with major depression alone. Only about half fully recover from dysthymic disorder alone and, if major depression occurs with dysthymia, only about one-third recover (Klein et al., 1988).

A 40-year-old married woman from a traditional Italian family sought treatment because "I'm anxious and shaky most of the time, especially at work. I can't be that way at home, ever since my mother-in-law moved in for good and I have to be on my best behavior when I'm around her." The patient said she'd been unhappy most of her life, but had felt much worse since her mother-in-law camped in 5 months ago. "She comes from the old country. She expects me to wait on her, but nothing I do ever satisfies her. She complains; otherwise she does nothing. I return exhausted from work and immediately prepare dinner; so what does she say? 'You made the carrots wrong; you should cut them at angles, not up-and-down.' When I ask my husband to do something about *his* mother, all he says is, 'You're overreacting.' I feel unappreciated and drained. I cry all the time, but only in private: I don't want anybody to see I'm weak."

For the first time, somebody did. Tears and words gushed out, as this woman revealed her darkest fear: "I'm terrified I'm turning into my mother. Our family lived near Rome, which is where my mother was hospitalized for shock treatment, but she was depressed most of her life. She would sit in the corner for hours and say nothing. At other times, she'd act crazy and speak nonsense; she'd talk to the dead and accuse the milkman of stealing. My mother wasn't mean to me; it was more like she was mentally absent. That's when I learned you can't rely on anybody to solve your problems but yourself. . . . When I was 16, my mother began to improve. Suddenly, I had the mother I always wanted. I loved it. Two years later, though, she died of cancer. I still miss her, and I know I can't expect my mother-in-law to replace her, yet sometimes I do, and *that's* nuts. Far worse is that I'm acting like my mother— snapping at people, never laughing, overly serious, avoiding people, not talking, and always hopeless. I'm frightened I'll be crazy like her."

The patient's marriage ("my ticket to America") was sexless and passionless ("all he does is eat"). Because of financial limitations, she quit premed and became a secretary. Over the years, she's been promoted to administrator, but far slower than "other women with less skill." She claimed to have "always" had initial insomnia and poor appetite. During the past year she has shed 25 pounds, felt increasingly sluggish and restless during the day, preferred being alone, and seemed immune to praise. She had no history of hypomania or mania, nor did she ever contemplate suicide.

Her dysthymic disorder was treated with an antidepressant, and after 2 weeks, her sleep and appetite normalized and her dysthymia lifted. She could laugh and enjoy people. Although she still felt just as unappreciated at home and at work, she stopped fretting about it. After a month of treatment, her symptoms abated completely, but she refused to have any of her family meet with the therapist, saying simply, "I will handle things myself." (Note: Another example of how Axis I problems resolve much easier than Axis II problems.) Two months after her first visit, she observed, "I must have been depressed my entire life. Until now, I didn't know what it was like *not* to be depressed. . . . I feel like a new person, and yet I still worry that someday I'll go crazy like my mother." It was only after 8 months of psychotherapy that this fear disappeared.

Cyclothymic Disorder

Patients with cyclothymic disorder have hypomanic *and* dysphoric periods that are not severe enough to qualify as a bipolar disorder. Moreover, whereas bipolar disorder is episodic, cyclothymic disorder is continual; it, like dysthymic disorder, must exist for at least 2 years without the patient being euthymic for more than 3 months. Diagnostic criteria for cyclothymic disorder are listed in Table 13-5.

Premenstrual Dysphoric Disorder

Premenstrual Dysphoric Disorder is a more recently established diagnostic entity characterized by sudden mood swings, irritability, and depressive symptoms that have onset following ovulation and remit shortly after menses. They occur regularly, more months than not, and cause significant distress or impairment in some important area of functioning.

Disruptive Mood Dysregulation Disorder

Disruptive mood dysregulation disorder is a new diagnostic category for individuals who have chronic non-episodic and severe irritability beginning before age 10 years. This is the person's baseline condition with little fluctuation. The elevated or expansive mood and grandiosity typical of a manic episode are not present. Children with disruptive mood dysregulation disorder have high risk for developing depressive and anxiety disorders which is why the condition is discussed here. This diagnosis was established to address concerns about the overdiagnosis of bipolar illness in children. In addition to the difficult baseline moods, there exists a high probability for extreme behavioral dyscontrol in these children as well. Consequently there is sub-

TABLE 13-5
Diagnostic Criteria for Cyclothymic Disorder

A. The essential feature is a **persistent instability of mood, involving numerous periods of mild depression and mild elation**, none of which has been sufficiently severe or prolonged to fulfil the mood criteria for even a mild major depressive disorder or hypomania (see criteria Tables 13-1, 13-3).

   DSM-5 specifies a duration of 2 years for adults and at least 1 year for children and adolescents.

B. This instability pursues a chronic course, and although at times the mood may be normal and stable for months at a time (*but not more than 2 months at a time*), **most of the time hypomanic and depressive periods are present**. The diagnosis is difficult to establish without a prolonged period of observation or an unusually good account of the individual's past behavior.

C. Individual episodes of mood swings **do not fulfil the criteria for any of the other diagnostic categories describing mania, hypomania, or depression**. The mood swings are usually perceived by the individual as being unrelated to life events.

D. The symptoms are **not better explained by another mental disorder**, particularly schizoaffective, schizophrenia, delusional disorder, or other psychotic thought disorders.

E. The disturbance is **not better explained by the direct physiological effects of a substance or another medical condition**.

F. The symptoms result in **significant distress or significant impairment** in personal, family, social, educational, occupational, or other important area of functioning. Because the mood swings last for years at a time, and sometimes for the greater part of the individual's adult life, they involve considerable subjective distress and disability.

Note: Adapted from *ICD-10* (p. 106) *and DSM-5* (p. 139)

---

stantial overlap with oppositional defiant disorder. This condition is distinguished from intermittent explosive disorder by being more continuously present than intermittent.

SUBTYPES

Types and subtypes of mood disorders are important to identify for several reasons. Some require different treatments; some often escape detection (and treatment) because they resemble other disorders; some suggest different etiologies; some of these have research implications. Some have already been mentioned: endogenous/reactive, primary/secondary, unipolar/bipolar, psychotic/neurotic. (Reader beware! The classifications presented above and below are commonly used but not fixed in stone.)

The most important subtypes of major depression are those with "psychotic," "melancholic," or "atypical features." (see Table 13-6) *Major depressive episode with psychotic features* displays either delusions or hallucinations. The delusions and hallucinations may be either *mood-congruent* ("the devil is taking me to hell") or *mood-incongruent* ("the FBI is trying to program my brain to become an informant"). Patients with depression rarely hallucinate without also having delusions. During the first 6 months, psychotic depressions are more severe than nonpsychotic depressions. The chief reason for distinguishing psychotic from nonpsychotic depressions is that they benefit from different treatments.

Major depressive episode with melancholic features is dominated by symptoms seen in endogenous depressions, but no attempt is made to include cause or lack of cause as a feature. These patients are both lucky and unlucky; they are *unlucky* because they feel awful, but *lucky* because they have a depression that has an especially good chance of responding to biological treatments (e.g., antidepressants and electroconvulsant therapy); better than to psychotherapy or placebo (Peselow et al., 1992).

Major depressive episode with atypical features is almost the opposite of melancholic depressions. Atypical episodes display reverse biological signs and an extreme reactivity to environmental events, which often manifest as "rejection sensitivity." The slightest rejection plunges these patients into dark despair, whereas the slightest good news induces ecstasy.

> An example of rejection sensitivity occurred when Mary Rae's fiancé met her at the airport. He casually remarked to Mary Rae that a passerby was "attractive." Mary Rae became incensed, opened her suitcase, threw clothes all over the place, spent 30 minutes screaming at him, and then left the airport by herself. By evening she had calmed down, yet for weeks she pouted that, "The cluck doesn't realize I'm sensitive about my looks. Why couldn't he say something nice about *my* body?"

Patients with atypical features don't respond very well to tricyclic antidepressants or electroconvulsive therapy, but do better on MAOIs and Selective Dopamine Norepinephrine Reuptake Inhibitors.

Bipolar disorder is divided into "bipolar I," which meets the full diagnostic criteria for a manic episode, and "bipolar II," in which there is a major depressive episode and hypomania, not mania; the patient's "highs" do not merit hospitalization (Table 13-7). Although bipolar II disorder is generally considered to be a milder version of bipolar I, it may be an intermediate entity between bipolar I and major depression, or a completely distinct entity. Many clinicians find it useful to conceptualize bipolar disorder as a

TABLE 13-6
Specifiers for Depression

A. Differentiation between mild, moderate, and severe depressive episodes rests upon a complicated clinical judgment that involves the number, type, and severity of symptoms present.

   1. In **mild** depression none of the symptoms should be present to an intense degree. An individual with a mild depressive episode is usually distressed by the symptoms and has some difficulty in continuing with ordinary work and social activities, but will probably not cease to function completely.

   2. An individual with a **moderate** depressive episode will usually have at least two of the three most typical symptoms plus at least 3 (and preferably 4) of the other symptoms along with considerable difficulty in continuing with social, work, or domestic activities.

   3. For depression to be of **severe** intensity, all three of the typical symptoms noted for mild and moderate depressive episodes should be present, plus at least 4 other symptoms, some of which should be of severe intensity. During a severe depressive episode it is very unlikely that the sufferer will be able to continue with social, work, or domestic activities, except to a very limited extent.

   4. A severe depressive episode **with psychotic features** exists when the above criteria for severe depression are met and delusions, hallucinations, or depressive stupor are present. The delusions usually involve ideas of sin, poverty, or imminent disasters, responsibility for which may be assumed by the patient. Auditory or olfactory hallucinations are usually of defamatory or accusatory voices or of rotting filth or decomposing flesh. Severe psychomotor retardation may progress to stupor. Delusions or hallucinations may be specified as mood-congruent or mood-incongruent

   These grades of severity are specified to cover a wide range of clinical states that are encountered in different types of psychiatric practice. Individuals with mild depressive episodes are common in primary care and general medical settings, whereas psychiatric inpatient units deal largely with patients suffering from the severe grades.

B. Specify whether the depression is **recurrent or single episode**.

C. With **atypical features**: Atypical depression is characterized by mood reactivity, hyperphagia, hypersomnia, leaden paralysis, and a pattern of hypersensitivity to rejection.

D. With **melancholic features**: Melancholic depression could also be referred to as "somatic," "vital," "biological," "vegetative," or endogenomorphic." These "somatic" symptoms and characteristic features may have special clinical significance: loss of interest or pleasure in activities that are normally enjoyable; lack of emotional reactivity to normally pleasurable surroundings and events; waking in the morning 2 hours or more before the usual time; depression worse in the morning; objective evidence of definite psychomotor retardation or agitation (remarked on or reported by other people); marked loss of appetite; weight loss (often defined as 5% or more of body weight in the past month); marked loss of libido. Usually, melancholic depression is not regarded as present unless about 4 of these symptoms are definitely present.

E. With a **seasonal pattern**

Note: Adapted from *ICD-10* (p. 99) *and DSM-5* (p. 184)

TABLE 13-7
Diagnostic Criteria for Bipolar II Disorder

A. Several of the features of mania, consistent with elevated or changed mood and increased activity, should be distinctly present for at least several (4) consecutive days, to a degree and with a persistence greater than described for cyclothymia. In addition to this **hypomanic episode** there must have been criteria met for **at least one major depressive episode** (See Table 13-1).

B. The **criteria for a manic episode have never been met** (see Table 13-3 Criterion B).

Hypomania is a lesser degree of mania characterized by a persistent mild elevation of mood (for at least several days on end), increased energy and activity, and usually marked feelings of well-being and both physical and mental efficiency. Increased sociability, talkativeness, overfamiliarity, increased sexual energy, and a decreased need for sleep are often present but not to the extent that they lead to severe disruption of work or result in social rejection. Irritability, conceit, and boorish behavior may take the place of the more usual euphoric sociability. Concentration and attention may be impaired, thus diminishing the ability to settle down to work or to relaxation and leisure, but this may not prevent the appearance of interests in quite new ventures and activities, or mild over-spending.

C. The disturbance is **not better explained by another mental disorder**, particularly schizoaffective, schizophrenia, delusional disorder or other psychotic thought disorders.

D. The symptoms of alternating hypomania and depression result in **significant distress or significant impairment** in personal, family, social, educational, occupational, or other important area of functioning.

Considerable interference with work or social activity is consistent with hypomania alone, but if disruption of these is severe or complete, mania should be diagnosed.

E. The hypomanic symptoms are **not accompanied by hallucinations, delusions, or other psychotic features**. Otherwise the symptoms would meet the threshold for mania.

F. The disturbance is **not better explained by the direct physiological effects of a substance or another medical condition**.

Note: Adapted from *ICD-10* (p. 97) *and DSM-5* (p. 132)

---

spectrum illness ranging from the narrow bipolar I definition to broader phenotypes that do not meet the strict diagnostic criteria for number of symptoms, episodic presentation, severity, or duration.

In *rapid cycling bipolar disorder*, patients have four or more episodes per year of mania, hypomania, or major depression. Each episode is followed by either remission or a switch into an episode of opposite polarity. This subtype represents a particularly severe form of bipolar disorder in which lithium is less effective than anticonvulsants.

Mood disorder with seasonal pattern, formerly called seasonal affective disorders (SAD) (or "the winter blues," as patients call it), refers to those depressions that invariably occur in the fall and winter; they improve within days of moving from cold to warm climates or from areas with short to long exposures to daylight. When depressed, these patients tend to eat more and sleep longer or later in the morning. SAD seems to be alleviated by artificial bright (at least 2500 lux) light, particularly if given in the early morning. Ordinary room light is 150–200 lux. If these patients develop hypomania or mania, it's usually in the summer. Clinicians should inquire about seasonal patterns of mood with every patient who presents with any type of mood disorder.

EPIDEMIOLOGY

Mood disorders are the most common mental disorders in outpatients treated by mental health professionals and comprise roughly one-quarter of a typical practice. However, in the general population mood disorders rank third behind anxiety and impulse control disorders. The 1-year prevalence rate for mood disorders in the United States using *DSM-IV* criteria is 9.5%, with the rate for major depression at 6.7%, for dysthymic disorder at 1.5%, and for bipolar disorder at 2.6%. When looking at the broader expressions of bipolar disorder (including cyclothymia and not otherwise specified), lifetime prevalence may be as high as 5%. Just one-third of those with bona fide bipolar illness have been diagnosed and fewer treated.

> In general, mood disorders strike twice as many women as men; however, this ratio varies depending on the disorder. Ninety percent of "atypical depressions" occur in women. Major depression and dysthymic disorder afflict two to three times more women than men. Bipolar disorder is closer to one and one-half times more common in women. During a lifetime, roughly 20% of women and 10% of men will suffer a major depressive episode; about a third of these patients will be hospitalized. Patients with recurrent depression have high rates of avoidant (30%), obsessive–compulsive (19%), and dependent (16%) personality disorders (Pilkonis & Frank, 1988). Contrary to popular belief, older adults do not have an increased risk for major depression. One high-risk group for depression is young women who have children and minimal support in child rearing (Ensel, 1982). It may be more common in divorced, separated, or single people.
>
> It appears that each successive generation since World War II has had an increased rate of depression and an earlier age of onset. Simultaneously, the rate of suicide, especially among youth, has also escalated with each generation. For instance, since the 1950s, the suicide rate for 15- to 24-year-olds has

tripled, replacing homicide as the second leading cause of death among youth. These increased rates of depression and suicide are distressingly genuine; they are not methodological artifacts. Why depression and suicide have increased is unknown. Nevertheless, despite suicide still being most prevalent among older adults, more than ever, today's clinician must be alert to teenage suicide. The prevalence of mood disorders varies widely from culture to culture.

DIFFERENTIAL DIAGNOSIS

Substance-Induced Mood Disorder

When mood disorders exist, clinicians should consider that medications, exposure to neurotoxic chemicals, or recreational drugs may have caused a mood disturbance. Before it can be assumed that a drug causes depression, it should be demonstrated that the drug increases the rate for a major depression over the prevalence in the general population. In most reports on drugs "causing" depression, there was no screening for depression when the drug was started. However, it is important to realize that any medication may have any side effect, including the side effect of depression. Retinoids for acne and interferon for hepatitis C are just two examples of nonpsychotropic medications recently suspected to cause depression.

Mania can be precipitated by stimulants such as *cocaine* and *dextroamphetamine*. Sometimes patients report frequent manic episodes that are really 2- to 4-day cocaine binges. When people abruptly stop using stimulants, they may appear depressed: They sleep a lot, are apathetic, and show extreme psychomotor retardation, but they might not actually *say* they are depressed. This phase of stimulant withdrawal usually passes in a few days. Antidepressants can induce mania—TCAs about 2% of the time and SSRIs about 1%. This rate is much higher in patients with a known bipolar disorder. A variety of other drugs (e.g., hallucinogens, corticosteroids) occasionally are associated with manic episodes. Agents frequently implicated in mood disturbance are listed below.

Oral contraceptives. Women on oral contraceptives (containing 50 mcg estrogen) in the 1970s appeared to have an increased rate of depression, with features such as hypersomnia, hyperphagia, and retardation. Half of the depressed women on oral contraceptives had an absolute pyridoxine (vitamin B$_6$) deficiency, secondary to estrogen's competitive effects with pyridoxine coenzyme systems. When they were treated with pyridoxine 50 mg bid, there was a 90% recovery rate. Women without a deficiency responded to pyridoxine about 30% of the time (placebo response rate). It seems that the new lower-estrogen oral contraceptives are safer in this regard. On the other hand, estrogens have been used to help treat depression in peri- and post-menopausal women.

Antihypertensives. Reserpine induces depression in about 15% of cases, probably through its ability to deplete biogenic amines. The beta-blocker propranolol increases the risk of depression twofold or at least creates a depression-like syndrome (insomnia, low energy, apathy). Less lipophilic beta-blockers such as atenolol have a lower depression risk because they don't reach the brain. Methyldopa has also been reported to induce depressions. In some instances, calcium channel blockers and ACE inhibitors have been reported to cause mild improvement in depressive symptoms and may be preferred treatments in people at risk for mood disorders.

Steroids. High doses of corticosteroids (>80 mg equivalent of prednisone) result in major psychiatric sequelae in about 20% of the cases; depression and mania are frequent among these.

Opiates. Produced naturally in the brain as endorphins but included in many pain preparations, opioids impact mood directly and profoundly through specific brain receptors. The opiates include morphine, oxycodone, fentanyl, methadone, and codeine. Initially mood improves, sometimes too much (to the point of euphoria), but after a few weeks tolerance develops and symptoms of withdrawal emerge. It is extremely difficult to successfully treat someone who is depressed and on opiate pain medications.

Hypnoanxiolytics. Although diazepam and chlordiazepoxide have often been touted to induce depression, there is little convincing evidence of this. Many patients with depression present with anxiety, which treatment with a benzodiazepine may relieve while unmasking the remaining depressive symptoms. In higher doses (>30 mg equivalent of diazepam) benzodiaze-pines, barbiturates, and alcohol all probably exacerbate or cause depression. A 25% depression rate has been reported in patients who were started on alprazolam 4 mg a day for panic disorder without depression. Diazepam 30 mg is equivalent to alprazolam 3 mg, clonazepam 1.5 mg, lorazepam 4–6 mg, or beer 5–6 bottles.

Stimulants. These include cocaine, amphetamines, methylphenidate, and xanthine derivatives (caffeine). All can transiently improve mood through outpouring of monoamine neurotransmitters, even to the point of mania. However, tolerance and withdrawal symptoms emerge within a couple of weeks causing rebound dysphoria and even severe depression.

Mood Disorder Due to a Medical Condition

Generally, medical illnesses (e.g., TB, hepatitis, mononucleosis, anemia, hypothyroidism) differ from depression in that fatigue tends to be associated with hypersomnia (rather than the insomnia of depression), and depressed mood increases as the day progresses, rather than peaking in the morning, as is typical in depression. In medical conditions that produce several "vegetative symptoms," such as cancer, psychological symptoms such as dysphoric mood, hopelessness, guilt, worthlessness, and suicidal ideation are the best indicators of a major depression. For unknown reasons, pancreatic cancer seems to be associated with higher depression rates than other cancers. Depression may be the first indication of an occult pancreatic carcinoma before any metabolic disturbance. Certain medical illnesses have higher depression rates than others; these include:

Neurological conditions such as multiple sclerosis, Parkinson's disease, and strokes (particularly in the frontal left hemisphere). Mania is also more frequent in multiple sclerosis.

Endocrine diseases such as hypothyroidism and Cushing's disease are associated with higher depression rates. Cushing's disease and hyperthyroidism have higher mania rates. Women with treatment-resistant depression have higher thyroiditis rates, but may have no other obvious thyroid abnormality.

The increased activity and restlessness (and often weight loss) of mania or hypomania must be distinguished from the same symptoms occurring in hyperthyroidism and anorexia nervosa;

Autoimmune disorders such as rheumatoid arthritis and systemic lupus all carry higher depression rates than nonautoimmune disorders that have the same degree of disability. For example, rheumatoid arthritis has a higher depression rate than osteoarthritis.

Other Conditions Related to Mood Disorders

• Uncomplicated bereavement may present with the biological signs and symptoms of depression. In normal grief reactions, self-esteem tends to be preserved and anhedonia fluctuates considerably. Severe motor retardation, diurnal variation of mood, suicidal ideation, and significant disturbance of functioning are more often characteristics of depression. During normal bereavement, mourners episodically fantasize about their own death, berate themselves for not visiting or saving the deceased, or feel guilty that the wrong person died (survivor guilt). But when bereavement evolves into major depression, people can think of nothing but their loss, themselves, and their depression. Normal mourners acknowledge the deceased's unfavorable traits; those with depression idealize the departed and repress their faults. Bereavement with symptoms of depression may be delayed, but it usually emerges within 2 or 3 months of the loved one's death. After 3 months, normal mourners have moments of grief, but gradually return to their usual activities and can sustain thoughts about matters unrelated to the death. In contrast, when bereavement is complicated by depression, the depression often persists for more than 3 months, may get more (instead of less) severe over time, presents with numerous biological signs, and prevents the person from getting back into the swing of things. In about 10% of individuals, bereavement becomes major depression. Those at highest risk have no, or minimal, support systems.

• *Secondary anorgasmia* or *secondary impotence* can occur with depression or as a result of a medical problem such as diabetes. In patients with depression these two symptoms are a result of the decrease in libido. In men, nocturnal erections can be lost in diabetes, whereas in depression, nocturnal erections usually occur. In diabetes, normal libido is initially present despite the impotence. Women who have had normal sexual desire and orgasms may become anorgasmic with depression.

• *Somatization* can be the result of depression or a disorder in its own right. Patients with a somatization disorder have had it, by definition, since at least the age of 30. In contrast, people with depression often start somatizing only when they get depressed; while depressed, they will double their doctor visits with an average of five to six visits a year. Before the depression and after treatment, somatic complaints and doctor visits return to normal levels. These patients may acknowledge anhedonia but deny depressed mood or blame depressive symptoms on their somatic complaint. For these reasons, they are often called "masked depressions."

• *Alcoholism or hypnoanxiolytic dependence* can cause depression or be a result of attempts to self-medicate depression. The diagnosis of depression should not be made until at least a 4- to 6-week trial of abstinence has been completed.

• *Pain* occurs in many depressed patients, with headache, back pain, or abdominal pain the most common. About a quarter of patients presenting with chronic pain have a diagnosis of major depressive disorder. Antidepressants have been effective in treating chronic pain with or without depression, particularly if a "pain lifestyle" has not yet been established.

• *Juvenile delinquents* have major depression about 25% of the time.

These are the youngsters who are treatable and much less likely to have antisocial personalities. They manifest classic vegetative signs of depression and, while possibly denying depression, will acknowledge persistent boredom (anhedonia). Another reason for boredom in this population is that many of these kids are high stimulus seekers (low basal dopamine in the frontal lobes, present in ADHD) who get into trouble as they impulsively chase excitement (unfortunately, incarceration can be boring). The girls may be promiscuous, but driven by a need for warmth and affection and not by increased libido. The boys frequently abuse drugs to escape their situation rather than for strictly recreational purposes. Sometimes these were the good kids in grade school who "went bad." Kids with depression commit antisocial acts in an effort to be accepted by other kids, whereas antisocial kids behave in this way no matter what the consequences to others.

• *Anxiety* is a presenting complaint for many patients, more than half of whom really have a major depression. All symptoms of depression are present, but patients attribute them to anxiety. Antidepressants are more effective than anxiolytics in treating this combination. Nearly 60% of patients with major depression have a comorbid anxiety disorder. Accumulating evidence indicates that in patients with comorbid depression and anxiety, there is a tendency toward greater illness severity and a lower treatment response than those with either illness alone. Also, social functioning and quality of life are more greatly impaired.

• Since *schizophrenia* and mood disorders can display psychotic, catatonic, and dysphoric features, the most likely diagnosis is the one that presents first, occurs in first-degree relatives, shows the characteristic natural history, and meets the diagnostic criteria. If catatonia is present and the patient is mute, an amytal interview or brief treatment with benzodiazepines may help with the diagnosis by allowing the patient to talk. Psychosis in depression and mania is usually briefer and less bizarre than in schizophrenia. If criteria for schizophrenia are met and there is an additional major depressive or manic episode, then the patient has a schizoaffective disorder (see Chapter 12).

ETIOLOGY AND PATHOGENESIS

Some mood disorders arise for no apparent reason; others are triggered by a precipitant. Unless the precipitant is blatantly obvious, clinicians should be cautious about attributing a depression to it. If clinicians look hard enough, they can always find a stressor to "explain" a depression. (Review your past month and you will surely discover some stressor to "account" for why you should be depressed.) Stress is the way of the world; therefore, the path toward depression must involve more than stress.

With or without environmental stressors as a triggering event ("situational" versus "nonsituational" or "reactive" versus "endogenous"), major depressions present with similar symptoms, overall clinical pictures, types and amounts of stress, premorbid social supports, and family psychopathology. The reason they present the same is because no matter how a depression begins, at some point a *final common pathway* of biological dysfunction is reached. In this way depression may be more like fever, for which there are many causes but a final common pathway and presentation. This commonality may explain why particular biological abnormalities are seen only in subgroups of mood disorders and usually in less than 60% of people with depression. The final common pathway may arise from many biological or psychosocial causes, a genetic vulnerability, a "depressogenic" medication, an early loss, a lack of positive reinforcement, and so on.

Biomedical Factors

Genetics. Because concordance rates for mood disorders in MZ and DZ twins are about 60% and 15%, respectively, genetic transmission is suspected. Severe endogenous depression and bipolar illness carry a higher genetic loading than milder forms. Families with predominantly unipolar depression are most likely to have relatives with unipolar depression, but they also have increased rates of bipolar disorders compared to the general population (and vice versa, in families with predominantly bipolar illness). The fact that bipolar and unipolar mood disorders do not breed absolutely true supports the notion that these conditions are not precisely distinct from each other. Genetic linkage studies have identified different sites of transmission in different families, so there is no one depression gene. Because genetic penetrance is incomplete, not all carriers of "depression" genes may get depressed.

Biochemistry. Many studies suggest that during depression, there is decreased serotonergic function and/or dysregulated noradrenergic function in the brain. The dysregulation involves a high basal (tonic) rate of firing but, when stimulated, a low response rate. In the noradrenergic system the result is like a TV with poor reception. There is a lot of "snow" in the picture (high basal rate of firing), and images come in weakly and poorly (low response). Most antidepressants normalize both the decreased serotonergic and dysregulated nonadrenergic function. It is thought that these abnormalities occur only during the depressive episode. Increased cholinergic sensitivity is found during and after many depressions (Dilsaver, 1986). Many of the relatives of depressed patients have this increased cholinergic sensitivity, including those who have never had depression. This cholinergic sensitivity may create a vulnerability to depression and underlie a trait abnormality in many people with depression.

Abnormalities in endocrine challenge tests (such as the dexamethasone suppression test and the TRH–TSH stimulation test) in patients with major depression occur 40–60% of the time. With a variety of endocrine challenges, a lack of the normal response occurs. If suppression normally occurs, nonsuppression or "escape" is seen, and if stimulation usually occurs, blunting of the stimulation manifests in depression. These probably are state abnormalities that normalize with recovery. One explanation for how stressful events may precipitate depression is through release of the hormone, cortisol. A persistent surge of cortisol may trigger or worsen depression in a person who is predisposed because of genetic or psychosocial factors.

Disruptions of the function of the hypothalamic-pituitary-adrenal (HPA) axis appear to be an important feature of mood disorders, and some work suggests that different types of HPA axis dysregulation may be present in different forms of depression. Melancholic depression appears to be associated with a relative hypercortisolism and overactivity of the HPA axis, while individuals with atypical depression may have lower cortisol levels and a relative underactivity of the HPA axis. These different neuroendocrine phenotypes are associated with different health risks and different symptom clusters. However, no routine evaluations of cortisol are recommended in screening for depressive disorders. Rather an awareness that different disease states may be associated with different neuroendocrine profiles may help providers in selecting treatments for patients and advising patients about other health risks. If features of an endocrine disorder are present in addition to depressive symptoms, then consultation with an endocrinologist is recommended.

A routine screening of thyroid stimulating hormone (TSH) and Free T4 (thyroxine) is recommended when patients present with new onset psychiatric symptoms. Treating hypothyroidism is recommended when this condition is discovered in a patient with a mood disorder. There is an association between mood disorders and a positive anti-thyroid antibody status. People who are positive for thyroperoxidase (TPO) antibodies are more likely to suffer depression and anxiety. If the TSH is normal, but symptoms consistent with hypothyroidism are present in a depressed patient (weight gain, fatigue, hair loss, etc.), it may be reasonable to assess the antibody status of the patient as there can be a wide range of subclinical hypothyroidism prior to a diagnosis of Hashimoto's disease, and some patients who are antibody positive but have normal TSH may still benefit from treatment.

Psychosocial Factors

The *loss of either the mother or father* during the first 5 years of life, or the loss of the father between the ages of 10 and 14, is associated with increased risk of adult depression. Losses during these time periods are also later associated with increased doctor visits (help-seeking behavior), whether or not the patient is depressed. In adulthood, although many different kinds of stressful events can contribute to depression, losses are most directly associated with increased risk for depression.

Little or no support system leads to a much higher risk for depression. Social support has been shown to mitigate the effects of negative stressors such as losses.

Sexual, physical, and/or emotional abuse leads to a much higher adult rate of major depression as well as to a variety of other psychiatric disorders. Children in environments in which their self-esteem is constantly threatened, or in which a very negative view of life is communicated, are more likely to become depressed as adults.

A *biopsychosocial continuum of response vulnerabilities* is always present. One person might carry a very high genetic biological risk for depression and need little environmental stress to precipitate the disorder, whereas another person may have a high psychological risk for depression and need little genetic predisposition. Most individuals are likely to fall between these two poles on the continuum.

Psychosocial Theories

Despite the variety of psychosocial theories of depression, their differences often rest more in language than content. Most of these theories involve the factors of *loss* and *self-esteem*. Many types of losses can trigger depression. Besides the obvious—deaths, separations—depression may occur after the removal of a bodily organ or on the anniversary of a personally significant loss. A manifestly good development may bring on a depression. For example, after winning a Pulitzer prize, a once-obscure writer is suddenly inundated with admirers—groupies, money-management types, the cocktail set, publishers—all wanting a "piece" of him. Unable to meet everyone's expectations, dissatisfied with his own inability to write another masterpiece, and missing his old friends, he becomes depressed. Loss can also trigger mania.

Psychoanalytic theories. Freud proposed that an *early severe loss* or trauma during childhood causes a vulnerability to depression. Although subsequent research has tended to support this hypothesis, the research has also raised doubts about how much and how frequently early loss contributes *specifically* to depression. Brown (1961) showed that the loss of a parent during childhood occurred in 51% of adults with depression and in 16% of controls. In contrast, Roy (1985) demonstrated that early parental separation and loss accounted for relatively few additional cases, that ages 5–11 were most crucial, and curiously, that loss of a father was slightly more psychonoxious than losing a mother.

In *Mourning and Melancholia* (1917), Freud observed that the normal mourner accepts both positive and negative feelings about the deceased, whereas the melancholic mourner cannot tolerate or consciously acknowledge any negative feelings toward the deceased; this *"ambivalence toward the lost object"* induces guilt and depression. Mourning is a reaction to a realistic loss, but melancholia may be a reaction to an imagined, or an unconsciously exaggerated, loss.

A controversial yet widely touted hypothesis is that depression results from "retroflexed anger"—that is, patients turn their rage against a lost object onto themselves. Today, hundreds of therapists hear a similar story: A patient's fiancé suddenly breaks their engagement, but rather than getting angry at the fiancé, the patient becomes depressed and says things like "This proves I'm unworthy." The concept of retroflexed anger neatly dovetails with the inverse relationship between suicide and homicide; it may also account for the low self-esteem of the depressed, for why some believe that they deserve punishment, and for why many are terrified of expressing and experiencing anger. The Catch-22 is, the more patients with depression express their fury, the more depressed they become—it's "proof" they're terrible people—and the more likely they are to commit suicide. Retroflexed anger may be germane to some depressions as either a contributor or a consequence; it may be more prominent in people who normally blame themselves for everything.

Ego psychologists initially claimed that many patients with depression were "mourning" more for their *loss of self-esteem* than for the loss of the object itself. Whether the object is a job or a lover, when patients believe their self-esteem is an extension of that lost object, then depression becomes increasingly likely. Later, ego psychologists stressed that depression arose from a discrepancy between the patient's actual and idealized self-esteem.

Many *behaviorists* view depression as a product of *"learned helplessness"*—that is, patients experience themselves as continually trying and failing. Repeated loss of positive reinforcement and concomitant increase of negative reinforcement results in discouragement, giving up (which further reduces rewards), and depression (Abramson, Seligman, & Teasdale, 1978; Beck, Rush, Shaw, & Emery, 1979).

The *cognitive theory* of depression emphasizes the patient's conscious thoughts. Patients with depression display the "cognitive triad": a negative view of self, the world, and their future. They think of themselves as inadequate, their world as unrewarding, their future as hopeless. Cognitive theory claims that these attitudes distort patients' perceptions of reality and cause depression; however, other studies suggest that the cognitive triad is a consequence of depression.

CLINICAL COURSE

Major Depression

The age of onset is equally distributed throughout the adult lifecycle; age 40 is the mean, and it can arise during childhood and infancy. Major depression usually appears over days or weeks, but it may erupt in a day or evolve over months or years. Anxiety, phobia, panic, or dysthymia may predate a major depression. The sequence of events leading to a depression should be precisely determined, since it is a mistake to assume that, for example, a person's termination from his job caused his depression, whereas it was actually his depression (and poor functioning) that caused the termination. Some depressions arise out of the blue, some after a precipitant. If untreated, major depression usually persists 6–13 months. By 1 year, 85% of major depressions have remitted. Most episodes of treated depression last about 3 months. As the course progresses, episodes tend to be more frequent and last longer. Recurrences are common and typically there will be six episodes over a 20-year period. Single and recurrent episodes of major depression may be slightly different species. Roughly half of all people with a major depression never have another episode. Of those having a second episode, 50% have a third one, and so on. People with recurrent major depressions continue to have about a 10% risk of their next episode being manic, no matter how many depressive episodes they have had. They also have more difficulties between depressive episodes. Recurrence rates are greatest during the first 4–6 months after recovery; thereafter, the further away from the episode, the lower the chance of a recurrence. For individuals with major (or bipolar) depression, the risk of future episodes increases if they have a history of dysthymic disorder, a persistent dysthymia after a major or bipolar depression, a substance abuse or anxiety disorder, an older age of onset, or a greater number of previous episodes. Roughly 20% of patients with major depression become chronically depressed. For the vast majority, major depression is an episodic condition where outside of distinct periods of illness, patients may be productive with few if any residual symptoms.

Bipolar Disorder

On average, bipolar disorder arises by age 30, although on rare occasions it may begin in octogenarians. First-onset mania in older adults is almost always associated with medical conditions, particularly neurological disease or medications. Mania more often precedes depression. Whereas most bipolar depressions emerge over days or weeks, mania can erupt suddenly. The most common prodromal symptoms of mania are increased activity, elevated mood, and a decreased need for sleep. On the average, these develop about 3 weeks prior to the manic episode (Molnar, Feeney, & Fava, 1988). If biologically untreated, bipolar depressions typically persist 6–9 months, manic episodes, 2–6 weeks. As with major depression, almost half of those with bipolar disorder experience more than one episode. One-third of all patients have chronic symptoms and evidence of social decline. However, good prognostic indicators are short duration of manic episodes, advanced age of onset, few suicidal thoughts, and few coexisting psychiatric or medical problems.

The sequence and frequency of manic and depressive episodes vary: Some patients have three or four depressive periods before exhibiting mania; others alternate between highs and lows. Some have an episode every 10 years, whereas others, known as "rapid cyclers," have four episodes of either mania or depression in a single year. The episodes of bipolar disorder tend to become more frequent and longer over time.

The term *bipolar* is misleading because it implies that mania and depression are opposites and that euthymia occurs between them. Yet careful observation reveals that mania and depression are closer to each other than to normality. For instance, it's common to see a depressive affect intrude on mania; a patient will be talking a mile a minute, when for no apparent reason he cries a eulogy to a long-departed mother, and then just as suddenly, starts imitating a famous entertainer. It is also common to see mania and depression alternate, with no intervening period of normalcy. There is also an increasingly recognized species of mania called "dysphoric mania" or mixed manic–depression, in which people have manic and depressive symptoms at the same time (or ultra-rapid cycling). Sometimes mixed episodes are misdiagnosed as treatment-resistant depression. Patients who experience mixed episodes have higher rates of suicidality or substance abuse.

Dysthymic Disorder

The persistent affective disorders are classified here because of evidence from family studies that they are genetically related to the mood disorders, and because they are sometimes amenable to the same treatments as mood disorders. This disorder typically emerges during early adult life, although it occurs in children and adolescents. Its onset is gradual and often hard to pinpoint. Its course is chronic, its symptoms fluctuating.

Cyclothymic Disorder

The age of onset for cyclothymic disorder is most often in early adulthood. It begins gradually and persists chronically. Intermixing or alternating hypomanic and dysphoric symptoms may fluctuate within hours, days, weeks, or months. Intermittent euthymic periods may exist for up to 2 months. Because the mood swings are relatively mild and the periods of mood elevation may be pleasant, cyclothymia frequently eludes medical attention. Also, in some cases the mood change, although present, is less prominent than cyclical changes in activity level, self-confidence, sociability, and goal-directed behavior. The mood swings may persist throughout adult life, cease temporarily or permanently, or develop into a more severe mood episodes. This disorder is common in the relatives of patients with bipolar disorder and so it is not surprising that some individuals with cyclothymia eventually develop bipolar illness.

COMPLICATIONS

Suicide is one of the leading causes of death worldwide, resulting in about 1 million deaths annually, and within the top 12 leading causes of death in the United States. Suicide is committed eventually by 15% of patients with severe depression, that is, major or bipolar depression. It rarely occurs with dysthymic and cyclothymic disorders. Men commit suicide nearly three times as often as women, whereas women make suicide attempts much more often than men. Some of these differences can be explained by the fact that men are more likely to choose violent, highly lethal methods (e.g., shooting, hanging, jumping, crashing), whereas women more often overdose. More than 90% of those who commit suicide have a diagnosable psychiatric disorder, with major and bipolar depressions accounting for 50–70%, making depression the chief cause of suicide. Alcoholism and schizophrenia are the second and third leading causes, respectively. Although the evaluation of suicide is discussed in Chapter 2, it's worth repeating that, contrary to myth, those who talk about suicide *are* more likely to commit suicide.

The pathophysiology of suicide (and depression) is likely to be related to serotonin depletion and reduction in the 5-HT receptors in the brain's limbic system and frontal cortex. Because of the favorable safety profile of these medications and effectiveness in treating depression, SSRI antidepressants have been increasingly prescribed and credited with the reduction in suicide rates over the last few years. After the recent advisories by the FDA that SSRIs may increase the risk of suicidal thoughts in youth and young adults, there has been a reduction in the use of these medications. This reduction in antidepressant prescriptions has coincided with an 8% increase in suicide in 10- to 24-year-olds for 2003–2004 after a 13-year decline. A causal relationship is suspected.

Substance abuse, particularly alcoholism, is a frequent complication in all mood disorders. Patients "medicate" their dysphorias with alcohol, cocaine, amphetamines, and less often with marijuana and hypnoanxiolytics. Convinced they're immune from danger and oblivious to their own limitations, patients with hypomania or mania take drugs to remain "up." *Death* from physical illness is four times more prevalent among patients with major depression. In adults, this prevalence is not accounted for by the increased suicide rate, but rather by a large increase in the usual "natural" deaths from illnesses such as cancer and cardiovascular disease (Murphy et al., 1987). The reasons for this increase are unknown, but it is known that impairments in the immune system and disturbances in heart rhythms are more likely to occur during depressive episodes.

Impaired judgment and *lousy decisions* are common. If a depressed patient thinks she's a terrible person or, because of anhedonia, feels "no love," she may try to divorce a loving spouse; if he's sure he's incompetent, he may quit a perfectly good job. People with bipolar disorder may also initiate divorce and quit work, thinking they are too good for their spouse or job. Clinicians should inform patients that their pathological moods are distorting their judgment and that they should postpone major decisions until they've recovered. *Occupational and academic failures* result from poor judgment, and more: Depressed patients function slowly, work inefficiently, and display little effort. Neuropsychiatric tests show that their abstract thinking abilities, attention spans, and short-term (but not long-term) memories are impaired. Patients with depression and/or mania often trap colleagues into covering for them.

Familial consequences, including an increased rate of marital difficulties, separation, and divorce, occur in major depression. Although the mechanisms are unclear, roughly 40% of children with a depressed parent develop major, longstanding impairments, especially mood, anxiety, and conduct disorders. Because of the increased risk of inheritance and the long-term burdens of serious mood disorders, some afflicted individuals consider not getting married or not having children.

In summary, mood disorders have an enormous impact on a person's life. When compared with 10 major medical disorders, including heart disease, diabetes, and back pain, depression and cardiac disease were tied for having the worst impact on social, occupational, familial, and physical function.

MANAGEMENT AND TREATMENT

The management and treatment of mood disorders employ one or more of the following interventions: (1) suicide prevention, (2) biotherapies, (3) psychotherapies, and (4) family involvement. These interventions tend to be used in this sequence; for example, preventing suicide precedes psychotherapy. However, these interventions are also interrelated such that, for example, suicide prevention often entails family involvement. Each of these interventions serves a different purpose: Biotherapies rectify symptoms by correcting biochemical abnormalities, psychotherapies address issues arising from and contributing to the disorder, and family involvement can be used to support patients or to remedy pathogenic family systems.

Regardless of the intervention, working with affectively disturbed patients is ultimately rewarding, since most patients recover—though in the short run, treatment may frustrate the most experienced of therapists and evoke considerable countertransference. Patients with depression frequently present with marked dependency, which they themselves disdain, expect others to meet, yet when this occurs, they get furious. Relatives may respond with pity, which patients will overtly reject yet feel they deserve. This dynamic of dependency strivings, anger over deprivation, anticipated rejection, and "entitled pity" leads clinicians to feel guilty, helpless, angry, and drained— feelings therapists should keep in check. Clinicians, often feeling that nothing they do for these patients is ever enough, should be careful not to try to run patients' lives. Therapists should avoid overpromising; they should dispense hope, not saccharine. Especially during the more impaired or serious periods of the disorder, therapists should be warm, "real," and accepting. To quote Sederer (1983):

> The therapist must be able to bear the patient's pain with him; extra time may be needed for this affect to emerge, especially in view of the depressed patient's psychomotor retardation. . . . The depressed patient feels unworthy of and unable to reciprocate excessive warmth and tends to withdraw and feel worse when this is offered. Excessive humor on the part of the therapist denies the patient his grief and is devaluing. (p. 22)

If therapists identify with patients who have depression, they will begin to feel depressed and trapped by the nihilistic view of the world. Instead, empathy is needed, allowing appreciation and acceptance of patients' feelings, but in the larger context of a more objective viewpoint.

Suicide Evaluation, Management, and Prevention

As indicated above, 15% of patients with severe depression will eventually die by suicide. This accounts for about 60% of all suicides. Approximately 80% of people who kill themselves have seen their physicians in the previous 6 months, often for symptoms of major depressive disorder (e.g., insomnia, decreased energy) or exaggerations of ongoing medical complaints. Therefore, all patients with depression should be asked about suicidal ideation. This can be done by approximations. One recommended questioning sequence follows:

1. "Do you sometimes have a feeling that life isn't worth living, or do you think about death much?"
2. "Do you sometimes think that if you died tomorrow from an accident or illness, that it just wouldn't matter?" (This is *passive* suicidal ideation.)
3. "Have you had thoughts of killing yourself?" (This is *active* suicidal ideation.)
4. "Have you thought of a way or plan to kill yourself?" (Is there a detailed plan, with the means to carry it out, and without the possibility of rescue?)

If patients answer yes to passive but not to active suicidal ideation, for now they are probably low risk, unless they are engaging in high-risk behavior (e.g., auto racing). If patients answer yes to the third question, further risk assessment is in order. Many patients who acknowledge ideation are at minimal risk if they have strong reasons for not committing suicide. Ask patients, "What has kept you from acting on your suicidal ideas?" Patients who respond that they could not actually do it because of their religious beliefs or because of their families are usually at lower risk. Similarly, patients who experience suicidal ideation as ego alien and frightening are at lower risk. The higher demographic risks are male, white, increasing age over 45 years, alone, socially alienated, with chronic disease, obsessive–compulsive or perfectionist tendencies, and/or substance abuse issues. People who have already made a suicide attempt are at higher risk, and, perhaps the best predictor of suicide is a prior attempt. The presence of a major psychiatric illness and family history of suicide are important risk factors.

How can actively suicidal patients be managed? Suicidal impulses, like alcoholic impulses, can be managed better 1 day or 1 week at a time. Many suicidal patients can agree to go for 1 or 2 weeks or a month without killing themselves, but cannot agree to *never* kill themselves. This "no suicide decision," which they make for themselves (and not as a promise to the clinician or anyone else), can help to buy time while treatment is started (Drye, Goulding, & Goulding, 1973). It should also include a "no-escape clause": that is, "no matter what happens." This allows for crisis situations (e.g., a cocaine-using boyfriend leaving the relationship). Suicidal ideation should be reassessed at least weekly and at the end of the agreed-upon time period, and if patients are still suicidal, a new "no suicide decision" should be made. Patients who are unreliable because of substance abuse or personality disorders, or who indicate that a week is too long to defer suicide, require expert evaluation and possible hospitalization.

The clinician's next priority is to prevent suicide, which in most cases entails breaking the patient's "inertia cycle." When they finally seek professional help, most suicidal patients have been mired in painful, unproductive ruminations that have intensified their helplessness. One way to avert suicide and to stop this inertia is to hospitalize the patient. This key decision may depend less on the patient's actual suicide potential and more on his or her network of support. It's crucial to immediately involve the patient's family or close friends, not only to determine how well they can care for the patient, but also to teach them how to be extensions of the treatment team—how to mobilize the patient, what warning signs to look for, what to do with medications, what to discuss (and not discuss) with the patient, and so on.

Interrupting the inertia cycle is the start to treatment, not its end, and a good place to start is to assign patients household chores. No matter how mundane this sounds, patients feel that "at last" something is happening, that they are a part of it, and that they are finally "giving" instead of just "getting." Outpatients should have follow-up appointments within days, not weeks. Until the first appointment, the therapist can have the patient telephone, if only for 3 minutes a day. Since a 10-day supply of tricyclic antidepressants ingested all at once can be lethal, only a few days' worth of pills should be prescribed, or low-lethality antidepressants such as SSRIs should be substituted. Two medications are reported in the literature to be antisuicidal. Clozapine carries an FDA-approved indication for preventing suicide in patients with schizophrenia or schizoaffective disorder. Lithium has been reported to reduce risk of suicide as well as suicide attempts by as much as 80% in patients with bipolar disorder.

Potentially suicidal patients might also be reminded that "suicide is a permanent solution to a temporary problem," and that patients with depression, after they are successfully treated, invariably stop feeling suicidal.

Biological Treatments

The biological treatment of mood disorders includes SSRIs, SNRIs, heterocyclic antidepressants (mainly TCAs), atypical antidepressants (bupropion, trazodone, mirtazapine), MAOIs, mood stabilizers (lithium and anticonvulsants), atypical or traditional antipsychotics, augmentation agents (e.g., triiodothyronine), electroconvulsive therapy (ECT), and vagal nerve stimulation (VNS). The therapeutic categories and side effects of medication are outlined in Chapter 6, and their applications are discussed below. Patients need to be told that none of these medications causes physical or psychological dependency. In regard to tolerance, over time these medications may "poop out" or stop working (tachyphylaxis) even though they are faithfully taken (adherence) and properly dosed.

Major depression. Considering patients with *all* types of major depression, 78% improve with ECT, 60–70% improve with antidepressants (heterocyclic, atypical, MAOIs, SNRIs, SSRIs), and 23% improve with placebo alone. Of the seven well-controlled studies comparing ECT and TCAs, four showed no difference and three favored ECT. Nonetheless, because ECT is more inconvenient to administer and ominous to laypeople, antidepressant medications are usually the first biological treatment for major depression. In general, patients who benefit from antidepressants have *biological signs* of depression, whereas those without biological signs do not.

• *TCAs.* The predictors of response to TCA antidepressants include insomnia, anorexia, psychomotor retardation, anhedonia, insidious onset, and one puzzling nonbiological predictor: guilt (Jewish, Catholic, or Protestant guilt— it doesn't matter). It also doesn't matter whether or not the depression has been environmentally triggered, or whether it is "understandable." If a patient lost her job and then developed major depression with its accompanying biological symptoms, antidepressants still work. One or more atypical and reverse biological signs, including hypersomnia, hyperphagia, profound anergy, mood reactivity, rejection sensitivity, and nocturnal worsening of mood, appear to reduce effectiveness of TCAs to 50%, whereas SSRIs and MAOIs may retain their 70% effectiveness.

• *SSRIs.* When choosing an antidepressants, it makes sense to begin with an SSRI because of lower side effects (tolerability), easy dosing, and safety even in overdose (high therapeutic index). The SSRIs (fluoxetine, sertraline, citalopram, paroxetine, fluvoxamine) usually don't have any of the tricyclic or heterocyclic side effects. Furthermore, the starting dose is often sufficient to treat a depression. The SSRIs may perform better than the tricyclics in patients with reverse vegetative symptoms and atypical depressions. When looking at the grouped data in clinical trials, no SSRI has demonstrated clear efficacy over another; however, individuals may respond much better to one antidepressant over another even in the same category. Often the initial choice of antidepressant is based on side effect profile or previous response by the person or a family member to the particular medication. Despite relative safety in overdose, SSRIs have been reported to increase suicidal thinking and impulsiveness, especially early in the treatment course, for a small (2%) but statistically significant number of adolescents and young adults. This observation may particularly apply to younger people whose depression may be of the bipolar variety but not yet accurately diagnosed, not fully developed, or otherwise undetected.

• *Monoamine-oxidase inhibitors.* MAOIs have the same efficacy as other antidepressants in treating typical depressions, but they do not lose efficacy in depressions with one or more atypical symptoms (hypersomnia, hyperphagia, mood worse at night, severe anergy, rejection sensitivity, mood reactivity, or in depression with panic attacks). But MAOIs are rarely chosen first because of dietary concerns: Patients on MAOIs who ingest tyramine-containing foods (e.g., herring, aged cheese, salami) or sympathomimetic drugs (e.g., cocaine, amphetamines, decongestants) can develop a "hypertensive crisis"—soaring blood pressure—that can be life-threatening. MAOIs should be stopped for 2 weeks before the initiation of another type of antidepressant.

In order for any antidepressant to work, patients must be on the *proper dose* for the *proper duration*. Therapeutically effective dosages of SSRIs and TCAs vary from one patient to another. For example, the typical adult dose for a TCA such as imipramine is usually 150–300 mg/day (a third to half this amount for older adults). Moreover, the patient's mood may not begin to lift until she's been on an adequate dose for at least a few weeks. Patients (and relatives) should be told, "Don't give up because you don't feel better in a day or so. Valium acts right away, but antidepressants don't; they usually take 4–6 weeks." Most patients on antidepressants show some improvement before 4 weeks but an adequate trial should last from 4 to 8 weeks.

Despite their overall effectiveness, antidepressants do not completely eliminate symptoms in 25% of patients with major depressions. If patients have not begun to improve after 4 weeks, the options include (1) increasing the dose of the currently prescribed antidepressant; (2) adding lithium or triiodothyronine (T3, a thyroid compound); (3) adding another antidepressant, particularly one that works on a different neurotransmitter system; (4) changing to another category of antidepressant; (5) adding an antipsychotic, especially when psychotic symptoms are present; (6) considering ECT.

Depressed patients without hypothyroidism or anti-thyroid antibodies sometimes benefit from treatment with thyroid hormone. Women may be slightly more likely to respond to augmentation of other mood medications with thyroid hormone. In unipolar depression, augmenting antidepressants with thyroid hormone may accelerate treatment response. In addition, supraphysiologic doses of thyroid hormone have been shown to aid with mood stabilization in rapid cycling bipolar disorder. Even when given in higher than usual amounts, thyroid treatment of mood disorders is generally well tolerated.

• *Antipsychotics.* Patients with psychotic depression respond only about one-third of the time to antidepressants alone and just under half the time to antipsychotics alone. Combining the two treatments results in 65–75% response rates. Failing this combination or if a faster response is necessary, ECT is the preferred treatment.

• *Benzodiazepines.* Supplemental low-dose benzodiazepines may initially alleviate prominent anxiety and insomnia, but typically should be discontinued after a couple of weeks because of tolerance to their beneficial effects and the risk for dependency.

Patients should remain on antidepressants until they have been symptom-free for at least 16–20 weeks and until stressors in their lives are down to manageable levels. Discontinuing medication at the time of a child-custody battle would be a bad idea. To encourage staying on medication, patients should be informed that there is a 50% chance of relapse if they stop sooner than 6 months after complete symptom resolution. Mild symptoms are just as predictive of relapse as major symptoms, so that even when major symptoms have disappeared, the presence of minor symptoms indicates that the disorder has not run its full course (Prien & Kupfer, 1986). This is all about homeostasis—the brain tends to maintain itself where it's at. If not given enough time to reset its neurotransmitters and receptors, it tends to revert to the previous settings. Antidepressants should be prescribed for longer periods in patients with more frequent depressive episodes, longer depressive cycles, and an older age of onset. If depression is severe and frequent enough (more than two episodes), prophylactic, long-term antidepressant therapy may be indicated.

TCAs should always be discontinued slowly—no faster than 25 mg/day; they should never be stopped abruptly. If they are, in two to four days patients may experience insomnia, nightmares, or nausea and a flu-like syndrome without a fever. Fluoxetine probably can be stopped all at once, because it stays in the blood for weeks. But when the shorter-acting SSRIs such as paroxetine are abruptly withdrawn, nausea and headache may ensue.

• *Electroconvulsive therapy.* ECT, as it is now administered, is the most effective of all the antidepressant treatments, with nearly 80% responding. Historically, ECT was frightening. Patients would receive over 20 treatments for just about any condition; they'd convulse wildly, fracture spines, lose memories, and be dazed silly. Those days are gone. Today ECT is a safe and effective treatment for severe depressions (and sometimes for life-threatening mania). Usually six to twelve treatments, one every other day, are given. Fractures and wild convulsions no longer occur; memory loss and confusion are either nonexistent or minimal and short-lived. ECT may work by massively discharging or releasing neurotransmitters throughout the cortex and subcortex. (It does not scare patients into getting better—sham ECT doesn't work.) Perhaps more importantly, the seizure stimulates the hypothalamus to discharge its hormones, which stimulate the anterior pituitary and inhibits the discharge of cortisol.

Now patients are given a short-acting anesthetic (about 10 minutes), oxygen, and a temporary muscle paralyzer to prevent fractures. The seizure is monitored with an EEG because the motor seizure is masked. The convulsion usually lasts from 25 to 60 seconds. Convulsions less than 25 seconds have less therapeutic effect. Several minutes later patients awaken from the anesthesia with no memory of the shock.

First-time observers of ECT invariably describe it as "underwhelming." Patients, too, are surprised they don't feel anything, and why should they?—

brain tissue is free of pain fibers. A survey of patients who received ECT revealed that two-thirds found going to the dentist more upsetting than getting ECT. The mortality rate from ECT is lower than for tonsillectomy, the former ranging from 0.008 to 0.05%. Indeed, the most dangerous aspect of ECT is not ECT per se, but the anesthesia. The main side effects of ECT are short-term memory loss and confusion; these may not occur or they may be so bad that the patient urinates in public or can't name his or her spouse. These problems, which are greatly minimized by unilateral ECT, significantly decrease within 2 weeks of the final treatment. When compared to bilateral, unilateral ECT is less effective when using the same amount of electrical energy. ECT does not cause any permanent brain damage or memory loss. Six months later, patients who have had ECT do as well on memory and other neuropsychological tests as do people who have never had ECT. It is considered a safe and effective treatment for major depression, mania, and schizophrenia. Relative contraindicators to the use of ECT include space-occupying lesions, increased intracerebral pressure, or recent myocardial infarction. Transcranial magnetic stimulation is still being studied as a possible alternative to ECT but is not consistently effective.

• *Vagal nerve stimulation (VNS)*. An electric device is surgically implanted and the left vagus nerve is electrically stimulated at the cervical level. This expensive FDA-approved procedure is reserved for patients with chronic or recurrent depression who are not responsive to all other treatments.

Bipolar disorder. Whether the patient presents manic or depressed, treatment should begin with a bone fide mood stabilizer, either lithium or an anticonvulsant. The use of antidepressants in bipolar disorder is controversial because they may be ineffective for depression and may actually increase cycling of moods, thereby worsening the long-term prognosis of this illness. If an antidepressant is prescribed during a depressive phase, it is generally recommended that it be tapered and discontinued once the depression is controlled. Lithium is effective in bipolar depression but has a more robust impact on mania. Lamotrigine may have more antidepressant activity than other anticonvulsants and is effective in both preventing and treating depressive episodes. Some of the newer antipsychotics seem to have some mood-stabilizing and antidepressant effects and may be used in combination with mood stabilizers. Quetiapine is currently the only second-generation (atypical) antipsychotic approved for depression.

For the manic phase, the effectiveness of lithium has been documented for about 50 years. Divalproex and carbamazepine have also been supported by about 20 years of clinical study (lamotrigine is the new kid on the block). The atypical antipsychotics (aripiprazole, olanzapine, quetiapine, risperidone, and ziprasidone) are FDA approved for acute mania. As in bipolar depression, lithium or divalproex sodium may be used in combination with an antipsychotic for severe mania, rapid cycling, or mixed states. Patients with mixed episodes respond more slowly to, and experience less improvement with, lithium, and divalproex sodium may be more effective in these instances. Benzodiazepines may be added temporarily for resting, sleep, or reducing anxiety. Once the acute episodes (mania, depressions, or mixed) are under control, the same medications are often continued to prevent return episodes (maintenance pharmacotherapy).

Lithium is a salt, much like table salt, except that lithium replaces sodium. The immediate predecessor to the beverage 7-Up contained lithium and was marketed as a lithium soda that took the "ouch out of the grouch." Trace amounts of lithium are in the water supply, a tidbit that encourages some patients to reason, "It's okay to take lithium because it is a natural substance and not a drug."

Lithium is best for preventing mania and usually effective for preventing bipolar depression. Acute bipolar depression is often treated with lithium and antidepressants, whereas acute mania responds best to lithium with the addition of benzodiazepines for agitation or antipsychotics for psychosis. Although lithium usually takes 10 days to take effect, the benzodiazepines and antipsychotics can calm people with mania within hours for up to a few days. One to three treatments of ECT can be effective in treating mania that does not respond quickly to medication. There is evidence that with each new episode, the bipolar disorder worsens both in frequency and severity. Some recommend that most patients should stay on lithium for life to prevent this deteriorating course.

Overall, a majority of patients with bipolar disorder substantially improve on lithium. A common problem, especially with "rapid cyclers," is the occurrence of mania or depression in lithium-treated patients. When this happens, first serum lithium levels are checked to see if patients are actually taking the drug and have a high enough lithium level to treat an acute episode. Bipolar patients often stop lithium because they miss their highs—can you blame them? Second, patients' thyroid functioning is checked, since hypothyroidism mimics the symptoms of depression and may result from prolonged lithium therapy. Third, if patients become depressed, an antidepressant may be added. Although usually helpful, giving antidepressants to patients with bipolar depression may increase the rapidity of cyclic mood changes or "switch" patients to mania. (Bupropion may have a lower risk of switching patients.) Fourth, if none of the above works, or if patients cannot tolerate lithium's side effects, anticonvulsants divalproex sodium, lamotrigine, or carbamazepine are prescribed. Divalproex sodium can significantly decrease mania in 5 days.

Psychotherapies

The psychotherapy of mood disorders can help patients to (1) learn the "facts" about their disorder, (2) feel less alone, (3) cope better with their disorder, (4) identify and avert situations likely to rekindle another episode, (5) abort episodes that have just begun by early symptom recognition, (6) view themselves and their world more rationally and constructively, (7) improve interpersonal relations, and (8) address the problems plaguing them.

Which of these goals are pursued depend primarily on patients' current mental state. If they are in an acute manic or depressive episode, psychotherapy should stress support more than insight, since they lack the attention span, abstract thinking abilities, and emotional perspective to use insight appropriately. For example, a man with major depression who "suddenly discovers" his sexual feelings toward his daughter will not apply this realization to understand his marital problem but to "prove his depravity." Patients with melancholia or psychotic depression are especially unable to profit from insight, and if anything, will use it for self-flagellation. Cognitive–behavioral or interpersonal psychotherapies benefit about 70% of patients with mild to moderate depression. These psychotherapies work as well but more slowly than antidepressants. Typically, 12–16 weeks are needed. Psychotherapy is indicated if patients with mild to moderate depression prefer this treatment. Patients with severe and/or psychotic depressions or with personality disorders don't do as well with psychotherapy and should be treated with antidepressants first. Among the more commonly used therapies are the following:

Interpersonal psychotherapy (ITP). This therapy is based on the theory that almost all people who become depressed have a major interpersonal problem — conflicts with a significant other, a boss, difficult role transitions, or deficient social skills and the consequent social isolation. These problem areas are identified and addressed. Instead of concentrating on intrapsychic material with a goal of personality change, ITP focuses on interpersonal matters, both inside and outside of therapy. Some studies have shown that combining ITP and medications yields superior results and lower dropout rates than either treatment alone especially in more seriously depressed patients (Schramm et al., 2007). By teaching patients how to cope with problems, ITP may reduce the risk of relapse. The conduct of ITP has been detailed in a manual (Klerman et al., 1984).

Behavior therapies. These approaches assume that depressed patients lack positive reinforcement and would benefit from being taught to identify the relation between events and feelings, to maximize praise from self and others, to avoid self-punishment, to set realistic goals, and to improve social skills. Behavior therapy for depression is detailed in a manual (Lewinsohn et al., 1984).

Cognitive therapy (CT). Because CT focuses on more accessible conscious and preconscious material, it can be used by many more patients with depression than can traditional psychoanalytic treatments. The actual technique of CT is summarized in Chapter 5, and its use for depression is best detailed by Beck et al. (1979). It is usually combined with behavioral therapy.

Group therapy. Group behavioral, cognitive, and psychodynamic therapy may be only slightly less effective than their individual versions.

Brief psychodynamic psychotherapy. The goal of this therapy is to resolve core conflicts based on personality and situational variables. Compared to the other therapies, it may be somewhat less effective for depression. Treatment manuals are available (Luborsky, 1984; Malan, 1979; Sifneos, 1979; Strupp & Binder, 1984).

Marital therapy. Marital therapy may treat both the depression and the marital and family problems by modifying negative interaction patterns and increasing mutually supportive aspects of the relationship (Barbato & D'Avanzo, 2007). Marital discord or separation often precedes depression, persists after depression, and frequently precedes relapses. In more than half of distressed couples who are considering, or are in the process of, separation and divorce, one spouse will be clinically depressed. This form of therapy might be considered as the main psychotherapy or as an adjunct with a patient who has both depression and marital discord.

Family Involvement

The importance of involving family members cannot be overemphasized. Like therapists, family members often feel that their advice and support are ignored, but unlike therapists, family members *live* with the relative who has depression, and doing so can drain the most caring and resilient of loved ones. Perhaps this accounts for higher divorce rates and higher rates of psychopathology in spouses of depressed patients.

There are three general therapeutic reasons for involving relatives: (1) to support the patient, (2) to support the family, and (3) to treat the family. During acute affective episodes, therapists should employ family members as extensions of the treatment. Relatives should be told the "facts" about mood disorders—their symptoms, natural history, genetic risks, prognosis, and treatment. They should be counseled on how to respond to the patient's disorder. They should be cautioned about getting sucked into the patient's pessimistic views, as well as to understand the limits of what they can do to alleviate their loved one's misery. By helping the family help the patient, the therapist helps support the family.

> Citing confidentiality, some patients with depression seek to prevent any family involvement. Although confidentiality is usually respected, when a patient's *judgment is impaired*, maintaining confidentiality may be senseless and harmful. Some patients exclude relatives so that the relatives "won't be contaminated by me"; others "use" confidentiality to deny that they are ill and need help; still others invoke confidentiality as a way of avoiding intimacy. In each case, the therapist must assess what information should be shared with the family and what should remain private. That a patient has sexual fantasies about aardvarks is nobody's business; that he's contemplating suicide or selling the family business is!
>
> After a severe episode has passed, there are times when it is best to examine the family's or couple's role in causing or aggravating the patient's depression. This possibility is especially important to consider with female patients, since they tend to assume full responsibility for the problem, which is actually the entire family's. As a result, these patients seek individual treatment when couple or family therapy would be more appropriate.
>
> Family treatment is also of special use for teenagers with depression, because they often come from families with a low tolerance for individuation and anger. The kid will rebel but succumb in despair. One parent might frequently abuse substances while the other is chronically depressed. A common pattern is for the parents to be furious with each other, yet bait their child by being "injustice collectors" and "grave-diggers"—that is, resurrecting past misdeeds and using them as accusations. Therapists should help these adolescents distinguish their problems from their parents', while also addressing the depression and substance abuse that usually afflict other family members. Adolescents with depression can be very convincing about the

utter malevolence of their parents. They often tell their own version of the Cinderella story, with them as the victims and the parents as the evil persecutors. This may be an example of the negative thinking of depression, and a face-to-face meeting with the family is needed to see where truth lies.

Finally, in the ultimate tragedy—suicide—clinicians should talk with the family to afford comfort, to prevent others from committing impulsive suicides, to minimize the self-blame of relatives (which might require pointing out to them that suicide is a hostile act because it hurts everyone), and finally, to learn from any therapy mistakes that might have been made. Sometimes lawyers recommend against this approach, but the chances of lawsuit are much higher if the family sees the clinician as cold, distant, or uncaring.

References

Abramson, L.Y., Seligman, M.E., & Teasdale, J. (1978). Learned helplessness in humans Critique and reformulation. *Journal of Abnormal Psychology, 87,* 49–79.

American Psychiatric Association. (2013). *Diagnostic and statistical manual of mental disorders,* 5th ed. Arlington, VA: American Psychiatric Association.

Barbato, A., & D'Avanzo, B. (2007). Efficacy of couple therapy as a treatment for depression. *Journal of Rehabilitation Research and Development, 44*(6), 775–784.

Beck, A.T., Brown, G., Berchick, R.J., Stewart, B.L., & Steer, R.A. (1990). Relationship between hopelessness and ultimate suicide: A replication with psychiatric outpatients. *American Journal of Psychiatry, 147,* 190–195.

Beck, A.T., Rush, A.J., Shaw, B.F., & Emery, G. (1979). *Cognitive therapy of depression: A treatment manual.* New York: Guilford.

Brown, F. (1961). Depression and childhood bereavement. *Journal of Mental Science, 107,* 754–777.

Degner, D., Haust, M., Meller, J., Rüther, E., & Reulbach, U. (2015). Association between autoimmune thyroiditis and depressive disorder in psychiatric outpatients. *European Archives of Psychiatry and Clinical Neuroscience, 265*(1), 67–72. doi: 10.1007/s00406-014-0529-1. Epub 2014 Sep 6.

Dilsaver, S.C. (1986). Cholinergic mechanisms in affective disorders: Future directions for investigation. *Acta Psychiatrica Scandinavica, 74,* 312–334.

Drye, R.C., Goulding, R.L., & Goulding, M.E. (1973). No-suicide decisions: Patient monitoring of suicidal risk. *American Journal of Psychiatry, 130*(2), 171–174.

Ensel, W.M. (1982). The role of age in the relationship of gender and marital status to depression. *Journal of Nervous and Mental Diseases, 170,* 536–543.

Freud, S. (1917). Mourning and melancholia. In E. Jones (Ed.), *Collected papers.* New York: Basic Books.

Gold, P.W., & Chrousos. G.P. (2002). Organization of the stress system and its dysregulation in melancholic and atypical depression: High vs low CRH/NE states. *Molecular Psychiatry, 7*(3), 254–275.

Keller, M.B., Lavori, P.W., Rice, J., Coryell, W., & Hirschfeld, R.M.A. (1986). The persistent risk of chronicity in recurrent episodes of nonbipolar major depressive disorder: A prospective follow-up. *American Journal of Psychiatry, 143,* 24–28.

Klein, D.N., Taylor, E.B., Harding, K., & Dickstein, S. (1988). Double depression and episodic major depression: Demographic, clinical, familial, personality, and socioenvironmental characteristics and short-term outcome. *American Journal of Psychiatry, 145,* 1226–1231.

Klerman, G.L., Weissman, M.M., Rounsaville, B.J., & Chevron, R.S. (1984). *Interpersonal psychotherapy of depression.* New York: Basic Books.

Lewinsohn, P.M., Antonuccio, D.A., Steinmetz, J., & Teri, L. (1984). *The coping with depression course: A psychoeducational intervention for unipolar depression.* Eugene, OR: Castalia.

Lieberman, P.B., & Strauss, J.S. (1984). The recurrence of mania: Environmental factors and medical treatment. *American Journal of Psychiatry, 141,* 77–80.

Łojko, D., & Rybakowski, J.K. (2007). L-thyroxine augmentation of serotonergic antidepressants in female patients with refractory depression. *Journal of Affective Disorders, 103*(1–3), 253–256. Epub 2007 Feb 7.

Luborsky, L. (1984). *Principles of psychoanalytic psychotherapy.* New York: Basic Books.

Malan, D.H. (1979). *Individual psychotherapy and the science of psychodynamics.* Boston: Butterworth.

Merikangas, K.R. (1984). Divorce and assortative mating among depressed patients. *American Journal of Psychiatry, 141,* 74–76.

Molnar, G., Feeney, M.G., & Fava, G.A. (1988). Duration and symptoms of bipolar prodomes. *American Journal of Psychiatry, 145,* 1576–1578.

Murphy, J.M., Monson, R.R., Olivier, D.C., Sobol, A.M., & Leighton, A.H. (1987). Affective disorders and mortality. *American Journal of Psychiatry, 44,* 473–480.

Peselow, E.D., Sanfilipo, M.P., DiFiglia, C., & Fieve, R.R. (1992). Melancholic/endogenous depression and response to somatic treatment and placebo. *American Journal of Psychiatry, 149*(10), 1324–1334.

Pilkonis, P.A., & Frank, E. (1988). Personality pathology in relationship to treatment response. *American Journal of Psychiatry, 145,* 435–441.

Prien, R.F., & Kupfer, D.J. (1986). Continuation drug therapy for major depressive episodes: How long should it be maintained? *American Journal of Psychiatry, 143,* 18–23.

Roy, A. (1985). Early parental separation and adult depression. *Archives of General Psychiatry, 42,* 987–991.

Schramm, E., vanCalker, D., Dykierek, P., Lieb, K., Kech, S., Zobel, I., et al. (2007). An intensive treatment program of interpersonal psychotherapy plus pharmacotherapy for depressed inpatients: Acute and long-term results. *American Journal of Psychiatry, 164,* 768–777.

Sederer, L.I. (1983). Depression. In L.I. Sederer (Ed.), *Inpatient psychiatry: Diagnosis and treatment* (pp. 2–27). Baltimore: Williams & Wilkins.

Sifneos, P. (1979). *Short-term dynamic psychotherapy, evaluation, and technique.* New York: Plenum Press.

Stamm, T.J., Lewitzka, U., Sauer, C., Pilhatsch, M., Smolka, M.N., Koeberle, U., Adli, M., Ricken, R., Scherk, H., Frye, M.A., Juckel, G., Assion, H.J., Gitlin, M., Whybrow, P.C., & Bauer, M. (2014). Supraphysiologic doses of levothyroxine as adjunctive therapy in bipolar depression: A randomized, double-blind, placebo-controlled study. *Journal of Clinical Psychiatry, 75*(2), 162–168. doi: 10.4088/JCP.12m08305.

Strupp, H.H., & Binder, J.L. (1984). *Psychotherapy in a new key: A guide to time-limited dynamic psychotherapy.* New York: Basic Books.

Ward, N.G. (1990). Pain and depression. In J.J. Bonica (Ed.), *The management of pain* (pp. 310–319). Malvern, PA: Lea & Febiger.

World Health Organization. (1992). *The ICD–10 classification of mental and behavioural disorders: Clinical descriptions and diagnostic guidelines.* Geneva: World Health Organization.

14

Anxiety Disorders

A nationwide study of mental disorders in the United States revealed the surprising fact that anxiety disorders, not depression, were the most prevalent psychiatric diagnoses. Anxiety disorders are seen in 18% of the population in a given 12-month period, and about 29% will meet criteria for an anxiety disorder over the course of their lifetime. In general, females seem to have increased prevalence for all anxiety disorders (2:1 ratio). Table 1-3 summarizes the epidemiology of the most frequent anxiety disorders and points to the fact that individuals who have one anxiety disorder are likely to meet criteria for another. This may represent diagnostic overlap as opposed to real co-occurring illness and suggests that certain categories may not be entirely valid discriminations. The various established anxiety disorders while highly comorbid can be distinguished by careful examination of the types of situations that provoke fear or avoidance behaviors and the associated beliefs and thoughts.

In the following discussions, it is assumed that anxiety is not a unitary phenomenon, but rather a complex and variable response that frequently co-occurs with other psychiatric disorders. When predominant, anxiety may define one of the three distinct types of disorders (panic, phobic, or generalized) covered in this chapter. Also covered are separation anxiety disorder and selective mutism that, along with many of the anxiety disorders, originate in childhood and are likely to persist in some form without effective treatment.

Subsequent chapters include other mental disorders with a foundation in anxiety. Obsessive-compulsive type disorders is a grouping based upon predominant repetitive thoughts and behaviors that accompany the anxiety. Anxiety can also manifest as primarily bodily concerns. Actual exposure to a trauma or severely stressful event can lead to another type of anxiety (fear-based). Moreover, if the anxiety (usually traumatic) is overwhelming, the predominant clinical picture can be one of dissociation where there is disrupted integration of memories and a loss of awareness in relation to identity, immediate sensations, and bodily control.

The majority of these anxious individuals are not seen by mental-health professionals, but present instead to medical-care settings with anxiety-related physical complaints or to substance abuse treatment settings. In medical settings, anxiety and anxiety-induced insomnia are the most common psychological complaints. People with anxiety-related problems represent approximately 30% of patients seeking help from primary-care physicians. Frequently, these patients complain about somatic symptoms related to anxiety—for example, heart racing, diarrhea, upset stomach, dizziness, chest tightness—rather than about the anxiety itself. When both the patient and physician maintain a strictly somatic orientation, the underlying anxiety frequently goes unrecognized.

NORMAL VERSUS PATHOLOGICAL ANXIETY

Although everybody experiences anxiety, only some are impaired by it. Anxiety in moderation can be highly adaptive, since optimal learning and adaptation to a variety of problems occur at moderate rather than high or low levels of anxiety/arousal. In addition to arousal, information about what to expect and how to cope with the situation increases adaptiveness. Thus it may be counterproductive for clinicians to provide blanket reassurance or to implore patients "not to worry."

While moderate levels of anxiety may be normal and adaptive, the ability to vary anxiety levels in response to different situations is also desirable. Most people have a characteristic range of anxiety responses that is relatively fixed and can be viewed as a personality trait. This is called "trait anxiety." In clinical settings, when trait anxiety is uniformly high and maladaptive, it is called "chronic anxiety." In contrast to trait anxiety, the anxiety response at a particular time and situation is called "state anxiety"; it is not fixed and is time-limited. In clinical settings, when state anxiety is high and maladaptive, it is referred to as "acute anxiety," which may continue beyond the particular stressful situation and become chronic anxiety.

How is pathological anxiety diagnosed? In diagnosing an anxiety syndrome, the presence of both psychological and physiological symptoms should be ascertained. Psychological symptoms include a subjective sense of apprehension, worry, tension, and uneasiness without a known object or event, or out of proportion to known specific events. Hypervigilance, in which the person becomes excessively attentive to the point of distractibility, irritability, or insomnia, is also frequently seen. Physiological symptoms include motor tension (tremors, twitches, muscle aches, jitters) and autonomic hyperactivity (sweating, heart racing, frequent urination, diarrhea, dizziness, hot or cold spells). For example, these autonomic symptoms are easily set off in most "normal" people without anxiety disorders by the appearance of flashing police car lights in the rearview mirror, combined with the sound of a siren. Making the diagnosis of anxiety can be difficult when patients present only with physiological symptoms, since each of these symptoms may stem from a host of other medical disorders. For example, if patients complain only of headache or diarrhea, direct but supportive questioning may reveal additional symptoms of an anxiety syndrome that they have been reluctant to reveal.

It is important to recognize anxiety in patients who are not complaining of it. High levels of anxiety can exacerbate a wide variety of medical conditions, including gastric and duodenal ulcers, ulcerative colitis, asthma, hypertension, hives, hypoglycemia, and some seizure disorders. It may also be an important component in the aggressive, pressured, "type A" cardiac personality, who is at increased risk for myocardial infarction.

Just eliciting reports of anxiety-related symptoms is not enough, however. Many of these symptoms may exist with normal anxiety. Normal and pathological anxieties are quantitatively and qualitatively different. In anxiety syndromes the anxiety is high and maladaptive; there is decreased functioning because of the anxiety; the physiological symptoms are distressing and disturb normal functioning, and/or the psychological symptoms interfere with the individual's ability to cope. Even when complete information is available, diagnosing anxiety is not a simple task. There are no concrete or cardinal signs; rather, clinicians have to exercise considerable judgment, for example, when concluding that the patient's emotional reactions are out of proportion to the situation.

That relatively few people with anxiety disorders seek treatment is unfortunate, since treatment is usually effective, and without it, less than a quarter of these patients fully recover. In general, the earlier in life patients receive treatment, the better their long-term outcome. Thus, early detection matters.

It may not be essential to distinguish between the terms "fear" and "anxiety." For all intents and purposes it is the difference between a real and an imagined danger. Anxiety is the anticipation of a perceived future threat that is unclear or uncertain. There is the apprehension about an unknown future threat or internal conflict, and the greater stress of not having control. Fear is the actual emotional response to a known or definite threat. There is clear focus on a real external danger—an object of fear that is present and imminent. Both anxiety and fear are alerting signals but they may prepare the person for different actions (preparation versus protection). Too much of either signal may be incapacitating.

THE CAUSES OF ANXIETY

Psychodynamic Theory

At first, Freud postulated that pathological anxiety resulted from a failure to repress painful memories, impulses, or thoughts. When the psychic energy used for this repression is particularly intense, the repressed material breaks into consciousness in a disguised form. For instance, after "discovering" that she was sexually molested as a child, a woman was flooded not with sexual thoughts but with anxiety, difficulty breathing, hyperventilation, and other symptoms of a panic attack. Later, Freud introduced the concept of "signal anxiety," the experience of which enables the person to avoid dangerous thoughts and impulses, through repression, phobic avoidance, compulsions, etc.

Behavioral Theories

In Pavlov's classic experiment, a dog salivated on repeated simultaneous exposure to food and the sound of a bell. When Pavlov removed the food, the dog had become conditioned to salivate on hearing the bell alone. When students walk into a classroom and hear the instructor say "Surprise exam!," immediately the effects of years of associating exams with anxiety trigger anxiety before the content of the exam is even glimpsed. Most behaviorists view conditioning as essential in perpetuating and intensifying anxiety. In the 1970s and 1980s, Kandel (1983) photographed the actual changes in nerve cells produced by behavioral conditioning.

Although many assume that psychic anxiety causes and conditions somatic anxiety, William James (1893) proposed the opposite: That is, subjectively experienced anxiety is a conditioned response to the physical signals of anxiety such as tachycardia and rapid breathing. When injected with norepinephrine (noradrenaline), people report feeling angry if they are watching a fight and more anxiety if they are watching a chase. Here there was no difference in the somatic symptoms but in how they were labeled. Under stress and at rest, anxious subjects have a higher rate of these bodily signals than do controls. Some evidence suggests that patients who report higher levels of psychic anxiety do so, not because they have greater physiological arousal, but because they are more sensitive to perceiving physiological arousal and are more likely to label it *anxiety* instead of *excitement* or *anger*.

Biological Theories

Whereas James, in what came to be known as the James–Lange theory, claimed that peripheral symptoms provoked central anxiety, Cannon (1932) argued that anxiety originates in the brain, which in turn produces peripheral symptoms. In Cannon's view, anxiety and panic are not consequences but causes of tachycardia, sweating, rapid respiration, etc. Yet if anxiety and panic tend to go from the brain to the body (and not vice versa), where and how do these reactions originate in the brain?

During the late 1970s, two major discoveries began to address this question. The first advance (Redmond, 1979) involved the locus coeruleus (LC), a dense cluster of neurons that produces 70% of the brain's norepinephrine. When the LC is stimulated electrically or by the drug yohimbine, anxiety increases; when the LC is inhibited by drugs called "adrenergic blockers" (e.g., clonidine, propranolol), anxiety diminishes. In addition, benzodiazepines and tricyclic antidepressants slow the LC's firing and reduce anxiety.

The second major advance (Skolnick & Paul, 1983) was the discovery of benzodiazepine (BZ) receptors in the brain. BZs (e.g., diazepam) appear to work by augmenting the antianxiety action of the GABA inhibitory system in different parts of the brain, including the limbic system (LS). There is evidence of neuronal connection between the LC and the LS. Many investigators suspect that the LC and BZ receptors pertain to different clinical syndromes—the very ones that Freud and the latest classification systems have characterized!—the LC to panic disorder and the BZ receptors to generalized anxiety disorders (GAD). When stimulated, the LC produces the symptoms and intense somatic signs characteristic of panic anxiety. In contrast, the BZ receptors may play more of a role in GAD.

The third major advance was the discovery that several drugs that primarily affect the serotonin system also affect anxiety disorders (Murphy & Pigott, 1990). Buspirone is mainly used for GAD, whereas the SSRIs are effective in panic, obsessive–compulsive disorder, and GAD. The cell bodies of the nucleus raphe (the brain's main group of serotonin neurons) send projections to the LC, LS, and prefrontal cortex. There are complex interactions among serotonergic, noradrenergic, and GABA-ergic neuronal systems within these brain areas that regulate anxiety.

From a neuroanatomical perspective the amygdala is a brain structure within the limbic system that is necessary for fear. The amygdala provides saliency to incoming stimuli. Fears are learned socially and stored with the assistance of the hippocampus. Once a memory is retrieved it must be stored again in a way that updates and strengthens the memory. Extinction of these fears involves the hippocampus and the ventral medial prefrontal cortex inhibition of the amygdala. Cognitive control for fear seems to be through the dorsolateral prefrontal cortex and is the basis for regulation of emotions through changing our thoughts (cognitive-behavioral therapy). Stress impairs the prefrontal cortex and interferes with attempts for cognitive control of fear and anxiety.

ANXIETY DISORDER DUE TO SUBSTANCES AND OTHER MEDICAL CONDITIONS

One of the first steps in the diagnosis of an anxiety disorder is to determine if it has a known specific cause. If it is caused by a medical condition or is substance-induced, treatment can then be directed at the underlying problem. Several medical conditions can mimic panic and generalized anxiety. Some salient examples follow.

Cardiopulmonary Disorders

(1) Recurrent pulmonary emboli (blood clots in the lungs) produce repeated episodes of acute anxiety with hyperventilation or dyspnea (shortness of breath) in conjunction with decreased oxygen concentration in the blood. Functional anxiety is associated with slightly increased oxygen concentrations. (2) Paroxysmal atrial tachycardia starts with a sudden increase in heart rate and then, unlike panic disorder, a sudden decrease. (3) Chronic obstructive pulmonary disease (COPD) can lead to symptoms of anxiety, which may then be exacerbated by bronchodilators. (4) Silent myocardial infarction, which more often occurs in people with diabetes, produces palpitations, sweating, and dyspnea in the absence of chest pains. (5) In mitral valve prolapse (MVP), diagnosed by auscultation and echocardiogram, the mitral valve doesn't close properly and produces a murmur or "systolic click." It is associated with panic disorder but is *not* a definite cause of panic. Because patients with panic attacks often think that something is wrong with their heart, they go see cardiologists, who on finding MVP, decide that this caused the panic. The evidence does not support this conclusion. MVP sometimes

improves after the panic is satisfactorily treated, suggesting that panic disorder may actually cause some forms of MVP. In others, the MVP remains unchanged, but the panic attacks remain successfully treated. Because the MVP does not need to be corrected in order for the panic attacks to get better, it is unlikely that MVP is the cause of the attacks.

Temporal Lobe Epilepsy

Sudden, paroxysmal episodes of fear accompanied by derealization, depersonalization, and epigastric discomfort often constitute the prodrome of a complex partial seizure in which chewing, lip smacking, or other automatisms occur without the patient remembering. When there is no grand mal seizure component in the patient's history, this can be a difficult differential diagnosis. Information from people living with the patient can be the key to diagnosis.

Pheochromocytoma

This is a rare (less than 1 in 10,000) catecholamine-secreting tumor that produces marked episodic elevations of blood pressure and vasomotor lability in conjunction with a wide array of anxiety symptoms. However, patients with this tumor do not usually complain of the psychological symptoms of anxiety. Blood pressure rises in panic disorder are modest by comparison.

Hyperthyroidism

In this syndrome, a fine tremor, heat intolerance, and weight loss—despite normal or increased appetite—usually accompany symptoms of generalized anxiety.

Hypoglycemia

A constellation of symptoms occur together, including hunger, weakness, headache, sweating, palpitations, and anxiety. The syndrome, including anxiety, is episodic, predictably occurring several hours after meals. It can be reversed by glucose ingestion (e.g., eating a candy bar). Differentiating anxiety from hypoglycemia is somewhat complicated by the fact that anxiety can worsen glucose tolerance. Generalized anxiety does not have predictable waves of anxiety associated with hunger, and panic attacks come on much faster and stronger. *Hypoglycemia is a very rare cause of anxiety* and is probably grossly overdiagnosed in patients actually suffering from anxiety disorders.

Postconcussion Syndrome

Anxiety frequently accompanies this medical condition for several months after the head trauma. This is not just a psychological phenomena. It is seen in people with no memory of the accident (secondary to the concussion), and usually the anxiety is not related to the traumatic event. Anticonvulsants sometimes are effective.

Delirium

Anxiety sometimes is the prominent feature in delirium, but unlike in anxiety disorder, fluctuations in alertness, interrupted attention, and problems in cognitive functioning are also always present.

Alcohol or Hypnoanxiolytic Withdrawal

Frequently, patients do not recognize alcohol as a cause of anxiety but, rather, see it only as a treatment for anxiety. Direct questioning about alcohol and hypnoanxiolytic use is necessary, as many patients may try to conceal this information. If patients have been using long-lasting medications such as diazepam or clonazepam, withdrawal symptoms might not appear for 4–7 days following drug discontinuation. In some anxiety disorders, even the ingestion of small amounts of alcohol can produce severe anxiety several hours later, as blood levels of alcohol fall (a "rebound" from the brief calming effect of alcohol). Thus, "social drinking," not just alcoholism, may cause anxiety.

Caffeine Overuse

This is frequently not recognized by patients as the cause of their anxiety symptoms. For example, increased sensitivity to caffeine can precipitate a new anxiety-like syndrome in an older adult who has maintained a constant intake over the years. Only a reduction in caffeine intake will relieve the symptoms. It has also been shown that patients suffering from certain anxiety disorders are more sensitive to caffeine. Some have discontinued use of caffeinated beverages on their own in an attempt to reduce their symptoms;

others, however, remain unaware of the link between caffeine and anxiety. Symptoms of caffeine intoxication—nervousness, irritability, agitation, headache, rapid heart rate, tremulousness, and occasional muscle twitches—can result from ingesting over 250 mg of caffeine a day (about 2 cups of coffee). These effects can last 7 hours. There are many other sources of caffeine, including tea, most soft drinks, pain relievers, and cold preparations.

Other Stimulants

Both legal and illegal stimulants can cause significant anxiety. Common illegal sources are methamphetamine and cocaine. Common legal sources are decongestants, over-the-counter diet pills, and antiasthmatic medications that rely on beta-adrenergic stimulation. One common symptom of anxiety, especially panic anxiety, is shortness of breath. A patient with the sporadic sensation of shortness of breath may be incorrectly diagnosed in primary care settings as having reactive airway disease. Upon using the prescribed albuterol inhaler, such a patient may experience an exacerbation of the anxiety symptoms.

Other Drugs

Yohimbine, marijuana, phencyclidine, and organic solvents have all been reported to increase anxiety and induce panic attacks.

PANIC DISORDER

Suddenly and without reason, panic attacks engulf the victim with a sense of imminent doom, death, or destruction. Since most victims have never heard of panic attacks, they fear that they're going mad and won't tell loved ones or physicians about them. Panic attacks are terrifying—"worse than Auschwitz," according to one concentration camp survivor.

Clinical Presentation

The essential feature of panic disorder is a history of *panic attacks*. These attacks affect women more often than men and strike outside the victim's home—most often in a store, sometimes on the street. The person feels she's in a life-threatening situation from which she must escape—immediately. She might fear an imminent stroke, heart attack, or nuclear explosion. Very often she can't pinpoint what she fears, but knows it's horrendous. Her imagination takes over: She might die right on the spot, go berserk, or be killed, butchered, or maimed. Her heart feels as though it is pounding so hard that it could bust or burst through her chest. She may scream or look blank, even though she's frozen in fear and unable to move. The woman from Auschwitz, now quite elderly, says she's terrified of falling and clutching onto strangers. Another woman described her arm turning to stone and people appearing miles away. Most patients gasp for air, hyperventilate, develop parethesias, or feel dizzy and lightheaded. They may race outside and only then will their breathing slow and their attack subside. Most attacks last 3–10 minutes, and rarely more than 30 minutes.

Many patients shrug off the first attack, but in several days, unprovoked attacks recur; these may be less intense but still frightening. Patients begin to dread future attacks. Although the timing of panic attacks is unpredictable, the locations may follow a pattern. A patient may panic in the same bank on three occasions, but not on the fourth nor in any other bank. A patient's attacks usually have their own symptom cluster: Some patients have primarily respiratory distress, some worry about going crazy, some fear death. Diagnostic criteria for panic disorder are listed in Table 14-1. Some patients have serious dysfunction from *limited-symptom anxiety* in which they experience fewer than four of the defining symptoms of panic attacks.

Panic attacks can occur in a variety of anxiety disorders (e.g., panic disorder, social phobia, simple phobia, generalized anxiety disorder, and posttraumatic stress disorder). In determining the differential diagnostic significance of a panic attack, it is important to consider the context in which the panic attack occurs. There are two prototypical relationships between the onset of a panic attack and situational triggers: (1) *unexpected* (uncued) panic attacks, in which the onset of the panic attack is not associated with a situational trigger (i.e., occurring "out of the blue"); and (2) situationally *bound* (cued) panic attacks, in which an attack almost invariably occurs immediately upon exposure to, or in anticipation of, the situational trigger (cue). The occurrence of unexpected panic attacks is required for a diagnosis of panic disorder, whereas situationally bound panic attacks are most characteristic of social and specific phobias. Moreover, there are panic attack presentations that do not conform to either of these prototypical relationships. These *situationally predisposed* panic attacks are more likely to occur upon exposure to the situational trigger (cue) but are not invariably associated with the cue. In addition, these panic attacks may not necessarily occur immediately after the exposure. Situationally predisposed panic attacks may be frequent in panic disorder but not diagnostic.

TABLE 14-1
Diagnostic Criteria for Panic Disorder

A. The essential features **are recurrent attacks of severe anxiety (panic)** which are not restricted to any particular situation or set of circumstances, and which are therefore **unpredictable**. Individual attacks have a sudden onset and usually last for minutes only, though sometimes longer; their frequency and the course of the disorder are both rather variable. As in other anxiety disorders, the dominant symptoms vary from person to person, but the following are common:

1. palpitations
2. choking sensations
3. chest pain
4. dizziness
5. feelings of unreality (depersonalization or derealization)
6. fear of dying
7. fear of losing control or going mad

DSM-5 specifies an additional 6 symptoms below and requires at least 4 of the total 13 to be present during a panic episode.

8. *sweating*
9. *trembling or shaking*
10. *shortness of breath or smothering sensations*
11. *nausea or abdominal distress*
12. *chills or flushing sensations*
13. *paresthesias*

B. For a definite diagnosis, **several severe attacks of autonomic anxiety should have occurred within a period of about 1 month** in circumstances where there is no objective danger, without being confined to known or predictable situations, and with comparative freedom from anxiety symptoms between attacks (although anticipatory anxiety is common).

1. A panic attack is often followed by a persistent fear of having another attack.
2. An individual in a panic attack often experiences a crescendo of fear and autonomic symptoms which results in an exit, usually hurried, from wherever he or she may be. If this occurs in a specific situation, such as on a bus or in a crowd, the patient may subsequently avoid that situation. Similarly, frequent and unpredictable panic attacks produce fear of being alone or going into public places.

C. The panic attacks are **not due to the direct physiological effects of a substance or another medical condition**.

D. The panic attacks are **not better explained by another mental disorder** such as depression or where there are responses to feared situations (Phobias, Obsessive–Compulsive Disorder, Posttraumatic Stress Disorder, and Separation Anxiety Disorder).

1. Panic attacks can be present across a variety of disorders and are an indication of severity.
2. Panic attacks may be secondary to depressive disorders, particularly in men, and if the criteria for a depressive disorder are fulfilled at the same time, the panic disorder should not be given as the main diagnosis.
3. A panic attack that occurs in an established phobic situation is regarded as an expression of the severity of the phobia, which should be given diagnostic precedence. Panic disorder should be the main diagnosis only in the absence of any of the phobias.

Note: Adapted from *ICD-10* (p. 115) and *DSM-5* (p. 208)

In time, instead of returning to their baseline state, most patients develop *anticipatory anxiety* in between panic attacks. This anxiety resembles that seen in GAD and includes continued motor tension, autonomic hyperactivity, apprehension, hypervigilance, and initial insomnia. Patients say this anxiety stems from a terror of having future attacks. This anxiety can be mild or severe; it may be the most dominant symptom, thereby misleading clinicians into diagnosing GAD.

Over time, a majority of patients with panic disorder will also develop situationally bound panic attacks. In some cases, these become the main form of panic attack. Subsequently, some patients—and there's no way of knowing which ones—develop *phobic avoidance*. They may be phobic for situations associated with the panic attacks. This avoidance may be based on the mistaken belief that the situation caused the attack or on the reality that many of the panic attacks have become situationally bound. For example, a patient may avoid driving because she thinks driving caused her to panic. More often, patients avoid situations in which they fear being trapped or unable to get help (e.g., buses, elevators, bridges, department stores). In lectures or movies they may take an aisle seat near the door to assure the possibility of escape. When restrictions on travel away from home significantly impair functioning, the additional diagnosis of *agoraphobia* is merited. The number of blocks a patient ventures away from home is a simple and reliable measure of impairment.

Epidemiology

The 1-year prevalence of panic disorder is 2.7% and lifetime prevalence is 4.7%. Two to three times more women than men get it, and it is most prevalent between the ages of 16 and 40. During pregnancy, the frequency of panic attacks appears to decline sharply. Severe separation anxiety or sudden object loss during childhood may predispose to panic disorder.

Differential Diagnosis

As discussed earlier, several medical conditions can mimic panic disorder. Differentiating *generalized anxiety disorder* from panic disorder may be complicated because anticipatory anxiety may be the dominant symptom of panic disorder, even when the patient has long forgotten that he or she ever had panic attacks. A history of repeated discrete attacks points to panic disorder. Several anxiety disorders, including *obsessive–compulsive, posttraumatic stress, separation anxiety,* and *social phobia,* have very specific fears that, in severe form, may look like a panic attack. Unlike panic attacks, however, these fears are *only* precipitated by very specific cues related to these disorders.

Panic attacks may occur during sleep. It is easy to confuse these with *nightmare disorder* and *sleep terror disorder*, but there are a few important differences. People with sleep panic attacks usually also have panic attacks during the day. Unlike nightmare disorder, there is no nightmare remembered and, unlike sleep terror disorder, the person with a panic attack remembers it well (does not have amnesia) and is quite responsive.

Etiology

Panic disorder runs in families. About 20% of these patients' first-degree relatives have panic disorder, in comparison to about 4% of first-degree relatives in unaffected individuals. Given an MZ to DZ twin ratio of 5:1 for panic disorder, genetics seem to play a major role in this familial transmission. (Knowing this, parents with panic disorder can spare their children considerable grief by ensuring that their kids know about the disorder and obtain early treatment.)

The initial panic attack, though not triggered by a specific stressor, usually occurs during an unusually stressful period. Relocation to new places commonly precede the onset of panic attacks (Roy-Byrne, Geraci, & Uhde, 1986). When repressed, unacceptable thoughts invade one's consciousness, panicky anxiety may ensue. For example, over the last 2 years, Sally provided round-the-clock care for her seriously injured son. She experienced anxiety attacks each time her unacceptable wish for her son's death threatened to break through into consciousness.

First attacks frequently happen in patients with thyroid disorders, during the immediate postpartum period, and after using marijuana, cocaine, or amphetamines. Caffeine produces panic attacks in up to 70% of patients with panic disorder, and stopping caffeine reduces the frequency and intensity of the attacks.

Lactic acid, which builds up in muscles during exercise and causes soreness and stiffness, plays a role in panic disorder. Intravenous infusions of sodium lactate trigger panic attacks in those with panic disorder but not in controls. Vigorous physical exercise, which produces lactic acid, can trigger panic attacks in some patients (Pitts & McClure, 1967). Yet if patients with panic disorder receive a tricyclic antidepressant (TCA) prior to being infused with lactate, they do not develop an attack. This finding is noteworthy, given that TCAs block panic attacks. Carbon dioxide may increase during vigorous exercise as well, and brainstem hypersensitivity to changes in CO_2 has been postulated as a trigger for panic. This is related to the panic people experience with air hunger and suffocation. In fact, lactate can create a sense of breathlessness. Donald Klein proposed two theories based on the idea that panic attacks are "normal" in little children who have been abandoned and in people of all ages who feel suffocated. The abnormalities that then predispose an adult to panic attacks would be fear of separation or an abnormally low "suffocation" alarm threshold.

Clinical Course

Panic disorder usually begins during the late teens and 20s (most commonly in the 20s and rarely after age 35). There is usually an initial discrete attack, although chronic anxiety, fatigue, or dizziness may precede it. Most patients originally consult a physician for difficulty breathing or chest discomfort, and less often, for abdominal distress or "irritable colon." In one survey, 70% of the patients had visited more than 10 physicians, 95% had had prior psychiatric treatment, and 98% had long and frequent use of hypnoanxiolytics.

Over time, the intensity of panic attacks, anticipatory anxiety, and phobic avoidance varies. Spontaneous remissions occur for months and sometimes for years. A patient may go 5–10 years without an attack, suddenly have three attacks in a month, and then not have another attack for a decade. In general, 5–20 years after the initial attack, 50–60% of patients will recover substantially, whereas 20% will remain moderately impaired. Some studies suggest bleaker prognoses with substantial rates of suicide.

The earlier patients get treatment, the better the outcome. If panic attacks can be squelched relatively early, anticipatory anxiety and phobia may be averted or minimized. Even if the latter stages occur, early treatment can reduce their incapacitations and complications.

Complications

Substance abuse is a frequent complication because patients discover that alcohol and benzodiazepines will temporarily calm their anticipatory anxiety. Unfortunately, tolerance develops resulting in overuse and chemical dependency. Occupational, social, and marital impairments are common, often compounded by the patient's concealment of the attacks and by others not knowing that panic disorder exists.

Depression may affect up to 50% of all patients with panic disorder. These depressions are usually mild, two-thirds last under 3 months, and most are associated with a precipitating stress, such as a divorce. Yet a third of patients with panic disorder have had a major depression years *before* having their first panic attack. This suggests that for some patients, depression is not a complication of panic disorder, but a second disorder.

Management and Treatment

From the start, clinicians should help patients and their families develop reasonable expectations of treatment. It should be pointed out that panic disorder is not a figment of the patient's imagination, but a genuine illness with biological components that often cause severe impairments. They should be told that panic disorder has a fluctuating course, and that patients should not feel that they, or the treatment, have failed if some symptoms persist or recur. They should know that improving the patient's ability to function and to travel are key goals of treatment.

Treatment of Mild Panic Disorder

Patients who have had only a few panic attacks or get them very intermittently but do not have much anxiety between episodes should be given an explanation of how the attacks occur, emphasizing that they are not life-threatening, dangerous to health, or a symptom of impending insanity. Cognitive–behavioral therapies aimed at changing patients' catastrophic thinking about attacks are highly effective in patients with infrequent attacks, especially if there is high anticipatory anxiety between attacks. These therapies have been systematized and are available in manual form.

Treatment of Moderate and Severe Panic Disorder

If attacks are occurring frequently (five to seven times a week) or there is significant anxiety between attacks and some disability, in addition to the cognitive–behavioral approach there are three classes of medications that can be considered. Imipramine at doses of 150 mg or higher has been shown to be effective about 70% of the time. Most other TCAs are probably equally effective, but there are fewer well-controlled studies on them. Imipramine, desipramine, or nortriptyline had been the first choice for treating panic disorder pre-SSRIs. Selective serotonin reuptake inhibitors (SSRI) such as fluoxetine, sertraline, citalopram, and paroxetine have become the treatment of choice, as they appear to be equally effective and better tolerated. Full response can take six to twelve weeks. Early overstimulation with exacerbation of panic may occur unless the initial doses are small (10 mg imipramine or 5 mg fluoxetine), and titration proceeds slowly.

Monoamine oxidase inhibitors (MAOIs) such as phenelzine appear to be effective in panic disorders about 75–80% of the time and are particularly effective in treatment-refractory cases. Because of the need to stay on a low-tyramine diet to avoid hypertensive crisis, these drugs are probably underutilized by most physicians.

Benzodiazepines in doses two to three times higher than usually used for simple anxiety have been reported to be effective in about 70–90% of panic disorder cases. There are many controlled studies supporting alprazolam's effectiveness, and a few for clonazepam, lorazepam, and diazepam. High doses of benzodiazepines present a risk of physical dependence, but nonetheless may be considered in patients who have not responded to, or cannot tolerate, antidepressants or who may be fearful of taking MAOIs because of the danger of dietary interactions. Response to benzodiazepines (days) is much faster than to antidepressants (weeks). Short-term use for a few weeks during administration of antidepressant treatment may be indicated to prevent early overstimulation and to provide more rapid relief of panic, especially in patients with occupational or familial dysfunction. Unfortunately, when attempts to withdraw the benzodiazepines are made, patients may not only experience a return of the original symptoms but also rebound withdrawal symptoms. During this withdrawal period, patients can have worse symptoms than when they started treatment ("rebound anxiety"). Neurontin (gabapentin) is an antiepileptic that may be used as a substitute for benzodiazepines without the significant risk of dependence. Beta-blockers have *not* been shown to effectively block panic attacks.

Long-term Management of Panic Attacks

When the *anticipatory anxiety* of having panic attacks continues for months or years, the anxiety that develops in anticipation of these attacks becomes entrenched and resistant to treatment. Although it may seem redundant to the therapist, repeatedly telling the patient that she will experience fewer and less severe panic attacks while on her medication goes a long way to quelling anticipatory anxiety. Cognitive–behavioral approaches for mild to moderate panic disorder can help to prevent further symptoms. Because medications have become the patient's "security blanket," stopping them is usually difficult. Extremely slow decreases are recommended. In the case of benzodiazepines, a slowly titrated decrease is also necessary to minimize withdrawal symptoms. Sometimes patients will get stuck on the last tiny dose which, though they know it is pharmacologically inactive, remains psychologically quite active for them.

The *agoraphobia* that frequently accompanies panic disorder is discussed below. In general, any treatment that eventually exposes patients to the phobic stimulus is likely to work, whereas any treatment that never exposes them to the stimulus is likely to fail.

PHOBIC DISORDERS

A phobia is an irrational dread of, and compelling desire to avoid, a specific object, situation, or activity. People with phobias know that their phobias are "crazy," unreasonable, or excessive. Unlike panic attacks, phobias are always anticipated and never happen spontaneously. Patients with both unpredictable panic attacks and phobias may be diagnosed as having both disorders.

The *original phobia* is usually followed by mild to severe *anticipatory anxiety*, although if the phobic stimulus is avoided, some patients will remain anxiety-free. Patients' degree of anticipatory anxiety depends primarily on their confidence in being able to avoid the phobic situation. The anxiety is not relieved by the knowledge that other people do not regard the phobic object or situation as dangerous. Patients who are phobic to unusual things, such as snakes, are generally calm in other circumstances; those who dread common things that might suddenly appear, such as pigeons, tend to be chronically anxious unless they're in a safe haven (e.g., home).

A set of *avoidant behaviors* often occurs. A person with a fish phobia is so uncomfortable around fish that before visiting new friends, he or she may phone ahead to make sure they won't serve herring and don't have goldfish. If the fish can't be hidden or trashed, the person with the fish phobia won't visit.

On occasion, virtually everyone, especially children, are bugged by some phobia—mice, snakes, insects, and so on. Phobic *symptoms* become phobic *disorders* when they cause undue distress and impair functioning. Roughly 20% of patients with phobic symptoms develop phobic disorders. Many phobias remit quickly without therapy, but if they endure for over a year, they're unlikely to remit spontaneously. Many childhood phobias vanish within a year; treatment hastens their disappearance. The prognosis is worse in adults: In a 5-year span, 50% of patients will improve, but only 5% will be symptom-free.

One medical dictionary lists 275 types of phobia; *DSM-5* lists three: agoraphobia (Table 14-2), social phobia (Table 14-3), and specific phobia (Table

TABLE 14-2
Diagnostic Criteria for Agoraphobia

A. The term "agoraphobia" is used here with a wider meaning than originally introduced and is now taken to include **fears not only of open spaces but also of related aspects where there is difficulty of immediate easy escape to a safe place (usually home)**. Therefore the anxiety must be restricted to (or occur mainly in) **at least two of the following situations**:

1. public places
2. open spaces
3. confined areas
4. crowds
5. traveling away from home
6. traveling alone

B. **Avoidance of the phobic situation** must be, or has been, a prominent feature. (It must be remembered that some agoraphobics experience little anxiety because they are consistently able to avoid their phobic situations.) *DSM-5 specifies that the phobic social situation consistently provokes anxiety or fear out of proportion to the actual danger.*

C. *DSM-5 specifies that the fear and/or avoidance have persisted for typically 6 months or longer.*

D. The above symptoms result **in significant distress or significant impairment** in personal, family, social, educational, occupational, or other important areas of functioning.

E. The disturbance **is not due to the direct physiological effects of a substance or another medical condition**. (Although the severity of the anxiety and the extent of avoidance behavior are variable, this is the most incapacitating of the phobic disorders and some sufferers become completely housebound; many are terrified by the thought of collapsing and being left helpless in public.)

F. The psychological, behavioral, or autonomic symptoms must be **primarily manifestations of anxiety and not secondary to other symptoms,** such as delusions or obsessional thoughts, so they are not better explained by another mental disorder.

The DSM-5 specifies that agoraphobia would not be diagnosed if the anxiety is better explained by a specific phobia or by posttraumatic, separation, or social anxiety. It is possible to have both panic disorder and agoraphobia.

The presence of other symptoms such as depression, depersonalization, obsessional symptoms, and social phobias does not invalidate the diagnosis, provided that these symptoms do not dominate the clinical picture. However, if the patient was already significantly depressed when the phobic symptoms first appeared, depressive episode may be a more appropriate main diagnosis; this is more common in late-onset cases.

Note: Adapted from *ICD-10* (p. 112) and *DSM-5* (p. 217)

TABLE 14-3
Diagnostic Criteria for Social Anxiety Disorder (formerly Social Phobia)

A. Anxiety must be **restricted to or predominate in particular social situations and be centered around a fear of scrutiny by other people** in comparatively small groups (as opposed to crowds). They may be discrete (i.e., restricted to eating in public, to public speaking, or to encounters with the opposite sex) or diffuse, involving almost all social situations outside the family circle.

B. The anxiety is about being **negatively evaluated by others** and associated with low self-esteem and fear of criticism.

C. **Avoidance of the social situation** is often marked, occurs whenever possible, and in extreme cases may result in almost complete social isolation. *DSM-5 specifies that the phobic social situation consistently provokes anxiety or fear that is out of proportion to the actual danger.*

D. *DSM-5 specifies that the fear and/or avoidance have persisted for typically 6 months or longer*

E. The above symptoms result **in significant distress or significant impairment** in personal, family, social, educational, occupational, or other important areas of functioning.

F. The disturbance **is not due to the direct physiological effects of a substance or another medical condition.**

G. The psychological, behavioral, or autonomic symptoms must be primarily manifestations of anxiety and not secondary to other symptoms such as delusions or obsessional thoughts, so they are **not better explained by another mental disorder.** *(The DSM-5 specifies panic, body dysmorphic disorder, or autism spectrum disorders.)*

1. Agoraphobia and depressive disorders are often prominent, and may both contribute to sufferers becoming "housebound." If the distinction between social phobia and agoraphobia is very difficult, precedence should be given to agoraphobia; a depressive diagnosis should not be made unless a full depressive syndrome can be identified clearly.

2. The sufferer of social anxiety may present with a complaint of blushing, hand tremor, nausea, or urgency of micturition, and is sometimes convinced that one of these secondary manifestations of anxiety is the primary problem; symptoms may progress to panic attacks.

Social phobias often start in adolescence and unlike most other phobias are equally common in men and women.

Note: Adapted from *ICD-10* (p. 113) and *DSM-5* (p. 202)

14-4). *Agoraphobia* literally translates to "fear of the marketplace," but now refers to fear of being in places or situations where escape might be difficult or, in cases involving panic attacks, of being where help is not available (e.g., shops, theaters, streets). The most severe of phobic disorders, agoraphobia accounts for about 60% of phobic disorders in clinical practice. *Social phobia* refers to the fear of being scrutinized and judged, as in "stage fright"; social phobias comprise 10% of all phobic disorders. *Specific phobia* encom-

TABLE 14-4
Diagnostic Criteria for Specific Phobia (Formerly Simple Phobia)

A. **Anxiety must be restricted to the presence of the particular phobic object or situation**. These are phobias restricted to highly specific situations such as proximity to particular animals, heights, thunder, darkness, flying, closed spaces, urinating or defecating in public toilets, eating certain foods, dentistry, the sight of blood or injury, and the fear of exposure to specific diseases.

DSM-5 notes that in children, the anxiety may be expressed by crying, tantrums, freezing, or clinging.

B. The **phobic social situation is avoided whenever possible**. *DSM-5 specifies that the phobic social situation consistently provokes anxiety or fear that is out of proportion to the actual danger.*

C. *DSM-5 specifies that the fear and/or avoidance have persisted for typically 6 months or longer*

D. The above symptoms result in **significant distress or significant impairment** in personal, family, social, educational, occupational, or other important areas of functioning. The seriousness of the resulting handicap depends on how easy it is for the sufferer to avoid the phobic situation.

E. The psychological, behavioral, or autonomic symptoms must be primarily manifestations of anxiety and not secondary to other symptoms such as delusions or obsessional thoughts, so they are **not better explained by another mental disorder**. (*The DSM-5 specifies panic, agoraphobic, posttraumatic, separation, or social anxiety.*) Although the triggering situation is discrete, contact with it can evoke panic as in agoraphobia or social phobias. It is usual for there to be no other psychiatric symptoms with a specific phobia, in contrast to agoraphobia and social phobias.

Specific phobias usually arise in childhood or early adult life and can persist for decades if they remain untreated. Fear of the phobic situation tends not to fluctuate, in contrast to agoraphobia. Radiation sickness and venereal infections and, more recently, AIDS are common subjects of disease phobias.

It is usual for there to be no other psychiatric symptoms, in contrast to agoraphobia and social phobias. Blood-injury phobias differ from others in leading to bradycardia and sometimes syncope, rather than tachycardia. Fears of specific diseases such as cancer, heart disease, or venereal infection should be classified under hypochondriacal disorder, unless they relate to specific situations where the disease might be acquired. If the conviction of disease reaches delusional intensity, the diagnosis should be delusional disorder. Individuals who are convinced that they have an abnormality or disfigurement of a specific bodily (often facial) part, which is not objectively noticed by others (sometimes termed dysmorphophobia), should be classified under hypochondriacal disorder or delusional disorder.

Note: Adapted from *ICD-10* (p. 114) and *DSM-5* (p. 197)

passes irrational fear and avoidance of specific objects or situations not covered by agoraphobia or social phobia. Simple phobias usually involve animals or insects (e.g., dogs, spiders), things (e.g., hypodermic needles), or places (e.g., heights, closed spaces). Whereas social phobias are normally confined to a few stimuli, simple phobias usually involve only one object. In comparison to social phobias, simple phobias begin earlier in life, rarely incapacitate, and have better prognoses. Among the phobias, simple phobias are most common in the population, but agoraphobias are most common in the office.

Clinical Presentation

Agoraphobia

The public places or open spaces typically feared by these patients include driving a car, riding a bus, crossing bridges, standing in lines, passing through tunnels, walking through crowds, or shopping. Exposure to the phobic stimulus often triggers intense somatic anxiety. Some patients with phobias fear going berserk in public—screaming without reason, propositioning strangers, guffawing nonstop, disrobing, or masturbating. Agoraphobia mushrooms: Fears of taking a bus may escalate to fears of going anywhere by any means. Because people with agoraphobia often become terrified of leaving safe places (e.g., home), of being without a familiar object (e.g., a cane), or of traveling alone, they become highly dependent on others. The fear of not having an immediately available exit is one of the key features of agoraphobia. Unless treated early, patients may increasingly restrict their activities and venture outside only with a trusted companion.

> When agoraphobia is not a sequela of panic attacks, it usually arises during the early 20s, even though it may begin at any age. Many patients delay getting treatment for a decade or more. Over time, symptoms typically fluctuate from mild to severe. Spontaneous remissions occur, but uncommonly. Without early treatment or a spontaneous remission, patients tend to get worse.
>
> Complications are frequent. If the patient is housebound, depression is common. Alcohol and hypnoanxiolytic abuse may result from patients medicating their anticipatory anxiety or from physicians incorrectly treating patients' depressions or anxieties. Many people with agoraphobia develop compulsions: They cannot leave home, for example, without repeatedly checking if the oven is turned off or the back door is locked. Marital and sexual problems may precede or follow agoraphobia.

Social Phobia

These patients have an irrational fear of being scrutinized, judged, or humiliated in public. It may be a dread of embarrassing oneself while speaking in public, eating in restaurants, or using public lavatories. People with social phobia tend to blush and twitch, whereas people with agoraphobia become dizzy, faint, short of breath, weak in the limbs, and have ringing or buzzing in their ears (Liebowitz et al., 1985). Social phobia is diagnosed if the fear or avoidant behavior interferes with occupational or social activities or relationships. The phobia may be discrete (public speaking) or extend to more widespread social situations. In the latter case, it is easily confused with panic disorder, unless patients are asked if they've ever panicked when *not* in social situations.

> With a mean age of onset of 19, social phobias usually begin before agoraphobia. Without early therapy, social phobia has an unremitting, chronic course. At some point, a third to a half will have depressive symptoms, a majority will stop work or school, 60% will abuse alcohol or drugs, and about half will avoid all social interaction outside the immediate family (and then may qualify for the diagnosis of avoidant personality disorder).

Specific Phobia

The most common, benign, and circumscribed of the phobias, these usually start in childhood or early adolescence and cease within 5 years in 50% of patients. Specific phobia is the elevation of a particular fear to phobic proportions. Animals and "creepy-crawlies" are the most common phobias for which treatment is sought. The more ubiquitous the phobic object, the more incapacitating the phobia. For example, phobias for common household pets are socially inconvenient, and discomfort may be excessive and frequent. Animal phobias almost always begin in childhood. Before puberty, specific phobias occur equally in males and females. It is not known why the animal phobias tend to persist in women and not men. Acrophobia (fear of heights) and claustrophobia (fear of closed spaces) are examples of other common specific phobias. Blood/injury/illness phobias are distinguished by their unique physiology (bradycardia, hypotension, and fainting, as opposed to tachycardia and hypertension) and may be encountered more often in medical settings. In the wild, this response would protect humans from profuse bleeding.

Epidemiology

Epidemiological surveys of phobias can yield very different results because what qualifies as a phobia can vary considerably. Is somebody phobic if she's queasy around snakes? Does one count phobias that appear with other disorders? In the general population, the lifetime prevalence for phobic *symptoms* is near 40%, whereas for phobic *disorders*, around 15%.

Although women have two to three times more agoraphobia and simple phobia than men, social phobias affect the sexes more equally. Adults who are phobic and nonphobic had the same rates (4%) of phobias during their childhoods. Separation anxiety during childhood and sudden loss of a loved one predispose to agoraphobia. Social phobia is a more common psychiatric precursor to schizophrenia than any other psychiatric disorder. Social phobia is also common in some alcoholic populations ("Have a few drinks to help your confidence").

Differential Diagnosis

Phobic anxiety may be indistinguishable subjectively, physiologically, and behaviorally from other types of anxiety. A phobic disorder should not be diagnosed when another mental disorder better accounts for the phobia. For example, fear of contamination may result from *obsessive–compulsive disorder,* and fear of a specific past stressor occurs with *posttraumatic stress disorder.* Whereas the feared object leads the person with an obsession to perform rituals or to block out intrusive thoughts, it primarily induces anxiety in the patient with the phobia. *Schizophrenia* may produce social withdrawal resembling agoraphobia and social phobia, but people with schizophrenia have many more symptoms and may avoid situations because of delusions, whereas people with phobias know that their phobia is absurd. *Paranoid disorders* can lead to avoidant behavior, but unlike the person with the phobia, the person with paranoia sees nothing irrational about his or her behavior.

Typically the phobic object or situation is external to the individual. When the fears are related more internally to the presence of disease (nosophobia) and or disfigurement (dysmorphobia), hypochondriasis and body dysmorphic disorders respectively would be the likely diagnoses. On the other hand fear of disease through possible exposure to infection or a simple fear of medical procedures would qualify as specific phobias.

Clinical presentations with a mixture of depression and anxiety frequently occur. Pre-existing phobias worsen during depression. Depression itself may be accompanied by temporary phobic anxiety. If the criteria for depressive disorder were met prior to the first appearance of phobic symptoms, then the former diagnosis should be given precedence. Because many patients with *depressive disorders* feel worthless, gradually restrict their activities, and become reclusive, they may appear agoraphobic. However, pervasive symptoms, biological signs of depression, and excessive guilt and shame point to depression rather than to an anxiety disorder.

Patients with *dementia* may withdraw to "think clearly," but this phobic-like avoidance is not associated with a specific feared stimulus; MSE testing will eliminate any remaining diagnostic confusion. Phobias commonly occur in patients with *borderline, paranoid,* and *avoidant personality disorders.*

Normal fears of public speaking should be distinguished from social phobia, as should "normal fears" of bugs or snakes from specific phobia. In these cases, the border between "normal" and pathological depends on the degree of distress and disability the phobia generates.

Etiology and Pathogenesis

As a general proposition, it can be said that unknown biological or psychosocial mechanisms cause patients with phobias to acquire an ingrained and unconscious stimulus–response association, which generates fear on subsequent exposure to the phobic stimulus. However, why some objects and not others are feared, and why some phobias vanish whereas others intensify, are unknown. The standard (tautological) explanations are: The phobic object is "chosen" because it carries enormous symbolic importance, of which patients are unaware; and repression and displacement are the chief defense mechanisms that cause phobias.

For example, a woman who was usually punished as a child by being locked in her bedroom may become claustrophobic when fired by her boss. If she has forgotten (or repressed) these childhood banishments, she will be unaware of having been conditioned to associate punishment with being locked in a room, and she will be puzzled by her current claustrophobia. As in any phobia, conditioning of the "sick role" through secondary gain may extend her claustrophobia into anticipatory anxiety and avoidant behaviors (e.g., not seeking jobs).

Agoraphobia runs in families; most social and simple phobias do not. Nevertheless, some studies show that children specifically phobic to insects and animals are likely to have mothers with similar phobias. This suggests that imitation, indoctrination, or identification may transmit phobias in some cases. Genetic factors may also play a role in the pathogenesis of phobia. Identical twins raised apart have a significantly increased chance of having a phobia and, not only that, but the *same* phobia.

Management and Treatment

> One can hardly master a phobia if one waits till the patient lets the analysis influence him to give it up . . . one succeeds only when one can induce them by the influence of the analysis to . . . go [about it alone] . . . and to struggle with their anxiety while they make the attempt.
>
> —Sigmund Freud (1919)

Essential in the treatment of phobias is exposing patients to the feared object or situation for an uninterrupted period of time. This principle applies to all treatment approaches, including psychoanalytic psychotherapy, behavior therapy, hypnosis, and medication. Historically, the preferred treatment for phobias was primarily behavior therapy involving relaxation training, mental rehearsal, and exposure, supplemented by supportive individual, family, and group therapy whenever appropriate. More recently, however, evidence suggests that supportive psychotherapy may be just as effective as behavior therapy, as long as patients encounter the feared situation. Freud believed that because phobias were based on underlying conflicts, just removing the symptom (the phobia), but not the underlying conflict, would result only in "symptom substitution"—another symptom popping up. On the contrary, eliminating phobias by "superficial" behavioral or pharmacological means rarely, if ever, leads to this substitution.

Biotherapies

Most studies show little use for TCAs and MAOIs in patients with phobias but without panic attacks or social phobia. Social phobias appear to respond well to MAOIs and more modestly to SSRIs and TCAs. In many cases in which the social phobia was so severe that the person developed avoidant personality disorder, a year on MAOIs produced such dramatic improvement that the avoidant personality disorder diagnosis no longer existed. Because beta-adrenergic blockers (e.g., propranolol) diminish somatic (but not psychic) anxiety, they may be useful for some social phobias, such as stage fright, in which somatic anxiety is paramount. Hypnoanxiolytics can be used temporarily to reduce anticipatory anxiety, but their long-term use risks habituation.

Behavior Therapies

Live exposure to the phobic stimulus—the essential therapeutic intervention—can be performed in three ways. First is *flooding*, in which patients are directly confronted with the phobic stimulus for sessions lasting from 30 minutes to 8 hours. Flooding may also involve bombarding the patient with the feared stimulus. One man was cured of his pillow phobia by sitting for two 45-minute sessions in a hospital room stuffed with 127 pillows. Second is a *graduated exposure*, in which patients initially confront the phobic object for a brief time, and then gradually in subsequent sessions escalate the duration of exposure. Therapist-aided graduated exposure seems to have nominal benefit and may actually "prolong the agony" for some patients. The third approach is *systematic desensitization*, usually involving progressive *muscle relaxation*, as described in Chapter 5. To be effective, this technique must be followed (at some point) by direct exposure to the phobic object.

Assertiveness training. Modeling, role-playing, behavioral rehearsal, and in vivo homework assignments may also be helpful for those with social phobias and those with chronic phobias who also have marked dependence needs.

Psychotherapies. Individual psychotherapy can supplement behavior therapy by encouraging patients to enter the phobic situation, by addressing any secondary gain that might perpetuate their avoidant behaviors, and by exploring the symbolic meaning of the phobic object. Group psychotherapy may help patients redevelop social skills, foster assertiveness, reduce or distribute dependency, and decrease loneliness. For some patients and their families, self-help groups for people with phobias are invaluable.

Virtual reality. By simulating exposure to the phobic object in a controlled and safe environment, the patient may be desensitized and learn to tolerate exposure to the phobic object. Some researchers have similarly applied virtual reality technology to trauma therapy by exposure to previous trauma in order to promote emotional processing of trauma-related memories.

GENERALIZED ANXIETY DISORDER

Persons with generalized anxiety disorder (GAD) tend to worry excessively, out of proportion to what the situation warrants. These patients are chronic "worrywarts." During a majority of their days, they are tense, highly distractible, irritable, restless, and so "on edge" that they're often fatigued and mildly depressed. Unrelenting anxiety is, by itself, very exhausting. The anxiety is diffuse, unfocused, free-floating, and ongoing; it may or may not be accompanied by prominent physical complaints such as sweating, dizziness, clammy hands, and tachycardia. When somatic symptoms dominate, patients tend to consult numerous medical specialists, chiropractors, physiotherapists, or nutritionists, which may lead them to fad diets and substance abuse. GAD also impairs social and occupational functioning. The diagnostic criteria are listed in Table 14-5. GAD occurs in persons of all ages and is believed to be twice as common in women as in men. Lifetime prevalence is estimated at over 5% and 12-month prevalence at over 3%. In practice, persons are frequently assigned to this diagnosis when they have some of the features of the other disorders, but do not meet diagnostic criteria.

Differential Diagnosis

As discussed earlier, drugs and medical conditions commonly mimic GAD. Patients with early *schizophrenia* and extensive anxiety also manifest disorganized thinking, will be suspicious and distrustful, and may appear to be emotionally remote, with very constricted affect. A *mood disorder* is the most common diagnosis (more than 50%) in patients presenting with anxiety. Differentiating anxiety from *depression* is somewhat difficult. Since the frequency of mixed anxiety and depression is perhaps as high as 50%, patients complaining mainly of anxiety who have definite symptoms of the depressive syndrome should be treated as having depression. Antidepressants have been shown to be more effective than antianxiety agents in this group. Although these anxious people with depression may not complain of depression, they usually do experience anhedonia, a distinct loss of pleasure in situations that were formerly enjoyable, along with other classic depressive symptoms such as insomnia, anorexia, and fatigue.

Panic disorder is the second most common diagnosis in patients presenting with anxiety. It may be confused with GAD, since chronic anxiety often occurs between panic attacks; yet unlike GAD, panic disorder has distinct episodes of intense anxiety. In *phobic disorder* the patient's anxiety is specific for the phobic stimulus, whereas in GAD it is unfocused and ongoing. The somatic complaints of GAD may resemble *hypochondriasis*, but the person with hypochondriasis more gravely exaggerates the danger of his or her symptoms and is a "specialist" in the fear of disease.

TABLE 14-5

Diagnostic Criteria for Generalized Anxiety Disorder

A. Primary **symptoms of anxiety are present most days for at least several weeks at a time**, and usually for several months. *DSM-5 specifies 6 month duration of symptoms.*

B. **Anxiety is generalized and persistent but not restricted to, or even strongly predominating in, any particular environmental circumstances** (i.e., it is "free-floating"). *DSM-5 specifies that the individual finds it difficult to control the worry.*

C. The dominant **symptoms are variable but should usually involve elements of apprehension, motor tension, and autonomic overactivity**.

Apprehension

    (1) Worries about a variety of future misfortunes

    *(2) Nervousness or feeling on edge

    *(3) Concentration difficulty

    *(4) *Irritability*

Motor Tension

    (5) Fidgeting

    *(6) Muscle tension and related headaches

    *(7) Fatigue

    (8) Inability to relax

    (9) Trembling

Autonomic Overactivity

    *(10) Sleep Disturbance

    (11) Lightheadedness or dizziness

    (12) Sweating

    (13) Tachycardia, palpitations, or tachypnea

    (14) Epigastric discomfort

In children, frequent need for reassurance and recurrent somatic complaints may be prominent.

DSM-5 requires 3 of the 6 symptoms indicated by asterisks for adults and a single symptom for children.

D. The above symptoms result **in significant distress or significant impairment** in personal, family, social, educational, occupational, or other important areas of functioning.

E. The disturbance **is not due to the direct physiological effects of a substance or another medical condition**.

F. The above signs and symptoms must not meet the full criteria for depressive episode, phobic anxiety disorder, panic disorder, or obsessive-compulsive disorder and are **not better explained by another mental disorder**. The transient appearance (for a few days at a time) of other symptoms, particularly depression, does not rule out generalized anxiety disorder as a main diagnosis. *In addition to these disorders DSM-5 specifically mentions that the patient's anxiety is not better explained by psychotic disorders, Separation Anxiety Disorder, Anorexia Nervosa, Somatic Symptom Disorder, Hypochondriasis, or Posttraumatic Stress Disorder.*

This disorder is more common in women, and often related to chronic environmental stress. Its course is variable but tends to be fluctuating and chronic.

Note: Adapted from *ICD-10* (p. 115) and *DSM-5* (p. 222)

Management and Treatment

Psychotherapies

Several studies show that psychotherapy of various kinds is as effective as medication for all but a minority of individuals. All psychotherapies seek to identify the stressors producing the anxiety, offer better means of handling stress, and eliminate dietary or physical sources of anxiety. Insight-oriented psychotherapies will explore the *unconscious* and symbolic meanings of the patient's anxiety and clarify its defensive and "signal" functions. In cognitive therapy, patients identify the precise events or circumstances that trigger *conscious* dysphoric "automatic thoughts" and then develop more rational ways of thinking and feeling in response to the same stressors.

Behavior Therapy

Muscle relaxation, meditation, biofeedback, and autogenic training are frequently employed either by themselves or as supplements to the previously mentioned therapies.

Pharmacotherapy

SSRIs, SNRIs, TCAs, and buspirone, an anxiolytic with no sedative or amnestic properties and no risk of dependence, are probably all reasonable and safe choices with which to treat chronic anxiety. Benzodiazepines can be used to treat acute, paralyzing exacerbations of anxiety. Generally, these should be prescribed for limited durations, such as 2–4 weeks, to avoid long-term physical and psychological dependence. Patients who are primarily distressed by the physiological symptoms of anxiety, such as increased heart rate or "butterflies," may respond well to beta-blockers. Several studies have reported that both sedating and nonsedating antidepressants are effective for GAD without depression.

An example of a treatment manual for GAD is *Mastery of Your Anxiety and Worry*, developed by Craske, Barlow, and O'Leary (1992).

SEPARATION ANXIETY DISORDER

Separation is too gentle a word for this disorder—*abandonment* is closer to the real issue. These children are the clingers; they are scared and miserable when they are away from the important people in their lives and appeased when they are with them. These kids don't fully outgrow normal separation anxiety. For them, going to a friend's house or being left with a babysitter or in a preschool is an ordeal. They can't wait to get back home. At times, the children may be generally anxious and worry about separations even when with those they love. They may worry about significant family members getting sick, hurt, or dying. Often these children prefer to have a parent fall asleep with them at night, preferably with a night light on. Bedtime can turn into 1 or 2 hours of nightly misery. Fear of the dark is common. Mythical nighttime monsters may be under the bed or in the closet. Mere mention of a possible separation sets off physical symptoms of anxiety: Stomachaches, nausea, vomiting, and headaches are typical. Parents often say that the child is deliberately making up these symptoms to avoid separating. The truth usually lies somewhere in-between. Real anxiety is always there to set off these symptoms, but these children have also learned that reporting symptoms staves off separation. Adolescents, but not usually younger children, may also have cardiovascular symptoms, including palpitations, dizziness, and fainting. In short, these children are on their way to panic disorder. Although most are demanding and intrusive, some adapt by being compliant and eager to please.

Most children with separation anxiety are never brought to clinicians unless they develop "school phobia" or "school refusal" and completely stop going to school. They either never leave home or pretend to go to school and, when the parents are gone, sneak home. The symptoms of separation anxiety disorder include two types of worries (harm to, or separation from, major attachment figures), three types of behaviors (school refusal, daytime and bedtime clinging), and three categories of symptoms related to anxiety (anxiety itself, nightmares, and physical symptoms). The diagnostic criteria for separation anxiety disorder are listed in Table 14-6.

Etiology and Pathogenesis

Frequently this disorder manifests after a life stress such as the loss of a relative or a pet, an illness in the child or a relative, or a change in the child's environment (e.g., a move to a new neighborhood or a school change). It rarely starts in adolescence. Separation anxiety tends to wax and wane throughout childhood with periods of remission. New stresses typically cause flare-ups. Boys and girls have an equal risk for this disorder. It is not a coincidence that kids with this disorder come from close-knit, caring homes. Such

TABLE 14-6
Diagnostic Criteria for Separation Anxiety Disorder

A. A focused **excessive anxiety concerning separation from those individuals to whom the child is attached** (usually parents or other family members), that is not merely part of a generalized anxiety about multiple situations. The anxiety may take the form of:

(1) **excessive, recurrent distress** (as shown by anxiety, crying, tantrums, misery, apathy, or social withdrawal) in anticipation of, during, or immediately following separation from a major attachment figure.

(2) an unrealistic, preoccupying **worry about possible harm befalling major attachment figures** or a fear that they will leave and not return;

(3) an unrealistic, preoccupying **worry that some untoward event**, such as the child being lost, kidnapped, admitted to hospital, or killed, **will separate him or her from a major attachment figure;**

(4) persistent **reluctance or refusal to go to school because of fear about separation** (rather than for other reasons such as fear about events at school);

(5) persistent **inappropriate fear of being alone**, or otherwise without the major attachment figure, at home during the day;

(6) persistent **reluctance or refusal to go to sleep** without being near or next to a major attachment figure;

(7) repeated **nightmares about separation;**

(8) repeated **occurrence of physical symptoms** (nausea, stomachache, headache, vomiting, etc.) on occasions that involve separation from a major attachment figure, such as leaving home to go to school;

DSM-5 *specifies at least three of the above.*

B. DSM-5 *specifies a minimum duration of 4 weeks in children and 6 months in adults.*

C. The above symptoms are the source of **significant distress or significant impairment** in personal, family, social, educational, occupational, or other important area of functioning.

D. The psychological, behavioral, or autonomic symptoms are **not better explained by another mental disorder** (e.g., psychotic disorders, autistic spectrum disorders, agoraphobia, or illness anxiety).

Note: Adapted from *ICD-10* (p. 214) and *DSM-5* (p. 190)

---

an environment is usually positive and creates strong bonds. On the negative side, however, children may have trouble forming bonds elsewhere. A general rule of preschool teachers and daycare workers is that separation anxiety problems are as much the parents' as the child's problem. A mother may have trouble letting go of her "baby" and experience distress at leaving him in the care of others. She may be a little overprotective, not wanting him to experience unpleasant feelings. When he cries, she stays or returns soon to check on him. Even if he had just settled down, he may cry after spotting Mom, reinforcing her belief that she should never have left. Her hovering and attempts to ensure that he never feels distress reinforce his perceptions that something dangerous is always about to happen.

Clinical judgment and familiarity with *normal separation anxiety* is necessary to diagnose this disorder. The extreme narrowness of the source of anxiety—*separation*—distinguishes it from other anxiety disorders, such as *generalized anxiety disorder* and *panic disorder with agoraphobia*, and from disorders in which anxiety is but one symptom, such as *schizophrenia, pervasive developmental disorder,* or *major depression*.

A child brought in for school refusal can be asked, "Why don't you want to go to school?" If she has separation anxiety disorder, she may say, "I want to be home with my mommy." The child with *conduct disorder* might say, "I don't feel like it—it's not fun"; the child with *oppositional defiant disorder* might say, "Nobody can make me go to school if I don't want to." Kids without a specific disorder might say, "I'm afraid of failing and looking stupid in class" or "Someone bullies me there."

A variety of approaches are used to treat children who have never successfully separated. Children should be allowed to have transitional objects such as blankets, stuffed animals, and pictures of family members with them in the new setting. Stretching the length of separation very gradually from minutes to hours can help children master the sensations of separation anxiety. Since children pick up their parents' anxieties, counseling parents to help reduce *their* anxiety about separation is very often needed, and has demonstrated efficacy in reducing the child's anxiety.

For children who have successfully separated but are currently experiencing a separation anxiety disorder after the death or illness of a family member, more specialized approaches (such as grief work) are recommended.

SELECTIVE MUTISM

Children with this rare disorder typically talk at home but refuse to speak at school or in social situations. Children who are socially withdrawn, oppositional, or have a speech disorder, are more prone to develop this disorder. Selective mutism generally starts before age 5 and typically lasts only a few weeks. It occurs with equal frequency for boys and girls. Major stresses such as immigration, hospitalization, or traumas before age 3 may predispose some children to mutism. This disorder would not be diagnosed in the presence of autism, schizophrenia, specific developmental disorders of speech

---

TABLE 14-7
Diagnostic Criteria for Selective Mutism

A. Marked, **emotionally determined selectivity in speaking,** such that the child demonstrates his or her language competence in some situations but fails to speak in other (definable) situations.

B. This condition is the source of **significant impairment** in personal, family, social, educational, occupational, or other important area of functioning

C. *DSM-5 specifies a duration of at least 1 month in addition to the first month of school.*

D. The diagnosis presupposes:
   (a) a normal, or near-normal, level of language comprehension;
   (b) a level of competence in language expression that is sufficient for social communication; and
   (c) demonstrable **evidence that the individual can and does speak normally or almost normally in some situations**.

E. The disturbance is **not better explained by another mental disorder** (e.g., psychotic disorders, autistic spectrum disorders, or communication disorder).

Note: Adapted from *ICD-10* (p. 218) and *DSM-5* (p. 195)

---

and language, or transient mutism as part of separation anxiety in young children. Table 14-7 lists the diagnostic criteria for selective mutism.

References

American Psychiatric Association. (2013). *Diagnostic and statistical manual of mental disorders*, 5th ed. Arlington, VA: American Psychiatric Association.

Bourne, E.J. (1995). *The anxiety and phobia workbook.* Oakland, CA: New Harbinger Workbooks.

Cannon, W.B. (1932). *The wisdom of the body.* New York: Norton.

Craske, M.G., Barlow, D.H., & O'Leary, T.O. (1992). *Mastery of your anxiety and worry.* Albany, NY: Graywind.

Dahl, S. (1989). Acute responses to rape: A PTSD variant. *Acta Psychiatrica Scandinavica, 80*(Supp), 355.

Freud, S. (1919). Lines of advance in psychoanalytic therapy. In J. Strachey (Ed. and Trans.), *The complete psychological works, the standard edition* (Vol. 17, pp. 157–168). New York: Norton.

James, W. (1893). *The principles of psychology.* New York: Hold & Co.

Jenike, M.A. (1993). Augmentation strategies for treatment-resistant obsessive–compulsive disorder. *Harvard Review of Psychiatry, 1,* 17–26.

Jenike, M.A., Baer, L., Ballantine, T., Martuza, R.L., Tynes, S., Giriunas, I., et al. (1991).

Cingulotomy for refractory obsessive–compulsive disorder. *Archives of General Psychiatry, 48*, 548–554.

Kandel, E.R. (1983). From metapsychology to molecular biology: Explorations into the nature of anxiety. *American Journal of Psychiatry, 140*, 1277–1293.

Klein, D.F. (1993). False suffocation alarms, spontaneous panics, and related conditions: An integrative hypothesis. *Archives of General Psychiatry, 50*, 306–317.

Liebowitz, M.R., Gorman, J.M., Fyer, A.J., & Klein, D.F. (1985). Social phobia: Review of a neglected anxiety disorder. *Archives of General Psychiatry, 42*, 729–736.

Maxmen, J. S. (1986). *A good night's sleep: A step-by-step program for overcoming insomnia and other sleep problems.* New York: Warner.

Murphy, D.L., & Pigott, T.A. (1990). A comparative examination of a role for serotonin in obsessive–compulsive disorder, panic disorder, and anxiety. *Journal of Clinical Psychiatry, 51*(4, Supp.), 53–60.

Pitts, F.N., & McClure, J.N. (1967). Lactate metabolism and anxiety neurosis. *New England Journal of Medicine, 277*, 1329–1336.

Redmond, D.E., Jr. (1979). New and old evidence for the involvement of a brain norepinephrine system in anxiety. In W.E. Fann, I. Karacan, A.D. Porkorney, & R.L. Williams (Eds.), *Phenomenology and treatment of anxiety* (pp. 153–203). New York: Spectrum.

Roy-Byrne, P., Geraci, M., & Uhde, T.W. (1986). Life events and the onset of panic disorder. *American Journal of Psychiatry, 143*, 1424–1427.

Skolnick, P., & Paul, S.M. (1983). New concepts in the neurobiology of anxiety. *Journal of Clinical Psychiatry, 44*, 12–19.

World Health Organization. (1992). *The ICD–10 classification of mental and behavioural disorders: Clinical descriptions and diagnostic guidelines.* Geneva: World Health Organization.

15

Obsessive–Compulsive Disorders

Being "obsessive" or "compulsive" is not the same as having *obsessions* or performing *compulsions*. The distinction between "obsessive" and "obsession" is the difference between a personality *style* with some adaptive features and a mental *disorder* that's often incapacitating.

Obsessions are persistent, disturbing, intrusive thoughts or impulses that the patient finds illogical but irresistible. Unlike delusions, patients consider obsessions absurd and actively resist them. Most of us have experienced these in a mild form when we have had an advertising jingle or catchy little song like "It's a Small World" take over our minds for a few hours or days. *Compulsions* are obsessions expressed in action. Obsessions and compulsions are methods for reducing anxiety. True obsessions and compulsions are the essential traits of obsessive–compulsive disorder (OCD), a surprisingly common disorder occurring in almost 3% of the population. This chapter considers a group of related disorders based upon predominant repetitive thoughts and behaviors that accompany the anxiety. It includes body dysmorphobia, hoarding, trichotillomania (hair-pulling), and excoriation (skin-picking).

OBSESSIVE-COMPULSIVE DISORDER

Clinical Presentation

The first and most important point to remember is that people with OCD rarely reveal their symptoms; they are too embarrassed and keep them a big secret. Clinicians usually must ask gently about the most common obsessions and compulsions and not wait for patients to offer the information on their own. Diagnostic criteria for OCD (Table 15-1) illustrate the many ways obsessions and compulsions can present. Obsessions may appear as *ideas—*

TABLE 15-1

Diagnostic Criteria for Obsessive–Compulsive Disorder

A. **Obsessional symptoms or compulsive acts, or both**, must be present on most days for at least 2 successive weeks and should have the following characteristics:

1. the thoughts, images, or impulses must be **unpleasantly repetitive**;

2. there must be at least **one thought or act that is still resisted unsuccessfully**, even though others may be present which the sufferer no longer resists;

3. the **thought of carrying out the act must not in itself be pleasurable** (simple relief of tension or anxiety is not regarded as pleasure in this sense);

4. they must be **recognized as the individual's own thoughts or impulses** (often considered repugnant).

B. The above symptoms must interfere with other activities and are a source of **significant distress or significant impairment** in personal, family, social, educational, occupational, or other important area of functioning.

C. The disturbance **is not due to the direct physiological effects of a substance or another medical condition**.

D. The above signs and symptoms are **not better explained by another mental disorder** (e.g., depression, schizophrenia, body dysmorphic disorder, or somatic symptom disorder).

Note: Adapted from *ICD-10* (p. 117) and *DSM-5* (p. 237)

---

words, rhymes, or melodies that annoyingly interrupt normal thought and are often considered nonsensical, obscene, or blasphemous by the patient; and they may appear as *images* that are usually violent or disgusting (e.g., children burning, rape).

Underlying most cases of OCD is some form of pathological doubting— "Something bad will happen unless I do this." If there is any possibility of something bad happening, these patients can rapidly elevate the possibility to a probability and, in many cases, to a near certainty. We all have some fears about contracting disease and even occasionally feel compelled to wash our hands, but a person with OCD is plagued by this dreaded possibility and may wash all day long. All patients with OCD have obsessions and a majority have compulsive rituals based on those obsessions. The compulsive rituals are either directly linked to the obsession (e.g., washing hands to prevent disease) or linked by magical thinking (e.g., "My parents might die if I don't wash my hands").

Most forms of OCD fall into the following five categories (most people with OCD have symptoms in more than one category):

1. *Washers* fear contamination and usually have cleaning compulsions (e.g., "If I don't clean this, something bad will happen").

2. *Checkers* repeatedly check things such as ovens ("Are they turned off?") and doors ("Are they locked?"), etc. Each time the pathological doubt recurs ("If I left the oven on, the house will burn down"), the person checks it again, up to 20 times a day or more.
3. *Doubters and sinners* fear that terrible things will happen if everything is not perfect ("Am I a good Catholic?"; "Did I do this job right?"). They are more likely to be paralyzed into inaction than to have compulsions.
4. *Counters and arrangers* are ruled by magical thinking and superstitions. Obsessions about order, symmetry, and number fuel the counting and arranging. Certain numbers or colors may be "bad," and asymmetry may lead to imagined catastrophes. Pencils all must face north or no work proceeds.
5. *Hoarders* cannot throw anything away because if they do, terrible things might happen. Not all hoarding is based on OCD, however. Some people are poorly organized and never get around to throwing things out; others intend to sort those piles but don't find the time. The important question to ask a hoarder is, "What would happen if all that stuff were thrown out?" A catastrophic answer suggests OCD. A more banal one—"Oh, well, I needed to get rid of stuff anyway"—suggests procrastination or poor organization. Hoarding disorder is now its own diagnostic category in *DSM-5*.

Epidemiology

The lifetime prevalence of OCD in the general population is 2.6% (see Table 1-3). The sexes are equally affected with onset usually in childhood or early adult life. The course is variable and more likely to be chronic in the absence of significant depressive symptoms. OCD is more common among the higher educated, higher socioeconomic groups, and those with higher IQ scores—three interrelated factors. Obsessive–compulsive personality disorder is not particularly more common in OCD, but avoidant and dependent personality disorders are. More recent data suggest that believing the thoughts or behaviors are real or reasonable does not indicate a poorer prognosis.

Differential Diagnosis

Normal obsessive thoughts and compulsive behaviors are not resisted or considered ridiculous by the person having them. Avoiding sidewalk cracks and other compulsive actions are common during childhood, but kids don't mind them; they do mind OCD. Kids have a lot of magical thinking and don't see the senselessness of their acts. Adults may feel that their obsessive brooding, ruminations, and preoccupations are annoying and excessive, yet they usually think they're meaningful; not being fully ego-dystonic, these are not the true obsessions of OCD. This disorder was once believed to be intimately related to *obsessive–compulsive personality disorder*, but more recent evidence suggests no real relationship between the two. The obsessive and compulsive traits in obsessive–compulsive personality disorder are ego-syntonic, whereas they are usually ego-dystonic in OCD; moreover, patients with obsessive–compulsive personality disorder do not have true obsessions or compulsions. Neither are so-called *compulsive gambling, eating, and sexual behaviors* true compulsions; the person usually enjoys doing them, does not imagine any disaster occurring if they are not done, and at least is temporarily distracted from unpleasant feelings.

OCD should not be diagnosed when specific obsessions and compulsions arise directly from other disorders. *Schizophrenic delusions* may resemble obsessions, but they are usually ego-syntonic and occur without patients' insight. Obsessions are overvalued ideas, not delusions; patients with OCD usually accept the fact that their obsessions are not realistic. Because *major depression* is often accompanied by ruminative, guilt-ridden, and self-critical obsessions, and since major depression and OCD both have episodic courses, differentiating the two can be difficult. In general, the diagnosis of OCD should be reserved when OCD clearly precedes major depression, or when the obsessions are not directly related to the depression. If the obsession or preoccupation is confined to body parts, somatic symptoms, or having an illness then body dysmorphic or somatic symptom disorders are diagnosed. Similarly, in disorders in which preoccupations normally occur, OCD is diagnosed only if the obsessions include other areas of concern.

Etiology and Pathogenesis

Freudian psychodynamic theory states that obsessions and compulsions develop in three phases: (1) an internally perceived dangerous impulse, (2) the threat of what would occur if this impulse were acted upon, and (3) the defenses to avert the threat. The most commonly used defenses are repression, reaction formation, isolation, and undoing.

Individuals with neurological disorders and brain insults due to trauma or infection are more prone to develop OCD. Research indicates that there are abnormalities in the frontal lobes, basal ganglia, and cingulus areas of patients with this disorder. Cingulotomy in extreme cases can substantially relieve or cure OCD. The basal ganglia is involved in overlearned routine behaviors such as grooming, and the prefrontal areas mediate planning and organizing behaviors. Because drugs that treat OCD all markedly affect serotonin transmission, the serotonin system is probably involved.

Psychopathology in general and obsessions in particular run in the families of people with obsessions. Given that concordance rates for OCD are 70% and 50% among MZ and DZ twins, respectively, genetic transmission is involved. A patient with OCD has a 25% chance of having a first-degree relative with this disorder.

Clinical Course

Two-thirds of patients with OCD have substantial symptoms before the age of 15 and almost all have some symptoms in childhood. On the average, men develop OCD 5 years earlier than women. It is rare to develop OCD after the age of 35 years. The first psychiatric contact is in the 20s and the first hospitalization (if any), during the 30s. Although it tends to begin gradually, OCD may erupt suddenly after a severe psychosocial stressor. In the average patient it is a chronic lifelong illness with waxing and waning of symptoms. Outcome is not related to the content of the obsessions; patients with milder symptoms, no compulsions, briefer duration of symptoms, and higher premorbid functioning have better prognoses.

Complications and Comorbidity

Attempts to resist an obsession or compulsion may produce anxiety of panic proportions; hence the inclusion of this disorder with the anxiety disorders. Depression is the most frequent (80% of patients) comorbidity for these patients. It may be difficult to sustain interpersonal relationships. Although going insane, being totally incapacitated, or permanently incarcerated are all common fears of people with obsessions, these fears rarely materialize. Despite much suicidal thinking, less than 1% of these patients commit suicide.

Several uncommon disorders may coexist with OCD about 10–15% of the time, but are not necessarily a result of it. These include anorexia and bulimia nervosa, trichotillomania, and Tourette's disorder. Body dysmorphic disorder (e.g., "My nose is too big, my lips too small")—sometimes called the "Michael Jackson syndrome"—often occurs with OCD. Underlying many of these conditions is pathological doubting (e.g., "I'm too fat" in the anorectic).

Management and Treatment

Medication

The only proven effective medication treatment for this disorder are the SSRIs (fluoxetine, sertraline, paroxetine, citalopram, escitalopram, fluvoxamine) and the highly serotonergic TCA clomipramine. As the chlorinated derivative of imipramine (itself ineffective), clomipramine must be given in an eventual dose of 150–250 mg after gradual titration. High doses of SSRIs (fluoxetine 60–80 mg, sertraline 150–200 mg, paroxetine 40–50 mg) may be required, although one recent study showed that doses traditionally effective for depression do work. Response can take 10–12 weeks, so premature termination of medication trials should be avoided. Although 70% of patients respond to some degree, most are left with residual symptoms. Only about 10–15% of patients have full remissions. The average partial responder has a 40% reduction in symptoms. In OCD, however, that may mean 3–5 more hours of good functioning each day—a big improvement. Most patients stay on medication chronically; about 85% relapse in a month or two after stopping medication.

Behavior Therapy

A combination of behavior therapy and antidepressants is generally recommended for OCD patients. Behavior-based approaches have been moderately successful, particularly with patients who have compulsions. Graded exposure and response prevention are usually used for the compulsions. For example, a hand-washer might be taken into a "contaminated" place and prevented from washing his hands for two minutes. Catastrophic thoughts are identified as the patient watches his anxiety peak and then subside. In another case, a woman who fears contamination if she touches anything without wearing gloves is directed to not wear gloves for half an hour and to touch a variety of feared objects (e.g., food, newspapers, silverware, old sweat socks). Eventually, she becomes desensitized to touching these objects.

Surgery

Stereotactic cingulotomy has been used occasionally for very severe, very treatment-resistant cases. About 25–30% of these patients substantially benefit from this procedure (Jenike et al., 1991). The non-invasive repetitive Transcranial Magnetic Stimulation (rTMS), by targeting magnetic waves to the caudate nucleus or prefrontal cortex, shows some promise in treating OCD.

BODY DYSMORPHIC DISORDER

Clinical Presentation

Body dysmorphic disorder (BDD), originally called "dysmorphophobia," is the preoccupation in a normal-appearing person with an imagined defect in appearance or a markedly excessive concern with a slight physical anomaly. People with this disorder complain, "My nose is too big," "My mouth is too small," or "My face is crawling with wrinkles." The preoccupation must also be very upsetting or impair some important areas of functioning, such as a job, marriage, or social situations. People with BDD run to their dermatologist or plastic surgeon, but almost never to a psychiatrist. Table 15-2 lists the DSM-5 diagnostic criteria for body dysmorphic disorder. This disorder is included in hypochondriasis for ICD-10 but will be included as a separate disorder for ICD-11.

The focus of concern can be virtually any area of the body or anything on the face. Frequent mirror checking, sometimes consuming hours each day, is common. Others *avoid* mirrors with equal passion and consequent distress. Because of embarrassment, it's usually a secret problem, shared only with doctors. Camouflage tactics are common and may include makeup, hats, or the use of hands or hair to cover the imagined defect, or countermeasures such as jutting forward a receding jaw.

TABLE 15-2
Diagnostic Criteria for Body Dysmorphic Disorder

A. **Preoccupation with at least one perceived defect in appearance** that is markedly excessive for any slight physical anomaly that may exist.

B. In response to the appearance concerns the individual has performed **repetitive mental actions or behaviors**.

C. The preoccupation is a source of **significant distress or significant impairment** in personal, family, social, educational, occupational, or other important area of functioning.

D. The above symptoms are **not better explained by another mental disorder** (e.g., psychotic disorders, depression, phobias, illness anxiety, or eating disorder).

Note: Adapted from DSM-5, p. 242–243.

Differential Diagnosis

Body dysmorphic disorder shouldn't be diagnosed in people who are concerned about minor defects if their concern is not excessive (e.g., typical adolescents). "Bad hair" days don't count! One study found that 70% of college students had at least some dissatisfaction with their appearance, and 46% were somewhat preoccupied with one particular aspect of their appearance (Fitts et al., 1989). If the preoccupation is about weight, the distorted body image is part of an *eating disorder*, not BDD. In BDD the belief is not delusional in intensity, as it is in a *delusional disorder, somatic type*. Patients recognize the possibility that they have exaggerated the extent of the defect or that there isn't a defect at all. Exaggerated concerns about appearance are common in *major depressive disorder, avoidant personality disorder, social phobia*, and *narcissistic personality disorder*, but unlike in BDD, they aren't the predominant feature.

Clinical Course and Complications

Body dysmorphic disorder affects women slightly more often than men, often begins in adolescence, can wax and wane for years, and if untreated, can go on for decades. Major depression and dysthymia are associated with this disorder, but probably as complications rather than causes. Usually the depression comes *after*, not *before*, the onset of BDD. Another complication is unnecessary plastic surgery. Obsessive–compulsive disorder has also been reported to travel with BDD. Nobody really knows what causes it. Sometimes it is acutely triggered by a chance remark such as "My, you have a small head," or "You're very handsome considering how big your nose is." Sometimes it comes after a threat to, or breakup of, a relationship.

Management and Treatment

The literature is full of reported successes and failures, often with the same purported treatment. Plastic surgery usually leads to new problems—the surgery wasn't quite right or there are other parts of the body that aren't right. Some people with BDD undergo as many plastic surgeries as Michael Jackson. *Behavior therapies*, using progressive exposure techniques, audiovisual self-confrontation, and systematic desensitization have all been successful. Psychodynamic approaches seek to uncover unconscious conflicts regarding patients' feelings of inadequacy.

A successful result is more often a response along the lines of "Who cares about my big nose?" rather than an all-out assertion, "My nose is normal." The *serotonergic antidepressants* clomipramine and fluoxetine work at least 50% of the time in depressed and nondepressed patients with BDD and occasionally even in the patient who has crossed the line into delusion. Responses with less selective antidepressants have been mixed. This pattern of treatment response parallels those for OCD, leading some to suggest that BDD is a variant of OCD.

TRICHOTILLOMANIA

Trichotillomania is the recurrent failure to resist pulling out one's own hair. Unlike the other impulse control disorders, it usually causes harm only to the individual affected. Trichotillomania is commonly associated with depressive and anxiety disorders, and may run in families. There has been some controversy surrounding the grouping of trichotillomania with the other impulse control disorders and the current prevailing view is that it may be a variant of obsessive–compulsive disorder.

The disorder causes distress because hair loss can be extensive, and the obvious hair loss can attract social scrutiny. Children with the disorder are often teased or ostracized. For many (but not all) individuals with trichotillomania, tension mounts before the moment of plucking and is reduced during or after the act. The majority pull out one hair at a time, concentrate on scalp hair, and report that pulling the hair out doesn't hurt. Some pull out clumps of hair, often by first twirling a group of hairs together and then pulling them out as a group.

> Hair loss varies from barely noticeable thinning to total loss. This loss usually occurs in patches, as individuals often have a preferred pulling spot, often the crown area or at the temples. Eyelashes (22%) and eyebrows (8%) are other favored sites. Multiple sites (two on average) are eventually used, and because it's easily concealed, even pubic hair (17%) is included. After pulling out the hair, many people with trichotillomania will manipulate or examine the hair in some way. They may put the hair in or around their mouths (25%), lick it (8%), and/or eat it (10%) (Christenson et al., 1991).

Most patients with trichotillomania are females with some studies reporting the female to male ratio to be as high as 10:1. This difference may reflect some bias in seeking treatment, but there does seem to be a greater occurrence of the disorder in females. Estimates from university surveys suggest

TABLE 15-3
Diagnostic Criteria for Trichotillomania

A. **Noticeable hair loss due to repeatedly pulling out hairs**.

B. **Attempts but recurrent failure to resist impulses**.

C. The repetitive impulses and hair-pulling are a source of **significant distress or significant impairment** in personal, family, social, educational, occupational, or other important area of functioning.

D. The above symptoms are **not better explained by another mental disorder** (e.g., a pre-existing inflammation of the skin, or if the hairpulling is in response to a delusion or a hallucination).

Note: Adapted from *ICD-10* (p. 167) and *DSM-5* (p. 251)

that 1.5% of males and 3.4% of females endorse significant hair pulling, and 0.6% of these university students met all diagnostic criteria for trichotillomania (Dell'Osso, 2006). Table 15-3 lists diagnostic criteria for trichotillomania. By replacing "hair-pulling" with "skin-picking" the same criteria would be used for excoriation disorder.

Many people with trichotillomania don't come in for treatment. A third of the women who came to a clinic for treatment said that they had the problem less than a year. A broader, nonclinic study (Christenson et al., 1991) found that most had started the behavior within 5 years before or after puberty and had had the problem for two decades. Only 18% did *not* have another acute mental disorder. The rest had a lifetime diagnosis of mood disorders (65%), anxiety disorder (57%), eating disorders (20%), and/or substance use disorder (22%). Within the anxiety disorders, 18% had panic disorder, 10% had obsessive–compulsive disorder, and another 18% had obsessions or compulsions but did not meet the full criteria for obsessive–compulsive disorder.

> Because people with trichotillomania are, at times, secretive about their pulling, a medical cause for their hair loss may be considered. With a biopsy, a dermatologist can easily distinguish between the medical condition of *alopecia areata* and hair loss from trichotillomania. If the patient insists to the clinician that she never pulls out her hair, and the dermatologist can verify that this is a lie, then the person really has a *factitious disorder* with physical symptoms. One important question is "What makes you pull out your hair, and how do you feel once you've done it?" People with *obsessive–compulsive disorder* will say that they are doing it to prevent or produce some future situation. Kids and adults with *stereotypic movement disorder* will say that they

don't know why they do it, they just do, and it doesn't bother them. Fiddling with the hair and occasionally pulling out a hair is normal; no tension–relief cycle is noted. Normals might say "I barely thought about it—I was spaced out." In contrast, individuals with trichotillomania will often describe urges to pull, and relief after, or pleasure during, pulling. The behavior often occurs during passive activities such as reading or TV viewing. Usually the individuals pull when they are alone, suggesting some degree of voluntary control. Sessions of pulling may last many minutes and result in the loss of significant (noticeable) amounts of hair. Other impulsive behaviors seen in individuals with trichotillomania include nail biting and excessive picking at skin.

Along with behavioral approaches, treatment with antidepressants may be helpful. As in obsessive–compulsive disorder, serotonin agents such as clomipramine and fluoxetine have shown efficacy. There are established cognitive–behavioral treatment models for the disorder, and these have also shown efficacy. There have also been reports of benefits from hypnosis.

References

American Psychiatric Association. (2013). *Diagnostic and statistical manual of mental disorders*, 5th ed. Arlington, VA: American Psychiatric Association.

Christenson, G.A., Mackenzie, T.B., & Mitchell, J.E. (1991). Characteristics of 60 adult chronic hair pullers. *American Journal of Psychiatry, 148*, 365–370.

Fitts, S.N., Gibson, P., Redding, C.A., & Deiter, P.J. (1989). Body dysmorphic disorder: Implications for its validity as a *DMS-III–R* clinical syndrome. *Psychological Reports, 64*, 655–658.

Phillips, K.A., Albertini, R.S., & Rasmussen, S.A. (2002). A randomized placebo-controlled trial of fluoxetine in body dysmorphic disorder. *Archives of General Psychiatry, 59*(4), 381–388.

World Health Organization. (1992). *The ICD–10 classification of mental and behavioural disorders: Clinical descriptions and diagnostic guidelines*. Geneva: World Health Organization.

16

Trauma and Stress Disorders

POSTTRAUMATIC STRESS DISORDER

Posttraumatic stress disorder (PTSD) occurs after a severe and extraordinary stressor: a massive fire, hurricane, holocaust, rape, mugging, military combat, or terrorist bombing. The stressful events are usually more than "normal" bereavement, chronic illness, business losses, divorce, and so forth. Hours or months following the stressor, patients waver between two main features of PTSD: reexperiencing (also called intrusion) and avoidance of the event. Often, *avoidance* or *denial* comes first, with prominent "psychic numbing." These individuals minimize the significance of the stress, forget it happened, feel detached from others, lose interest in life, display constricted affect, daydream, and abuse drugs or alcohol. In reexperiencing the trauma, patients are flooded by intrusive recollections while awake (flashbacks), while asleep (nightmares), or while waking up (hypnopompic hallucinations). They may then manifest the third cardinal feature of PTSD, which is autonomic arousal (e.g., being hypervigilant and "on edge"). They cannot sleep or concentrate; they ruminate about the stressor, cry "without reason," show emotional lability, are startled or upset by the slightest reminders of the trauma, and develop somatic anxiety. Patients compulsively relive the stressful event, are often unable to think about anything else, and fear "going crazy." In the diagnostic criteria for PTSD (Table 16-1), the reexperiencing phase is generally covered under criterion B, the avoidance phase under criterion C, and hyperarousal under E.

Normal and pathological responses to traumatic events are usually, but not always, easy to distinguish (see Figure 4-5). Normal responders react with sadness or anxiety and find it harder to acknowledge guilt, rage, or shame. They may undergo periods of denial and intrusion. They often go through stages similar to those associated with grief, but without resolution. Indeed, this is one of the few times that producing symptoms is healthy.

TABLE 16-1
Diagnostic Criteria for Posttraumatic Stress Disorder

A. Evidence for **a traumatic event of exceptional severity** to which the person was exposed within the last 6 months (rarely longer).
   1. The trauma was exceptionally threatening or of a catastrophic nature likely to cause pervasive distress in almost anyone (e.g., natural or manmade disaster, combat, serious accident) or it involved
   2. Witnessing the violent death of others, or
   3. Being the victim of torture, terrorism, rape, or other crime.
B. **Repetitive, intrusive recollection or reenactment of the event** in memories, daytime imagery, or dreams.
   1. Typical symptoms include episodes of repeated reliving of the trauma in intrusive memories ("flashbacks") or dreams.
   2. Rarely, there may be dramatic, acute bursts of fear, panic or aggression, triggered by stimuli arousing a sudden recollection and/or reenactment of the trauma or of the original reaction to it.
C. **Avoidance of stimuli that might arouse recollection of the trauma** are often present. Commonly there is fear and avoidance of cues (activities and situations) reminiscent of the original trauma.
D. *Negative alteration of mood and cognitions.**
E. **Autonomic disturbance**—there is usually a state of autonomic hyperarousal with hypervigilance, an enhanced startle reaction, and insomnia.
F. *The symptoms have persisted for at least one month.**
G. This condition is the source of **significant distress or significant impairment** in personal, family, social, educational, occupational, or other important area of functioning.
H. The symptoms are **not due to the direct physiological effects of a substance or another medical condition**.
I. The psychological, behavioral, or autonomic symptoms must be primarily manifestations of anxiety and not secondary to other symptoms such as delusions or obsessional thoughts. The symptoms are **not better explained by another mental disorder**.

Specify whether dissociative symptoms are present, i.e., conspicuous emotional detachment, sense of "numbness" and emotional blunting, detachment from other people, depersonalization, derealization, and unresponsiveness to surroundings.

**DSM-5 specifies criteria D and F as well as modified criteria for children under the age of 6 years to reflect the developmental differences in symptom manifestation.*

Note: Adapted from *ICD-10* (p. 118) and *DSM-5* (p. 271)

There is a very brief (less than 1 month) variation of PTSD called Acute Stress Disorder that emphasizes dissociative symptoms. There exists an immediate and clear temporal connection (usually within a few minutes) between the onset of symptoms and the impact of an exceptional traumatic event. The mixed and usually changing picture of symptoms resolves rapidly (usually within hours) and includes intrusive memories, avoidance, arousal, negative emotions, and dissociation. Dissociation as an early symptom may predict the development of PTSD. The risk of developing an acute stress disorder increases with the presence of physical exhaustion of other biological factors (e.g., in the elderly).

Rarely, PTSD may have a *delayed onset* that emerges at least 6 months past the trauma. This delayed expression of the disorder has the worst prognosis with frequent development of mood and substance use disorders. Anxiety and depression are commonly associated with posttraumatic stress, and suicidal ideation is not rare. These comorbid disorders may be both different manifestations and sequelae of the same underlying illness of PTSD. Excessive use of alcohol or drugs may be a consequence or a complicating factor. Perhaps two-thirds of these individuals had family members with a psychiatric disorder, usually substance abuse or an anxiety disorder, suggesting an underlying predisposition. In general, a previous history of mood and anxiety disorders, along with certain personality traits may predispose one to developing a posttraumatic syndrome or aggravate its course.

> After spending 16 months on active duty in Iraq, a 29-year-old soldier returned to his home in the rural Midwest. He found a job at a nearby factory. He was doing reasonably well adjusting to civilian life, when fireworks on the 4th of July unleashed memories of being fired at, explosions from rocket-propelled grenades, and helping transport dead bodies. This was accompanied by withdrawal from family, easy irritability, episodes of crying, nightmares of seeing people die, and being easily startled. Cognitive–behavioral therapy (described in Chapter 5) aimed at normalizing his reactions, relaxation techniques, and the use of an SSRI, helped decrease the severity and frequency of his symptoms, enabling him to return to work in 6 weeks.

In both acute and chronic forms, encountering a circumstance similar to the original stressor often aggravates or rekindles symptoms. Many persons with PTSD continue to experience intermittent and residual symptoms throughout life. The intensity and duration of symptoms are usually less severe if the trauma is caused by nature (e.g., hurricane) rather than by people (e.g., rape, torture). *Single-event traumas* are less likely to cause PTSD than *complex traumas* that repeat and persist. However, many single-event traumas (e.g., hurricanes) are associated with secondary adversities, such as loss of home, school, friends, and income, which transform them into complex traumas with indistinguishable clinical results.

Epidemiology

The lifetime prevalence of PTSD in the general population is approximately 7% with females being twice as likely to meet the diagnostic criteria. This disorder can occur at any age, but children and older adults generally have a more difficult time coping with traumatic events. There is a latency period of a few weeks to months (rarely more than 6 months) prior to the onset of symptoms following the trauma. The course is fluctuating but in the majority of cases recovery can be expected. In a small proportion of patients the course becomes chronic and over many years the condition transitions to more enduring personality change.

Studies conducted after the San Fernando earthquake of 1971 and the Chowchilla bus kidnapping in 1976 demonstrated the effects of significant trauma on children. In the latter instance, all 25 kidnapping victims who had been held for 27 hours (for 16 of those hours, they were buried in their school bus) demonstrated pessimism, shame, increased fearfulness, repeated nightmares, and related symptoms 4 years after the trauma. Frequently, traumatized children stop thinking about the future, feeling that they have none. Trauma in childhood more often than in adults, results in dissociative experiences, self-injurious behavior, difficulties with impulse control, traumatic reenactments, "repetition compulsions," social isolation, and profound restrictions in emotional responsiveness (Terr, 1991).

Differential Diagnosis

On one hand, PTSD may go undiagnosed in patients because (1) they don't report the initial trauma or the subsequent symptoms, (2) substance abuse masks the symptoms, or (3) their traumatic visual imagery is misattributed to schizophrenia, LSD intoxication or flashbacks, temporal lobe epilepsy, or a dissociative disorder. On the other hand, when PTSD is used to justify financial compensation, malingering might be the diagnosis. Differentiating PTSD from *malingering* can be difficult, partly because the patient may no longer be able to distinguish reality from fabrication. People who deliberately malinger may not present with the specific diagnostic criteria, but rather display their own version of what they (or television) consider madness. Careful coaching by an attorney or others may later help them get the symptoms "right." The differential diagnosis includes the other *anxiety disorders, major depression,* and *adjustment disorder. Adjustment disorder with anxiety* should not be confused with PTSD. Adjustment disorders are triggered by more ordinary stressors (e.g., exams to graduate from college, a court hearing, or divorce). Over 95% of patients with PTSD have a past psychiatric disorder of some kind and over 50% have an additional current diagnosis.

Etiology

To qualify for diagnosis of PTSD, the etiology must include a sufficiently traumatizing event.

> In men, military trauma is the most common cause of PTSD; and in women rape and/or physical abuse are the most common causes. Men entering the military who are most likely to get PTSD are younger, have had less military training, were previously emotionally or physically abused, or already have had some psychiatric symptoms. Particularly severe traumas involving witnessing the death or dismemberment of buddies, witnessing or participating in atrocities, and physical injury with permanent disability are more likely to cause chronic and severe PTSD (Kulk et al., 1990). Soldiers who had been deployed to Iraq more than once were 1.6 times more likely to have PTSD than those deployed only once. Soldiers deployed for more than six months were also 1.5 times more likely to have PTSD than those deployed for less than 6 months.
>
> Women who have been raped are more likely to develop PTSD if physical force, display of a weapon, or injury to the victim occurred (Bownes et al., 1991). They also tend to have more acute guilt, shame, and suicidal ideation (Dahl, 1989). A woman who was sexually abused in childhood by a male is less likely to develop PTSD if she had a supportive mother who intervened and an overall positive family environment. Later, a gentle, caring boyfriend can help a woman desensitize to her trauma and to men in general. Women with PTSD from childhood sexual abuse may display less obvious but highly related symptoms, such as going to bed fully clothed with a night light on, having insomnia until dawn comes, and then sleeping well. These are all understandable responses to being regularly sexually abused at bedtime or during the night. A dissociative disorder more often accompanies PTSD induced by childhood versus adult trauma.

Perhaps 20% of those exposed to such an event develop PTSD, which means that the vast majority do not. Risk factors include proximity to the trauma, prolonged exposure, complex trauma, previous psychiatric history, minimal support network, and early dissociative symptom response. Sustained hyperarousal seems to elevate cortisol levels and thereby alter the hypothalamic–pituitary–adrenal axis. Chronically high cortisol may damage the hippocampus (reducing its volume), which, along with the anterior cingulate, are involved with cognitive memory. The amygdala (a major member of the limbic system), which controls emotional memory, is overactive in PTSD. The essence of treatment is to help the person suffering from PTSD to move from pure emotional to cognitive memory of the event and essentially reverse these neurophysiological concomitants. The noradrenergic and serotonergic neurotransmitter systems have been implicated in this disorder.

Management and Treatment

Debriefing immediately after the trauma may actually worsen outcome by unwittingly reinforcing overwhelming feelings through forced disclosure of events and exploration of feelings. There is general agreement that immediate interventions should include ensuring safety while addressing concerns of the moment and practical needs; encouraging use of the existing natural supports (family and friends); expressing hope while tolerating the person's expressions of emotion; expecting recovery and providing reassurance for successful coping; educating on common and maladaptive responses to trauma; and evaluating mental status, especially for dissociative symptoms and other risk factors. Often the trauma victim will accept support only from a person who has experienced a similar trauma. This is based on the mistaken belief that a person who has had the same experience will automatically understand and empathize with the victim. A well-functioning support group can be especially helpful for those temporarily overwhelmed by the trauma by providing practical support that reinforces the victim's reactions as "normal"; addressing common fears, concerns, and traumatic memories; increasing the capacity to tolerate disturbing emotions; and sharing strategies for coping. Unfortunately, some support groups may encourage endless catharsis and a posttraumatic group identity without treatment progress or improvement in adaptive functioning.

Acute PTSD may remit spontaneously, and mild and acute cases may respond to supportive psychotherapy. Most chronic (more than 5 months) and severe cases do not remit spontaneously or with supportive approaches alone and require more intensive and specialized psychotherapy. Individual or group therapy for chronic and severe cases involves active confrontation of feared topics and memories, examining misinterpretation of the events, and developing better methods of coping with the trauma. However, treatment occurs in carefully orchestrated phases, and its ultimate success is measured by restored relationships and community integration. Although eventually returning to the trauma is considered necessary, former adaptive defenses are restored and a safe therapeutic environment is established before traumatic memories are gradually and gently explored. Typically one works through the trauma by creating a narrative account with an understanding of its personal meaning and its proper context.

In cognitive–behavioral therapy, exposure approaches are used to reduce fear responses to both the original trauma and present reminders. Cognitive restructuring methods focus on distorted views of the original trauma and the subsequent changes in basic assumptions regarding self-invulnerability, self-esteem, and life meaningfulness. Even with successful treatment, symptoms of PTSD may resurface in response to stress from life events and developmental stages and require intermittent psychotherapy (preferably with the same therapist). If untreated, the syndrome continues for decades or a lifetime and spawns associated substance abuse; mood, panic, or phobic disorders; and occupational and interpersonal impairments. These must also be a focus of therapy. Medications are often indicated, since phobic and anxiety symptoms and major depressive disorder are typically dominant features that interfere with psychotherapy.

Medications for PTSD can be used adjunctively for some symptoms. There is some evidence to suggest that early treatment of hyperarousal with adrenergic blockers may reduce the risk of developing the full syndrome. In addition to reducing the physiological arousal (e.g., excessive hypervigilance and startle response), the adrenergic blockers such as propanol and clonidine can decrease anger. SSRIs, TCAs, and MAOIs are useful in treating PTSD. These drugs can reduce symptoms such as nightmares, flashbacks, and intrusive recollections. An 8-week trial might be needed to show full effect. Anticonvulsants increase behavioral control, particularly for irritability and aggression. Prazosin has been shown to decrease flashbacks, and cyproheptadine to improve nightmares in war veterans. Benzodiazepines have not been shown to work and may disinhibit. MAOIs should not be used in substance abusers because of the risk of hypertensive crisis from a drug–MAOI interaction. Trazodone can be used safely for insomnia in this population.

ATTACHMENT DISORDERS

The profound disturbance in social relatedness of these disorders is usually associated with grossly pathogenic, neglectful care during infancy. Because of this early trauma, social milestones such as smiling with pleasure by 2 months or shared laughter at 3 months are missed. The neglected infant typically appears apathetic, staring vacantly and moving little. They often fail to thrive physically. Placement in a more positive environment may lead to normal physical growth, but may only partially correct the disturbed social relatedness. As they grow older some children may exhibit a pattern of indiscriminate sociability with strangers. Attachment anxiety is associated with the child's inability to trust and is magnified in situations that promote intimacy.

Reactive attachment disorder represents grossly underdeveloped attachment characterized by emotional withdrawal and minimal social responsiveness. The child does not seek or respond to comfort. This behavior is sometimes described as "frozen watchfulness." In contrast, *disinhibited social engagement disorder* represents insecure attachment as manifest by the child being indiscriminately friendly, socially disinhibited, and attention-seeking. Both of these disorders require evidence of insufficient care that did not meet basic emotional and physical needs or evidence of limited opportunities for a selective attachment to form (e.g., discontinuities with caregivers).

Children with attachment disorders differ from those with autistic spectrum disorders in having the preserved hard-wired capacity for normal social responsiveness and reciprocity. This is evident once the child is placed in a more nurturing environment. Also, children with attachment disorders usually have normal cognitive development and communication abilities. They do not have the more restricted interests and stereotypies of autism.

ADJUSTMENT DISORDERS

Adjustment disorders are a large part of clinical practice and often the most rewarding conditions to treat. Using *DSM-IV*, clinicians diagnosed adjustment disorders in about 10% of adults and 32% of adolescents. Adjustment disorders can be disruptive and distressing, yet with time and treatment, they resolve; in fact, many patients emerge healthier and wiser.

Adjustment disorders are the most benign of mental disorders, but more severe than "normal" problems in living (e.g., uncomplicated bereavement, marital problems). Thus, adjustment disorders *are* psychopathology and their diagnoses *are* critical. When adjustment disorders are dismissed as normal problems in living, clinicians risk underestimating the seriousness of the patient's difficulties, whether it be truancy, financial disaster, or suicidal intent. On the other hand, when adjustment disorders are misdiagnosed as a more ominous condition, the patient may receive inappropriate medication, psychotherapy, or even hospitalization.

Clinical Presentation

Adjustment disorders involve maladaptive reactions to psychosocial stressors occurring within 3 months of their occurrence. It is presumed that the clinical condition would not have arisen without the stressful event, situation, or life crisis. Undoubtedly a person's individual vulnerabilities will predispose to and influence the expression of adjustment disorders. These disorders are self-limiting (less than 6 months) and are not due to another mental disorder. In other words, these are relatively benign, transient, but maladaptive situational reactions. Table 16-2 lists diagnostic criteria for adjustment disorders.

To qualify as maladaptive, a reaction must impair function, or it must be stronger or last longer than a "normal" person's reaction to the same stressor. These reactions constitute relatively persisting patterns of behaviors, not single acts. On watching his house burn down, a frightened man starts smashing his neighbor's windows. His reaction, although excessive, is lim-

---

TABLE 16-2
Diagnostic Criteria for Adjustment Disorders

A. **Emotional or behavioral reactions occurring within 3 months of the onset of a stressful event, situation, or life crisis**. There is strong evidence to support that the symptoms would not have arisen without the stressor.

B. The symptoms result in **marked subjective distress or significant impairment** in personal, family, social, educational, occupational, or other important area of functioning.

C. The symptoms are **not better explained by another mental disorder** and do not simply represent an exacerbation of a preexisting mental disorder.

D. The symptoms are **not the result of normal bereavement reactions or appropriate to the culture** of the individual concerned, and not usually exceeding 6 months in duration.

E. The duration of symptoms **does not exceed 6 months after the stressor is removed**. If the symptoms persist beyond this period, the diagnosis should be changed according to the clinical picture present.

Specify clinical form based upon predominant features: depression, anxiety, conduct, mixed reaction with anxiety and depression, mixed reaction with emotions and conduct.

Note: Adapted from ICD-10 (p. 121) and DSM-5 (p. 286)

---

ited to this outburst; subsequently, he experiences nothing but the expected sadness and frustration. This man does *not* have adjustment disorder.

> Steve Walsh did have an adjustment disorder. Extremely bright and bored by school, at 16 Steve began to skip classes and to peddle marijuana and cocaine. Prior to these behaviors, he had been a good student and had never sold drugs. School officials and the police dragged in Steve, who dragged in his parents. While upstairs in his room one evening, Steve overheard one of his parents' many screaming matches. Steve says that his mother yelled at her husband, "My psychiatrist says I need tranquilizers because you're such a bastard," to which his father replied, "At least I didn't breed that delinquent bastard son of yours." Although Mrs. Walsh tried hushing her husband so Steve wouldn't hear, it was too late. Stunned at first, Steve turned up his stereo earphones to blast and empty his mind. At three in the morning, Steve quietly emerged, grabbed his mother's barbiturates, fled Dayton, drove to Cleveland, and began selling the barbiturates on the street. Steve hated living on the street, but had no place to go. He felt unloved and unwanted; Steve wanted his parents, but refused to call them. Five days later, his father tracked him down, scooped him up, and returned him to Dayton on the condition that the entire family would get therapy. Steve desperately wanted to get away from home and attend a challenging private school. The parents agreed, partly for Steve's sake, but also because they wanted to improve their relationship without Steve's acting up constantly (and "conveniently") distracting them. The plan worked.

Adjustment disorders present with *generalized* symptoms (e.g., disruptions of mood or conduct) as opposed to *specific* ones (e.g., hallucinations, delusions, phobias, and panic attacks). There are a variety of emotional and behavioral manifestations and some resulting degree of disability in performing normal daily activities. Depression and anxiety are the most frequent mood disturbances. Except for suicide attempts, depressive symptoms are more common in adults (87%) than adolescents (64%), whereas conduct (or behavioral) problems are more prevalent in adolescents (77%) than adults (25%). Suicidal thoughts are more often reported by adults (36% vs. 29%), but among those having these thoughts, adolescents (86%) attempt suicide more than adults (47%). Conduct problems among adolescents may include truancy, drinking, temper outbursts, vandalism, school suspension, persistent lying, and repeated arrests, among others. Aggressive or dissocial behavior may be an associated feature, particularly in adolescents. In children, regressive phenomena such as return to bed-wetting, baby talk, or thumb-sucking would qualify.

> The stressor can be just about anything: It may be short-lived or ongoing, single, or multiple, affect individuals or groups; it may be associated with a specific event or a developmental stage. The stressor's impact varies according to its duration, timing, context, and meaning, and so the severity of any particular stressor depends on the particular individual. The nature of the stressor may be indicated on Axis IV. For adults, the most common stressors are marital problems (25%), separation or divorce (23%), relocation (17%), finances (14%), and work (9%). For adolescents, they are school problems (60%), parental rejection (27%), substance abuse (26%), parental separation or divorce (25%), boyfriend–girlfriend problems (20%), and parental marital problems (18%). Death of a loved one affected a mere 3% of the adults and 11.5% of the adolescents (Andreasen & Wasek, 1980).

As seen in criterion E of Table 16-2, the diagnosis of an adjustment disorder requires an assumption, or a reasonable prediction, that the patient's symptoms will remit within 6 months after the stressor has ended. If not, a more severe diagnosis is presumably more appropriate.

The beginning clinician's most common mistake is to diagnose *adjustment disorders* with depressed mood when the person really has a *major depressive disorder*. If a patient meets criteria for major depression following a major stressor such as being fired from work, the diagnosis is still major depression. Even if it seems like the depression was entirely caused by the stressor, people with this form of major depression are more likely than normals to have major depression in their families, in their pasts, and in their futures.

Epidemiology

Although adjustment disorders are common, few epidemiological studies have been conducted. In a study of 1,264 Operation Iraqi Freedom/Operation Enduring Freedom (OIF/OEF) service members evacuated from the theater of operations, 34.1% were diagnosed with adjustment disorders. They were also found to be more likely female, under the age of 31 years, and enlisted, that is, without a college degree (Rundell, 2006). Adjustment disorders are more commonly diagnosed in younger persons and females, but the actual prevalence according to situation, gender, race, and class is unknown. However, clinicians may overdiagnose adjustment disorders because of their benign connotations. Their prevalence among various races and classes is unknown, but a 2:1 female to male ratio is common.

Differential Diagnosis

Adjustment disorder should not be diagnosed until "normal problems in living" and other mental disorders have been ruled out. The DSM-5 includes these normal problems in living under "Other Conditions that May Be a Focus of Clinical Attention," and they are outlined in Chapter 3. Adjustment disorders differ from these conditions either by impairing functioning or by exceeding the normally expected reactions to a particular stressor. These distinctions are relative and require clinical judgment.

> Unlike *posttraumatic stress disorder* which has a delayed onset subtype, adjustment disorder must occur within 3 months of the stressor. The stressors producing adjustment disorder are "typical" (e.g., marital problems, retirement), whereas those that generate acute stress disorder and PTSD involve actual or threatened death or serious injury to self or others (e.g., 9/11, school shootings, suicide bombers, plane crashes, combat experience, earthquakes). Adjustment disorder is briefer and less severe than PTSD.

When a psychosocial stress exacerbates a medical illness, instead of adjustment reaction, the preferred diagnosis is *psychological factors affecting physical condition*. If a stressor aggravates a *personality disorder*, an adjustment disorder is diagnosed only when a new symptom appears that is not central to the personality disorder. For example, after her last child leaves home for college, a mother with a histrionic personality disorder becomes uncharacteristically withdrawn.

Etiology and Pathogenesis

When *normal* responses to stress are intensified, prolonged, or blocked, they produce either (the milder) adjustment disorders or (the more severe) mood or anxiety disorders. Responses to stress—normal or pathological—evolve in stages, as previously described (see Figure 4-5). A common adjustment disorder that follows this sequence is the classic "midlife crisis" (Getz, 1974). People may emerge from such a crisis better off than before depending upon inherent strengths of the person and availability of assistance in their crisis. They may develop greater maturity, ego strength, wisdom, or self-confidence.

It's unknown why some patients react to a stressor with an adjustment disorder, some with a more severe disorder, and some with no difficulties at all. Only a few clues exist: neurological and personality disorders may predispose patients to developing adjustment disorders. Vaillant's (1971) lifetime study of Harvard graduates indicated that those who started with more primitive defenses (e.g., denial and projection) fared more poorly with life crises than those with more adaptive defenses (e.g., sublimation). Interacting variables of neurodevelopment, biological predisposition, early life experiences, delayed or arrested psychosocial development, temperament, and personality structure contribute to either resilience or vulnerability to psychopathology.

Clinical Course

In most cases, once the precipitating stressor disappears, so does the adjustment disorder. In nearly every respect, adults fare better than adolescents. Adjustment disorders in adolescents are more severe, last longer, require more treatment, and ultimately are associated with more psychopathology and worse outcomes. Three- to five-year follow-ups revealed 59–71% of adults functioning well, but only 44% of adolescents doing so. Among those doing poorly in both groups mood, antisocial personality, and substance use disorders were common, but suicide was rare (2–4%). Overall, the most reliable predictors of poor outcome were the chronicity of the adjustment disorder, being younger, the frequency of misconduct symptoms, and the number of stressors. Depressive symptoms do *not* appear to predict outcome.

Management and Treatment

The main controversy concerning the treatment of adjustment disorders is whether to treat them at all. Although most patients recover fully without therapy, many do not. The arguments against treatment are that because (by definition) adjustment disorders are time-limited, treatment wastes the patient's time, money, and effort. Patients may be harmed by interfering with the natural recovery process (at least in theory). Additional problems might be generated: patients may become "therapy addicts"; or they may be unable to cope with a newly discovered set of difficulties—how much they hate their fathers, how little they love their spouses; or, if therapy is a bust, they may terminate more discouraged than ever.

The arguments in favor of therapy contend that, because clinicians can never really know in advance whether patients will fully recover, if nothing else, treatment can minimize adverse consequences, such as preventing patients from making ill-advised, spur-of-the-moment, irreversible decisions. Therapy could also hasten recovery, stop patients from blowing matters out of proportion, and enable them to avert similar crises in the future.

Experts generally believe that treatment should be based on a crisis intervention model. Accordingly, the primary goal of treatment is to have patients return to baseline. The secondary goal, or possibility, is to capitalize on the emotional turmoil of the crisis to change some longstanding maladaptive patterns into more useful and self-satisfying ones. In this model, treatment is brief, time-limited, and focused exclusively on problems linked to the stressor. (About half the patients who enter brief psychotherapy for adjustment disorders finish in 4 weeks.)

> The most frequently used treatment is *individual psychotherapy*, which identifies the stressor, examines how it affects the patient, and discusses how the patient could deal with it. The therapist typically supports defenses, reinforces existing coping skills, or suggests new strategies. *Family therapy* is the second most widely used treatment. When the family plays a major role in the adjustment disorder, family treatment can follow the same principles of crisis intervention. Supportive *psychotherapy groups* for common stressors are present in many communities. *Medications* might be used temporarily as long as there is a clear target symptom (e.g., insomnia, anxiety), which impairs functioning or slows recovery.

References

American Psychiatric Association. (2013). *Diagnostic and statistical manual of mental disorders*, 5th ed. Arlington, VA: American Psychiatric Association.

Andreasen, N.C., & Hoenk, P.R. (1982). The predictive value of adjustment disorders: A follow-up study. *American Journal of Psychiatry, 139*, 584–590.

Andreasen, N.C., & Wasek, P. (1980). Adjustment disorders in adolescents and adults. *Archives of General Psychiatry, 37*, 1166–1170.

Bownes, I.T., O'Gorman, E.C., & Sayers, A. (1991). Assault characteristics in post-traumatic stress disorder in rape victims. *Acta Psychiatrica Scandinavica, 83*, 27–30.

Getz, W., Wiesen, A.E., Sue, S., & Ayers, A. (1974). *Fundamentals of crisis counseling*. Lexington, MA: D.C. Heath & Co.

Gil, E. (2006). *Helping abused and traumatized children, integrating directive and nondirective approaches*. New York: Guilford.

Kulk, R.A., Schlenger, W.E., Fairbank, J.A., Hough, R.L., Jordan, B.K., Marmon, C.R., et al. (1990). *Trauma and the Vietnam War generation*. New York: Brunner/Mazel.

Mental Health Advisory Team (MHAT) IV Operation Iraqi Freedom 05-07 Final Report: 23–24. Available at: http://www.armymedicine.army.mil/news/mhat/mhat_iv/MHAT_IV _Report_17Nov06.pdf.

Rundell, J.R. (2006). Demographics of and diagnoses in Operation Enduring Freedom and Operation Iraqi Freedom personnel who were psychiatrically evacuated from the theater of operations. *General Hospital Psychiatry, 28*, 352–356.

Solomon, S.D., Gerrity, E.T., & Muff, A.M. (1992). Efficacy of treatment for posttraumatic stress disorder. *Journal of the American Medical Association, 268*, 633–638.

Terr, L. (1991). Childhood traumas: An outline and overview. *American Journal of Psychiatry, 148*, 10–20.

Vaillant, G.E. (1971). Theoretical hierarchy of adaptive ego mechanisms. *Archives of General Psychiatry, 24*, 107–118.

World Health Organization. (1992). *The ICD–10 classification of mental and behavioural disorders: Clinical descriptions and diagnostic guidelines.* Geneva: World Health Organization.

17

Dissociative Disorders

How come dissociative disorders, although relatively uncommon, are of such uncommon interest? *Sybil, The Three Faces of Eve*, the Boston Strangler, and (if brainwashed) Patty Hearst fascinate many because they are very ordinary individuals who have made an extraordinary transformation. And if these people can become completely different people, then couldn't we? If such strangeness can lurk within them, why not within us?

Dissociative states refer to the "splitting off" from conscious awareness of some ordinarily familiar information, emotion, or mental function. In other words, selected mental contents are removed or dissociated from conscious experience but continue to produce motor or sensory effects. These are the *elsewhere* disorders: Part of the person (e.g., memory, identity) is elsewhere and not available at the present time. In dissociative states, people can appear unconscious and focus selectively on the environment (e.g., sleepwalking, trance), act bizarrely (e.g., running "amok," going "berserk"), lose their identity and wander away from home (e.g., fugue), lose memory without wandering away from home (e.g., amnesia), assume an alien identity (e.g., multiple personality, witchcraft, possession), or be brainwashed.

Some dissociative states are not pathological, and to some extent, some are highly adaptive. We all forget things. We all switch states of consciousness, from meditating to sleeping to working to daydreaming, and to do so, sets of memory and attitudes must also switch. Dissociation also may occur in crystal gazing, intense prayer, "mass hysteria," religious revivals, healing ceremonies (e.g., Holy Spirit possession, glossolalia ["speaking in tongues"]), and hypnosis. Amazingly enough, it can even occur during lectures or while reading textbooks (other than this one)—"I blanked out on what he said" or "I spaced out on that page—I'll have to read it again."

Most dissociative states are activated by a psychosocial trigger, arise suddenly, and end abruptly. During normal intervals, people are partly or totally amnestic for their dissociative episodes. For example, using *posthypnotic suggestion*, a hypnotist may instruct a hypnotized subject, "After you awaken, you'll sing 'God Save the Queen' when I scratch my head but not remember that I told you to." Ten minutes after the subject awakens, the hypnotist scratches and the subject wails "God Save the Queen." Ask why she's singing, she may confess she doesn't know or confabulate, "I thought people would like the music."

Dissociative experiences are common. On the Dissociative Experience Scale, 29% of the general population agreed that the following happened to them in almost one-third of their conversations: "Some people find that sometimes they are listening to someone talk and they suddenly realize that they did not hear part or all of what was said" (Ross, Joshi, & Currie, 1990). In the same study, 5% scored over 30, a score highly associated with having a dissociative disorder. There were no differences in scores based on gender, income, occupation, education, or religion. However, dissociative experiences (e.g., hypnotizability, a phenomenon highly correlated with dissociation) decrease with age (Frischholz et al., 1992). Men and women differed only on two items. Men more often endorsed the statement, "Some people find that they have no memory for important events in their lives, for example, a wedding or graduation" (until now, something women had suspected was happening but couldn't prove), while women more often endorsed the statement, "Some people sometimes find that when they are alone, they talk out loud to themselves."

Dissociative disorders are defined as conditions whose predominant feature is a disturbance or alteration in the normal integrative functions of consciousness, identity, or memory (see Table 17-1). The type of alteration dictates the type of dissociative disorder: In *dissociative amnesia*, consciousness is altered and significant personal events forgotten. In *dissociative fugue*, identity and motor behavior are altered; patients unexpectedly travel far from home, assume a new identity, forgetting their old one. In *dissociative identity disorder* (multiple personality disorder), numerous identities arise. In *depersonalization-derealization disorder*, patients feel as if they are outside of their mind or body, as an observer. Other dissociative conditions include *brainwashing,* dissociative trance disorder, and derealization without depersonalization.

CLINICAL PRESENTATIONS

Dissociative Amnesia

These patients are suddenly unable to remember significant personal information, which is far in excess of ordinary forgetfulness. Patients know they've

---

TABLE 17-1
Common Diagnostic Criteria for Dissociative Disorders

A. The common theme shared by dissociative disorders is a **partial or complete loss of the normal integration between memories of the past, awareness of identity, immediate sensations, emotions, behavior, and control of bodily movements**.

B. Presumed **impairment in the ability to exercise conscious and selective control** to a degree that can vary from day to day or even from hour to hour.

C. The symptoms intrude into awareness or behaviors resulting **in significant distress or significant impairment** in personal, family, social, educational, occupational, or other important areas of functioning.

D. The symptoms are **not better explained by another mental disorder**.

E. The disturbance **is not due to the direct physiological effects of a substance or another medical condition** (e.g., head trauma or temporal lobe epilepsy).

F. **Evidence for psychological causation**, in the form of clear association in time with traumatic events, insoluble and intolerable problems, or disturbed relationships (even if denied by the individual). Convincing evidence of psychological causation may be difficult to find, even though strongly suspected.

Note: Adapted from *ICD-10* (p. 122) *and DSM-5* (p.291)

---

forgotten something, but don't know what. Often they don't seem to care. Feeling perplexed, disoriented, and purposeless, they're often picked up by the police as lost or for wandering aimlessly. During their amnesia, patients are able to perform relatively simple tasks (e.g., taking a bus) and, less often, more complicated ones (e.g., shopping, cooking).

Most often, patients' amnesias are *localized* to several hours or days during and after a highly disturbing event and are only rarely *generalized* for an entire life. They may be *selective* for only some events, usually the most traumatic. An uninjured person may remember driving and talking to staff at a hospital, but not the car accident itself. Rare is *continuous* amnesia, wherein patients forget everything from the time of the stress until the present. (Some politicians have been accused of selective amnesia because they seem unable to remember any promises they made from before the election to the present.)

An example of localized amnesia is the case of a photojournalist in Vietnam who, confused and bewildered, strolled into the office of Army Intelligence. He had no recollection of the past 3 days, but his camera did. It showed photographs of a Buddhist monk immolating himself. Like most dissociative amnesias, his completely cleared within 24 hours of being discovered.

Dissociative Fugue

These patients flee from home or their customary locale, forget (or are confused about) their previous identity, and adopt a partial one. During a fugue, patients usually behave with sufficient skill to go unnoticed by most casual observers. Fugues typically are precipitated by an acute stressor and consist of a several-day excursion with minimal social contact. Perplexity and disorientation may occur in some fugues, but if they dominate, the condition is diagnosed as dissociative amnesia and not fugue. Other fugues are more elaborate, lasting weeks to months: Previously quiet and very ordinary people may establish a new residence, fashion a completely new, more gregarious identity, have a full social calendar, and appear no different than any other colorful new arrival in town. Patients have traveled thousands of miles and passed numerous customs officials without detection. A rare few are violent. Afterward, patients can't remember what transpired during the fugue. In contrast to amnesia patients, who are aware of their memory loss, fugue victims are usually not aware. Most patients with dissociative fugue recover rapidly. Specific diagnostic criteria for dissociative amnesia and dissociative fugue are presented in Table 17-2.

TABLE 17-2
Specific Diagnostic Criteria for Dissociative Amnesia and Fugue

Dissociative Amnesia

A. Amnesia, usually partial and selective, for recent events that are of a traumatic or stressful nature (these aspects may emerge only when other informants are available); the failure to recall information is too extensive to be explained by ordinary forgetfulness or fatigue.

B. The absence of another medical condition including brain disorders, intoxication, or excessive fatigue.

Dissociative Fugue

A. All the diagnostic features for dissociative amnesia are present.

B. An apparently purposeful travel beyond the usual everyday range (the differentiation between travel and wandering must be made by those with local knowledge);

C. Maintenance of basic self-care (eating, washing, etc.) and simple social interaction with strangers (such as buying tickets or gasoline, asking directions, ordering meals).

D. In some cases, a new identity may be assumed, usually only for a few days but occasionally for long periods of time and to a surprising degree of completeness.

E. Although there is amnesia for the period of the fugue, the individual's behavior during this time may appear completely normal to independent observers.

Note: Adapted from ICD-10 (pp. 123–124) and DSM-5 (p.302)

TABLE 17-3

Diagnostic Criteria for Dissociative Identity Disorder

A. The apparent existence of **two or more distinct personalities within an individual,** with only one of them being evident at a time. Each personality is complete, with its own memories, behavior, and preferences; these may be in marked contrast to the single premorbid personality.

B. **One personality is usually dominant but none has access to the memories of the others** and the different personalities are almost always unaware of one another's existence (consequently there are apparent recurrent lapses in memory and information recall).

C. **Change from one personality to another in the first instance is usually sudden and closely associated with stressful events or traumatic reminders.**

D. *DSM-5 specifies that the disturbance is not better explained by behavior that is a normal part of broadly accepted cultural or religious practice.*

Note: Adapted from *ICD-10* (p. 128) *and DSM-5* (p.292)

Dissociative Identity Disorder

Dissociative Identity Disorder is the new name for "multiple personality disorder." The most common and fundamental alteration in this disorder is the presence of more than one discrete identity, that is, what the person calls herself and believes herself to be. The quiet, careful guy at the lab who is a "wild man" at parties may look to others like a multiple personality, but he sees these ways of being as different aspects of his identity and does not suffer from dissociative identity disorder. Specific diagnostic criteria for dissociative identity disorder are presented in Table 17-3.

These patients have two or more distinct identities or personality states, each dominant at a particular moment. Each identity is a complex, integrated being with its own name, memories, behavioral traits, emotional characteristics, social relations, employment histories, mental and physical disorders, and psychological test responses. Even rates of cerebral blood flow and evoked electrical potentials differ between the identities. Needing to eat for three identities, one patient ate nine meals a day! The average number of identities is 8–13, but more than 50 have been reported. Sybil had 16 personalities, and Eve, 22 faces.

Transitions from one identity to another are usually sudden, follow a stressor, and catch most observers off-guard. They're spooky to watch, since the "new" person seems to have taken over the patient's body and soul. Dress, speech, gait, and facial expressions may change so much the person goes unrecognized. The original (or primary) personality is usually unaware of the other (or secondary) personalities, but most secondary personalities are aware of the primary personality. The secondary personalities generally have some inkling of the others; they converse with each other, protect each other, or one may act while others watch. Secondary personalities are often extreme caricatures of the original personality. A shy, conventional primary personality may have secondary personalities as a whore, drag queen, devil, and social worker. Secondary personalities may have a different sex, race, or age from the original personality.

> Clinicians are frequently unaware that they're treating a multiple identity, since these patients are tough to detect. One psychiatrist reported that 7 years had passed before he realized his patient had this disorder. Few enter treatment complaining of a multiple personality, and if they come at all, it's usually for depression. These patients may reveal themselves through memory lapses, time distortions ("lost weekends"), using "we" rather than "I" in conversations, being charged for items they don't remember buying (imagine the Visa bills!), and encountering friends who act like strangers and strangers who act like friends. If asked to write their thoughts freely for a half-hour, another personality may emerge. Another personality breaks through half the time in psychotherapy (Harvard, 1985).
>
> Dissociative identity, and the proliferation of new identities, often continues for life, making this condition the worst of the dissociative disorders. These patients are frequently depressed, abuse substances, mutilate themselves, attempt suicide, and have psychotic episodes, tension headaches, phobias, conversion symptoms, and hypochondriasis. "Hallucinated" voices in "psychotic" episodes are often one or more other personalities talking.

Depersonalization-Derealization Disorder

Depersonalization is a common perceptual distortion in which the person experiences his body, or mental processes, as if he were a detached, outside observer. The person may feel anesthetized or wooden; a sense of unreality or self-estrangement may confound him. The size and shape of objects may seem altered. Although the person feels, and indeed fears, that he's not in full control, gross reality testing is *not* impaired. See diagnostic criteria for depersonalization-derealization disorder in Table 17-4.

Because temporary depersonalization frequently occurs during normal, psychopathological, or physiologically altered states, depersonalization *disorder* is only diagnosed in the absence of another mental disorder, a general medical condition, or a direct effect of a substance, and when it's so persistent or recurrent that it significantly interferes with social or occupational

TABLE 17-4
Specific Diagnostic Criteria for Depersonalization-Derealization Disorder

A. Persistent complaints that mental activity, body, and/or surroundings are changed in their quality, so as to be unreal, remote, or automatized.

    1. (**depersonalization symptoms**) Individuals feel that their own feelings and/or experiences are detached, distant, not their own, or lost. They may feel that they are no longer doing their own thinking, imaging, or remembering; that their movements and behavior are somehow not their own; that their body seems lifeless, detached, or otherwise anomalous.

    2. (**derealization symptoms**) Objects, people, and/or surroundings seem unreal, distant, artificial, colorless, or lifeless. Individuals may experience that their surroundings seem to lack color and life and appear as artificial, or as a stage on which people are acting contrived roles.

B. During these experiences there is an acceptance by the individual that this is a subjective and spontaneous change, not imposed by outside forces or other people (i.e., insight with intact reality testing);

C. There is a clear sensorium and absence of toxic confusional states or epilepsy.

D. Only limited aspects of personal identity are usually affected, and there is usually no associated loss of performance in terms of sensations, memories, or movements.

Note: Adapted from *ICD-10* (p. 135) *and DSM-5* (p. 302)

---

functioning. Depersonalization episodes can last for seconds, minutes, days, or years. The course is chronic, but its severity fluctuates over time.

Other Dissociative Disorders

Brainwashing intentionally disrupts the normal integration of consciousness, memory, and identity toward the desired end of controlling another person.

> Three myths about brainwashing abound: (1) that it doesn't exist; (2) that it's no different from education, advertising, and psychotherapy; and (3) that it's an irresistible method that robs people of their beliefs and personalities. Instead, brainwashing can be defined as a "comprehensive, systematic, and total program using psychological techniques, to stress *confession* and then *reeducation* in order to change fundamental beliefs. During confession, the subject admits to past errors and renounces past affiliations; during reeducation, the subject is refashioned to conform to the idealized image of the brainwasher" (Lifton, 1963, p. 5).

Dissociative trance disorder applies to the person who feels she has been taken over by a new identity attributed to the influence of a spirit, power,

---

TABLE 17-5

Specific Diagnostic Criteria for Trance and Possession Disorders

A. A **temporary loss of both the sense of personal identity and full awareness of the surroundings**; in some instances the individual acts as if taken over by another personality, spirit, deity, or "force."

B. Attention and awareness may be limited to or concentrated upon only one or two aspects of the immediate environment, and there is often a **limited but repeated set of movements, postures, and utterances**.

C. Only trance disorders that are **involuntary or unwanted, and that intrude** into ordinary activities by occurring outside (or being a prolongation of) religious or other culturally accepted situations are included here.

D. Trance disorders occurring during the course of schizophrenic or acute psychoses with hallucinations or delusions, or dissociative identity disorder, should not be included here.

E. This category does not apply if the trance disorder is judged to be closely associated with any physical disorder (such as temporal lobe epilepsy or head injury) or with psychoactive substance intoxication.

Note: Adapted from ICD-10 (p. 125) and DSM-5 (p.307)

---

deity, or other person (see Table 17-5). Running "amok" in Malaysia is an example. To be called a disorder, the patient's symptoms can't be part of a broadly accepted culture or religious practice. Therefore, "speaking in tongues" when "possessed" by the Holy Spirit would not be classified as a disorder if the person is a "Holy Roller"—but might be if the person is a Unitarian!

EPIDEMIOLOGY

Dissociative disorders were once thought to be rare but recently there have been reports of increased incidence and prevalence. Few studies have investigated the epidemiology of dissociative amnesia. Increases in the case reports of dissociative amnesia can be due to increased awareness of the diagnosis among physicians or overdiagnosis in individuals who are highly suggestible.

Dissociative fugue has been reported in 0.2% of the general population. Although there are no conclusive studies on the epidemiology of Dissociative Identity Disorder (DID), the estimate on prevalence can range from rare to 1 in 100. The prevalence of depersonalization disorder is not known. Half of all individuals can experience depersonalization at some time in their lives at a time of increased stress.

TABLE 17-6
**Studies of the Prevalence of Dissociative Disorders
among Psychiatric Inpatients**

STUDY	YEAR	LOCATION	PATIENTS COMPLETING A DISSOCIATIVE EXPERIENCES SCALE	PATIENTS COMPLETING A STRUCTURED INTERVIEW	PATIENTS WITH A DISSOCIATIVE DISORDER (%)	PATIENTS WITH DISSOCIATIVE IDENTITY DISORDER (%)
Ross et al.	1991	Canada	299	80	21	3–5
Saxe et al.	1993	Massachusetts	110	20	13	4
Horen et al.	1995	Canada	48	11	17	6
Latz et al.	1995	North Carolina	176[a]	176[a]	15	4
Knudsen et al.	1995	Norway	85	23	8	5
Lussier et al.	1997	Connecticut	—	70[b]	9	7
Tutkun et al.	1998	Turkey	116	40	10	5
Rifkin et al.	1998	New York	—	100	?	1
Friedl and Draijer	2000	Netherlands	122	56	8	2
Gast et al.	2001	Germany	115	15	4–8	1–2

[a]Female patients only.
[b]Acute day hospital patients.
Adapted from Foote et al., 2006.

Psychogenic amnesia and fugue are common during war and natural disasters. In battle, young males are at highest risk. Away from battle, adolescent and young adult women have slightly more dissociative disorders. In psychiatric populations, DID is reputed to affect four times as many women as men, but if prison populations were included, the sex differential would narrow. Except for the variable age of onset of psychogenic fugue, dissociative disorders rarely begin after the age of 40 and almost never originate in older adults. Prevalence studies of dissociative disorders over a 15-year period are summarized in Table 17-6.

DIFFERENTIAL DIAGNOSIS

Neurological disorders can simulate dissociative amnesia, except that the memory loss is more recent than remote and usually unrelated to a specific stressor. Most neurological disorders arise slowly, rarely improve, and are accompanied by other signs, such as confusion, disorientation, attention deficits, and clouding of consciousness. Delirium may arise quickly but will also have all of these other signs and symptoms. Unlike those with dissociative fugue, most patients with neurological disorders who wander off are unable to perform complex, purposeful tasks.

Substance-induced intoxications can produce *hypnoanxiolytic* and *alcoholic* *"blackouts,"* an amnesia for events occurring while intoxicated. In blackouts, the history of drinking and the lack of a complete recovery exclude psychogenic amnesia. In *alcohol amnestic disorder*, 5-minute (not immediate) memory is lost. *"Dissociative" anesthetics*, primarily phencyclidine (PCP), frequently cause depersonalization, but a drug history and urine screen are sufficiently diagnostic.

Acute stress disorder emphasizes dissociative symptoms in response to a traumatic event. It differs from a dissociative disorder in occurring within 4 weeks of the traumatic event and being time-limited to 4 weeks of symptoms. *Posttraumatic stress disorder* may have some persistent dissociative symptoms (e.g., flashbacks, amnesia for the trauma, feelings of detachment) but also requires others such as increased arousal for the diagnosis.

In *postconcussion amnesia*, patients generally have a retrograde memory loss for the period before the head trauma, whereas in psychogenic amnesia there's generally an anterograde memory loss for the period since the precipitating stress. Hypnosis and amytal interview can usually retrieve lost memories in psychogenic amnesia, but not in concussion. In dissociative amnesias, memory loss tends to be global and total; after concussion, it tends to be spotty and patchy. Patients with concussive amnesia do not form new identities. In psychogenic amnesia patients retain prior skills, have little difficulty conducting current tasks, and apparently benefit from secondary gain; patients with postconcussion amnesia lose some prior skills, have problems coping with present tasks, and do not appear to acquire secondary gain (Ludwig, 1985).

Partial complex seizures (PCSs) may cause sudden memory loss and flight, but unlike psychogenic fugue, patients can't perform complex tasks or form a new identity; they often have stereotyped movements, such as lip smacking, and about half the time there's an abnormal EEG. Sometimes PCS is hard to distinguish from dissociative amnesia. Because people with severe dissociative disorders often were physically abused as children, including being knocked unconscious many times, they may have both PCS and dissociative amnesia. A trial of anticonvulsants may be useful. Many who exhibit PCSs but have a normal EEG during the seizures (called a pseudo-seizure) are found to have dissociative symptoms often precipitated by guilt-laden grief (Ramchandani & Schindler, 1993).

Malingering must always be considered, especially if there's obvious secondary gain. Attorneys are seeing many more claims of multiple identity by criminals: "Hey, judge, it's not *me* who slaughtered the guy, it's that *other* personality." Kiersch (1962) found that in 32 cases of suspects with alleged amnesia who were standing trial, 21 subsequently confessed to lying about their memory loss. Patients with dissociative conditions usually recover during hypnosis and amytal interviews, but malingerers do not. Remember, amytal is not truth serum. Liars can keep on lying under amytal.

Descriptively and psychodynamically, dissociative (multiple) identity disorder often resembles *borderline personality disorder*. Emotional lability, low self-esteem, impulsivity, substance abuse, chronic boredom, identity confusion, temper tantrums, manipulative interpersonal relations, and suicide attempts characterize both disorders. In fact, in one investigation (Horevitz & Braun, 1984), 70% of patients with multiple personality were also diagnosed as borderline. Observing the patient's abrupt personality changes settles the diagnosis.

Distinguishing among dissociative disorders is usually easy. When a person forgets *and* travels to another locale, the diagnosis is psychogenic fugue; when the person "merely" forgets, it's psychogenic amnesia. Patients with dissociative amnesia look more befuddled, rarely conduct complex tasks, and are more readily spotted by lay observers. Awareness of one's original identity is absent in psychogenic amnesia and fugue, but present in multiple personality.

ETIOLOGY AND PATHOGENESIS

Because dissociative states induced by substances or medical conditions are excluded by definition, dissociative disorders are produced psychosocially. Most often, the immediate precipitating factor is an imminent threat of injury or death, the performance of a guilt-provoking act (e.g., an affair), or a serious auto accident.

Psychoanalytic theory suggests that dissociative states protect the individual from experiencing painful sexual or aggressive impulses. With amnesia, one forgets what's painful; with fugue, one runs away from it; with multiple personality, one displaces it onto a new identity; with depersonalization, one abandons it.

Almost all patients with DID report being physically or sexually abused as children (Ross, Miller et al., 1990). (However, most abused children do not appear to develop dissociative disorders.) Sybil's mother tortured her as a child; Billy Milligan's father frequently raped him from the ages of 9 to 16 and threatened to kill him if he told anybody. These children have been cannon fodder in custody fights, raised as the opposite sex, had their genitals squeezed in a vice, and kidnapped by parents. Dissociation into different identities defends against these trauma by isolating the horror, sectioning off the child's negative self-images, and permitting a modicum of self-control. By compartmentalizing emotions, the child says, in effect, "I can't deny that this is happening, but I can deny that it's happening to me" (Harvard, 1985).

Several studies suggest an association between attachment difficulties and dissociation. Ogawa et al. (1997) demonstrated in a longitudinal study that avoidant and disorganized patterns of attachment were predictors for dissociation. There has been little research in the neurobiological mechanisms of dissociation, but several studies report impairment in thalamic–limbic–cortical feedback networks. Inability of the prefrontal cortex to integrate perceptual, cognitive, and emotional process results in dissociation. One recent study found that patients with DID had smaller hippocampal and amygdalar volumes.

MANAGEMENT AND TREATMENT

The treatment of dissociative disorders is still mainly anecdotal. Patients with these disorders present with challenging symptomatology that can overwhelm experienced clinicians. A summary of treatment follows:

> *Dissociative amnesia and fugue.* Because of the relatively acute onset, brief duration, and high rate of spontaneous recovery of these states, this sequence of interventions is recommended: (1) *Evaluate* patients, allowing a few days for a spontaneous remission. Suggest that they might find their memory returning slowly day by day. If patients do not fully recover, (2) provide *discussion, support,* and *persuasion.* Encourage them to talk freely of recent events, periodically suggest avenues for exploration, and gently persuade them to keep looking for lost memories. If these methods are not sufficient, (3) employ an *associative anamnesis* by having patients free-associate to events surrounding the amnesia. (4) Use *hypnosis*; amnestic patients, as most patients with dissociative disorders, are extremely good subjects. Instruct

them to give a running commentary of known past incidents, which usually leads to abreaction. Once these emotions calm, patients are told to keep talking and then to wake up. When awake, patients are surprised to find themselves recounting past events and their amnesia ends. If it doesn't, (5) administer an *amytal interview* and then gently prod them to review events around the forgotten period. The closer in time to the onset of the amnesia, the more effective the interview. (6) If memory still hasn't returned, reconsider *neurological causes*, and if none is found, (7) gather a more exhaustive *psychological history* with antennae attuned to possible secondary gain (Coombs & Ludwig, 1982).

Dissociative Identity Disorder

Only very experienced therapists should treat this disorder. Initially these patients fascinate, but then soon overwhelm and exasperate therapists. As soon as psychotherapy with the primary identity is underway, a secondary identity (often referred to as an "alter") takes over, and then another, and another, and another. Many are hostile, seductive, and manipulative; some will bait the primary identity, try blocking alliances with the therapist, or act out by drug-taking and wrist-slashing. All resist recalling traumatic events. These patients sense the therapist's fascination with the drama and may try to please him or her by exaggerating past horrors, which were already bad enough. Because these patients are very suggestible, leading questions must be avoided, such as, "Don't you think your parents may have been involved in a Satanic cult?" (something the FBI and police have seldom been able to prove), or "Aren't there many more personalities in there?" Too often, leading questions are experienced as new suggestions which are dutifully followed.

Hypnosis may engage certain personalities, but it should not be introduced too early, since the patient may experience it as an emotional assault. *Group therapy* often backfires (unless all participants share the same diagnosis), because the others consider the patient a fraud. An intriguing approach is "internal group therapy" in which the therapist "moderates" a discussion between the patient's personalities and facilitates the quiescent ones to speak via hypnosis. *Videotaping* early in treatment may help personalities get acquainted. *Family counseling* should also be considered. Medications (SSRIs, clonidine, and benzodiazepines) can be helpful in reducing anxiety and arousal symptoms. SSRIs are the antidepressants most often used to treat co-occurring depression. Often it is tempting to use neuroleptics for "the voices," but those are other personalities and not usual hallucinations.

References

American Psychiatric Association. (2013). *Diagnostic and statistical manual of mental disorders*, 5th ed. Arlington, VA: American Psychiatric Association.

Coombs, G., & Ludwig, A.M. (1982). Dissociative disorders. In J.H. Greist, J.W. Jefferson, & R.L. Spitzer (Eds.), *Treatment of mental disorders* (pp. 309–319). New York: Oxford University Press.

Foote, B., Smolin, Y., Kaplan, M., Legatt, M.E., & Lipschitz, D. (2006). Prevalence of dissociative disorders in psychiatric outpatients. *American Journal of Psychiatry, 163*, 623–629.

Frischholz, E.J., Lipman, L.S., Braun, B.G., & Sachs, R.G. (1992). Psychopathology, hypnotizability, and dissociation. *American Journal of Psychiatry, 149*, 1521–1525.

Harvard Medical School Mental Health Letter. (1985). Multiple personality. *1*(10), 1–6.

Horevitz, R.P., & Braun, B.G. (1984). Are multiple personalities borderline? *Psychiatric Clinics of North America, 7*, 69–87.

Kiersch, T.A. (1962). Amnesia: A clinical study of ninety-eight cases. *American Journal of Psychiatry, 119*, 57–60.

Lifton, R.J. (1963). *Thought reform and the psychology of totalism: A study of "brainwashing" in China*. New York: Norton.

Ludwig, A.M. (1985). *Principles of clinical psychiatry*, 2nd ed. New York: Free Press.

Ogawa, J.R., Sroufe, L.A., Weinfield, N.S., Carlson, E.A., & Egeland, B. (1997). Development and the fragmented self: Longitudinal study of dissociative symptomatology in a nonclinical sample. *Development and Psychopathology, 9*, 855–879.

Ramchandani, D., & Schindler, B. (1993). Evaluation of pseudoseizures: A psychiatric perspective. *Psychosomatics, 34*, 70–79.

Ross, C.A., Anderson, G., Fleisher, W.P., & Norton, G.R. (1991). The frequency of multiple personality disorder among psychiatric inpatients. *American Journal of Psychiatry, 148*, 1717–1720.

Ross, C.A., Joshi, S., & Currie R. (1990). Dissociative experiences in the general population. *American Journal of Psychiatry, 147*, 1547–1552.

Ross, C.A., Miller, S.D., Reagor, P., Bjornson, L., Fraser, G.A., & Anderson, G. (1990). Structured interview data on 102 cases of multiple personality disorder from four centers. *American Journal of Psychiatry, 147*, 596–601.

World Health Organization. (1992). *The ICD–10 classification of mental and behavioural disorders: Clinical descriptions and diagnostic guidelines*. Geneva: World Health Organization.

18

Somatoform Disorders

DOCTOR: It's all in your head.
PATIENT: But it's *not* in my head; it's in my stomach.

What the doctor considers reassurance, the patient may consider an accusation. The doctor says that nothing is *physically* wrong with the patient, but the patient hears that *nothing* is wrong. Yet there *is* something wrong: The patient's stomach hurts. Even when psychological factors produce the pain, for the patient that pain is just as real and just as miserable. When the physician ignores this central fact, the patient feels accused of being a fake or crazy.

Patients with psychogenic physical symptoms frustrate professionals because they don't have "real" illnesses, don't respond to conventional medical treatments, shop around for doctors, are stubbornly unpsychological, and dwell on their physical complaints. The professional claims that the patient's physical problems are psychogenic, and because the patient disagrees, he or she is, in essence, rejecting the professional's expertise.

Consequently, these patients receive poor care. Not knowing what else to do and succumbing to these patients' demands for medication, physicians often prescribe drugs, expecting them not to work. These medications are frequently hypnoanxiolytics or opioids, and patients become addicted. (At least now they have a "real" problem!) These patients undergo countless tests, procedures, and operations. In comparison to controls, patients with *somatoform disorders* have three times the weight of body organs removed surgically (Cohen et al., 1953). Sensing, often correctly, that doctors consider them "crocks" and "gomers," these patients distrust doctors and don't follow their advice. Yet they also feel helplessly dependent on doctors and glom onto them, causing further alienation. In a "no-win situation," these patients distrust the very doctors on whom they must rely.

Somatoform disorders include those in which patients have physical symptoms that cannot be fully explained by medical findings or known physiological mechanisms; if there are medical findings, these patients' complaints or impairment exceed what would be expected. There is positive evidence, or at least a strong presumption, that psychological factors play an important role in the onset, severity, exacerbation, or maintenance of symptoms. These symptoms are not under voluntary control.

Somatoform disorders differ from *malingering* and *factitious disorders* where patients deliberately make and fake symptoms of physical illness. In *psychological factors affecting physical conditions*, often called "psychosomatic disorders," emotional factors trigger, aggravate, or exacerbate a clearly existing medical condition, such as ulcers or hypertension, through a known pathophysiological mechanism. In many somatoform disorders, however, there is no identifiable medical disease or any known pathophysiological mechanism to account for the patient's symptoms.

This chapter considers the following somatoform disorders: *somatization (somatic symptom) disorder, somatoform pain disorder, hypochondriasis (illness anxiety disorder), conversion disorder*, and *psychological factors affecting other medical conditions (psychosomatic disorders)*.

It is appropriate that the consideration of these disorders immediately follows the dissociative disorders. In essence the somatoform disorders seem to share the common dissociative theme of a partial or complete loss of the normal integration functions between conscious awareness, emotions, somatic sensations, and motor control. Selected mental contents are removed or dissociated from conscious experience but continue to produce physical symptoms. The term "conversion" actually refers to how unpleasant emotions, related to problems and conflicts that an individual is unable to solve, are somehow transformed into physical symptoms.

SOMATIZATION (SOMATIC SYMPTOM) DISORDER

Clinical Presentation

Somatization disorder—also named "Briquet's syndrome" after the French physician who first described it in 1859—is a chronic condition featuring multiple, unexplained somatic symptoms in numerous organ systems. Vomiting, aphonia (inability to produce sounds), painful limbs, muscle weakness, dizziness, painful menstruation, burning sensations in sex organs, paralyses, and conversion symptoms are common. Table 18-1 presents diagnostic criteria for somatization disorder.

TABLE 18-1
Diagnostic Criteria for Somatic Symptom Disorder
(formerly Somatization Disorder)

A. **Multiple and variable physical symptoms** that are distressing or result in some degree of impairment of social and family functioning. *DSM-5 allows a single symptom.*

Symptoms may be referred to any part or system of the body, but gastrointestinal sensations (pain, belching, regurgitation, vomiting, nausea, etc.), abnormal skin sensations (itching, burning, tingling, numbness, soreness, etc.), skin blotchiness, and sexual and menstrual complaints are among the most common.

B. Persistent **refusal to accept the advice or reassurance of several doctors**.
DSM-5 emphasizes excessive time and energy, persistent anxiety, and disproportionate thoughts about the seriousness of the somatic symptoms or associated health concerns.

C. The symptoms have been present for at least 2 years and **no adequate physical explanation** of the symptoms has been found. *DSM-5 specifies 6 months.*

By specifying if pain is predominant, the previous separate diagnosis of *somatoform pain disorder* is subsumed under somatic symptom disorder.

Note: Adapted from *ICD-10* (p. 129) and *DSM-5* (p. 311)

The number of unexplained or excessive symptoms distributed in the right way to qualify a person for somatization disorder has dropped from over 12 in *DSM-III*, to 8 in *DSM-IV*, and down to just a single symptom in *DSM-5*. *DSM-5* places more emphasis on how much time, thought, energy, and anxiety is devoted to somatic concerns. This makes sense considering the myriad constellations of bodily symptoms. For clinical convenience, Othmer and DeSouza (1985) found that the presence of any two out of seven specific symptoms predicted the correct diagnosis of *DSM-III* somatization disorder in 80–90% of cases; they incorporated this finding into the screening test outlined in Table 18-2.

Everyone has physical symptoms, but they mostly ignore them. Not so for patients with somatization disorder. For every ache and pain they will see a doctor, want a complete workup, and expect a prescription. (Any patient who enters a doctor's office with three dozen medications has a somatization disorder till proven otherwise.) These patients don't just present symptoms, they dramatize them: "I'm puking like a volcano." "I almost fainted in front of a bus." "I'm breathing so hard, I'm going to suffocate." Hyperbole is their norm: Headaches aren't headaches, they're "the worst headaches ever." Their histories are vague; it's never clear when their symptoms began, why

TABLE 18-2
Screening Test for Somatization Disorder

MNEMONIC	SYMPTOM	ORGAN SYSTEM
S omatization	Shortness of breath	Respiratory
D isorder	Dysmenorrhea	Female reproductive
B esets	Burning in sex organs	Psychosexual
L adies	Lump in throat	Pseudoneurological
A nd	Amnesia	Pseudoneurological
V exes	Vomiting	Gastrointestinal
P hysicians	Painful extremities	Skeletal muscle

Questions used to assess the presence of the seven symptoms of the screening test for somatization disorder:

S. Have you ever had trouble breathing?

D. Have you ever had frequent trouble with menstrual cramps?

B. Have you ever had burning sensations in your sexual organs, mouth, or rectum?

L. Have you ever had difficulties swallowing or had an uncomfortable lump in your throat that stayed with you for at least an hour?

A. Have you ever found that you could not remember what you had been doing for hours or days at a time? If yes, did this happen even though you had not been drinking or taking drugs?

V. Have you ever had trouble from frequent vomiting?

P. Have you ever had frequent pain in your fingers or toes?

If any 2 of the above 7 questions are answered affirmatively, this *screening* test is positive; a positive test simply means that the patient *might* have a somatization disorder. To confirm the diagnosis, the patient should meet the diagnostic criteria in Table 18-1.

Note: This table is adapted from Othmer & DeSouza (1985).

they seek help now, and what they want. On repeated tellings, symptoms "change": One day a backache is dull, the next day it's sharp; one day it began 12 months ago, on the next visit it started a month ago. Symptoms never end; as soon as the clinician thinks he's heard them all, another pops up. However, these histrionics should not mislead clinicians into underestimating these patients' genuine discomfort.

Epidemiology

Somatization disorder is rarely diagnosed in men. Reported lifetime prevalence rates range widely from 0.1% to 2.0% (Mai, 2004). Its frequency among general psychiatric patients is reported to range from 1.1% to 6.0%, whereas among medical/surgical patients referred for psychiatric consultation, it may be as high as 14%. In outpatient primary-care settings, 5–10% may meet the diagnostic criteria for somatization disorder. In the United States it tends to be more common among African-Americans, lower socioeconomic groups, and less formally educated people.

Differential Diagnosis

Hypochondriasis and somatization disorder share many features, including an early and gradual onset. However, in somatization disorder patients focus on *symptoms* of disease, whereas hypochondriacs are preoccupied with a *fear* of disease. Hypochondriasis may appear in somatization disorder, but not as the dominant symptom.

A patient with *schizophrenia* or a *psychotic depression* with multiple somatic delusions—for example, "Insects are eating my liver"—may appear to have a somatization disorder, but patients who truly have a somatization disorder specialize only in nondelusional complaints. Patients with *dysthymia, generalized anxiety, major depression,* and *panic disorder* all complain about physical symptoms more than normal, but they rarely meet full criteria for somatization disorder; most do not have a pseudoneurological symptom. However, somatization disorder can be diagnosed concurrently with any of these psychiatric disorders and it is commonly comorbid with anxiety and depressive disorders. In *factitious disorder* and *malingering,* symptoms are intentionally produced. It can be quite difficult to ascertain the extent to which the physical symptoms and loss of function might be under voluntary control for some secondary gain. For somatoform disorders it is often presumed that the suffering individual may be dealing with some intolerable stress through the unconscious motivation to escape an unpleasant conflict or indirectly express dependency and resentment.

Certain *medical conditions* mimic somatization disorder and need to be ruled out. For example, multiple sclerosis, systemic lupus erythematosus, porphyria, hemochromatosis, and hyperparathyroidism can all cause vague, multiple, and confusing somatic symptoms. Patients may have a variety of syndromes, including atypical chest pain, fibromyalgia, premenstrual syndrome, temporomandibular joint dysfunction, and "syndrome that incorporates many unexplained symptoms." (Having a name to describe a nebulous constellation of symptoms may help the patient to feel better but may not improve functioning.)

Diagnostic criteria for chronic fatigue syndrome (neurasthenia) are included in Table 18-3 but not in *DSM-5.* The characteristic features are either fatigue after mental effort or weakness after minimal physical effort. Many diag-

---

TABLE 18-3
Neurasthenia (Chronic Fatigue Syndrome)

A. **Either persistent and distressing complaints of increased fatigue after mental effort, or persistent and distressing complaints of bodily weakness and exhaustion after minimal effort;**

B. At least **two of the following**:
  1. feelings of muscular aches and pains
  2. dizziness
  3. tension headaches
  4. sleep disturbance
  5. inability to relax
  6. irritability
  7. dyspepsia

C. Any autonomic or depressive symptoms present are **not sufficiently persistent and severe to fulfill the criteria for any of the more specific mental disorders**, particularly depressive illness or an anxiety disorder.

Note: Adapted from *ICD-10* (p. 134)

---

nosed cases may actually meet the criteria for depressive or anxiety disorders. Actual cases of chronic fatigue seem to be more frequent in certain cultures than in others.

Features of somatization disorder useful in discriminating from general medical conditions include (1) involvement of multiple organ systems, (2) early onset and chronic course without the development of physical signs or structural abnormalities, and (3) absence of characteristic laboratory abnormalities for the suggested physical disorder.

Etiology and Pathogenesis

About 20% of first-degree female relatives of these patients will have a somatization disorder—that's roughly 20 times the normal frequency for women in the general population. Somatization disorder appears to be genetically and environmentally linked to antisocial personality disorder and alcoholism. Adopted children have a higher risk for alcoholism, antisocial personality disorder, and somatization disorder if they have a biological parent or an adoptive parent with any of these disorders.

Family studies reveal a high prevalence of antisocial personality disorder and alcoholism among the *male* relatives of patients with somatization disorder.

Conversely, there's an increased prevalence of somatization disorder among the *female* relatives of convicted male felons. Many delinquent girls develop somatization disorder as adults, and adult female felons have an increased prevalence of medical contacts (Goodwin & Guze, 1989).

Somatization is often considered a defense mechanism in which the patient unconsciously avoids painful affects by experiencing physical discomfort. Supposedly, the central defense mechanism is somatization and the painful affect, depressive. Indeed, alexithymia, the inability to recognize and express feelings, has been especially associated with somatization disorder. Other studies reveal that patients with somatization disorder are more troubled by confused and negative self-identities (Oxman et al., 1985) and have higher rates of childhood sexual abuse. For some, somatization may be learned from a parent with somatization. In others, physical symptoms may have been the only or best way to get attention or escape abuse.

Clinical Course

Somatization disorder usually arises during adolescence, but always before age 30. It is far more common in women and its course is fluctuating, lifelong, and exacerbated by environmental stressors—a fact deemed irrelevant or accusatory by the patient. Hardly a year passes without intense discomfort and medical treatment. Frequent complications are substance abuse, excessive laboratory tests and numerous fruitless surgeries (and their complications), work and social impairment, chronic demoralization, dysthymia, anxiety, marital problems, and divorce. The disorder is important to diagnose, if only to reduce these complications. Depression and anxiety are frequently present and these patients commonly attempt suicide, but rarely commit it. Addiction to analgesics and sedatives is another complication.

Management and Treatment

Since most of these patients are leery of psychiatry, they rely on nonpsychiatric, especially primary-care, physicians. Doctors can greatly help these patients if they remember to do the following: (1) Repeatedly check their own annoyance. Somatization disorders are chronic, lifelong conditions, and being angry at these patients for complaining about symptoms is akin to being angry at diabetics for having uncooperative blood sugars. (2) The primary goal of treatment is not to eliminate patients' physical complaints but to improve their functioning. (3) Avoid raising false hopes or promises, such as, "You're going to feel completely better." (4) Protect patients from needless laboratory tests, medical treatments, and surgical interventions. (5) Relate to patients "as they are": Try changing their personality and the only change will be you having one less patient. (6) Offer positive reinforcement for "non-complaining behaviors," ignore complaining behaviors, and teach the families to do likewise.

> More specifically: On her first visit to the doctor, a patient with somatization disorder should receive a thorough history and physical. Assuming this examination is "negative," the doctor should tell her, "I'm pleased there is nothing *seriously* wrong with you, but I know you're experiencing considerable discomfort. So I want to follow you carefully and see you in a (week, 2 weeks, or a month—doctor's choice)." An appointment is made, whether or not the patient has symptoms; therefore, the patient doesn't *have* to get sick to see the doctor. The scheduled interval between visits should coincide with doctor-going frequency, but as-needed visits should be discouraged. At the next appointment, the doctor conducts a briefer exam, repeats the same message, and schedules another appointment. Each week, the doctor devotes full attention to the patient for 15 minutes, telling her how marvelously she's doing despite her symptoms, lauds her planned trip to Arizona, restates that she doesn't have cancer and that nothing else is seriously wrong. Eventually, the patient not only *complains* less about symptoms, but actually *experiences* fewer symptoms.
>
> Typically these patients are avoided by all because of their incessant complaining. They then become socially isolated, more miserable, and complain more. One approach may be to have a family meeting to establish a very specific goal: From then on, the patient should not talk to family members or friends about her symptoms but only to an expert, her doctor. For a while she will not know what to talk about, but over time, normal social conversation gradually replaces the medical litany. After a good physician–patient alliance has been established, some instructions about symptoms and explanations may help; for example, informing the patient that the average person has 1.7 weird-but-temporary symptoms a week.

In addition to improving the patient–physician relationship, especially by recognizing and controlling the negative reactions (countertransference), other elements of treatment include addressing the underlying or co-occurring mood and anxiety disorders. SSRIs, SNRIs, and TCAs are prescribed for that purpose; polypharmacy (multiple medications) should be minimized, and addictive drugs avoided. Social reintegration, relaxation therapy, meditation, physical reactivation, and therapy using graded exercise and biofeedback are some examples of the specific therapies that can be provided when appropriate. Individual psychotherapy that includes psychoeducation, cognitive and behavioral approaches, and support appears to improve functioning. Group psychotherapy may be useful to reduce dependency upon, and confrontation with, the therapist.

HYPOCHONDRIASIS (ILLNESS ANXIETY DISORDER)

Clinical Presentation

Hypochondriasis is an overwhelming, persistent preoccupation with physical symptoms based on unrealistically ominous interpretations of physical signs or sensations. (The Greeks believed that the seat of these troubles was the *hypochondrion*, the area between the rib cage and the navel.) Hypochondriacs may have a physical disease, but what distinguishes them is their unrealistic and dire interpretation of it. As noted in the previous section, patients with somatization disorder worry about *symptoms*, whereas hypochondriacs *fear* a serious disease—the symptoms being only harbingers. The somatizing patient who coughs complains that it hurts; the patient with hypochondriasis who coughs concludes he has lung cancer. To this person, a skipped heart beat is a heart attack; a headache, a brain tumor. People with hypochondriasis may present with many symptoms in many organ systems, or they may have a single preoccupation, as does the "cardiac neurotic." Diagnostic criteria for hypochondriasis are listed in Table 18-4.

Epidemiology

Hypochondriasis affects the sexes equally and usually begins between ages 20 and 30. One recent study reported a 6-month prevalence of 4–6% in the general medical clinic population but it could be as high as 15%. At least two-thirds of these patients meet the criteria for mood and anxiety disorders, which suggests that, in many cases, it may be a variant of those diagnoses. The severity of hypochondriasis fluctuates over time but rarely stops completely or permanently. It may or may not impair occupational and social functioning, but almost always strains patients because needless operations and tests occur.

Differential Diagnosis

The differential diagnosis for hypochondriasis is the same as for somatization disorder. Unlike the delusions of *schizophrenia* or *psychotic depression*,

TABLE 18-4

Diagnostic Criteria for Hypochondriasis (Illness Anxiety Disorder)

A. **Persistent preoccupation with the possibility of having one or more serious and progressive physical disorders.**

    Persistent belief in the presence of at least one serious physical illness underlying the presenting symptom or symptoms, even though repeated investigations and examinations have identified no adequate physical explanation.

B. **Normal or commonplace sensations are often interpreted by a patient as abnormal and distressing,** and attention is usually focused on only one or two organs or systems of the body.

C. Persistent **refusal to accept the advice and reassurance of several different doctors** that there is no physical illness or abnormality underlying the reported symptoms. *DSM-5 adds that the individual is easily alarmed about personal health status.*

D. **The individual performs excessive health-related or maladaptive avoidance behaviors.**

E. Illness preoccupation is **present for over 6 months.**

F. The persistent preoccupation with illness is **not better explained by another mental disorder** such as other somatoform disorders, delusional disorder, body dysmorphia, obsessive-compulsive disorders, or panic and generalized anxiety disorders.

Note: Adapted from *ICD-10* (p. 131) and *DSM-5* (p. 315)

in hypochondriasis the patient will entertain the possibility that another interpretation of the symptoms is valid. This individual has an overvalued idea but not a delusion. In *mood* and *anxiety disorders*, dread or misinterpretation of disease is not a central feature, nor is it usually a longstanding preoccupation. Individuals with fears of the presence of one or more diseases (nosophobia) share the feature of repetitive thoughts and behaviors with obsessive-compulsive disorders.

Etiology and Pathogenesis

Little is known about the etiology of hypochondriasis, but it probably arises for a number of reasons: For some patients, secondary gain is crucial (e.g., repressed desire to escape insurmountable stressors through assuming the sick role); for others the disorder may be a defense against low self-esteem or a fear of being defective; for still others, introjection may be paramount purpose—these patients "prefer" punishing themselves over being angry at others. Given the higher incidence of painful injuries and diseases among close relatives of people with hypochondriasis, identification may be a key influence on some patients. A previous legitimate medical illness also predisposes to hypochondriasis. The prevalence of this disorder does not appear to be elevated in relatives of patients with hypochondriasis.

Management and Treatment

Investigations of treatment for hypochondriasis are few and rarely controlled. Although hypnoanxiolytics diminish somatic symptoms in anxious patients, and TCAs diminish somatic complaints in patients with depression, most clinicians find that neither class of drugs lessens hypochondriasis. Most of the treatment principles outlined above for somatization disorder apply.

Some researchers (Fallon et al., 1993) have redefined hypochondriasis as a variant of obsessive–compulsive disorder: The patient has a symptom, then obsessively thinks about it with catastrophic expectations (obsession), and then goes to the doctor (the compulsion) to receive temporary reassurance. As with OCD, the relief is fleeting. Armed with this theory, patients with hypochondriasis have been successfully treated with high doses of fluoxetine (40–80 mg) given over 8–12 weeks. As with most cases involving OCD, response speed is slow, but in the end, more than 70% improve with serotoninergic antidepressants in higher doses. They still thought about their bodies excessively, but they were no longer driven by obsessive fears and the need to see a doctor. Cognitive–behavioral therapy may reduce symptoms by up to 80% (Abramowitz, 2005).

In Kellner's (1982, 1987) literature reviews, the beneficial interventions for hypochondriasis included *repeatedly* (1) giving patients the facts about their difficulties, (2) clarifying the difference between pain and the *experience* of pain, (3) describing how emotions affect the *perception* of physical sensations (e.g., "real" pain is experienced as more painful when one is anxious than when one is calm), (4) demonstrating how selective attention and suggestion contribute to overestimating a symptom's seriousness, (5) stressing that "life can go on" despite physical symptoms, (6) conveying acceptance and empathy for the hypochondriasis, and (7) applying the approach described for treating somatization disorder. Several studies indicate that these strategies yield complete or vast improvement in roughly 75% of people with hypochondriasis for 1–3 years, and for over 3 years in a third of the patients. In view of the generally unfavorable prognosis of this condition, these results are striking, even if they reflect nothing more than a more invested physician.

CONVERSION DISORDER (DISSOCIATIVE MOVEMENT AND SENSORY DISORDER)

Clinical Presentation

The cardinal feature of a conversion disorder is an involuntary loss or alteration of a function, which, although resembling a physical disorder, appears to arise from psychological mechanisms. Conversion disorders usually consist of a single motor or neurological symptom (e.g., blindness, paralysis). Also common are tunnel vision, seizures, coordination disturbances, akinesia, dyskinesia, anosmia (no smell), anesthesia, and paresthesias. A single nonneurological symptom may arise, such as pseudocyesis (false pregnancy). Diagnostic criteria are listed in Table 18-5.

The strong psychological evidence required for the diagnosis can assume various forms. The conversion symptom may have symbolic meaning to the patient: For example, pseudocyesis may represent a fear of, and wish for, pregnancy. Psychogenic vomiting may symbolize revulsion or disgust. Conversion symptoms may arise from unconscious mechanisms. (Freud was right some of the time.) For instance, a man developed paralysis of his right arm after discovering his wife in bed with his best friend. The arm had normal nerve conduction and muscle tone. During a sodium amytal interview, the patient revealed that he used to be a fighter but quit after badly injuring a man in a bar fight. When asked what would happen if his arm still worked, he thrust his "paralyzed" arm out and said, "I'd kill the bastard, but then I could never live with myself."

TABLE 18-5
Diagnostic Criteria for Conversion Disorder
(Dissociative Movement and Sensory Disorder)

A. In these disorders there is a **loss of or interference with voluntary movements or loss of sensations**. The patient therefore presents as having a physical (neurological) disorder.

B. **There is no evidence of a physical disorder that might explain the symptoms**. The symptoms can often be seen to represent the patient's concept of physical disorder, which may be at variance with physiological or anatomical principles. Convincing evidence of psychological causation may be difficult to find, even though strongly suspected.

C. The symptoms are not better explained by another mental disorder.

D. The above symptoms result **in significant distress or significant impairment** in personal, family, social, educational, occupational, or other important area of functioning.

Note: Adapted from *ICD-10* (p. 126) and *DSM-5* (p. 318)

Often the conversion is a medical impossibility. "Glove anesthesia," in which sensation is felt to stop evenly at the wrist, is neurologically impossible (unless one's wrist is slashed!), but it conforms to the patient's conception of the nervous system. (Remember Frankenstein?) Soon after the swine-flu vaccine was found to produce Guillain-Barré syndrome, an ascending paralysis *arising* from the feet, cases presented in the emergency room. Patients with "Guillain-Barré" had a "paralysis," but they misread the newspapers: Their "paralysis" spread *downward*!

Although patients with conversion disorder are often said to have histrionic personalities, many do not. Typically patients are interested in their symptoms, but they also may display *la belle indifference* — a nonchalance to their impairment — which has the paradoxical effect of making the impairment more noticeable. This trait is of little diagnostic value, because it is also found in seriously ill medical patients who are stoic about their situation.

Conversion symptoms may begin at any age, but usually surface during adolescence and early adulthood. An acute psychosocial stressor generally triggers the symptom, which will arise suddenly, last for several days or weeks, and then stop abruptly. Conversion symptoms can persist for months or years. When this occurs, organic pathology must be reevaluated, since many of these patients turn out to have neurological disease. Long-term conversion symptoms may cause disuse atrophy and muscle contractures. "Psychological contractures" also occur: Patients become so mired in the sick role that after a conversion symptom disappears, work and social functioning may remain impaired.

Epidemiology

Conversion disorder presents far less today than during Freud's time; back then, it mainly afflicted women. Today, it appears more around battlefronts and in military hospitals; its sex distribution is now equal, although globus hystericus (a discomfort in swallowing) is more common in females. Conversion symptoms are reported to be twice as prevalent among African-Americans as among European Americans; they are also more common in lower socioeconomic classes, and they occur more commonly in those less psychologically sophisticated or in subcultures that consider these symptoms expectable, not crazy. Perhaps 1–3% of psychiatric outpatients and 5–15% of psychiatric hospital consults have conversion disorder.

Differential Diagnosis

Conversion disorder typically involves one symptom, whereas other *somatoform disorders* usually present with many symptoms in numerous organ systems. If pain is the predominant symptom, the diagnosis is psychogenic pain disorder (or somatic symptom disorder, with predominant pain); if the only disturbance is psychosexual, a psychosexual disorder is the more likely diagnosis. Patients with conversion disorders tend to minimize their problems; those with other somatoform disorders dramatize them. Conversion disorders arise suddenly, whereas *somatization disorder* and *hypochondriasis* emerge gradually. Unlike conversion disorders, there is no loss of function in hypochondriasis. Unlike *unspecified somatoform disorders*, symptoms tend to be dramatic and discrete, not vague and/or subjective (e.g., fatigue, loss of appetite).

Physical disorders, especially those with vague, episodic, and hard-to-document symptoms, must be considered, such as *multiple sclerosis* and *systemic lupus erythematosus*. Because it is common for a neurological disorder to be uncovered a full decade after symptoms first present, *all* patients with a long-standing conversion symptom should be evaluated *repeatedly* for underlying medical conditions.

Etiology and Pathogenesis

A conversion symptom affords patients either *primary gain*—that is, it *protects* them from experiencing a painful underlying feeling—or *secondary gain*—that is, it *gratifies* them by enabling them to receive concern and support from others. For example, a nurse who cared for her dying father became "blind" immediately after his death. The psychological evidence for a conversion disorder was the temporal relation between the death and the symptom's onset. The primary gain from this "blindness" was that it prevented her from seeing her father dead; the secondary gain was the added sympathy she would receive. Moreover, because she interpreted her father's death as a profoundly personal/ professional failure, her "blindness" unconsciously relieved her of guilt (primary gain) and protected her from others' blame (secondary gain). In the military, a "paralyzed" hand usually serves a secondary gain—to circumvent any demand to fire a gun.

Clinicians should be careful in deciding what constitutes psychological evidence. Because environmental stressors occur all the time, only those of obviously substantial impact on the patient should qualify. Furthermore, if clinicians want to find something, almost anything can have unconscious significance. Consider psychogenic vomiting: If the reader tries, he or she surely can find something in his or her psyche to explain psychogenic vomiting.

Management and Treatment

Because many conversion symptoms spontaneously disappear within a few weeks to months of their onset, very early treatment may be unnecessary. Therapy aims to temporarily remove patients from the situation that has overwhelmed their usual coping mechanisms, to reassure them that they will soon recover, to minimize any secondary gain that may prolong recovery, and to reinforce alternative coping strategies. Occasionally hypnosis, with posthypnotic suggestions of recovery, is helpful. Sometimes suggestions without hypnosis can be helpful, such as, "How much better are you today?" or "Let's see how quickly you get better."

SOMATOFORM PAIN DISORDER

Eighty percent of all patients who consult physicians do so for pain-related problems. Low back pain alone disables 7 million Americans and prompts more than 8 million doctor visits a year. Estimated health care and indirect (loss of work days, compensation litigation, and quackery) costs for chronic pain exceed $100 billion. The percentage of these patients having a psychogenic pain disorder is unknown but substantial.

Not all patients with psychogenic pain have a pain *disorder*. For instance, among patients hospitalized in a 3-week program for chronic pain, 32% had a major depression, and over half had had a psychiatric disorder before their chronic pain developed (Katon et al., 1985). In fact, chronic pain may be a symptom of major depression. Pain disorder is not diagnosed if the pain is due to a mood or psychotic disorder. *DSM-5* subsumes somatoform pain disorder under somatic symptom disorder (somatization disorder) with predominant pain.

Clinical Presentation

Pain disorder is characterized by a predominant complaint of significantly distressing or impairing pain in which psychological factors play an important role. The pain can have a medical cause but is not totally explainable on a medical basis. Table 18-6 lists diagnostic criteria for pain disorder. The following case is typical.

TABLE 18-6
Diagnostic Criteria for Somatoform Pain Disorder

A. **Persistent, severe, and distressing pain, which cannot be explained fully by a physiological process or a physical disorder and is not intentionally produced.**

    1. A variety of aches and pains are common in somatization disorders but are not so persistent or so dominant over the other complaints.

    2. The result is usually a marked increase in support and attention either personal or medical.

B. The pain results **in significant distress or significant impairment** in personal, family, social, educational, occupational, or other important area of functioning.

C. Pain **occurs in association with emotional conflict or psychosocial problems** that are sufficient to allow the conclusion that they are the main causative influences.

D. Pain presumed to be of **psychogenic origin** occurring during the course of depressive disorder or schizophrenia should not be included here.

Note: Adapted from *ICD-10* (p. 133)

Carol, a 45-year-old high school teacher, was standing outside her classroom when three students began taunting her with lewd remarks. When she objected, one picked her up, wheeled her around, and threw her to the ground, breaking her left arm and causing numerous facial contusions. The next day Carol developed sharp pains radiating up her neck and both arms, across her chest, and toward her pelvis. After a month, her arm and face had mended, but her radiating pains continued, even though no medical explanation could account for this pain. Although Carol was medically approved to return to work and was eager to do so—she needed the money—her pain kept her home. She then sued the school for not protecting its teachers. Carol frequently expressed her rage about these students, not just for hurting her, but especially because of their sexual innuendos.

On psychiatric examination, Carol wore a neck brace and made sure one noticed how slowly she sat down. While her flitting forefinger pointed to every radiating pain in her body, she said, "The pain just zaps you like shock waves. It attacks your entire body. If I touch anything, it triggers another shooting pain." Initially she denied any psychiatric problems, but later admitted that for months before her injury, her boyfriend had been "trying real hard to get me into the sack, and when I refused he'd always call me a prude." However, since her pains developed, "he's been a prince—he's stopped pushing me sexually and has been very considerate."

Carol's case raises three questions: First, is there sufficient physical evidence to explain her pain? No. Second, is she faking the pain? Probably not.

As with many pain patients, possible compensation suggests malingering, but the apparent genuineness of Carol's pain and her eagerness to return to work suggest otherwise. Third, is there psychological evidence to account for her pain? Yes. Her pain affords the secondary gain of cooling her boyfriend's sexual advances while eliciting his support and affection. There is also temporal and psychodynamic evidence: When she was having sexual conflicts with her boyfriend, the students' sexual insults especially hit "below the belt," just where her pains were shooting. Therefore, the most likely diagnosis was pain disorder. With the treatment described below, her pain gradually disappeared in 3 months and she returned to school.

Although pain disorder may arise any time in life, it especially surfaces during young to middle adulthood. Symptoms are usually initiated by an acute stressor, erupt suddenly, intensify over the next several days or weeks, and subside when the acute stressor is gone. Less often, presumably because of secondary gain, the pain persists long after the acute stressor, waxes and wanes for months or years, worsens under stress, and may continue indefinitely. These patients "doctor-shop," become demoralized, abuse analgesics, undergo unnecessary surgery and tests, get stuck in the sick role, restrict social and occupational functioning (some are bedridden for years), and develop secondary muscle spasms and pins-and-needles sensations around painful areas.

Epidemiology

In the absence of proper epidemiological study, it appears that pain disorder more often afflicts women and is common in clinical practice. However, surveys might find that after disorders associated with psychogenic pain (e.g., major depression) are eliminated, pain disorders may be less frequent.

Differential Diagnosis

The dramatic presentation of organic pain may appear excessive, but this alone does not qualify as a pain disorder. Dramatic presentations may reflect a person's normal or cultural style of communicating. To qualify as a pain disorder, pain must be severe, and psychological factors must play an important role. Patients with pain disorder may or may not have a medical condition. If a patient's pain is produced by another mental disorder, pain disorder is not diagnosed.

Etiology and Pathogenesis

In a study of hospitalized patients with all types of chronic pain, about 60% had a first-degree relative with chronic pain, 38% with alcohol misuse, and 30% with a mood disorder (Katon, 1985). These figures may be high, but many believe that they suggest a link—psychological or biological—between chronic pain, alcoholism, and depression. Given that pain runs in families, identification with a family member may also play an etiological role for some patients. That roughly 50% of patients with chronic pain improve with antidepressants fuels the old speculation that chronic pain is a "depressive equivalent." However, antidepressants also help chronic arthritis pain and work in a variety of nondepressive disorders such as panic.

Pain patients may repress intense affects and conflicts, or their cognition or perception of internal feeling states may be greatly distorted. Pain disorder may allow some patients to escape an unpleasant situation such as work (secondary gain). People without physical abnormalities who work in dangerous, exhausting jobs (e.g., coal mining) more often stop working because of a pain disorder then those in less physically taxing jobs.

Management and Treatment

Acute Pain Management

It is important that hospitalized medical or surgical patients in acute pain receive adequate doses of analgesics to maximize their comfort. The main reasons (rationalizations) doctors and nurses give for underusing narcotics is a fear of "addicting" and "overdosing" patients. Another common excuse is that "patients don't really hurt *that* much." Since nobody can know how much pain another person feels, it's never clear how patients are supposed to *prove* the extent of their pain. Professionals may point to the fact that patients *demand* narcotics as evidence of being "manipulative." This may be a false premise because many patients in severe pain just want narcotics because they're in pain!

When given as needed (or prn), the pain medication may arrive late and the patient may become conditioned to associate complaining of pain with getting a drug-induced euphoria. Thus, for hospitalized medical/surgical patients in acute pain, narcotics are given freely and on a regular schedule, without patients having to ask for them. Unfortunately if opioid pain medications are given regularly for several days, the patient may develop a tolerance to the analgesic effects and require increasingly higher doses. This tolerance accompanied by the often extreme discomfort from withdrawal of the medication, may lead to rebound pain and serious addiction.

Chronic Pain Management

There are few studies of pain disorder per se, but many of chronic pain in general. Research demonstrates that patients with all kinds of chronic pain clearly benefit from antidepressants, behavior and activity therapy, couple therapy, and supportive group therapy. Individual psychotherapy seems less useful. These treatments are effective (or ineffective) whether or not the patient's pain has a physical basis. Group therapy for inpatients hasn't been studied systematically, but with outpatients it reduces their perception of pain and their use of medication; dysthymia is alleviated and employment increases. These groups provide support, ventilation, education about pain mechanisms, relaxation techniques to reduce the experience of pain, and reinforcement of nonpain behaviors.

A wide variety of antidepressants is effective in chronic pain for patients with and without depression. For most types of pain the results are modest, with about 50–55% of patients getting 50% (or more) pain reduction. For migraine and neuropathy, 60–70% response rates are seen. Benzodiazepines afford little benefit, and opioids should be avoided on a long-term basis because of tolerance to their therapeutic effects and rebound pain. Opioids may adversely impact mood and anxiety when used chronically. ECT helps patients with severe depression and chronic pain. Most patients with chronic pain deserve a trial on antidepressants, usually an SNRI or TCA. Some antiepileptic drugs (e.g., gabapentin, pregabalin) are beneficial.

Pain clinics employ a multidisciplinary team to provide antidepressants, behavior therapy, and group psychotherapy. In a typical program, Fordyce et al. (1973) treated 36 patients whose pain had lasted an average of 7 years and who did not improve from conventional medical treatments. Patients were hospitalized 1–3 months and continued as outpatients for another 3 weeks. The program's aims and methods were: (1) To decrease the patient's use of medication, drugs were given at regular intervals and not "on demand"; over time, drugs were tapered. Frequently, chronic pain improved when hypno-anxiolytics and opiates were stopped. (2) To diminish pain behavior, the staff praised patients for conducting non–pain-related activities; when patients exhibited pain-related behavior (e.g., not going to movies on account of pain), the staff ignored them. (3) To increase functioning, patients were rewarded for participating in a tailored program of gradually increasing physical activity. Rest was contingent on performing the activity, not on complaining of pain. (4) To maintain the patient's gains after discharge, the staff trained relatives to reinforce nonpain, instead of pain, behaviors.

At discharge, there was a 50% increase in time spent sitting, standing, walking, and exercising; most patients were taking little or no medication. At other pain centers, 60–80% of patients have shown similar gains in functional activity, decreased medication, and improved quality of life for at least 3–5 years. These improvements occurred regardless of whether patients were still in pain. What's more, most patients not only *talked* less about pain, they *experienced* less pain (Ochitill, 1982).

References

Abramowitz, J.S. (2005). Hypochondriasis: Conceptualization, treatment, and relationship to obsessive–compulsive disorder. *Annals of Clinical Psychiatry, 17*(4), 211–217.

American Psychiatric Association. (2013). *Diagnostic and statistical manual of mental disorders,* 5th ed. Arlington, VA: American Psychiatric Association.

Barsky, A. (2001). The patient with hypochondriasis. *New England Journal of Medicine, 345,* 1395.

Barsky, A.J., & Ahern, D.K. (2004). Cognitive–behavior therapy for hypochondriasis: A randomized controlled trial. *Journal of the American Medical Association, 291*(12), 1464–1470.

Barsky, A.J., Orav, E.J., & Bates, D.W. (2005). Somatization increases medical utilization and costs independent of psychiatric and medical comorbidity. *Archives of General Psychiatry, 62,* 903–910.

Bleichhardt, G., Timmer, B., & Rief, W. (2004). Cognitive–behavioural therapy for patients with multiple somatoform symptoms—a randomised controlled trial in tertiary care. *Journal of Psychosomatic Research, 56*(4), 449–454.

Cohen, M.E., Robins, E., Purtell, J.J., Altmann, M.W., & Reid, D.W. (1953). Excessive surgery in hysteria. *Journal of the American Medical Association, 151,* 977–986.

Fallon, B.A., Liebowitz, M.R., Salman, E., Schneier F., Jusino, C., Hollander, E., et al. (1993). Fluoxetine for hypochondriacal patients without major depression. *Journal of Clinical Psychopharmacology, 13,* 438–441.

Fordyce, W.E., Fowler, R.S., Lehmann, J.F., DeLateur, B.J., Sand, P.L., & Trieschmann, R.B. (1973). Operant conditioning in the treatment of chronic pain. *Archives of Physical Medicine and Rehabilitation, 54,* 399–408.

Goodwin, D.W., & Guze, S.B. (1989). *Psychiatric diagnosis,* 4th ed. New York: Oxford University Press.

Katon, W., Egan, K., & Miller, D. (1985). Chronic pain: Lifetime psychiatric diagnoses and family history. *American Journal of Psychiatry, 142,* 1156–1160.

Kellner, R. (1982). Hypochondriasis and atypical somatoform disorder. In J.H. Greist, J.W. Jefferson, & R.L. Spitzer (Eds.), *Treatment of mental disorders* (pp. 286–303). New York: Oxford University Press.

Kellner, R. (1987). Hypochondriasis and somatization. *Journal of the American Medical Association, 258,* 433–437.

Mai, F. (2004). Somatization disorder: A practical review. *Canadian Journal of Psychiatry, 49*(10), 652–662.

Ochitill, H. (1982). Somatoform disorders. In J.H. Greist, J.W. Jefferson, & R.L. Spitzer (Eds.), *Treatment of mental disorders* (pp. 266–286). New York: Oxford University Press.

Othmer, E., & DeSouza, C. (1985). A screening test for somatization disorder (hysteria). *American Journal of Psychiatry, 142,* 1146–1149.

Oxman, T.E., Rosenberg, S.D., Schnurr, P., & Tucker, G.J. (1985). Linguistic dimensions of affect and thought in somatization disorder. *American Journal of Psychiatry, 142,* 1150–1155.

Smith, G.R., Jr., Rost, K., & Kashner, T.M. (1995). A trial of the effect of a standardized psychiatric consultation on health outcomes and costs in somatizing patients. *Archives of General Psychiatry, 52*(3), 238.

Smith, R.C., Gardiner, J.C., Lyles, J.S., et al. (2005). Exploration of *DSM-IV* criteria in primary care patients with medically unexplained symptoms. *Psychosomatic Medicine, 67*(1), 123–129.

World Health Organization. (1992). *The ICD–10 classification of mental and behavioural disorders: Clinical descriptions and diagnostic guidelines.* Geneva: World Health Organization.

19

Factitious Disorders

Factitious disorders are rare conditions in which patients feign physical or psychological symptoms with the sole intent of being a patient. Their "symptoms" so closely resemble known illnesses that they trick doctors into hospitalizing them, conducting numerous tests, and performing unnecessary surgeries. Little is known about these patients, because when they're finally detected, they flee the hospital and are lost to follow-up. They will repeat their charade at many hospitals.

These patients create symptoms *intentionally*, in the sense of feeling that they control their production. Clinicians infer this intentional quality from the adeptness at simulating illnesses. However, although these patients intentionally generate symptoms, they are also driven to do so. Their fakery is compulsive; they can't refrain from subjecting themselves to procedures they know are dangerous and needless. Their illness-feigning behavior is deliberate and purposeful, but their motivations are not; for reasons beyond their control, they are impelled to be a patient.

Factitious disorders lie in the middle of a continuum between the outright fakery of physical symptoms (malingering) and their unconscious production (somatoform disorders). Unlike patients with factitious disorders, *malingerers* fabricate symptoms for reasons other than being a patient, such as draft evasion, drugs, disability payments, or missing classes. The malingerer's behavior *and* motivations are conscious, deliberate, and easily understandable. Unlike patients with factitious disorders, those with somatoform disorders are not consciously faking illness.

Factitious disorders have been divided into those with *psychological signs and symptoms* and those with *physical signs and symptoms*. In both, symptoms can't be explained by another mental disorder, but are often superimposed on one. In the latter, the patient's physical "symptoms" result in multiple hospitalizations. Table 19-1 lists diagnostic criteria for factitious disorder.

TABLE 19-1
Diagnostic Criteria for Factitious Disorder

A. The individual **intentionally produces or feigns physical or psychological symptoms** repeatedly and consistently.

B. The imitation and insistence of symptoms (e.g., pain and bleeding) may be **so convincing and persistent** that repeated investigations and operations are performed at several different hospitals or clinics, in spite of repeatedly negative findings.

   For physical symptoms this may even extend to self-infliction of cuts or abrasions to produce bleeding, or to self-injection of toxic substances.

C. The **motivation for this behavior is almost always obscure and presumably internal** (no obvious external rewards), and the condition is best interpreted as a disorder of illness behavior and the sick role.

D. The falsified symptoms occur in **the absence of a confirmed physical or mental disorder**, disease, or disability such as delusional or some other psychotic disorder.

Note: Adapted from *ICD-10* (p. 174) and *DSM-5* (p. 324)

CLINICAL PRESENTATION

With Predominantly Physical Signs and Symptoms

Asher (1951) coined the name "Munchausen syndrome" to designate patients who travel from hospital to hospital, dramatically presenting plausible histories and receiving surgery. Their stories are so elaborate that Asher named their condition after Baron Karl Friedrich Hieronymus Freiherr von Munchausen (1720–1797), a German cavalry officer and world-class liar. Munchausen syndrome equates to chronic factitious disorder with physical symptoms.

These patients' "symptoms" are limited only by their creativity and medical knowledge; many work in hospitals as nurses or technicians; some study medical texts and speak "medicaleze." Most will dramatically enter an emergency room with a classical description of a disease (e.g., crushing chest pain, sudden loss of breath, convulsions). Once hospitalized, they may insist on narcotics or tell staff which lab tests and procedures to perform.

Their *pièce de résistance* is feigning objective physical signs and abnormal laboratory findings. One patient "raised" his rectal temperature by relaxing and contracting his anal sphincter. Another swallowed blood, strolled into the ER, and puked. Patients will spit saliva into urine samples to elevate urinary amylase, or they may prick a finger and squeeze a little blood into their urine to "develop" hematuria. Self-injecting insulin will produce hypoglycemia. Fecal bacteria will somehow find their way into urine. Patients have swallowed nails, fish hooks, and paint. By self-inducing disease, some of these patients become genuinely sick, although death is rare.

Factitious patients often spin intriguing yarns ("pseudologia fantastica") —false accounts of famous parents, financial wizardry, or show-biz exploits; they might be still another bastard descendant of Aaron Burr or claim a surgical scar came from battlefield heroics. For all their "accomplishments" or "notoriety," the staff begin to wonder why they have so few visitors, phone calls, or friends. Further clues to this diagnosis are extensive travel, self-mutilation, *la belle indifference* to pain and painful procedures, drug abuse (in 50% of cases), ever-changing medical complaints, and substantial evidence of prior treatment (e.g., venous cutdown scars), signs of recent cardioversion, or a "gridiron abdomen" from multiple operations (Sussman & Hyler, 1985).

When the staff becomes suspicious, these patients become increasingly strident and may present new evidence of illness. Any suggestions of a psychiatric consult are angrily rejected. If confronted with their contradictory stories or inconsistent findings, instead of recanting or displaying embarrassment, factitious patients will question the staff's competence or threaten litigation. Once these ploys fail, patients will sign out of the hospital against medical advice or leave surreptitiously. A few days later they may pop up at another hospital, recycling the same saga.

> Factitious disorder usually begins during early adulthood, but can start during childhood. Although initially these patients may receive medical care for a real illness, they then develop a pattern of repeated ambulatory treatments and hospitalizations. The prognosis worsens as patients escalate from (1) giving a fictitious history, to (2) simulating signs of illness, to (3) inducing pathological states.

With Predominantly Psychological Signs and Symptoms

These factitious patients will fake several, often psychotic-like symptoms, which laypeople would take as a mental illness, but professionals would realize are inconsistent with any known psychiatric disorder. Patients may complain of hallucinations, erratic memory loss, itchy feet, facial twitches, and episodic blindness—a symptom cluster that, although inventive, doesn't exist. They're also highly suggestible: If told that hallucinating patients don't sleep, these patients don't sleep. When observed, their symptoms get worse. Some are negativistic and refuse to answer questions. Many have a (genuine) borderline personality disorder.

Some present with overwhelming grief instead of psychosis (Phillips, Ward, & Ries, 1983). Invariably, many family members have been killed, usually by dramatic means (train wrecks, murders). Authenticity of the story is rarely questioned because these patients are already enduring enough suffering and need support rather than suspicions. They differ from those really grieving in not having any family members ("they all died") or friends who can be contacted to verify the story. The best way to confirm suspected factitious mourning is to ask for the place and date of the alleged death(s) and call the appropriate coroner.

Others, especially prisoners, may have Ganser syndrome, whose chief symptom is *vorbeireden*—that is, giving approximate answers, near misses, or talking past the point. They appear to understand questions, but to deliberately give false answers: Ask when Santa comes, and they'll say Halloween; ask them to subtract 7 from 100 and they'll respond, "92, 84, 76," and so on. *Vorbeireden*, however, is also found in other disorders and malingering.

EPIDEMIOLOGY

Factitious disorder is rare, but its true prevalence is unknown: The rate may be underestimated, because patients don't stay around to be detected or counted; or overestimated, since patients move from hospital to hospital and the same patient may be reported many times. One patient had over 420 documented hospitalizations. Epidemiological figures from university populations may be inflated, since these patients are drawn to these facilities. Perhaps 1% of inpatients referred for psychiatric consultation have factitious disorders. Males seem to have more factitious disorders than females.

DIFFERENTIAL DIAGNOSIS

The main reason for identifying factitious disorder is to spare patients from unnecessary hospitalizations and potentially harmful medical procedures and operations. The chief diagnostic problem is to distinguish factitious disorder from *true medical illness*. Factitious disorders should be considered when patients stage their history as high drama, exhibit pseudologia fantastica, disrupt a ward and break hospital rules, argue continuously with staff, show off medical jargon and knowledge, demand narcotics, "advertise" signs of numerous prior medical treatments and surgeries, give contradictory histories, develop frequent or inexplicable medical complications, present new symptoms after every negative workup, or become hostile when questioned about their medical history or personal background.

As discussed previously, factitious disorder should be distinguished from *somatoform disorder* and *malingering*. *Antisocial personality disorder* may be misdiagnosed on account of these patients' pseudologia fantastica, impostership, lying, drug abuse, and lack of close relations. Sociopaths, however, usually avoid painful tests and hospitals, unless these might get them out of a jail sentence; Munchausen patients "attract" them. Some people with *schizophrenia* self-induce physical symptoms, but secondarily to a specific delusion or command hallucination.

Diagnosing factitious disorder with psychological symptoms is especially difficult, because most psychological symptoms can't be objectively verified. Whenever symptoms don't fit the pattern of a *known mental disorder*, factitious disorder merits consideration. Factitious disorder with psychological symptoms *and* another mental disorder can both be diagnosed, as long as the factitious symptoms are produced without an external incentive or ulterior motive (as in malingering). For a malingerer whose motive is as simple as "three hots and a cot" (three meals and a bed), a psychiatric hospitalization with its "painless patienthood" may seem like a good alternative for the patient (but not for anyone else). Other common external motives for malingering are obtaining narcotics, evading criminal prosecution, improving living conditions, and disability benefits. Compared to civilian life, malingering is much more common in the military and legal settings.

ETIOLOGY AND PATHOGENESIS

What causes factitious disorders is unknown, but they probably develop from a confluence of factors, which vary depending on the patient. People with factitious disorder with physical symptoms are more likely to have had physical disorders (often requiring extensive treatment) while growing up; a close relationship with a doctor in the past, such as having a doctor in the family or having been sexually abused by a doctor; or a grudge against the medical profession, sometimes based on bad past medical care. A severe personality disorder—often borderline, dependent, or antisocial—is a predisposing factor for factitious disorders.

All patients with factitious disorders engage in "inappropriate care-getting behavior." They probably want care and attention but can't or don't know how to get it in usual, healthy ways. Given their self-destructiveness, *masoch-*

istic impulses may feed on a *love–hate relationship* with health-care professionals. If they could say it, their underlying message might be, "Help me, you bastard." These patients often suffer from *childhood deprivation, neglect, and abuse,* which may steer them into dependent roles even as they expect health professionals to make up for lost parenting. This need also might account for factitious disorder *"by proxy,"* a rare phenomenon in which a parent induces symptoms in his or her child in order to live vicariously through the child as he or she receives the parental affection of doctors and nurses. Some Munchausen patients *identify* with health-care professionals, while enjoying a *sense of mastery and control* from learning about illness, coping with pain, and outwitting physicians.

MANAGEMENT AND TREATMENT

Wilhelm Kaiser claimed the only requirement for successful therapy is that two people be in a room. And since patients with factitious disorders don't stay in the room, the only thing that's clear about treating them is that nothing is known to work. Failed treatments include hypnosis, medications (of all kinds), ECT, insulin coma, and lobotomy. Several authors advocate psychotherapy, but have too few treatment cases to establish its efficacy. Even when physicians gently confront these patients with their true diagnoses, patients usually react with hostility and reject any offer of help.

Despite the absence of any clearly effective treatment, experts generally recommend that, once the diagnosis of factitious disorder is established, clinicians should (1) be careful not to overlook genuine medical disease; (2) keep patients in the hospital—for once out, always out—to begin to involve them in extended psychiatric treatment; (3) if necessary to ensure safety, commit children with factitious disorders by proxy to hospitals, and report the caregiver to child protective services; (4) carefully check annoyance with these patients, avoid power struggles and public humiliations, and be ever alert to the behaviors and dynamics (including splitting) commonly associated with borderline personality disorder; (5) if outsmarted by these patients, do not get bent out of shape; and (6) track these patients through electronic health records and funding databases to effectively coordinate care.

References

American Psychiatric Association. (2013). *Diagnostic and statistical manual of mental disorders*, 5th ed. Arlington, VA: American Psychiatric Association.

Asher, R. (1951). Muchausen's syndrome. *Lancet, 1,* 339–341.

Phillips, M.R., Ward, N.G., & Ries, R.K. (1983). Factitious mourning: Painless patienthood. *American Journal of Psychiatry, 140,* 420–425.

Pope, H., Jonas, J.M., & Jones, B. (1982). Factitious psychosis: Phenomenology, family history, and long-term outcome of nine patients. *American Journal of Psychiatry 139,* 1480–1483.

Wang, D., Nadiga, D.N., & Jenson, J.J. (2005). Factitious disorders. In B.J. Sadock & V.A. Sadock (Eds.), *Comprehensive textbook of psychiatry,* 8th ed. (pp. 1829–1843). Philadelphia: Lippincott, Williams & Wilkins.

World Health Organization. (1992). *The ICD–10 classification of mental and behavioural disorders: Clinical descriptions and diagnostic guidelines.* Geneva: World Health Organization.

20

Eating and Elimination Disorders

In 1689, Dr. Richard Morton described a self-starving 18-year-old female who looked like a "skeleton only clad with skin." He called her condition "nervous consumption"; in 1874, Sir William Gull called it "*anorexia nervosa*." This disorder is characterized by an irrational dread of becoming fat, a zealous pursuit of thinness, massive weight loss, a disturbed body image, and an almost delusional belief of being too fat. *Bulimia*, which wasn't recognized until the 1950s, is characterized by binge-eating and self-induced vomiting. Unlike anorexia nervosa, bulimia usually afflicts individuals with normal, or slightly excessive, weight. Preoccupation with weight and the use of pathological approaches to losing weight are shared by the two disorders.

The frequency of eating disorders has leveled off in Western nations after rapidly escalating. For example, in Rochester, Minnesota, the incidence of anorexia nervosa among women ages 10–19 jumped a walloping 375% between 1950 and 1954 and 1980 and 1984 (Lucas et al., 1991); similar increases have been reported in Zurich and London. These dramatic increases, which initially mainly occurred in the most vulnerable group (teenage girls) were genuine and not merely the result of greater awareness. More recently, anorexia nervosa has also been increasing in young and middle-aged women, many of whom suffer from chronic anorexia nervosa (Strober et al., 1997). Anorexia nervosa is also *lethal*, with its mortality rate ranging from 5 to 10%. The combined prevalence of anorexia nervosa and bulimia in the highest risk group, adolescent and young adult women (mainly upper- and middle-class students), has ranged between 1 and 4% over the past 10 to 20 years and has become more evenly distributed worldwide (Yager et al., 2006).

This chapter discusses only anorexia nervosa and bulimia, but there are other eating disorders that occur during infancy and childhood: *pica*, in which children persistently ingest nonnutritive substances (e.g., lead paint chips, hair, dirt; *pica* is the Latin word for "magpie," a renowned avian scavenger); and *rumination disorder* of infancy, or merycism, a rare and some-times fatal disorder of repeated regurgitation. Some minor feeding difficulties are common during infancy and early childhood. They only receive clinical attention when food refusal (including extreme pickiness) leads to failure to gain weight or weight loss over a 1 month period of time. *Obesity* isn't a mental disorder because it lacks a consistent psychological pattern. When psychological forces promote obesity, they should be indicated as "psycho-logical factors affecting physical condition." *Binge-eating disorder*, in which the individual engages in binge eating but without compensatory purging, may accompany obesity. The prevalence of binge eating disorders is esti-mated to be 2% in community samples and accounts for 1.3 to 30.1% of patients seeking medical treatment for obesity (Fairburn, Marcus et al., 1993; Dingemans et al., 2002).

ANOREXIA NERVOSA

Clinical Presentation

The essential features of anorexia nervosa are a dread of being fat and a com-pulsion to be thin, substantial weight loss, refusal to maintain a healthy weight despite being very thin or even emaciated, distorted internal and external perceptions of one's body as fat despite being underweight, and in women, amenorrhea. Table 20-1 lists diagnostic criteria for anorexia nervosa.

In the typical individual with anorexia nervosa—a teenager or woman in her early 20s, formerly a "model child"—starts dieting due to mild over-weight; this weight gain may occur after a stressor (e.g., puberty, a broken romance, a family divorce) or for no apparent reason. After shedding a few pounds, she decides that's not enough. This cycle repeats itself until she virtually stops eating. Only in the most severe stages (near emaciation) does she lose her appetite (hence the term *anorexia* nervosa is a misnomer). Most of the time she has a raging appetite and constantly thinks about food. Unfortunately, her food choices are very restricted ("Romaine versus iceberg lettuce? With or without lemon juice?"). She may memorize the calorie content of foods and prepare meals for everyone but herself. She may hide food, steal it, or play with it, but avoids eating in public and often consumes what little she eats in secrecy. To lose weight, she exercises frenetically, goes on fad diets, abstains from carbohydrates and fats, takes laxatives and diuret-ics, and gorges food then induces vomiting (i.e., episodes of binge eating).

TABLE 20-1
Diagnostic Criteria for Anorexia Nervosa

A. **Deliberate weight loss** induced or sustained by the person so that body weight is maintained at least 15% below that expected, or **body-mass index is 17.5 or less**. (Prepubertal patients may show failure to make the expected weight gain during the period of growth.)

B. Weight loss may be **self-induced** by
   1. Avoidance of "fattening foods"
   2. Self-induced vomiting
   3. Self-induced purging
   4. Excessive exercise
   5. Appetite suppressants and/or diuretics

C. There is **body-image distortion** in the form of a specific psychopathology whereby a dread of fatness persists as an intrusive, overvalued idea and the patient imposes a low weight threshold on himself or herself.

D. Endocrine abnormalities involving the hypothalamic-pituitary-gonadal axis are manifest in women as **amenorrhea** and in men as a **loss of sexual interest and potency**.
   1. There may also be elevated levels of growth hormone, raised levels of cortisol, changes in the peripheral metabolism of the thyroid hormone, and abnormalities of insulin secretion.
   2. If onset is prepubertal, the sequence of pubertal events is delayed or even arrested (growth ceases; in girls the breasts do not develop and there is a primary amenorrhea; in boys the genitals remain juvenile).

DSM-5 *specifies two subtypes: restricting type and binge-eating/purging type*

Note: Adapted from *ICD-10* (p. 138) and *DSM-5* (p. 338)

At first, she's energetic, enthusiastic, and pert, but then depressive symptoms set in, especially dysthymia, insomnia (or hypersomnia), social withdrawal, and decreased libido. She's usually perfectionistic and introverted. She'll have stomach pains, nausea, constipation, cold intolerance, headaches, frequent urination, low blood pressure, and diminished secondary sex characteristics. Vomiting that started intentionally may become automatic. As teenagers, female anorectics may shy away from boys and sex. Normal overt anger is curiously lacking in many anorectics (i.e., in those with the "restricting type" not the "binge-eating/purging type").

The anorectic's family members are usually described as being "as nice as you could find." However, they frequently speak for the patient and avoid any sort of disagreement or conflict to an extreme degree ("No, you [to the patient] don't get angry, do you?"). They proudly tell you that "before this all started, we never fought." Efforts to get her to eat have backfired—she just starves herself more.

Epidemiology

The typical female with anorexia is a white, teenage girl from the middle or upper classes, who will attend college. However, there is an increasing prevalence of anorexia nervosa in females in minority populations in the United States (Latina and Asian-American teens and adults, and African-American adult women). There also is a major worldwide increase in this disorder among residents of Third World nations and Third World immigrants in Europe. This increased prevalence of anorexia nervosa is associated with the increased adoption of European/Western body image ideals of thinness as required for attractiveness in women, either in the nations of origin or by acculturating immigrant groups (Pumariega, 1986; Pumariega et al., 1994; Miller & Pumariega, 2001). Given that 90–95% of anorectics are female, the diagnosis should be made extra cautiously in males, where it is frequently associated with homosexual orientation, serious personality disorders, or psychosis (Andersen & Holman, 1997). Dancers, modeling students, and athletes (e.g., gymnasts, marathon runners) have a higher incidence of anorexia nervosa, but only *after* they began these activities. Individuals with chronic illnesses where food or nutrition is affected (e.g., cystic fibrosis or diabetes) are at higher risk (Pumariega et al., 1986). Eating disorders have also been found in male athletes, especially wrestlers and racehorse jockeys, who learned to starve and vomit "to get down to weight." Males with anorexia often don't say that they started dieting because they were too fat but rather to get "better muscle definition." All in all, the prevalence of anorexia nervosa is between 0.2 and 0.3% for females and is 0.02% for males. Rates for teenage girls are around 0.5–0.8%.

Differential Diagnosis

Anorexia nervosa is easy to distinguish from other disorders, primarily *schizophrenia* and *depression*, in which significant weight loss is also found. Besides lacking the common symptoms seen in these disorders, those with anorexia of either type (restricted or binge-eating/purging) misjudge their body image, misperceive internal body cues, may binge and purge, and display hyperactivity, inordinate cheerfulness, a zealous preoccupation with food, and a dread of obesity. These distinctions also apply for *malnutrition* and *starvation* (e.g., as may occur in *tuberculosis, Crohn's disease, ulcerative colitis, extreme poverty*), as well as various *neurological diseases* (e.g., *epilepsy, brain tumors*). One question can usually distinguish a very thin person from a person with anorexia: "What is your ideal body weight?" Almost all people with anorexia will say something less than their current weight, whereas all others will say, "I need to gain weight, I'm too thin."

Etiology and Pathogenesis

Psychologically, individuals with anorexia share three cardinal features: perfectionism, dread of losing control, and the distorted perception of their own bodies. Before becoming ill, the typical patient is a "model child"; afterward, everything's a power struggle. Superficially strong and defiant, she's devoid of self-confidence, paralyzed by helplessness, and terrified by her lack of self-control. This individual reacts to gaining a pound with the same distress that the reader might have if she gained 50 pounds overnight. When frantic parents fight with her about eating, they merely feed the patient's stubbornness, since to her, the issue isn't health or even love, but control.

Struggles over control are inflamed by the patient's internal and external misperceptions of her own body. She minimizes internal stimuli: In comparison to normals, she says she feels less hunger after not eating and feels less exhaustion after exercising. Externally, she sees her body differently from the way others see it. Precise measuring shows that anorectics greatly overestimate their front profile width (often twofold), yet correctly estimate their height, the height and width of female models, and the size of physical objects. However, such body misperception (and extreme "black–white" perfectionism) has been seen in experimentally starved individuals, so the cognitive effects of starvation may also fuel these characteristics.

Psychosocial Theories

Biopsychosocial. Our culture has an absurd thinness ideal for females but not for males. This thinness ideal is a historical and cultural aberration, largely confined to Western civilization of the mid- to late-20th century. Prior to this, more rounded and filled-out women were the ideal. Examples include the women in Ruben's paintings in the 1800s and movie stars such as Marilyn Monroe in the 1950s. By today's standards these women would be labeled "too fat." In countries where food is not plentiful, such as China, India, and parts of Africa, being thin means not getting enough food. Anorexia and bulimia had been very rare in these settings, but as these world regions have overcome food shortages, there has been increasing adoption of Western body image ideals. The proportions of representatives of feminine beauty—Miss America contestants (and winners), *Playboy* centerfolds, movie stars, models, and even department store mannequins—have been getting progressively thinner and are now typically below ideal body weight. In modern Western civilization, a woman's appearance tends to be scrutinized and evaluated more than a man's, with a high premium placed on youthfulness and attractiveness. All this is happening during a time when young American women are actually becoming heavier in relation to their height, apparently owing to improved nutrition, creating a progressively greater discrepancy between the real situation and the so-called ideal. The increasing pressure to conform to the ideal drives many to diet. In one study of normal-weight adolescents, 80% of the girls "felt fat," compared to 20% of the boys. The women's popular press responds to this pressure by publishing increasing numbers of articles featuring reducing diets (more than 100 per year). Two theoretical perspectives address this phenomenon: (1) The feminist perspective proposes that as women become more socially autonomous, there is added pressure to conform to ideals imposed by male-dominated society (explaining the increased prevalence in women); and (2) the ethological perspective proposes that dieting in the face of plenty serves to rein in fertility and excessive population growth (Gustavson et al., 1991; Miller & Pumariega, 2001).

In spite of strong societal influences on the development of eating disorders in women, only a minority of women actually develop eating disorders. Therefore, individual factors in those women must play a role. Adolescents have several daunting developmental tasks to perform, including developing and solidifying their own identities, individuating from their families, coming to terms with their sexuality, and feeling accepted by peers. Adolescents who have greater difficulty accomplishing these goals are vulnerable to developing anorexia. At highest risk are those with low self-esteem (individuals with anorexia have high rates of depression), rigid approaches in dealing with problems (25% also have obsessive–compulsive personality disorder), overcontrolling (or, in some cases, undercontrolling) families in which problems don't get worked out, and those with serious conflicts about sexuality. In some, the initial massive weight loss may alter their biological homeostatic mechanisms in such a way as to maintain the anorexia.

Psychodynamic. Analysts blame "domineering" parents for preventing the young person with anorexia from the two chief psychosocial tasks of adolescence: separating and individuating. Adolescents with anorexia demand independence even as they cling to their parents. Yet with these, as with most etiological theories of anorexia nervosa, what's purported to be a cause of the disorder may be both a cause and consequence of it.

Family. Many papers describe the father of the affected youngster as ineffective, her mother as overbearing, and both parents as intrusive. The family system is dysfunctional—but, once again, is this cause or effect? Though some family theorists proposed that this was causative (Minuchin et al., 1978), others (Amdur et al., 1969) proposed that once the disorder has arisen, family psychopathology was more a reaction to the patient's difficulties than a cause for them. Such reactions surely aggravate and perpetuate matters and merit addressing in treatment.

Biological Theories

A major debate in recent biological research has been whether or not eating disorders share common biological pathways with depression. The affirmative side points to the high frequency of depression in people with anorexia (40–75%), and the higher prevalence of mood disorders in close relatives of those with anorexia and especially those with bulimia. The negative side points out that eating and depressive disorders are more different than alike. Although the question remains open, anorexia nervosa might be a heterogeneous disorder, with some cases having, and other cases not having, a biological link to depression.

> *Genetic.* Family and twin studies suggest a high heritability of anorexia and bulimia, and researchers are searching for genes that confer susceptibility to these disorders. Scientists suspect that multiple genes and gene combinations may interact with environmental and other factors to increase the risk of developing these illnesses. Identification of susceptibility genes will permit the development of improved treatments for eating disorders (Ramoz, Versini, & Gorwood, 2007).

> *Neurobiological and anatomical.* Investigations of the neurobiology of emotional and social behavior relevant to eating disorders and the neuroscience of feeding behavior have revealed that both appetite and energy expenditure are regulated by a highly complex network of nerve cells and molecular messengers called neuropeptides. These discoveries and follow-up research will provide potential targets for the development of new pharmacologic treatments for eating disorders (Torsello et al., 2007; Baranowska et al., 2008). Other studies are investigating the role of gonadal steroids. Their relevance to eating disorders is suggested by the clear gender effect in the risk for these disorders, their emergence at puberty or soon after, and the increased risk for eating disorders among girls with early onset of menstruation (Lawson & Klibanski, 2008). Gustavson et al. (1991) also found a major increase in diagnosed anorexia nervosa or unexplained weight loss in the offspring of women who took diethylstilbestrol (DES), with a higher

risk than the reproductive cancer risk associated with DES exposure. They suggested that androgenic exposure in utero might explain increased risk for women, who may develop conditioned aversions to their own estrogen after puberty (thus starve to reduce it). More recently, a study suggested that the rate of anorexia was higher in males born from opposite sex fraternal twin pairs than in monozygotic same-gender twin pairs, suggesting hormonal exposure in utero as a factor (Procopio & Marriott, 2007). Perinatal complications have also been associated with higher prevalence of anorexia nervosa and bulimia, suggesting that impairments in neurodevelopment could be factors in their development (Favaro, Tenconi, & Santonastaso, 2006).

Clinical Course and Complications

Although milder anorexia nervosa may stop within 12 months, it usually persists for years, punctuated by remissions and exacerbations. About half of these patients have intermittent bulimic symptoms of binge-eating and purging. Nutritionally, patients usually recover in 2–3 years, but even then about half continue to have menstrual problems, sexual and social maladjustment, massive weight fluctuations, or disturbed appetite, and two-thirds continue to fret over their weight and body image. In terms of their overall prognosis, on average 44% recover completely (weight 85% or more of recommended weight), 28% improve considerably, 24% remain unimproved or severely impaired (weight never approaches 85% of recommended weight), and 5% die prematurely. About half die from medical complications (such as cardiac arrest secondary to electrolyte imbalance from vomiting or purging), but the other half die from suicide (Hsu, 1986, 1990; Norman, 1984). In the past, death rates reached 20% among patients followed for 20 years (Theander, 1985). Because many patients with chronic anorexia nervosa develop osteoporosis leading to pathological fractures, complaints of bone or back pain should be investigated. The bone calcium lost may never be regained. Brain mass decreases in 50% of patients, a loss that also may be permanent. An increasing number of people with chronic anorexia nervosa is chronically incapacitated by the disorder and end up in a state of disability. Table 20-2 summarizes the medical complications of anorexia.

Predictors of a favorable outcome include onset in the early teen years, good premorbid functioning, more education, being single, less weight loss, less denial of illness, overactivity, greater psychosexual maturity, and feeling hunger when hospitalized. Indicators of a poor prognosis are the opposite of

TABLE 20-2
Medical Complications of Anorexia

Endocrine/Metabolic

Amenorrhea*	Decreased somatomedin C
Constipation*	Elevated growth hormone
Osteoporosis*	Decreased or erratic vasopressin secretion
Lanugo hair*	Hypercarotenemia
Abnormal temperature regulation (hypothermia)*	Hair loss
Euthyroid sick syndrome	Abnormal glucose tolerance test
Decreased norepinephrine secretion	Elevated cortisol and abnormal dexamethasone tolerance test

Cardiovascular

Bradycardia*	Arrhythmias
Hypotension*	Impaired cardiac function with normal EKG (with increased sudden death)

Renal

Increased BUN (blood urea nitrogen)	Renal calculi
Decreased glomerular filtration rate	Pedal edema (also caused by decreased albumin)

Hematologic

Anemia*	Leukopenia
Thrombocytopenia	

*Most common complications.

above, plus premorbidly disturbed family relationships, perinatal complications, bingeing, self-induced vomiting and purging, longer duration of illness, longer delay in initially obtaining treatment, failure to respond to previous treatment, severe dysthymia and obsessions, severe personality disorder, and greater exaggeration of body size.

Management and Treatment

The legacy of Karen Carpenter, the young pop singer who died from anorexia nervosa (most likely cardiotoxicity from Ipecac/emetine), should remind clinicians that the first goal in treatment is always to (1) keep the patient alive. Beyond this, the goals are (in order of priority and treatment focus) (2) establish adequate nutrition, (3) treat physical complications, (4) correct abnormal eating habits, (5) supplant family overinvolvement with more appropriate intrafamilial relationships, (6) enhance self-control, identity, and autonomy,

(7) identify and begin correcting dysfunctional thoughts, attitudes, and beliefs, and (8) correct defects in affect and behavioral regulation.

Hospitalization and Behavior Therapy

If the patient's weight is *medically precarious*, hospitalization is mandatory. If matters have so deteriorated that the patient is in danger of losing her life, professionals must take charge. Once hospitalized, treatment follows the same principles set down in 1874 by Sir William Gull, who named the disorder. Patients should be fed at regular intervals and surrounded by persons who would have "moral control" over them; relatives and friends generally are the worst attendants.

> Behavior therapy is used first to prevent starvation, restore nutritional balance, and increase weight. Programs can vary as to whether a prescribed minimum weight goal or a minimum caloric goal (using a prescribed diet) must be met to gain privileges or reinforcers. Dietician consultation can be useful, though individuals with anorexia are usually experts on caloric content and daily requirements, albeit distorting these as applying to all except them. The patient may request liquid nutritional supplements because she has difficulty with solid foods. She's weighed every morning in the nude or in a hospital gown, a half hour after voiding, since these patients are pros at adding extra weight in the heels of shoes, hems of nightgowns, by water loading, etc. Bed rest can be a natural consequence of not taking in sufficient calories to burn in daily activities. Tube feeding is used only when the patient goes below a critical weight associated with medical complications (usually 30% below ideal body weight). All efforts are made to help the patient begin to regain weight naturally, since extended tube feeding not only has medical complications but reinforces feelings of loss of control. Consequences are sometimes built in for bingeing weight gains, e.g., more than 1 pound a day. This program is continued until the patient reaches medically safe weight, usually within 10–15% of the norm. Discharging only at an acceptable weight (below 15% of norm) is risky. After discharge medical personnel, *not the family*, should follow her weight, typically at weekly intervals. Nursing and therapy staff members can offer reassurance to patients by helping them resist the urge to binge and even by assuring them that they (the staff) will not allow the patients to gain excessive weight. Staff members show that they understand her dread of becoming fat and are allies *with* her, not *against* her. This approach undercuts the rebellious aspect of the disorder and circumvents power struggles and fears of loss of control.

Family Therapy

Early on, parents should not have any responsibility for the patient's care. This approach diffuses family tension, permits autonomy for the patient, and gracefully lets the parents "off the hook." In some programs, either a week after admission or once the patient begins to gain weight, informal lunches with the entire family are held to evaluate family interactions at mealtime, to reduce intrafamilial power struggles, and to promote more helpful behavior around the table. These family therapy lunches are continued after discharge to establish more balanced family relationships. Most programs just use traditional family therapy.

Psychotherapy

Psychotherapies are no substitute for proper nutrition and weight gain, and nutrition must be established for the patient to have sufficient cognitive function to be able to utilize psychotherapy. Individual psychotherapy focuses on helping the patient learn to abandon her self-destructive approach to establishing autonomy and find more enduring sources of self-worth and self-control. Variations on assertiveness training are helpful so that patients can learn to say "no" in family conflicts without undercutting or capitulation. *Group therapy* helps patients reestablish lost social skills and view themselves in a more normative manner. Many locales offer self-help groups for patients with eating disorders; these groups are helpful adjuncts, especially when they include consulting professionals.

Medication

Many patients with anorexia have comorbid depression, which sometimes improves with weight restoration. Between 40 and 60% of patients benefit from antidepressants. Malnourished patients are especially sensitive to drugs, so lower doses may be indicated. Orthostatic hypotension and arrhythmias are the biggest risk with the tricyclic antidepressants in malnourished or dehydrated patients. The SSRIs are recommended as a first choice because they don't cause orthostatic hypotension and have minimal effects on heart rhythms. Cyproheptadine (Periactin), a serotonin antagonist and antihistamine, is a useful adjunct for weight restoration, primarily if the patient has lost her appetite and can view appetite as a cue to eat and not exercise or play with her food or feel that she is losing control.

BULIMIA NERVOSA AND BINGE-EATING DISORDER

The word *bulimia* means "the hunger of an ox" from the Greek: *bous* = ox, *limos* = hunger. Binge-eating is the central feature of *bulimia*. People with bulimia view their bingeing as pathological, dread their inability to control their eating, and become unhappy and self-deprecating after bingeing. Because they're ashamed, a majority try to hide their problem from those close to them and even clinicians. Although self-induced vomiting occurs in 88% of patients, it is not a diagnostic requirement. In contrast to anorexia nervosa, severe weight loss is uncommon, and amenorrhea is less common (40%). Diagnostic criteria for bulimia are listed in Table 20-3.

Eating binges last a few minutes to 2 hours. People with bulimia may binge twice a week or over 10 times a day, but between binge episodes they typically engage in food restriction or dieting. Dysphoria usually precedes a binge and is relieved by it. Patients typically give more than one reason for bingeing: feeling anxious or tense (83%), craving certain foods (70%), feeling unhappy (67%), "can't control appetite" (59%), hunger (31%), and/or insomnia (22%) (Mitchell et al., 1985). Those with bulimia are more likely to binge as the day goes on. While gorging themselves, most patients aren't

---

TABLE 20-3
Diagnostic Criteria for Bulimia Nervosa

A. There is a persistent preoccupation with eating, and an irresistible craving for food; the patient succumbs to **episodes of overeating** in which large amounts of food are consumed in short periods of time.

B. The patient attempts **to counteract the "fattening" effects of food by one or more of the following**:
   1. self-induced vomiting;
   2. purgative abuse (emetics, laxatives);
   3. alternating periods of starvation;
   4. excessive exercise
   5. use of drugs such as appetite suppressants, thyroid preparations, or diuretics.

C. *DSM-5 specifies that both the binge eating and inappropriate compensatory behaviors occur, on average, at least once a week for 3 months.*

D. The psychopathology consists of a **morbid dread of fatness** and the person sets herself or himself a sharply defined weight threshold, well below the premorbid weight that constitutes the optimum or healthy weight in the opinion of the physician.

Binge Eating Disorder is binge eating associated with marked distress but not with the recurrent use of inappropriate compensatory behaviors.

Note: Adapted from *ICD-10* (p. 139) and *DSM-5* (p. 345)

---

aware of hunger and don't stop even when satiated. They don't chew, they gobble, preferably foods high in calories and carbohydrates, and easy to devour. Three thousand calories is an average binge, but calorie consumption ranges from 1,200 to 11,500 calories (not a normal portion of food or "three carrots," as a person with anorexia might report). These individuals might binge on 3 pounds of chocolate, popcorn for an army, and 4 pints of ice cream; they might spend well over $100 a day on food; some steal food. To avoid detection, most binge in secrecy, with windows covered and the telephone disconnected.

Bingeing typically stops when the patient is discovered, falls asleep, develops stomach pain, or induces vomiting. By diminishing abdominal cramps and distention, this self-induced vomiting permits further binges. People with bulimia continue to binge in order to delay the inevitable postbinge dysphoria. This dysphoria is described as guilt (87%), feeling too full (64%), worrying (53%), still feeling hungry (22%). (This dysphoria is also associated with a drop in blood sugar associated with the rush of insulin stimulated by carbohydrate bingeing.) A minority feels relaxed (23%) or satisfied (15%). In therapy, patients with bulimia describe their bingeing as "disgusting" but irresistible. When having a normal meal, they fear bingeing again or gaining weight.

These patients are preoccupied with their appearance, body image, and sexual attractiveness, as well as how others, men especially, perceive and respond to them. By using various techniques—binge eating (100%), fasting (92%), exercise (91%), vomiting (88%), spitting out food (65%), laxatives (61%), diet pills (50%), diuretics (34%), saunas (12%)—patients with bulimia can readily add or shed 10 pounds a day. These patients are rarely underweight, and 5% are overweight. Prior to their bulimia, 14% were underweight, and 56% were overweight. They frequently have problems controlling their impulses in other areas. About a third have abused drugs and alcohol and about a fifth have received treatment for it. A minority will steal, engage in self-mutilation, or attempt suicide. To look thin and sexually attractive— a redundancy to bulimics—and to alleviate sadness, they'll go on clothes-buying sprees ("retail therapy"). Unlike those with anorexia, people with bulimia are usually sexually active, and some are promiscuous.

Individuals with *binge-eating disorder* have similar characteristics as those with bulimia but also some differences. They engage in binge eating to a similar extent (though less intensely), but do not engage in compensatory purging behaviors. They have some tendencies toward impulsive behaviors, but not as extreme, with lower association with substance abuse, stealing, and self-mutilation. They are almost always overweight, are less preoccupied with their bodies, and have somewhat of a "hopeless" attitude about their appearance and weight, often shunning sexual activity. They may engage in dieting over a period of weeks or months, only to fall back into binge-eating behaviors (Fairburn et al., 1993).

Epidemiology

Like the young woman with anorexia, the prototypic youngster with bulimia is a white, adolescent girl from the middle or upper class, who attends a university. However, bulimia has been increasing among Latinas and African-Americans of college age and young adulthood, and in people of lower socioeconomic status, as they increasingly adopt Western and upwardly mobile body image ideals. Ninety to 95% of people with bulimia are female. The prevalence of bulimia varies enormously depending on the particular subpopulation. Although the prevalence is less than 0.5% in the general population, in a survey of 500 college students, 4.4% reported eating disorders; 86% of these had bulimia using the less restrictive *DSM-III* criteria, whereas only 14% had anorexia nervosa (Strangler & Printz, 1980).

Binge eating disorder has a higher male representation, approximately 30% though it too is seen predominantly in women. It is seen in greater frequency in people of lower socioeconomic status. It may also have an overall greater prevalence in the general population (2%) and is common (about 30%) in patients seeking treatment for obesity at university-affiliated weight programs (Dingemans, Bruna, & van Furth, 2002). One characteristic in common between individuals with bulimia and binge eating disorders is a personal history of sexual abuse, which may explain both their impulsivity and ambivalence about their bodies and sexuality.

Differential Diagnosis

Distinguishing between anorexia nervosa and bulimia is the only common diagnostic difficulty. Few people make a habit of bingeing and vomiting, except for those with bulimia and 40–50% of those with anorexia. There is a continuum between the two disorders, with pure "restricting type" of patients with anorexia at one end and "pure bulimics" at the other. Those with anorexia who binge and purge are in the middle of that spectrum. Those with anorexia who binge (the binge/purge subtype) are more akin to normal-weight individuals with bulimia than to those with anorexia who don't binge (the restrictive subtype). In comparison to those with restrictive anorexia, normal-weight individuals with bulimia and those with bingeing anorexia perceive more family conflict and are more impulsive, outgoing, sexually active, and emotionally disturbed; they may be more prone to depression and have twice as many relatives with mood disorders.

Etiology and Pathogenesis

Very little is known about the causes of bulimia. Descriptive and biological psychiatrists have noted a relationship between bulimia and other psychiatric disorders. About 75% of individuals with bulimia develop major depression; 43% have anxiety disorders; 49% have substance disorders; and 50–75% have personality disorders or trait disturbances (usually in cluster B). First-degree relatives of people with bulimia have a higher frequency of mood disorder, substance abuse, and obesity (Yager, Devlin et al., 2006). A similar association exists between binge-eating disorders and mood, anxiety, and personality disorders or traits—clusters B and C (Dingemans, Bruna, & van Furth, 2002).

Families in which a member has bulimia appear enmeshed but disengaged. In comparing 105 bulimic with 86 control families, Johnson and Flach (1985) found that the former set high expectations, but placed small emphasis on their daughter's intellectual, cultural, or recreational activities. Despite the fact that the overall structure and rules of families with a bulimic member resembled those in normal families, the "bulimic families" were more disorganized, showing lack of ability to solve problems, manage crises, or get things done. A high prevalence of domestic violence and abuse is found in these families. Although high expectations were also seen in the control families, the disorganization and lack of concern for patients' activities in the affected families best correlated with the severity of the patients' symptoms. The families of individuals with binge-eating disorder have been found to be disorganized, but more neglectful than abusive.

Clinical Course and Complications

Bulimia and binge-eating disorder both usually arise later than anorexia, during the late teens or 20s, and rarely after 30. The first episode commonly follows a traumatic event or a period of stringent dieting. Bulimia and binge-eating disorder are chronic disorders, with fluctuating intensity and alternating periods of normal and binge eating. Less often, normal eating doesn't occur; the patient cycles between periods of bingeing and fasting. Anecdotally, patients with bulimia generally improve or completely recover. Death, usually from hypokalemia (low potassium) in people with bulimia, is rare.

During periods of rapid weight gain, the hands, feet, and ankles of people with bulimia often swell from a "refeeding edema." These patients endure weakness (84%), abdominal bloating (75%), stomach pain (63%), headaches, and dizziness. They get sore throats from the vomiting (54%), painful swellings of salivary and parotid glands (called "chipmunk" or "puffy" cheeks) (50%), dental caries from loss of enamel (37%), and finger calluses (on their gagging fingers). Menstrual irregularities are common, and 40% have intermittent or sustained amenorrhea. If they use Ipecac to make them vomit, they are at risk of death from cardiomyopathy. Individuals with binge-eating disorder suffer more from the complications of obesity, often morbid obesity.

Dehydration is common in underweight patients with bulimia who use diuretics or vomit after bingeing. Electrolyte imbalance, most often hypokalemic alkalosis, occurs in about half of these patients. It can result from vomiting as well as from diuretic and laxative abuse. The hypokalemia can cause patients to feel lethargic and cognitively dulled and may even lead to serious or life-threatening cardiac conduction abnormalities. Because of the problems in thinking, hypokalemia should be corrected before psychotherapy is attempted. Patients report problems with intimate or interpersonal relations (70%), family (61%), finances (because of food purchasing) (53%), and work (50%).

Management and Treatment
Medical Complications

The medical complications associated with bulimia are related to the individual aspects of the illness. These must always be addressed first in evaluation and treatment because several are life-threatening and disabling.

Electrolyte imbalance, resulting from vomiting as well as diuretic and laxative abuse, occurs in about half of patients with bulimia. Hypokalemic alkalosis is particularly common. The hypokalemia (low potassium) can lead to serious, even life-threatening cardiac conduction abnormalities. This condition can cause patients to feel lethargic, weak, and cognitively dulled.

Patients with bulimia who use diuretics may experience dehydration and rebound edema as well as the electrolyte disturbances mentioned earlier. Some patients use syrup of Ipecac to induce vomiting. Its active ingredient, emetine, can produce myopathies, both generalized and cardiomyopathy. This is a particularly insidious complication because the effect of the emetine is cumulative. Patients with bulimia who misuse laxatives are at risk for laxative dependency, steatorrhea, protein-losing gastroenteropathy, and gastrointestinal bleeding. Laxatives will cause the person with bulimia to lose only 3% of calories consumed. Many individuals with bulimia, when informed of this fact, quit this dangerous method. To avoid an atonic bowel, excessive laxatives should be slowly tapered, not stopped abruptly.

Parotid gland enlargement (chipmunk cheeks) is common among patients with bulimia, but the mechanism for this is unknown. As many as a third of these patients may have elevated serum amylase levels; however, this does not appear to be correlated with the presence of parotid gland enlargement, and both salivary and pancreatic isoenzyme may be involved. Dental erosion and numerous cavities are common with vomiting. Menstrual irregularities are also common in these patients, even those of normal weight. Gastric or esophageal rupture (which can be fatal) is a rare complication of binge eating, whereas acute gastric dilation is a common and a painful result of it.

Hospitalization

Most patients with bulimia are best treated as outpatients, but four conditions warrant the intervention of hospitalization: (1) to manage a medical emergency (electrolyte imbalances, severe orthostatic hypertension, or precipitous weight loss); (2) to break a severe, recalcitrant binge–starve cycle; (3) to evaluate diagnostically or deal with a family crisis; or (4) to respond to a suicidal crisis.

Medication

Bulimia, or at least bingeing, is moderately responsive to antidepressants (TCAs, SSRIs, and MAOIs) over 6–8 weeks (Yager, Devlin et al., 2006). On average, antidepressants decrease binge frequencies of patients with bulimia by 50%, with 20% achieving complete recovery. Both depressed and nondepressed patients with bulimia show equally effective responses. Higher doses (approximately 60 mg) of fluoxetine, work better than the usual antidepressant dose (20 mg). When patients with bulimia are treated with antidepressants alone for 6 months or more, there are many dropouts, and by 12 months, antidepressants do no better than placebo (Walsh, 1991). When antidepressants are combined with cognitive–behavioral therapy, there are fewer dropouts and possibly an additive effect of the therapy (Abbot & Mitchell, 1993). Patients who don't respond to the usual antidepressants still may respond to MAOIs. Antidepressants may be most useful in "jumpstarting" a person's recovery while awaiting the delayed positive effects of psychotherapy. Those who are excellent responders could elect to stay on their medication, but antidepressants could also be reserved for patients who aren't progressing with psychotherapy alone. Similar results are reported with binge eating disorder in terms of antidepressant responsiveness and the benefits of combined pharmacological and psychotherapeutic approaches.

Psychotherapy

Individual and group therapy using either cognitive–behavioral or psychodynamic (particularly, interpersonal) approaches are quite effective in treating bulimia and binge eating disorders. Generally there are two phases to the treatment. Phase 1 focuses on breaking the binge–purge cycle in the case of bulimia (for binge eating disorders the focus is on the binge eating triggers)—a behavioral approach can quickly reduce bingeing and purging. The patient keeps a careful record of food intake, vomiting, purgative abuse, and the context of bingeing (time, place, mood, etc.). The abnormal pattern of eating is then shaped into a more normal pattern by avoiding precipitants of binges and substituting alternative pleasurable activities (e.g., showers, baths, walks, talk to a friend on the phone). Patients are also instructed to practice delaying (but not necessarily stopping) vomiting, especially if it happens after normal meals. For example, they may try to wait 30 minutes before vomiting, having succeeded at waiting 25 minutes the day before.

Phase 2 focuses on broad areas of behavior and attitudes—cognitive–behavioral therapy (CBT) appears to be best. CBT is as effective as behavioral and interpersonal therapy at reducing bingeing and depression and more effective in modifying disturbed attitudes toward shape, weight, dieting, and the use of vomiting to control shape and weight (Agras, 1991; Yager, Devlin et al., 2006). Patients who participate in CBT show greater overall improvement. Dietary management helps further. One goal is eating for weight maintenance to break the binge–fast roller coaster. Group therapy works at least as well as individual therapy in this phase. Behavioral therapy is particularly effective in reducing binge eating in individuals with binge eating disorder, but interpersonal psychotherapy may be equally effective after binge control is established, given its focus on reducing interpersonal isolation (Dingemans, Bruna, & van Furth, 2002).

Mortality for bulimia is 1% within 10 years of diagnosis (Sullivan, 1995) and is largely associated with suicide over medical complications. The overall short-term prognosis is about 70% reduction in bingeing and purging, with reasonably good maintenance of gains over 6 years. The mortality for binge eating disorder is not known.

ELIMINATION DISORDERS

Elimination disorders are very common and are discussed in most pediatric and child-care books. Both *encopresis* (soiling of pants with stool) and *enuresis* (soiling of pants with urine) are more common in boys. They should not be diagnosed until the developmental age is 4 years for encopresis, and 5 years for enuresis. One-fourth of children with encopresis also have enuresis. Physical causes for both disorders should be ruled out.

Encopresis

Generally, the two types of kids that are more prone to *encopresis* are the anxious and the oppositional. The anxious ones develop a vicious cycle: They are afraid to use toilets in public places, develop constipation, and then may develop involuntary overflow incontinence. Soiling almost always occurs during waking hours. For them, the encopresis does not feel under control. The oppositional ones do it deliberately, don't usually have constipation, and to rub their defiance in further, may smear their feces. Occasionally the anxious ones smear their feces in a botched attempt to hide their accidents. Table 20-4 lists the diagnostic criteria for functional encopresis. About 1% of 5-year-olds have this disorder.

A history of constipation, developmental delays in other areas, ADHD, or coercive or premature bowel training each increases the risk for encopresis. Toilet phobia can also lead to encopresis and may develop if the available facilities are particularly gruesome or if fantasies about the toilet, such as being drowned or bitten by snakes, take over. Secondary encopresis (resumption of accidents after a period of successful toilet training) may begin with stressful events, often with separation themes such as birth of a sibling, starting school, or mom starting a full-time job. School-age children can successfully retain feces at school only to soil at home. The ones who don't are usually ridiculed by peers. Encopretic children usually can't explain their behavior.

To avoid the retention-leakage cycle of laxatives, stool softeners are used to evacuate the colon. Children are then scheduled to have regular periods on the toilet for the purpose of muscle retraining and are given responsibility

TABLE 20-4
Diagnostic Criteria for Encopresis and Enuresis

Encopresis

A. **Repeated voluntary or involuntary passage of feces, usually of normal or near-normal consistency, in places not appropriate for that purpose in the individual's own sociocultural setting**. The condition may:

1. represent an abnormal continuation of normal infantile incontinence (**failed toilet training**),
2. involve a loss of continence following the acquisition of bowel control (**physiological retention**), or
3. involve the deliberate deposition of feces in inappropriate places in spite of normal physiological bowel control (**psychological resistance** to conforming with societal norms)

B. *DSM-5 specifies at least one such event occurs each month for at least 3 months.*

C. *DSM-5 specifies that the chronological age (or equivalent developmental level) of the individual is at least 4 years.*

D. The behavior is **not due to the direct physiological effects of a substance** (e.g., laxatives) and is **not a consequence of another medical condition** such as anal fissure, gastrointestinal infection, or fecal blockage resulting in "overflow" fecal soiling of liquid or semiliquid feces.

When there exists smearing of feces over the body or over the external environment there is usually some degree of associated emotional/behavioral disturbance.

Enuresis

A. **Repeated involuntary voiding of urine, by day and/or by night** (*DSM-5 allows intentional voiding as well*).

B. *DSM-5 specifies that the voiding behavior manifests at least twice a week for at least 3 consecutive months or results in significant distress or impairment in personal, family, social, educational, occupational, or other important areas of functioning.*

C. The voiding behavior is **abnormal in relation to the individual's mental age** (not ordinarily diagnosed in a child under the age of 5 years or with a mental age under 4 years).

1. Enuresis present from birth is called **primary**.
2. Enuresis arising following a period of acquired bladder control is termed **secondary**.

D. The behavior is **not due to the direct physiological effects of a substance** (e.g., diuretics) and is **not a consequence of the lack of bladder control due to another medical condition** such as any neurological disorder, epileptic attacks, or any structural abnormality of the urinary tract.

Enuresis sometimes occurs in conjunction with encopresis; when this is the case, encopresis should be diagnosed.

Note: Adapted from *ICD-10* (pp. 223–224) and *DSM-5* (pp. 355–357)

for cleaning themselves and any soiled clothing. The parents are helped to develop a matter-of-fact approach in helping their children.

Enuresis

Enuresis is a more biologically based disorder than encopresis, as 75% of these children have a first-degree relative who has had it. At age 5, 3% of girls and 7% of boys have enuresis. All but 1% of males and almost all females outgrow it by age 18. Nocturnal enuresis is much more common than diurnal (daytime) enuresis. Nocturnal enuresis usually occurs in the first third of the night. Very stressful events can trigger it in children who had previously been continent. When this happens, the enuresis is described as secondary enuresis.

Children with enuresis should be evaluated for potential medical causes, such as urinary tract infection, minor neurological impairment, structural anomalies, and medical illness. If no medical problems are found, a variety of treatment options are available: (1) In *retention control* training, children drink a large amount of liquid and gradually delay the time to voiding. Token or social reinforcement can be used to amplify the rewards for success. This method works much better for daytime than for nighttime enuresis. (2) *Conditioning devices*, which set off an alarm when urine contacts the bed, can be highly effective, at least initially. Over 1–3 months, about 75% of children succeed with this approach, but about 35% relapse when it is stopped. Repeat trials are then used. (3) *Tricyclic antidepressants* (usually imipramine or an *antispasmodic* such as oxybutynin), have also been used to treat this disorder. Although up to two-thirds of children have a reduction in wetting with 25–75 mg of imipramine, almost all relapse when the medication is stopped. Another useful medication is DDAVP (a synthetic version of antidiuretic hormone), but again, symptoms resume when treatment is stopped.

A popular but unproven technique for nocturnal enuresis involves eliminating fluid intake after dinner, having children void before bedtime, and carrying the sleepy child to the toilet once during the night. This may keep the bed dry, but may not lead to enduring results.

References

Abbott, D.W., & Mitchell, J.E. (1993). Antidepressants vs. psychotherapy in the treatment of bulimia nervosa. *Psychopharmacology Bulletin, 29,* 115–119.

Agras, W.S. (1991). Nonpharmacologic treatments of bulimia nervosa. *Journal of Clinical Psychiatry, 52,* 29–33.

Amdur, M.J., Tucker, G.J., Detre, T.D., & Markhus, K. (1969). Anorexia nervosa: An interactional study. *Journal of Nervous and Mental Diseases, 148,* 559–566.

American Psychiatric Association. (2013). *Diagnostic and statistical manual of mental disorders,* 5th ed. Arlington, VA: American Psychiatric Association.

Andersen, A.E., & Holman, J.E. (1997). Males with eating disorders: Challenges for treatment and research. *Psychopharmacology Bulletin, 33*(3), 391–397.

Baranowska, B., Baranowska-Bik, A., Bik, W., & Martynska, L. (2008). The role of leptin and orexins in the dysfunction of hypothalamo-pituitary-gonadal regulation and in the mechanism of hyperactivity in patients with anorexia nervosa. *Neuro Endocrinology Letters, 29,* 37–40.

Dingemans, A., Bruna, M., & van Furth, E. (2002). Binge eating disorder: A review. *International Journal of Obesity and Related Metabolic Disorders, 26,* 299–307.

Fairburn, C.G., Jones, R., Peveler, R.C., Hope, R.A., & O'Connor, M. (1993). Psychotherapy and bulimia nervosa. *Archives of General Psychiatry, 50,* 419–428.

Fairburn, C.G., Marcus, M., & Wilson, G. (1993). Cognitive–behavioral therapy for binge eating and bulimia nervosa: A comprehensive treatment manual. In C. Fairburn & G. Wilson (Eds.), *Binge eating: Nature, assessment, and treatment* (pp. 361–404). New York: Guilford.

Favaro, A., Tenconi, E., & Santonastaso, P. (2006). Perinatal factors and the risk of developing anorexia nervosa and bulimia nervosa. *Archives of General Psychiatry, 63,* 82–88.

Gustavson, C., Gustavson, J., Noller, K., O'Brien, P., Melton, L., Pumariega, A., et al. (1991). Increased risk of profound weight loss among women exposed to diethylstilbestrol in utero. *Behavioral and Neural Biology, 55,* 307–312.

Hart, K.J., & Ollendick, T.H. (1985). Prevalence of bulimia in working and university women. *American Journal of Psychiatry, 142,* 851–854.

Hsu, L.K.G. (1986). The treatment of anorexia nervosa. *American Journal of Psychiatry, 143,* 573–581.

Hsu, L.K.G. (1990). *Eating disorders.* New York: Guilford.

Johnson, C., & Flach, A. (1985). Family characteristics of 105 patients with bulimia. *American Journal of Psychiatry, 142,* 1321–1324.

Lawson, E.A., & Klibanski, A. (2008). Endocrine abnormalities in anorexia nervosa. *Nature Clinical Practice Endocrinology & Metabolism, 4,* 407–414.

Lucas, A.R., Beard, C., O'Fallon, W., & Kurland, L. (1991). Fifty-year trends in the incidence of anorexia nervosa in Rochester, Minn.: A population-based study. *American Journal of Psychiatry, 148,* 917–922.

Miller, M., & Pumariega, A.J. (2001). Eating disorders: A historical and cross-cultural review. *Psychiatry: Interpersonal and Biological Processes, 64*(2), 93–110.

Mitchell, J.E., Hatsukami, D., Eckert, E.D., & Pyle, R.L. (1985). Characteristics of 275 patients with bulimia. *American Journal of Psychiatry, 142,* 482–488.

Minuchin, S., Rosman, B.L., & Baker, L. (1978). *Psychosomatic families.* Cambridge, MA: Harvard University Press.

Norman, K. (1984). Eating disorders. In H.H. Goldman (Ed.), *Review of general psychiatry* (pp. 464–480). Los Altos, CA: Lange.

Procopio, M., & Marriott, P. (2007). Intrauterine hormonal environment and risk of developing anorexia nervosa. *Archives of General Psychiatry, 64,* 1402–1408.

Pumariega, A.J. (1986). Acculturation and eating attitudes in adolescent girls: A comparative and correlational study. *Journal of the American Academy of Child Psychiatry, 25*(2), 276–279.

Pumariega, A.J., Gustavson, C.R., Gustavson, J.C., Motes, P., & Ayers, S. (1994). Eating attitudes in African American women: The *Essence* Eating Disorders Survey. *Eating Disorders: The Journal of Treatment and Prevention, 2*(1), 5–16.

Pumariega, A.J., Pursell, J., Spock, A., & Jones, J.D. (1986). Eating disorders in adolescents with cystic fibrosis. *Journal of the American Academy of Child Psychiatry, 25*(2), 269–275.

Ramoz, N., Versini, A., & Gorwood, P. (2007). Eating disorders: An overview of treatment responses and the potential impact of vulnerability genes and endophenotypes. *Expert Opinion on Pharmacotherapy, 8,* 2029–2044.

Strangler, R.S., & Printz, A.M. (1980). *DSM-III:* Psychiatric diagnosis in a university population. *American Journal of Psychiatry, 137,* 937–940.

Strober, M., Freeman, R., & Morrell, W. (1997). The long-term course of severe anorexia nervosa in adolescents: Survival analysis of recovery, relapse, and outcome predictors over 10–15 years in a prospective study. *International Journal of Eating Disorders, 22,* 339–360.

Sullivan, P.F. (1995). Mortality in anorexia nervosa. *American Journal of Psychiatry, 152,* 1073–1074.

Theander, S. (1985). Outcome and prognosis in anorexia nervosa and bulimia. *Journal of Psychiatric Research, 19,* 493–508.

Torsello, A., Brambilla, F., Tamiazzo, L., Bulgarelli, I., Rapetti, D., Bresciani, E., & Locatelli, V. (2007). Central dysregulations in the control of energy homeostasis and endocrine alterations in anorexia and bulimia nervosa. *Journal of Endocrinology Investigations, 30,* 962–976.

Walsh, B.T. (1991). Psychopharmacologic treatment of bulimia nervosa. *Journal of Clinical Psychiatry, 52,* 34–38.

Walsh, B.T., Hadigan, C.M., Devlin, M.J., Gladis, M., & Roose, S.P. (1991). Long-term outcome of antidepressant treatment for bulimia nervosa. *American Journal of Psychiatry, 148,* 1206–1212.

World Health Organization. (1992). *The ICD–10 classification of mental and behavioural disorders: Clinical descriptions and diagnostic guidelines.* Geneva: World Health Organization.

Yager, J., Devlin, M., Halmi, K., Herzog, D., Mitchell, J., Powers, P., & Zerbe, K. (2006). *Practice guidelines for the treatment of patients with eating disorders*, 3rd ed. Washington, DC: American Psychiatric Association. http://www.psychiatryonline.com/praGuide/pra GuideHouse.ASPX (Accessed on August 10, 2008).

21

Sleep Disorders

Mind and body come together in a complex interaction during sleep. Sleep is a fragile state that is easily disturbed by anxiety, mania, psychosis, drugs, and physical illness. Conversely, disrupted sleep may predispose to mental disorders and exacerbate medical conditions.

> Sleep issues are common in people with psychiatric disorders, and the interaction is complex. Sleep disorders, particularly insomnia, can precede and predispose to psychiatric disorders, can be comorbid with and exacerbate psychiatric disorders, and can occur as part of psychiatric disorders. Sleep disorders can mimic psychiatric disorders or result from medication given for psychiatric disorders. Impairment of sleep and of mental health may be different manifestations of the same underlying neurobiological processes. (Sutton, 2014)

NORMAL SLEEP

For the most part, physical activity is suppressed during sleep. By contrast the brain alternates periods of neurologic quiet with cerebral activation, as in rapid eye movement (REM) sleep. The purpose of sleep and the mechanisms by which we are refreshed and sleepiness is decreased are not clearly understood.

The modern study of sleep began with the development of the electroencephalograph (EEG) in the late 1920s. Dr. Robert Schab opened the first clinical department for EEG services in the United States at Massachusetts General Hospital in 1937. Before the development of the EEG, sleep was assumed to be a uniform state of cortical suppression, and sleep stages were unknown. Sleep can be divided into discrete stages based on EEG, occulographic (EOG), and myographic (EMG) criteria. See Figure 21-1. These

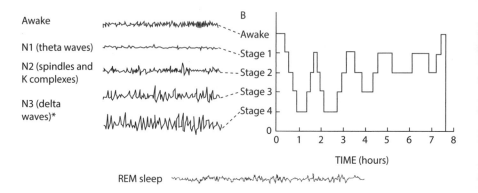

FIGURE 21-1
Stages of Sleep
*The more recent classification of deep sleep combines stages 3 and 4 into one stage N3.

parameters and other physiologic phenomenon are juxtaposed in real time in a recording referred to as a polysomnogram (PSG).

EEG uses differential amplifiers to measure voltage differences across the scalp. These voltages are produced by membrane currents that pass through the cerebral extracellular space. The potential difference recorded reflects electrical fields generated by neurons relative to a ground or reference electrode. Scalp electrodes are placed in a set pattern that covers the cortex. The EMG uses surface electrodes to measure action potentials in superficial skeletal muscles. Activities in these muscles as well as eye movements help distinguish sleep stages. The technical aspects of polysomnography which combines EEG, EMG, and eye movements are standardized in the Practice Parameters of the American Academy of Sleep Medicine's (AASM) and the Manual for the Scoring of Sleep and Associated Events Version 2.0 (Berry et. al., 2012). A 30 second segment of sleep is referred to as an "epoch" and is the unit whereby sleep is staged and events are quantified. Staging is predicated on visual voltage amplitude and frequency analysis. Delta waves are 0.5–2 cycles/second (Hz); theta are 3–7 Hz; alpha are 8–13 Hz; and beta are greater than 13 Hz.

In the awake state with eyes closed, the predominant rhythm seen over the central scalp electrodes is an 8–12 Hz alpha rhythm. It is accompanied by rapid and slow eye movements and high amplitude EMG activity. The alpha rhythm is not evident when the eyes are open. The subject is lucid and interactive.

Stage I sleep (N1) is the first stage of sleep. It is indistinguishable from wakefulness for some subjects. Some partially lucid thought is possible. Drowsy individuals can alternate between drowsy wakefulness and Stage I without realizing it. This is dangerous for individuals performing tasks that require vigilance such as driving. Interrupted Stage I sleep may be confused ("misperceived") as wakefulness. This is common in patients with chronic insomnia who overreport wakefulness during the night. Slow, rolling eye movements occur during Stage I sleep. Less than 50% of an epoch contains alpha rhythm with the remainder of the EEG being a low-frequency 4–7 Hz (theta) rhythm. Vertex sharp waves are sharply contoured waves seen in the central scalp electrodes. EMG activity declines minimally.

Stage II sleep (N2) is associated with K complexes and sleep spindles. K complexes are waves comprised of sharp spikes upward and then downward. They are best seen in the frontal leads and often linked to "spindles"—trains of distinctive waves 11–16 Hz lasting at least 0.5 seconds. These are best seen in the central head electrodes. Spindle prominence and amplitude decline in the elderly. The EMG amplitude declines relative to awake. Eye movements are not specific to N2.The patient is unequivocally asleep and more difficult to arouse than when in stage I sleep.

Slow wave sleep (N3) is a very deep sleep from which it is most difficult to awaken. This is particularly the case in children. It is typified by stage N2 figures (spindles and K complexes) but each epoch must contain at least 20% or more delta waves which are slow (0.5–2 Hz) and tall (75 Hz in amplitude). EMG and EOG findings are not specific to N3. Breathing is particularly regular and the heart rate slows.

Rapid eye movement (REM) sleep was also previously called paradoxical or active sleep. The EEG is of low amplitude and mixed frequency, as in an awake person, and there may be vivid mental imagery (dreaming). At the same time the EMG is at its lowest point and the patient has skeletal muscle atonia and minimal movement. (The diaphragm and sphincters are the only skeletal muscles that continue to function.) There are rapid eye movements and concurrent skeletal twitches. Stage N2 figures are lacking. Dreaming may occur in other stages of sleep but much less frequently. Sleep onset (N1) dreaming is seen in sleep-deprived individuals. There are strict criteria for differentiating sleep stages, their onset and termination.

Sleep architecture refers to the distribution of the sleep stages across the sleep period. Sleep architecture changes with age, disease, and certain medications. Alterations in sleep architecture produce nonrefreshing sleep and daytime sleepiness. Non-REM sleep (NREM) comprises 75% of all sleep time in adults. As sleep deepens, the brain waves become slower and of higher amplitude, and the patient becomes harder to rouse. Older children and adults doze off into NREM sleep, descending from light stages (N1) to intermediate (N2) sleep, and N2 comprises about 50% of the total sleep time. Stage (N3) is about 20% of the sleep period in adults, but is much more predominant in children less than 10 years old. The greatest percentage of delta, or deep, sleep is in the first third of the sleep-period time, and most REM sleep is in the last third. About 70–90 minutes after sleep onset, the first REM episode occurs. REM recurs nearly every 90 minutes. As the night proceeds, the duration of REM episodes increases. The initial REM period lasts a few minutes whereas the final REM episode may last about 20–30 minutes. Sleeping individuals who awaken during a dream will likely recall the dream. If there is no arousal, dream recall is unlikely.

Sleep architecture is age dependent. Newborns sleep 14 to 18 hours each day and spend 50% of total sleep time in REM sleep. By 6 months, the total sleep time declines to about 14 hours, and REM sleep time declines to about one-third of the sleep time. NREM sleep time increases to two-thirds and reaches adult percentages by adolescence. Between ages 20 and 60, the average total sleep time decreases from 9 to 7 hours, and delta sleep declines from 23 to 8% of the total sleep time. Elderly patients spend less time in bed asleep, take longer to fall asleep, have less slow-wave sleep and less REM. Arousals are more frequent. Age-related changes in sleep quality and continuity can be perceived as insomnia in older individuals, leading to inappropriate use of hypnotics.

How much sleep people need to feel refreshed depends on their age and individual requirements (Table 21-1). Short sleepers are often more efficient at sleeping and have higher percentages of N3 and REM sleep. Thomas Edison was said to sleep less than 4 hours a night with no ill effects. Alterna-

TABLE 21-1
Average Amount of Sleep per Day

AGE	SLEEP IN HOURS
Newborn	Up to 18
1–12 months	14–18
1–3 years	12–15
3–5 years	11–13
5–12 years	9–11
Adolescents	9–10
Adults, including elderly	7–8
Pregnant women	variable

tively, excessive daytime sleepiness (EDS), a hallmark of sleep pathology, can result merely from inadequate sleep time. The difference between the amount of quality sleep obtained and sleep needed is referred to as "sleep debt." The debt is paid with excessive sleepiness, impaired performance, and altered mood. Some individuals require more than 8 hours to feel refreshed. This is problematic in our society, where sleep is undervalued and encroached upon by multiple demands for our attention.

SLEEP ASSESSMENT

Three sources are available to diagnose sleep disorders: patients, bed partners, and sleep clinics. Each has its own limitations and advantages. Self-reports of sleep may be inaccurate. Insomniacs typically overestimate the time it takes them to fall asleep and underestimate their total sleep time. Bed partner reports can provide key facts that the sleeping patient may not perceive, such as snoring, sleep apnea, leg movements, and unusual behaviors. More objective measurements of sleep are best made using accredited sleep laboratories. Access to such sleep centers has improved dramatically across the country, providing help to patients for a variety of sleep disorders. Clinics accredited by the American Academy of Sleep Medicine offer four forms of tests: unattended portable monitoring for home use, polysomnogram (PSG), multiple sleep latency test (MSLT), and maintenance of wakefulness test (MWT).

Unattended Portable Monitoring (PM) testing has become more widespread. PM offers both convenience and thrift. PM is useful, however, only for patients with a high likelihood of obstructive sleep apnea. It does not include EEG monitoring and cannot clearly distinguish sleep from wakefulness (Collop et al., 2007).

Continuous pulse oximetry, electrocardiography; capnography to track carbon dioxide levels, airflow, and pressure at the nose; thoracic and abdominal impedence plethysmythography; and surface electrodes to detect periodic leg movements can be added to EEG and EMG. All parameters are continuously and concurrently recorded as a display called a montage. Extended EEG montages can be added when a seizure disorder is suspected. Video monitoring helps in the diagnosis of nocturnal seizure and parasomnias. Studies are scored manually and every epoch of the PSG is reviewed by the interpreting physician according to strict AASM criteria. The care with which all this is performed is critical to the quality of the report and is a quality-assurance check to all technical aspects of the sleep laboratory. Referring practitioners should enquire whether their sleep physicians adhere to the practice parameters and guidelines of the AASM and if their facility is accredited for in-lab and at-home testing.

Indications for PSG include: suspected obstructive or central sleep apnea, periodic breathing, REM and non-REM parasomnias (sleepwalking, -talking, etc.), periodic limb movements of sleep, narcolepsy syndrome, and, *rarely*, insomnia. Insomnia is diagnosed historically: PSG is only performed if a concurrent sleep disorder contributing to the insomnia is suspected. Insomniacs should not be routinely referred for PSG.

PSG and PM (home sleep tests) are NOT screening tools for sleep-disordered breathing. Sleep apnea is most appropriately screened for historically or by using validated screening tools such as the Stop Bang or Berlin Questionnaire (Pataka et al., 2014). These are inexpensive and sensitive tools that can be used quickly as part of a clinic check-in process (e.g., Table 21-2). PM are being inappropriately marketed by some entrepreneurial entities for screening populations considered to be at risk for sleep apnea (the obese, diabetics, those with difficult-to-control hypertension). The accuracy of some of these instruments can be as low as 59% in patients who do not meet basic screening measures for sleep apnea.

The Multiple Sleep Latency Test (MSLT) measures daytime sleepiness. The patient is given five 20-minute nap opportunities every 2 hours throughout the day. Using EEG criteria for sleep staging, the time to sleep onset (sleep latency), and the number of REM periods are noted. A mean sleep latency of less than 10 minutes is considered "pathologic sleepiness." REM sleep normally does not occur in adults until 70–90 minutes after sleep onset. The appearance of REM sleep in a 20-minute nap—a sleep onset REM (SOREM)—is abnormal and suggests narcolepsy, a hypersomnolent condition, or prior REM sleep deprivation.

Narcolepsy is diagnosed if the mean sleep latency over the five naps is less than 10 minutes, and if there are two SOREM periods in 5 naps. In a recent change, a SOREM period on the previous night PSG may be used as one of the 2 required REM periods if the MSLT has only one SOREM. There are other hypersomnolence syndromes to consider (after encephalitis or post-concussive) with short sleep latency and no SOREM. Drugs can alter the results of the test by suppressing REM or by causing REM rebound when withdrawn. Tricyclic antidepressants, benzodiazepines, narcotics, SSRIs, and

TABLE 21-2
Berlin Questionnaire—Sleep Evaluation

1. Complete the following:

Height: _____   Weight: _____

Age: _____   Gender: ___M ___F

2. Do you snore?

_____ **Yes**

_____ No

_____ Don't know

If you snore:

3. Your snoring is . . .

_____ Slightly louder than breathing

_____ As loud as talking

_____ **Louder than talking**

_____ **Very loud**

4. How often do you snore?

_____ **Almost every day**

_____ **3–4 times a week**

_____ 1–2 times a week

_____ never or almost never

5. Has your snoring ever bothered other people?

_____ **Yes**

_____ No

6. Has anyone noticed that you quit breathing during your sleep?

_____ **Almost every day**

_____ **3–4 times a week**

_____ 1–2 times a week

_____ never or almost never

7. Are you tired after sleeping?

_____ **Almost every day**

_____ **3–4 times a week**

_____ 1–2 times a week

_____ never or almost never

8. Are you tired during waketime?

_____ **Almost every day**

_____ **3–4 times a week**

_____ 1–2 times a week

_____ never or almost never

9. Have you ever nodded off or fallen asleep while driving a vehicle?

_____ **Yes**

_____ No

_____ If yes, how often does it occur?

_____ Almost every day.

_____ 3–4 times a week

_____ 1–2 times a week

_____ 1–2 times a month

_____ never or almost never

10. Do you have high blood pressure?

_____ **Yes**

_____ No

_____ Don't know

BMI (Body mass index) **=** _____

$$BMI = \frac{\text{Weight in Pounds} \times 703}{\text{Height in inches}}$$

BMI is also defined as weight (kg) divided by height (m) squared, i.e., kg/m^2).

Scoring Categories: Your risk for sleep apnea is high if you check one of the boxes below

_____ **Category 1** (questions 2–5): if a total of 2 or more answers in **bold** are positive

(question 6): if either of the answers in **bold** are positive

_____ **Category 2** (questions 7–9): if a total of 2 or more answers in **bold** are positive

_____ **Category 3** (question 10) if **yes** response to question 10 and/or a **BMI > 30**

Note: Adapted from Netzer, Stoohs, Netzer, Clark, & Strohl (1999)

TABLE 21-3
International Classification of Sleep Disorders–3

I. Insomnia

II. Sleep-related breathing disorders (snoring, sleep apnea)

III. Central disorders of Hypersomnia (disorders of excess sleepiness, includes narcolepsy)

IV. Circadian rhythm sleep-wake disorders

V. Parasomnias (sleep behaviors)

    1. Non–Rapid Eye Movement sleep arousal (sleep walking and sleep terrors)

    2. Rapid Eye Movement sleep behaviors (nightmares)

VI. Sleep-related movement disorders (e.g., Periodic Limb Movements of Sleep, Restless Legs Syndrome)

Sateia (2014)

alcohol all interfere (ruinously) with the MSLT and should be withdrawn about 2 weeks before the test if possible. Urine toxicology is performed with the MSLT to exclude malingering and drug seeking.

The maintenance of wakefulness test (MWT) measures a patient's ability to stay awake. This is required by some regulatory agencies for truck drivers, railroad engineers, and pilots. This test is similar to the MSLT except that the subject is instructed to stay awake rather than try to sleep. Although there is less normative data for the MWT than the MSLT, the MWT is more predictive of road accidents then the MSLT in patients with sleep apnea (Saaspe, 2007). An abnormal test may disqualify the person from their occupation until sleepiness is objectively corrected.

Understanding sleep disorders requires a familiarity with, but not necessarily a mastery of, their classification. Table 21-3 lists the latest classification by the *International Classification of Sleep Disorders–3* (ICSD-3) published by the American Academy of Sleep Disorders in 2014. It is compatible with *ICD-10* and *DSM-5*.

INSOMNIA

ICSD-3 defines *insomnia* as "a persistent difficulty with sleep initiation, duration, consolidation, or quality that occurs despite adequate opportunity and circumstances for sleep, and results in some form of daytime (perceived) impairment" (Sateia, 2014).

Clinical Features of Insomnia

Insomnia is characterized by trouble getting to sleep (*sleep initiation insomnia*), trouble staying asleep (*sleep maintenance insomnia*), or waking too early (*late insomnia*). Daytime symptoms are prerequisite to a diagnosis. Insomnia may be expressed as feelings of fatigue, altered mood, and lack of energy or focus. Rarely does the insomniac report excessive daytime sleepiness or inopportune sleep to the extent that patients with sleep apnea, narcolepsy, or sleep deprivation do. Insomnia is a state of persistent hyperarousal throughout the entire 24-hour period. The EEG shows arousal with less delta (deep) sleep and frequent awake (alpha) rhythm intrusions into sleep.

The nosology for insomnia has recently been simplified (see Table 21-4 for the diagnostic criteria). Previously, insomnia was thought to be a primary

---

TABLE 21-4
Diagnostic Criteria for Insomnia Disorder

A. The patient reports or the patient's caregiver observes one or more of the following
  1. difficulty initiating sleep
  2. difficulty maintaining sleep
  3. waking up earlier than desired
  4. resistance to going to bed on appropriate schedule
  5. difficulty sleeping without parent or caregiver intervention
B. The patient reports or the patient's parent or caregiver observes, one or more of the following related to the night time sleep difficulty:
  1. fatigue/malaise
  2. attention, concentration, or memory impairment
  3. impaired social, family, occupational, or academic performance
  4. mood disturbance/irritability
  5. daytime sleepiness
  6. behavioral problems (hyperactivity, impulsivity, aggression)
  7. reduced motivation/energy/initiative
  8. tendency to errors/accidents
  9. concerns about or dissatisfaction with sleep
C. The reported sleep/wake complaint cannot be explained purely by inadequate opportunity or inadequate circumstances for sleep.
D. The sleep disturbance and associated daytime symptoms have been present for at least 3 months (**Chronic Insomnia**) or less than 3 months (**Short-term Insomnia**) and causes significant distress or impairment in some area of functioning.
E. The sleep/wake disorder is not better explained by another sleep disorder, substance use, another mental disorder, or other medical condition.

Sateia (2014)

---

disorder or the consequence of other secondary medical, psychiatric, or medication-related problems. This simplification was done by "lumping" rather than "splitting" some diagnoses into chronic insomnia, short-term insomnia, and other insomnia.

> This simplification was done for several reasons. First, there was a concern that many subtypes of insomnia represented generic manifestations of insomnia. The clinical features of secondary insomnia could exist concurrently and with overlapping symptoms. Second, a sense existed of limited clinical utility in specifying secondary causes of insomnia and that treatment targeting these entities was felt to be not useful. Also, a secondary insomnia from some other medical or psychiatric issue could develop its own natural history and require a specific treatment apart from the primary cause of the insomnia. Hence, insomnias were divided into those lasting less than 3 months (short-term) or longer (chronic) insomnia.

Despite the more simple classification, chronic insomnia is nearly always a multifactorial problem. The practical treatment of insomniacs requires systematic identification and rectification of all the contributing problems. There is a considerable body of literature addressing the subclasses of clinical and pathophysiologic types of insomnia and their specific treatments. A careful history will often discern maladaptive psychological and behavioral responses to the perceived stress of "unsatisfactory" sleep (psychophysiologic insomnia). Cognitive behavioral therapy has been shown to be efficacious in these settings (Sato, 2010). Patients often have poor bedtime habits or sleep hygiene, which contribute to poor quality sleep. Improving sleep hygiene is an important feature of the nonpharmacologic treatment of chronic insomnia (Andrew, 1999). Rebound insomnia can result from withdrawal of hypnotics and benzodiazepines and can be addressed by a slow taper of longer acting drugs. Prescribing sedative hypnotics to a patient with significant misperception of his or her own sleep is not logical. Overtly psychotic and manic patients simply don't sleep without effective treatment of the primary psychiatric illness.

Short-term insomnia is the most common type of insomnia and is familiar to most adults. Precipitating causes are numerous—anticipation of an important activity, relationship problems, illnesses, and so on. Short-term insomnia usually lasts a month or less and in the *ICSD-3* is specified as less than 3 months' duration. There must be some daytime distress associated with poor sleep and there must be adequate opportunity for sleep to occur. Once the problem has resolved, the person regains his or her normal sleep pattern. A person who frets about difficulty initiating sleep is even less likely to fall asleep, leading to a chronic problem. The devolution of a situational insomnia into a chronic one can often be prevented by short-term use of hypnotics or anti-anxiety medications under close supervision, tapering the medication quickly when indicated. Counseling can be helpful as well. Patients who do not come to their health care providers for situational insomnias may begin to self-medicate with over-the-counter medications and alcohol leading to rebound insomnia when not taking the medication and then dependency. A progression to chronic insomnia is most unfortunate as the chance of cure decreases as the duration of insomnia increases.

Epidemiology

The overall prevalence of insomnia in the United States varies from 8 to 18% in primary care settings and may be higher in people over 60 years old. Insomnia occurs more often in women (1.4:1), the unemployed, and unmarried individuals. People with insomnia tend to have higher depression, hypochondriasis, and hysteria scales on the Minnesota Multiphasic Personality Inventory (Healey, 1981). Insomnia occurs initially in young adults; some patients recall childhood problems sleeping. "Limit-setting insomnia" in children is caused by a lack of structure around bedtime and can start as early as 6 months. Insomnia can occur initially in menopause and persist even after the characteristic vasomotor instability (hot flashes) has resolved.

Differential Diagnosis

Difficulty falling asleep (sleep initiation insomnia) has a broad differential diagnosis. Sleep initiation insomnia is seen in delayed sleep phase syndrome, a circadian rhythm disorder in which the patient's biological rhythm for sleep initiation is delayed relative to clock time. These "night owls" perceive their inability to fall asleep at normal hours as insomnia though they usually have normal sleep continuity, normal amounts of wakefulness after sleep onset (WASO), and usually get adequate and restorative sleep if allowed to sleep until late morning. Use of hypnotics and alcohol to force earlier sleep can lead to habituation. Delayed sleep phase syndrome is common in adolescents and is worsened by the use of light emitting electronics prior to bed time and other issues (Owens, 2014). Night shift workers trying to fall asleep during the day, while their body temperature is rising often cannot initiate sleep without hypnotics. Periodic limb movements of sleep and upper airway resistance syndrome (snoring leading to arousals without high grade airway obstruction) can interrupt sleep onset by causing repeated arousals as the patient drifts off into Stage N1 sleep. This is misperceived as frank wakefulness. Sleep state misperception is common in chronic insomnia and the extent of objective sleepiness is over reported. Generalized anxiety and sympathetic activation caused by performance anxiety about sleep can perpetuate sleep initiation insomnia—so-called psychophysiologic insomnia. Chronic alcoholics in remission and people withdrawing from hypnotics and benzodiazepines can also have difficulties with sleep initiation. Bupropion and the dopaminergic agonist Levodopa, among many other medications, can cause sleep onset insomnia.

Middle insomnia involves frequent awakenings during the night. Depression, pain, medical illness, obsessive compulsive disorder, anxiety, obstructive sleep apnea, periodic limb movements, and withdrawal from the effects of drugs and alcohol can cause arousals and prolonged wakefulness after sleep onset. Late insomnia (early morning awakening) is a prominent finding in some patients with major affective disorder. This may improve with treatment but is often the last symptom of depression to abate. Elderly patients with advanced sleep phase syndrome go to bed early and wake early. They perceive the earlier than desired awakenings as insomnia. Arousals occurring roughly at 90-minute intervals throughout the night and in the early morning suggest REM-related disorders such as sleep apnea and REM behavior disorder.

There must be a report of sleep dissatisfaction affecting daytime functioning for a diagnosis of insomnia; expressed as feelings of fatigue, altered mood, and or frustration. Seldom do insomniacs report excessive daytime sleepiness to the extent reported by individuals with sleep apnea, narcolepsy, or temporary sleep deprivation. People with chronic insomnia are seldom able to nap, although they report feeling very fatigued. Patients with insomnia and sleep deprivation have increased sensitivity to pain, increased reaction time, and decreased attention span and memory. Less time spent in deep sleep (delta) and frequent awakenings with alpha rhythm intrusions are commonly seen in insomniac tracings. Elevated heart rate, body temperature, cortisol levels, and body temperature reflect a state of sympathetic hyperarousal which may be part of the pathophysiology of insomnia.

Management and Treatment

Some tips for sleep hygiene are listed in Table 21-5. In some cases those simple interventions take care of the insomnia. If unsuccessful one can progress to sleep therapies.

TABLE 21-5
Sleep Hygiene

1. Keep a fairly regular sleep onset and awakening schedule.
2. Avoid excessive napping, especially in the evening.
3. Make your sleep environment as noise- and light-free as possible. Pets and children sleep in another room. Cooler room temperatures may help.
4. Avoid watching television in bed. If some activity is preferred before lights out, read or listen to music. Sexual activity usually promotes sleep.
5. Regular exercise is helpful if not too close to bedtime. Otherwise, it may be stimulating.
6. Avoid caffeine, nicotine, and alcohol 4 hours before bedtime.
7. Do not watch the clock if you awaken at night. Setting the alarm eliminates worry about oversleeping.
8. Winding down 1 to 2 hours before bedtime with a warm shower or bath as well as stretching exercises is encouraged. Cooling off promotes sleep.
9. Avoid upsetting discussions just before bedtime.

Cognitive and Behavioral Treatment

Cognitive therapy challenges misconceptions and unreasonable expectations about sleep and insomnia. The goal is to decrease the anxiety, preoccupation, and worry about sleep quality, onset, and duration, and to modify the maladaptive behaviors that arise out of these exaggerated concerns that in themselves interfere with sleep. A Pavlovian-like conditioned response linking bedtime with frustration arises. Frustration associated with the sleep process perpetuates insomnia. The patient becomes paradoxically hyperaroused at bedtime and is unable to fall asleep. The classic history given is of the insomniac who more easily falls asleep when away from her own bedroom on vacation—where the association of sleepless nights and frustration are lacking.

Sleep restriction therapy (SRT) limits time in bed to decrease insomnia. SRT makes the patient more fatigued so they are more likely to fall asleep when they go to bed, thus removing the negative association of bed with frustration. Stimulus control therapy (SCT) attempts to limit the negative association of time spent awake in bed by establishing fixed schedules for sleep and arising, limiting the bedroom to sleep and sex only, and being in bed only when sleepy. Americans are inculcated in hard work and perseverance, not in how to relax. Relaxation training specifically teaches reducing somatic tension through techniques such as progressive muscle relaxation, imagery training, and meditation. Cognitive Behavioral Therapy (CBT) combines SCT, sleep hygiene, SRT, and cognitive techniques together. CBT for insomnia is becoming well established in the literature.

Pharmacologic Therapy

When given the choice between the above cognitive–behavioral approach that involves several sessions and the expense of the program, some patients may choose the route of taking a sleeping pill at bedtime. Historically, physicians prescribed hypnotics liberally for insomnia. Hypnotics may be appropriate for situational short-term insomnia, some shift worker disorders, and in the overtly psychotic and manic. Due to the development of tolerance, the efficacy of these drugs can be lost with chronic use. Rebound insomnia makes it difficult to stop these agents. The use of a drug for a chronic condition equates to chronic use of the drug. Two-thirds of all hypnotics go to chronic users (Kripke, 2000). Progressively more potent agents are requested as the drug loses its effectiveness. Medicated sleep is not the same as normal sleep. Hypnotic agents do increase total sleep time and shorten sleep onset latency (SOL), but detrimentally affect sleep architecture by suppressing REM and N3 sleep. Impaired daytime performance, auto accidents, falls, and hip fractures are more common with chronic hypnotic use. Yet, patients clamor for these drugs, often because they have become dependent on them. Steering patients away from hypnotics is time consuming and difficult and comes as a responsibility to primary care providers who are the most likely to be asked to prescribe them.

Relatively newer, benzodiazepine receptor agonists are now available and offer some advantages over older benzodiazepine hypnotic drugs. Because of specific agonist effects on gamma-aminobutyric acid (GABA) receptors, the newer drugs promote sleep but do not have muscle relaxant or anticonvulsive properties, as do older benzodiazepines. These newer drugs have less effect on the sleep architecture and produce less rebound insomnia but still should probably not be used as a long-term strategy. Three are available in the United States and differ mainly in their durations of action: Zaleplon (Sonata) is rapidly absorbed and has a half-life of about 1 hour, making it useful for patients with sleep-onset insomnia or for the troublesome older-age problem of awakening too early in the morning. In either situation, lingering side effects are not very prevalent in the morning. Zolpidem (Ambien) is also rapidly absorbed and has a half-life of 2–3 hours, so it should be taken at sleep-onset only. A longer-acting preparation with both fast-release and delayed-release properties is available as Ambien CR. Recently small dose, ultra-rapid onset, short-duration sublingual zolpidem has become available for those with middle insomnia who wish to go back to sleep. Eszopiclone (Lunesta), which has a longer half-life, is also suited for sleep-onset and sleep-maintenance insomnias, and should definitely be given only at sleep onset. Eszopiclone received approval for longer-term use, a change from the short-term usage recommended for earlier drugs. Rameltron (Rozerem) differs by being a melatonin agonist and targeting the circadian sleep–wake cycle.

There are numerous benzodiazepines and other hypnotic agents include both prescription and over-the-counter preparations. Hypnotic benzodiazepines (temazepam, triazolam, flurazepam) have been on the market for many years. They differ mainly from the newer benzodiazepine receptor agonists in their effect on sleep architecture. With chronic usage they reduce delta or slow-wave sleep (N3) at the expense of increasing intermediate stage sleep (N2). Some REM suppression also occurs with chronic usage. These changes in sleep architecture often result in morning reports of nonrefreshing sleep. However, the discomfort of tapering the drugs is often worse than continuing them, and so dependence develops.

Trazodone, an older, inexpensive sedating antidepressant, is the most prescribed prescription agent for sleep that is not FDA-approved as a hypnotic agent. It is given in lower doses for hypnotic effects than for antidepressant usage. Some studies report favorable effects on sleep architecture and patient satisfaction. Undesirable side effects are infrequent but should be noted and include arrhythmias and priapism. Other sedating antidepressants, such as amitriptyline and mirtazepine, are also frequently used for sleep. None of the sedating antidepressants have FDA approval as hypnotic agents. Antihistamines, melatonin, chamomile, and valerian are popular nonprescription drugs widely marketed to the public. They have not been approved by the FDA, but their low expense and easy availability have made them frequent first choices of patients having a variety of sleep problems. These agents have different proposed mechanisms of action. Histamine is a naturally occurring cerebral neurotransmitter with strong wake-promoting properties; so it makes sense that the older antihistamines that cross the blood-brain barrier would promote sleepiness. However, many of these drugs also have strong anticholinergic effects like tachycardia and urinary retention that can be especially hazardous in the eldery. Tryptophan, an amino acid precursor of serotonin, was commonly used as a sleep promoting agent in the 1980s and has seen some resurgence. Its use was associated with eosinophilic–myalgia syndrome (due to contaminants) but it is once again available. Chamomile tea is advertised as an herbal natural substance promoting sleep, but can be an abortifacient in pregnant women.

SLEEP-RELATED BREATHING DISORDERS

A person who is unable to breathe regularly will unsurprisingly have problems sleeping. Breathing problems may arise from control failure in the central nervous system or from restrictions in air flow. The most common cause of sleep disordered breathing is obstructive sleep apnea (OSA). Central sleep apnea is a non-obstructive sleep-associated breathing disorder of central nervous system control of breathing such as caused by brainstem injury, neuromuscular diseases, and medication-induced hypoventilation. Congestive heart failure can manifest with Cheyne–Stokes respiration, a periodic form of breathing due to an overly sensitive chemoreceptor (carotid body) and an unstable central respiratory controller.

OSA is a recurrent upper airway obstruction occurring when relaxation of the soft palate during deep sleep allows it to collapse over the airway and either partially or completely block air flow. Partial airway obstruction causes hypopnea or decreased breathing. When insufficient air is moved in and out of the lungs, blood oxygen drops (hypoxemia) and carbon dioxide climbs (hypercapnia) causing partial wakening and fitfull sleep. Prior to complete airway obstruction, vibration of the tissues causes snoring. Simple snoring exists without OSA or arousals; it is unfortunate for the bedfellow but generally asymptomatic. When crescendo snoring leads to arousals without a frank airway obstruction, the patient is said to have upper airway resistance syndrome (UARS). UARS may present with excessive daytime sleepiness or insomnia complaints. Complete airway obstruction causes apnea (absence of breathing). The current prevalence of OSA in affluent, mostly white countries is about 8% but 15% in Sao Paulo and Hong Kong (Santos-Silva, 2009).

During arousals, upper airway muscle tone (which declines during sleep) briefly improves as the soft tissues of the throat move back out of the way. The patient is now able to breathe a few breaths and reverts to stage I or II sleep which persists only until the next obstructive event. The arousals are usually not appreciated as such by the patient. Arousals are common with central apneas and periodic breathing also. Fragmented sleep from frequent arousals cause nonrestorative sleep and adversely affects sleep architecture. Though in bed and apparently asleep, the patient actually develops sleep deprivation which causes drowsiness, impaired daytime function, and cognitive changes over time. The end result of sleep-related breathing disorders is excessive daytime sleepiness. Sleep latencies become very short in patients with sleep disordered breathing. The patient is said to be pathologically sleepy when their mean sleep latency falls below 10 minutes. These individuals can drift into stage I sleep when left quietly to themselves. Peeking into the exam room, a physician may find a waiting (untreated) patient asleep in a chair. This sleepiness becomes very dangerous with activities that require vigilance such as driving. Sleep deprivation causes irritability and increased pain sensitivity, and worsens symptoms of anxiety and depression.

In OSA airway obstruction may occur at different anatomical levels. In children the obstruction often occurs at the level of the palatine tonsils or adenoids. In adults it is mostly palatal, retrolingual, or even retronasal. Most patients with OSA are overweight. Obesity causes deposition of fat and narrowing of the airway which predisposes to obstruction during sleep. Thin, micrognathic patients or those with high arched palates may also develop OSA and are often missed clinically as they do not have the typical body habitus. Drugs such as benzodiazepines, narcotics, and alcohol decrease upper airway tone, alter vagally mediated reflex that causes arousal during airway obstruction and alter ventilatory thresholds for carbon dioxide/pH, worsening the severity of the apnea. These agents should be used cautiously if at all until the apneas are corrected.

Sleep specialists distinguish apnea from hypnoapnea. Apneas last longer than 10 seconds with absent airflow. A "hypopnea" occurs when a partial airway obstruction produces a 50% decrement in airflow lasting at least 10 seconds and resulting in oxygen desaturation of 3–4%. Both apneas, hypopneas and even crescendo snoring may result in arousals, which may be unappreciated by the patient but are evident on EEG.

There is growing evidence that untreated sleep apnea leads to significant cardiovascular morbidity. Cyclic, frequent, oxygen desaturations and reoxygenation causes a free radical injury to the endothelial lining of blood vessels. This activates soluble cytokines, producing inflammatory changes in the vessel walls that predispose to subsequent deposition of lipid (athersosclerosis) and apoptosis of endothelial cells. Leukocytes become more adherent to the endothelium and nitric oxide (a vasodilator) levels decrease (Atkeson, 2008). There is a well-known association between OSA and increased risk for coronary artery disease and cerebrovascular accidents (Yumino, 2006). Activation of the autonomic nervous system predisposes to hypertension; a prospective cohort study in Spain showed hypertension was more common in patients with OSA than in those without (Marin, 2012). More severe apneics have more severe hypertension. Insulin resistance from OSA may cause more weight gain in patients making the sleep apnea worse. Most of these abnormalities can be ameliorated with treatment of OSA (Buchner, 2007).

Predisposing factors for OSA are obesity, increased neck circumference, age, male gender, anatomical structures of nasal and oral passages, and family history. Medical conditions may also predispose to OSA including hypothyroidism, neuromuscular disorder with bulbar weakness such as strokes and Parkinsonism, Down's syndrome, and kyphoscoliosis. OSA is suspected when there is a history of snoring, witnessed apnea, and daytime sleepiness. Obesity (body mass index >30) increased neck circumference of more than

17 inches in males and 15 inches in females, and reduction in space between the soft palate and base of tongue fit the "usual" clinical picture. The "Mallampati classification" (Figure 21-2) describes the tongue–soft palate relationship and is helpful for determining a patient's likelihood of having obstructive sleep apnea.

In central sleep apnea, the respiratory drive center in the medulla has diminished function. These patients may not snore, have more insomnia than hypersomnia, and are less apt to be obese than patients with OSA. The basic difference between obstructive and central sleep apnea is that the upper airway is obstructed in OSA and open in CSA. The diaphragm and intercostal muscles contract against a closed upper airway in OSA but are noncontractile in CSA, with a patent upper airway. This difference in muscle effort is useful in the sleep laboratory to distinguish obstructive from central apneas.

With OSA the astute clinician at the bedside, or the beleaguered bed partner, will notice snoring and cessation of breathing punctuated by snorts and gasping. A formal diagnosis of sleep apnea is accomplished by polysomnography either in a sleep center or with portable equipment at home. The number of apneas and hypopneas per hour divided by the time the patient sleeps is the Apnea Hypopnea Index (AHI). In portable studies there is no formal way to assess sleep duration so the number of events is divided by the recording time to give the Respiratory Disturbance Index (RDI). The RDI may underestimate severity of sleep apnea if the patient spent part of the night awake.

It is considered normal for adults to have an AHI/RDI of fewer than 5 events an hour; 5–15 is considered mildly severe sleep apnea; 15–35, considered moderate; and >35, severe sleep apnea. The AHI does not always correlate with symptoms of sleepiness as measured by the Epworth Sleepiness Scale (Bausmer, 2010). Some people with truly awful apnea have no symptoms, and conversely some patients bitterly complain of sleepiness with nearly normal AHI.

Management and Treatment

Treatment of sleep apnea depends on the severity and type of apnea. Weight loss, nonsupine sleep (not sleeping on one's back), and avoiding hypnotics and alcohol near bedtime improve sleep breathing in patients with milder obstructive apnea. There are oral appliances which pull the lower jaw forward—opening the airway. These are helpful with mild apnea in patients who are not terribly obese.

The Mallampati classification relates tongue size to pharyngeal size. This test is performed with the patient in the sitting position, the head held in a neutral position, the mouth wide open, and the tongue protruding to the maximum. The subsequent classification is assigned based upon the pharyngeal structures that are visible.

Class I = visualization of the soft palate, fauces, uvula, anterior and posterior pillars
Class II = visualization of the soft palate, fauces, and uvula
Class III = visualization of the soft palate and the base of the uvula
Class IV = soft palate is not visible at all

The classification assigned by the clinician may vary if the patient is in the supine position (instead of sitting). If the patient phonates, this falsely improves the view. If the patient arches his or her tongue, the uvula is falsely obscured. A class I view suggests ease of intubation and correlates with a laryngoscopic view grade I 99–100% of the time. Class IV view suggests a poor laryngoscopic view, grade III or IV 100% of the time. Beware of the intermediate classes, which may result in all degrees of difficulty in laryngoscopic visualization.

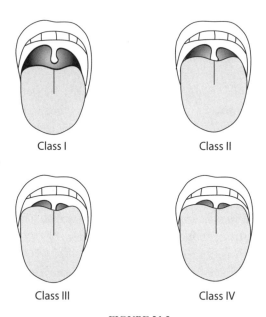

Class I   Class II

Class III   Class IV

FIGURE 21-2
Mallampati Classification
Although originally presented as predicting difficulty with intubation, the classification is also used in the examination of patients to predict the likelihood of obstructive sleep apnea. From Mallampati et al. (1985), 429–432.

Surgery for OSA has largely fallen out of favor. Tracheotomy is reserved for critically ill, super-morbidly obese patients with cardiopulmonary collapse. Uvulopalatoplasty (UVPP) and related techniques treat obstructive sleep apnea but generally decrease the AHI only about 50%. Pain, expense, and nasal reflux during swallowing are drawbacks to this procedure. These surgical procedures may be useful for milder apnea cases, simple snoring, and when continuous positive airway pressure (CPAP) is not tolerated by the patient.

> Adenotonsillectomy in children with OSA, is however, equally effective as CPAP and easier for children (Sudarsan, 2014). Children and young adults may not complain of excessive sleepiness as prominently as older adults and are more likely to have behavioral or cognitive problems resulting from their sleep apnea. Children with attention deficit disorder have improved school performance and behavior with treatment of OSA (Consantin, 2014).

With moderate to severe OSA CPAP is the standard of care. A CPAP machine produces positive pressure through a tight-fitting mask to prevent soft tissue from collapsing over the airway and keeping the passages open. CPAP and its variations are more effective than surgery for obstructive sleep apnea because they tend to correct airway obstruction without regard to the nature or location of the obstruction. CPAP treatment benefits include:

1. elimination of snoring;
2. reduction of sleep fragmentation from arousals;
3. prevention of nocturnal hypoxia and hypercarbia;
4. reduction in the incidence of hypertension, cardiac arrhythmia, myocardial infarction, stroke, congestive heart failure;
5. improvement in insulin resistance;
6. reduction of number of automobile accidents; and
7. improved job performance, depression, cognitive function and quality of life.

The use of continuous positive airway pressure leads to a more variable response in cases of central sleep apnea. Some patients respond to CPAP, whereas others require bi-level pressure settings with automatic backup rates (essentially nasal ventilators) to deliver breaths during long apneic periods. CPAP probably works in central sleep apnea by stimulating upper airway reflexes that promote breathing. If the central sleep apnea is related to respiratory center depression from medications, removal of the offending drug is essential. One example might be a patient on both a benzodiazepine and an opioid that act in tandem to depress respiratory drive. Sometimes patients with obstructive sleep apnea syndrome develop transient central sleep apneas (complex sleep apnea) after being placed on positive airway pressure. These central apneas are seldom clinically significant and usually disappear with time and treatment of the OSA. Successful treatment of congestive heart failure may often eliminate central apneas of the Cheyne–Stokes type. Central apnea may occur in the presence of brainstem pathology such as Arnold Chiari Syndrome, multiple sclerosis, and cerebrovascular infarction. A high clinical suspicion in such settings is required as these patients have other reasons to feel fatigued and do not as a rule snore as would other patients with OSA.

NARCOLEPSY

A person suffering from narcolepsy has compelling and persistent daytime sleepiness that is not related to breathing. In its full expression, it may be accompanied by poor quality sleep, cataplexy (sudden loss of voluntary muscle control provoked by emotion), hypnagogic hallucinations, and sleep paralysis. Understanding narcolepsy and associated symptoms had to await the discovery of REM sleep in 1951 by a physiology graduate student, Eugene Aserinsky, working in Chicago. He, along with Dr. William Dement, were studying sleep in infants and noted the periodic bursts of REMs and the appearance of low-amplitude faster cortical waveforms. Variations in autonomic functions, such as respiration, temperature, heart rate, blood pressure, and skeletal muscle tone, were also observed. Later, reports of dreaming in REM sleep, along with penile and clitoral erections in adults, were documented.

These REM-related changes contrasted with non-REM sleep patterns of slower cortical rhythms and eye movements, and a more stable autonomic state. Further investigation showed that cataplexy, sleep paralysis, and hypnagogic hallucinations coincide with an intrusion of REM sleep into the waking or near-wakeful state accounting for skeletal muscle hypotonia (cataplexy) and visual imagery (dreaming or hallucinations). People with narcolepsy often enter REM sleep within 5 minutes of dozing off during the day. The history of the elucidation of the clinical and laboratory findings of narcolepsy by the researchers at Stanford University was recently reviewed and is fascinating reading (Mignot, 2014).

Narcolepsy may present initially with hypersomnolence and no other

TABLE 21-6
Diagnostic Criteria for Narcolepsy
Type 1

A. The patient develops periods of irrepressible need to sleep or daytime lapses into sleep occurring for at least 3 months.

B. The presence of one or both of the following:

1. Cataplexy* and a sleep latency of <8 min with 2 sleep-onset REM periods. A sleep-onset REM (within 15 min of sleep onset) on the previous night polysomnogram may replace one sleep-onset REM on the MSLT.

   *Cataplexy is defined by brief episodes of sudden bilateral loss of muscle tone, most often in association with intense emotion.

2. Cerebrospinal fluid (CSF) hypocretin-1 concentration is <110 pg/ml.

Type 2

A and B (above) are reiterated

C. Cataplexy is absent. If it develops later Narcolepsy is redefined as Type 1

D. Either CSF hypocretin was not measured or CSF hypocretin-1 concentration is >110 pg/ml.

E. Hypersomnolence is not explained by other causes.

Sateia (2014)

features. Diagnostic criteria are included in Table 21-6. Cataplexy may develop later or be entirely absent. Sleepiness is grinding and persistent but typically improved by daytime naps. Nocturnal sleep is unsatisfactory and many patients paradoxically complain of insomnia. The time between development of initial symptoms to diagnosis is often delayed by as much as 10 years. Sleepy people get little sympathy and these patients' symptoms are attributed to depression, attention deficit disorder, various medical illnesses, malingering, and laziness. Jobsite and relationship problems are frequent. Lack of worth, frustration, and a sense of being misunderstood are common feelings these patients experience prior to diagnosis. Making a bona fide diagnosis is a liberating and life-changing event for narcoleptics.

Cataplexy is more than one episode of bilateral, symmetric loss of muscle tone with retained consciousness. The loss of muscle tone is REM skeletal muscle atonia, which intrudes upon a period of wakefulness. Deep tendon reflexes are lost during the attack and return after the spell, which lasts for several minutes. Areflexia is helpful in distinguishing cataplexy from conversion reactions or malingering. Strong emotions trigger cataplexy. In dramatic cases, the patient will fall to the ground, immobile. More subtle cataplexy with perhaps inability to lift a hand or maintain upright posture can occur. Children and some adults may develop facial hypotonia without strong emotions preceding the events. Cataplexy occurs in 60–70% of narcoleptics. Hypnopompic hallucinations (on sleep onset) or hypnogogic hallucinations (on awakening) are typical and disturbing to the patient. On arousing from sleep the patient may be temporarily unable to move (sleep paralysis). Sleep paralysis can also occur in severe sleep deprivation or sleep apnea. Once again, not all of these associated narcolepsy features are present in every patient. The *forme fruste* is more the rule than the exception with narcolepsy.

Epidemiology

The incidence of narcolepsy is 1 in 2,500 in the United States; it occurs more frequently in Japan. A weak familial association exists, as does a link to human leukocyte antigens, especially in patients who have narcolepsy with cataplexy. More than 90% of patients with narcolepsy and cataplexy are positive for the human leukocyte antigen variant HLADQB1*0602, reaching nearly 100% in African-Americans. Human leukocyte antigens cannot be used as an independent diagnostic test because about 20% of normals without narcolepsy are also HLADQB1*0602 positive. The antigen's presence is neither adequate nor sufficient for making the diagnosis. The onset of symptoms occurs usually between ages 15 and 25 years. There is another peak of incidence between 34 and 45 years of age, and it may accompany onset of menopause (Ohayon, 2005).

Differential Diagnosis of Hypersomnolence

Post concussive hypersomnolence, Von Economo's Syndrome of *encephalitis lethargica* (post encephalitic Parkinsonism), bipolar depression, and major affective disorder may present with hypersomnia. Myriad medical illnesses present with lassitude and fatigue. Cataplectic attacks may resemble epileptic psychomotor seizures. However, seizures usually have perserverative motor movements, such as repeated swallowing, hand rubbing, head turning, or eye deviation. Malingering and drug seeking should be considered.

Management and Treatment

Narcoleptic individuals tolerate sleep deprivation poorly. Regular sleep hours and a daily nap are essential parts of the treatment of narcolepsy. Scheduling a morning and/or afternoon nap may obviate the need for a higher dose of an alerting medication. Any other concurrent sleep disorder should be corrected and sleep hygiene reviewed.

There are several choices of FDA-approved medications for hypersomnolence. Amphetamine preparations (e.g., Dexedrine) were the first compounds to be used and remain important. They are well absorbed and have a favorable peak onset of action of 2 hours. They activate the dopaminergic system to enhance wakefulness. Methylphenidate (Ritalin) has a similar action. Several long-acting, once-daily preparations of amphetamines and methylphenidate are available. All are Schedule Class II drugs and apt to possible dependency and abuse. Well-read scoundrels will occasionally feign narcoleptic symptoms to obtain these medications, mandating a strict adherence to diagnostic criteria before prescribing.

Modafinil (Provigil) is a newer agent; it is a Class IV drug with less abuse potential than amphetamines. The mode of action is unknown. It is not a dopamine reuptake inhibitor as are amphetamines; it is a long-acting, well-absorbed medication. Side effects are infrequent and include headache, which subsides with time and lower dose. The efficacy of oral contraceptives may be reduced. Modafinil has become the drug of choice for treating hypersomnolence due to narcolepsy. Unfortunately, modafanil and its newer congener armodafanil are extraordinarily expensive.

Orexin (hypocretinin) is an alerting substance produced in cells of the ventrolateral hypothalamus and is responsible for alertness (and probably other important functions). In narcolepsy with cataplexy the orexin-producing cells no longer produce orexin, leading to sleepiness. The neurons producing orexin may be damaged through an autoimmune mechanism. An orexin receptor antagonist, Suvorexant, has recently been released. The hypnotic effect of Suvorexant comes from antagonizing these orexin receptors. In an industry funded, double-blind, placebo-controlled trial, Suvorexant improved total sleep time by 38.7 min—versus 16 min with placebo. The main side effect was drowsiness. There was no clear difference in incidence of side effects between the active drug and placebo, but 64% of the placebo group had some side effect (Michaelson et al., 2014).

Cataplexy must be treated separately from narcolepsy as most medications that control hypersomnolence in narcolepsy do not work for cataplexy. In some patients, cataplexy may be so mild and infrequent that additional medications are not required. Cataplexy is more common than other symptoms accompanying narcolepsy, such as sleep paralysis or hypnagogic hallucinations. REM-suppressant medications have been the mainstay of treatment for cataplexy in the past; tricyclic antidepressants are effective, but anticholinergic and sedating side effects limit their tolerance. Protryptiline was the classically used agent, but fluoxetine and venlafaxine have gained in popularity and are effective in modest doses—venlafaxine inhibits reuptake of both noradrenalin and serotonin and is effective in reducing cataplexy. Sodium oxybate (Xyrem) is the only medication that is FDA-approved for the treatment of cataplexy; none of the SSRI drugs are. Sodium oxybate is the sodium salt of gamma-hydroxybutyrate (GHB), which became infamous as a "date-rape drug." Xyrem is effective in controlling daytime sleepiness as well as cataplexy; it probably improves sleep quality. Xyrem requires in-depth knowledge of its prescribing method and potential side effects, but it is an option for those few patients with cataplexy and excessive sleepiness who fail to respond to other medications. Hypnotics are sometimes used since narcoleptics sleep poorly at night and do not tolerate sleep deprivation.

Hypnopompic hallucinations are experienced upon awakening, whereas *hypnagogic hallucinations* appear when dropping off to sleep. Narcoleptic hallucinations can be alarming: Professionals should counsel patients that these images are not part of a mental illness and are a normal variation of "premature dreaming" or "dreaming while awake." Approximately 10% of the nonnarcoleptic U.S. population has experienced these pre- and post-sleep hallucinations. Treatment of these hallucinations or illusions consists of reassurance.

Idiopathic hypersomnia is a term reserved for patients who have no demon-strable cause for their sleepiness and do not fit the criteria for narcolepsy. The histories are of long duration and consist of inappropriate sleepiness in spite of long periods of nocturnal sleep. The patients seem never to satisfy their sleepiness, even for short periods. People with narcolepsy, by contrast, may awaken quite refreshed after a nap but show signs of sleepiness in a few hours. The idiopathic group will show a short-mean sleep latency but no sleep-onset REM periods on MSLT, even after a full night's sleep. Given that CSF orexin levels require a lumbar puncture and are not readily avail-able, this diagnosis may be difficult to distinguish from Narcolepsy Type II.

Treatment is much like that for narcolepsy except the idiopathic group does not have associated features of cataplexy, hypnagogic hallucinations, or sleep paralysis. Alerting medications are used for these patients as in narco-leptics. Stimulant medications doses are titrated to minimize sleepiness and improve wake function. However, particularly for sympathomimetic stimu-lants, there are troubling side effects and toxicities. Tachycardia, tremor, insomnia, activation of mania, and anxiety are side effects that have to be balanced against residual sleepiness. The very long term consequences of stimulant medication have not been well studied. There is an association of pulmonary hypertension with some anorexant stimulants. The lowest effec-tive dose for a reasonable level of alertness is the goal. Nonpharmacologic measures such as napping, keeping regular hours, and sleep hygiene may allow for dose reduction. Such "reasonable accommodations" to help hyper-somnolent workers can be requested vis-a-vis the Americans with Disabili-ties Act.

Safety and Sleepiness

Special care should be used to counsel sleepy patients about safety. Patients with hypersomnia from any cause can lapse into Stage 1 sleep without realizing it. In a study of long-haul truck drivers using portable EEG monitored over four 13-hour shifts there was a total of 3.83 hours of bona fide sleep noted (Miller, 1997). Being sleepy at the wheel increases 8-fold the risk of accidents. The subjective sensation of sleepiness at the wheel is a better predictor of accidents than the Epworth Sleepiness Score (Sagaspe, 2010). A near-miss accident in the past from sleepiness increases the risk for subsequent driving accidents. Most accidents occur close to home, in a city, and involve younger drivers. In patients with sleep disorders the relative risk of an accident is nearly 4 times that of controls, with narcoleptics leading the way. The Epworth Sleepiness Scale and MSLT do not predict the risk of driving accidents, but some studies show the MWT does. CPAP decreases driving risks in OSA.

Likely, all activities requiring vigilance are impaired similarly by sleepiness. The Exxon Valdez wreck, Bhopal catastrophe, *Challenger* explosion, and a recent train derailment in New York City are examples of catastrophic events that involved sleepy individuals making poor decisions or functioning inadequately. It is highly advisable to have an informative handout available to give sleepy patients about drowsy driving and other activities that require vigilance. A moment to discuss safety and liability issues is well spent. Such advice should be documented in the medical record. Consider referring treated patients to a sleep specialist for a consultation and MWT to ensure they are no longer hypersomnolent.

SLEEP-RELATED MOVEMENT DISORDERS

Restless Legs Syndrome

Restless legs syndrome (RLS) is classified under sleep-related movement disorders. RLS presents as an uncomfortable, usually painless sensation in the legs, extending occasionally into the thighs and less often occurring in the arms. The RLS patient complains of an urge to move the limbs. The symptoms are always worse later in the evening. Symptoms are relieved by activity and worsen with inactivity. Symptoms differ from the restlessness of neuroleptic drugs, termed *akathisia*, which remains throughout the day and is not as well relieved by activity. The circadian activity of RLS is very notable and helps to distinguish it from other movement disorders. *DSM-5* requires the presence of symptoms 3 days a week for more than 3 months, as well as a requirement for distress from the symptoms and disruption of social, educational, or other important area of function.

Periodic Limb Movement Disorder

Periodic limb movement disorder (PLMD) was initially called nocturnal myoclonus. This term was given to patients because they kicked and moved their legs rhythmically every 20–40 seconds during sleep, often without realizing it. The motor activity may last for several minutes, and then subside, only to recur in one or both legs or the arms. Stereotypical movements are the extension of the toes and feet (as seen with a positive Babinski sign) with hip flexion. Most complaints come from the bed partner, although some patients are aware of disturbed sleep. Nonrestorative sleep, daytime fatigue, and early or middle insomnia are common. Symptoms wax and wane over time. More than half of patients with RLS also have PLMD, but PLMD may occur without the discomfort of restless legs while awake. Patients with PLMD usually complain more of fatigue, whereas those with RLS alone complain of insomnia. RLS/PLMD is diagnosed clinically and PSG is typically not necessary. A careful examination of the limbs for reflexes or sensory deficits is indicated as neuropathic problems can mimic RLS in some ways. RLS may affect 10% of people with chronic insomnia who consult sleep clinics. PLMD afflicts both sexes and increases with age.

RLS/PLMD may be familial, secondary to other causes, or sporadic. When familial, the onset occurs earlier in life and behaves like an autosomal dominant trait. Isolated or sporadic cases usually appear beyond middle age, and no family history or identifiable cause is apparent. Secondary RLS/PLMD is seen with iron deficiency, pregnancy, and chronic renal failure on dialysis. The association of iron deficiency is an important clue. PLMD/RLS is due to relative decrease in dopamine. Iron is a cofactor of dopamine decarboxylase, an enzyme in the synthesis of dopamine. A serum ferritin level identifies the presence of iron deficiency. If iron deficiency is present, replacement of the mineral is therapeutic. A ferritin level greater than 50ng/ml is the goal.

Dopaminergic agents have been found to improve symptoms of RLS. Carbidopa-levodopa (Sinemet), the mainstay of Parkinson's treatment, is noted to be beneficial for RLS/PMLD. It improves both the urge to move the extremities and the periodic limb movements at night when asleep. The dopaminergic agonists ropinirole (Requip) and pramipexole (Mirapex) are the current treatment of choice and less likely to cause rebound symptoms

TABLE 21-7
Agents and Conditions Affecting RLS and PLMD

IMPROVES	WORSENS
Dopamine agonists:	Iron deficiency
Pramipexole (Mirapex)	Dopamine antagonists
Ropinirole (Requip)	Antipsychotics (e.g., haloperidol)
Carbidopa-levodopa	Antidepressants (e.g., TCAs)
Narcotics:	Antiemetics (e.g., metoclopramide)
Codeine	Pregnancy
Hydrocodone	Renal failure on dialysis
Tramadol	Propoxyphene
Benzodiazepines, less effective	
Sleep hygiene measures, with avoidance of caffeine, alcohol, and tobacco	

in the night or *augmentation*. Augmentation occurs when the restless legs occurs earlier in the daytime. This is much more common with cardiodopa-levadopa. Rarely, these agents can cause impulsive behaviors to worsen (gambling, excessive shopping, etc.).

Regular exercise and stretching the limbs offer some benefit, although it is transient. Caffeine, TCAs, serotonin reuptake inhibitors, and agents with strong dopamine antagonistic properties such as metoclopramide (Reglan) make RLS/PLMD worse. Table 21-7 summarizes agents and conditions that worsen or improve sleep-related movement disorders.

Other sleep-related movement disorders include *nocturnal leg cramps*, *bruxism*, and *rhythmic movement disorder*. Nocturnal leg cramps are sudden, painful muscle spasms that occur during the night, usually in the calves and/or small muscles of the feet, which are acutely relieved by stretching or massaging the affected areas. They may be followed by a vague, uncomfortable sensation and can be very disruptive to sleep. The etiology of leg cramps is not always apparent, and treatments are imprecise.

Bruxism consists of clenching and grinding motions of the jaw, and disturbs sleep of the bed partner more often than the patient. Worn occlusive surfaces of the teeth are often noted by the dentist. More commonly occurring in children, the condition usually subsides with age. Bruxism may occur in anxious adults and require oral appliances to lessen the wear on permanent teeth. Bruxism can be a side effect of SSRI medication.

Rhythmic movement disorders in sleep are mainly limited to infants and children. Other descriptive terms are head banging (*jactatio capitis nocturna*) and body rocking. These are large, rhythmic muscle movements that begin at sleep onset and persist into Stage 2 sleep for about 15 minutes then subside. PSG shows rhythmic muscle artifact that corresponds to video evidence of rhythmic movement. Most cases cease by age 5. Rarely does head banging/body rocking cause injury or important sleep disturbance other than worry for the parents.

PARASOMNIAS

Parasomnias are undesirable events during sleep. The sleep architecture itself is usually not affected, except by an arousal. Parasomnias may occur during entry into sleep, within sleep, or during arousals from sleep. They can be divided into REM-related and non–REM-parasomnias. Parasomnias are well-known sleep disorders because they are both prevalent and attract the attention of bed partners. They may be more prevalent in certain age groups; for example, confusional arousals, sleepwalking, and sleep terrors are normal events in childhood but unusual in adults. Among the REM-sleep–related parasomnias, nightmares are present in childhood and adults. REM behavior disorder is a disease of the elderly.

A distinction should be made between night terrors and nightmares. Children with *night terrors* suddenly awaken from N3 sleep in the first third of the sleep period with a cry or scream. The child shows increased autonomic activities such as tachypnea, tachycardia, diaphoresis, and dilated pupils. The child is hard to awaken from the episode and when awakened, there is no dream recall. Night terrors occur from ages 4 to 12, are not associated with any behavioral or physical abnormality, and resolve with age. Like sleepwalking, there can be an autosomal dominant inheritance. By awakening the child just prior to the usual time these spells occur, these parasomnias are averted. Medications that reduce N3 delta-wave sleep, such as benzodiazepines, will reduce or eliminate the behavior. Sleep-talking (somniloquy) is a common benign related NREM sleep phenomenon which may occur alone or accompany sleepwalking.

Sleepwalkers are often confused, bump into objects, and are not well-coordinated. Somnambulists can be dangerous and leap from windows, fall down stairs, or wander outside the home. A typical episode starts with the patient sitting up and repeating acts, such as picking at pajamas or bedsheets. More complicated behaviors follow, including dressing, eating, and urinating. With blank and staring faces, these patients are rarely affected by those who attempt to contact them. Episodes typically persist for several minutes to half an hour. Sometimes patients don't walk but just fret in bed. They have no recollection of their walking. Hostility is uncommon among sleepwalkers. Security of the bedroom is important. Sleepwalkers may need to sleep on the ground floor, have the outside doors securely locked, and have the car keys unavailable.

Nightmares are REM-associated parasomnias that occur universally, but in excess constitute a sleep disorder. Commonly present in preschool children, nightmares may overlap with night terrors but are very different from them. Nightmares are more common in the last third of the night. They are associated with visual imagery, which can be recalled, especially if the individual awakens close to the time the dream is occurring. Nightmares in the young are more colorful, action-packed, and contain more sexual content than in older individuals. The content of nightmares is mostly random, although usually threatening, such as being chased. The recurrent nightmares that follow a traumatic event may contain related content; in nondepressed persons nightmare content is random. Occurring frequently after stress, nightmares cause a sleep-onset insomnia condition in patients due to fear of experiencing another bad dream. This is seen in some patients with posttraumatic stress disorder. The central-acting alpha blocker prazosin has been used to block the sympathetic discharge and fright that occurs with nightmares. Medications such as thioridazine, TCAs, SSRIs, and benzodiazepines may trigger nightmares by reducing NREM deep sleep. Suddenly withdrawing REM-suppressant medications and drugs such as alcohol, TCAs, and MAOIs causes REM rebound, which can likewise result in nightmares.

REM behavior sleep disorder (RBSD) occurs when the usual muscle atony of REM sleep is lost and patients act out dreams. RBSD is more common in older men. The initial complaint is an increase in dream frequency and content after many years of less-frequent, bland dreams. The dreams are often action filled and contain imagery of fighting, being chased, or being threatened by another person or an animal. The bed partner is awakened by vocal and motor activity, and may flee from the bed to avoid violent arm flailing and kicking. When awakened, patients will recount vivid dreams of violent encounters that are completely out of character, and they are embarrassed by their actions. The embarrassment often causes them to delay evaluation. The activity usually occurs in the latter half of the sleep period when REM sleep and dreaming are most common. After several years of this activity, nearly half of the affected patients may develop a neurodegenerative disorder such as Parkinson's disease, multisystem atrophy, or Lewy body dementia.

Dreams and motor activity respond to low doses of clonazepam (Klonopin, 0.5 mg) better than any other treatment. As with sleepwalking safety issues in the bedroom require attention. Polysomnograms during these episodes fail to show any epileptiform activity, but there is, paradoxically, increased motor activity in REM sleep. Video monitoring during PSG shows the patient moving in a purposeful way during REM. RBSD may be caused by antidepressants and chronic alcohol abuse. Brainstem tumors have caused nocturnal behavior similar to RBSD. These diverse situations all have in common interference with REM sleep generation in the brainstem.

CIRCADIAN RHYTHM DISORDER

The supra chiasmatic nucleus of the hypothalamus programs biologic systems over a cycle that lasts about 24 hours (*circa diem*). These circadian rhythms control many automatic mechanisms including core body temperature, which fluctuates from higher during the day to lower at night; cortisol secretory patterns, which are characteristically lower at sleep onset and increase by early morning; and growth hormone secretion, which is higher in slow-wave sleep. These three markers are among the strongest of the 24-hour body rhythms. External stimuli which synchronize our circadian rhythms are called "zeitgebers." Sunlight is the strongest one exerting its effect through the anatomical pathway that carries input from light receptors in the retina to the hypothalamus. Exercise and meals synchronize circadian rhythm to a lesser extent than light.

Sleep disorders arise when there is a misalignment between the patient's circadian sleep–wake pattern ("biological clock"), and clock time. This misalignment may be transient, as in jet lag, or persistent, as in shift-work sleep disorder. The patient may complain of sleepiness at work or inability to sleep when off work. The sleep–wake cycle is one of the body's circadian rhythms, and it is strongly entrained in most individuals to the light–dark cycle. The duration and quality of sleep are unaffected, but sleep is out of phase with the environmental time in circadian sleep disorders.

One example of a circadian rhythm disorder is the delayed sleep phase syndrome (DSPS). This entity is prevalent in adolescence, and defined by staying up late and desiring to sleep late into the mornings. An individual with a normal sleep–wake pattern can develop DSPS because of late-night activities, such as those that occur in a college setting. Once DSPS is established, it may be difficult to phase-advance the person so that he or she goes to bed at a reasonable hour. Many college students do not take morning classes because of this tendency. The sensation of initial insomnia can lead to overuse of hypnotics and other substances in an attempt to initiate sleep.

Establishing a rigid wakeup time followed by exposure to early-morning light or use of a bright (2500–10,000 lux) full spectrum light box for 30–60 minutes in the morning may correct the phase delay. Melatonin in small doses, about 5 hours prior to desired bedtime causes a phase advance. A more rapid way to correct this delayed sleep phase tendency is to have the individual remain awake the entire night and the following day, and then go to sleep at a more reasonable hour, that is, 11:00–12:00 midnight. Alternatively, sleep onset is delayed for 3 hours each night. After several days, the time of sleep onset is chosen to be around 11:00 P.M., and the patient goes to bed at that time thereafter. A fixed wakeup time is essential for maintaining the normal pattern. Timed light exposure, melatonin, and morning exercise help phase-advance these individuals, but it requires weeks for this to work and is difficult to do.

With advancing age, sleep phase tends to advance. The patient will go to bed earlier and earlier and awake earlier than desired. This is treated with late-evening exercise and bright light exposure to move the bedtime to a later time.

Shift Work

Artificial light and 24-hour factories have changed sleep schedules for millions. Nocturnal sleep time has declined since the invention of the electric lightbulb in 1879. An estimated 20 million Americans are involved in shift work. There are numerous variations in shift-work schedules: Some workers have fixed nighttime hours whereas others rotate shifts, which is a more difficult situation in which to adapt. Common to night or rotating shift workers is changing sleep times whenever the individual is off work and trying to accommodate their family and home schedules. Complaints of insomnia are common during the hours the patients try to sleep during periods when normal circadian rhythms would have them awake. Sleep without hypnotics is difficult in these situations. Sleepiness during work periods may interfere with productivity and workplace safety. Shift work is less well tolerated by older workers. Alerting and/or hypnotic medications can be helpful if needed. Avoiding bright, full spectrum light before bedtime is very important. Time-zone changes, or *jet lag*, have some features in common with shift work, but are usually of shorter duration. Jet lag is also better tolerated by younger individuals. The body's circadian system is out of synchrony with the environmental time and may take several days to adjust; approximately 1 hour of adjustment per day, per time zone crossed, seems to fit most travelers.

Irregular sleep–wake pattern is not a rarity in psychiatric practice. The usual patient with this problem has a cognitive dysfunction and is often a resident of a nursing home. Sleep disturbances are very common in nursing home patients because of inactivity and constant low-level light. "Sundowning" leads to the use of sedatives that can cause paradoxical agitation and confusion. Adverse drug effects may occur with increased frequency due to potential hepatic interactions of multiple drugs, decreased renal clearance with age, and decreased volume of distribution.

References

American Psychiatric Association. (2013). *Diagnostic and statistical manual of mental disorders*, 5th ed. Arlington, VA: American Psychiatric Association.

Andrew, L. (1999). Practice parameters for non-pharmacologic treatment of chronic insomnia. *Sleep*, 22(8), 1128–1133.

Atkeson, A. (2008). Mechanisms of endothelial dysfunction in obstructive sleep apnea. *Vascular Health and Disease Management*, 4(6), 1327–1335.

Bausmer, U. (2010). Correlation of the Epworth Sleepiness Scale with respiratory sleep parameters in patients with sleep-related breathing disorders and upper airway pathology. *European Archives of Otorhinolaryngology*, 267(10), 1645–1648.

Berry, R., Vaughn, B., et al. (2012). *The AASM manual for the scoring of sleep and associated events*. Darien, IL: American Academy of Sleep Medicine.

Blagrove, M. (1994). The effects of chronic sleep reduction on the performance of cognitive tasks sensitive to sleep deprivation. *Applied Cognitive Psychology*, 9, 21–40.

Buchner, N. (2007). Continuous positive airway pressure treatment of mild to moderate obstructive sleep apnea decreases cardiovascular risk. *American Journal of Respiratory and Critical Care Medicine*, 176(12), 1274–1280.

Collop, N., Schwab, R., et al. (2007). Clinical guidelines for the use of unattended portable monitors in the diagnosis of obstructive sleep apnea in adult patients. *Journal of Clinical Sleep Medicine*, 3(7), 737–747.

Consantin, E. (2014). Association between childhood sleep-disordered breathing and disruptive behavior disorders in childhood and adolescence. *Behavioral Sleep Medicine*, Aug 7, 1–13.

Healey, E., & Kales A. (1981). Onset of insomnia: Role of life stress events. *Psychosomatic Medicine*, 43, 439–451.

Jacobs, G.D. (2004). Cognitive behavioral therapy and pharmacotherapy for insomnia. *Archives of Internal Medicine*, 164, 1888–1896.

Kripke, D. (2000). Chronic hypnotic use: Deadly risks, doubtful benefit. *Sleep Medicine Reviews*, 4(1), 5–20.

Mallampati, S. (1985). A clinical sign to predict difficult tracheal intubation: A prospective study. *Canadian Anesthesia Society Journal*, 32(4) 429–434.

Marin, J. (2012). Association between treated and untreated obstructive sleep apnea and risk of hypertension. *Journal of the American Medical Association*, 307(20), P2169–P2176.

Michaelson, D., et al. (2014). Safety and efficacy of suvorexant during 1-year treatment of insomnia with subsequent abrupt treatment discontinuation: A phase 3 randomized, double-blind, placebo-controlled trial. *Lancet Neurology*, 13(5), 461–471.

Mingot, E. (2014). The history of narcolepsy at Stanford University. *Immunology Research*, 58(2–3), 315–339.

Mitler, M. (1997). The sleep of long-haul truckers. *New England Journal of Medicine*, Sep 11, 337(11), 755–761

Morin, C.M., Hauri, P.J., Espie, C.A., Spielman, A.J., Buysse, D.J., & Bootzin, R.R. (1999). Nonpharmacologic treatment of chronic insomnia. An American Academy of Sleep Medicine review. *Sleep*, 22(8), 1134–1156.

Morin, C., Bootzin, R.R., Buysse, D.J., Edinger, J.D., Espie, C.A., & Lichstein, K.L. (2006). Psychological and behavioral treatment of insomnia: An update of the recent evidence (1998–2004). *Sleep*, 29(11), 1398–1414.

Netzer, N.C., Stoohs, R.A., Netzer, C.M., Clark, K., & Strohl, K.P. (1999). Using the Berlin Questionnaire to identify patients at risk for the sleep apnea syndrome. *Annals of Internal Medicine, 131*(7), 485–491.

Ohayon, M. (2005). How age influences the expression of narcolepsy. *Journal of Psychosomatic Research, 59*, 399–405.

Owens, J. (2009). Neurocognitive and behavioral impact of sleep disordered breathing in children. *Pediatric Pulmonology, 44*(5), 417–422.

Owens, J. (2014). Insufficient sleep in adolescents and young adults: An update on causes and consequences. *Pediatrics, 134*(3), e921032.

Pataka, A., Argyropoulou, P., et al. (2014). Evaluation of five different questionnaires for assessing sleep apnea in a sleep clinic. *Sleep Medicine, 15*(7), 776–781.

Sagaspe, P. (2010). Sleepiness, near-misses and driving accidents among a representative population of French drivers. *Sleep Research, 19*, 578–584.

Sagaspe, P, Talliard. J, Guillminault, C. (2007). Maintenance of wakefulness test as a predictor of driving performance in patients with untreated sleep apnea. *Sleep*, 30, 327–330.

Santos-Silva, R. (2009). Sao Paulo Epidemiologic Sleep Study: rationale, design and sampling procedures. *Sleep Medicine, 10*, 679–685.

Sateia, M. (2014). *International classification of sleep disorders.* Darien,IL: American Academy of Sleep Medicine.

Sato, M. (2010). Clinical efficacy of individual cognitive behavior therapy for psychophysiological insomnia in 20 outpatients. *Psychiatry Clinical Neuroscience, 64*(2), 187–195.

Sudarsan, S. (2014). Comparison of treatment modalities in syndromic children with obstructive sleep apnea—a randomized cohort study. *International Journal of Pediatric Otorhinolaryngology, 78*(9), 1526–1533.

Sutton, E.L. (2014). Psychiatric disorders and sleep issues. *Medical Clinics of North America,* 98(5), 1123–1143.

World Health Organization. (1992). *The ICD–10 classification of mental and behavioural disorders: Clinical descriptions and diagnostic guidelines.* Geneva: World Health Organization.

Yumino, D. (2006). Impact of obstructive sleep apnea on clinical and angiographic outcomes following percutaneous coronary intervention in patients with acute coronary syndrome. *American Journal of Cardiology, 99*(1), 26–30.

22

Sexual and Gender Identity Disorders

Sex plays a uniquely pervasive role in people's lives; it influences how we think, feel, dress, flirt, play, mate, and love. Thus, when individuals experience a psychosexual disorder, it can produce a pervasive sense of discomfort, conflict, and distress for that person and/or for others around them. The DSM-5 covers these disorders in three sections: *sexual dysfunctions, paraphilias (sexual preference disorders)*, and *gender dysphoria (gender identity disorders)*. At the outset, some basic terms and concepts need clarification.

DEFINITION OF TERMS

A person's *anatomical sex* is his or her biological sex as determined by whether he has XY, or she has XX, chromosomes. *Intersex conditions* occur when one or more of the physical variables of biological sex—including chromosomal status, external genitals, internal sexual anatomical structures, sex hormonal status, and/or secondary sex characteristics—are discordant (e.g., partial androgen insensitivity syndrome or congenital adrenal hyperplasia). The medical conditions of intersex variations, by themselves, are not considered sexual or gender identity disorders, but can be a contributing factor in the development of a sexual or gender identity disorders.

Gender identity is the individual's *internal* feelings or self-perception as to whether he or she is a male or a female.

Gender role refers to whether a person wishes to be seen by others (or by oneself) as a male or as a female; or it refers to role behaviors empirically associated predominantly by most individuals to one biological sex while observed in only a small minority of the other sex. Gender role involves the person's *external* appearance and behavior, including sexual behavior.

Sexual orientation describes a person's erotic attraction and preference for partners of the same (homosexual) or opposite (heterosexual) sex or for both (bisexual). Only about 1% of adult females and 2–3% of adult males report homosexual orientation expressed in enduring homosexual or bisexual behavior.

DIAGNOSTIC CATEGORIES

The major groupings of sexual and gender disorders are considered in this chapter according to the descending order of their prevalence: sexual dysfunctions (common), paraphilias (less common), and gender identity disorders (rare).

The general category of *sexual dysfunctions* includes disturbances in the human sexual response cycle or disturbances involving pain associated with sexual intercourse. The phases of the sexual response cycle are as follows: (1) desire; (2) excitement or arousal; (3) orgasm; and (4) resolution. *Sexual desire disorders* refer to excessive interest in, or aversion to, sexual activity. *Sexual arousal disorders* refer to the inability to attain or maintain gender-normal psychophysiological changes during sexual activity. *Orgasmic disorders* involve either delays or absence of orgasm in men and women after normal sexual excitement, or in men, the opposite: premature ejaculation. *Sexual pain disorders* are characterized by the chronic presence of genital pain or spasms during sexual activity. *Sexual dysfunctions* may be due to substance use or another medical condition such as diabetes or hypothyroidism.

Paraphilias are persistent patterns of sexual arousal in response to atypical or bizarre stimuli and include the following subtypes classified by the stimulus (noted in parentheses): *exhibitionism* (exposing one's genitals), *fetishism* (material object), *frotteurism* (touching and rubbing against a nonconsenting individual), *pedophilia* (a prepubescent child), *sexual masochism* (being humiliated, beaten, bound, or other suffering), *sexual sadism* (causing physical or psychological suffering of a victim), *transvestic fetishism* (cross-dressing), *voyeurism* (observing unsuspecting naked or sexually involved individuals), and related conditions that are diagnosed as *other specified paraphilic disorder.*

Gender identity disorders (now called gender dysphoria in *DSM-5*) are characterized by discomfort with one's anatomical sex to such an extent that one adopts the behavioral patterns and identity associated with the other sex. Although some advocate for the removal of "transgendered" conditions from diagnostic nomenclature, gender identity disorders are recognized diagnostically because they almost always cause significant distress. Although variations in *gender role* are not listed as distinct disorders, "transient, stress-related cross-dressing behavior" would fall under the diagnostic category of *other specified gender dysphoria*.

SEXUAL DYSFUNCTIONS

Sexual dysfunctions are disturbances in a phase of the human sexual response cycle. Table 22-1 defines the four phases of this cycle.

Nine specific sexual dysfunctions are outlined in Table 22-2. In each of these the problem (1) is persistent or recurrent; (2) is not better explained as exclusively occurring during the course of another acute mental disorder (other than another sexual dysfunction) such as major depressive disorder and is not due to the direct physiological effects of a substance (e.g., a drug of abuse, a medication) or a general medical condition; and (3) causes marked distress or interpersonal difficulty. In describing a sexual dysfunction, clinicians also should indicate if it's *acquired* or *lifelong* (with or without previously normal functioning); if it's *generalized* or *situational* (only under certain conditions or with a particular partner); or if it's due to *psycho-*

TABLE 22-1
The Human Sexual Response Cycle

PHASE	KEY FEATURES
I. DESIRE	Fantasies about sexual activity and the desire (i.e., libido) to have it.
II. EXCITEMENT	Subjective sense of sexual pleasure with accompanying physiological changes in the male leading to erection, and in the female leading to vaginal lubrication and expansion, vasocongestion in the pelvis, and swelling of the external genitals. Associated with "foreplay" and mediated by the parasympathetic nervous system, this phase includes the "excitement" and "plateau" stages described by Masters and Johnson (1970) and the "vascular" stage described by Kaplan (1974).
III. ORGASM	The peaking of sexual pleasure and the release of sexual tension. This phase is mediated by the sympathetic nervous system and called the "muscular" stage by Kaplan. During it, males sense an inevitable ejaculation, which is followed by intense muscular contractions that emit semen. In a more variable response, females contract the outer third of their vagina.
IV. RESOLUTION	There is a generalized and muscular relaxation, during which males are physiologically refractory to further erection or orgasm, whereas females may be able to respond immediately to additional sexual stimulation for multiple orgasms.

TABLE 22-2
Sexual Dysfunctions

SEXUAL DESIRE DISORDERS (Occurring in Phase I of the sexual response cycle)

Hypoactive sexual desire disorder is a deficiency (or absence) of sexual fantasies and desires for sexual activity. It is the most common sexual dysfunction in women and is often accompanied by other sexual dysfunctions.

Sexual aversion disorder is an extreme aversion to and avoidance of all (or almost all) genital sexual contact with a partner. This may occur in those sexually victimized as part of a posttraumatic stress disorder.

SEXUAL AROUSAL DISORDERS (Occurring in Phase II of the sexual response cycle)

Female sexual arousal disorder and *male erectile disorder* are persistent conditions in which there is a partial or complete failure in women to attain or maintain the lubrication-swelling response, or in men to attain or maintain an erection (impotence) prior to the sexual act being completed.

ORGASMIC DISORDERS (Occurring in Phase III of the sexual response cycle)

Female and male orgasmic disorders are persistent or recurrent conditions in which there is a delay in or absence of orgasm following a normal sexual excitement phase.

Premature ejaculation is a persistent or recurrent condition in males in which ejaculation occurs with minimal sexual stimulation before, on, or shortly after penetration and before the person wishes it. The clinician must take into account factors such as the person's age and the frequency and duration of coitus.

SEXUAL PAIN DISORDERS

Dyspareunia (not due to another medical condition) is recurrent or persistent genital pain (usually in women, but sometimes in men) that occurs before, during, or after sexual intercourse.

Vaginismus (not due to another condition) is recurrent or persistent involuntary muscular spasm of the outer third of the vagina that interferes with sexual intercourse by making penetration difficult, painful, or impossible. Vaginismus may be secondary to pain or vice versa.

Note: Adapted from *ICD-10* (pp. 150–152) and *DSM-5* (pp. 423–450)

---

logical or *combined* (psychological and medical or substance) factors. Clinicians should also note its frequency, setting, duration, degree of sexual impairment, level of subjective distress, and effects on other areas of functioning (e.g., social, occupational).

Most sexual dysfunctions arise during young adulthood or with first sexual encounters. The overall clinical course is highly varied; a disorder may be brief, recurrent, smoldering, or permanent. Patients usually delay seeking treatment for 3–12 years and then do so only after several years of a prolonged problematic sexual relationship. Dysfunctions also may arise later in life; for males, inhibited sexual desire and excitement is more common in middle adulthood. Women tend to have increasing sexual responsiveness until their 30s and often maintain their responsiveness into old age. Men often retrospectively report that their peak sexual responsiveness was in their teens or early 20s.

Some sexual dysfunctions tend to be associated with specific psychiatric traits. For example, women with histrionic personalities are more likely to have inhibited sexual desire and inhibited orgasm. Men with obsessive–compulsive personalities are prone to inhibited sexual desire and excitement. Anxiety predisposes one to premature ejaculation and also impotence.

A patient's dysfunction will involve one or more etiological factors. These may be (1) *intrapsychic*, such as "performance anxiety," guilt, low self-esteem, denial, undue self-monitoring, or prior learning and conditioning effects; (2) *interpersonal*, such as fear of abandonment, power struggles, lack of trust, failure to explicitly inform partners about one's particular sexual needs and specific pleasures, a "sex manual mentality," displaced anger, or past experience of sexual victimization; (3) *cultural*, such as sexual myths, insufficient or incorrect information, and negative attitudes about sex learned from parents or others; (4) *medical*, such as drugs, alcohol, or illness; or (5) *psychiatric*, such as depressive and obsessive–compulsive disorders.

> A 38-year-old man sought psychotherapy for his inability to obtain an erection during sexual activity with his wife without viewing a new female pornographic video. Reviewing a recently viewed pornographic video would not suffice, but using a video that he had not seen for a couple of years would work. As a result, he had an entire double garage full of pornographic videos that he would "recycle" to view before sex in order to be able to attain an erection. The only other way he could become sexually aroused would be to bring another woman to join him and his wife in a "threesome." He reported that his wife enthusiastically went along with the "threesomes." However, later in marital therapy, his wife made it clear that it repulsed her; she had complied only because she knew her husband would be impotent without another person or yet another pornographic video. In this case, the man's self-described "liberal" sexual practices eventually contributed to a sexual dysfunction through a conditioning process in which the man consciously disassociated sex from love through years of pairing sexual arousal with pornographic stimuli.

The most common failure in treating sexual dysfunctions is overlooking the presence of another mental disorder, medical illness, or a drug effect. No matter how obviously emotional problems are affecting the patient, no sexual dysfunction should be treated until *after* the patient has had a complete medical workup, preferably by a physician well versed in the medical causes of sexual dysfunction. A common example is a 55-year-old man with impotence. Diabetes is the most likely cause and loss of nocturnal erections is the best clue. In addition, almost all psychiatric and many nonpsychiatric drugs can cause sexual side effects (over 30% of those taking SSRIs are affected). When a sexual dysfunction is clinically determined to be the direct effect of a medical condition, it is diagnosed as one of the "sexual dysfunctions due to another medical condition," in which the type of dysfunction and specific medical condition are identified. If the sexual dysfunction is clinically attributed exclusively to the direct effects of a substance (whether a medication, toxin exposure, or abused substance), then the condition is specifically diagnosed as one of the "substance-induced sexual dysfunctions," in which the type of dysfunction and specific substance are identified.

Sex therapies are short-term and experiential, aim for behavioral improvement, focus on the here-and-now sexual interactions of a couple, and combine treatments such as education, couple therapy, cognitive–behavioral therapy, directed masturbation exercises, Kegel exercises, homework assignments, desensitization, the squeeze technique, stop–start (actually, start–stop) technique, and sensate focus exercises. The squeeze and stop–start techniques are used mainly to treat premature ejaculation, which is the most common male sexual dysfunction (30% of men). Patients concentrate on arousal while the penis is stimulated, and then stop stimulation just before ejaculatory inevitability. With the stop–start ("pause") technique, control quietly returns. With the squeeze technique, the partner squeezes the penis below the corona until the erection slumps, after which stimulation is resumed. Sensate focusing teaches partners to enjoy sexual activity that is not intended to lead to intercourse. Instead of emphasizing performance, sexual pleasure is separated from intercourse. Pharmaceutical interventions that may delay ejaculation include applying anesthetic to the coronal ridge or prescribing daily paroxetine.

Fifty years ago using what were then the latest sex therapies, Masters and Johnson (1970) reported an 80% overall success rate, with 5% of patients having a recurrence of symptoms within a 5-year period. In general, male dysfunctions respond best, with success rates highest for (in declining efficacy) premature ejaculation, retarded ejaculation, secondary impotence, and primary impotence. Treatment is reputed to reverse vaginismus virtually

100% of the time, with less success for generalized unresponsiveness and inhibited orgasm among women. Anal stimulation may improve anorgasmia. Medications that have been reported to enhance responsiveness include testosterone (in men), yohimbine (α_2-presynaptic antagonist), L-arginine (nitrous oxide precursor), and cyproheptadine (serotonin antagonist).

Primary erectile dysfunction (primary impotence) affects less than 1% of men under 35 years. *Primary* refers to the fact that these men have never been able to attain or maintain an erection. On the other hand, secondary erectile dysfunction (i.e., having lost the ability) is common and occurs in about 40% of males over 60 years old. A physical cause for impotency is present 75% of the time. If the patient is able to have erections in sleep or with masturbation, then the cause is psychological. The medical workup for this condition may include the measurement of nocturnal penile tumescence, penile blood pressure with penile plethysmography or Doppler flow meter, pudendal nerve latency time, dorsal nerve somatosensory evoked potentials, and blood parameters (glucose, thyroid, liver function, prolactin, testosterone, luteinizing and follicle stimulating hormones). Correcting hormonal deficiencies and other medical conditions is the first treatment step. A vacuum pump with ring, penile implants (inflatable or bendable rods) are mechanical interventions. Prostaglandins (PGE1), particularly alprostadil, relax smooth muscle and can be delivered by intercavernosal injections (Caverject) or more comfortably by gel (Topiglan) or urethral suppository (MUSE). Phosphodiesterase (PDE5) inhibitors amplify the natural effects of nitrous oxide in relaxing smooth muscle and increasing penile blood flow. These medications include sildenafil (Viagra), vardenafil (Levitra), and tadalafil (Cialis), which are taken orally and have half-lives ranging from a couple hours to about 3 days, respectively. Because they potentiate nitrates, these medication may cause severe hypotension in those already taking nitroglycerin or related medications.

PARAPHILIAS

Derived from the Greek meaning "along side of" and "love," a paraphilia is the involuntary and repeated need for unusual or bizarre imagery, acts, or objects to induce sexual excitement. Paraphilias involve either (1) inanimate objects, (2) suffering or humiliation, or (3) sexual activity with nonconsenting partners. To qualify as a disorder, the patient's sexually arousing imagery, sexual urges, or actions must be intense and recurrent over a period of at least

6 months. Individuals with paraphilias are rarely self-referred and paraphiliac disorders are rarely diagnosed, but judging from the sales of pornographic magazines, movies, and paraphernalia, they may be more common in the community than we know. They almost always occur in men. Although some people enjoy their paraphilias, others feel guilty, develop psychosexual dysfunctions, or end up behind bars. The common paraphilias are described in Table 22-3.

The diagnoses of pedophilia, exhibitionism, voyeurism, and frotteurism are made if the individual has *either* acted on these urges *or* experiences marked distress or interpersonal difficulties associated with the urges. The diagnosis of sexual sadism is made if the individual has acted on the urge *or* experiences marked distress or interpersonal difficulties associated with the

---

TABLE 22-3
The Paraphilias

Any one of these must occur over a period of several months and involve recurrent, intense sexual urges and sexually arousing fantasies or behaviors regarding the paraphilia. They should be diagnosed only if the paraphilia is the most important source of sexual stimulation or essential for satisfactory sexual response.

Sexual fantasies are common, but they do not amount to a disorder unless they lead to rituals that are so compelling and unacceptable as to interfere with sexual intercourse and cause the individual or others distress.

Exhibitionism involves achieving sexual excitement through a recurrent or persistent tendency to expose the genitalia to strangers (usually of the opposite sex) or to people in public places, without inviting or intending closer contact. The act is commonly followed by masturbation. Exhibitionism is almost entirely limited to heterosexual males who expose to females, adult or adolescent, usually confronting them from a safe distance in some public place. Most exhibitionists find their urges difficult to control and ego-alien. If the witness appears shocked, frightened, or impressed, the exhibitionist's excitement is often heightened.

Fetishism involves reliance on some non-living object as a stimulus for sexual arousal and sexual gratification. Many fetishes are extensions of the human body, such as articles of clothing or footware. Other common examples are characterized by some particular texture such as rubber, plastic, or leather. Fetish objects vary in their importance to the individual: in some cases they serve simply to enhance sexual excitement achieved in ordinary ways (e.g., having the partner wear a particular garment). Fetishism is limited almost exclusively to males.

Transvestic fetishism occurs when wearing clothes of the opposite sex principally to obtain sexual excitement. The disorder is to be distinguished from simple fetishism in that the fetishistic articles of clothing are not only worn, but worn also to create the appearance of a person of the opposite sex. Usually more than one article is worn and often a complete outfit, plus wig and makeup.

Pedophilia involves fantasizing about or engaging in sexual activity with a prepubescent child or one of early pubertal age. Some pedophiles are attracted only to girls, others only to boys, and

TABLE 22-3
Continued

others again are interested in both sexes. Often sexually abused as children, these patients usually turn on to pedophilia in midlife during a setback in marriage or in another close relationship. Most people with pedophilia are males with low self-esteem, who enjoy a sense of mastery and safety when fondling children. Pedophilia is usually a chronic disorder with frequent relapses and is resistant to therapy. Pedophilia is rarely identified in women. A persistent or predominant tendency is required for the diagnosis.

Sadomasochism is a preference for sexual activity that involves bondage or the infliction of pain or humiliation. If the individual prefers to be the recipient of such stimulation this is called *masochism*; if the individual is the provider, *sadism*. Often an individual obtains sexual excitement from both sadistic and masochistic activities. Mild degrees of sadomasochistic stimulation are commonly used to enhance otherwise normal sexual activity. This category should be used only if sadomasochistic activity is the most important source of stimulation or necessary for sexual gratification. Sexual sadism is sometimes difficult to distinguish from cruelty in sexual situations or anger unrelated to eroticism. Where violence is necessary for erotic arousal, the diagnosis can be clearly established. Masochistic fantasies often arise during childhood, but are not acted on until early adulthood. Some men engage in sexual masochism, but the ratio is 20 females to each male. Unintentional deaths have resulted from sexual masochism. Sexual sadism may involve a consenting or nonconsenting partner. Although sexual sadism may lead to murder and rape, few rapists are sexual sadists.

Voyeurism involves a recurrent or persistent tendency to look at people engaging in sexual or intimate behavior such as undressing. This usually leads to sexual excitement and masturbation and is carried out without the observed people being aware. Most "Peeping Toms" are more erotically stimulated by watching than by other sexual acts. They typically don't wish to have sex with the observed and would be frightened if it were offered. They prefer to masturbate while observing or to fantasize about the observed woman feeling helpless, mortified, or terrorized if she knew "Tom" was observing her.

Frotteurism involves touching and rubbing against a nonconsenting person. It is the touching, not the coercive nature of the act, that is sexually exciting.

Other Paraphilias is a residual category for sexual preferences not meeting criteria for any of the specific paraphilias. Erotic practices are too diverse and many too rare or idiosyncratic to justify a separate disorder for each. Examples include *coprophilia* (feces); *klismaphilia* (enemas); *mysophilia* (lying in filth); *partialism* (exclusive focus on part of the body, such as the feet); *zoophilia* (sexual activity with animals); *necrophilia* (sexual activity with a corpse); *telephone scatologia* (making lewd phone calls); *urophilia* (urinating on others or observing someone urinating), and *asphyxiophilia* (inducing oxygen deprivation through temporary strangulation by a rope around the neck or a plastic bag over the head in order to induce sexual arousal or to enhance sexual excitement and orgasm).

Note: Adapted from *ICD-10* (pp. 170–172) and *DSM-5* (pp. 685–705)

sadistic urges. The diagnoses of fetishism, transvestic fetishism, and sexual masochism are made only if the sexual fantasies, urges, or behavior result in clinically significant distress or impairment in social, occupational, or other important areas of living.

Persons with transvestic fetishism are generally heterosexual men (or less commonly, bisexual men) who derive erotic pleasure from dressing as women. Usually beginning during childhood or adolescence, these individuals first experiment with cross-dressing in private (typically becoming paired with masturbation at some point) and then increase the frequency and number of worn items. They may join a transvestite subculture wherein they experience acceptance and encouragement for public cross-dressing. In time, cross-dressing may no longer provide erotic stimulation, but they continue it because it relieves anxiety and/or depression. When not cross-dressing, transvestites look like regular guys. Although heterosexual, their sexual experiences are typically limited, involving few heterosexual encounters and may include occasional homosexual activity. Some people with transvestic fetishism claim that during childhood, they were punished and humiliated by mothers or sisters who forced them to put on female attire. Others begin with masturbating to images or fantasies of the scantily clad female body to finding the female garments themselves becoming sexually arousing.

In pedophilia, the erotic stimulus is a prepubescent child (generally age 13 or younger), of either the same or opposite sex. The offender must be at least 16 years old and at least 5 years older than the child. A late adolescent involved in an ongoing sexual relationship with a 12- or 13-year-old does not count. Pedophiles are almost always male. Heterosexual pedophilia is twice as common as homosexual pedophilia, even though heterosexual men outnumber homosexual men approximately 35:1 in the general population. Thus, on a percentage basis, disproportionately higher rates of pedophiliac behavior occur in homosexual men compared to heterosexual men. Certain subtypes of pedophilia should be noted: (1) Is the *sexual attraction to males, females, or both*? (2) Is the pedophilia *limited to incest*? (3) Is the person *exclusively* or *nonexclusively* attracted to children?

For the most part, the person with pedophilia engages in genital petting or oral–genital contact. Physical aggression against children in such situations is relatively rare, although because of the publicity when this happens, the public has come to associate pedophilia with murderous violence. Probably between a quarter and a third of the sexual offenses committed by adults against children are committed by true pedophiles. Most sexual offenses against children are committed by individuals with mental retardation, psy-

chosis, neurological disease, sociopathy, or (occasionally) males who impulsively approach children while under the influence of drugs or alcohol.

In sharp contrast with common belief, most men with pedophilia are
mild-mannered and innocuous appearing, with profound feelings of masculine inadequacy. They are often adults who are unable to relate comfortably
to the opposite sex and have turned to children instead. Many were sexually
abused as children; as teenagers, they were frequently shy and awkward. In
their relations with mature women, they typically suffer from inadequate
sexual performance or impotence, all of which reinforces their profound
sense of masculine inadequacy and impaired self-esteem.

Individuals with pedophilia are notorious rationalizers, using excuses
such as "It has educational value for the child," "The child gets rewarded
with sexual pleasure," or "The child was sexually provocative and wanted it."
Methods of preventing the child's disclosure range from direct threats to
being very generous and attentive to the child's needs.

Not all paraphilias are impulsive. Exhibitionism usually is, but pedophilia
is often planned. Arrest for paraphilia typically occurs after the average pedo-
phile has committed 30 or more molestations and after the exhibitionist has
committed hundreds of exposures.

Paraphiliac-related problems can cause much distress, break up marriages, and end jobs. They are sometimes referred to as "sexual addictions,"
because like "real" addictions, these behaviors have a compulsive, repeti-
tious, and ultimately unsatisfying quality.

Men with paraphilia in stable relationships often experience paraphiliac
fantasies that intrude during sexual activity with their partners, and paraphiliac behaviors typically replace most normal sexual behaviors. They usually do not specialize in one paraphilia, but rather have two or more during
a lifetime. If they have another Axis I diagnosis, it is usually dysthymic disorder (but with more libido, not less) or substance abuse (most commonly, the
typical disinhibitor—alcohol).

> A 63-year-old man initially sought treatment, referred by his physician, for
> help coping with the impact of a medical condition on his physical activity
> level. In addition, he had been treated for years with medication for a bipolar
> mood disorder. Within a few sessions, he began talking about dissatisfaction
> in his relationship with his wife. Tearfully, he described his loneliness, stat-
> ing that his wife had not kissed him on the lips in years. She had reportedly
> started rejecting him sexually long ago, no longer willing to wear the lingerie
> he bought for her. Early in the relationship, she had complied, to his delight.
> The client explained his desire for his wife to dress "ultrafem" like the women

and men he frequently viewed on Internet sites. He was especially aroused sexually by seeing men dressed as women in "ultrafem." Without this visual stimulation, he is impotent. More recently, even hugs and hand-holding have ceased. The client stated that he longs and "begs" for physical affection from his wife. His wife was invited to counseling, but refused. The couple had attended marital counseling once previously, but did not find it to be helpful. Currently, the client masturbates to completion while on the Internet. He hides this almost-nightly behavior from his wife, who has been sleeping in a separate bedroom for years. Again, this case illustrates the multidimensional impact that a paraphilia can have on the individual, on their marital relationship, and on their sexual behavior pattern.

Management and Treatment

A good way to assess sexual functioning is to ask (without apologies or embarrassment), *"What is the total number of behaviors in a week that culminate in orgasm?"* Kinsey referred to this number as the "total sexual outlet." Only 5% of men have an outlet of seven or greater, whereas a majority of men with paraphiliac disorder have persistent hypersexual desire and tie or exceed this number. A good way to find out what abnormal and normal sexual behaviors are occurring is to ask, *"What are the different ways that you become aroused to the point of orgasm?"* Honest answers to this question will reveal paraphilias and paraphiliac-related behavior problems such as promiscuity, dependence on pornography, and compulsive masturbation.

Few individuals with paraphilia seek treatment, and if they do, it's usually to extricate themselves from secondary legal or marital difficulties. Many males with paraphiliac disorder are shy or immature and have difficulty establishing mature heterosexual relations. For them, the paraphilia becomes the main sexual outlet. Therapy attempts to (1) diminish sexual arousal in response to the paraphilia, (2) increase normal heterosexual arousal, (3) teach appropriate assertiveness and social skills (since many of these patients have trouble simply talking to the opposite sex), (4) provide sex education, (5) treat psychosexual dysfunctions, (6) modify distorted thinking and rationalizations with cognitive therapies, and (7) prevent relapse. Also, 12-step programs (modeled on Alcoholics Anonymous), which combine group support, cognitive restructuring, and spiritual resources, are offered for persons with paraphilias.

Older behavior therapy methods paired shock or noxious odors with pictures or fantasies of the arousing stimuli. More recently imaginal covert sensitization techniques coupled with deliberate fantasizing only about heterosexual activity during masturbation, can help reduce the power of the paraphilia. Cognitive-behavioral treatments focus on relapse prevention by identifying high-risk thoughts, feelings, and situations. If possible, the patient tries to avoid these. When avoidance isn't possible, cognitive restructuring strategies are implemented to address the faulty thinking used to justify the problematic behaviors.

Pharmacological approaches include drugs that reduce libido, such as medroxyprogesterone acetate at 100–400 mg each day (long-acting Depo-Provera at 200–400 mg is injected into muscle every 7–10 days) or luprolide (a luteinizing hormone releasing hormone agonist) at 7.5 mg intramuscular every month. Triptorelin, another gonadotropin releasing hormone analog, is now available in the United States. These medications are usually reserved for men who have exhibited violent or illegal paraphilic behaviors and are essentially forms of "chemical castration" by lowering testosterone levels. Naltrexone, an opiate receptor blocker, has been prescribed by some clinicians in an attempt to interfere with the biological reinforcement (reward) of the paraphilia. High doses of SSRIs (e.g., 40–80 mg fluoxetine) have been reported to decrease paraphilic fantasies, aberrant sexual urges, and compulsions while sparing conventional sexual behaviors (Kafka, 1993). The total number of sexual outlets also decreases from hypersexual to normal levels.

GENDER IDENTITY DISORDER (GENDER DYSPHORIA)

Gender identity disorder (also called *gender dysphoria*) involves a profound disturbance in a person's sense of being a male or a female in concordance with his or her sexual anatomy—in other words, a conflict between a person's anatomical sex and his or her gender identity. A person with a gender identity disorder has both (1) intense and persistent cross-gender identification, and (2) a persistent discomfort with one's sexual anatomy or its associated gender role. This class of disorders can be diagnosed in childhood, adolescence, or adulthood. Formerly called "transsexualism" in adult cases, gender identity disorder is such a persistent feeling of severe discomfort with one's own anatomical sex, strong wish to be rid of one's genitals, and wish to live as the opposite sex, that anatomical males with the condition often say, "I'm a woman trapped in a man's body," and anatomical females with the condition similarly complain, "I'm a man trapped in a woman's body."

Table 22-4 presents diagnostic criteria for gender dysphoria in children. The adolescent and adult criteria naturally focus more on secondary sex characteristics, identifying with feelings and reactions of the opposite gen-

TABLE 22-4
Diagnostic Criteria for Childhood Gender Identity Disorder (Gender Dysphoria)

A. An **intense and persistent cross-gender identification** as manifested by the following (*DSM-5 specifies a marked incongruence between expressed and assigned gender that requires at least six of the following*):

1. the pervasive and persistent desire to be (or insistence that he or she is of) the opposite gender to that assigned or a repeatedly stated desire to be, or insistence that he or she is, another gender

2. an intense rejection of the attire of the assigned gender and persistent preoccupation with the dress of the opposite gender

3. an intense rejection of the attributes and behavior (roles) of the assigned gender

4. a very strong desire to participate with the games, toys, and pastimes stereotypically of the other gender

5. preferred playmates are of the opposite gender

6. an intense rejection of participation with the games, toys, and pastimes stereotypically of the same gender

7. repudiation of the anatomical structures specific to their own gender

8. a strong desire for the sexual anatomy of the other gender

In adolescents and adults, the disturbance is manifested by symptoms such as a stated desire to be the other sex, frequent passing as the other sex, desire to live or be treated as the other sex, or the conviction that one has the typical feelings and reactions of the other sex.

B. **Persistent and intense distress** about one's assigned gender **or significant impairment** in personal, family, social, educational, occupational, or other important areas of functioning.

Note: Adapted from *ICD-10* (pp. 168–170) and *DSM-5* (pp. 452–459)

der, and a strong desire to dress, behave, and be treated as the other gender. In all ages, the strong desire to be the other gender must be present to reduce the possibility of overdiagnosing individuals with extreme gender-variant behavior. Gender identity disorder is rare, with an estimated prevalence among men of 1 in 25,000; among women, 1 in 100,000.

To make the diagnosis of gender dysphoria, the intrapsychic gender conflict must not be the product of psychosis. With a psychotic delusion, an individual may truly *believe* he or she is a member of the other sex, but an individual with a gender identity disorder strongly *feels* like a member of the other sex rather than believing it is factually true. Perhaps 30% of individuals with gender dysphoria have an anxiety disorder. About 10% have a co-occurring autistic spectrum disorder. This association may help explain the propensity for obsessions and restricted interests in many who suffer from gender identity disorder. Those individuals with congenital sexual anomalies, such as occurs in a hermaphrodite who has both testicular and ovarian tissues (but ambiguous genitalia), may develop an accompanying gender dysphoria. Intersex conditions are most often caused by congenital adrenal hyperplasia or 5-alpha-reductase deficiency. Prenatal sex hormones (androgen exposure) may affect gender role behavior and sexual orientation in adulthood.

Those with gender identity disorder usually cross-dress to be in accord with their own gender identity. The patient's family members typically recollect that as a child *he* wanted to be a *she*, or vice versa, even as early as 3 years old. This cross-gender identification perplexes and frustrates the child as well as his or her family and peers. While growing up, these children often experience correction, criticism, ostracism, and/or marginalization by peers and some relatives. These interpersonal difficulties, combined with the person's own strong and disturbing intrapsychic cross-gender conflicts, result in high rates of oppositional and antisocial behavior, self-mutilation (frequently of the genitals), attempted suicide, and completed suicide. For example, a 24-year-old anatomical male with gender identity disorder was referred for psychotherapy after he had medically recovered from a self-inflicted injury in which he had deliberately sliced off his unwanted penis with a kitchen knife and flushed it down the toilet. This tragedy is extreme, but the intensity of the distress and unhappiness is unfortunately typical for individuals with gender dysphoria.

Males with *gender identity disorder* differ from males with *transvestic fetishism* in that the former have female gender identities and don't experience sexual excitement by wearing women's clothes, and the latter have male gender identities and do not wish to get rid of their genitals. (Don't confuse "trans-*vest*ism" with "trans*sexual*ism": The former changes his vest, the latter, his sex.) Interfering with cross-dressing frustrates males with transvestic fetishes and is a useful diagnostic clue for this differential diagnosis. However, if a man with transvestic fetishism develops a persistent discomfort with the male gender role or identity, the diagnosis is transvestic fetishism with gender dysphoria. When transvestic fetishism occurs in conjunction with the full criteria for gender identity disorder, both diagnoses are given. When *male homosexuals* dress as "drag queens" — for a goof, for masquerade, or for attracting another man — there's typically no erotic sensation in conjunction with the cross-dressing. Also, *female impersonators* are not typically sexually aroused by cross-dressing.

For prepubescent children, gender identity is fluid. At least 80% of childhood gender dysphoria resolves by adulthood. However, if present after puberty it rarely resolves. The child seems best served by achieving congruence with anatomy and gender identity. One approach to early treatment attempts to lessen the dysphoria by helping the child accept his biological sex through expanding the sex-role stereotypes to accommodate the child's preferences. Others have had success with specifically developed child behavior therapy.

> Eight-year-old Carl talked with a pronounced high feminine voice inflection, with his conversation dominated by topics such as cosmetics, female roles, dresses, female undergarments, and delivering babies—a pattern that began at the age of 4. His gestures were exaggerations of an effeminate swishy gait and arm movements. He preferred playing with girls and assumed a female role frequently. He preferred girls' toys, particularly dolls, avoiding boys' toys and games. Other boys teased him and called him "sissy" and "queer." Fearing getting hurt, he repeatedly feigned illnesses and injuries to avoid playing with other boys. He repeatedly referred to himself with a girl's name, and even called himself a "sissy" and "fag." On the school playground, the other boys fought over who "had to take Carl" on their team.
>
> Carl's mother sought psychological treatment for him. Carl was behaviorally treated in the clinic, at home, and at school. His mother was trained to administer a token economy program in the home, and his schoolteacher was taught to apply a response–cost procedure in the classroom. As a result of treatment, Carl's gender role behaviors became normal compared to other boys, and he developed a normal male identity. But he still retained his negative reputation among his peers. So his mother and therapist arranged for him to be transferred to a different school; at the new school, Carl was elected captain of the sports team with the opportunity to pick other boys for his team. This was a defining moment for Carl, solidly confirming his male identity. On follow-up in his adolescence, Carl was not experiencing any gender dysphoria (Rekers et al., 1990).

For those with persistence of gender identity disorder into adulthood, another approach encourages a transition to the cross-gender role. As they try to live as if they belong to the opposite sex, many successfully hide their gender from co-workers and friends. Sexual intimacy is restricted and a majority of transsexuals don't marry. Because they experience themselves as members of the opposite sex, they prefer normal heterosexual partners of the same biological sex, but they do not view themselves as "homosexual" because of their cross-gender identity. Although not altering the transsexual's cross-gender identification, psychotherapy can help alleviate emotional problems arising from the transsexualism.

Because there are no randomized controlled trials addressing efficacy of treatment, it is not possible to endorse any one intervention for reducing gender discordance. The following treatment principles are proposed according to the best evidence (Kilgus, 2014).

1. Achieving greater gender flexibility is a major treatment goal and the clinician should offer education and resources toward that end.
2. It follows that psychotherapy would initially explore assisting the individual with establishing gender identity that is congruent with biological and anatomical sex.
3. Especially early in development, one should avoid definitive labels on a person's cross-gender identity because it is still evolving.
4. There should be careful assessment and treatment of any co-occurring psychiatric diagnoses!
5. Ongoing support should be provided for the youth and the parents through the therapeutic treatment relationship.
6. Sex reassignment surgery (also referred to as normalizing or gender-conforming procedures) is controversial and typically follows three phases: diagnostic phase, real-life experience as the other gender with prescribed hormones, and surgery to change the genitals and other sex characteristics.

A majority of adults with cross-gender identity express the strong desire to change their sex permanently. In the United States, two to eight times more men than women seek surgical sex reassignment. To qualify for a surgical sex transformation, surgeons often require that patients live as the opposite sex for at least 2 years, during which time they should demonstrate minimally adequate social and occupational functioning, be able to sustain enduring friendships, and be free of major psychopathology. However, some individuals with gender identity disorder seek surgery in foreign countries at a lower cost, where psychiatric evaluations are rare. Surgical procedures are accompanied by prescriptions for estrogen or testosterone to induce the secondary sex characteristics of the other sex. The surgical transformation is more successful for males than females. The man's genitals are amputated, an artificial vagina is constructed from existing fascial planes, and the urethra is moved to feminine location. Bladder infections are the most common postoperative physical complication. Most individuals with cross-gender identities do not regret having the surgery although many sexual, personal, and occupational problems persist after sex reassignment. In fact, psychological, relational, and vocational adjustment of individuals with gender identity disorder who obtain sex reassignment surgery are not significantly different from those who do not, and some individuals regret the irreversible surgery. In terms of a cost–benefit analysis, surgical sex reassignment is difficult to justify. However, many adults with gender identity disorder continue to work for years to save up money to pay for this surgery (because it is not typically covered by health insurance) for the gender satisfactions they anticipate.

This chapter began with the observation that sex plays a uniquely profound role in people's lives, influencing their thoughts, their emotions, their social relationships, and their ability to express love. Because sexual maladjustment can have such a pervasive, troublesome impact on people's lives, patients can be especially appreciative of mental health care professionals who can accurately diagnose their sexual disorder, explain the disorder to them in lay terms, answer their pressing questions, and then either skillfully provide empirically validated treatment or refer them to another professional who has the specialized clinical skills to provide this care.

References

American Psychiatric Association. (2013). *Diagnostic and statistical manual of mental disorders* (5th ed.). Arlington, VA: American Psychiatric Association.

Barlow, D.H., Reynolds, E.J., & Agras, W.S. (1973). Gender identity change in a transsexual. *Archives of General Psychiatry, 28,* 569–576.

Kafka, M.P. (1993). Update on paraphilias and paraphilia-related disorders. *Currents in Affective Illness, 12,* 5–13.

Kaplan, H.S. (1974). *The new sex therapy.* New York: Brunner/Mazel.

Kinsey, A., Pomeroy, W., & Martin, C. (1948). *Sexual behavior in the human male.* Philadelphia: Saunders.

Kinsey, A., Pomeroy, W., Martin, C., & Gebhard, P. (1953). *Sexual behavior in the human female.* Philadelphia: Saunders.

Masters, W.H., & Johnson, V.E. (1970). *Human sexual inadequacy.* Boston: Little, Brown.

Kilgus, M.D. (2014) Dysphoria about gender. In M.D. Kilgus and W.S. Rea (Eds.), *Essential psychopathology casebook* (pp. 367–399). New York: Norton.

Rekers, G.A., Kilgus, M.D., & Rosen, A.C. (1990). Long-term effects of treatment for childhood gender disturbance. *Journal of Psychology and Human Sexuality, 3*(2), 121–153.

Rekers, G.A. (1995). *Handbook of child and adolescent sexual problems.* New York: Lexington Books.

World Health Organization. (2007). International statistical classification of diseases and related health problems (10th ed.). Available at http://www.who.int/classifications/apps/icd/icd10online/.

World Health Organization. (1992). *The ICD–10 classification of mental and behavioural disorders: Clinical descriptions and diagnostic guidelines.* WHO.

23

Disruptive and Impulse Control Disorders

CONDUCT DISORDER

Clinical Presentation

Kids with conduct disorder violate norms and the rights of others. Conduct disorder is usually a boy's disorder, with about 9% of boys and 2% of girls having it. They're always in trouble, be it with parents, peers, or teachers. They often try to place blame on others. Lying and cheating are typical; some children are called "pathological liars." Physical aggression and cruelty to other people or to animals is common with these children, or they may destroy others' property (e.g., by setting fires). Stealing is common and can range from "borrowing" other people's possessions to shoplifting, forgery, and breaking into someone's house. These children are often truant from school and may run away from home. Drug use is common, especially use of tobacco, liquor, or street drugs. They begin sex at an early age and often have multiple partners. Self-esteem is low, despite the image of "toughness" presented to the public. Poor frustration tolerance, irritability, temper outbursts, and recklessness are common. Table 23-1 lists diagnostic criteria for conduct disorder.

Differential Diagnosis

Conduct disorder continues over 6 months or more, so isolated acts of anti-social behavior do not count. Children with *oppositional defiant disorders* may look like children with a conduct disorder with their temper outbursts, curfew violations, running away, playing hooky, being spiteful and vindictive, and generally showing disobedience and opposition to authority figures.

TABLE 23-1
Diagnostic Criteria for Conduct Disorder

A. A repetitive and **persistent pattern of dissocial, aggressive, or defiant conduct** with duration of at least 6 months. These are **major violations of age-appropriate social expectations** so it is necessary to take into account the child's developmental level.

The following behaviors are more severe than ordinary childish mischief or adolescent rebelliousness:

1. bullying
2. excessive levels of fighting
3. unusually frequent and severe temper tantrums, uncontrolled rages
4. cruelty to people
5. cruelty to animals
6. extortion or violent assault (in older children)
7. defiant provocative behavior
8. fire-setting
9. severe destructiveness to property
10. repeated lying
11. excessive levels of disobedience, rudeness, uncooperativeness, and resistance to authority
12. stealing
13. running away from home
14. truancy from school
15. cruelty to animals and other children

DSM-5 requires at least three example behaviors and adds to the above list the use of a weapon that can cause serious physical harm to others, forcing someone into sexual activity, often staying out at night despite parental prohibitions, and beginning before 13 years of age.

Isolated dissocial or criminal acts are not in themselves grounds for the diagnosis, which implies an enduring pattern of behavior.

The disorder is usually pervasive across situations but it may be most evident at school.

B. The behaviors result in **significant impairment** in personal, family, social, educational, occupational, or other important area of functioning.

C. The disturbance is **not better explained by another medical disorder including** schizophrenia, mania, autistic spectrum disorder, attention-deficit hyperactivity disorder, and depression.

Specify whether **unsocialized**: the lack of effective integration into a peer group constitutes the key distinction and has precedence over all other differentiations. Disturbed peer relationships are evidenced chiefly by isolation from and/or rejection by or unpopularity with other children, and by a lack of close friends or of lasting empathic, reciprocal relationships with others in the same age group. Relationships with adults tend to be marked by discord, hostility, and resentment. Good relationships with adults can occur (although usually they lack a close, confiding quality) and, if present, do not rule out the diagnosis. Offending is characteristically (but not necessarily) solitary. The nature of the offense is less important in making the diagnosis than the quality of personal relationships. There is a lack of remorse, guilty feelings, empathy, effort in performance, or emotional expression. In general, a marked lack of concern for the well-being and feelings of other people is demonstrated.

Note: Adapted from *ICD-10* (pp. 209–210) and *DSM-5* (pp. 469–475)

However, they don't violate the basic rights of others or major age-appropriate societal norms or rules, as do kids with conduct disorders. Adolescents with *major depression* can suddenly engage in antisocial behavior, but they will also meet major depression criteria and, when asked why they behaved so badly, they will say for social approval or to distract themselves from pain. Kids with conduct disorders will answer "because it's fun" or "I don't know, I just felt like doing it." Children with *ADHD* or *specific developmental disorders* are more likely to develop conduct disorder. Each of these diagnoses should be given, if present.

Etiology and Pathogenesis

Some children have cognitive predispositions that lead them to conduct disorder. Despite normal IQs, they often are 2 or more years behind on academic (particularly verbal) skills and have difficulties with abstract reasoning (in particular, understanding complex directions and social interactions). However, they often have excellent manipulative, problem-solving abilities. It is not a coincidence that many a delinquent has failed reading and writing in school but can work magic on cars or in picking a lock. Parents who decide that their child is inherently bad can send him down the road to jail; those who have the patience to view this child as having academic and educational problems can sometimes prevent a deteriorating course by working with the child and his school to help him overcome these problems.

Other risk factors for conduct disorder include family history of antisocial personality disorder or substance dependence; sexual, physical, or emotional abuse; a learning disorder that makes school an ordeal (especially reading problems); parenting issues such as a young mother, large family, inadequate supervision, inconsistent disciplining, or neglect; and/or an immediate environment that offers more temptations to get into trouble. These issues are discussed in more depth in Chapter 24 under antisocial personality disorder.

Clinical Course

Onset is typically prepubertal for the "unsocialized (solitary aggressive)" type. The group or gang of delinquents often starts at puberty. They usually show loyalty to the gang's members and norms but to no one else. Postpubertal onset is more typical of females who meet diagnostic criteria. Conduct disorder is the forerunner of adult antisocial personality disorder. Fortunately, only about half of all children with conduct disorder go on to develop antisocial personality disorder. Those with milder forms, a later start, or simple peer-pleasing motives are less likely to become tomorrow's criminals.

Management and Treatment

Although conduct disorder is often difficult to treat, one intensive intervention, multisystemic therapy (MST), provides some evidence for effective treatment. The *multisystemic* part of the name refers to the capacity of the intervention to simultaneously address multiple risk factors for identified youths. Any coexisting problems such as ADHD, major depression, drug abuse, or learning problems should be addressed initially.

> MST is a coordinated effort to provide efficacious and evidence-based mental-health services throughout the continuum of care. Important principles include the therapist's assuming responsibility for the identified patient across the continuum of care, from residential facilities to acute hospitalization to therapeutic foster care and intensive home-based services, with the latter being the preferred venue. MST therapists work in teams of two to four clinicians and a supervisor. MST emphasizes accountability of clinicians to their supervisors, expert consultants, and patients. Therapists are available at times convenient for the patient, rather than the other way around. The typical duration of treatment is 3–5 months but may continue for as long as necessary to reach desired goals. Caseloads do not exceed six families and are usually three or four. MST is labor intensive, for example, requiring daily supervision during crisis stabilization.

Medications for aggression, hyperarousal, and behavioral dyscontrol, including lithium, anticonvulsants (e.g., carbamazepine), antipsychotics (e.g., risperidone), clonidine, hydroxyzine, and propranolol, are sometimes helpful adjuncts to treatment. Receiving tutoring for developmental problems may make it easier for these children to progress in school. If possible, children are removed from significantly abusive home environments. The parent(s) are coached to develop realistic rules and consequences and consistently enforce them. Too often these children are rescued from the consequences of their actions or, alternately, beaten and ignored. Commands should be clear but not hostile. When noncompliant, enforcing "time-outs" or loss of privileges is appropriate; when compliant and prosocial, give social rewards such as time with a friend or going on a recreational outing with the family. Objects and money (all too easily stolen) should not be the reward, and the punishment should not be too harsh and overwhelming. For example, grounding a child for 2 months almost never works.

Children who are truly led astray by the boy (gang) "down the block" can be helped to develop prosocial rather than antisocial alternatives by, for example, participating in community programs that structure their time in positive ways. No parent will admit that his or her child is the one who led others astray, but in this situation, even though the prognosis is much grimmer, prosocial programs can be attempted. Variations on "tough love" approaches have been touted to have some success. Ideally, all of these treatments should be implemented as soon as the symptoms appear and not years later, after the symptoms have become ingrained behaviors.

OPPOSITIONAL DEFIANT DISORDER

This disorder is displayed by the quintessential angry child who is chronically argumentative, volatile, spiteful, and vindictive. Children with this disorder ignore or openly defy adults' requests and rules, finding ways to annoy others. Some are more passive—"I wasn't doing anything"—and others more active—"You deserved it, hate you." They blame others for their own mistakes or difficulties. In spite of all these behaviors, they do not have a conduct disorder because they don't seriously violate the basic rights of others. They don't steal, destroy property, force people to do things, or engage in cruel activities. Table 23-2 lists diagnostic criteria for oppositional defiant disorder.

These behaviors are almost invariably present in the home, but not always at school or with other adults or peers. In some kids, the behaviors are displayed outside the home from the beginning, whereas in others, the behaviors start at home and are later shown outside. Typically, these children reserve their awful behaviors for adults and peers they know well. Without a good history, children with this disorder are hard to diagnose because they often show little or no sign of the disorder in the clinician's office. When asked why they are so oppositional and defiant, they answer that they are merely responding to unreasonable rules, demands, and requests. Sometimes they are very convincing—so convincing that the naive clinician decides that the problem must be with the parents, and perhaps a "parentectomy" is in order.

Oppositional defiant disorder (ODD) typically begins by age 8 years and usually not later than early adolescence (Rey, 1993). With the right (or wrong, depending on how one looks at it) family environment, the child with a "difficult-child" temperament frequently goes on to become ODD (Maziade et al., 1990). Boys more often have this disorder before puberty, but after puberty the sex ratio is equal. These kids often have low self-esteem, mood lability, low frustration tolerance, and temper outbursts; they may abuse psychoactive substances, including tobacco, alcohol, and cannabis.

TABLE 23-2
Diagnostic Criteria for Oppositional Defiant Disorder

A. A pattern of **persistently negativistic, hostile, defiant, provocative, and disruptive behavior**, which is clearly outside the normal range of behavior for a child of the same age in the same sociocultural context, and which does not include the more serious violations of the rights of others as reflected in the aggressive and dissocial behavior specified in conduct disorder. Children with this disorder

1. possess low frustration tolerance and readily lose their temper
2. are easily annoyed by other people
3. have a tendency to be angry and resentful
4. initiate confrontations and generally exhibit excessive levels of rudeness, uncooperativeness, and resistance to authority
5. defy adult requests or rules
6. deliberately annoy other people
7. blame other people for their own mistakes or difficulties
8. *DSM-5 adds being spiteful or vindictive*

DSM-5 specifies that four of the above symptoms have been present for at least 6 months

Frequently, these behaviors are most evident in interactions with adults or peers whom the child knows well, and signs of the disorder may not be evident during a clinical interview.

B. The behaviors result in **significant distress for the individual or others and/or significantly disrupts** personal, family, social, educational, occupational, or other important area of functioning.

C. The disturbance is **not better explained by another medical disorder including conduct, substance use, psychotic, or mood disorders.**

   The definite presence of any behavior that violates the law and the basic rights of others, such as theft, cruelty, bullying, assault, and destructiveness would exclude the diagnosis.

Note: Adapted from *ICD-10* (pp. 212–213) and *DSM-5* (pp. 462–466)

Often ADHD is also present. Some kids with ODD later develop a conduct disorder, but most just maintain their ODD behaviors, no matter what happens.

The symptoms of ODD usually occur in *conduct disorder*, sometimes occur in the prodromal phase of *psychotic disorders*, and may also occur during the course of *mood disorders*. When this happens, these other disorders are diagnosed and not ODD.

Unfortunately, little is known about the cause or effective treatment of ODD, except that the outcome of treatment is usually poor. Sometimes family therapy can help. The therapist must work very hard at not assigning blame to the child or parents. *Parenting with Love and Logic* can help (Faye & Cline, 2006). Some clinicians have suggested the use of "paradoxical approaches." For example, the therapist assigns the child the task of having one temper tantrum next week, when asked to go to bed. In order to show defiance toward the therapist, the child may have to *not* have the temper tantrum next week. This approach should be used only by highly trained clinicians.

IMPULSE-CONTROL DISORDERS

On occasion, everyone is impulsive, many like to gamble, and some may follow fire engines to a fire. Almost everyone has impulsively eaten a sweet at some time. Unlike these normal behaviors, however, people with impulse control disorders experience three essential features: (1) They *can't resist* an impulse or drive to do something that they know will be harmful to themselves or others. (2) They experience increasing *tension* before performing (or while attempting to resist performing) the act. (Patients often describe this tension as "pressure," "restlessness," "anxiety," or "discomfort.") (3) They feel *relief*, gratification, or satisfaction when committing the act. Whereas acting on the impulse is momentarily ego-syntonic, later these individuals might feel guilt, self-reproach, or regret. They may act in haste and repent at leisure. However, repenting is not a necessary part of these diagnoses. Patients may or may not be aware of their impulses, and their deeds may or may not be premeditated. Patients with impulse control disorders may portray themselves as weak souls who readily cave into temptation or are easily overwhelmed by external forces. In a way, they're right, in that pathological impulsivity stems less from deliberate intent and more from an irresistible urge to discharge tension. People with impulse control disorders share two historical features: (1) onset in childhood, adolescence, or early adulthood (except for gambling, which doesn't start as early as childhood), and (2) associated psychopathology and family history—mood disorders and substance-use disorders are frequent (McElroy et al., 1992). The disorders considered here are grouped together because of the broad descriptive similarities.

Four defined disorders of impulse control are pathological gambling, kleptomania, pyromania, and intermittent explosive disorder. Impulse-related disturbances also occur in other mental illnesses such as attention-deficit/hyperactivity disorder, bulimia, mania, substance abuse, paraphilias, and also in borderline and antisocial personality disorders. This chapter highlights pathological gambling as a prototypic impulse disorder; the other specific impulse disorders are briefly described.

PATHOLOGICAL GAMBLING

Distinguishing "social" from pathological gambling is akin to differentiating the social drinker from the alcoholic. Social gambling, like social drinking, is done for pleasure, with friends, and feels optional. Pathological gambling, like alcoholism, is done because the person can't stop, excludes friends, and feels obligatory. In most respects, pathological gambling, like alcoholism, is an *addiction*. Unlike alcoholism and drug dependence it does not involve an exogenous substance, so gambling disorder will be presented here with the other disorders of habit and impulse control.

Clinical Presentation

People with gambling addictions feel unable to resist gambling, despite knowing that they'll lose and can't afford it. As one patient explained, "I've placed hundreds of bets, not caring whether I win or lose. Why? Because, I love the action. I'm drawn to the excitement. When I bet, I feel good and important."

Like other addictions, pathological gambling begets further gambling, which goes on to disrupt and damage every aspect of a person's life. Gambling debts take precedence over grocery bills. Forgery, fraud, arrests, tax evasion, excessive borrowing, stealing from friends, defaulting on loans, juggling financial obligations, lying, and forgetting who's owed what—they are all part of the disorder. Obligations to family and friends are supplanted by obligations to loan sharks and pawnbrokers. Even when these patients are not gambling, they're preoccupied with gambling. Everything they do is a result of gambling. They may sneak away from home to borrow money or to place a bet. Some people who gamble compulsively develop a perverse thrill or pride in the creativity of their reasons for why their debts aren't being paid and why their "big winnings" aren't paying off. Short of violence, anything will be done for money. As a "big game" approaches, these individuals reach an intolerable level of tension, which only the game relieves. Winning or losing has no effect on their gambling; they gamble as long as people will let them. Table 23-3 presents diagnostic criteria for pathological gambling; the problems listed under criterion A highlight the disorder's chief problems.

TABLE 23-3
Diagnostic Criteria for Gambling Disorder (Pathological Gambling)

A. The disorder consists of **frequent, repeated episodes of gambling which dominate the individual's life** to the detriment of social, occupational, material, and family values and commitments. Features of the disorder include:

1. persistently repeated gambling, which continues and often increases despite adverse consequences
2. an intense urge to gamble
3. difficult to control
4. preoccupation with ideas and images of the act of gambling and the circumstances that surround the act
5. preoccupations and urges often increase at times when life is stressful
6. unlikely to curb the habit when confronted with heavy losses (chasing losses)
7. lie or break the law to obtain money or evade payment of debts
8. put jobs and relationships at risk by acquiring large debts
9. rely on others to pay the debt

DSM-5 specifies at least four of the above over a 12-month period.

B. Pathological gambling **should be distinguished from excessive gambling by manic patients and gambling by sociopathic personalities**.

Note: Adapted from *ICD-10* (pp. 165–166) and *DSM-5* (pp. 585–589)

The person who gambles compulsively turns every nongambling situation into a gamble. Explains such a person, "When a normal person is driving with a quarter tank of gas on a highway and spots a sign saying that the next gas station is 50 miles away, she'll stop for gas. The gambler won't. He'll make a bet with himself that he can reach the next station without stopping for gas. This is a typical 'mind bet,' and when I'm not making a real bet, I'm making a mind bet."

Gambling, or talk of gambling, tends to dominate conversation; it's as if every social skill has atrophied, except for gambling or talking about gambling. Damon Runyon's characters might be fiction, but his descriptions of the gambler's mentality are not. For instance, a Runyon character says that whenever Feet Samuels—so-named because his feet are always at 90° angles—stands at a corner, gamblers will bet on which way Feet Samuels will go. In *Guys and Dolls*, Nathan Detroit calls Sky Masterson "the highest player of them all. . . . Another time he was sick and would not take penicillin because he bet his fever would go to 104°."

Generalizations surely, but people who gamble impulsively tend to be "big talkers" and "big spenders." Normally overconfident, self-centered, abrasive, energetic, and jovial, their moods reflect their earnings: On winning, they're temporarily elated; on losing, they're moody and anxious.

Epidemiology

With the growth of legalized gambling in the United States, the number of people who gamble pathologically has climbed from 4 million in 1976 to 12 million in 1990—which is about 2% of the population. A 2000 study of gambling in U.S. adolescents and young adults found a similar prevalence of 2.1%. A parallel pattern has occurred in Great Britain, suggesting that legalized gambling may promote pathological gambling. Nearly two-thirds of Americans patronize legalized gambling such as casinos, horse racing, dog racing, church bingo, and state-run lotteries. Their promoters don't call it "gambling" but run ads imploring listeners to "Get where the action is!"—a most telling phrase, given the gambler's thirst for excitement.

In a New York State study (Volberg & Steadman, 1988), 1.4% of the population was classified as pathological gamblers. Men outnumbered the women at least 2 to 1. A 2005 review of pathological gambling noted that the prevalence of pathological gambling in the United States is between 1 and 2%, but the prevalence is twice as high in areas located within a 50-mile radius of a casino. Gambling affects all social classes, though it is more common in those making under $25,000 a year than in those earning more. However, this yearly income figure may be a *result* of gambling and not a cause of it.

Differential Diagnosis

When a patient's chief complaint is *depression*, pathological gambling can be overlooked. If seeking treatment during the desperation or hopeless phases, the gambler may be so ashamed of his "moral weakness" that he avoids the topic, complaining instead of hopelessness, helplessness, suicidal thoughts, insomnia, and other depressive symptoms. Since clinicians rarely ask patients with depression if they gamble excessively, the disorder can elude diagnosis. Unlike people with *antisocial personality disorder*, most people who gamble pathologically have good work records prior to their serious gambling, and they steal solely to pay debts or to have money for gambling.

Pathological gambling may be confused with *manic* or *hypomanic episodes*, since (a) mania often leads to outrageous betting, (b) both conditions involve poor judgment and little foresight, and (c) euphoria usually follows a gam-

bler's winning streak. The presence of other manic behaviors, however, easily rules out pathological gambling. Pathological gambling is distinguished
from *social gambling*, which occurs between friends, limits potential losses,
and does not cause substantial harm.

Etiology and Pathogenesis

Little is known about the etiology of pathological gambling; a combination
of psychological and psychosocial factors is generally cited. The typical person who gambles impulsively comes from a family in which social gambling
was at least condoned, or in which a parent of the same sex was a compulsive
gambler or an alcoholic.

Several studies report that physiological arousal reinforces and maintains
pathological gambling. High-sensation seekers and extraverts may be particularly vulnerable. In general, the trait "sensation seeking" is correlated
with bigger bet size and higher heart rate in casino gamblers and also with
how extensive their gambling is. People who gamble pathologically have
higher levels of norepinephrine and dopamine than normals do during
gambling, suggesting they experience greater "reward" than do nonproblem
gamblers who show more modest increases in these neurotransmitters when
gambling (Meyer, 2004). In the past decade, newer, dopamine enhancing
treatments for Parkinson's disease have been associated with the untoward
side effect of inducing problem gambling, lending further support to the
idea that the behavior is mediated through specific neurotransmitter systems.

Other lines of research suggest that pathological gambling may belong to
the depressive spectrum disorders. People who gamble pathologically have
more first-degree relatives with mood and substance-use disorders (McElroy
et al., 1992).

Clinical Course and Complications

While still teenagers, future pathological gamblers bet socially. Their gambling usually becomes serious by early adulthood, often after some modest
winnings and during some stressful period.

Gamblers Anonymous (discussed later) describes four phases in the deterioration of people who gamble pathologically. First is the *winning phase*, in
which they gamble occasionally, fantasize about winning, escalate their bets,
and win big. Next comes the *losing phase*, in which they gamble alone, skip

work, lie, borrow heavily, don't pay debts, and return the next day to win back losses ("chasing"). Third is the *desperation phase,* during which they are filled with remorse and their reputation suffers: They become separated from family and friends, get fired, blame others, panic, and steal. Last is the *hopeless phase,* in which they feel utterly futile, may get arrested and divorced, may drink heavily and abuse drugs, and typically become depressed. On hitting "rock bottom," up to 20% contemplate or attempt suicide.

Pathological gambling impairs most aspects of the person's life: Lost jobs, broken marriages, imprisonment, financial ruin, and attempted suicide are common. While stressing the many similarities between pathological gambling and alcoholism, a "reformed" gambler aptly pointed out a big difference: "If you're an alcoholic with $1,000, you'll drink $50 worth of booze and fall asleep; when you awake, you've still got $950. If you're a druggie and shoot up $400 worth, you'll drift off and still awake with $600. But if you're a gambler, you'll blow all $1,000 and end up with *nothing!*"

Management and Treatment

Many people with gambling problems enter treatment simply to get relatives off their back; once things cool down, gambling resumes. If they remain in treatment, four attitudes frequently undermine their progress: (1) Lack of money is seen as *the* problem; (2) an instant or miraculous cure is expected; (3) life without gambling is inconceivable; and (4) repaying debts is desirable but impossible (Custer, 1979). Denying these attitudes during treatment, especially near the beginning, may raise doubts about the authenticity of the patient's commitment to change. Since these patients are often bright and have a gift of gab, place little stock in what they *say* and far more in what they *do.* Treatment should be judged on the duration of gambling-free intervals, on debts being paid, and on developing interests other than gambling.

The last goal, often overlooked, is crucial, since substitute excitements and pleasures must eventually replace gambling; hence, vocational counseling and recreational therapy may be invaluable adjuncts to therapy. Meeting periodically with relatives is also important, as much for the relatives as for the person with the gambling problem. Clinicians should remind themselves and the patient's loved ones that pathological gambling is a *chronic* disorder in which lapses are expected and do not necessarily mean that therapy is a bust.

If the patient is on trial for problems secondary to his or her gambling, such as tax evasion, the best sentence might involve an extended probation *contin-*

gent on the patient's participating fully in therapy, repaying all debts on schedule, not gambling, being employed regularly, and periodically showing financial accountability. Imprisonment is only useful when the person doesn't fulfill this program.

Founded in 1957, Gamblers Anonymous (GA) is modeled after Alcoholics Anonymous (AA), claims 12,000 members, and affiliates with Gam-Anon, which is similar to Alanon in that it is for relatives of gamblers. (Contact GA's National Service Office, P. O. Box 17173, Los Angeles, CA 90017, 213/386–8789. www. gamblersanonymous.org). Only 5–8% of people who gamble and join GA stop gambling, but if GA is combined with comprehensive care, half who complete the program refrain from gambling for a year, and a third do so for several years (Kellner, 1982). Given the similarities between gambling and alcoholism and between GA and AA, if a GA chapter isn't available, attending AA may be a good substitute.

KLEPTOMANIA

Kleptomania is the recurrent failure to resist impulses to steal objects that are not for immediate use or for economic gain. People with kleptomania typically have enough money to buy the objects, and once possessing them, they have no use for them; they are likely to give the objects away, return them, or forget them. Unlike other thieves or shoplifters, people with kleptomania experience mounting tension before stealing and a gratifying relief of tension afterward; they steal by themselves, spontaneously, and without compatriots. Because they steal to alleviate tension, when that tension becomes unbearable, they're more concerned with discharging anxiety than with taking precautions. Hence, people with kleptomania make lousy thieves: Their bounty isn't worth much, and they're frequently caught. Contrary to myth, people with kleptomania do *not* want to be caught: What they *do* want is the thrill of discharging that tension. Table 23-4 presents the criteria for kleptomania.

Kleptomania is more common among women, seems to wax and wane over time, and often decreases with age. Four percent of apprehended shoplifters are people with kleptomania. Because most patients aren't people with kleptomania, the best question to ask to make the diagnosis is "Why did you do it?" People with kleptomania will give their own version of the tension and relief cycle. People with *psychosis* will tell you things like "The CIA made me do it." People with *antisocial and conduct disorders* will say "I wanted it," unless they are *also malingerers* and have learned to give the "right" answers for kleptomania. Then you have to see what was being stolen—pencils, lipstick?—or what really counts—jewelry, money, or valuable

---

TABLE 23-4
Diagnostic Criteria for Kleptomania (Pathological Stealing)

A. **Repeated failure to resist impulses to steal objects that are not acquired for personal use or monetary gain**

   Although some effort at concealment is usually made, not all the opportunities for this are taken.

B. **Increasing sense of tension before** the act of stealing

C. A **sense of gratification during and immediately after** the act of stealing

   The individual may express anxiety, despondency, and guilt between episodes of stealing but this does not prevent repetition.

D. The theft is a **solitary act**, not carried out with an accomplice

E. The disturbance is **not better explained by another mental disorder** including depression, psychosis, sociopathic personality, conduct disorder, substance intoxication, neurodevelopment, or neurocognitive disorder.

Note: Adapted from *ICD-10* (pp. 167) and *DSM-5* (pp. 478–479)

---

electronics (*antisocial*). People with *mania* will say it was the fun thing to do and have all the other symptoms of mania. Other people without kleptomania may admit doing it out of anger or for revenge.

Kleptomania is associated with extraordinarily high rates of other psychiatric disorders. In one study using *DSM-III-R* lifetime diagnosis (McElroy, 1992), 100% had a mood disorder, 80% had at least one anxiety disorder, 60% had an eating disorder (most often bulimia), 50% had a substance disorder, 45% had obsessive–compulsive disorder, and 40% had some other impulse control disorder. Similarly high rates of these disorders were found in the patients' families. In a majority of cases, one of the other psychiatric disorders came first.

> Almost nothing is known about the specific treatment of kleptomania. However, treating the other disorders associated with it is essential. Bulimia and obsessive–compulsive disorders, and to some extent substance abuse, also share the tension–relief cycle, so approaches to this cycle, such as response prevention, alternative forms of tension release, and antidepressants (particularly the SSRIs) may be helpful.

PYROMANIA

Pyromania is the recurrent failure to resist setting fires, along with an intense fascination with igniting and watching them. Setting fires is gratifying because it discharges mounting tension. People with pyromania thrill at seeing flames leap up and destroy things; by definition, these individuals do not set fires for any other reason (e.g., greed, revenge, politics). They rarely feel remorse or regret, despite knowing that they've destroyed property, maimed victims, or even murdered. Even planning arson, which they do far in advance, brings pleasure. This planning feature makes pyromania different from the other impulse disorders. Table 23-5 lists diagnostic criteria for pyromania.

Case studies show that as children, most future pyromaniacs are fascinated by fires, fire engines, firefighters, and any firefighting equipment. They have pulled many a false alarm and relished the sight of firefighters rushing to the scene; orchestrating this whole to-do may afford children an enormous sense of power, control, and mastery, which they probably lack in other areas of life.

People with pyromania are drawn to any huge fire (which is the first place police look to nab a firesetter). Since most people with pyromania come to psychiatrists via the courts, the literature about them is skewed. They are often diagnosed with alcohol abuse (91%), mood disorder (95%, usually dysthymia), and intermittent explosive disorder (68%). Also associated with pyromania is a higher rate of borderline personality disorder, attention-deficit/hyperactivity disorder, and learning disabilities. In one study, impulsive firesetters were found to be low in serotonin metabolites (Virkkunen et al., 1989). Low serotonin has been correlated with increased aggression and impulsivity.

Pyromania is a rare disorder. Firesetters are men 90% of the time; females tend to set fires in their own homes and to experience marital discord and

---

TABLE 23-5
Diagnostic Criteria for Pyromania (Pathological Fire-Setting)

A. **Repeated fire-setting**

B. Reported feelings of **increasing tension before** the act of fire-setting

C. An **intense interest** in watching fires burn and a persistent preoccupation with subjects related to fire and burning

D. **Intense excitement immediately after** fire-setting

E. **Without any obvious motive** such as monetary gain, revenge, or political extremism

F. The disturbance is **not better explained by another mental disorder** including mania, psychosis, sociopathic personality, conduct disorder, substance intoxication, neurodevelopment, or cognitive disorder.

Note: Adapted from ICD-10 (pp. 166–167) and DSM-5 (pp. 476–477).

depression. Pyromania in children differs from *normal childhood fascination with fires*, in that the latter is less frequent, pernicious, and all-consuming. Although patients with *antisocial personality disorders* sometimes set fires, their reasons are not limited to being gratified by the fire. Deliberate sabotage, as "paid torches," political terrorism, and good old-fashioned revenge must be ruled out. Individuals with psychotic symptoms may set fires, but they do so in response to delusions or hallucinations. Unlike people with pyromania, patients with dementia may accidentally set fires, always without planning and without realizing the consequences of the act.

There are no controlled studies assessing treatment. Anecdotal reports indicate that most child pyromaniacs recover fully, whereas adults do not. With the majority having mildly low intelligence and ingrained impulsiveness, few people with pyromania benefit from insight-oriented psychotherapy. Behavior therapies might be more useful by substituting healthy gratifications, by improving social skills, or by applying aversive techniques. Perhaps the most useful intervention is to ensure that these individuals don't drink or use other substances that might further impair judgment and enhance impulsivity.

INTERMITTENT EXPLOSIVE DISORDER

This very rare disorder is characterized by infrequent discrete episodes of violence based on little or no provocation. The outbursts, which start and stop abruptly, usually last several minutes but may last for several hours. The person suddenly breaks windows, throws chairs, and so on. The "seizures" or "spells" may be immediately preceded by a rapid mood change, flushing, tachycardia, or altered sensorium (e.g., confusion, amnesia). Patients then describe an "irresistible impulse that comes over them" to smash everything in sight. Afterward, most assume responsibility for the act and express genuine remorse.

This disorder primarily affects men; age of onset may be in childhood to the early 20s. Individuals with intermittent explosive disorder may have childhood histories of attention-deficit/hyperactivity disorder, and may also have some mild neurological abnormalities.

In the past, people with this disorder have been labeled "explosive characters" and "epileptoid personalities" because their explosive rages may resemble seizures. Despite this, their EEGs are usually normal or have only nonspecific changes that cannot be attributed to a known medical disorder.

At times there may be historical evidence of delayed development (e.g., speech delay, coordination delay) in people who suffer from intermittent explosive disorder.

The "mean drunk" may seem explosive, but shows "intermittent" violence only when intoxicated. Intoxication with any psychoactive substance and any neurological condition (e.g., head trauma) must be ruled out as the cause of the violent episodes, before a diagnosis of intermittent explosive disorder is given. *All the disorders associated with increased violence and outbursts must be excluded to make sure they aren't the main source of the destructive behavior.* Keep in mind that many people with intermittent explosive disorder also have a personality disorder; separating out the two diagnoses is not an easy task. As with pyromania, people with intermittent explosive disorder have been found in some studies to have signs of altered serotonin metabolism.

There is no clearly effective treatment, although some patients have been helped by anticonvulsant medications (e.g., carbamazepine), beta-blockers (e.g., propranolol, metoprolol), lithium, antipsychotics, and anti-depressants. Benzodiazepines (e.g., diazepam, lorazepam, clonazepam) may worsen the condition by disinhibiting the individual. Group therapy is claimed to be more useful than individual therapy.

References

American Psychiatric Association. (2013). *Diagnostic and statistical manual of mental disorders*, 5th ed. Arlington, VA: American Psychiatric Association.

Custer, R.L. (1979). "An overview of compulsive gambling." Paper presented at South Oaks Hospital, Amityville, New York.

Dell'Osso, B., Altamura, A.C., Allen, A., Marazziti, D., & Hollander, E. (2006). Epidemiologic and clinical updates on impulse-control disorders: A critical review. *European Archives of Psychiatry and Clinical Neuroscience, 256*(8), 464–475.

Fay, J., & Cline, F. (2006). *Parenting with love and logic: Teaching children responsibility* (updated and expanded version). Colorado Springs, CO: NaviPress.

Kellner, R. (1982). Disorders of impulse control. In J.H. Greist, J.W. Jefferson, & R.L. Spitzer (Eds.), *Treatment of mental disorders* (pp. 398–418). New York: Oxford University Press.

McElroy, S.L., Hudson, J.I., Pope, H.G., & Keck, P.E. (1991). Kleptomania and associated psychopathology. *Psychological Medicine, 21*(1), 93–108.

McElroy, S.L., Hudson, J.L., Harrison, G.P., Jr., Keck, P.E., Jr., & Aizley, H.G. (1992). The *DSM-III-R* impulse control disorders not elsewhere classified: Clinical characteristics and relationship to other psychiatric disorders. *American Journal of Psychiatry, 149*, 318–327.

Meyer, G., et al. (2004). Neuroendocrine response to casino gambling in problem gamblers. *Psycho-neuroendocrinology, 29*(10), 1272–1280.

Petry, N.M. (2007). Gambling and substance use disorders: Current status and future directions. *American Journal of Addictions, 16*(1), 1–9.

Roy, A., Adinoff, B., Roehrich, L., Lamparski, D., Custer, R., Lorenz, V., et al. (1988). Pathological gambling. *Archives of General Psychiatry, 45*, 369–373.

Roy, A., DeJong, J., & Linnoila, M. (1989). Extraversion in pathological gamblers. *Archives of General Psychiatry, 46*, 679–681.

Stein, D.J., Christenson, G., & Hollander, H. (Eds.). (1999). *Trichotillomania.* Washington, DC: American Psychiatric Association.

Sumitra, L.M., & Miller, S.C. (2005). Pathologic gambling disorder: How to help patients curb risky behavior when the future is at stake. *Postgraduate Medicine, 118*(1), 31–37.

Virkkunen, M., DeJong, J., Bartko, J., & Linnoila, M. (1989). Psychobiological concomitants of history of suicide attempts among violent offenders and impulsive fire setters. *Archives of General Psychiatry, 148*, 652–657.

Volberg, A., & Steadman, H.J. (1988). Refining prevalence estimates of pathological gambling. *American Journal of Psychiatry, 145*, 502–505.

Voon, V., & Fox, S.H. (2007). Medication-related impulse control and repetitive behaviors in Parkinson disease. *Archives of Neurology, 64*(8), 1089–1096.

Welte, J.W., Barnes, G.M., Tidwell, M.C., & Hoffman, J.H. (2008). The prevalence of problem gambling among U.S. adolescents and young adults: Results from a national survey. *Journal of Gambling Studies, 24*(2), 119–133.

World Health Organization. (1992). *The ICD–10 classification of mental and behavioural disorders: Clinical descriptions and diagnostic guidelines.* Geneva: World Health Organization.

24

Personality Disorders

"Personality" or "character" *traits* are ingrained, enduring patterns of behaving, feeling, perceiving, and thinking that are prominent in a wide range of personal and social contexts. Personality is the psychological equivalent of physical appearance: We grow up with both, and although we can adjust each, they remain essentially the same and affect the rest of our lives. As Heraclitus observed, "A man's fate is his character." An individual's personality has been compared with the body's immune system. Just as the immune cells protect us against viruses and bacteria, so does the individual's personality enable him or her to cope with life challenges (Millon, 2004). Personality may be understood as composed of *character*, which is the component of the personality evolving from upbringing, and *temperament*, which is composed of those features of the personality that have biological bases and are often inherited.

Personality features may or may not be adaptive. Compulsiveness in a student is adaptive when it promotes orderly study habits, but it's maladaptive when the student spends hours sharpening pencils instead of studying. Personality traits turn into personality *disorders* when they (1) become inflexible and maladaptive, and (2) significantly impair social and occupational functioning or cause substantial subjective distress. People with personality disorders are not always in significant emotional distress. Often, the people they are living or working with are more distressed. Freud once defined a successful mature adult as someone "who is able to love and to work." People with personality disorders frequently fail at both.

In general, personality disorders first become apparent during adolescence or earlier, persist through life, and become less obvious by middle or old age. The diagnosis is not typically made until adulthood, since behavioral disorders of childhood and adolescence are frequently transient. Personality disorders are more pronounced during periods of high energy (as in adolescence) and under stressful conditions; they should be diagnosed only when they cause lifelong problems, not just discrete periods of dysfunction. Except for schizotypal, borderline, and antisocial personalities, hospitalizations are rare.

Using a multiaxial approach to diagnosis, personality traits and disorders are listed on Axis II, whereas mental disorders are indicated on Axis I. This separation distinguishes patients' current and more florid mental disorders from their ongoing, baseline personalities; this distinction should result in more *realistic* treatment goals. Since Axis I mental disorders are more responsive to treatment than Axis II personality disorders, a realistic treatment goal may be to remedy the former but not the latter. For instance, it may be unrealistic to expect a dependent personality who develops a major depression to be rid of both after a brief hospitalization. The symptoms of a chronic Axis I disorder, undiagnosed or incompletely treated, may negatively influence personality so that over time the individual develops a more pervasive manner of interacting with the environment that is characteristic of a personality disorder. For example, someone with social phobia develops an avoidant personality or someone with rapidly cycling bipolar disorder develops a borderline personality. Table 24-1 lists the general diagnostic criteria for a personality disorder.

> Kahana and Bibring (1964) show how identifying medical patients' personality types may alter how clinicians relate to patients. For example, when a doctor pats Mr. Moscowitz on the shoulder and says, "Don't worry, everything will be fine," a dependent patient will be greatly relieved; do the same with a paranoid patient and he'll draw away and think, "How does he know I'll be okay? Why's he being so chummy? How dare he touch me?" Paranoid patients feel safer with clinicians who keep their distance. Thus in many settings, clinicians should not attempt to change the patient's personality, but rather should adjust their own behavior to fit the patient's. When treatment for a personality disorder is attempted, the goal is not to reverse a constitutional defect but to help the person live more comfortably and efficiently within his or her limitations; treatment can help modify and reduce the defect. The task of therapists who treat individuals with personality disorders is to help them (and others around them) recognize and accept their defects, and having done so, to organize their lives in such a way that their defects are minimized and their remaining talents and strengths maximized.
>
> Understanding a patient's personality traits can guide psychotherapy, medication use, family involvement, nurses' monitoring, and so on. To illustrate: During group therapy, Mrs. Grant suddenly asked to see her hospital chart. If Mrs. Grant had a paranoid personality, the group therapist could be

TABLE 24-1
General Diagnostic Criteria for a Personality Disorder

A. **Severe disturbance in the characterological constitution and behavioral tendencies** of the individual, usually involving several areas of the personality, and nearly always associated with considerable personal and social disruption, meeting the following criteria:

1. markedly disharmonious attitudes and behavior, involving usually several areas of functioning, e.g., affectivity, arousal, impulse control, ways of perceiving and thinking, and style of relating to others

2. the abnormal behavior pattern is enduring, of long standing, and not limited to episodes of mental illness

3. the abnormal behavior pattern is pervasive and clearly maladaptive to a broad range of personal and social situations

4. the above manifestations always appear during childhood or adolescence and continue into adulthood

5. the disorder leads to considerable personal distress but this may only become apparent late in its course

6. the disorder is usually, but not invariably, associated with significant problems in occupational and social performance

B. The condition is **not directly attributable to gross brain damage or disease, or to another psychiatric disorder.**

C. For diagnosing most of the specific personality disorders that follow, clear evidence is usually required for the **presence of at least three of the traits or behaviors** given in the clinical description.

For different cultures it may be necessary to develop specific sets of criteria with regard to social norms, rules, and obligations.

Note: Adapted from ICD-10 (pp. 157–158) and DSM-5 (pp. 646–647)

fairly sure she wanted to uncover malicious information that the staff were writing about her. However, Mrs. Grant is not paranoid; she has an avoidant personality, and as such, the therapist can reasonably guess that she wanted to know whether the therapist liked her—a proposition he raised for the group's consideration. Another illustration: If during a highly stressful period, a patient asked for a 3-day supply of sleeping pills, all things being equal, a patient with a borderline personality would be far more likely to abuse the pills than would a patient with a schizoid personality. Or, if a psychiatric nurse has to leave patients in the care of another patient, she would much prefer an obsessive–compulsive to an antisocial personality.

Physicians must be aware that patients with personality disorders may be less compliant with their medicines (Colum et al., 2000; Herbeck, 2005) and thus require more attention to their medical management. Patients with personality disorders have more troubled lives, as evidenced by more contact with police (Gandhi et al., 2001), increased use of medical services (Reich et al., 1989), and more suicide attempts (Pirkis et al., 1999). Substance-abuse disorders were the most common Axis I diagnosis found among those with personality disorders (Koeningsberg et al., 1985).

Personality disorders are not uncommon. Lenzenweger et al. (1997) report that about 11% of the general population suffers from a personality disorder. In a retrospective chart review, 36% of 2,462 psychiatric patients had personality disorders. Borderline personality disorder was diagnosed most frequently (12% of total); next (at 10%) was the residual category of "mixed, atypical, or other personality disorder." The other personality disorders were diagnosed in under 3% of the patients.

The etiology of personality disorder is probably multifactorial. Analytic theory strongly implicates environmental factors such as how the individual is raised. Others, such as Torgersen et al. (2000), suggest more biological factors. The answer is most likely a combination of environmental and genetic components.

Differential Diagnosis

In general, never diagnose a personality disorder in the midst of an episode of a major psychiatric illness without having information about the person's behavior before this episode. Too often, molehills in a personality become mountains during an acute psychiatric episode. Minor traits such as dependency may look like full-blown personality disorders during the acute stress. Consider the following:

1. *Neurosis* (i.e., nonpsychotic mood and anxiety disorders) *versus personality disorder.* Patients who develop a nonpsychotic mood or anxiety disorder regard their anxious behavior as uncharacteristic of their usual self, as different for them (i.e., a transient *state*). In contrast, the pathological behavior exhibited by patients with personality disorders is in character—in other words, usual for them, a *trait*. Anxiety disorders may develop at any time; personality disorders are longstanding. Anxious individuals are usually uncomfortable with their symptoms, whereas individuals with personality disorders often justify and rationalize their behavior.

2. *Personality trait versus disorder.* Diagnosing a personality disorder depends the most on whether there is evidence for the enduring and stable maladaptive traits that impair functioning. Some people have only one or two characteristics of a disorder, which do not significantly impair functioning like the full-blown disorder.

3. *Major mood disorders and schizophrenia versus personality disorders.* Impairment in functioning is seldom as profound in personality disorders as in major mood disorders and schizophrenia. Individuals with personality disorders seldom require hospitalization; they are not psychotic.

4. *Late-onset mental disorder.* Late-onset (adulthood) personality changes suggest the presence of a major mental or medical disorder.

One method for understanding and evaluating criteria for a personality disorder involves making a categorical decision. Personality disorders in the *DSM* have been divided into a taxonomy of three clusters: *Cluster A* consists of paranoid, schizoid, and schizotypal personality disorders, characterized by an odd or eccentric interpersonal style. *Cluster B* includes histrionic, narcissistic, antisocial, and borderline personality disorders, characterized by a dramatic or emotionally reactive interpersonal style (externalizing). *Cluster C* harbors the avoidant, dependent, and obsessive–compulsive personality disorders, characterized by a highly anxious and fearful interpersonal style (internalizing).

As opposed to a categorical approach to classifying personality disorders, there are ongoing attempts to identify fundamental personality dimensions across a continuum. *DSM-5* proposes an alternative dimensional model that includes the goal of integrating categorical descriptions of impaired personality functioning with pathological personality traits across five broad domains and twenty-six trait facets. The proposed trait domains include negative affectivity, detachment, antagonism, disinhibition, and psychoticism. The major focus is on how these traits impact one's experience of the self (identity and self-direction) and others (empathy and intimacy). So these dimensions of personality traits run across all of the ten personality disorders (and in "normal" people) and contribute to the level of self or interpersonal functioning.

PARANOID PERSONALITY DISORDER

"I only trust me and thee and I'm not so sure of thee."

—Anonymous

The essential features of a paranoid personality disorder (PPD) include: (1) pervasive and unwarranted suspiciousness and mistrust of people, (2) hypersensitivity, and (3) emotional detachment. None of these features should stem from another mental disorder, such as schizophrenia or paranoid disorder. Table 24-2 lists the diagnostic criteria for PPD.

TABLE 24-2
Diagnostic Criteria for Paranoid Personality Disorder

A. Personality disorder characterized by at least four of the following:

1. preoccupation with unsubstantiated "conspiratorial" explanations of events both immediate to the patient and in the world at large
2. excessive sensitiveness to setbacks and rebuffs
3. tendency to experience excessive self-importance, manifest in a persistent self-referential attitude
4. suspiciousness and a pervasive tendency to distort experience by misconstruing the neutral or friendly actions of others as hostile or contemptuous
5. tendency to bear grudges persistently, e.g., refusal to forgive insults and injuries or slights
6. a combative and tenacious sense of personal rights out of keeping with the actual situation
7. recurrent suspicions, without justification, regarding sexual fidelity of spouse or sexual partner

B. The condition is not directly attributable to gross brain damage or disease, or to another psychiatric disorder.

Note: Adapted from ICD-10 (p. 158) and DSM-5 (p. 649)

"Paranoids have enemies" mainly because they're paranoid. Paranoid people are very unpleasant, always blaming and suspicious of others. In general, suspicions may be justified and adaptive from time to time, but when contradictory evidence is presented, most people abandon them. People with PPD do not, but rather view the evidence as further proof that the person intends to harm them. The world of the person with PPD is hostile, devious, and dark, filled with persecutory forces for which he must be eternally vigilant. On entering a restaurant, the person will scan the room to ensure that no enemies are present and then sit with his back to the wall so that nobody can sneak behind him. Highly secretive, he may hide behind dark glasses. People with PPD bristle at the slightest contradiction or criticism, distrust other's loyalty, and misconstrue what is said to them. When a coworker congratulated a man with paranoia on plans to buy a home, he snapped, "It's mine! You can't have it!" These individuals may be ambitious and bright, yet they are also stubborn and defensive. They're quick to argue and find fault. They'll seize an alleged injustice, blow up its significance, and distort the facts to fit their suspiciousness.

An English professor with PPD discovered that a classroom he had reserved was occupied by another faculty member. The professor became enraged, citing it as "this draconian administration's efforts to drive me from the university." The next day, after learning that the university press would not publish his definitive study of Iago, he launched a $3 million lawsuit against the university. Four months later, the university threatened not to renew his contract. He dropped the suit but then instigated student protests against the university for "stifling academic freedom."

People keep their distance from people with PPD, which merely confirms the validity of these individuals' general distrust. People with PPD are pathologically jealous, tense, rigid, unwilling to compromise, moralistic, always detecting ill intent and special messages, litigious, humorless, coldly objective, overly rational, haughty, and distant. That's why "paranoids have enemies," have few friends, and fewer, if any, intimate relationships. They have contempt for weakness in others and disdain the sickly, defective, and imperfect—that is, everybody, but themselves. They think in hierarchical terms: Who's superior to whom? Who controls whom? With their egocentricity and exaggerated self-importance, they make a great show of self-sufficiency. They're drawn to politics, history, science, and technology; to them, the arts are for sissies. As unpleasant as these individuals can be, it's possible to muster compassion by remembering that it's a terribly uncomfortable existence for them.

PPD is more common in men than women. The prevalence of PPD is estimated at 2% of the general population, 20% among those in inpatient psychiatric settings, and 5% among those in outpatient psychiatric clinics. Social relations and job advancement are often severely impaired. Unlike paranoid disorders and paranoid schizophrenia, paranoid personalities are *not* psychotic. When a person with paranoid disorder is challenged about the certainty of his allegations, he will say, "I'm quite sure," or "It's highly probable." If pushed further about alternative explanations, he might say, "Yes, those alternatives are possible but highly unlikely." The psychotic will say, "It is fact and there are no alternative explanations." People with PPD can become psychotic when highly stressed. A person with PPD has overvalued ideas, not delusions.

These patients seldom come for psychiatric treatment since they do not perceive weaknesses or faults in themselves. They may be sent by bosses or wives under threat of the loss of a job or marriage, but the relationship they form with a therapist tends to be adversarial rather than collaborative and thus is often doomed to failure. They do, of course, need medical treatment from time to time, and when this happens, they interact with their physicians in the same manner as they interact with others. They tend to be guarded in giving information about themselves, suspicious of the intent behind the questions asked, and distrustful of examinations, procedures, and treatments. They often question the training and qualifications of those who treat them. They are particularly apt to bring suit. It is therefore important that clinicians who deal with this group of people do so in an honest and comprehensive fashion. They should be thoroughly informed and their consent obtained for whatever is done. Further, careful documentation of both the information given and the informed consent is advised.

In psychological treatment, the therapist's main task is to minimize the patient's distrust of the therapist and of therapy. It often takes months before the patient feels at all relaxed in treatment. Clinicians should be respectful and business-like, avoiding intimacy and too much warmth, which people with PPD experience as invasive. Deep psychological interpretations are verboten, since people with PPD are already leery of "shrinks who read people's minds and trick them." What is insight to a therapist is "messing with my mind" to a person with PPD. In the office, clinicians should *not* sit between the patient and the door; the person feels far less threatened if nobody "blocks" her exit way. What's an office to a therapist is an observation chamber to a person with PPD. When clinicians err, they should admit the mistake, apologize, and get on with it; overapologizing fosters distrust. Nor should clinicians ask these individuals to trust them, since to them, that's like a Nazi guard asking a Dachau inmate to trust him. Being straightforward and "professional" is the most reassuring approach. When starting medications, these patients should be given detailed and accurate side-effect information. They already expect the worst but feel better knowing about it.

SCHIZOID PERSONALITY DISORDER

The central features of a schizoid personality disorder (SDPD) include: (1) minimal or no social relations, (2) restricted expression of emotion, (3) a striking lack of warmth and tenderness, and (4) an apparent indifference to others' praise, criticism, feelings, and concerns. Unlike schizotypal personalities (see below), patients with SDPD do *not* exhibit eccentricities of speech, behavior, or thinking. Table 24-3 lists diagnostic criteria for SDPD.

Patients with SDPD are often "in a fog," absentminded, loners, detached from others, self-involved, "not connected." What appears as aloofness is actually profound shyness. Often dull and humorless, they will disavow feelings of anger or interest in sex; they prefer solitary activities and daydreaming to friendships. Dating is painful, marriage rare. Although SDPD greatly impedes social relationships and professional advancement, these patients

TABLE 24-3
Diagnostic Criteria for Schizoid Personality Disorder

A. Personality disorder characterized by at least four of the following:

    1. lack of desire for close relationships

    2. almost invariable preference for solitary activities

    3. little interest in having sexual experiences with another person (taking into account age)

    4. few, if any, activities, provide pleasure

    5. lack of close friends or confiding relationships (or having only one)

    6. apparent indifference to either praise or criticism

    7. emotional coldness, detachment, or flattened affectivity

    8. limited capacity to express either warm, tender feelings or anger toward others

    9. excessive preoccupation with fantasy and introspection

    10. marked insensitivity to prevailing social norms and conventions

B. The condition is not directly attributable to gross brain damage or disease, or to another psychiatric disorder particularly autistic spectrum disorders.

Note: Adapted from ICD-10 (pp. 158–159) and DSM-5 (pp. 652–653)

can excel if permitted minimal interpersonal contact. The prevalence of SDPD is unknown, though these individuals may be common on Skid Row. SDPD is diagnosed slightly more often in males, who seem to suffer more impairment from the disorder than their female counterparts.

SDPD resembles *avoidant personality disorder*, since both display prominent social isolation. Whereas the avoidant personalities want friends, people with SDPD don't; whereas those who are avoidant are alone because they're afraid people won't like them, people with SDPD have no interest in personal involvement. Once considered a prodromal phase of *schizophrenia*, SDPD and schizophrenia are now considered to be unrelated (see below). Few patients with SDPD become psychotic.

Little is known about the treatment of this disorder; most persons with this condition probably do not seek professional help or do so only when seeking help for depression, substance abuse, or other problems. Most undoubtedly these people lack the insight or motivation for individual psychotherapy and probably would find the intimacy of typical group therapy too threatening. If the patient is motivated, behavioral techniques may be helpful, such as graded exposure to a variety of social tasks. For example, the clinician might encourage the patient to attend a concert, then join a bridge club, and eventually enter a dance class. Long-term group psychotherapy with other patients who have SDPD has also been reported to be successful (Yalom, 2005). Some clinicians have postulated that schizoid personality may be a variant of high-functioning autism.

SCHIZOTYPAL PERSONALITY DISORDER

The essential feature of a schizotypal personality disorder (STPD) is eccentric behavior prompted by oddities in thought and perception. These patients have few friends because they appear very strange, almost schizophrenic. They seem to live in a different dimension filled with weird thoughts, ideas of reference, paranoid ideation, illusions of telepathy, and "magical thinking"—for example, "If I think hard enough, I can make the wind blow," or "My teeth itch." Their speech may be hard to follow, although without loose associations or incoherence. Their affect is flat or inappropriate. Sloppy, unkempt, giggling for no reason, and often talking to themselves, they are hypersensitive to criticism nd dreadfully anxious around people, especially if more than three are together. Table 24-4 lists the full diagnostic criteria for STPD.

TABLE 24-4
Diagnostic Criteria for Schizotypal Disorder

A. A disorder characterized by **eccentric behavior and anomalies of thinking and affect** which resemble those seen in schizophrenia, though no definite and characteristic schizophrenic anomalies have occurred at any stage. There is no dominant or typical disturbance, but at least five of the typical features listed below should have been present, continuously or episodically, for at least 2 years:

1. occasional transient quasi-psychotic episodes with intense illusions, auditory or other hallucinations, and delusion-like ideas, usually occurring without external provocation
2. odd beliefs or magical thinking, influencing behavior and inconsistent with subcultural norms
3. unusual perceptual experiences including somatosensory (bodily) or other illusions, depersonalization, or derealization
4. vague, circumstantial, metaphorical, overelaborate, or stereotyped thinking, manifested by odd speech or in other ways, without gross incoherence
5. suspiciousness or paranoid ideas
6. inappropriate or constricted affect (the individual appears cold and aloof)
7. behavior or appearance that is odd, eccentric, or peculiar
8. poor rapport with others and a tendency to social withdrawal (**DSM-5** *adds excessive social anxiety that does not improve with familiarity*)
9. obsessive ruminations without inner resistance, often with dysmorphophobic, sexual, or aggressive content

B. The condition is not directly attributable to gross brain damage or disease, or to another psychiatric disorder. In particular the individual must never have met criteria for schizophrenia. However, a history of schizophrenia in a first-degree relative gives additional weight to the diagnosis (but is not a prerequisite) as it is believed to be part of the genetic spectrum of schizophrenia.

Note: Adapted from *ICD-10* (pp. 83–84) and *DSM-5* (pp. 655–656)

Unlike *schizoid* personalities, *schizotypal* personalities are more likely to (1) display bizarre and peculiar traits, (2) develop fanatic, eccentric, or racist beliefs, (3) become dysthymic and anxious, (4) have an accompanying borderline personality disorder, (5) become transiently psychotic under stress, (6) evolve into schizophrenia, (7) run in families (Baron, Guren, Asnis, & Lord, 1985), and (8) have a relative with schizophrenia. Unlike STPD, patients with *schizophrenia, residual type* would have previously displayed a florid schizophrenic psychosis. If schizophrenia develops in a patient with STPD, the schizotypal diagnosis is dropped. Indeed, schizophrenia should always be suspected in these patients if they are under 35.

Treatment of patients with schizotypal personality disorder often centers on the issues that led them to seek treatment. These issues may include feelings of alienation due to paranoid ideation or ideas of reference. A supportive approach has been recommended, whereas exploratory and group psychotherapies are felt to be overly threatening. Social skills training may be useful in helping eccentric, odd persons to feel more comfortable with others. Lower doses of antipsychotics have been recommended to alleviate some of the intense anxiety and cognitive symptoms, such as odd speech and unusual perceptual experience; this approach has some empirical support. However, enthusiasm for using these medications must be tempered by their tendency to induce troublesome and potentially irreversible side effects.

BORDERLINE PERSONALITY DISORDER

Don't Leave Me, I Hate You
—Title of book on borderlines by Jerold Kreisman, M.D.

Borderline personality disorder (BPD) is characterized by the following criteria: (1) impulsivity, (2) unstable and intense interpersonal relations, (3) inappropriate or intense anger, (4) identity confusion, (5) affective instability, (6) problems being alone, (7) physically self-destructive acts, and (8) chronic feelings of emptiness and boredom. Table 24-5 lists diagnostic criteria for BPD.

In 1938 the term *borderline* was introduced to describe those patients who straddled the border between neurosis and psychosis. The diagnosis of "borderline schizophrenia," used widely until the mid-1970s, assumed that borderline disorders were a type of "latent schizophrenia." Most authorities now believe that borderline conditions are personality disorders. What nobody disputes is that people with BPD *look much better than they are*—a fact that continually deceives professionals as well as laypeople.

TABLE 24-5
Diagnostic Criteria for Borderline Personality Disorder

A. Personality disorder in which there is a marked tendency to **act impulsively** without consideration of the consequences, together with **affective instability** characterized by at least five of the following:

   1. excessive efforts to avoid abandonment
   2. intense and unstable relationships may cause repeated emotional crises
   3. the patient's own self-image, aims, and internal preferences (including sexual) are often unclear or disturbed
   4. ability to plan ahead may be minimal
   5. series of suicidal threats or acts of self-harm (these may occur without obvious precipitants)
   6. emotional instability
   7. chronic feelings of emptiness
   8. outbursts of intense anger may often lead to violence or "behavioral explosions" easily precipitated when impulsive acts are criticized or thwarted by others
   9. *DSM-5 adds stress-related dissociation or paranoia*

B. The condition is not directly attributable to gross brain damage or disease, or to another psychiatric disorder (particularly mood or psychotic disorders).

Note: Adapted from *ICD-10* (p. 160) and *DSM-5* (p. 663)

Clinical Presentation

Feeling chronically bored and empty, people with BPD desperately seek stimulation: They might gamble, act out sexually, abuse drugs, overdose, instigate brawls, or attempt suicide. Many slash their wrists or douse lit cigarettes on their arms, not to kill or to hurt themselves, but to *feel* something ("I feel so dead, cutting myself is the only way I know I'm alive") or to relieve tension. Their moods are always reactive, intense, and brief; trivial problems mushroom into calamities. They have been well portrayed in movies such as *Fatal Attraction, A Streetcar Named Desire*, and *Young Adult*.

The interpersonal relations of people with BPD swing between suffocating dependency and mindless self-assertion. They hate being alone and latch onto others to avoid feeling abandoned. For example, such an individual will call a recently made friend every day about a "disaster" needing immediate attention. Initially, the friend is flattered by the new friend's "idealization" of her, yet she soon finds herself sucked into a gooey, all-consuming relationship. When she tries to cool things, the person with BPD denigrates her ("devaluation") with a vengeance, pouring ink on her couch, demanding money, and accusing her of "being miserly," calling her at 3 a.m. to complain that she's a "bitch," and so on. The digs contain just enough truth to fester under the friend's skin, which eventually leads the friend to apologize.

Borderline relationships, be they platonic or romantic, are all-or-nothing endeavors. People with BPD are in love with love, not people. Anything less than total love is hate; anything less than total commitment is rejection ("rejection sensitivity"). They expect—nay, *demand*—that others do for them what they cannot do for themselves. Chronically sad and demoralized, they adopt friends not because they like them but because they expect the friends to rid them of unhappiness. When the friends fail at this unknown and undoable task, the person with BPD dumps them, looks for another savior, and repeats the cycle. Unable to figure out who or what they are ("identity diffusion"), these individuals glom onto others so as to acquire an identity by osmosis. A 25-year-old with BPD said that she dresses like the rock star Madonna "to express my individuality." Whereas she's convinced that nobody ever does enough for her, others find her exhausting and draining—an "empty gas tank" in need of constant refueling.

People with BPD are notorious for *splitting*—that is, they view people as *all good* or *all bad*—and then get others to act out these roles. Everywhere they go, they set people against each other, create havoc, and walk away without anybody realizing until later who caused the chaos.

Mary Rae, an inpatient with BPD, superficially slashed her wrist, squeezed the blood, and showed it dripping to her psychiatrist. As anyone would have predicted, he canceled her weekend pass. This infuriated Mary Rae. She then "confided" in Nurse Peter:

"You're the only person who understands me. My doctor and everyone else here hate me. . . . When I cut my wrist I realized I should tell my doctor. So I did, and right away. I *thought* that was the right thing to do. So what does Dr. Jerk-ass do? He locks me up. I don't get it: Staff says we're supposed to be open with them. Well, I was! From now on, I keep everything to myself. I wasn't suicidal—I would hardly tell people if I was. Peter, if only *you* would have been here. Then I could have gone to you and never have cut myself at all. As it is, I'm stuck here all weekend: Just thinking about it makes me suicidal. Can't you help me?"

Flattered that Mary Rae had confided in him, Peter campaigns to restore her weekend pass. He doesn't realize that Mary Rae has similarly "confided" in five other staff members, each thinking they have a "unique and confidential relationship" with her, which must be kept secret. The unit's staff soon splits between those who feel Mary Rae has been victimized for "being honest" and those who think she's a manipulator and should be shipped to a state hospital. Very quickly, both sides cease squabbling about Mary Rae and instead attack each other as insensitive or naive. Meanwhile, as if she's an innocent bystander, Mary Rae fiddles while the staff burns.

Patients with BPD may have many "neurotic" symptoms—panic attacks, phobias, anxiety, somatic complaints, conversion symptoms, dysthymia. Under stress, some become *briefly* psychotic. Highly characteristic of people with BPD is their ability to give sane answers on structured psychological tests (e.g., Wechsler Adult Intelligence Scale; WAIS), but bizarre, psychotic responses on unstructured tests (e.g., Rorschach). Where most people might see a bat or a butterfly on a Rorschach inkblot, one patient with BPD saw "the insides of a cow's stomach run over by a car."

BPD has a chronic, fluctuating course which, although it does *not* lead to schizophrenia, nonetheless significantly impairs social and occupational functioning. A 5-year follow-up showed that people with BPD function at pretty much the same poor level. Those with higher premorbid levels of functioning have better prognoses.

Epidemiology

Twice as many people with BPD are women than men. Using strict diagnostic criteria, 1.6–4% of the general population has BPD. The frequency of this diagnosis may be as high as 11% of psychiatric outpatients, and 19% of psychiatric inpatients (Linehan, 1993).

Differential Diagnosis

Known as the "disorder that doesn't specialize," BPD presents with such variegated symptomatology that it appears in many patients' lists of differential diagnoses. BPD may coexist with *schizotypal, histrionic, narcissistic,* or *antisocial personality disorders.* What usually distinguishes people with BPD are chronic feelings of emptiness and anger, self-mutilation, transitory psychoses, manipulative suicide attempts, intensely demanding relationships, and superficial intactness. The sadness common to people with BPD is short-lived and highly reactive. Still, *major depression* and *dysthymic disorder* can coexist with BPD or be confused with it. Because anger and irritability can be symptoms of major depression, some patients with depression may look like a person with BPD. However, they see their reactive behavior as different from usual for them, and friends usually confirm this observation. *Cyclothymic disorder,* like BPD, has roller-coaster mood swings, but BPD doesn't have true hypomanic periods. When briefly psychotic, people with BPD may be labeled *schizophrenic* but, unlike most with schizophrenia, they use logical sentences and demonstrate considerable affect in describing their psychotic experiences.

Etiology and Pathogenesis

Kernberg (1975) hypothesized that people with BPD have a "constitutional" inability to regulate affects, which predisposes them to psychological disorganization under specific adverse conditions during childhood. Zanarini and Frankenburg (1997) describe a tripartite model of borderline development. They present a hypothesis embracing three elements: a labile temperament, early childhood trauma, and a triggering event.

BPD runs in families. First-degree relatives of people with BPD have 10 times the rate of BPD and three times the rate of alcoholism than do controls. These relatives also have higher rates of mood disorders but normal rates of schizophrenia and bipolar disorder. While the mode of this familial transmission is unclear, most investigations have focused on psychosocial determinants.

Mahler, Pine, and Bergman (1975) proposed that borderline conditions stem from a disturbance in the "rapprochement sub-phase of the separation–individuation" process—from 18 to 36 months. During this period, the child, having experimented with separating self from mother, tries returning to mother for approval and emotional "refueling." These mothers, however, have had their own difficulties with separation, and so they resent the child's "clinging," as if to say, "Before you wanted me, now you don't. So get lost!" These mothers experience their child's attempts at autonomy as abandonment (e.g., "How dare you leave me!"). As the child grows up, she replays these dependence–independence conflicts with others. This style of parenting sets up a vicious, out-of-control feedback loop. Fear of separation or abandonment is not met with comfort but rather rejection. Thus, fear becomes a cue for abandonment, which leads to more fear, and so on.

Along similar lines, Masterson (1976) contended that the essence of the borderline dilemma is a conflict between a desire for autonomy and a fear of parental abandonment. He claimed that mothers of children with BPD reward their children's regressive behaviors and discourage their individuation.

A majority of people with BPD were physically, sexually, and/or emotionally abused by their caregivers at times; at other times these caregivers may have been adequate or even nurturing. This vacillation creates the problem of both hating and loving the caregiver.

Splitting is a healthy and normal defense in 18- to 36-month-old children. For example, a 2 1/2-year-old boy with a 6-month-old sister said to his father, "No like sister's daddy, like *my* daddy." Yes, this was the same daddy, but this splitting permitted the little boy to like his father while still feeling jealous that his sister was getting a lot of attention. Only later, when his mind is able to handle greater complexity, will this good–bad dichotomy diversify into more ambiguous shades of gray in which the good and bad coexist—the stuff of most adult experience. People with BPD don't accomplish this developmental task. Clinicians find themselves worshipped on an altar some days and vilified in an earthly hell on others. The clinician hasn't changed, but the patient's opinion has.

Strip aside everything people with BPD do and say and what remains is an underlying dread, or perhaps a conviction, of being *bad*—or as one patient remarked, "Underneath madness lies badness." These individuals typically disown this badness by projecting it onto others ("projective identification"), act out to escape feeling this "badness," employ reaction formation (as when romanticizing ideal love—e.g., Blanche DuBois), or may behave self-destructively. Similar defenses are used by people with BPD who feel that they are *nothing* inside, mere shells of humanity, scarecrows masquerading as people. Perhaps 10% of patients with BPD will commit suicide and 75% will engage in at least one episode of self-injurious behavior. Self-injurious behavior may decline over time, but the feelings of emptiness often persist (Zanarini et al., 2007).

Management and Treatment

Clinicians working with patients with BPD must walk a narrow path between giving support without rescuing and encouraging independence without signaling abandonment. When patients with BPD are doing better, praise for their improvement is often interpreted as "You do not need to see me anymore"—another abandonment. With BPD, emphatic and supportive statements should be combined: "You still have a lot of pain, but you are handling it better. There is a lot of work still ahead, but I see progress." Structure and consistency are also very important. During a crisis, a scheduled phone check-in works much better than waiting for an emergency.

Only well-trained professionals should consider attempting to treat these most difficult of patients. *Long-term, psychodynamic psychotherapy* has demonstrated some positive impact and is the often-recommended treatment for BPD (Bateman & Fonagy, 2001). One approach starts with fostering the patient's trust in treatment so that exploration of unconscious wishes and fantasies can follow. Another approach stresses reality testing, providing structure, and avoiding overly stimulating "depth interpretations" that may induce psychological disorganization. A *cognitive–behavioral approach*, which stresses integrating adaptive coping skills with intense affective reactions and cognitively fusing opposites, has been successful when used over several years (Linehan, 1993). Linehan's therapy model, dialectical behavior therapy (DBT), combines manualized group training of patients with individualized therapy that focuses on empathy and validating the patient. DBT places the focus on stopping self-destructive behavior, whereas psychodynamic therapies focus on the underlying issues in hopes that once the psychic conflicts are resolved, then the suicidal thinking will subside. There is solid evidence demonstrating efficacy of DBT in reducing dysfunctional parasuicidal behavior, substance abuse, and hospitalization.

Drug treatment may utilize MAOIs for depression and rejection sensitivity and low doses of antipsychotics for brief reactive psychoses and irritability (Cornelius et al., 1993). Anticonvulsants such as divalproex sodium may decrease impulsive self-destructive behavior. Benzodiazepines may disinhibit behavior and create drug dependence and therefore are not usually recommended. Tricyclic antidepressants have a poor record in treating a BPD-related depression, *and* they are lethal in overdose. Lithium does help stabilize mood and reduce impulsive behaviors but is also dangerous in overdose. In certain patients selective serotonin reuptake inhibiters (SSRIs) may share the efficacy of MAOIs with a better safety and side-effect profile.

HISTRIONIC PERSONALITY DISORDER

"Make me the center of all your attentions."

—Millon (2004)

Individuals with histrionic personality disorder (HPD) are lively, overdramatic, and always calling attention to themselves. Their behavior is overreactive, with minor stimuli giving rise to emotional excitability such as irrational outbursts or temper tantrums. Individuals with HPD crave novelty, stimulation, and excitement and become quickly bored with normal routines. Though they are often creative and imaginative, they seldom show interest in intellectual achievement and careful, analytic thinking. Table 24-6 lists the diagnostic criteria for HPD.

In relationships, these individuals are perceived as shallow and lacking in genuineness, though charming and appealing. They are quick to form friendships, but once a friendship is established, they become demanding, egocentric, and inconsiderate. Because of feeling helpless and dependent,

TABLE 24-6

Diagnostic Criteria for Histrionic Personality Disorder

A. Personality disorder characterized by at least five of the following:

    1. continual seeking for excitement and activities in which the patient is the center of attention

    2. inappropriate seductiveness in appearance or behavior

    3. shallow and labile affectivity

    4. overconcern with physical attractiveness

    5. egocentricity and self-indulgence

    6. self-dramatization, theatricality, exaggerated expression of emotions

    7. suggestibility, easily influenced by others or by circumstances

    8. continuous longing for appreciation and feelings that are easily hurt

B. The condition is not directly attributable to gross brain damage or disease, or to another psychiatric disorder

Note: Adapted from *ICD-10* (p. 160) and *DSM-5* (p. 667)

they make continuous demands for reassurance and manipulative suicidal threats, gestures, or attempts. Typically attractive and seductive, people with HPD attempt to control the opposite sex or to enter into dependent relationships. Although flights into romantic fantasy are common, their sexuality is often constricted or unsatisfying. They experience periods of intense dissatisfaction and unhappiness, usually related to external changes such as a breakup with a lover.

This disorder is common and diagnosed more frequently in females than in males. The prevalence of HPD in the general population may be about 2–3% with rates of about 10–15% in inpatient and outpatient psychiatric settings. It occurs more frequently among family members than in the general population. A frequent complication is substance use disorder. A codiagnosis of narcissistic, dependent, or borderline personality disorder is common. Although the cause of HPD is unknown, the disorder has been linked through family studies to somatization disorder and antisocial personality. Research has suggested that histrionic and antisocial personalities may be sex-typed phenotypic variants of the same underlying genetic diathesis. It has also been suggested that histrionic personality is a sex-biased diagnosis that merely describes a caricature of stereotypic femininity.

> If one talks about personality *styles* rather than *disorders*, "hysterics" and "compulsives' are cognitive opposites. Hysterics think in impressions, compulsives in facts. If Holly Go-Lightly, the Hysteric, and Carl Compulsive

were to describe a person they recently met, Holly would exclaim, "He's just a darling, and such thrilling eyes. He must've murdered somebody. Either that or he's a poet. Did you see how he looked straight through me? I loved it." Carl would say, "He's about 5 feet, 11 inches tall, weighs 160 pounds, has black hair, bushy eyebrows, a Southern accent. . . ." Compulsives present exhaustive, and ultimately boring, details; hysterics make global comments that lack specificity and focus. Compulsives are too mired in detail to make hunches, whereas hysterics base all their decisions on hunches, eschewing logic and information. Most people invoke hunches as temporary hypotheses, but hysterics use them as final conclusions (Shapiro, 1999). Because they so complement each other, it's not uncommon for compulsive professionals to marry histrionic artists. Such a marriage offers drama for the compulsive and stability for the histrionic.

In clinical interviews, it is very difficult to get detailed information from patients with HPD. It's like trying to nail gelatin to a wall. Asking a patient *how long* she has been feeling badly might evoke a response such as, "Forever, a very long time" (in reality, it started 12 days ago). If asked *how badly* she feels, the patient might say, "The worst ever. I can't take the pain." The patient is not deliberately creating a smoke screen or being passive–aggressive; she stores *impressions* in her brain, not details. To adapt to the histrionics' style, clinicians may fare better by using more global wording than usual (most clinicians tend more to the compulsive side). If medications are prescribed, the generalities about side effects may suffice, since the details will be lost anyway.

Interventions have not been clearly studied, but psychoanalytic psychotherapy has a long tradition in the treatment of this and related syndromes, and for that reason is considered by some the treatment of choice. However, others advocate a more supportive, problem-solving approach or a cognitive approach to deal with distorted thinking (i.e., inflated self-image) and to minimize the counterproductive effects of frequent excessive emotional outpouring. Interpersonal approaches tend to focus on uncovering conscious (or unconscious) motivations for seeking out disappointing lovers and being unable to commit to stable, meaningful relationships. Group therapy may be useful in addressing provocative and attention-seeking behavior. Because patients may not be aware of their behaviors, it can be helpful for others to point out these traits to them. A condition that may be related—*hysteroid dysphoria*, described in depressed women who have a history of sensitivity to rejection in relationships—is reportedly responsive to MAOIs (e.g., phenelzine).

NARCISSISTIC PERSONALITY DISORDER

"Please get me a tissue, I have a runny nose."
—Patient asking a nurse, who is attempting to resuscitate
a collapsed patient in the hallway

Narcissus was the mythological Greek youth who fell so in love with his own reflection that he pined away and died. In 1898 Havelock Ellis used this myth to describe a case of male autoeroticism in his essay on Casanova. Twelve years after this, Freud introduced the term *narcissism*. Narcissism has been defined in many ways; in *DSM-5* essential features for narcissistic personality disorder (NPD) include: (1) grandiose self-importance, (2) preoccupation with fantasies of unlimited success, (3) driven desire for attention and admiration, (4) intolerance to criticism, and (5) disturbed, self-centered interpersonal relations.

These patients' *grandiosity* manifests as an exaggerated sense of self-importance or uniqueness. Others call them "conceited." They greatly overestimate not only their accomplishments and abilities, but their failures as well. For example, at age 30, Isaac described himself as "the greatest actor since Edmund Kean." When he failed to land a part in a major motion picture, he insisted that "everyone in Hollywood will think I'm washed up."

Fantasies of fame substitute for actual achievements. Everyone daydreams, but true narcissists are preoccupied with brilliance, wealth, ideal love, beauty, copping an Oscar (or two), or whatever. In real life, most people enjoy reaching these goals, but narcissists don't. Their ambition is driven, their pursuit of recognition is a burden, their accomplishments don't satisfy. Isaac will perform in front of his own mirror, but not at an audition. He takes a role only if his agent gets him one, but even then, he loves the applause but hates the acting.

The narcissistic personality craves *attention* and universal admiration. Appearance is more important than substance. Being seen with the "right" people is more important than liking them. People with NPD are preoccupied with their physical image; they seek not merely to look attractive but to appear godlike. Isaac's home is a museum studded with photographs of Isaac, mostly in the nude.

Intolerance to criticism arises from the low self-esteem of these individuals. When their grandiosity is doubted, they respond with "narcissistic rage": cool disdain, anger, humiliation, extreme boredom, pessimism, negativism, and shame. Depressed moods result when they're rejected, neglected, or frustrated. When Isaac missed a key while playing the piano, he blamed the piano tuner for not doing his job correctly. At a party, Isaac was regaling his audience with show-biz stories, but when another actor joined in, Isaac became stone silent.

Interpersonally selfish, people with NPD act with a sense of entitlement, as if they are the masters and everyone else, servants. Arriving an hour late on the set, Isaac doesn't apologize ("Why should I? I rushed like hell to get here. If anything, they should thank me"). Narcissists do not sustain genuine, positive regard for anyone. Some alternate between idealization and devaluation ("splitting"), worshiping an individual one moment and despising him or her the next. While there may be many people in their lives, they are all "insignificant others."

Narcissistic and *histrionic personalities* are both self-centered, but the narcissist is more grandiose, egotistical, arrogant, vigorous, and selfish, whereas the hysteric is more overdramatic, flighty, and apprehensive. People with *mania* are grandiose, but episodically and often with psychosis, whereas the narcissist's grandiosity is continual and nonpsychotic. Few patients with NPD become psychotic, and when they do, the episodes are brief. Wilhelm Reich (1949/1972) described the "phallic-narcissistic character" whose "penis is not in the service of love but is an instrument of aggression and vengeance" (p. 203). Indeed, some narcissism creates many a business tycoon, surgeon, trial lawyer, politician, movie producer, actor, and orchestra conductor. Great accomplishments require great egos.

At about 4 years of age, narcissism is quite normal. All boys are "Superman" (or some other hero) and want everybody to watch them do their next stunt. Girls are vying for the highest social standing, all wanting to be the queen or prima donna. The boy's parents either "pound it out of him, so he doesn't get too big for his britches," or the opposite, indulge his every whim so as "not to frustrate and upset him." The girl's parents might constantly tell her that she is pretty or cute, but pay little attention to her real accomplishments or ignore her because they really wanted a boy. Either approach can warp progress toward a normal narcissism that is healthy and has realistic limits on it: "I am unique and special, but so are others and I need to respect their rights."

NPD is probably more common in men. Estimates of prevalence are less than 1% in the general population and range from 2 to 16% in the clinical population. NPD may be associated with anorexia nervosa and substance-related disorders (especially cocaine). Individuals with NPD may have more trouble as they age and their body loses its youthful form and their role in society changes. Positive changes can occur as the person with NPD faces various life events such as experiencing achievements or enduring relationships (Ronningstam et al., 1995).

Patients with NPD seek treatment infrequently ("Why should I? There's nothing wrong with me."). But when they do, it's usually because depression or a medical illness threatens their grandiosity. Successful short-term management of these patients includes acknowledging their "specialness," setting some reasonable limits, and allowing them to conclude that their therapist or M.D. is also special and therefore able to appreciate their "special" problems. Long-term psychotherapy is usually recommended, even though its chance of inducing major change is low. When their invincibility is exposed, patients with NPD project their resentment onto their therapists, who should try to respect their patients' exaggerated self-importance while gently placing it into perspective. Group therapy should usually be avoided, because these individuals will monopolize the group until either everybody quits or group members run them out (Yalom, 2005).

ANTISOCIAL PERSONALITY DISORDER

"Why do I rob banks? Because that's where the money is."
—Willy Sutton, professional bank robber

The essential feature of antisocial personality disorder (ASPD) is continuous and chronic antisocial behavior that violates the rights of others without the person expressing or demonstrating any remorse or concern (see Table 24-7 which lists the full diagnostic criteria). This condition is also called "sociopathy."

Clinical Presentation

Although many sociopaths are charming and resourceful, they're without enduring or intimate relationships. Friendships, even with fellow crooks, are opportunistic alliances to be broken whenever it's convenient. With radar for people's vulnerabilities, people with ASPD can readily manipulate, exploit, control, deceive, and intimidate. Unlike other criminals, these individuals enjoy "making suckers" of people. Their sexual relations are thrilling conquests and nothing more—and that includes marriage.

Emotionally shallow, people with ASPD seem incapable of shame, guilt, loyalty, love, or any persistently sincere emotion; although quick to anger, they don't even sustain hatred. One moment they'll proclaim how deeply they feel about someone, and momentarily, they might believe themselves. These feelings are at most fleeting. Expressions of guilt and remorse don't affect future conduct.

TABLE 24-7
Diagnostic Criteria for Antisocial (Dissocial) Personality Disorder

A. Personality disorder, usually coming to attention because of a gross disparity between behavior and the prevailing social norms, and characterized by at least five of the following:
1. disregard for social norms, rules and obligations
2. marked proneness to blame others, or to offer plausible rationalizations for the behavior that has brought the patient into conflict with society (*DSM-5 specifies deceitfulness*)
3. very low tolerance to frustration (*DSM-5 adds poor impulse control and failure to plan ahead*)
4. persistent irritability
5. low threshold for discharge of aggression, including violence
6. gross and persistent attitude of irresponsibility
7. callous unconcern for the feelings of others (indifference and lack of remorse)
8. incapacity to maintain enduring relationships, though having no difficulty in establishing them
9. incapacity to experience guilt or to profit from experience, particularly punishment
B. Must be 18 years or older.
C. Conduct disorder during childhood and adolescence, though not invariably present, may further support the diagnosis.
D. The condition is not directly attributable to gross brain damage or disease, or to another psychiatric disorder particularly schizophrenia, bipolar mania, or a substance use disorder.

Note: Adapted from *ICD-10* (p. 159) and *DSM-5* (p. 659)

Like some addicts crave heroin, individuals with ASPD crave stimulation. Excitement alone medicates their allergies to boredom, depression, and frustration. They can't hold a job; it would be too dull. They are always on the move, "making deals," bumming around, picking fights, raping people, or killing them. They live solely in the present; the past is a dim memory and the future a fiction. Unconcerned with the consequences of their actions and unable to learn from experience, these individuals are not restrained by the threat of punishment. Rewards must come now, not later; gratification cannot be delayed. Sociopaths are said to have "superego lacunae," that is, they are virtually without conscience. Expediency, immediate pleasure, and "stimulus hunger" override all other restraints.

Epidemiology

In the general population ASPD affects about 5% of men and nearly 1% of women. Among psychiatric populations ASPD affects up to 15% of men and 3% of women. ASPD is more prevalent in lower socioeconomic groups and among urban dwellers.

Differential Diagnosis

ASPD should be diagnosed *unless* the antisocial behavior only occurs during the course of *schizophrenia* or a *manic episode*. Schizophrenia preempts ASPD because it's hard to know what is producing the antisocial conduct. Mania is easy to differentiate because its antisocial behavior is episodic, time-limited, and rarely occurs during childhood. People with ASPD often abuse drugs and alcohol, but a *substance use disorder* should be diagnosed only when the patient meets the full criteria for it. Some people with substance use disorders displayed no antisocial behavior before they became addicted (Gerstley et al., 1990). After the addiction had taken hold, they lied, stole, and killed for their drugs. Treating the addiction in some cases may reverse this behavior.

Etiology and Pathogenesis

One should distinguish the "habitual" criminal (i.e., someone with ASPD) from the "occasional" criminal. Habitual antisocial behavior stems from genetic *and* psychosocial factors, whereas occasional antisocial behavior seems to arise more from psychosocial causes. This is a big generalization, but in large measure, habitual criminals are born whereas occasional criminals are made. This section only discusses the "habituals."

Psychosocial Factors

Sociological

Poverty contributes to ASPD, but it's hardly the sole cause. In a study of Philadelphia inner-city youth, 35% of males under 18 had at least one contact with the police, but only 6% caused half of all delinquencies and two-thirds of all violent crimes. These data confirm the distinction between habitual and occasional criminals. These data suggest that despite substantial economic deprivation, the vast majority of the poor do *not* develop sociopathic behavior.

Additional evidence demonstrates that factors other than poverty must be involved. First, ASPD also arises in middle and upper socioeconomic groups. Second, ASPD is becoming more prevalent worldwide, even where there is increasing wealth. Third, the childhood behaviors of adults with ASPD are remarkably similar regardless of economic class. Fourth, these childhood antisocial behaviors emerge so early, it's improbable that sociological factors are a primary cause.

Familial

Sociopaths generally grow up amid considerable parental discord (e.g., desertion, separation, divorce, custody fights) and family disruption (e.g., early deaths, frequent moves, brutal discipline). Mothers of children with ASPD often do not provide consistent affection or discipline (Glueck & Glueck, 1959; Rutter, 1981). Also common during their childhoods are maternal neglect, indifference, and alcoholism (perhaps leading to poor attachment). Instead of the mother, Robins (1966) found that the best predictor of ASPD was having a father with sociopathy or alcoholism. The children grew up to become delinquents whether or not their fathers had reared them. Was the father's absence or inconsistency the culprit? Or was sociopathy inherited from these fathers? The evidence is inconclusive. Many individuals with ASPD are also reared in stable families with loving parents and normal siblings. ASPD probably has multiple etiologies.

Biomedical Factors

On neuropsychological tests, individuals with ASPD frequently do better on performance than on verbal tests. When younger, they have trouble interpreting and abstracting verbal information. Tell a 6-year-old with incipient ASPD, "Do not get near the stove," and he will not understand *near* and continue approaching it from different directions until he is told *no*. He may appear to be "testing limits," but in reality he may be trying to figure out what was meant by *near*. It is not a coincidence that many fail reading and writing but excel at working on their cars or assault rifles.

> Studies of male felons, most having ASPD, revealed that 20% of their first-degree male relatives had ASPD and 33% had alcoholism. Among female felons, half being habitual criminals, a third of their male relatives had ASPD and half had alcoholism. Although most research demonstrates higher concordance rates for ASPD among identical (36%) than fraternal (12%) twins, these different rates are not as eye-popping as those with other mental disorders. One small study reported that the prefrontal lobes of people with ASPD had an 11% reduction in the gray matter volume and a lower autonomic response to social stress as compared with normal healthy controls

(Raine et al., 2000). Adopted-away research suggests that genetic factors play some etiological role, but that environmental factors are also important.

Clinical Course

Antisocial personalities have "always" been up to "no good"; they are not "good kids" who simply "fell into a bad crowd." ASPD emerges in boys during early childhood, in girls, around puberty.

As children, individuals with ASPD habitually lie, steal, skip school, and defy authority. They conceal feelings and talk to parents only when they want something. Exploiting parental affection, using siblings, running away from home, delighting in forbidden acts, and hanging around with older delinquents are common.

A mother describes her delinquent son: "He's always been different from my others, as if he's possessed. What kind of 5-year-old steals from his mother's purse? Once I caught him hammering a squirrel to death, and when I yelled at him to stop, he just smiled. He enjoyed taunting me."

As adolescents, these individuals abuse substances, gamble heavily, and display unusually early or aggressive sexual behavior. They mock rules, cut class, cause fights, and get expelled; their grades plummet. They're "pathological liars"—they lie without reason—and they delight in terrorizing others. For example, a delinquent youth pulled out a pistol, aimed it at his teacher's head, and demanded he undress. Once the teacher was nude, the youth nudged the teacher's testicles with his gun and fired. The gun wasn't loaded. Only the youth laughed.

By age 30, the promiscuity, fighting, criminality, and vagrancy of people with ASPD tend to diminish. They "burn out." Some find they no longer have the energy required for a shiftless life and try to go "straight." Some succeed partially but few completely. Some end up on skid row, some are chronic substance abusers, some die by violence; in many prisons up to 75% of the inmates are sociopaths. Many subsist from one low-paying job to another and from one town to another. Only 2% of cases with full-blown ASPD remit after age 21.

Alcoholism and depression are the mental disorders that most often affect people with ASPD and, thus, the most common reasons they seek treatment. They often have conversion symptoms, especially when stressed or arrested. Many delinquent teenage girls develop somatization disorder as adults. Most sociopaths have low-to-normal IQs; a few have significant mental deficiency (IQ < 70). Early-onset conduct disorder (before age 10 years) increases the likelihood of developing ASPD in adulthood.

Complications

ASPD markedly impairs social and occupational functioning. Plagued by infidelity, jealousy, and child abuse, marriages usually end in separation and divorce. These individuals tend to marry young, beat their wives, and marry women with ASPD. Besides getting murdered, they have unusually high rates of venereal disease, out-of-wedlock pregnancies, injuries from fights and accidents, substance dependence, and gun wounds—which all lead to their shorter life expectancies. Major depression, suicidal threats, and gestures are common; about 5% commit suicide.

Management and Treatment

No psychotherapy has been found to really help these individuals. ASPD is egosyntonic, and its bearers have no desire to change, consider insights to be excuses, have no concept of the future, resent all authorities (including therapists), view the patient role as pitiful, detest being in a position of inferiority, and deem therapy a joke and therapists as objects to be conned, threatened, seduced, or used. A "tough love" approach reduces some of these problems by showing that the therapist cares but is not a patsy. It is important to remember that individuals with ASPD are human beings with feelings. Frequent confrontation is expected. They want to do things for themselves, but they need to see that the way they are doing things isn't working. If they finally "burn out," become depressed, or experience incarceration, they may find themselves willing to try the "straight" way.

Judges are as stuck as psychotherapists. They know that "rehabilitation" does not help the "hard-core criminal." Judges should know that sentencing individuals with ASPD to psychotherapy wastes everybody's time. Those made to enlist in the military can't tolerate the discipline, go AWOL, and are dishonorably discharged. So what can be done? Not much. But consider the following:

1. *Prevention* is the most important intervention medical and mental health professionals can make. Early detection of antisocial behavior in children and young teenagers should be treated promptly before it gets out of hand. Many teenage gang members are not sociopathic; they want the respect of other members. Youngsters with ASPD don't do well in gangs

because they try to take advantage of their own fellow members. Getting the nonsociopathic members out of gangs and finding alternative ways for them to gain "respect" may prevent them from pursuing a life of crime.

2. *Family counseling* is critical. Therapists may not do much for individuals with ASPD, but they may help their families. Manipulated so often, family members swing from hate to guilt, never knowing what to feel. Because they are so close to the problem, common-sense guidelines from an objective outsider/professional can help them place matters into perspective.

3. *Treating substance misuse* is also critical, since antisocial acts increase during intoxication. Sociopathic behavior has gradations from milder to severe. Drug use may push someone with a milder ASPD into becoming a thief and murderer.

4. *Counseling should be independent of punishment and parole*, whenever possible. If sociopathic individuals know that therapists exert no influence on their sentence, they may be a bit more likely to use treatment constructively.

AVOIDANT PERSONALITY DISORDER

The essential feature of avoidant personality disorder (APD) is extreme social discomfort because of a pervasive fear of being judged negatively. More specifically, the diagnostic criteria in Table 24-8 include these characteristics: (1) hypersensitivity to potential rejection, humiliation, or shame; (2) only entering relationships in which uncritical acceptance is virtually guaranteed; (3) social withdrawal; (4) a desire for affection and acceptance; and (5) low self-esteem.

Schizoid and avoidant personalities are loners, but the person with SDPD doesn't want friends and the person with APD does. These are the painfully shy people, permeating Garrison Keillor's Lake Woebegone radio show. They want affection, but not as much as they fear rejection. Because they dread the slightest disapproval and will misconstrue people's comments as derogatory, they have few, if any, friends. Angry and upset at their own inability to relate, they'll try to prevent rejection by ingratiating themselves to others.

Children as young as 4 months of age have been described as fearful, withdrawn, and shy. These children with behavioral inhibitions possess the temperament most associated with APD in adults. A friendly, gentle, reassuring approach is the best way to manage people with APD. Most children and teens with APD can't avoid becoming avoidant adults. Virtually all

TABLE 24-8
Diagnostic Criteria for Avoidant (Anxious) Personality Disorder

A. Personality disorder characterized by at least four of the following:

1. avoidance of social or occupational activities that involve significant interpersonal contact because of fear of criticism, disapproval, or rejection
2. unwillingness to become involved with people unless certain of being liked
3. persistent and pervasive feelings of tension and apprehension
4. excessive preoccupation with being criticized or rejected in social situations
5. hypersensitivity to rejection and criticism
6. belief that one is socially inept, personally unappealing, or inferior to others
7. restrictions in lifestyle because of need to have physical security

B. The condition is not directly attributable to gross brain damage or disease, or to another psychiatric disorder. Social phobia is an antecedent.

Note: Adapted from ICD-10 (p. 161) and DSM-5 (pp. 672–673)

people with APD have social phobias, but a majority of people with social phobias do not have APD. Social phobias are responses to *specific* situations (e.g., public speaking), whereas APD pervades all social relations. APD may have started out as a social phobia that kept getting worse and involving more situations. One twin study strongly suggests that APD and social phobia share a common genetic vulnerability (Reichborn-Kjennerud et al., 2007). The prevalence of APD in the general adult population is estimated at 2.5%.

MAOIs are the most effective medication for social phobias and may also be indicated for APD. In one study, 75% of patients with APD who were treated for a year with MAOIs were so improved that they no longer qualified for the diagnosis. If this treatment proves to be that highly effective, the diagnosis of APD may become obsolete. After all, part of the definition of personality disorder is an enduring pattern of behavior. SSRIs and selective serotonin and norepinephrine reuptake inhibitors (SNRIs) are also proving to have therapeutic benefit with social phobia and thus might be useful in the treatment of APD. The use of caffeine and other stimulants may heighten anxiety and actually interfere with the avoidant person confronting his fears—a necessary step for any clinical improvement. Cognitive–behavioral therapies are effective when they focus on assertiveness, desensitization in the situations, and cognitive change. Group therapy can also be helpful as patients with APD tend to be well liked and get much support in therapy groups. The use of alcohol (and benzodiazepines) can become a maladaptive coping behavior to free inhibitions and is best avoided.

DEPENDENT PERSONALITY DISORDER

The essential features of people with dependent personality disorder (DPD) include (1) passively allowing others to assume responsibility for major areas in their lives because (2) they lack self-confidence or the ability to function independently; (3) they then subordinate their needs to those of others, (4) become dependent on them, and (5) avoid any chance of being self-reliant. Table 24–9 lists the diagnostic criteria for dependent personality disorder.

Everybody has dependent traits and wishes. What distinguishes the dependent personality is that the dependency is total, pervading all areas of life. People with DPD dread autonomy; they may be productive, but only if supervised. They are likely to view themselves as inept or stupid. When pressed to name redeeming qualities, they might reluctantly confess to being good companions, loyal and kind.

> Ethel is prototypical. She refers to herself as "man's best friend." Her man is Mitch, a husband who schedules her days, tells her what foods to eat, picks her doctors, chooses her clothes, and selects her friends. Explains Ethel: "He likes to think, and I don't. Why should I decide things, when he'll do it for me?" This arrangement pleased both for years until Mitch announced he

---

TABLE 24-9
Diagnostic Criteria for Dependent Personality Disorder

A. Personality disorder characterized by at least five of the following:
  1. limited capacity to make everyday decisions without an excessive amount of advice and reassurance from others
  2. encouraging or allowing others to make most of one's important life decisions
  3. unwillingness to make even reasonable demands on the people one depends on
  4. perceiving oneself as helpless, incompetent, and lacking stamina
  5. subordination of one's own needs to those of others on whom one is dependent, and undue compliance with their wishes
  6. feeling uncomfortable or helpless when alone, because of exaggerated fears of inability to care for oneself
  7. preoccupation with fears of being abandoned by a person with whom one has a close relationship
  8. fear of being left alone to care for oneself
B. The condition is not directly attributable to gross brain damage or disease, or to another psychiatric disorder.

Note: Adapted from ICD-10 (p. 161) and DSM-5 (p. 675)

was going to China for 3 weeks on business. Ethel was frantic and sought treatment. Like most dependent personalities, she wanted help not for dependency, but for losing it.

Historically, DPD was known as "passive–dependent" personality, and dependent personalities were known as "oral characters." This label referred to their most striking clinical feature — the insistence on being "fed" or taken care of; it also suggested the etiology of overindulged or frustrated wishes during the oral stage of psychosexual development. More recently, the role of maternal deprivation during the oral stage has been stressed. Oral features include a constant demand for attention, passivity, dependency, a fear of autonomy, a lack of perseverance, dread of decision making, suggestibility, and oral behaviors (e.g., thumb-sucking, smoking, drinking). Oral traits are common in "normals," but even more so in psychiatric patients.

The 1963 Midtown Manhattan survey showed that 2.5% of the residents had passive–dependent personalities. DPD is more prevalent in women and in the youngest sibling. Prolonged physical illness during childhood may predispose to DPD. *Histrionic, schizotypal, narcissistic, and avoidant personality disorders* often coexist with DPD, and *dysthymic disorder* and *major depression* are frequent complications. Although dependent traits are common in *agoraphobia*, the person with agoraphobia will *actively* insist that others assume responsibility, whereas the person with DPD *passively* abdicates control to others.

Management and Treatment

Patients with DPD will call the office incessantly asking for advice or clarifications and regularly to schedule extra appointments. From the start firm limits (e.g., no calls to home, clear expectations: "Let's schedule an appointment every 2 weeks") and information are important. If medications are being initiated, it is best to give out information sheets to reduce the calls with questions. If "emergency" appointments are happening too regularly, temporarily increase the frequency of scheduled visits. Sometimes knowing an appointment is coming soon is very reassuring to people with DPD, and they won't feel the need to call regularly. If clear limits are not established in the beginning, it is nearly impossible to establish them later without the patient experiencing a lot of anger or hurt.

More insightful patients may benefit from *psychodynamic psychotherapy*. Often addressed (in this sequence) are the patient's (1) low self-esteem and its origins, (2) fears of harming others by seeking autonomy, (3) dependency on the therapist, and (4) the experience of termination as it relates to dependency. Less psychologically minded patients or those not wanting psychodynamic therapy may benefit from supportive *group therapy* or *assertiveness training*.

OBSESSIVE–COMPULSIVE PERSONALITY DISORDER

"Are you sure there is a hyphen in *obsessive–compulsive*?"
—Anonymous medical student

The essential features of obsessive–compulsive personality disorder (OCPD) include (1) a restricted ability to express warm and tender emotions, (2) a perfectionism that interferes with the ability to grasp "the big picture," (3) an insistence that others submit to his or her way of doing things, (4) an excessive devotion to work and productivity to the exclusion of pleasure, and (5) indecisiveness. Table 24-10 lists diagnostic criteria for OCPD, also referred to as Anankastic Personality Disorder.

Wilhelm Reich called these patients "living machines." People with OCPD are highly productive but never enjoy what they produce. Everything is a chore, nothing is effortless. Every decision demands exhaustive

---

TABLE 24-10
Diagnostic Criteria for Obsessive–Compulsive (Anankastic) Personality Disorder

A. Personality disorder characterized by at least four of the following:
1. preoccupation with details, rules, lists, order, organization, or schedule
2. perfectionism that interferes with task completion
3. undue preoccupation with productivity to the exclusion of pleasure and interpersonal relationships
4. excessive conscientiousness, scrupulousness
5. feelings of excessive doubt and caution
6. unreasonable insistence by the patient that others submit to exactly his or her way of doing things, or unreasonable reluctance to allow others to do things
7. excessive pedantry and adherence to social conventions
8. rigidity and stubbornness
9. intrusion of insistent and unwelcome thoughts or impulses

B. The condition is not directly attributable to gross brain damage or disease, or to another psychiatric disorder.

Note: Adapted from *ICD-10* (p. 160) and *DSM-5* (pp. 678–679)

---

analysis. Everything must be right, and nothing must be left to chance. They won't follow hunches, since hunches may be wrong. They are perfectionists: Carrots must be sliced exactly one-quarter wide or a meal is ruined. Cleanliness *is* Godliness. These individuals excel at concentrating, and they never stop concentrating (Shapiro, 1999). They can't skim a page; they must scrutinize every word. Their focus is sharp, yet narrow; they see the parts, but never the whole. They are interpersonally obtuse, boring, and annoying; they subject people to endless irrelevant details, refuse to make decisions, are moralistic and hyper-critically self-righteous, insist on conformity (from others), and never get to the point.

> Harold, a compulsive accountant, spent 8 years obsessing over whether to leave his wife and three kids for his mistress-secretary. "I stay only for the kids," he insisted, but in truth, he never saw them. Repeatedly calculating the pros and cons—even devising a mathematical formula—Harold would ask a friend for advice, promptly reject it, criticize the friend for not helping him enough, and cap it off by complaining that his friend doesn't donate enough money to the synagogue. Like most people with OCPD, Harold considered himself an intellectual, while others considered him rigid.

OCPD is diagnosed more often in men and in the oldest sibling. The prevalence in the general population is estimated at 1%; in psychiatric clinical populations around 6%. Frequent complications are major depression, dysthymia, and hypochondrias. Only 6% of patients with obsessive–compulsive disorder also have OCPD (Baer et al., 1990).

Laypeople call these patients "tight-assed"; psychoanalysts call them "anal characters" because, theoretically, they have arrested at the anal stage of psychosexual development. The anal character is known for having problems with control, authority figures, autonomy, shame, and self-doubt. OCPD runs in families, but it's unclear how much this results from the emotionally constipated climate of the anger-suppressing parents who often rear these patients or from heredity, as suggested by several twin and adoption studies.

Management and Treatment

Patients with OCPD prefer clinicians who are like themselves. To form an alliance with them, clinicians must demonstrate that they are careful and attend to detail. The patient with OCPD, like the patient with paranoia, must have complete explanations of what will happen during evaluation and treatment. These patients may require long-term therapy since they resist exploring their emotions and have trouble developing close relationships. They are lethal when they become suicidal because they will be sure to complete it with much planning and perfection. Though they are often bright, they do not use insight to instigate change, only to avoid it. Psychology is abstract, whereas patients with OCPD are concrete. They swamp therapists with details. Simply asking a person with OCPD if he's reviewed the want-ads can result in a critique of every ad in the paper. If interrupted, he becomes angry; if allowed to continue, 10 minutes later he will blame the therapist for wasting time. Consequently, therapy should focus on the here-and-now and stress feelings instead of thoughts. Cognitive–behavioral therapy may be effective since it focuses on the here-and-now. Psychodynamic psychotherapy will require long-term management, and will need to focus on the psychic defenses, soften the severe superego, and uncover unconscious conflicts. Progress should be measured in terms of changed behavior, not insight. Perry et al. (2005) have demonstrated that both cognitive–behavioral therapy and psychodynamic psychotherapy have beneficial effects on patients with cluster C personality disorders, including OCPD. Group therapy may help those with serious interpersonal problems.

Additional categories of personality disorders have been defined but are not specifically included in the latest nosologies as they await further study. For example, depressive personality disorder is defined as "a pervasive pattern of depressive cognitions and behaviors beginning by early adulthood." The passive–aggressive or negativistic personality disorder is described as "a pervasive pattern of negativistic attitudes and passive resistance to demands for adequate performance in social and occupational situations that begin by early adulthood." The apparent demarcation of clear boundaries defining the various categories is somewhat arbitrary. In reality, there is a continuum ranging between normal and abnormal personalities. For example, the ruthless but very successful businessman may have many antisocial traits but function exceptionally well in the modern-day competitive world. The detailed-oriented and hard-working physician is well-appreciated by her patients, yet he or she embodies many traits of an OCPD. As mentioned near the beginning of this chapter, an alternative method of classifying personalities according to a continuum of personality traits is offered in *DSM-5*.

References

American Psychiatric Association. (2013). *Diagnostic and statistical manual of mental disorders* (5th ed.). Arlington, VA: American Psychiatric Association.

Baer, L., Jenike, M.A., Ricciardi, J., Holland, A.D., Seymour, R.J., Minichiello, W.E., et al.

(1990). Personality disorders in patients with obsessive–compulsive disorders. *Archives of General Psychiatry, 47*, 826–832.

Bateman, A., & Fonagy, P. (2001). Treatment of borderline personality disorder with psycho-analytically oriented partial hospitalization: An 18-month follow-up. *American Journal of Psychiatry, 158*, 36–42.

Colom, F., Vieta, E., Martinez-Aran, A., Reinares, M., Benabarre, A., & Gasto, C. (2000). Clinical factors associated with treatment and noncompliance in euthymic bipolar patient. *Journal of Clinical Psychiatry, 61*, 549–555.

Cornelius, J.R., Soloff, P.H., Perel, J.M., & Ulrich, R.F. (1993). Continuation pharmacotherapy of borderline personality disorder with haloperidol and phenelzine. *American Journal of Psychiatry, 150*, 1843–1848.

Ellis, H. (1915). *Affirmations,* 2nd ed. (pp. 86–130). Boston: Houghton Mifflin.

Gandhi, N., Tyrer, P., Evans, K., McGee, A., Lamont, A., & Harrison-Read, P. (2001). A randomized controlled trial of community oriented and hospital oriented care for discharged psychiatric population: Influence of personality disorders on police contracts. *Journal of Personality Disorders, 15*, 94–102.

Gerstley, L.J., Alterman, A.I., McLellan, A.T., & Woody, G.E. (1990). Antisocial personality disorder in patients with substance abuse disorders: A problematic diagnosis. *American Journal of Psychiatry, 147*, 173–178.

Glueck, S., & Glueck, E. (1959). *Predicting delinquency and crime.* Cambridge, MA: Harvard University Press.

Herbeck, D.M., Fitek, D.J., Svikis, D.S., Montoya, I.D., Marcus, S.C., & West, J.C. (2005). Treatment compliance in patients with comorbid psychiatric and substance use disorders. *American Journal of Addictions, 14*(3), 195–207.

Kahana, R.J., & Bibring, G.L. (1964). Personality types in medical management. In N.E. Zinberg (Ed.), *Psychiatry and medical practice* (pp. 108–123). New York: International University Press.

Kernberg, O. (1975). *Borderline conditions and pathological narcissism.* New York: Aronson.

Kessler, R.C., McGonagle, K.A., Ahzo, S., Nelson, C.H., Hughes, M., Eshleman, S., et al. (1994). Lifetime and 12-month prevalence of *DSM-III-R* psychiatric disorders in the United States. Results from the National Comorbidity Survey. *Archives of General Psychiatry, 51*, 8–19.

Koeningsberg, H.W., Kaplan, R.D., Gilmore, M.M., & Cooper, A.M. (1985). The relationship between syndrome and personality disorder in *DSM-III*: Experience with 2,462 patients. *American Journal of Psychiatry, 142*, 207–212.

Koerner, K., & Linehan, M.M. (2000). Research on dialectical behavior therapy for patients with borderline personality disorder. *Psychiatric Clinics of North America, 23*(1), 151–167.

Lenzenweger, M.F., Loranger, A.W., Korfine, L., & Neff, C. (1997). Detecting personality disorder in nonclinical populations. *Archives of General Psychiatry, 54*, 345–351.

Linehan, M.M. (1993). *Skills training manual for treating borderline personality disorder.* New York: Guilford.

Linehan, M.M., Armstrong, H.E., Suarez, A., Allmon, D., & Heard, H.L. (1991). Cognitive–behavioral treatment of chronically parasuicidal borderline patients. *Archives of General Psychiatry, 48,* 1060–1064.

Mahler, M., Pine, F., & Bergman, A. (1975). *The psychotherapy and the science of psychodynamics.* Boston: Butterworth.

Masterson, J.F. (1976). *Psychotherapy of the borderline adult: A developmental approach.* New York: Brunner/Mazel.

Millon, T. (2004). *Personality disorders in modern life,* 2nd ed. New York: Wiley.

Perry, J.C., & Bond, M. (2005). "Defensive functioning" in Gabbard's treatments of psychiatric disorders. In J. Oldham, A.E. Skodol, & D. Bender (Eds.), *American Psychiatric Publishing Textbook of Personality Disorders* (pp. 523–540). Washington, DC: American Psychiatric Association.

Pirkis, J., Burgess, P., & Jolley, D. (1999). Suicide attempts by psychiatric patients in acute inpatient, long stay inpatient and community care. *Social Psychiatry, 34*(12), 634–644.

Raine, A., Lencz, T., Bihrle, S., LaCasse, L., & Colletti, P. (2000). Reduced prefrontal gray matter volume and reduced autonomic activity in antisocial personality disorder. *Archives of General Psychiatry, 57,* 119–127.

Reich, J., Boerstler, H., Yates, W., & Nduaguba, M. (1989). Utilization of medical resources in persons with DSM-III personality disorders in a community sample. *International Journal of Psychiatry Medicine, 19*(1), 1–9.

Reich, W. (1972). *Character analysis,* 3rd. ed. New York: Noonday Press. (Original work published 1949)

Reichborn-Kjennerud, T., Czajkowski, N., Torgersen, S., Neale, M., Orstavik, R.E., Tambs, K., et al. (2007). The relationship between avoidant personality disorder and social phobia: A population-based twin study. *American Journal of Psychiatry, 164*(11), 1722–1728.

Robins, C.J., & Chapman, A.L. (2004). Dialectical behavior therapy: Current status, recent developments, and future directions. *Journal of Personality Disorders, 18,* 73–89.

Robins, L.N. (1966). *Deviant children grown up.* Baltimore: Williams & Wilkins.

Ronningstam, E., Gunderson, J., & Lyons, M. (1995). Changes in pathological narcissism. *American Journal of Psychiatry, 152*(2), 253.

Rutter, M. (1981). *Maternal deprivation reassessed,* 2nd ed. London: Penguin Books.

Shapiro, D. (1999). *Neurotic styles.* New York: Basic Books.

Svartberg, M., Stiles, T.C., & Seltzer, M.H. (2004). A randomized, controlled trial of the effectiveness of short-term dynamic psychotherapy and cognitive therapy for cluster C personality disorders. *American Journal of Psychiatry, 161*(5), 810–817.

Torgersen, S., Lygren, S., Oien, P.A., Skre, I., Onstad, S., Edvardsen, J., et al. (2000). A twin study of personality disorders. *Comprehensive Psychiatry, 41*(6), 416–425.

Trull, T.J., Tragesser, S.L., Solhan, M., & Schwartz-Mette, R. (2007). Dimensional models of personality disorder: *Diagnostic and Statistical Manual of Mental Disorders* fifth edition and beyond. *Current Opinions in Psychiatry, 20,* 52–56.

Whisman, M.A., Tolejko, N., & Chatav, Y. (1993). Social consequences of personality disorders, probability and timing of marriage and probability of marital disruption. *Journal of Personality Disorders, 7,* 44–62.

World Health Organization. (1992). *The ICD–10 classification of mental and behavioural disorders: Clinical descriptions and diagnostic guidelines.* Geneva: World Health Organization (WHO).

Yalom, I.D. (2005). *The theory and practice of group psychotherapy,* 5th ed. Basic Books: New York.

Zanarini, M.C., Frankenburg, F.R., Reich, B., Silk, K.R., Hudson, I., & McSweeney, L.B. (2007). The subsyndromal phenomenology of borderline personality disorder: A 10-year follow-up study. *American Journal of Psychiatry, 164,* 929–939.

25

Neurodevelopmental Disorders

The disorders included in this chapter invariably begin during infancy or childhood and demonstrate a delay or functional impairment in normal development. The functions affected often include language, visual-spatial, and motor coordination. Because development of these skills is strongly related to biological maturation of the central nervous system, it is characteristic for the deficits to become progressively milder. Usually, the history is of an early delay or impairment with no prior period of normal development, and a steady course without the typical remissions and relapses that are characteristic of many mental disorders. Most of the developmental disorders are multiple times more common in boys than in girls and are primarily influenced by genetic versus environmental factors. Commonly there is a family history of similar or related disorders.

Children may have many of the disorders already discussed in other chapters, such as mood, eating, and sleep disorders. But kids can have other problems too, and development may complicate their diagnosis. Behavior within the range of normal may become confused with psychopathology. The best way to minimize this confusion is to have a good understanding of normal development, so that any deviations can be recognized and addressed. Many disorders of childhood occur when development deviates from normal, is in some way impeded or delayed, or regresses. This chapter does not focus on normal development, but an understanding of normal child development is an essential prerequisite for those who recognize and treat disorders of childhood. Table 25-1 lists a number of normal developmental milestones for children.

INTELLECTUAL DEVELOPMENT DISORDER (FORMERLY MENTAL RETARDATION)

The diagnosis of an intellectual development disorder (formerly referred to as mental retardation) is not based on IQ alone but also includes deficits in

TABLE 25-1
Childhood Development

AGE	MOTOR AND COGNITIVE FUNCTIONS
1 month	Roots, sucks, and grasps
2 months	Social smile
5 months	Sits and grasps objects
7 months	Crawls (6–8 months)
8 months	Stranger anxiety
10 months	Object permanence (will look for an object hidden from view)
11 months	Walking (10–14 months)
15 months	Imitation
18 months	Talking (few words)
19 months	Preoperational thought
22 months	Toilet training (wide range of normal; 22–48 months)
6 years	Shift to verbal memory
7 years	Concrete operational thought
12 years	Formal operational thought, beginnings of abstract reasoning

adaptive functioning. IQ tests mainly measure potential ability to perform in school and were not specifically developed to measure ability to perform life functions. Adaptive behavior is always impaired, but in protected social environments with high levels of support, mild impairment may not be obvious. Intelligence is not a unitary characteristic but is based upon a large number of different skills. For each individual there is a general tendency for all these skills to develop to a similar level. However, there may be one particular area of higher skill level or one particular area of significant impairment. The assessment of intellectual functioning should be based on as much information as is available, including clinical findings, adaptive behavior, and psychometric testing (see Table 2-5).

Intellectual disability (ID) is not a single disease, syndrome, or symptom, but rather a state of impairment that is identified by the behavior and abilities of the individual. Contrary to popular impression, many people with intellectual disabilities are not immediately detectable. They can look, act, and talk normally. Table 25-2 lists the diagnostic criteria for intellectual development disorder (also commonly referred to as intellectual disability). The diagnosis, which is usually made before 7 or 8 years of age, describes an individual's current level of thinking and behavior, but does not necessarily give an accurate prognosis. People may be classified as ID at one time during their lives and not at another. How a particular child will eventually turn out depends more on coexisting handicaps, resources, motivation, educational and training opportunities, and treatment than on the intellectual disability

---

TABLE 25-2
Diagnostic Criteria for Intellectual Developmental Disorder
(formerly Mental Retardation)

Intellectual Developmental Disorder (also called Intellectual Disability) is a condition of arrested or incomplete development of the mind, which is especially characterized by impairment of skills manifested during the developmental period, which contribute to the overall level of intelligence, i.e., cognitive, language, motor, and social abilities. To establish a diagnosis the following 3 criteria must be met:

A. A **reduced level of intellectual functioning** (usually an IQ lower than 70) exists based upon global assessments of ability and not on any single area of specific impairment or skill.
  1. Intelligence testing should be individually administered and adjusted for local cultural norms.
  2. The intelligence test selected should be appropriate to the individual's level of functioning and additional specific handicapping conditions, e.g., expressive language problems, hearing impairment, physical involvement.

B. A **diminished ability to adapt to the daily demands of the normal social environment.**
  1. Scales of social maturity and adaptation should be locally standardized.
  2. Assessment should involve interviewing a parent or care-provider who is familiar with the individual's skills in everyday life.

C. Onset of the reduced intellectual and adaptive functioning is **during early development**

Without the use of standardized instruments and procedures, the diagnosis must be regarded as a provisional estimate only.

Note: Adapted from *ICD-10* (p. 176–180) and *DSM-5* (p. 33)

---

itself. Indeed, people with ID frequently have coexisting handicaps that are more incapacitating than the intellectual deficits.

The history of mental retardation is a checkered one. In Europe during the 14th and 15th centuries, those with mental retardation were regarded superstitiously as blessed "infants of the good God." However, during the "Enlightenment" Martin Luther referred to the "feebleminded" as "Godless" and thought society should rid itself of them. It was not until Binet developed psychometric tests so that schools could "track" schoolchildren into special programs that the range of human intellectual capacity became evident. In spite of noble intentions, these IQ tests were often used to exclude many children from school and to identify "imbeciles" in need of sterilization so that mental retardation would not be propagated. Only with Folling's discovery in 1934 of phenylketonuria, a treatable cause of mental retardation, did the study and treatment of mental retardation become respectable.

TABLE 25-3
Levels of Intellectual Disability

CATEGORY	PERCENTAGE OF THE INTELLECTUALLY DISABLED	IQ*	MENTAL AGE FOR ADULTS (IN YEARS)
Borderline			70–85
Mild	89.0	50–55 to 69	8.5 to 11.0
Moderate	6.0	35–40 to 50–55	6.0 to 8.5
Severe	3.4	20–25 to 35–40	3.75 to 6.0
Profound	1.6	below 20–25	0 to 3.75

*The IQ levels are provided as a guide and should not be applied rigidly.

Epidemiology

The adult prevalence of intellectual disability is generally lower than in childhood and estimates vary between 1 and 3% depending on criteria used. The vast majority of people with ID are only mildly impaired. Most people with ID can hold a job and live on their own, with perhaps some support from family members. Table 25-3 lists the levels of intellectual disability by degree of severity in the adult population.

Different IQ tests are scaled with different standard deviations: This variation is reflected in IQ *ranges* rather than fixed points. Between 70 and 84 IQ is defined as borderline intelligence and not intellectually disabled. Individuals in this range may struggle with some aspects of independent living but generally are not considered mentally impaired. However, because of the range of error on standard IQ tests, a person with an IQ of 75 and significant adaptive deficits could be classified as intellectual disabled. However, another individual with an IQ of 75 who does not have adaptive deficits would be considered to have borderline intellectual functioning. People with mild intellectual impairment are considered "educable" and can master some school subjects such as basic reading and simple arithmetic. People with moderate ID are termed "trainable" because they can learn simple basic tasks but usually cannot master most subjects taught in schools.

Intelligence in the general population does not follow a normal bell-shaped curve; rather, there are a larger number of cases than would be expected at the lower end of the IQ range. Specific pathological processes, such as major genetic abnormalities or brain injuries, probably cause this bulge at the lower end.

Differential Diagnosis

In general, the more severe the intellectual disability, the earlier the diagnosis is made. Children with mild ID often do well enough that they aren't detected until they are in kindergarten or first grade. Typically it is a primary-care physician who makes the first professional assessment. Table 25-4 outlines key areas that should be evaluated in conjunction with the following helpful tips:

1. When you see a child with some unusual features, do not immediately assume an intellectual disability associated syndrome. Check both parents' appearances—they may have similar features with very normal IQs.
2. If the mother of a child with intellectual disability has had multiple spontaneous abortions, then the child is more likely to be at risk for a chromosomal abnormality.
3. If the child has a selective delay in only one area, such as math or reading, it is not a disorder of intellectual development but rather a *learning disorder*.
4. If the child progressed normally for some time and then stopped or slowed, a specific *medical cause* is more likely.

The Denver Developmental Screening Test is an excellent tool for identifying developmental problems in infants and preschool children. A child with *developmental delays* may not be intellectually disabled but instead have hearing or visual impairment. If this is suspected, an audiologist or ophthalmologist skilled in the evaluation of infants and difficult children should evaluate the child. *Chromosome studies* should be done if the child with developmental delays has any *congenital defects, multiple minor malformations, or a combination of minor and major defects*. Any child with develop-

---

TABLE 25-4
Assessing a Child with Intellectual Disability

Pregnancy Lack or loss of fetal growth, abnormal weight gain by mother, particularly minimal fetal movement, maternal drug or alcohol ingestion, illness during the pregnancy (particularly rubella, syphilis, and HIV)

Birth Low birth weight, birth complications, abnormalities at birth (floppy, unresponsive)

Infancy Head size or head growth too small or too large; delay in developmental milestones; abnormal muscle tone, reflexes, postures, and movements

---

mental delays without a known specific diagnosis may have an *inborn error of metabolism* and should undergo appropriate metabolic studies.

Other mental disorders are at least three to four times more prevalent in the intellectually disabled than in the general population. Although individuals with intellectual disability can experience the full range of mental disorders, communication difficulties are likely to make diagnosis more difficult. It becomes necessary to rely more than usual upon objectively observable symptoms. For example, in the case of a depression, the clinician would look for psychomotor retardation, loss of appetite and weight, and sleep disturbance. One additional consideration is that individuals with intellectual impairment are more likely to be exploited and abused.

Etiology

The specific cause of intellectual disability can be identified in only 25–50% of affected children. In general, the more severe the ID, the more likely a specific cause can be found. In mild intellectual impairment there is usually a mix of cultural and multigenetic factors; such kids often have parents with borderline intelligence, and some may be raised in unstimulating environments or have neglectful early care. However, many children with mild ID are born to parents of normal intelligence and receive good and loving care. In those cases, the cause of their delays may be due to genetic factors, prenatal insults, or birth complications. Most often, no specific cause is identified.

> More often a cause usually can be established in cases of moderate and severe intellectual impairment. The general frequencies of the known causes are (1) *prenatal* (includes genetic), 80–85%; (2) *perinatal* (most often asphyxia), 5–10%; and (3) *postnatal*, 5–10%. Public health measures have substantially reduced two main perinatal causes of intellectual disability. Testing babies at birth for *hypothyroidism* (1 in 4,000 births) and *phenylketonuria* (PKU, 1 in 12,000), which is an inability to metabolize the amino acid phenylalanine, has essentially eliminated these causes. Newborn screening in the United States now tests for numerous rare but devastating metabolic disorders, thereby allowing these infants to be quickly identified and treated. Hypothyroid babies are treated with thyroid hormone, and PKU babies are put on very low phenylalanine diets.
>
> The three most common *chromosomal causes* of intellectual disability are *Down's syndrome, fragile* X, and *trisomy* 18. The most common *genetic causes* are *Prader–Willi syndrome* and *Wilson's disease*.

Down's syndrome, usually the result of an extra 21st chromosome, is also called trisomy 21 and accounts for approximately 10% of the individuals institutionalized with intellectual impairment. Its risk is higher with increasing maternal age and probably paternal age. People with Down's syndrome have a broad IQ range with a mean IQ of 47–50. They share numerous physical characteristics: high cheekbones, flat nasal bridge, large protruding tongue, microcephaly, small round ears, hypotonic muscles, and hyperflexibility. They are very susceptible to infections, particularly respiratory, and 30–50% have congenital heart defects. Many don't survive childhood, and few reach 50 years old. They generally have friendly temperaments and love music. Parents of children with Down's syndrome can contact the National Down Syndrome Congress, a parent organization, at www.ndsccenter.org or (800) 232–6372.

In *fragile* X *syndrome* intellectual disability varies from severe to mild, with a few in the borderline IQ range. Children with fragile X tend to do particularly badly in math and block designs and have a specific developmental language disorder. Females are the carriers, and males are affected. Males are short with long ears, a long narrow face, and sunken chest (*pectus excavatum*).

Almost all of the chromosomal and genetic causes of intellectual disability are associated with physical anomalies and most with short stature. Some have specific behavioral abnormalities, such as binge eating in Prader–Willi syndrome.

Prenatal brain and head malformations usually result in severe intellectual disability. Many of these are caused by autosomal recessive genes. Approximately a third of the population carries one of these genes, but because each is rare, the chances of two parents both having the same gene is small.

Brain abnormalities include *anencephaly*, in which parts of the brain and skull are missing (usually fatal); *hydroencephaly*, in which the cranium is filled with fluid instead of with brain tissue; and *porencephaly*, characterized by large fluid-filled cysts in the brain. *Skull abnormalities* include *microcephaly*, which is an abnormally small head, and *hydrocephalus*, in which pressure from excess cerebrospinal fluid destroys brain tissue. Skull abnormalities can be caused by a variety of sources other than an autosomal dominant gene.

The most common *preventable cause* of intellectual disability is *fetal alcohol syndrome*. The CDC estimates the prevalence of FAS at 0.2–1.5 per 1,000 live births (www.cdc.gov/ncbddd/fas). Other causes of intellectual disability include *asphyxia* from maternal hypertension, toxemia, or placenta previa, and *intrauterine infections* such as cytomegalovirus (CMV) rubella, and toxoplasmosis (often acquired from cats). Anoxia during delivery can also lead to intellectual deficits.

Fetal alcohol syndrome (FAS) usually results in mild intellectual disability with mean IQs in the 60s and a range of 25–120. The three hallmark signs of FAS are (1) CNS deficits (most often with lower IQ) and symptoms of attention-deficit/hyperactivity disorder (ADHD); (2) faces with small eyes and drooping upper lids, flat cheeks, short nose, thin upper lip, and flat philtrum (the two vertical ridges between the upper lip and nose); and (3) growth retardation.

Children with FAS are often frustrating to their parents and teachers because they develop adequate verbal skills and sound normal but have serious attention and math deficits. They can often mimic words well but don't fully understand or comprehend their meaning. They can "talk a good line," but don't understand basic cause–effect relationships; hence, behavioral approaches utilizing positive and negative reinforcement don't work. When told to do a task, they may indicate that they fully understand but then perform disastrously because of very poor comprehension, judgment, and attention span. They do best with structure and repetition. Some mothers find that they must put up the same "to do" list every day for their grade-school children or they won't brush their teeth, get dressed, take a shower, and so on. Fetal alcohol effect (FAE), which is a milder variation of FAS, has only two of the three hallmarks and is more common (1 in 200 to 300 births) than FAS; these children have somewhat higher IQs. Very low social drinking levels during pregnancy (e.g., one drink a day) are associated with high frequencies of attention and math deficits.

> Parents desiring support and information about FAS can contact NOFAS (National Organization on FAS) at www.nofas.org or 800-66-NOFAS. Two books—*The Broken Cord* by Michael Dorris, a gripping account of raising a child with FAS, and *Fantastic Antone Succeeds: Experiences in Educating Children with Fetal Alcohol Syndrome* by Judith Kleinfell and Siobhan Westcott, a more upbeat "how-to" book for parents and educators—are must reading for parents with FAS children.

The most common *postnatal causes* of intellectual disability are *meningitis, head trauma, encephalitis,* and *anoxia.* A child with physically abusive parents may be knocked unconscious and suffer enough brain damage to become intellectually disabled.

Management and Treatment

Attempts should be made to make a diagnosis because the intellectual impairment may be treatable and, if not, a reasonable prognosis can still be established. If discovered early enough, the progression of some cases of ID can be arrested, slowed, or partially reversed. The most dramatic examples of successful treatment are giving thyroid hormone to a hypothyroid infant, performing a shunt in a case of early hydrocephalus, and introducing a low-phenylalanine diet to a baby with phenylketonuria. Unfortunately, in most cases, the intellectual disability doesn't have a specific cause or, if it does, it is not specifically treatable.

> The clinician's ability to understand and provide direct management for these children and their parents may determine the child's eventual fate. Questions that parents frequently ask clinicians include (1) "Is our child mentally slow?"; (2) "What caused it?"; and (3) "What can we do about it?"
>
> When told that their child is intellectually disabled or developmentally delayed, parents might deny the clinical finding, which may lead to medical shopping—looking for a physician who will disagree with the original diagnosis or who will say the coveted words, "Your child will outgrow it." A second reaction, which is always present to some degree, is guilt. Since guilt is emotionally painful, parents may deal with it by projecting blame for the retardation on someone else, such as their spouse, their ancestors, their obstetrician, their pediatrician, or even on an event that occurred during the pregnancy. The guilt often results in frustrations for the parents and may be manifested by hostility directed toward the clinician. A third response is to rid themselves of the problem. Since this is socially and personally unacceptable, parents may hide these feelings from themselves and others by publicly demonstrating the opposite reaction of overprotection and oversolicitous care. Many parents of children with mental retardation become great advocates for their children and work effectively with schools and care providers to give their child every possible advantage. Support groups exist in many communities.

Clinicians caring for children with intellectual disability must recognize the multifaceted problems facing the family and be able to deal with the parents at their level by helping them accept the diagnosis, cope with their feelings of guilt and disappointment, and by working with them to develop and implement a management plan for the child. Clinicians must avoid removing all hope for parents, and at the same time be realistic in terms of expectations for their child. Above all, clinicians should avoid making decisions for parents based on their own reactions and attitudes. For example, even though a clinician may feel that a baby would be better off if he or she succumbed at birth, the parents may not share this feeling. Most children with ID have the best chance of reaching their full potential in a caring, supportive home wherein caregivers convey realistic expectations and provide training and care from specialists in intellectual disability.

Because individuals with ID have incurred some form of brain damage, it makes sense that they are more susceptible to other forms of mental illness than the general population. Specific accompanying diagnoses, such as ADHD, seizures (especially subtle partial seizures), and mood disorders should be vigorously treated. Anticonvulsants and lithium may improve aggression and impulse control. Children with mild intellectual impairment usually respond better to stimulants than children with severe ID (Handen et al., 1992). Clomipramine and SSRIs may be helpful in reducing anxious, obsessional, or self-injurious behavior. Buspirone, starting at low doses (2.5 mg three times a day), has been used for agitation and aggression in children with mental retardation. Naltrexone, an opiate blocker, is prescribed in instances where there are repetitive harmful behaviors such as head-banging or self-mutilation. Sedating antipsychotics probably have been overused for behavioral control in this population.

DISORDERS OF SCHOLASTIC SKILLS (LEARNING DISORDERS)

These disorders of scholastic skills, characterized by serious deficits in one or even two specific areas, do not imply intellectual disability. Children with these disorders can function adequately in other areas. Three specific learning disorders are reading, written expression, and mathematics. Diagnostic criteria for these disorders are listed in Table 25-5. As with most other developmental disorders, the impairment is evident in some way during the early school years and is much more common in boys. In many instances these disorders may persist in some form through adolescence and into adulthood.

Reading disorders (sometimes referred to as dyslexia) usually start before age 7 with difficulties in learning to read and then include *spelling problems* by age 7 and *writing problems* by age 8. From 3 to 10% of schoolchildren have a reading disorder, and boys have it more often than girls. It is the most common type of learning disorder. There are associations with attention deficits and hyperactivity. Complications include academic failure, poor school attendance, social struggles, and conduct problems. This condition is

TABLE 25-5
Diagnostic Criteria for Developmental Disorders of Scholastic Skills
(Learning Disorders)

A. There must be a clinically **significant degree of impairment in the specified scholastic skill**. The scholastic skills deficits are associated with factors intrinsic to the child's development.

   The severity of specific learning disorders may be defined in scholastic terms (i.e., a degree that may be expected to occur in less than 3% of schoolchildren); on developmental precursors (i.e., the scholastic difficulties were preceded by developmental delays or deviance—most often in speech or language—in the preschool years); on associated problems (such as inattention, overactivity, emotional disturbance, or conduct difficulties); on pattern (i.e., the presence of qualitative abnormalities that are not usually part of normal development); and on response (i.e., the scholastic difficulties do not rapidly and readily remit with increased help at home and/or at school).

B. The child's level of specified **scholastic skills attainment must be very substantially below that expected** for a child of the same mental age and school placement.

   Standardized tests of achievement and IQ that are appropriate for the relevant culture and educational system should be used in connection with statistical tables that provide data on the average expected level of achievement for any given IQ level at any given chronological age.

C. The impairment must be developmental, in the sense that it must have been **present during the early years of schooling** and not acquired later in the educational process.

   The history of the child's school progress should provide evidence on this point.

D. These impairments in learning are **not the direct result of other disorders** such as intellectual disability or lesser impairments in general intelligence, gross neurological deficits, uncorrected visual or auditory problems, other mental disorder, or another medical condition, although they may occur concurrently with such conditions.

E. There must be **no external factors that could provide a sufficient reason** for the scholastic difficulties such as inadequate learning opportunities or psychosocial distractions.

Reading Disorder (Dyslexia)

A. The child's **reading performance** as assessed through standardized testing of reading accuracy and comprehension should be **significantly below the level expected** on the basis of age, general intelligence, and school placement. Reading comprehension skill, reading word recognition, oral reading skill, and performance of tasks requiring reading may all be affected.

   1. **Accuracy** issues include:
      a. omissions, substitutions, distortions, or additions of words or parts of words;
      b. slow reading rate;
      c. false starts, long hesitations or "loss of place" in text, and inaccurate phrasing; and
      d. reversals of words in sentences or of letters within words.

   2. **Comprehension** deficits include:
      a. inability to recall read facts;
      b. inability to draw conclusions or inferences from material read; and
      c. use of general knowledge as background information rather than of information from a particular story to answer questions about a story read.

TABLE 25-5

Continued

It is characteristic that the spelling difficulties in reading disorder often involve phonetic errors, and it seems that both the reading and spelling problems may derive in part from an impairment in phonological analysis.

Children with specific reading disorder frequently have a history of specific developmental disorders of speech and language,

Spelling Disorder (Written and Oral Expression)

A. This disorder is a specific and **significant impairment in the development of spelling skills which is not solely accounted for by low mental age, visual acuity problems, or inadequate schooling.**

The ability to spell orally and to write out words correctly are both affected. Children whose problem is solely one of handwriting should not be included, but in some cases spelling difficulties may be associated with problems in writing. Unlike the usual pattern of specific reading disorder, the spelling errors tend to be predominantly phonetically accurate.

B. The child's **reading skills (with respect to both accuracy and comprehension) should be within the normal range and there should be no history of previous significant reading difficulties**.

Disorder of Arithmetical Skills (Math)

A. This disorder involves a **specific impairment in arithmetical skills, which is not solely explicable on the basis of general intellectual disability or of grossly inadequate schooling**.

The deficit concerns mastery of basic computational skills of addition, subtraction, multiplication, and division (rather than of the more abstract mathematical skills involved in algebra, trigonometry, geometry, or calculus).

B. **Reading and spelling skills should be within the normal range** expected for the child's mental age, preferably as assessed on individually administered, appropriately standardized tests.

Note: Adapted from *ICD-10* (pp. 188–195) and *DSM-5* (pp. 66–68)

---

observed with all known languages but it is not clear whether the same children would have difficulty with non-phonetic languages with non-alphabetic scripts. Although treatment can significantly help children with reading disorders, most will still have some problems in adulthood. Children given proper help and treatment can attain careers comparable to their peers with similar IQs.

A *mathematics disorder* is often not detected until rote memorization and primitive counting strategies no longer work. About 5% of schoolchildren have this disorder with inconsistent gender differences. Some children may be diagnosed mistakenly with this disorder because of poor teaching in their schools. Early signs of a mathematics disorder include a failure to name and count numbers or to use or understand numbers in simple, everyday activities (e.g., unable to comply with instruction to "Give Jim two candies and Jennifer three candies"). Children with this disorder tend to have impaired visual-spatial and visual-perceptual skills but normal auditory-perceptual and verbal skills (in contrast to many children with reading disorders).

Management and Treatment

Clinicians untrained in these areas too often assume that they can give professional advice about learning disorders. However, the causes of these disorders are myriad. One part of the brain may be functioning abnormally and the rest normally. Each of these abilities requires a complex integration of several subsets of abilities. Ideally, a child neuropsychologist or educational psychologist specializing in this area should evaluate children with these disorders to see which subset abilities are intact and which are not. Then a learning program can be prescribed that capitalizes on the child's strengths and circumvents the weaknesses. Treatment consists of remediating weak skills (through extra practice), compensation for a weak skill by relying more on a stronger skill, or complete substitution of the weak skill with another. As an example of compensation, a child with very good auditory memory and integration skills who has difficulties in complex visual integration might learn reading more easily by reading a book with a tape of the book playing in the background at the same time. Then the correct sounds are systematically paired with the words. More complex problems may merit a variety of special interventions. Reading disorder is probably not a unitary disorder but caused by a variety of deficits that need to be individually assessed. Current treatment of mathematics disorders focuses on acquiring basic arithmetic skills and speed training. Giving attention primarily to underlying perceptual– motor–cognitive abilities has yielded poorer results.

COMMUNICATION DISORDERS

Communication disorders can be very specific and may not involve other areas of function. Unlike the learning disorders, they can be diagnosed as accompanying intellectual disability if the language difficulties appear to be excessive for the level of ID. Three main categories of communication disorders are *language disorder, articulation disorder,* and *fluency disorder* (stuttering and cluttering).

Kids with *expressive language disorder* understand what they are told but can't express what they want to communicate. Those with *mixed receptive–expressive language disorder* have problems with both areas—understanding and communicating. *Articulation disorder* (speech sound disorder) creates a problem with speech, but not necessarily a problem in communication or understanding. Disorders of speech pronunciation are best assessed by trained speech pathologists. Pronunciation difficulties are normal in young children and are often defined as abnormal only if they persist past a certain age. Lisps and other kinds of pronunciation difficulties are often very treatable. Varying pronunciations due to regional accents or dialects are not considered disorders of speech. Dropping the *r* in water would be a problem in Seattle but normal in Boston. In *stuttering*, the sounds are accurately made, but the fluency and time patterning are frequently disrupted.

The sooner the more severe forms of these disorders are detected and treated, the better the outcome. Referral to a speech pathologist and therapist specializing in children's speech disorders is essential, and for the language disorders, a psychologist or neuropsychologist. The family and teachers should be educated about the diagnosis and taught how best to work with the child. Frequently, children with receptive language disorders are mistakenly accused of hearing but "not listening." Table 25-6 lists diagnostic criteria for the communication disorders.

Language disorders affect 3–10% of school-age children, while stuttering and articulation disorders each affect about 5%. Fortunately, these disorders usually are either outgrown or can be treated successfully. About 50% of children with expressive language disorder catch up to their peers before they reach school and do not need treatment. Those with more severe forms should get treatment before school-age. Many children who also have receptive language problems will eventually acquire normal language abilities, but some of the more severely affected do not. Children with language disorders often have other disorders suggesting developmental delay (e.g., enuresis, and/or articulation, motor coordination, and reading disorders).

With speech therapy almost all children recover from articulation disorder; the milder cases often recover by age 8 without speech therapy. Stutterers typically (80%) recover before age 16, 60% spontaneously. The disorder has strong biological and genetic association. Approximately 60% of those who stutter have a family member who stutters. The boy to girl ratio is about 3:1. Children with these disorders and their families often benefit from counseling to help them deal with the social repercussions from peers (teasing) and with low self-esteem from being criticized by parents and teachers.

TABLE 25-6
Diagnostic Criteria for Communication Disorders
Language Disorder

A. The **understanding and/or expression of language are impaired across settings**.
   1. **Understanding (Receptive) language deficits** include:
      a. failure to respond to familiar names (in the absence of nonverbal clues) by the first birthday
      b. inability to identify at least a few common objects by 18 months
      c. failure to follow simple, routine instructions by the age of 2 years (should be taken as significant sign of delay)
      d. inability to understand grammatical structures (negatives, questions, comparatives, etc.)
      e. lack of understanding of more subtle aspects of language (tone of voice, gesture, etc.)
   In almost all cases of receptive language deficits, the development of expressive language is also markedly disturbed and abnormalities in word-sound production are common
   2. **Expressive language deficits** include:
      a. the absence of single words (or word approximations) by the age of 2 years
      b. the failure to generate simple two-word phrases by 3 years
      c. restricted vocabulary development
      d. overuse of a small set of general words, difficulties in selecting appropriate words, and word substitutions
      e. short utterance length
      f. immature sentence structure
      g. syntactical errors, especially omissions of word endings or prefixes
      h. misuse of or failure to use grammatical features such as prepositions, pronouns, articles, and verb and noun inflexions
      i. incorrect overgeneralizations of rules
      j. lack of sentence fluency
      k. difficulties in sequencing when recounting past events
      l. delays or abnormalities in word-sound production
B. Receptive or expressive **language is below the appropriate level for mental age**.
   1. The diagnosis of a specific developmental language disorder implies that the specific delay is significantly out of keeping with the general level of cognitive functioning. As a general rule, a language delay that is sufficiently severe to fall outside the limits of 2 standard deviations may be regarded as abnormal. Most cases of this severity have associated problems that interfere with effective communication, social interaction, education or occupation.
   2. Attention should be paid to the functioning; if the pattern of speech and language is abnormal (i.e., deviant and not just of a kind appropriate for an earlier phase of development), or if the child's speech or language includes qualitatively abnormal features, a clinically significant disorder is likely.
C. Normal patterns of language acquisition are **disturbed from the early stages of development**.
   1. The impairment in spoken language should have been evident from infancy without any clear prolonged phase of normal language usage.
   2. The use of nonverbal cues (such as smiles and gesture) and "internal" language as reflected in imaginative or make-believe play should be relatively intact, and the ability to

TABLE 25-6
Continued

communicate socially without words should be relatively unimpaired. The child will seek to communicate in spite of the language impairment and will tend to compensate for lack of speech by use of demonstration, gesture, mime, or nonspeech vocalizations. However, associated difficulties in peer relationships, emotional disturbance, behavioral disruption, and/or overactivity and inattention are not uncommon, particularly in school-age children.

D. The conditions are **not directly attributable to neurological or speech mechanism abnormalities, sensory impairments, environmental factors, autistic spectrum disorders, intellectual disability, or global intellectual delays**.

Partial (often selective) hearing loss, inadequate involvement in conversational interchanges, or more general environmental deprivation, may play a major or contributory role in the impaired development of language.

Speech Articulation Disorder (Speech Sound Disorder)

A. Despite a normal level of language skills, the **use of speech sounds is below the appropriate level for mental age**.

1. Abnormalities include omissions, distortions, or substitutions of speech sounds; and inconsistencies in the co-occurrence of sounds (i.e., phonemes are correct in some word positions but not in others).

2. By the age of 11–12 years mastery of almost all speech sounds are normally acquired. At the age of 4 years, errors in speech-sound production are common, but the child is able to be understood easily by strangers. By the age of 6–7, most speech sounds will be acquired. Although difficulties may remain with certain sound combinations, these should not result in any problems of communication.

B. The misarticulations in speech consequently create **difficulties in understanding for others** and in turn interfere with effective communication, social interaction, education, or occupation.

C. Articulation issues are **present from the early stages of development**.

D. Articulation abnormalities are **not directly attributable to a sensory, structural, or neurological abnormality; and the mispronunciations are clearly abnormal in the context of colloquial usage in the child's subculture. In addition nonverbal intelligence is within the normal range**.

Fluency Disorder (Stuttering and Cluttering)

Stuttering (stammering) is speech characterized by frequent repetition or prolongation of sounds, syllables, or words; or by frequent hesitations or pauses that disrupt the rhythmic flow of speech. Minor dysrhythmias of this type are quite common as a transient phase in early childhood, or as a minor but persistent speech feature in later childhood and adult life. They should be classified as a disorder only if their severity is such as markedly to disturb the fluency of speech. There may be associated movements of the face and/or other parts of the body that coincide in time with the repetitions, prolongations, or pauses in speech flow.

Cluttering is a rapid rate of speech with breakdown in fluency, but no repetitions or hesitations, of a severity to give rise to reduced speech intelligibility. Speech is erratic and dysrhythmic, with rapid, jerky spurts that usually involve faulty phrasing patterns (e.g., alternating pauses and bursts of speech, producing groups of words unrelated to the grammatical structure of the sentence).

Note: Adapted from ICD-10 (p. 184–187) and DSM-5 (pp. 42–47)

AUTISTIC SPECTRUM DISORDER

Clinical Presentation

Children diagnosed with autistic disorders may have intellectual delays but are more prominently delayed in areas of social reciprocity and interest. These children often make poor eye contact, have limited interest in reciprocal social interactions, and may have very restricted repetitive interests that seem odd or obsessive to others. One father observed about his autistic child, "He lives according to a beat, but I have no idea what the beat is." Emerging between 6 and 30 months after birth, autistic symptoms do *not* include hallucinations, delusions, or paranoia, which partly explains why autism is not classified as schizophrenia. Autistic spectrum disorder was previously referred to as "pervasive developmental disorders" and now encompasses Rett's disorder, childhood disintegration disorder, Asperger's disorder, and classic autism.

> Soon after birth, children with autism develop abnormally. Within the first 3–6 months of their lives, their parents may note that they do not develop a normal pattern of smiling or responding to cuddling. As they grow older, they do not progress through developmental milestones such as learning to say words or speak sentences. Instead, they may seem aloof, withdrawn, and detached. Instead of developing patterns of relating warmly to their parents, they may engage in stereotyped behavior such as rocking, clapping, whirling, or head-banging. Children with this disorder are referred to as "autistic" because they appear to be withdrawn and absorbed into themselves. In the movie *Rain Man* Dustin Hoffman portrays most of the characteristics of high-functioning autistic disorder, except most autistic people are not savants.

The impairment in social interaction is usually the first obvious sign of the disorder and persists throughout life. These children may struggle with not understanding social cues and expectations and may seem less interested in relationships than other children. Most children with autistic spectrum disorders do form attachments to parents and caregivers, but even within these attachments may show lack of social understanding and empathy. Interactions, when they occur, have a mechanical quality. When stressed, their behavior typically becomes strange, difficult, or overactive. Individuals on the autistic spectrum may be intensely bothered by changes in routine or schedule and may react to transitions with resistance, fear, and anger. Their verbal impairments range from the complete absence of speech to mildly deviant speech and language patterns. Their speech is often odd: These children may exhibit echolalia, misname objects, invoke words only known to family members, hum monotonous sounds, or have an unusual intonation to their voices. Some examiners have described a monotonous pattern of speech that lacks expression, but this characteristic is not universal.

> Even children who develop good facility in verbal expression produce speech that has a repetitive, sing-song, and monotonous quality to it. They may become obsessed with counting things or totally absorbed by spinning things (e.g., whirling fans, water fountains). There is an intense and rigid commitment to maintaining specific routines, and extreme distress if routines are interrupted.
>
> Higher-functioning individuals with autistic spectrum disorder, including those formerly given the diagnosis of Asperger's disorder, may have special skills, though rarely. They may display a superb remote memory, remembering lyrics of songs heard years ago. They may recite schedules, TV programs, historical dates, math equations, and restaurant menus. At times, they may share this material out of context and inappropriately. Their savant skills—those islets of precocity or special capacities—can occur in music, drawing, calculating, and calendar dates. As preschoolers, a few can teach themselves to read (hyperlexia) without comprehending anything.

Children with autism may underreact or overreact to sensory stimuli. Sometimes smells enrapture them; they may ignore people speaking to them, suggesting deafness, but then respond to the tick of a watch or metronome. Because they might experience pain but react minimally, these kids occasionally can injure themselves and not cry. Table 25-7 lists diagnostic criteria for autistic spectrum disorder.

Most children with classic autism also have intellectual deficits: 40% score an IQ under 50, 30% between 50 and 70, and 30% can top 70. Only 20% have a normal nonverbal intelligence. "Elevated" IQs pop up, but often with inconsistent subscores, enormous "scattering," and considerable variation over time. In general, the lower the IQ, the worse the autism. Psychological tests show that verbal sequencing and abstraction are more disturbed than rote memory or visuospatial skills. These patients often have primitive neurological reflexes, "soft" neurological signs, mixed laterality of their hands, and physical anomalies.

Epidemiology

The prevalence of all pervasive developmental disorders (i.e., autistic spectrum disorder) is estimated at almost 1.5%. Among kids under 15, the prevalence of classic autism is near 0.25%. Boys have it three times as often as

TABLE 25-7
Diagnostic Criteria for Autistic Spectrum Disorder

A. **Qualitative abnormalities in reciprocal social interactions and in patterns of communication**. These qualitative abnormalities are a pervasive feature of the individual's functioning in all situations, although they may vary in degree.

B. **Restricted, stereotyped, repetitive repertoire of interests and activities**. *DSM-5 also mentions sensory differences.*

C. In most cases, development is **abnormal from infancy** and, with only a few exceptions, the conditions manifest during the first 5 years of life.

D. The above symptoms result in **significant impairment in personal, family, social, educational, occupational, or other important areas of functioning**. Severity level is based upon the degree of impairment and how much support is required.

E. The above symptoms are **not better explained by an intellectual developmental disorder**. It is usual, but not invariable, for there to be some degree of general cognitive impairment but the autistic spectrum disorders are defined in terms of behavior that is deviant in relation to mental age (whether the individual has intellectual disability or not).

F. In some cases the disorders are associated with, and presumably due to, some other medical condition, of which infantile spasms, congenital rubella, tuberous sclerosis, cerebral lipidosis, and the fragile X chromosome anomaly are among the most common. (The disorder is diagnosed on the basis of the behavioral features, irrespective of the presence or absence of any associated medical conditions.)

Manifestations of autistic spectrum disorder include formerly described conditions: Rett's, Childhood Disintegrative Disorder, Asperger's, and classic autism (severe verbal language deficits).

Note: Adapted from *ICD-10* (p. 198) and *DSM-5* (pp. 50–51)

girls. Mild autism outnumbers serious autism. Lower socioeconomic groups may produce more autism, but this finding may actually reflect inadequate research.

Autism has some genetic basis. Identical twins have 64% concordance rates; fraternal twins, 9% concordance rates. Other siblings are at a higher risk for cognitive and language problems. Fragile X syndrome may produce 2–5% of autism cases in kids; polygenetic factors may produce other cases. Parents of one child with autism have about a 4% risk of future children having autism. Some studies have shown even higher recurrence risks.

At birth, autistic children have more perinatal complications and congenital malformations. The disorder can also stem from specific diseases or conditions—e.g., tuberous sclerosis, anoxia during birth, intrauterine infections (rubella, cytomegalovirus herpes simplex), postnatal neurological infections, encephalitis, infantile spasms, untreated phenylketonuria, and drug exposure (thalidomide) during pregnancy. Neuroimaging studies in individuals with autism have demonstrated some regional brain size abnormalities with the most consistent finding being enlargements of temporal and frontal lobes. The increased size seems to be related to white matter versus gray matter and shorter versus longer neuron connections (Hazlet et al., 2006). This may account for the poor cognitive integration seen clinically with these patients. The underactivity of the amygdala, which has been implicated in autism, may also be related to this reduction in functional neuronal connectedness. Abnormalities in neurotransmitter systems have been discovered (especially dopamine, serotonin, and glutamate) and afflicted individuals more frequently carry polymorphisms of monoamine oxidase.

Differential Diagnosis

Children with intellectual disability and without autism are more extraverted, act more like their age, and exhibit more normal language; they also demonstrate broad intellectual deficits without any of the savant's math, music, or other specialized skills. When both mental retardation and autism clearly coexist, both are diagnosed. The stereotyped movements that occur in *tic* and *stereotypic movement disorders* lack the numerous other features of autism.

Unlike patients with autistic disorders, patients with *hearing, language,* and *speech disorders* can read lips, perform sign language, relate to parents, and, over time, display emotional and social appropriateness. Children who are deaf babble normally at birth but much less by 6–12 months, and if at all would respond only to loud sounds. In contrast, children with autism usually ignore both loud and normal tones, but will react to soft and low sounds. Auditory-evoked potentials can be used to diagnose deafness. Those children with *visual impairments* actively engage others, despite their poor eye contact and constant staring at people in motion.

Schizophrenia in children is extremely rare, and mental retardation or seizures do not typically accompany it. Development is usually normal prior to the onset of psychotic symptoms. Even for the most bizarre or shy person with autism, one would not give adult diagnoses of *schizoid* or *schizotypal personality disorder*. From inadequate parenting, social isolation, or "hospitalitis," *psychosocial deprivation* can induce apathetic, withdrawn children who display delayed language and motor skills because of poor attachment (*reactive attachment disorder*); yet, unlike autism, these patients markedly improve with an improved environment.

Clinical Course

Parents may not recognize the first signs of autism, especially if the affected child is their first. Parents may blame the unusual behavior on deafness, until they see their child respond to music, echo sounds, or react to softly spoken words. In desperation, parents may point to a particularly irrelevant event, such as a grandfather's death or a neighborhood fire, as the "cause" of their child's problems. Recently, there has been a great deal of controversy about whether or not childhood vaccinations may cause or contribute to autism in some cases. Many parents of children with autism advocate for this position, but the medical evidence has not been robustly supportive.

Although autism lasts the lifetime, slow gains can be made. A supportive home certainly helps. Even when socially awkward and egocentric, 15–30% of adults with autism can live alone and work, but only 2% reach a normal status and gainful employment. As these children become adolescents, depression may emerge. As the years continue, their speech and understanding may improve, despite continued perseveration, restricted interests, and stereotyped motor movements. Marriage is rare.

Medical illness, puberty, and major stresses can trigger temporary regressions. Over 25% of these children, especially those with IQs below 50, exhibit major or partial complex seizures. From 4 to 32% develop grand mal seizures in late childhood, which makes their prognosis very poor.

Management and Treatment

Two related goals guide treatment of autism disorders are reducing the child's symptoms and supporting constructive efforts. Initially, clinicians should assess patients' language, cognition, social interactions, and consider inborn metabolic disorders, degenerative diseases, EEGs, chromosomes, and psychological tests to determine if any treatable cause of symptoms exists.

Medications

Neuroleptics (e.g., risperidone) may decrease aggression, agitation, labile affect hyperactivity, and stereotyped movements (Parikh, MS). Social interaction, eye contact, anxiety, and learning may also improve with neuroleptics. If the autism is accompanied by hyperactive features, treatment with stimulants may be beneficial. Anticonvulsants curtail 35–50% of seizures, and lithium may reduce self-inflicted injuries. As with children with intellectual disability, SSRIs may reduce anxious, obsessional, and self-injurious behaviors but may more often have side effects in people with autism and are therefore used at very low doses (Kolevzon, 2006). Buspirone may reduce agitation and aggression (Buitelaar, 1998).

Social Therapies

Well-controlled studies suggest that structured classrooms and active behavioral programs encourage language, cognition, and appropriate behavior. Many children with autism benefit from picture schedules that visually reflect their daily activities and help them to mentally prepare for transitions. Parents should become adept at implementing these time-consuming behavioral techniques and providing highly structured routines. In addition, family life will be enhanced if parents pay attention to healthy siblings, collaborate with public agencies, and if necessary, arrange for long-term care. At some point, clinicians and family, working together, may want to evaluate whether well-supervised residential living would be better for the child with severe autism than living with parents.

> A form of behavioral modification that is founded upon the principles of social learning theory has been applied to increase socially significant behaviors in autism. Applied behavior analysis (ABA) focuses upon the observable relationship of targeted behavior to the environment, including antecedents and consequences. This functional analysis is without regard to any other hypothetical constructs to explain behavior (Dillenburger, 2009).

Asperger's Disorder

The now-supplanted diagnosis of *Asperger's disorder* is essentially a form of high-functioning autistic disorder. Kids with this disorder are impaired (although usually less severely) in social interaction and have the restricted, repetitive, and stereotyped behaviors and interests seen in autism, but without the delays in cognitive development and language. These children have normal intelligence and language skills but often demonstrate the lack of social reciprocity, restricted interests, and difficulty with transitions seen in children with more severe autism.

Childhood Disintegrative Disorder

In the rare *childhood disintegrative disorder* ("Heller syndrome"), afflicted children are normal in every way for at least 2 years and then disaster strikes in at least two major areas: (1) social interaction, communication, or restricted receptive language, and (2) stereotyped patterns of behavior. Some also lose bowel or bladder control. In its worse form, children with this disorder closely resemble children with autism. Most, fortunately, are less severely impaired.

Rett's Disorder

In *Rett's disorder*, seen only in girls, everything is normal for the first several months of life, but then they develop the stereotyped movements, poor social interaction, and impaired communication seen in autism. These girls have marked impairment of expressive and receptive language, severe psychomotor retardation, poorly coordinated gait or trunk movements, and deceleration of head growth. They may lose functional use of their hands (wringing and rubbing motions). Rett's syndrome is caused by a specific gene abnormality on the X chromosome.

ATTENTION-DEFICIT/HYPERACTIVITY DISORDER

Clinical Presentation

The cardinal features of attention-deficit/hyperactivity disorder (ADHD) are short attention span, hyperactivity, and impulsivity that are developmentally inappropriate and endure at least 6 months. Typically, this condition is recognized before or during early elementary school, although it can manifest from birth and perhaps before (some mothers report that their child was a nonstop womb kicker). Because younger children naturally have more ADHD features, kids diagnosed at age 4 are more likely to be "the little terrors" who wear out their parents. Historically ADHD was known as "minimal brain dysfunction," "hyperactive syndrome," and "minor cerebral dysfunction." The current name has been chosen because attention difficulties are prominent and virtually always present among children with these diagnoses. The primary characteristics are lack of persistence in activities that require cognitive involvement, bouncing from one activity to the next without completion of any task, and poorly organized behavior.

Children with this diagnosis are a caricature of the "active" child. They are physically overactive, distracted, inattentive, impulsive, and hard to manage. In classrooms, these children can't pay attention; they fidget and fuss, fall off inanimate objects such as chairs, and disrupt conversations. Some even get expelled and require private tutoring. Their headlong dive into life seems determined *for* them and not *by* them.

Impatient and frustrated, even intelligent children with ADHD may get lower grades. They'll attack an exam but get bored or distracted after a few questions. They don't wait their turn; answers precede questions. When they zoom into a room, everybody notices them. Their world is a bang, not a whimper. They're constantly interrupting, screaming, and chattering. Minor events become major cataclysms.

Children with ADHD may exhibit a depressed mood with or without chronic "body anxiety." The constantly tapping foot is not driven by anxiety but rather by overactivity itself; ask the child why he does that and he might say, "I don't know—my legs just gotta move." Many children with ADHD also demonstrate social immaturity and/or impairments in motor, math, or reading skills. Although lacking overt vision or hearing difficulties, their hearing gets tested regularly, only to find that they hear well but listen poorly. They may have subtle impairments in copying age-appropriate figures; executing rapid alternating movements; making left–right discrimination; and showing reflex asymmetries, ambidexterity, and numerous "soft" neurological signs. In short, there's something wrong with these children, but nothing *that* wrong. Table 25-8 lists diagnostic criteria for ADHD.

Epidemiology

The prevalence rate of ADHD is 3–7% in school-age children. Lower prevalence rates have been reported in several countries, which might be due to the use of different diagnostic criteria and cultural expectations. ADHD afflicts boys far more than girls, even though the precise ratios depend on the study. One investigation indicated that ADHD occurs six to nine times more often in boys than girls, whereas a community survey found a 3:1 ratio. The disorder is more common in firstborn boys. Among hyperactive ADHD kids 40% have oppositional defiant disorder. Depression and anxiety are also often co-morbid with ADHD (Elia, 2008).

Differential Diagnosis

Since many children seem fated to have at least some ADHD symptoms (especially high activity or low attention span), careful differential diagnosis is crucial. It is important to know what is normal at each age level and how children behave in a variety of environments. Inexperienced parents may

TABLE 25-8
Diagnostic Criteria for Attention-Deficit/Hyperactivity Disorder

A. A combination of **overactive, poorly modulated behavior with marked inattention and lack of persistent task involvement**. Both impaired attention and overactivity are necessary for the diagnosis:

1. **Inattention**

   Impaired attention is manifested by prematurely breaking off from tasks and leaving activities unfinished. The children change frequently from one activity to another, seemingly losing interest in one task because they become diverted to another. These deficits in persistence and attention are excessive for the child's age and IQ (developmental level). For other evidence of inattention see the SNAP-IV questions 1–9 at the end of this chapter.

2. **Overactivity**

   Overactivity implies excessive restlessness, especially in situations requiring relative calm. The standard for judgment should be that the activity is excessive in the context of what is expected in the situation and by comparison with other children of the same age and IQ. This behavioral feature is most evident in structured, organized situations that require a high degree of behavioral self-control.

   (a) fidgeting and wriggling

   (b) getting up from a seat when he or she was supposed to remain seated

   (c) running and jumping around (recklessness in situations involving some danger)

   (d) noisiness (even in leisure activities)

   (e) *is often "on the go" or often acts as if "driven by a motor"*

   (f) excessive talkativeness

   (g) prematurely answering questions before they have been completed

   (h) difficulty in waiting turns

   (i) intruding on or interrupting others' activities (disinhibition in social relationships, impulsive flouting of social rules)

   DSM-5 specifies that at least six of the above symptoms have persisted for at least 6 months. If fewer than six symptoms of overactivity then the presentation is predominantly inattentive type.

B. Symptoms always **arise early in development**, usually in the first 5 years of life (before age 6 years). *DSM-5 specifies prior to age 12 years.*

C. The impaired attention and overactivity should be **evident in more than one situation** (e.g., home, classroom, clinic) and persist over time.

D. The above **symptoms interfere with personal, family, social, educational, occupational, or other important areas of functioning.**

E. This disturbance is not diagnosed in the presence of schizophrenia spectrum or other psychotic disorders and is **not better explained by another mental disorder** (e.g., autistic spectrum, mood, anxiety, dissociative, or substance use disorders).

Note: Adapted from *ICD-10* (pp. 206–208) and *DSM-5* (pp. 59–61)

conclude that their children's age-appropriate activity is highly pathological, but their children's teachers, who have experience with many children, may view the behavior as normal. The SNAP-IV Rating Scale, when completed by teachers, assists the clinician in diagnosis and monitoring treatment effectiveness. The scale is provided at the end of this chapter and may be reproduced without copyright infringement.

Separating ADHD from *conduct disorder* can be tricky. Children with conduct disorder alone are often misdiagnosed as having ADHD. Because they exhibit many bad and unacceptable behaviors, they may be labeled "hyperactive." However, most are no more active than their normal peers. In contrast, most kids with ADHD don't specialize in bad behaviors but rather exhibit *all* behaviors at high rates, including positive ones such as petting animals, joking with friends, and helping out little kids. Children with conduct disorders flaunt their meanness to people and animals; they intend bad outcomes and may not repent. Kids with ADHD can act in haste but tend to show remorse for wrongdoing.

Etiology and Pathogenesis

Despite the absence of specific brain damage, ADHD is mainly a *biological disorder.* In many cases genetics has a major role with heritability accounting for 75% of cases. In comparison to controls, the family members of these children have more ADHD; their brothers display ADHD three times more often. As mentioned above, other psychiatric disorders tend to travel with ADHD. The male relatives of children with ADHD have a higher incidence of substance abuse, alcoholism, and antisocial personality disorder, whereas their female counterparts have more somatization disorder and histrionic personality disorder. These various disorders are also more frequent in the biological parents of adopted-away children with ADHD. Newer evidence indicates that these other disorders may not be *genetically* linked to ADHD but are nonetheless linked: An adult with ADHD is more likely to marry a person with one of these other disorders (Faraone et al., 1991). Similarly, learning disorders (e.g., dyslexia) are more common in kids with ADHD and in their first-degree relatives, but this is due to the fact that a parent with ADHD is more likely to have married a spouse with a learning disorder (Faraone et al., 1993). Parents with *only* ADHD are more likely to have children with *only* ADHD, unaccompanied by conduct or learning disorder. Neurochemical studies of ADHD indicate multiple neurotransmitter involvement, including dopamine and norepinephrine. Structural brain imaging studies in children with ADHD found significantly smaller volumes in the prefrontal cortex, caudate, pallidum, corpus callosum, and cerebellum.

Possible *perinatal* risk factors for ADHD include poor maternal nutrition, maternal smoking, maternal substance abuse, birth complications, infections, and exposure to toxins such as lead. There is no specific neurobiological marker. Frontal lobe hypofunction may be a part of the pathology. Hyperactive parents of hyperactive children metabolize glucose in the brain at a level 8% lower than control parents. Chaotic families and child abuse may cause children to exhibit symptoms consistent with ADHD, but their cause may be trauma related. Some "experts" claim that food additives and sugar cause ADHD; yet after withdrawing these chemicals, in a placebo controlled fashion, mothers could not appreciate any change. Social class and ADHD appear unrelated.

Clinical Course

Half of the youngsters with ADHD symptoms come to clinical attention before age 4, whereas the rest do so in early elementary school. Gross agitation is more frequent in preschool children, finer degrees of restlessness, later on. The overall course of ADHD is unpredictable: Symptoms may continue into adulthood or remit at puberty. They usually persist through the school years and into adult life, although many affected individuals show gradual improvement. If any symptom disappears it is usually the hyperactivity that improves first. If ADHD subsides during adolescence, the kids may become productive, develop relationships, and launch serious adult plans. Despite the common association of reading difficulties, about half of children with ADHD have a good outcome, completing school on schedule with acceptable grades. If childhood ADHD is severe, the chances of it persisting into adulthood are high. Around 60% of children with ADHD continue to have symptoms into adulthood. Adult ADHD symptoms mostly include inattention, disorganization, and failure to finish things. Other difficulties in adults associated with ADHD include frequent job changes, partner changes, and driving accidents.

ADHD commonly occurs with other psychiatric disorders, especially oppositional defiant disorder, conduct disorder, learning disorders, and substance use disorders. Kids with both ADHD and conduct disorder have a much worse prognosis than those with ADHD alone. Roughly 25% of adolescents with ADHD in combination with conduct disorder also develop antisocial personality disorder. These antisocial adults with ADHD complete fewer years of school, have a higher rate of substance abuse, more arrests, more car accidents, and more suicide attempts. Adults who had ADHD as children are more prone to mood disorders, perhaps secondary to both biological vulnerability and the constant assaults on self-esteem during childhood.

Hank got to school a little late. Getting ready for school that morning, he had spilled a glass of milk while gesturing with his hand, had fallen off the dining room chair twice, and while looking for a school book, had become distracted by five other things in his bedroom. Then he tripped a girl on the school bus as she was walking down the aisle because, for a moment, it seemed like a fun thing to do. He saw, he did, he thought—in that order.

At last Hank made it into the classroom, whereupon he dumped his books and homework into his messy desk. The class clown had arrived. While fidgeting at his desk, he chatted excitedly with his friend next to him, but the teacher was talking to the class and told him to stop. He tried paying attention to the teacher, and when the teacher asked the class a question, Hank answered it in the instant that five other hands went up. He thought, "Uh-oh, I got to remember to raise my hand next time," but at the next opportunity he blurted out the answer again. He was a smart kid who often knew the answer but got C's because he didn't finish assignments, lost homework, skipped items on exams, did 10 other things instead of studying for a test. The principal's office was all too-familiar a place. He was sent there mostly for talking, but also for the stunts he performed to get laughs—he had learned to capitalize on his hyperactivity and impulsiveness by getting laughs from his friends. They liked him but also found him intrusive, annoying, and distracting.

Hank's parents were worn out by him and were reduced to hollow "don't-do-that-stop-that" interchanges that almost never netted the desired consequences. They regarded him like the family Labrador retriever: hyper, friendly—and untrainable.

Hank's fourth-grade teacher finally persuaded the parents to have Hank assessed. ADHD was diagnosed and in a week's time, he was responding to 30 mg/day of dextroamphetamine. His father was stunned by the rapid and very noticeable response. Hank's restlessness diminished, his concentration improved, and he began getting A's and B's. His parents were taught to deliver consistent, appropriate consequences for Hank's behavior. Hank remained the class clown, but slowly discovered that he could get positive attention in other ways—by helping someone out, doing well on a test or homework assignment, and working *with*, not against, other kids on a group project.

Management and Treatment

The American Academy of Child and Adolescent Psychiatry has collected the latest evidence and clinical experience on ADHD and other childhood disorders in its published Practice Parameters (updated 2007 for ADHD). Because other conditions frequently occur with ADHD, referral for IQ, psychological, speech, language, and learning disabilities should be made if clinically indicated. Restlessness can also be caused by chronically used medications, such as anti-asthmatics, sympathomimetics, steroids, and decongestants. Some medications adults find sedating may cause a paradoxical response in children (e.g., phenobarbital or antihistamines).

Parent education, appropriate classroom placement, academic remediation, behavioral interventions, and medication are important components of treatment of ADHD. Stimulants, atomoxetine, guanfacine, and clonidine are FDA approved treatments for ADHD. Most children respond either to methylphenidate or amphetamine salts. Several long-acting preparations of stimulant medications are available with benefits of once/day dosing. Atomoxetine and buproprion are nonstimulants which improve ADHD symptoms less robustly than stimulants but without the risk of developing tolerance or dependency.

Medications

A child given separate trials of dextroamphetamine and methylphenidate has a greater than 90% chance of responding to one or the other. In trials of a single stimulant, roughly 30% of patients exhibited marked improvement, 40% received some benefit, and 10–30% were unaffected. If both drugs are equal, methylphenidate is preferred because of fewer cardiac effects (Sylvester, 1993). An EKG is now recommended prior to starting a stimulant if there is a history of cardiac issues. Optimal intellectual improvement and adequate behavioral control may be best at lower doses of methylphenidate. Methylphenidate's effects last from 3 to 6 hours; dextroamphetamine lasts somewhat longer. Stimulants diminish overactivity, impulsiveness, irritability, and emotional fluctuations; they increase vigilance, attention span, and general sociability. These medications don't facilitate learning per se, but when attention span lengthens and reduced criticism enhances self-esteem, learning accelerates.

These pharmacological agents can work immediately, but may require 1–2 weeks. Children with ADHD rarely develop tolerance and drug abuse, although stimulants might temporarily suppress growth slightly. If there is any question that the stimulant being used has little or no effect, the child should be placed on a different stimulant. While on these medications, blood pressure, pulse, height, weight, appetite, mood, and side effects (e.g., tics) should be regularly monitored. Common side effects of stimulants include loss of appetite, insomnia, headaches, stomachaches, and tics; less common but more serious side effects include psychosis, depression, suicidal ideation, and possibly stroke or sudden cardiac death.

Because as children mature they may no longer meet ADHD criteria, monitored trials of no medication can be conducted annually to see if they still need it. As alternatives to stimulants, antidepressants (e.g., imipramine, desipramine) help some kids with ADHD, particularly with depression, anxiety, and tics. However, the tricyclic antidepressants must be used very cautiously because they are more likely to cause cardiac arrhythmias in kids. Buproprion is an antidepressant that also has shown efficacy in ADHD. Atomoxetine is a nonstimulant medication that increases norepinephrine in the brain and is considered a first-line treatment for ADHD. Unlike stimulants, it is not a controlled substance. However, it carries a black box warning for possibly inducing suicidal ideation. In adults and adolescents with ADHD who are likely to abuse stimulants, atomoxetine or buproprion might be a good choice. Other medications that can be effective for hyperactivity and impulsivity in ADHD are the α-2 agonists, clonidine and guanfacine which are now available in immediate and extended release forms.

Environment

Medication, individual tutoring, family counseling, behavior therapy, and educational training may be helpful. Children with ADHD should be helped to understand that drug-taking does not mean that they're crazy, that *some* impaired behavior does not permit *all* poor behavior, that "unstructured permissiveness" is not good for them, and that genuine praise usually arises from jobs well done. They do best with a consistent, supportive, moderately structured environment.

The American Academy of Child and Adolescent Psychiatry recommends (1) family therapy if there is family dysfunction; (2) individual and/or group therapy for poor self-esteem and peer problems; (3) social skills training (including empathy training) and cognitive therapies for attention/impulsivity symptoms (one goal is to teach these children to verbalize/think *before* acting); and (4) parent behavior training to develop appropriate, consistent, limit-setting abilities and behavior modification programs for behavior problems. Too often, parents who are at their wits' end can no longer see anything positive about their children. Books such as *Raising Your Spirited Child* (1991, Mary Sheedy Kurcinka) and *Meeting the Challenge with Love and Logic* (2000, Jim Fay, Foster Cline, Bob Sorinson) help them recognize and harness their children's energy and "spiritedness" for positive purposes.

DISORDER OF MOTOR FUNCTION (DEVELOPMENTAL COORDINATION DISORDER)

Developmental disorders of motor skills include what has been called "developmental coordination disorder." The very clumsy child typically shows delays in gross motor skills (e.g., sitting and walking) and fine motor skills (e.g., self-feeding, zipping, or buttoning). The reported boy:girl ratio for this disorder varies between 2:1 and 4:1. These children break things often, though accidentally, and are called "destructive" or, refusing to attempt frustrating tasks such as writing, are called "lazy." Their peers have endless insulting names for them (e.g., "spaz," "klutz"). Academic performance is usually normal, but self-esteem is often affected. Kids with ADHD appear clumsy from excessive motor activity and inattention, and this disorder must be ruled out. The diagnostic criteria for developmental coordination disorder are listed in Table 25-9.

STEREOTYPIC MOVEMENT DISORDERS

Unlike the tic disorders, the repetitive behaviors in this disorder are intentional. It occurs in 10–23% of institutionalized children with moderate or severe intellectual impairment. It is also more common in deaf or blind children. The child's primary goal may be to use self-stimulation as an antidote to an otherwise impoverished, low-stimulation environment. Table 25-10 lists diagnostic criteria for stereotypic movement disorder.

TIC DISORDERS

Although anywhere from 5 to 24% of schoolchildren have some kind of tic, most fortunately do not have a tic disorder. A tic is defined as an involuntary, sudden, rapid, recurrent, nonrhythmic, stereotyped movement or vocalization. If they weren't normal, eyeblinks could be thought of as tics. Tics (like eye-blinks) are automatic, but can be voluntarily suppressed for varying lengths of time. Stress makes them worse; sleep and absorbing activities make

TABLE 25-9
Diagnostic Criteria for Developmental Disorder of Motor Function
(Developmental Coordination Disorder)

A. **Motor coordination, on fine or gross motor tasks is significantly below the level expected on the basis of age and general intelligence**. This is best assessed on the basis of an individually administered, standardized test of fine and gross motor coordination.

   1. The young child may be awkward in general gait, being slow to learn to run, hop, and go up and down stairs. There is likely to be difficulty learning to tie shoelaces, to fasten and unfasten buttons, and to throw and catch balls. The child may be generally clumsy in fine and/or gross movements—tending to drop things, to stumble, to bump into obstacles, and to have poor handwriting. Drawing skills are usually poor, and children with this disorder are often poor at jigsaw puzzles, using constructional toys, building models, ball games, and drawing and understanding maps.

   2. In most cases a careful clinical examination shows marked neurodevelopmental immaturities such as choreiform movements of unsupported limbs, or mirror movements and other associated motor features, as well as signs of poor fine and gross motor coordination (generally described as "soft" neurological signs because of their normal occurrence in younger children and their lack of localizing value). Tendon reflexes may be increased or decreased bilaterally but will not be asymmetrical.

B. Serious impairment in motor coordination that **may delay developmental motor milestones and may have some associated speech deficit**s (especially involving articulation), scholastic difficulties, or associated socio-emotional-behavioral problems. It is usual for the motor clumsiness to be associated with some degree of impaired performance on visuo-spatial cognitive tasks.

C. The difficulties in coordination should have been **present since early in development** (i.e., they should not constitute an acquired deficit).

D. The motor coordination deficits are **not solely explicable in terms of general intellectual disability or of any specific congenital (such as cerebral palsy or muscular dystrophy) or acquired neurological disorder** (other than the one that may be implicit in the coordination abnormality).

Note: Adapted from *ICD-10* (pp. 196–197) and *DSM-5* (p. 74)

them better. *Motor tics* may be simple (e.g., neck jerking, shoulder shrugging) or complex (e.g., facial gestures, grooming behavior). *Verbal tics* can also be simple (e.g., coughing or barking) or complex (e.g., words or whole phrases spoken out of context). The three tic disorders—*Tourette's, chronic motor or vocal tic disorder,* and *transient tic disorder*—are probably variations on the same genetic abnormality. Chronic motor or vocal tic disorder and transient tic disorder may be thought of as partial forms of Tourette's disorder. Chronic motor or vocal tic disorder meets all of the criteria for Tourette's, except only motor *or* only vocal tics are seen, but not both in the same per-

TABLE 25-10
Diagnostic Criteria for Stereotyped Movement Disorders

A. **Voluntary, repetitive, stereotyped, nonfunctional (and often rhythmic) movements that do not form part of any recognized psychiatric or neurological condition**.

　1. noninjurious movements include body-rocking, head-rocking, hair-plucking, hair-twisting, finger-flicking mannerisms, and hand-flapping.

　2. self-injurious movements include repetitive head-banging, face-slapping, eye-poking, and biting of hands, lips, or other body parts.

B. All the stereotyped movement disorders occur most frequently in association with intellectual disability and **interfere with personal, social, educational, or other important activity or functioning**.

C. The repetitive movements must be **present early in development**.

D. The disturbance is **not due to the direct physiological effects of a substance, neurological condition, mental disorder, or another medical condition**.

Note: Adapted from *ICD-10* (pp. 226–227) and *DSM-5* (pp. 77–78)

son. In transient tic disorder, a child has motor and/or vocal tics for at least 4 weeks but not longer than 12 consecutive months.

Boys have these disorders at least three times more often than girls. Half develop tics by 7 years and the majority by age 14. Tourette's, the worst form, is rare: 1 in 2,000. No other neurological or psychiatric disorder has the vocalizations heard in Tourette's and these related tic disorders. A triad of disorders that seem to occur together are ADHD, obsessive–compulsive disorder, and Tourette's. Some cases of Tourette's disorder and other tic disorders may be related to streptococcal infections (pediatric autoimmune neuropsychiatric disorders associated with streptococcus—PANDAS). Children with these disorders should be screened for this cause of the illness, which is potentially treatable with antibiotics. Table 25-11 lists diagnostic criteria for Tourette's and other tic disorders.

TABLE 25-11
Diagnostic Criteria for Tic Disorders

A. The predominant manifestation in these syndromes is some form of tic. **A tic is an involuntary, rapid, recurrent, nonrhythmic motor movement (usually involving circumscribed muscle groups), or vocal production, that is of sudden onset and serves no apparent purpose.**

　1. Simple motor tics include eye-blinking, neck-jerking, shoulder-shrugging, and facial grimacing. Complex tics (involving more than one muscle group) include hitting one's self, jumping, and hopping.

TABLE 25-11
Continued

2. Simple vocal tics include throat-clearing, barking, sniffing, and hissing. Complex vocal tics include the repetition of particular words, and sometimes the use of socially unacceptable (often obscene) words (coprolalia), and the repetition of one's own sounds or words (palilalia).

B. Tics tend to **wax and wane**. They are mostly experienced as irresistible but they can usually be suppressed for varying periods of time.

C. The disturbance **is not due to the direct physiological effects of a substance, neurological disorder, or another medical condition**.

Transient tic disorder

Meets the general criteria for a tic disorder, but tics do not persist for longer than 12 months. This is the commonest form of tic and is most frequent about the age of 4 or 5 years; the tics usually take the form of eye-blinking, facial grimacing, or head-jerking. In some cases the tics occur as a single episode but in other cases there are remissions and relapses over a period of months.

Chronic motor or vocal tic disorder

Meets the general criteria for a tic disorder, in which there are motor or vocal tics (but not both); tics may be either single or multiple (but usually multiple), and last for more than a year.

Combined vocal and multiple motor tic disorder (de la Tourette's syndrome)

A form of tic disorder in which there are, or have been, multiple motor tics and one or more vocal tics, although these need not to have occurred concurrently. Onset is almost always in childhood or adolescence. A history of motor tics before development of vocal tics is common; the symptoms frequently worsen during adolescence, and it is common for the disorder to persist into adult life. The vocal tics are often multiple with explosive repetitive vocalizations, throat-clearing, and grunting, and there may be the use of obscene words or phrases. Sometimes there is associated gestural echopraxia, which also may be of an obscene nature (copropraxia). As with motor tics, the vocal tics may be voluntarily suppressed for short periods, be exacerbated by stress, and disappear during sleep.

Note: Adapted from ICD-10 (p. 221–223) and DSM-5 (p. 81)

References

American Psychiatric Association. (2013). *Diagnostic and statistical manual of mental disorders* (5th ed.). Arlington, VA: American Psychiatric Association.

Cantwell, D.P., & Baker, L. (1989). Stability and natural history of *DSM-III* childhood diagnoses. *Journal of American Academy of Child and Adolescent Psychiatry, 28*, 691–700.

Dillenburger, K., & Keenan, M. (2009). "None of the As in ABA stand for autism: Dispelling the myths." *Journal of Intellectual and Developmental Disability, 34*(2), 193–195.

Faraone, S.V., Biederman, J., Keenan, K., & Tsuang, M.T. (1991). Separation of *DSM-III* attention deficit disorder and conduct disorder: Evidence from a family-genetic study of American child psychiatric patients. *Psychology of Medicine, 21*, 109–121.

Faraone, S.V., Biederman, J., Lehman, B.L., Keenan, K., Norman, D., Seidman, L.J., et al. (1993). Evidence for the independent familial transmission of attention deficit hyperactivity disorder and learning disabilities: Results from a family-genetic study. *American Journal of Psychiatry, 150*(6), 891–895.

Fay, J., Cline, F., & Sorinson, B. (2000). *Meeting the challenge with love and logic.* Golden, CO: Love and Logic Press.

Handen, B.L., Breaux, A.M., Janosky, J., McAuliffe, S., Feldman, H., & Gosling, A. (1992). Effects and noneffects of methylphenidate in children with mental retardation and ADHD. *Journal of the American Academy of Child Adolescent Psychiatry, 31,* 455–461.

Kurcinka, M.S. (1991). *Raising your spirited child.* New York: HarperCollins.

Maziade, M., Caron, C., Côté, R., Mérette, C., Bernier, H., Laplante, B., et al. (1990). Psychiatric status of adolescents who had extreme temperaments at age 7. *American Journal of Psychiatry, 147*(11), 1531–1536.

Practice Parameters for the Assessment and Treatment of Children and Adolescents with Attention-Deficit/Hyperactivity Disorder. (2007). *Journal of the American Academy of Child and Adolescent Psychiatry, 46*(7), 894–921.

Rey, J.M. (1993). Oppositional defiant disorder. *American Journal of Psychiatry, 150*(12), 1769–1778.

Smalley, S.L., Asarnow, R.F., & Spence, M.A. (1988). Autism and genetics. *Archives of General Psychiatry, 45,* 953–961.

Strayhorn, J.M. (1988). *The competent child: An approach to psychotherapy and preventive mental health.* New York: Guilford.

Swanson, J.M., Lerner, M.A., March, J., & Gresham, F.M. (1999). Assessment and intervention for attention-deficit/hyperactivity disorder in the schools: Lessons from the MTA study. *Pediatric Clinics of North America, 46,* 993–1009.

Sylvester, C. (1993). Psychopharmacology of disorders in children. *Psychiatric Clinics of North America, 16*(4), 779–791.

World Health Organization. (1992). *The ICD–10 classification of mental and behavioural disorders: Clinical descriptions and diagnostic guidelines.* WHO.

SNAP-IV RATING SCALE

Name of child _____ Date _____

Age _____ Sex _____ Grade _____ Rating period_____

Completed by _____

Relation to child: Mother _____ Father _____ Teacher _____ Other _____

Check the column that best describes this child:	Not at All	Just a Little	Quite A Bit	Very Much
1. Often fails to give close attention to details or makes careless mistakes in schoolwork, work, or other activities	____	____	____	____
2. Often has difficulty sustaining attention in tasks or play activities	____	____	____	____
3. Often does not seem to listen when spoken to directly	____	____	____	____
4. Often does not follow through on instructions and fails to finish schoolwork, chores, or duties in the workplace (not due to oppositional behavior or failure to understand instructions)	____	____	____	____
5. Often has difficulty organizing tasks and activities	____	____	____	____
6. Often avoids, dislikes, or has difficulties engaging in tasks that require sustained mental effort (such as schoolwork or homework)	____	____	____	____
7. Often loses things necessary for tasks or activities (e.g., toys, school assignments, pencils, books, or tools)	____	____	____	____
8. Is often easily distracted by extraneous stimuli	____	____	____	____
9. Often forgetful in daily activities	____	____	____	____
10. Often fidgets with hands or feet, squirms in seat	____	____	____	____
11. Often leaves seat in classroom or in other situations in which remaining seated is expected	____	____	____	____
12. Often runs about or climbs excessively in situations where it is inappropriate (in adolescents or adults, may be limited to subjective feelings of restlessness)	____	____	____	____
13. Often has difficulty playing or engaging in leisure activities quietly	____	____	____	____
14. Is always on the go or often acts if driven by a motor	____	____	____	____
15. Often talks excessively	____	____	____	____
16. Often blurts out answers to questions before the questions have been completed	____	____	____	____
17. Often has difficulty awaiting turn	____	____	____	____
18. Often interrupts or intrudes upon others (e.g., butts into conversations or games)	____	____	____	____
19. Often stares into space and reports daydreaming	____	____	____	____
20. Often appears to be low in energy level, sluggish, or drowsy	____	____	____	____

Check the column that best describes this child:	Not at All	Just a Little	Quite A Bit	Very Much
21. Often appears to be apathetic or unmotivated to engage in goal-directed activities	____	____	____	____
22. Often engages in physically dangerous activities without considering possible consequences	____	____	____	____
23. Often shifts from one uncompleted activity to another	____	____	____	____
24. Often fails to finish things he or she starts	____	____	____	____
25. Has difficulty concentrating on schoolwork or other tasks requiring sustained attention	____	____	____	____
26. Has difficulty sticking to a play activity	____	____	____	____
27. Frequently calls out in class or in other situations when silence is expected	____	____	____	____
28. Needs a lot of supervision	____	____	____	____
29. Moves about excessively (e.g., even during sleep, at home, or during quiet time at school)	____	____	____	____
30. Often acts before thinking	____	____	____	____
31. Often loses temper	____	____	____	____
32. Often argues with adults	____	____	____	____
33. Often actively defies or refuses adult requests or rules	____	____	____	____
34. Often deliberately does things that annoy other people	____	____	____	____
35. Often blames others for his or her mistakes or misbehavior	____	____	____	____
36. Often touchy or easily annoyed by others	____	____	____	____
37. Is often angry and resentful	____	____	____	____
38. Is often spiteful or vindictive	____	____	____	____
39. Often swears or uses obscene language	____	____	____	____
40. Often manifests provocative behavior	____	____	____	____
41. Often shows excessive stubbornness	____	____	____	____

Adapted from Swanson, Nolan, and Pelham (1983)

SCORING INSTRUCTIONS FOR THE SNAP-IV RATING SCALE

James M. Swanson, PhD, University of California, Irvine

The SNAP-IV Rating Scale, a revision of the Swanson, Nolan, and Pelham (SNAP) Questionnaire (Swanson et al., 1983), consists of 41 items. The first 18 items (#1–#18) are from the *DSM-IV* (1994) criteria for ADHD; the next 12 items (#19–#30) are from prior *DSM* definitions of ADD; the last 11 items consist of the 8 items (#31–#38) from the *DSM-IV* (1994) criteria for oppositional defiant disorder (ODD) plus the 3 items from prior *DSM* definitions of ODD. The SNAP-IV is based on a 0–3 rating and scoring scale (Not at All = 0, Just a Little = 1, Quite A Bit = 2, and Very Much = 3) that has been used by many questionnaires (e.g., the Conners Questionnaire and the Sattereld Questionnaires from the 1970s). Subscale scores on the SNAP-IV are calculated by summing the scores on the items in the subset and dividing by the number of items in the subset. The three subsets are ADHD-I (Inattentive Type), ADHD-HI (Hyperactive-Impulsive Type), and ODD (Oppositional Defiant Disorder). The score for any subset is expressed as the average rating per item, as shown below for hypothetical rating on the ADHD-inattentive (ADHD-1) subset: Scoring templates for the two sets of ADHD symptoms and for the set of ODD symptoms as below:

DSM-IV subscales:	ADHD-I Item Rating	ADHD-HI Item Rating	ODD Item Rating
#1 ____	#10 ____	#31 ____	
#2 ____	#11 ____	#32 ____	
#3 ____	#12 ____	#33 ____	
#4 ____	#13 ____	#34 ____	
#5 ____	#14 ____	#35 ____	
#6 ____	#15 ____	#36 ____	
#7 ____	#16 ____	#37 ____	
#8 ____	#17 ____	#38 ____	
#9 ____	#18 ____		
Total item ratings	= ____/9	= ____/9	= ____/8
Average rating per item	= ____	= ____	= ____

In general, scores over 1.65 are moderately high (M + 1SD) and scores over 2.0 are extremely high (M + 2SD).

Index